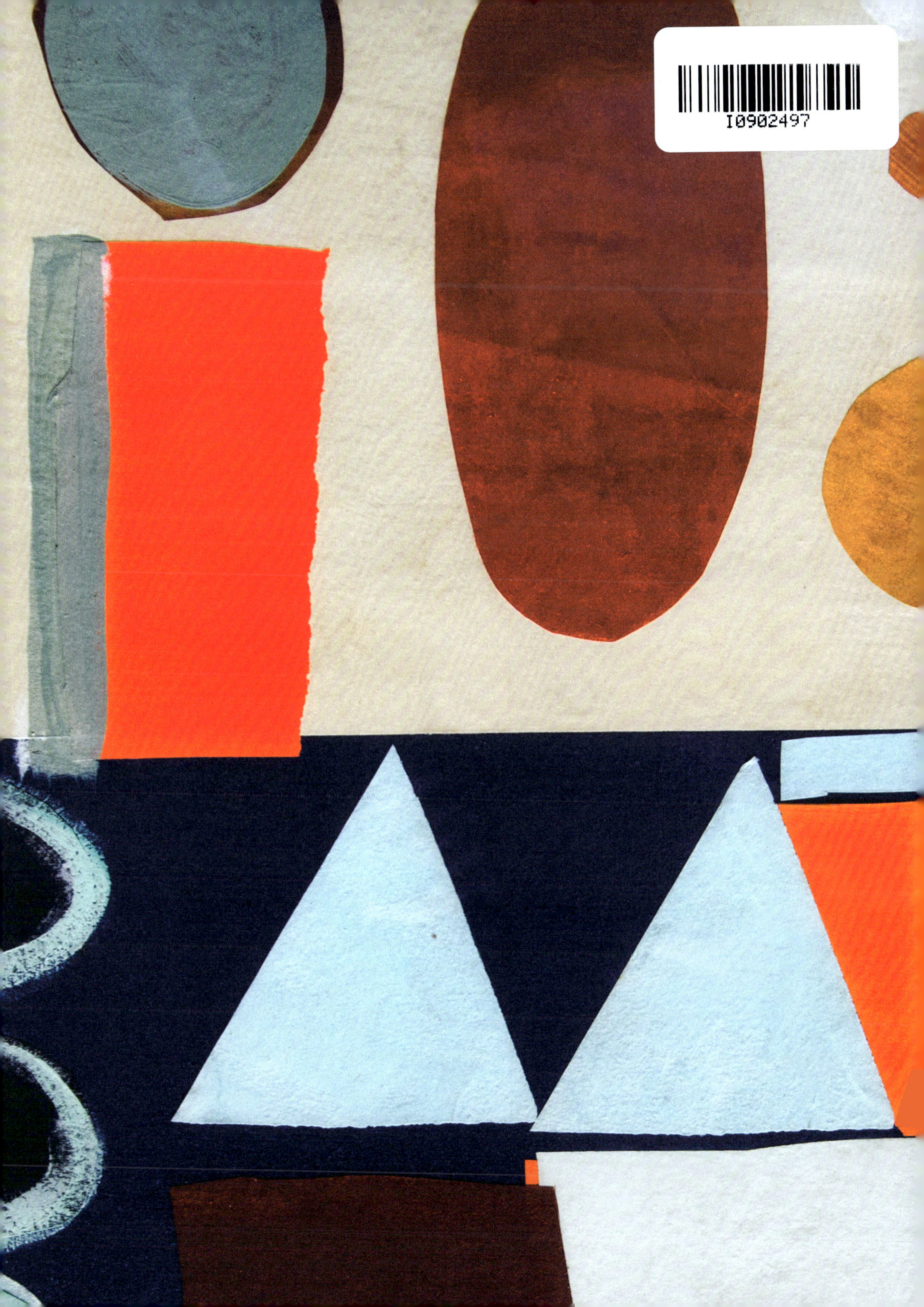

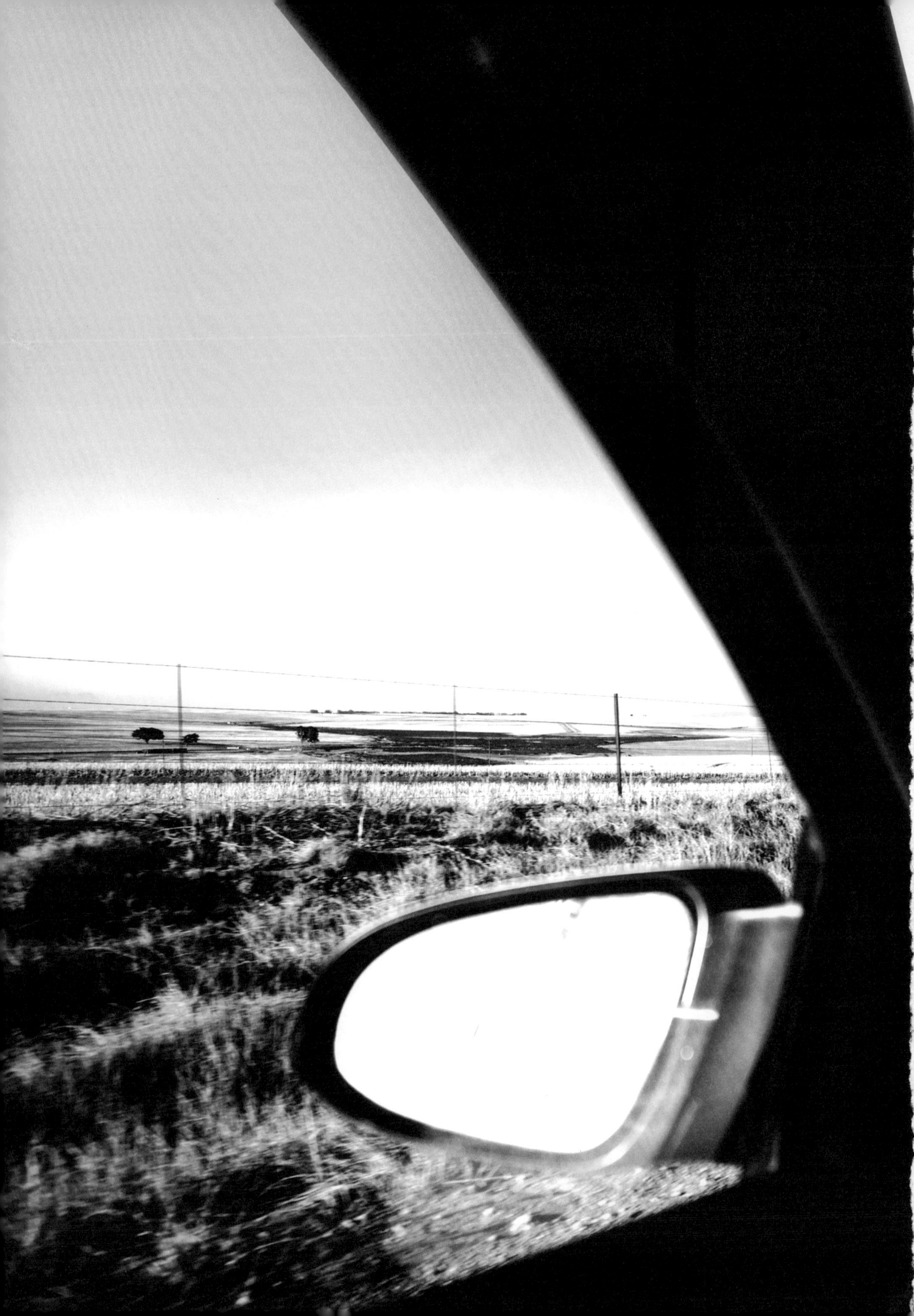

South Africa is an incredibly vast country with many different facets, and we realise that we have only glimpsed a small part of its soul.

This book documents our journey through the country by car, our walks exploring its cities, the many special encounters we had with its people and the beautiful places and homes we visited.

Travelling through a country is essentially a series of trips from one place to sleep to another. In the big cities we stayed with friends or booked a hotel in the most bustling neighbourhoods, where we danced the night away in the bar next door. We slept in a cabin right by the ocean, where the rotating light of the lighthouse kept us up all night. Other nights we spent in the middle of nowhere, with bats fluttering through our room.

But no matter where we slept, we felt like the luckiest people on earth. We had the chance to experience the beauty of Mother Nature in every aspect, becoming part of the breathtaking surroundings and experiencing how the scenery changed with the light and the weather. Nature's grandeur can be quite humbling.

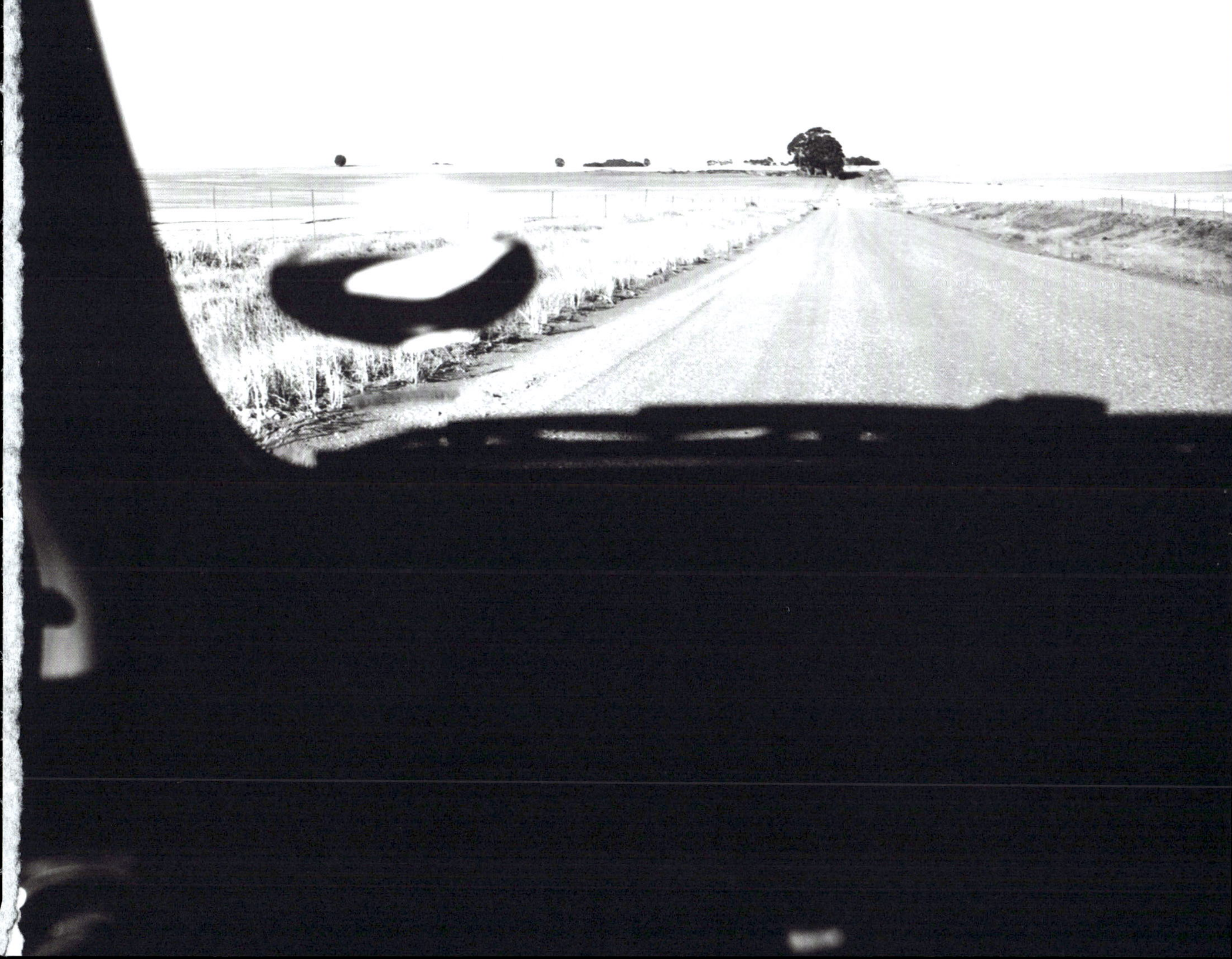

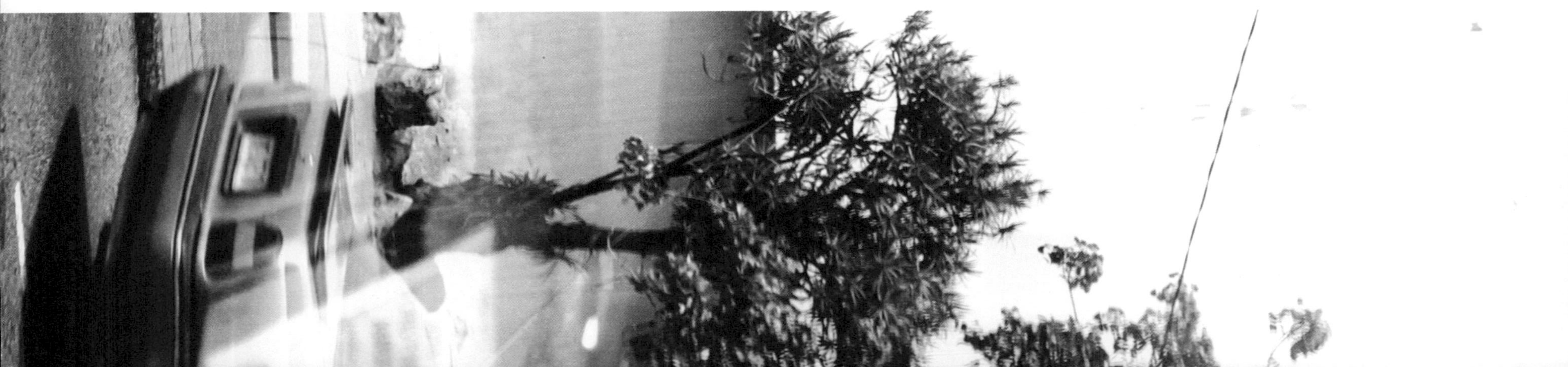

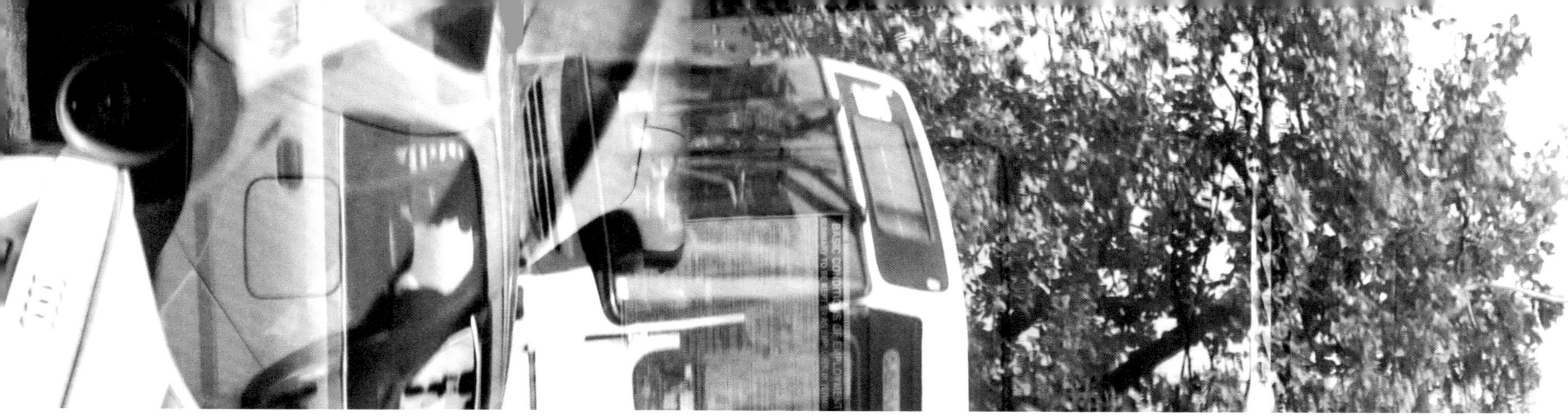

1

Cape Town

4

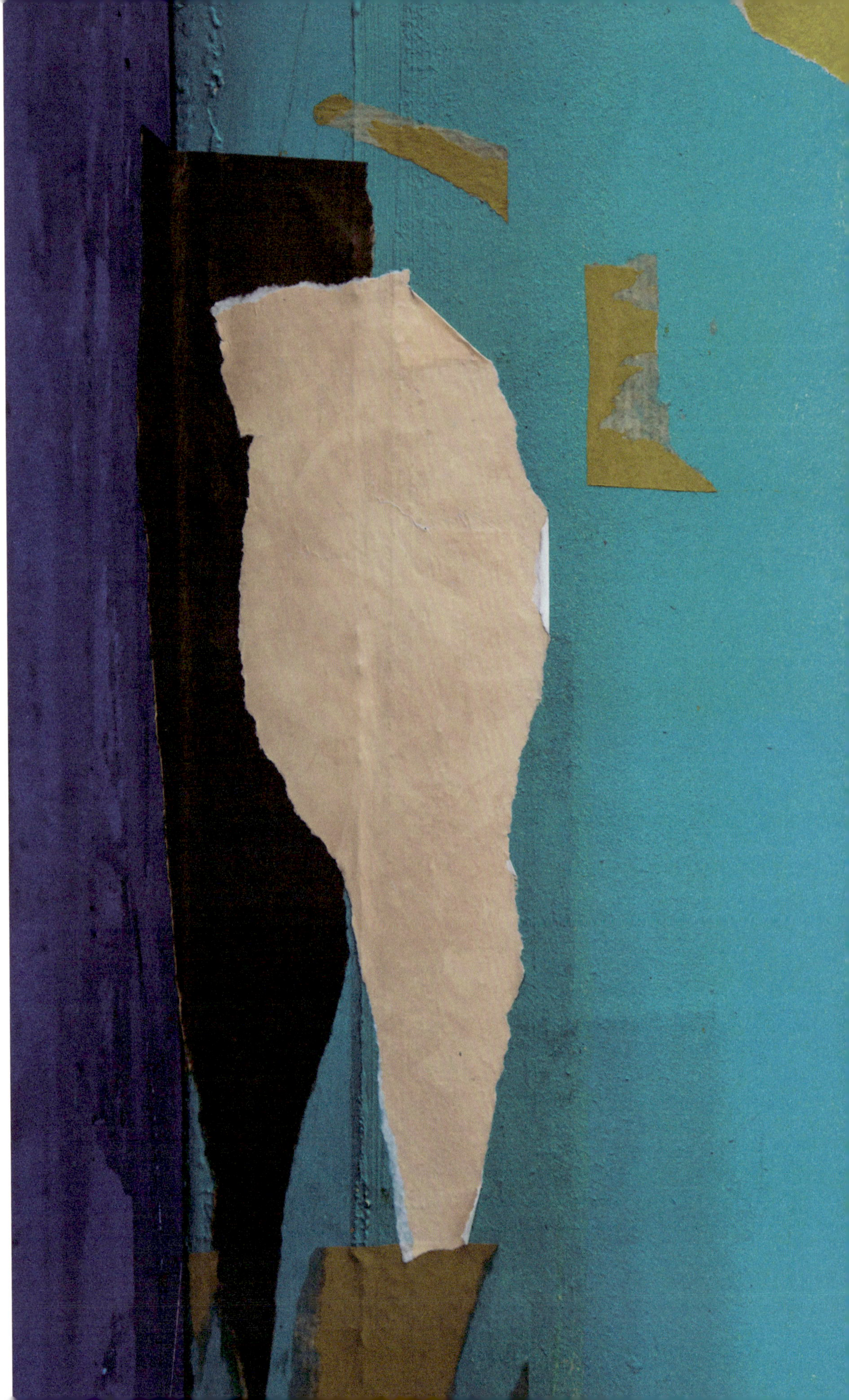

Cape Town, the most southern city of the African continent, is the kind of place you can't help but fall in love with. There are very few cities around the world where the impact of nature on the city's layout and development is so tangible, and where the environment has such a strong influence on the everyday experiences of both residents and visitors. The iconic Table Mountain dominates the Mother City, but wherever you look, you are struck by the stunning ocean, the strong winds, the intense sunlight, the impact of the dry climate and the vegetation.

At the same time, Cape Town is known for its dark history. The city's past has become synonymous with colonisation and exploitation, and unfortunately this is still very tangible in today's South Africa. Nevertheless, we decided to look on the bright side, discovering and showcasing a city where different cultures and colours live together, and one where ultimately wealth will hopefully be distributed more fairly.

Cape Town has also become a surprising rainbow hotbed, giving rise to exciting new developments in different fields, such as cuisine, fashion, and music. Now all that remains is for others to follow this positive trend, so this city can really become a city of 'good hope' for everyone!

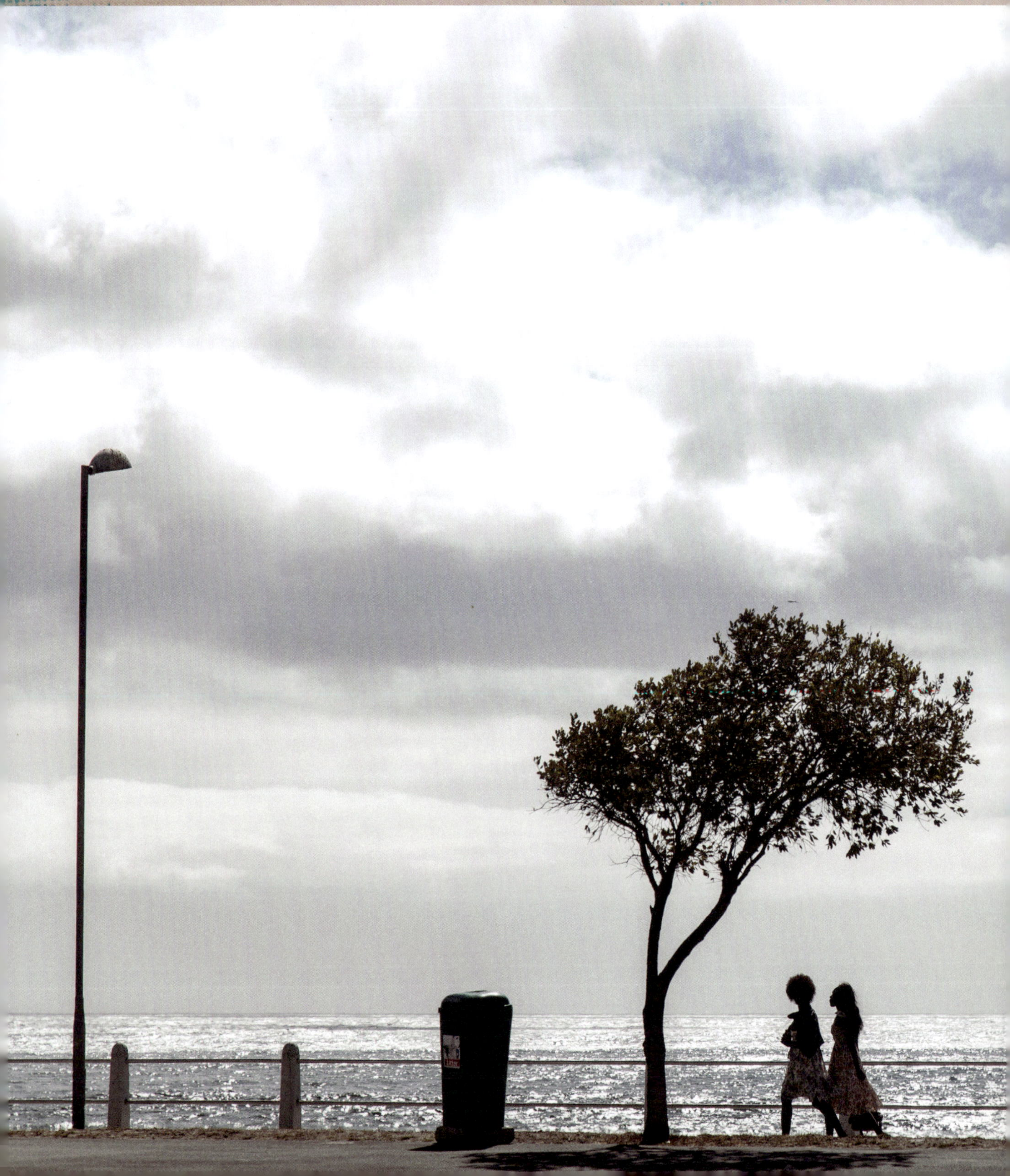

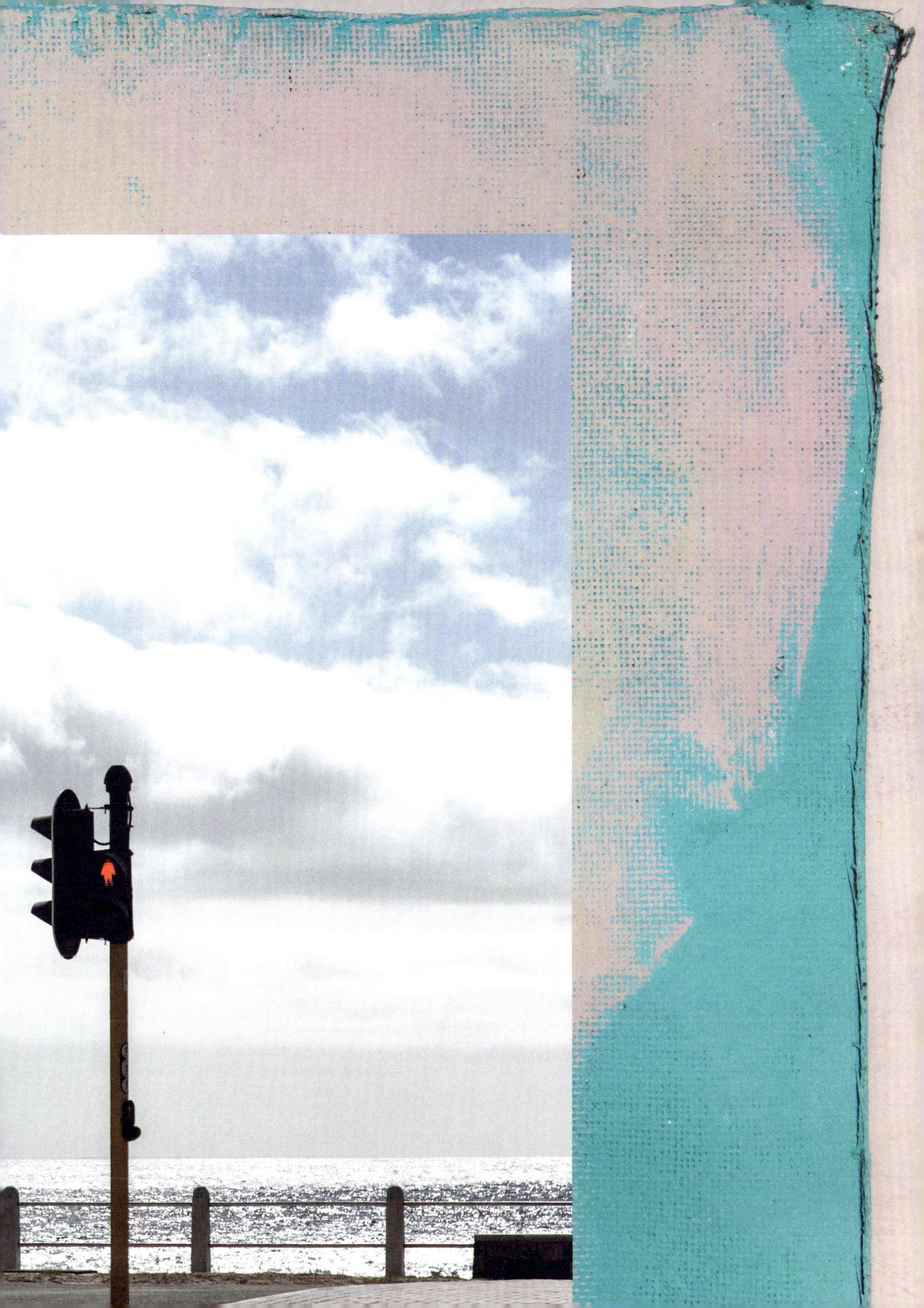

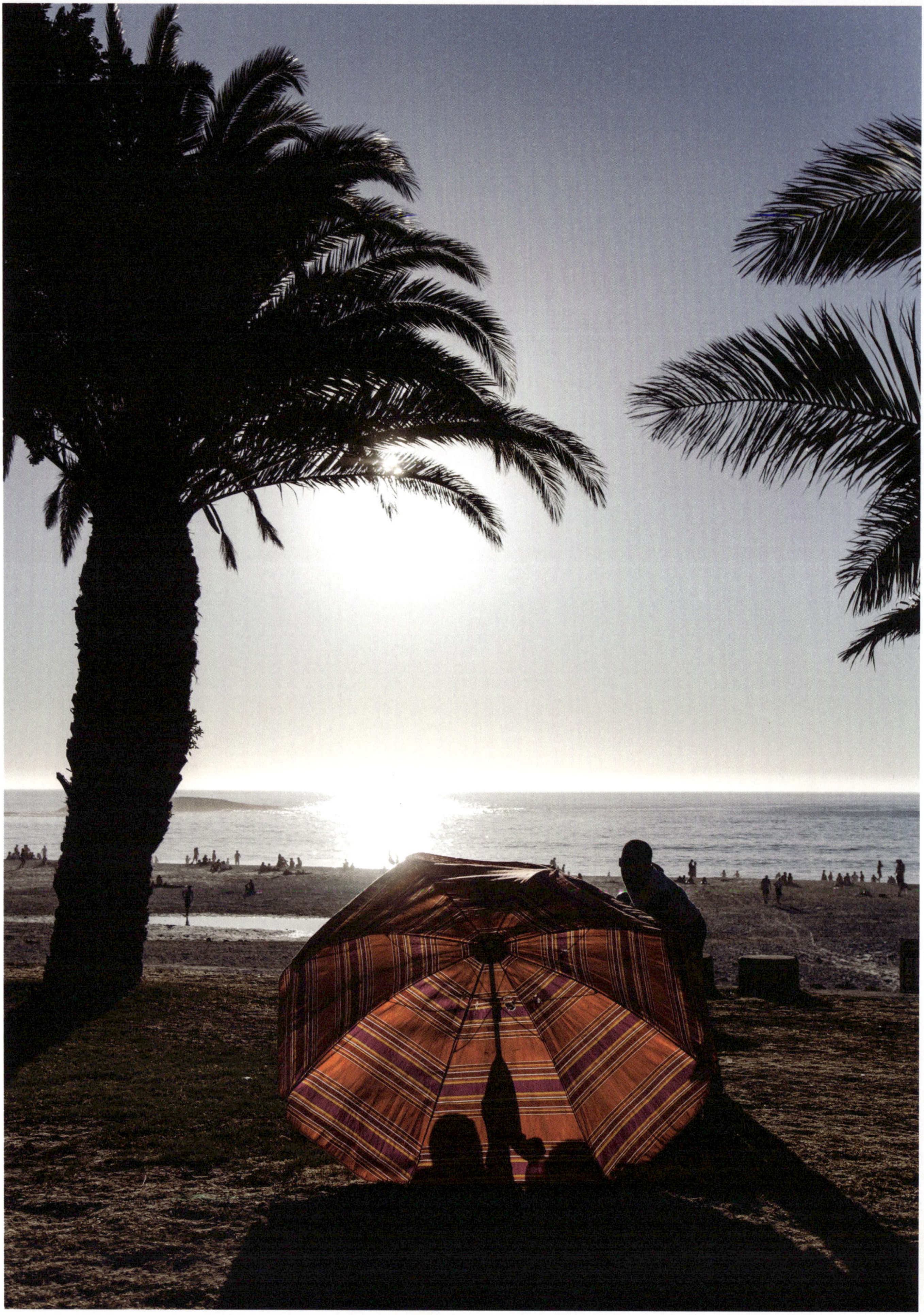

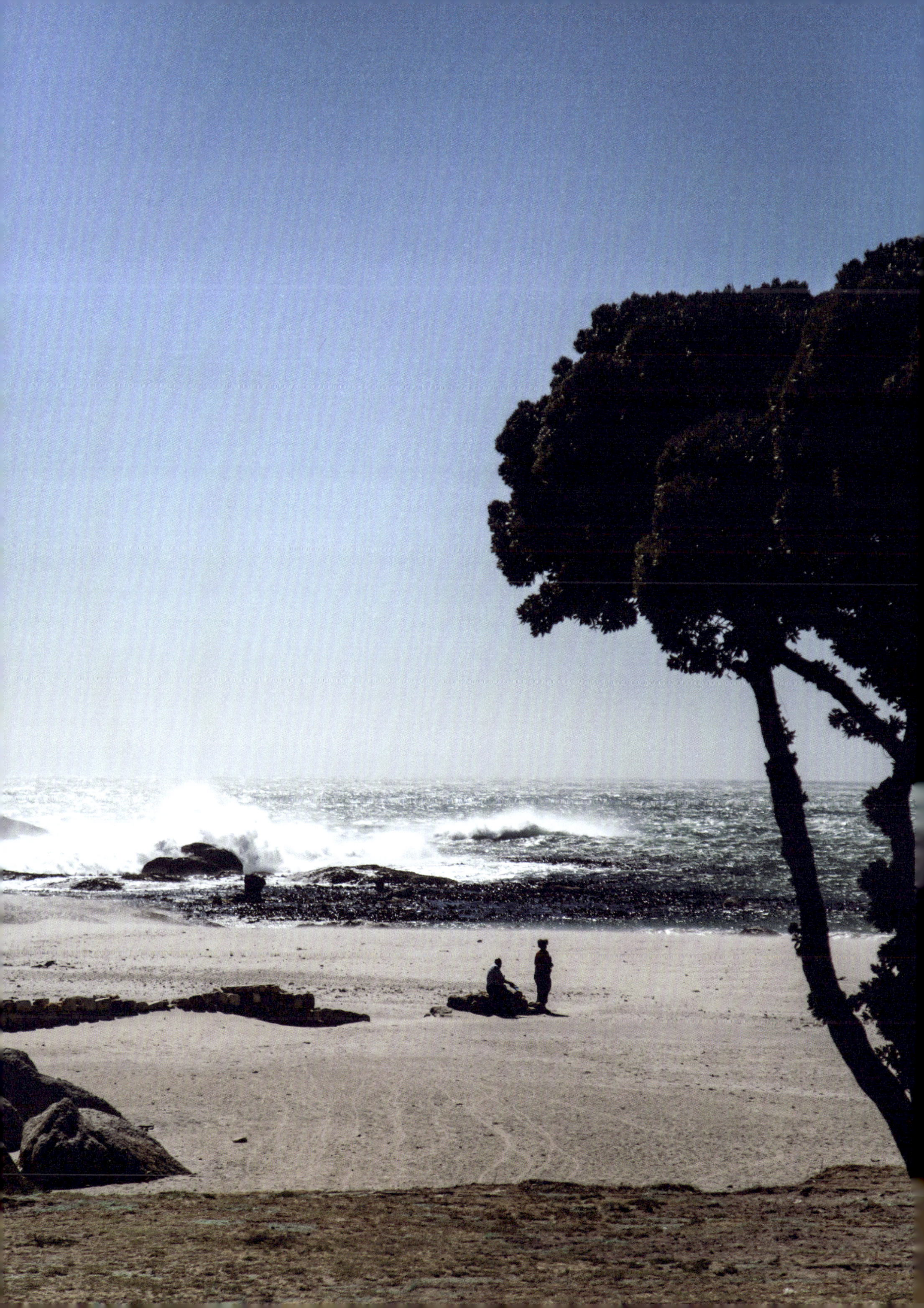

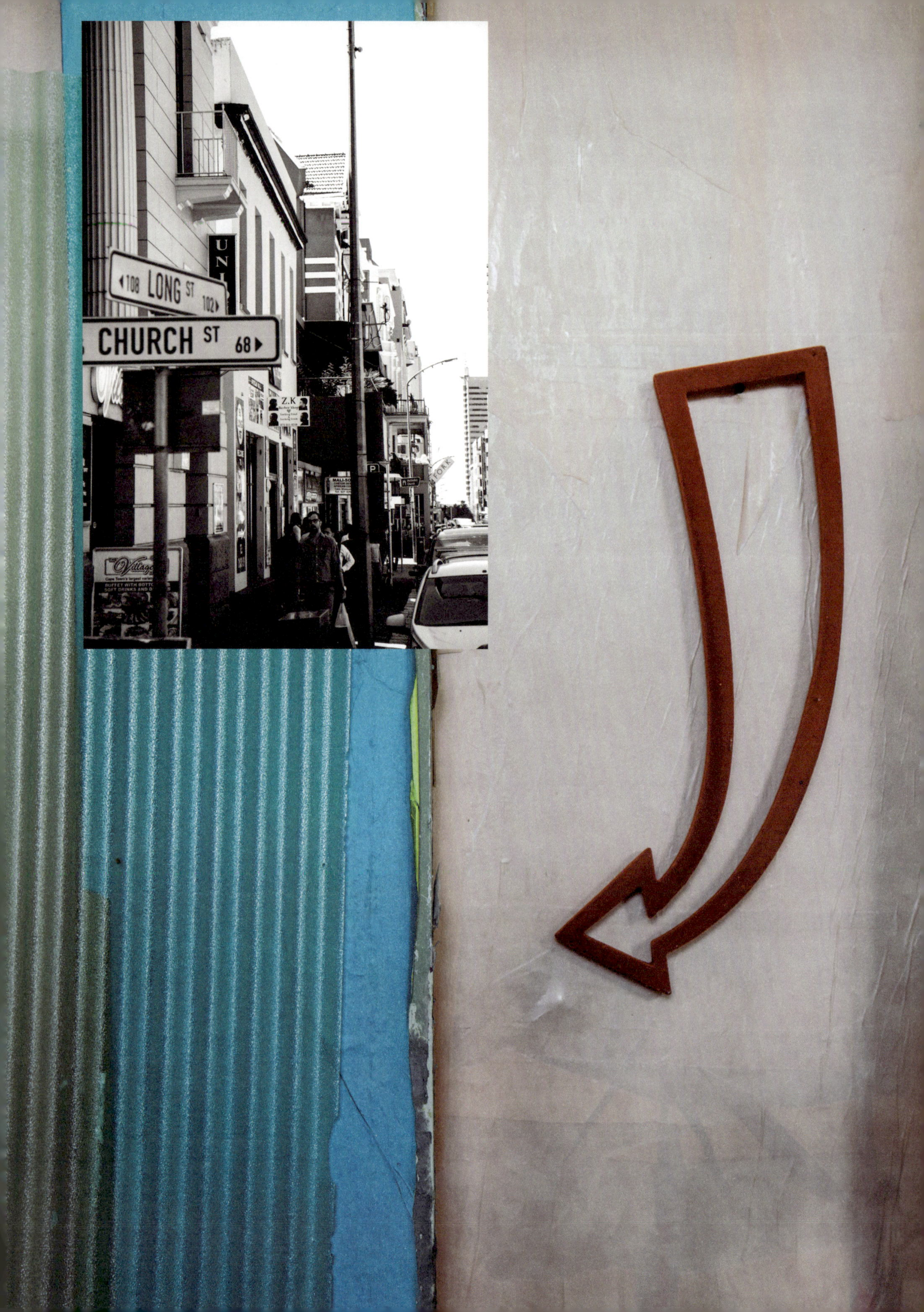
108 LONG ST 102
CHURCH ST 68
Z.K

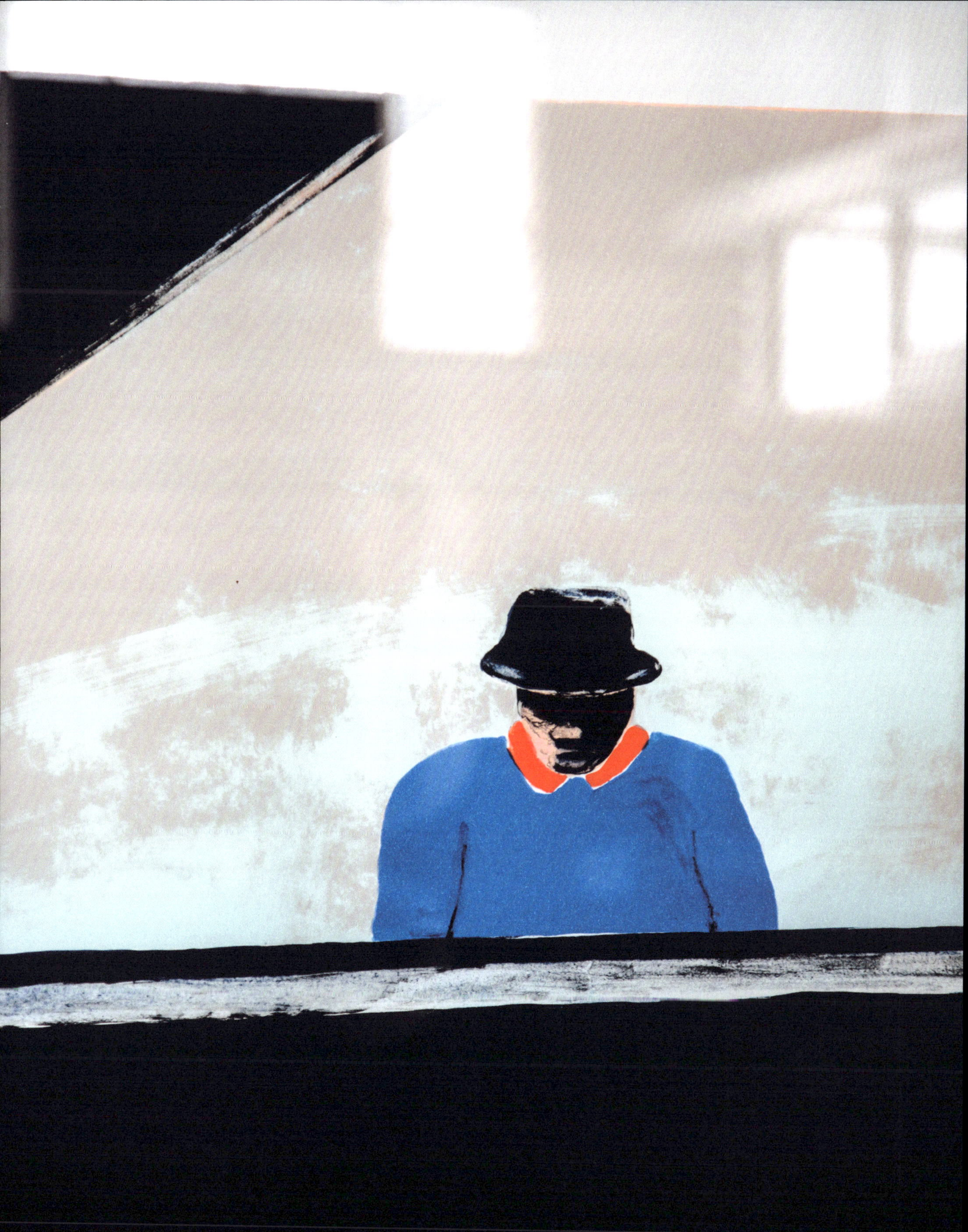

Endlessly entertaining

All day long and well into the night, there is plenty to see and do in Long Street, the street that never sleeps.

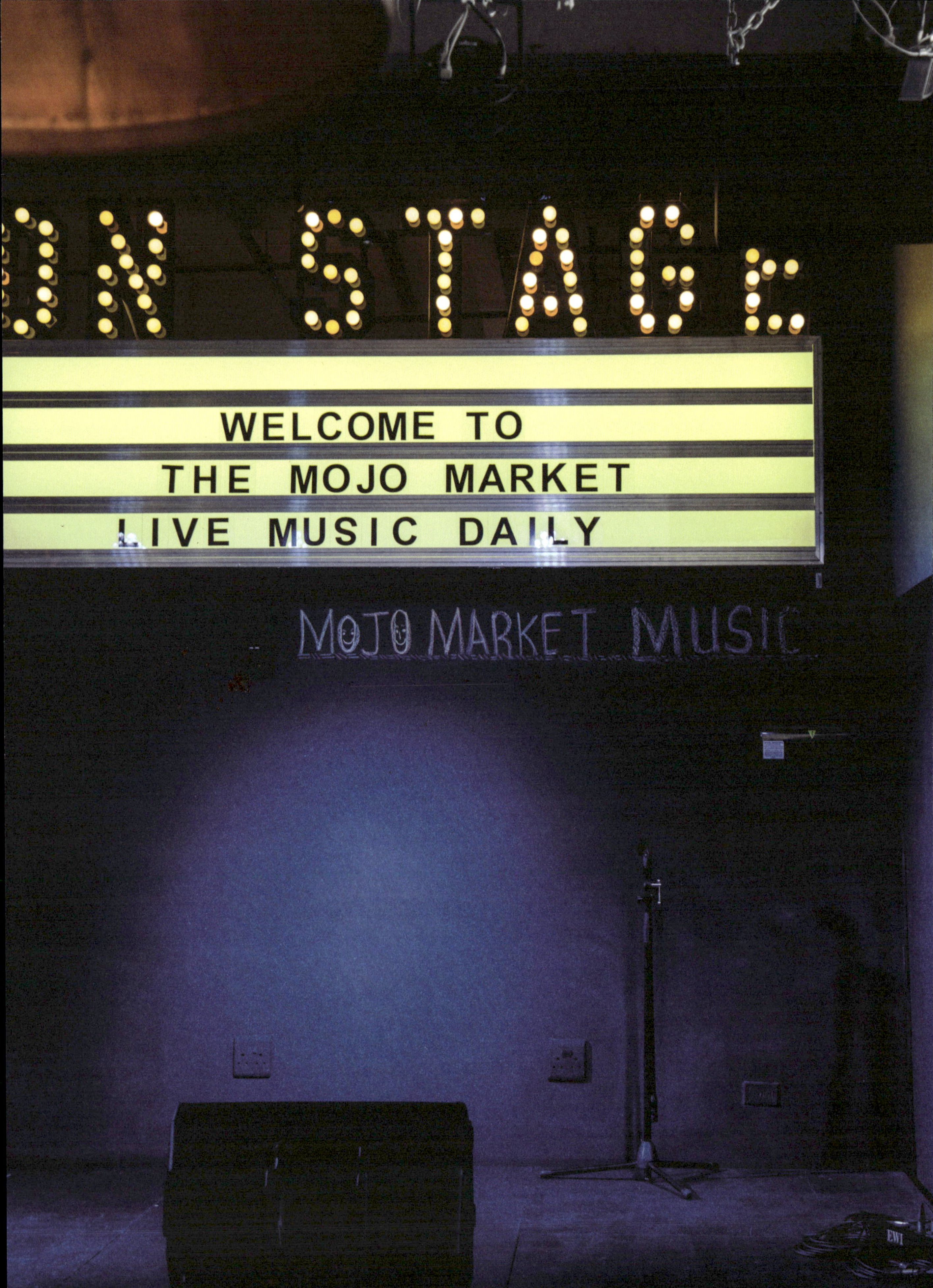
ON STAGE
WELCOME TO
THE MOJO MARKET
LIVE MUSIC DAILY
MOJO MARKET MUSIC

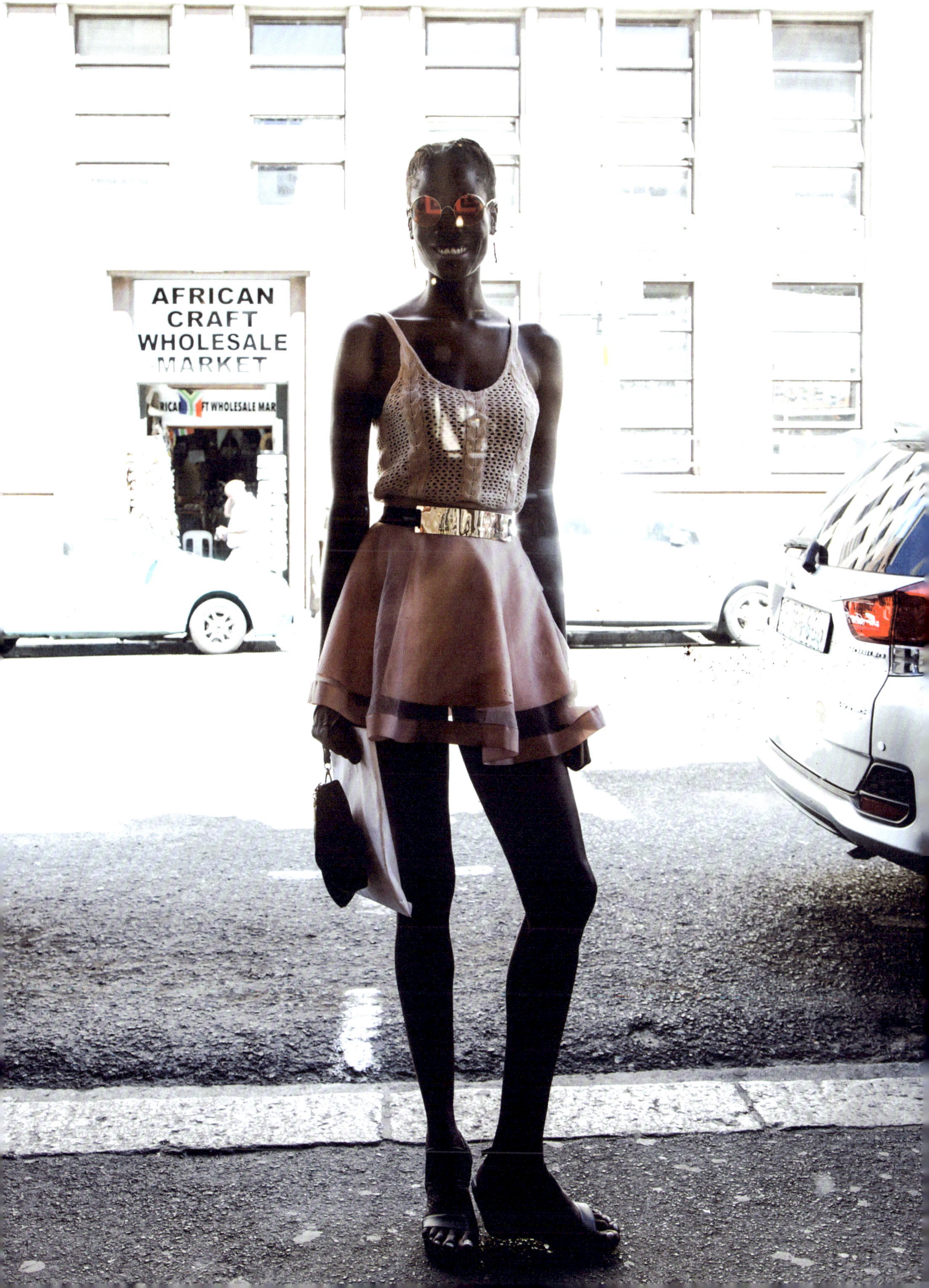
AFRICAN
CRAFT
WHOLESALE
MARKET

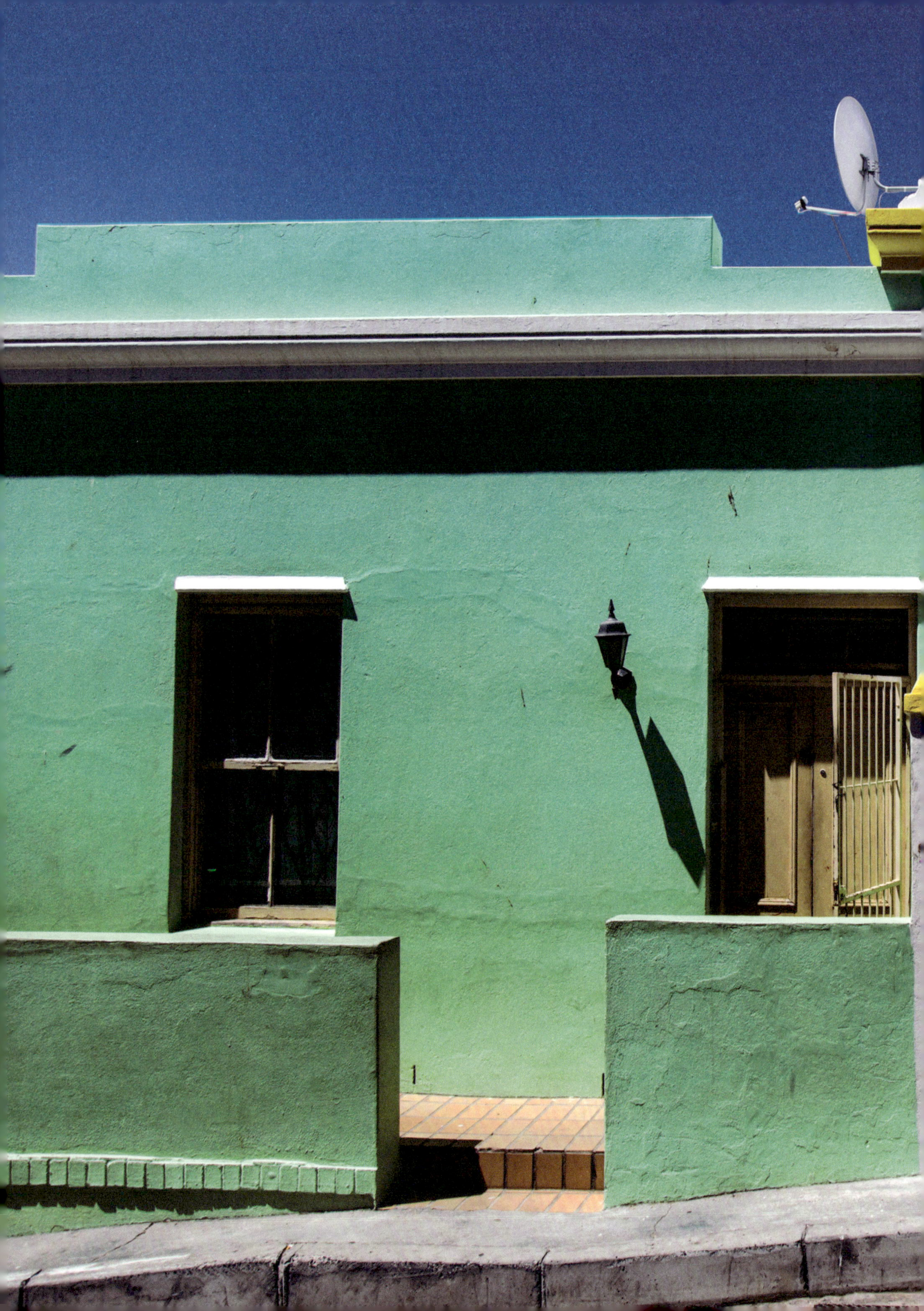

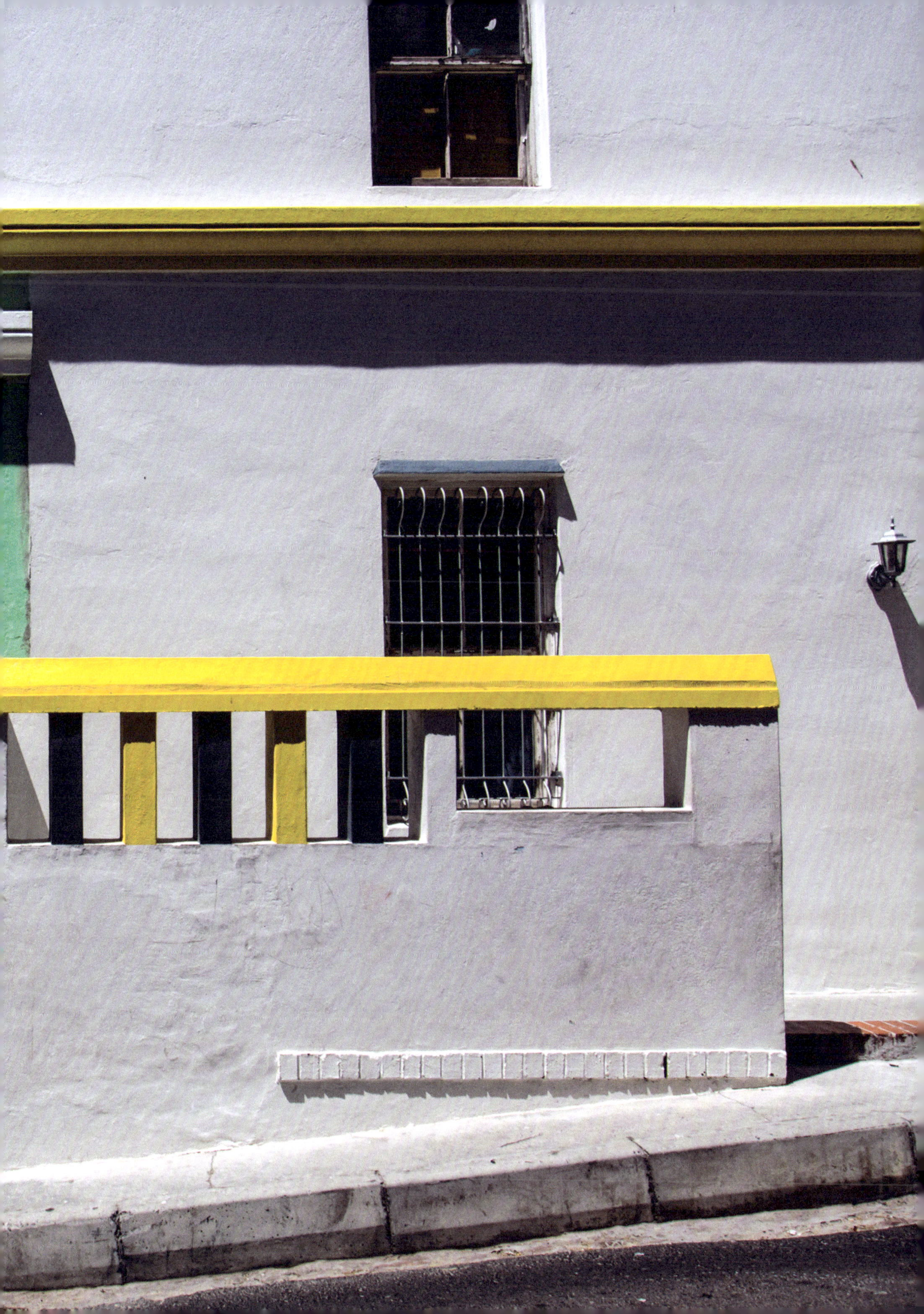

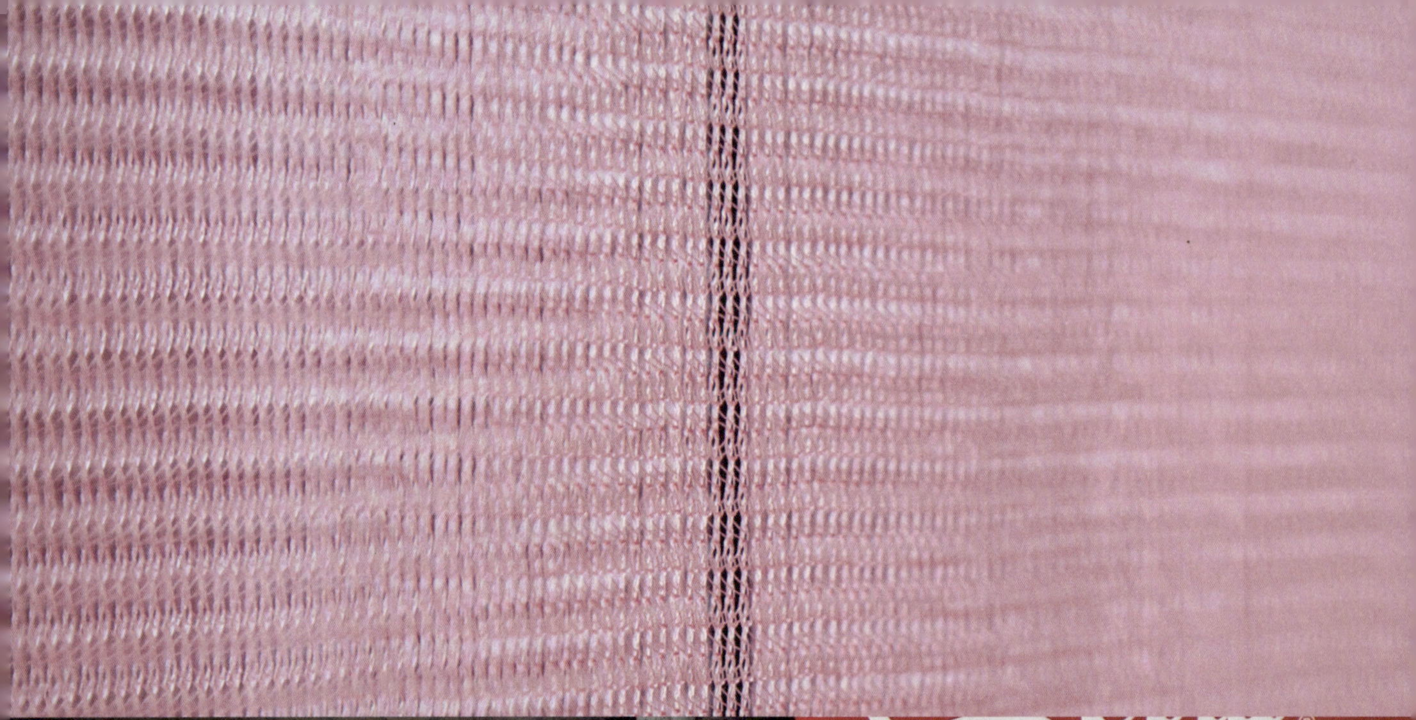

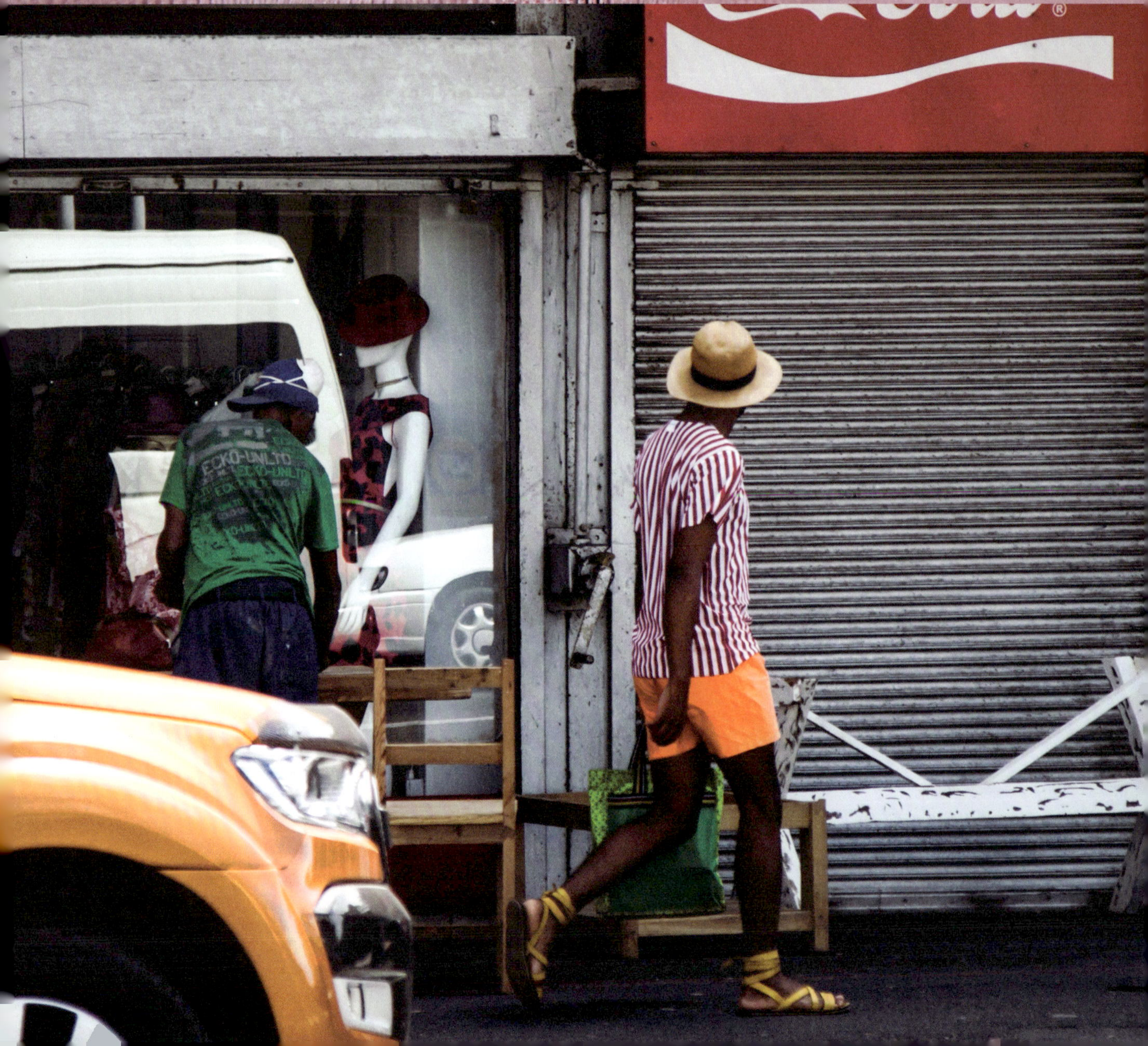

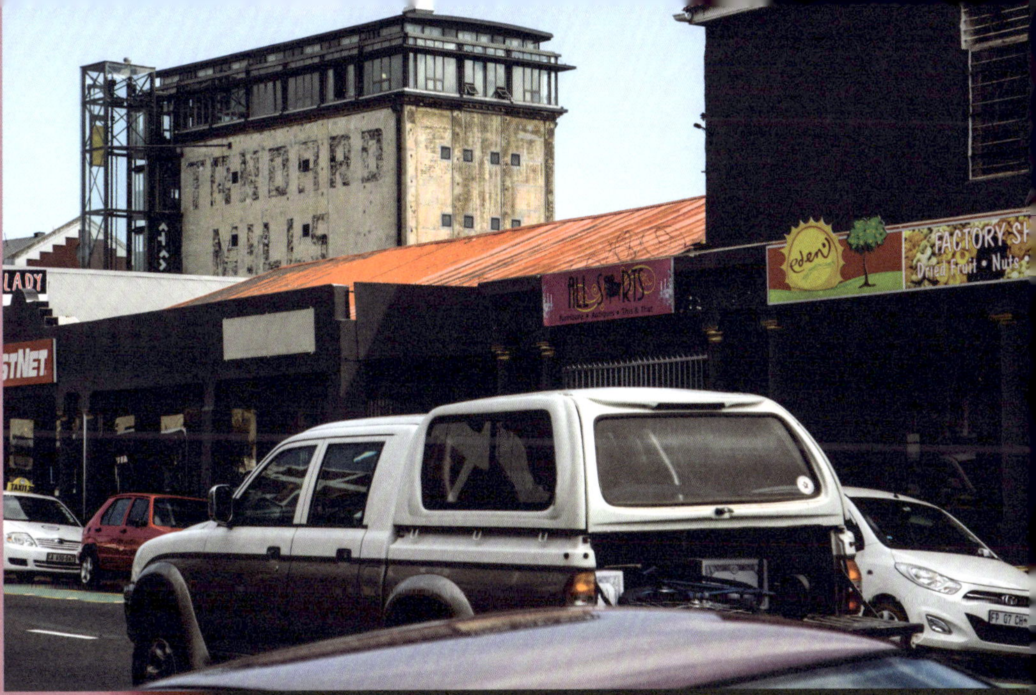

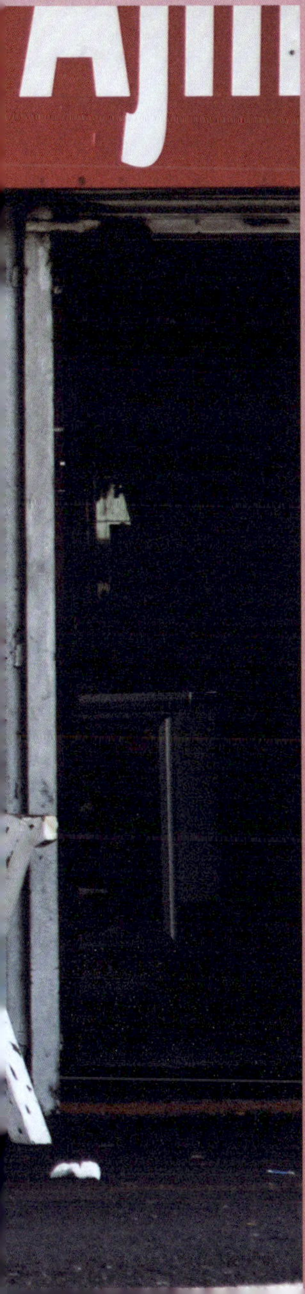

Combining the old with the new, hipsters and blue-collar workers, trendy boutique-style art shops and wholesale fabric outlets, healthy fruit and ginger juices and greasy burgers with lashings of sauce, Woodstock has it all. It is both boiling hot and cool, both elegant and raw.

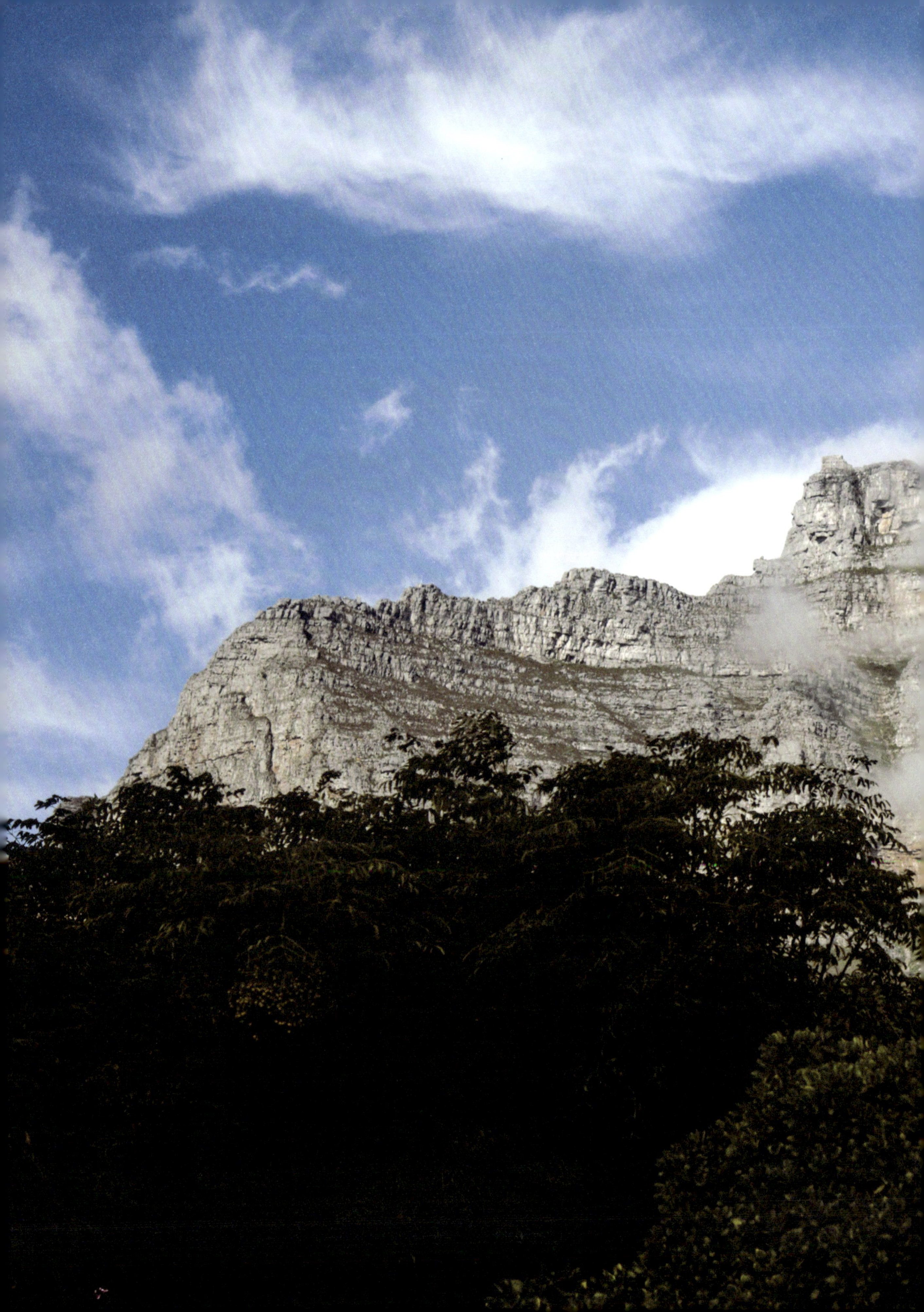

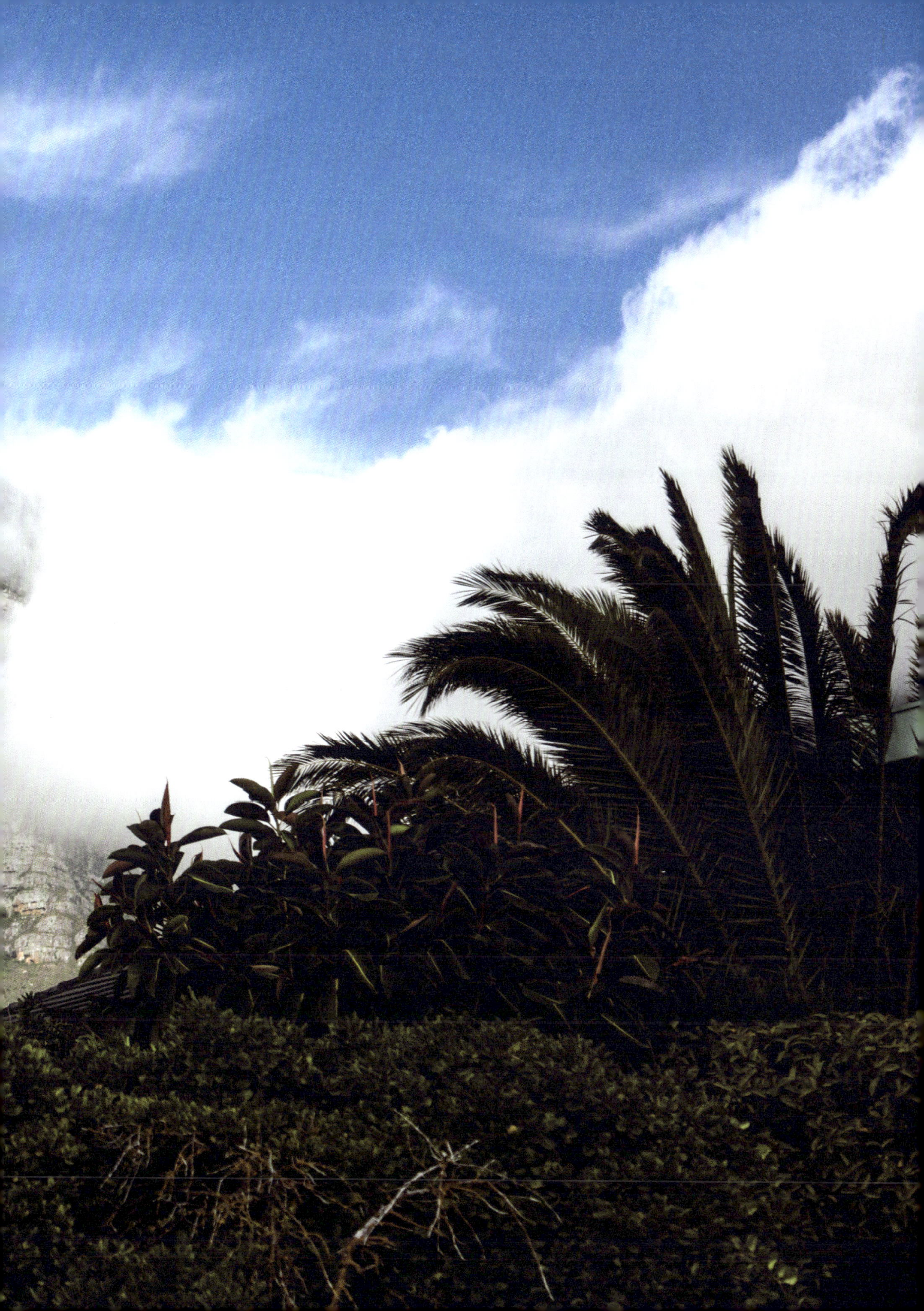

The small house stands peacefully between two overwhelming natural phenomena: Table Mountain and the Atlantic Ocean.

The home of Thirza Schaap and Braz Feskens is one of the few remaining older houses in Camps Bay. It is a modest 50s bungalow that was restored by Thirza and Braz in a seemingly effortless way. It was primarily a serious paint job that gave the house its current charm.

Thirza, Braz, and their son Bruin left the Netherlands seven years ago. They had felt the need for a change for quite a while. In search of a new adventure and a different lifestyle, the family ended up in Cape Town. Working as a photographer and digital operator respectively, Thirza and Braz had travelled quite a lot for their jobs, and they had gotten to know Cape Town fairly well during earlier work trips.

For the first six months after the move, they rented a house in Camps Bay to see if they were ready to say goodbye to their lives in Amsterdam. Soon it became clear that their new way of living made them happy. Bruin, then 15, quickly grew accustomed to his new school and made new friends.

Not much later they found this house. It was love at first sight, and they decided to buy the house almost overnight. For Thirza and Braz being so close to the ocean is an everyday luxury. The beach is just five minutes from their house and early morning walks along the coast are a daily routine.

Thirza also found a new goal and art project here in Camps Bay. Shocked by the amount of plastic waste that pollutes the oceans around the world, she began to collect washed-up plastic from the beach. Back at the house, she creates small installations using the plastic waste and takes beautiful photos of the results. Thirza realises that this does not solve the problem. But it is her way of making people aware of the impact that the intensive use of plastic has on our environment, and how our great oceans suffer from all the plastic we are thoughtlessly throwing away.

The kitchen overlooks the massive Table Mountain and the open living room has a beautiful view of the wild ocean. Both sights provide the residents with a set of breathtaking and ever-changing visual spectacles: whether it is the thin clouds hovering over the Table Mountain like a white tablecloth, the dolphins leaping up from the waves or the spectacular sight of big whales swimming close to the coast.

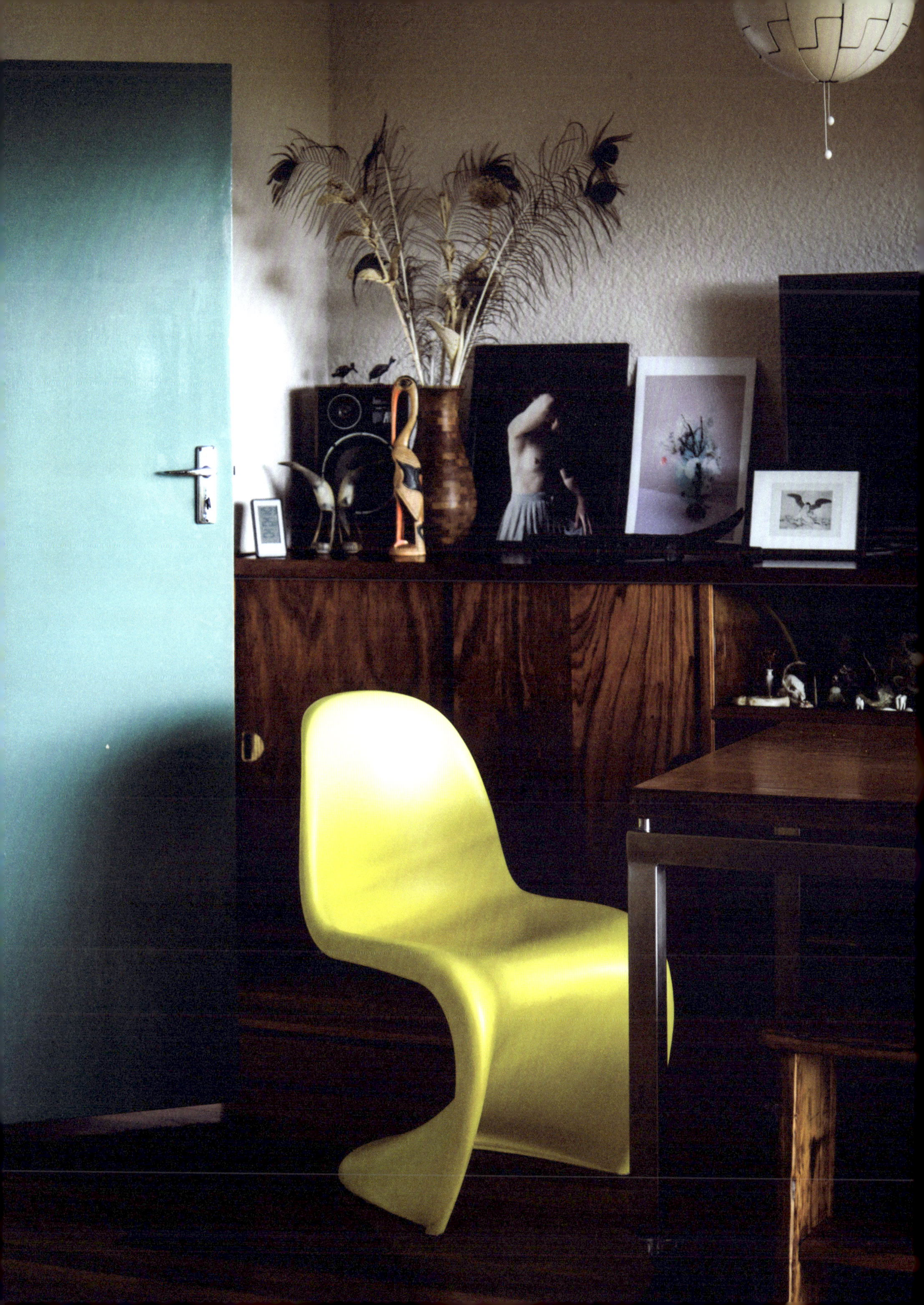

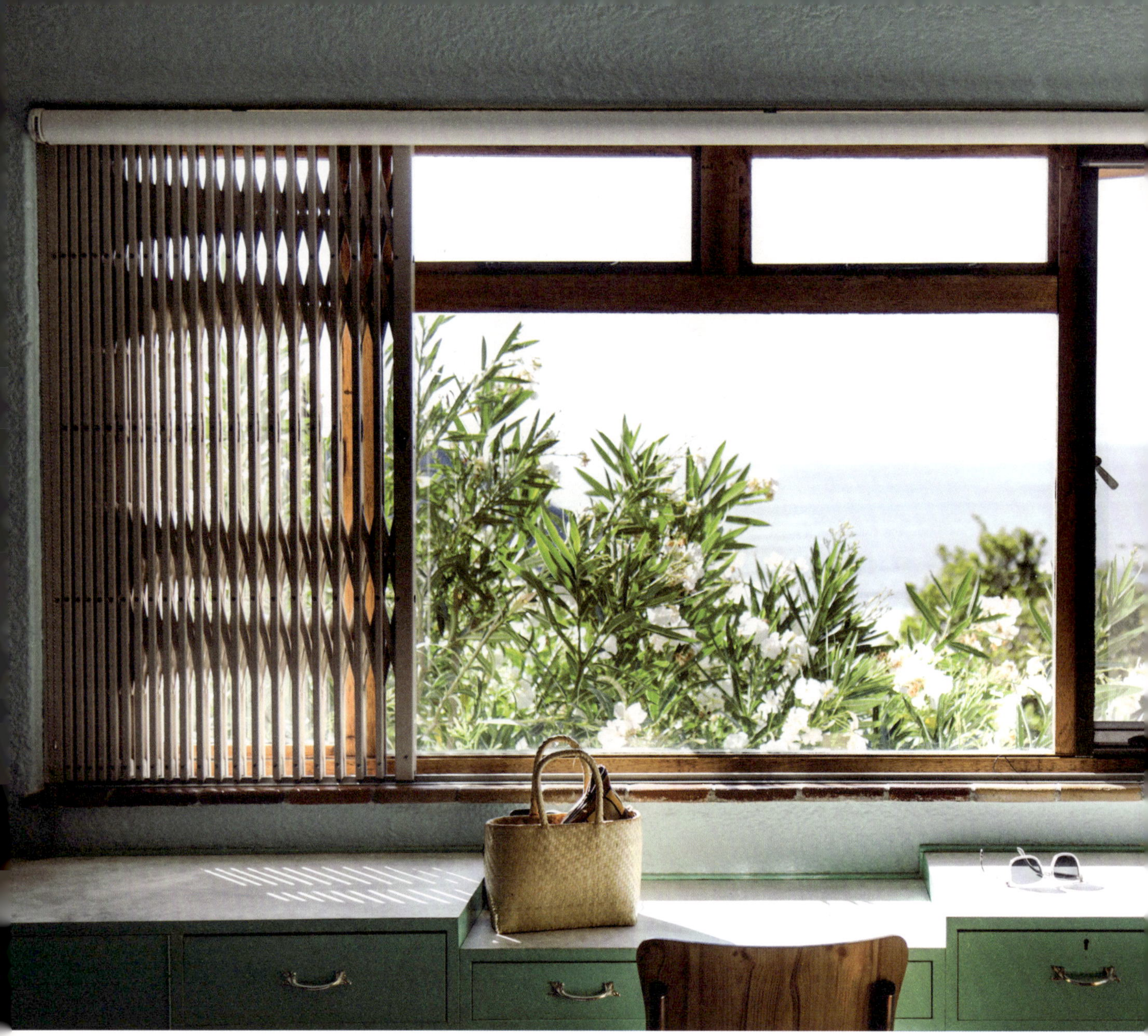

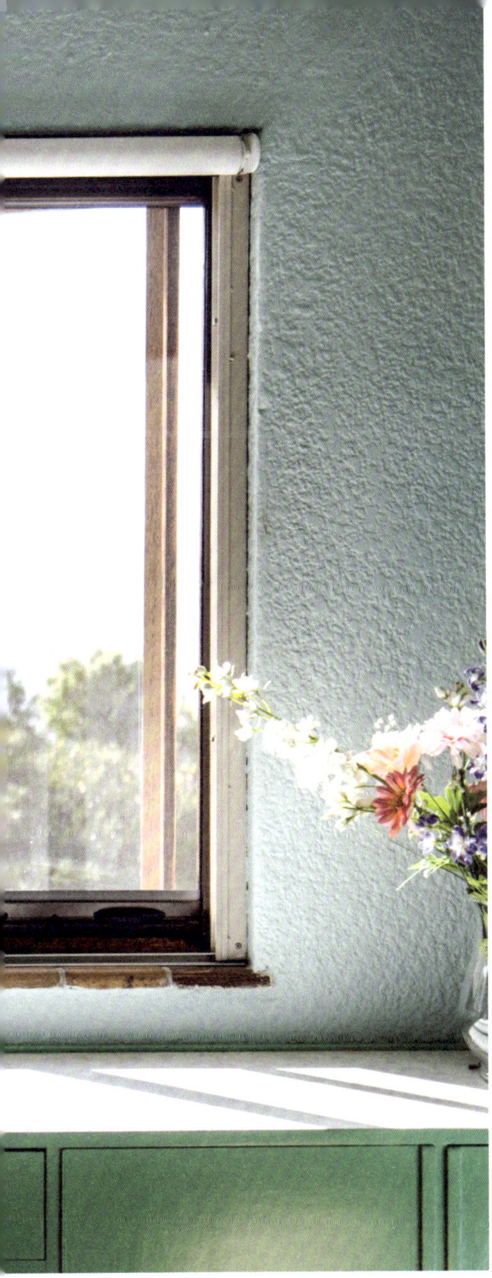

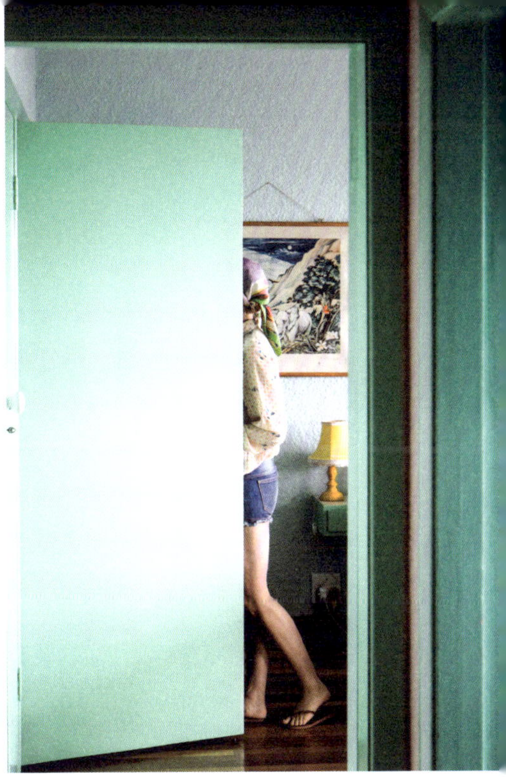

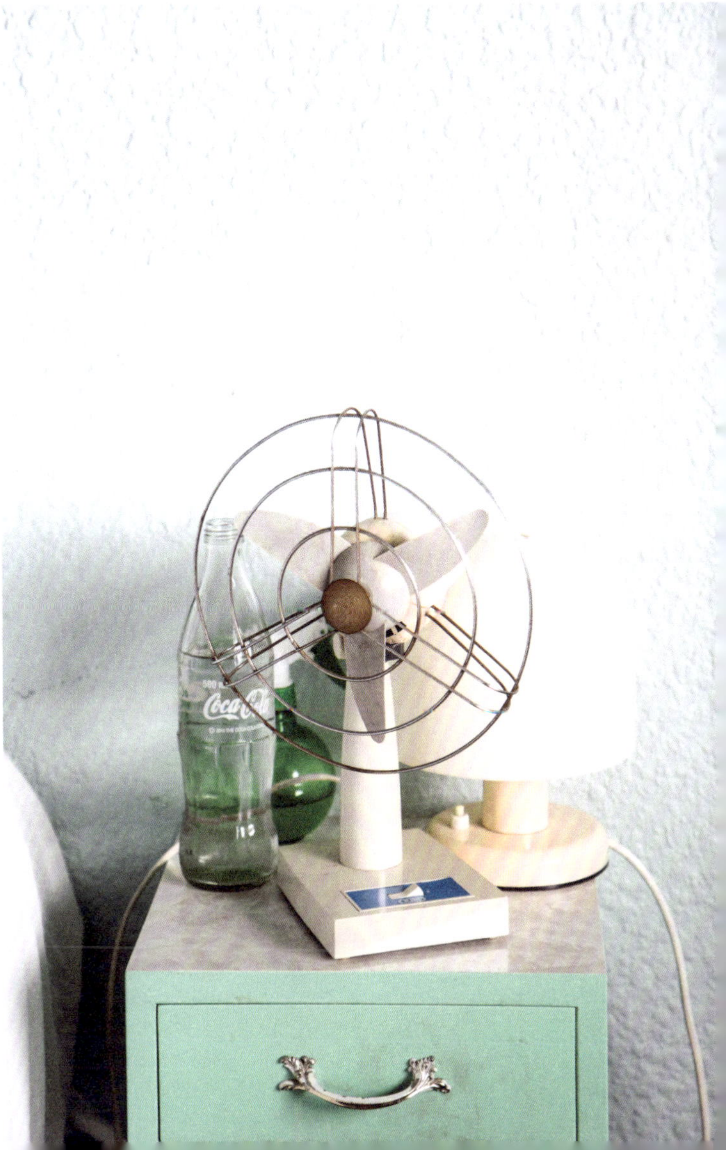

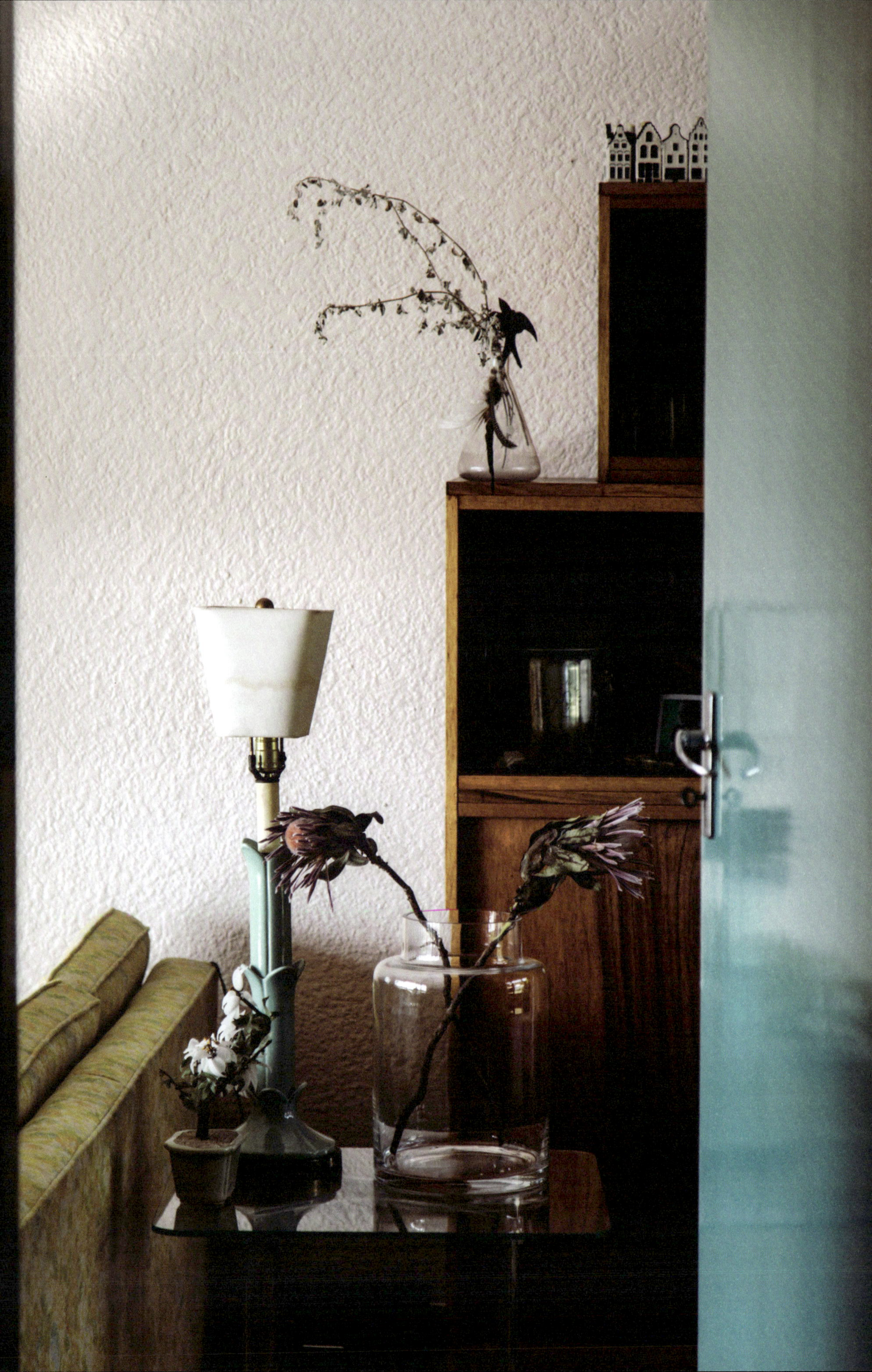

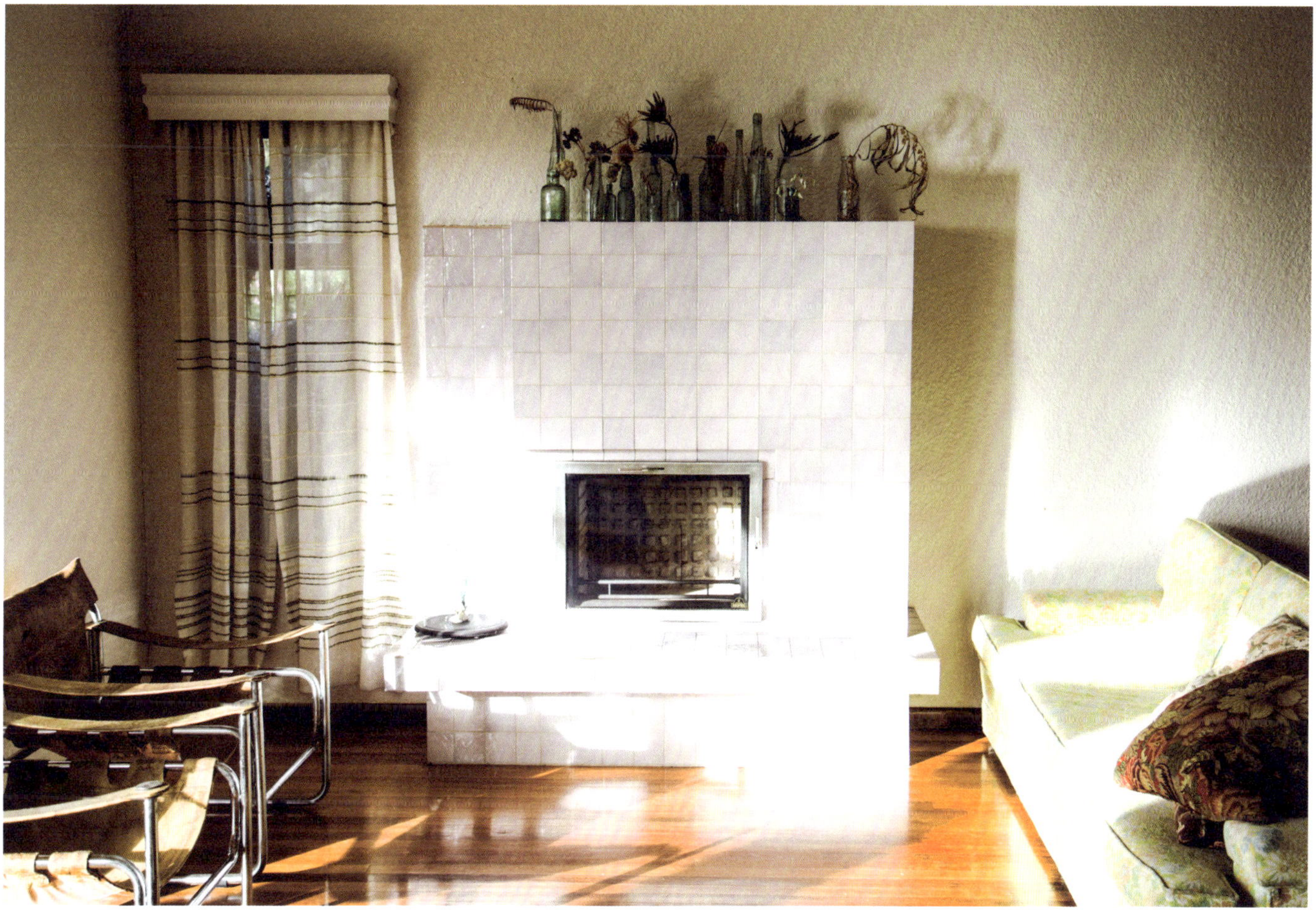

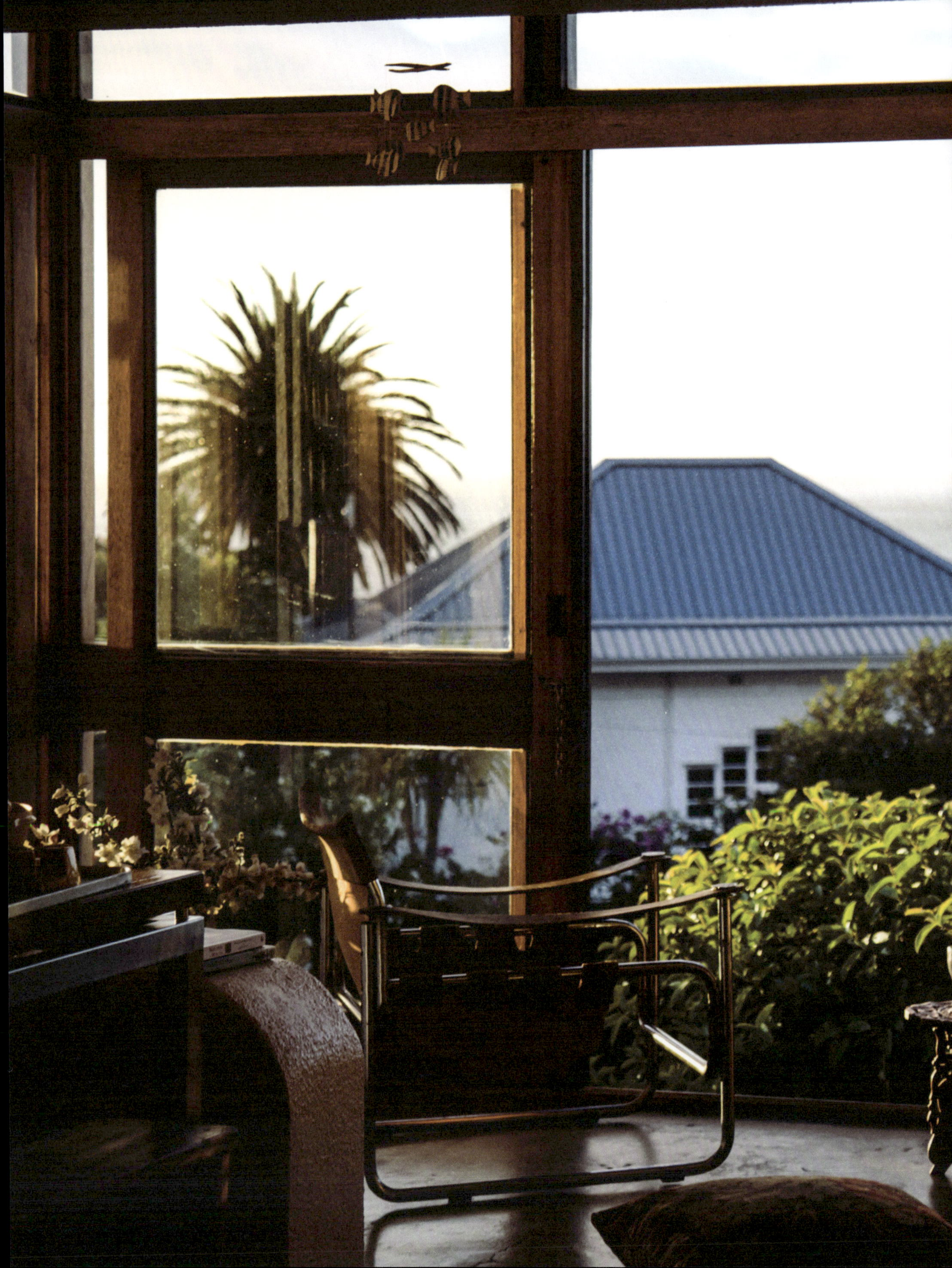

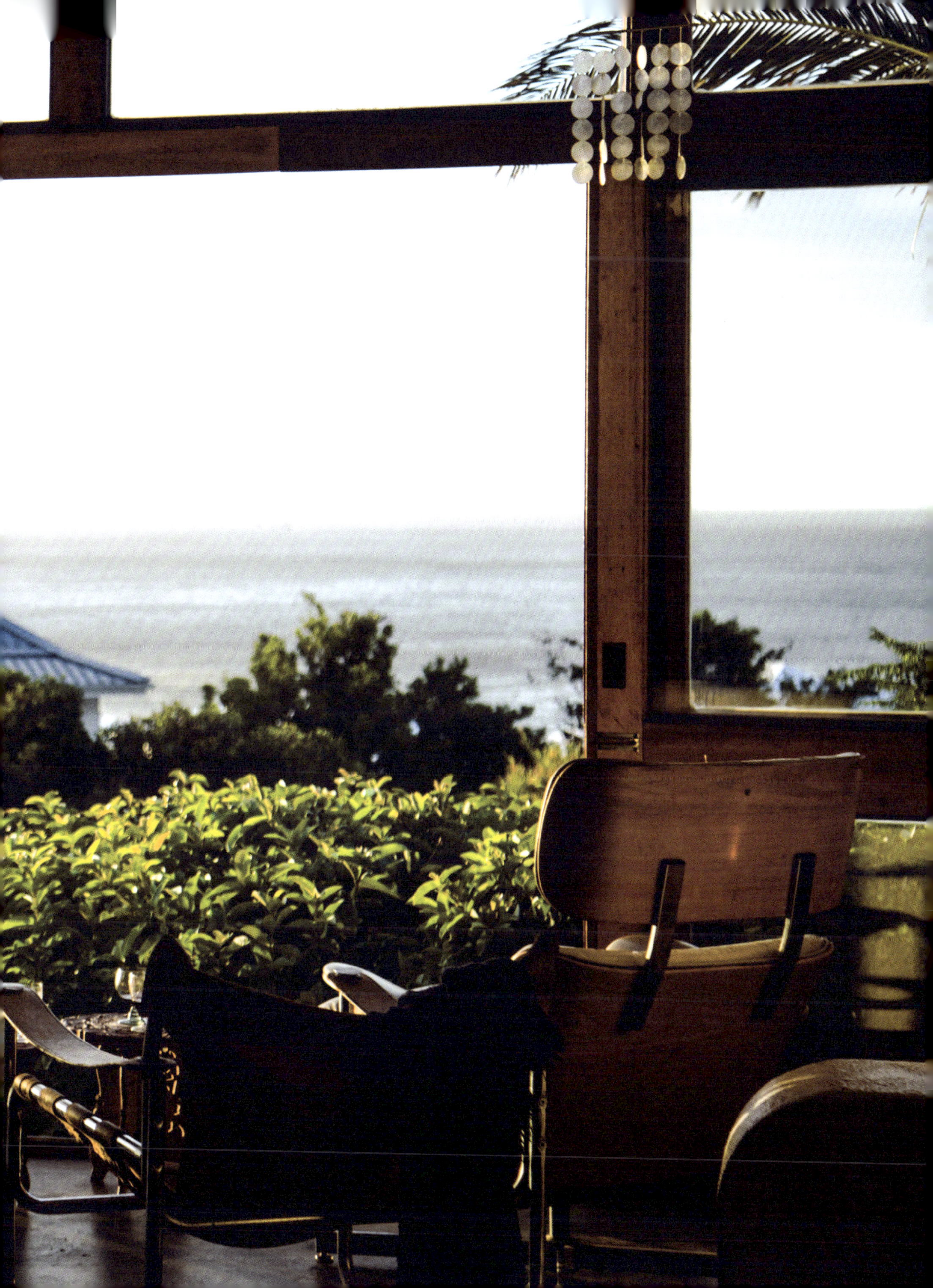

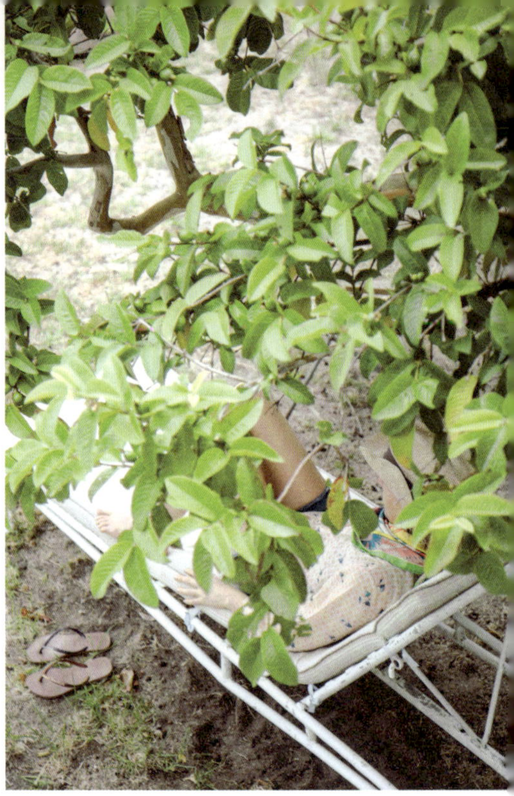

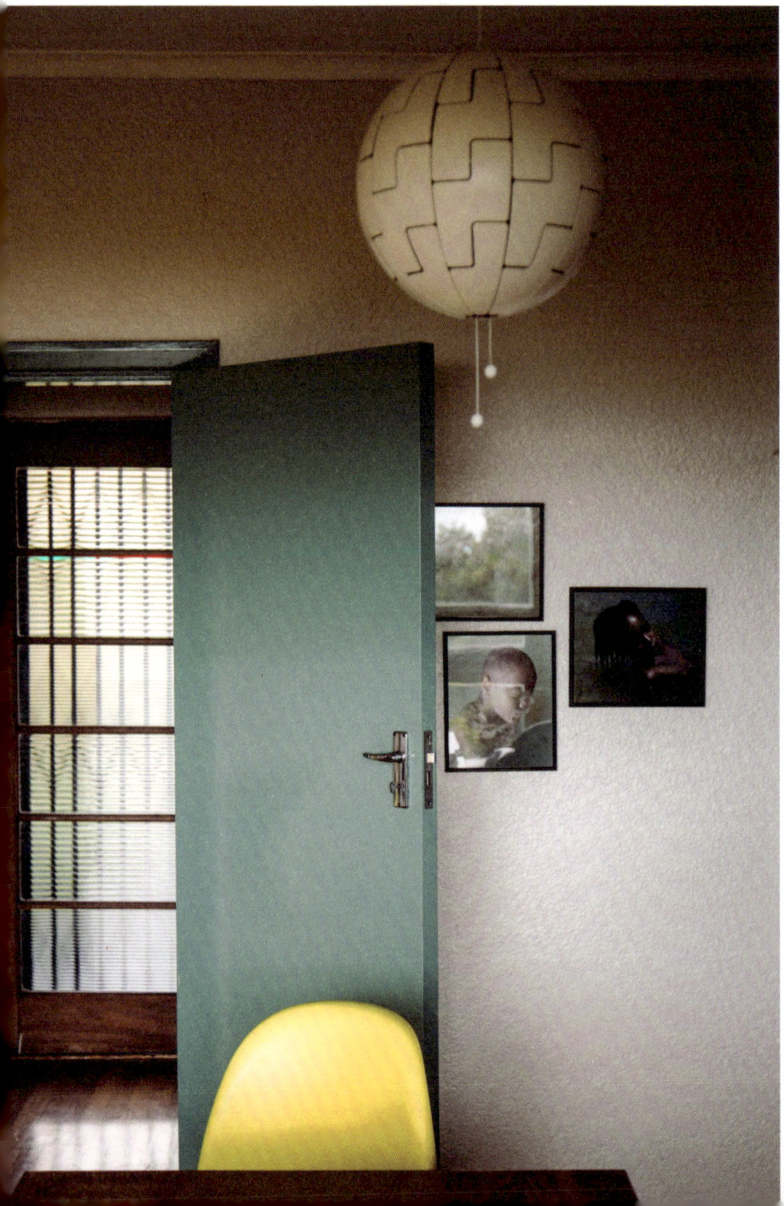

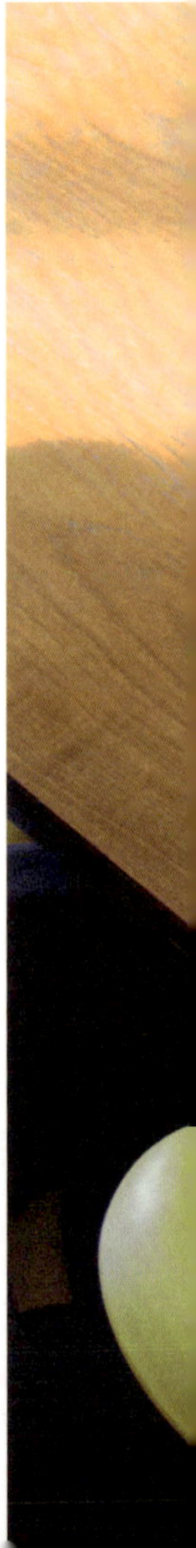

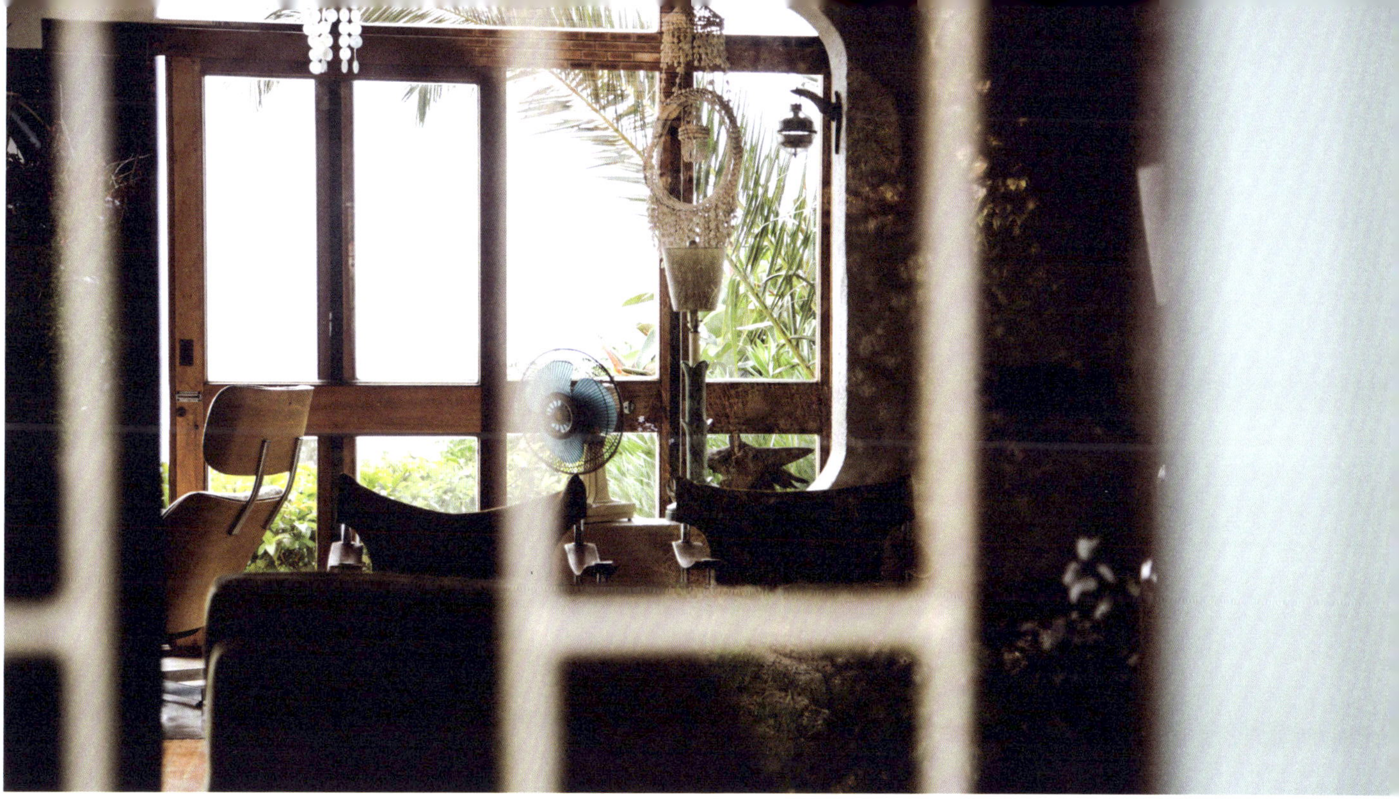

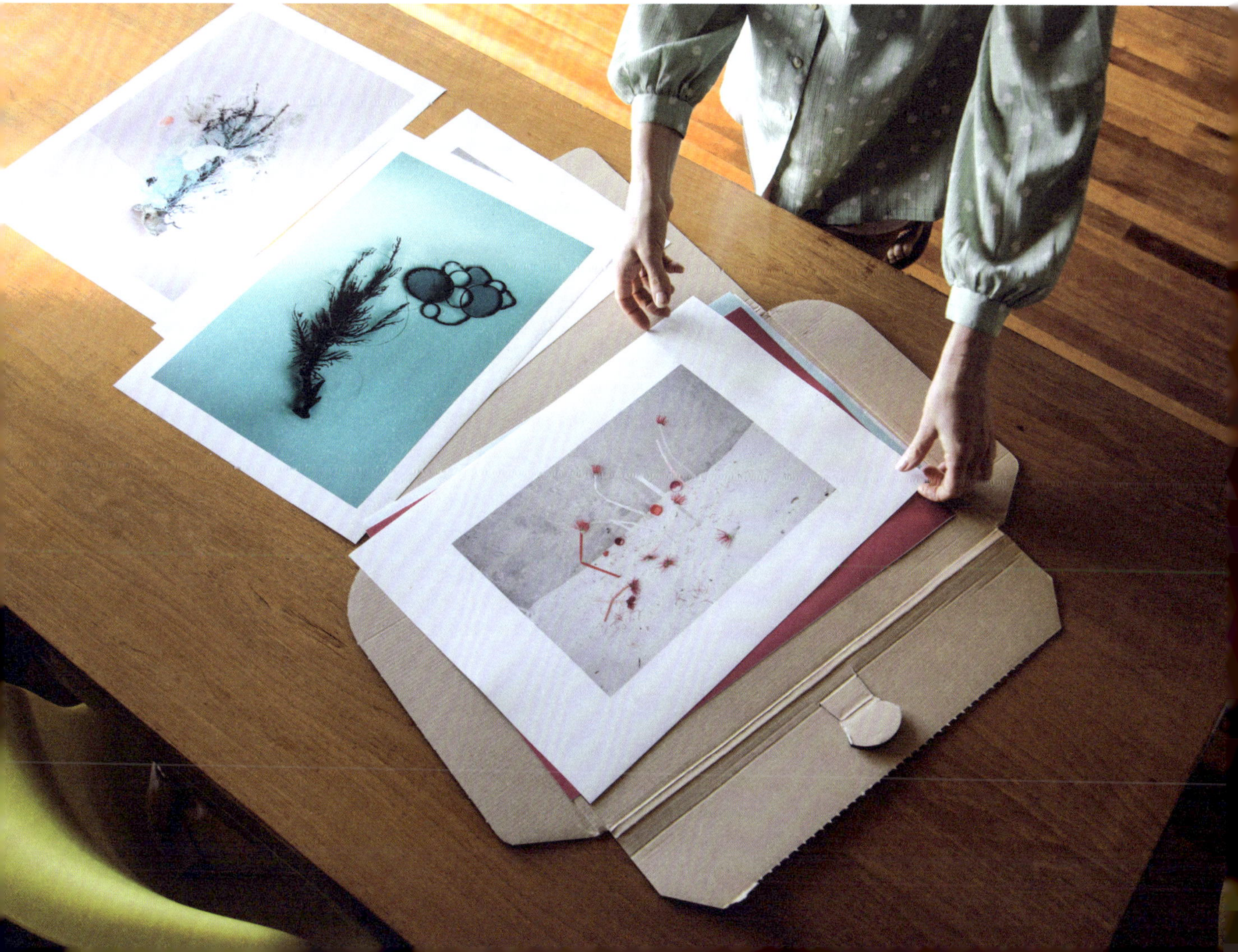

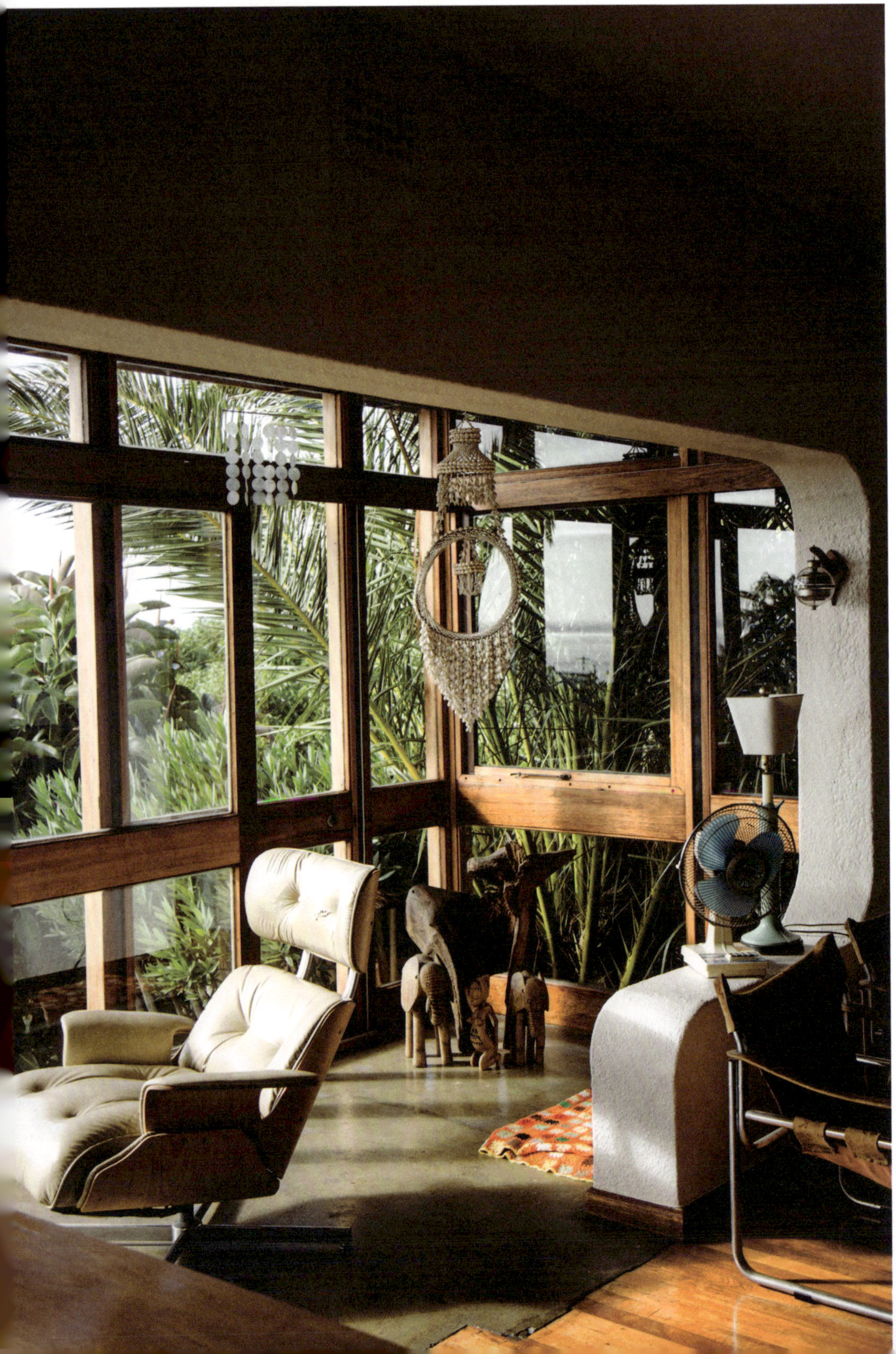

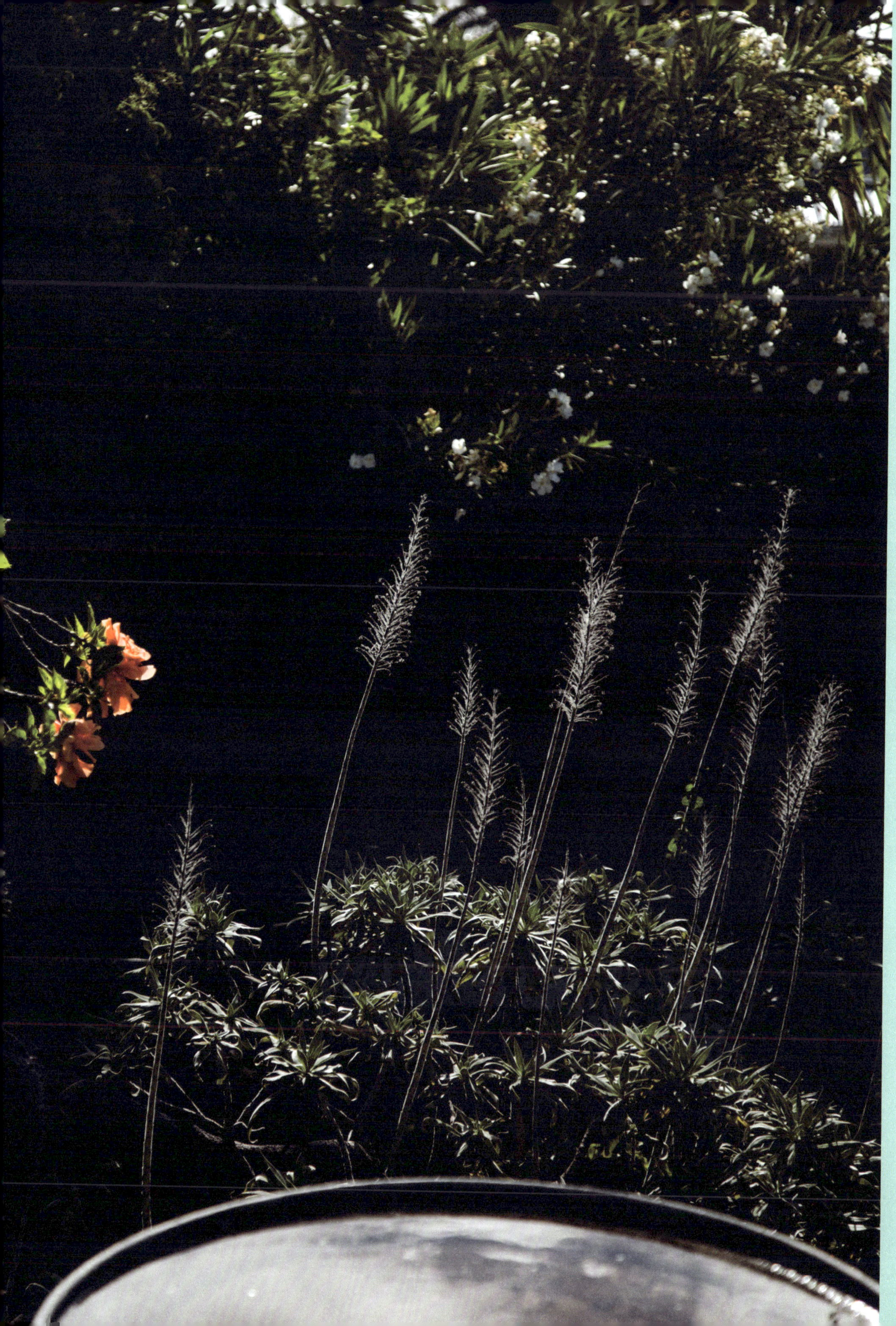

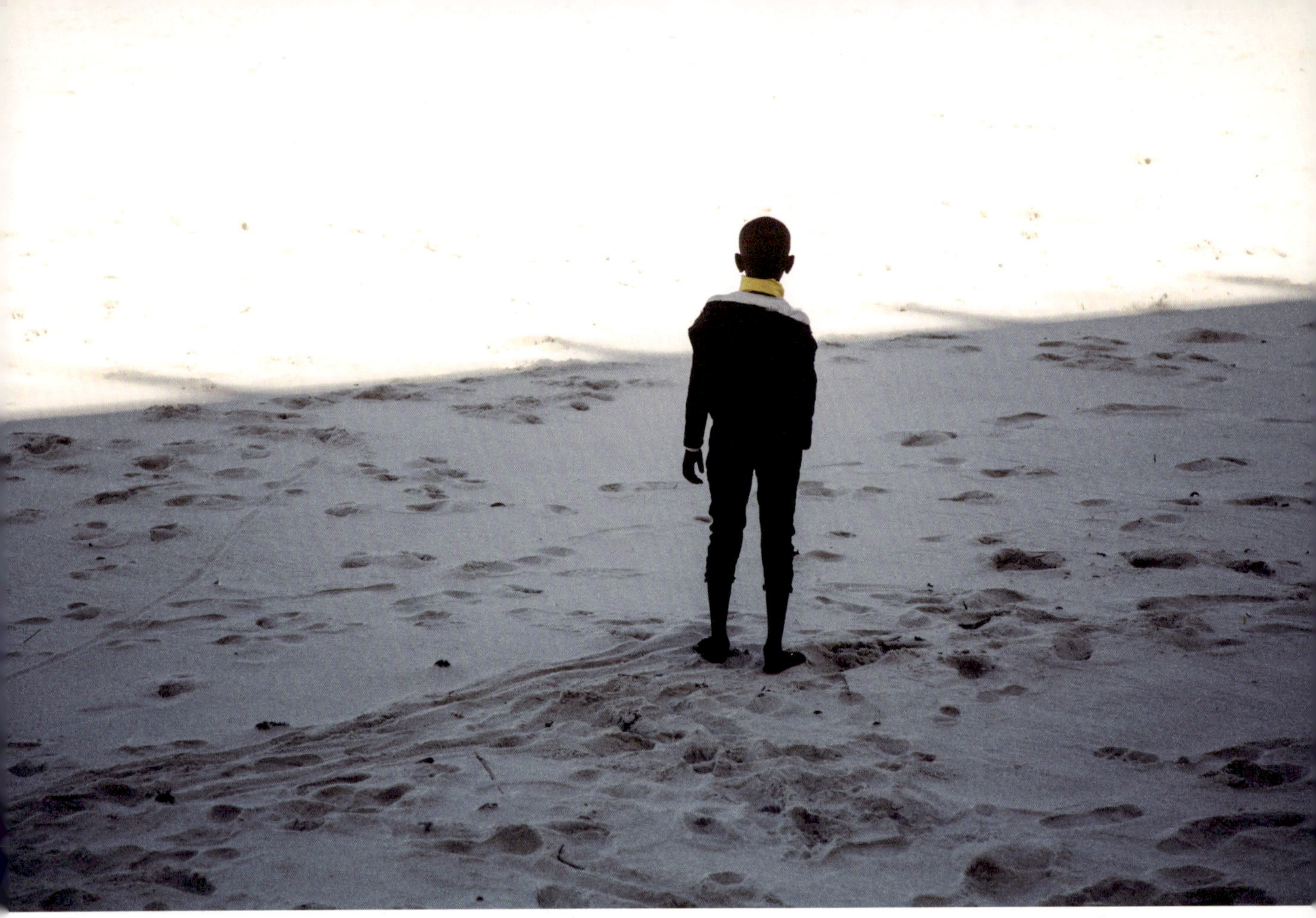

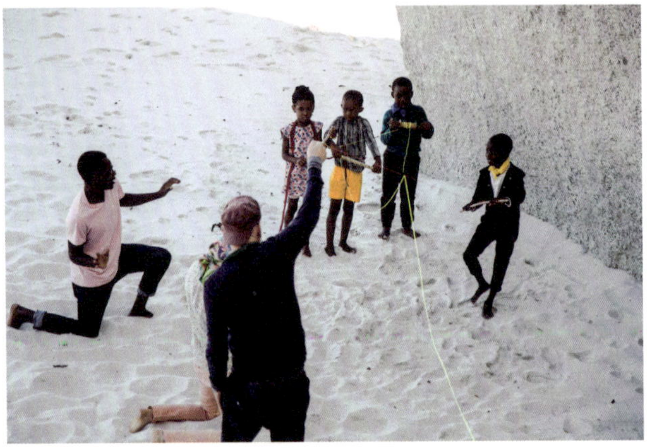

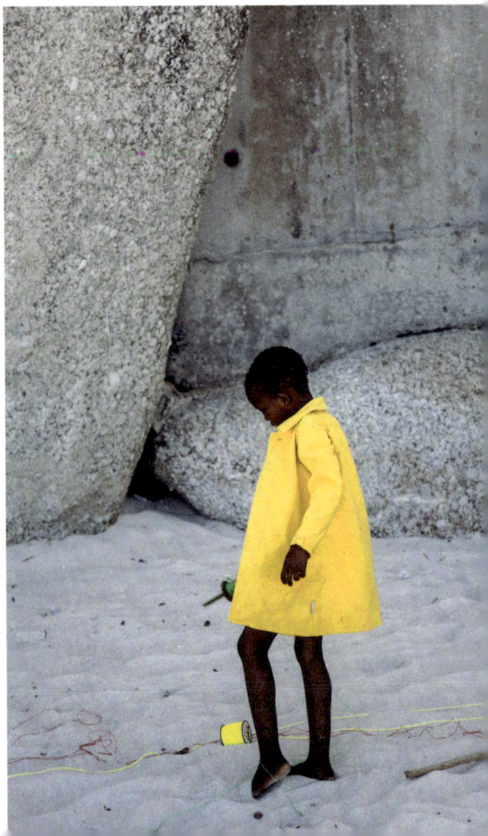

Backstage at a Sunday photoshoot

On our Clifton Beach set, we pulled out the clothes and large handmade kites shaped like eyes and other colourful figures that we brought with us from the Netherlands. We were shooting a fashion story for Milk Magazine, which we organised together with Thirza Schaap. A group of friends from the nearby town of Hout Bay were our models, and their playful imagination proved a valuable contribution to the story we wanted to tell. We all had a wonderful Sunday afternoon.

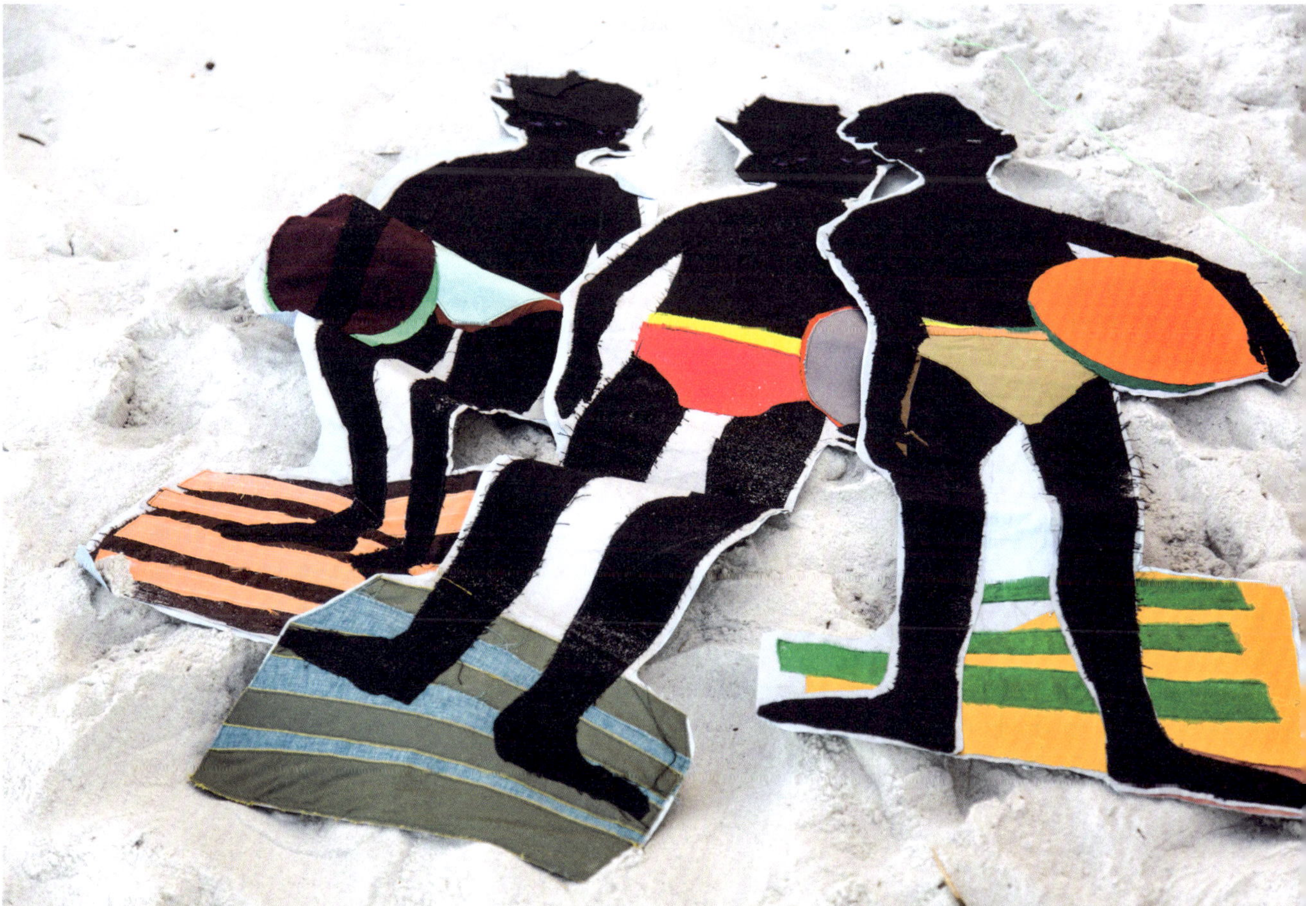

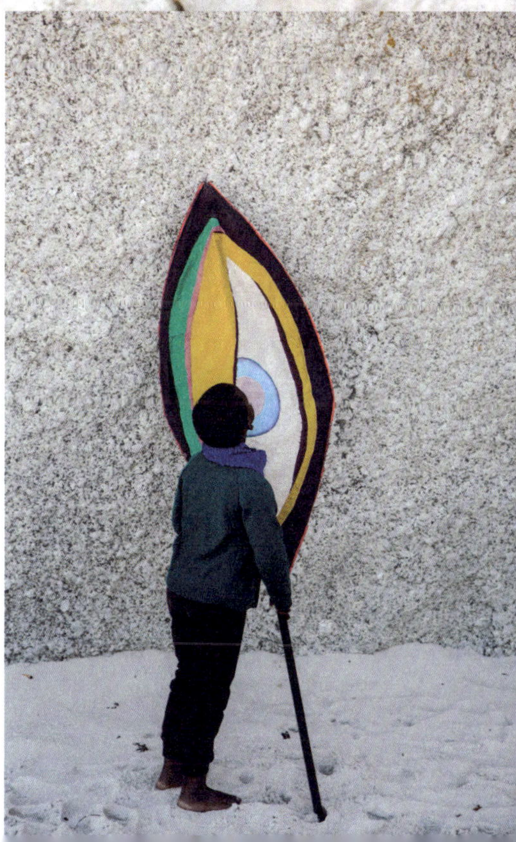

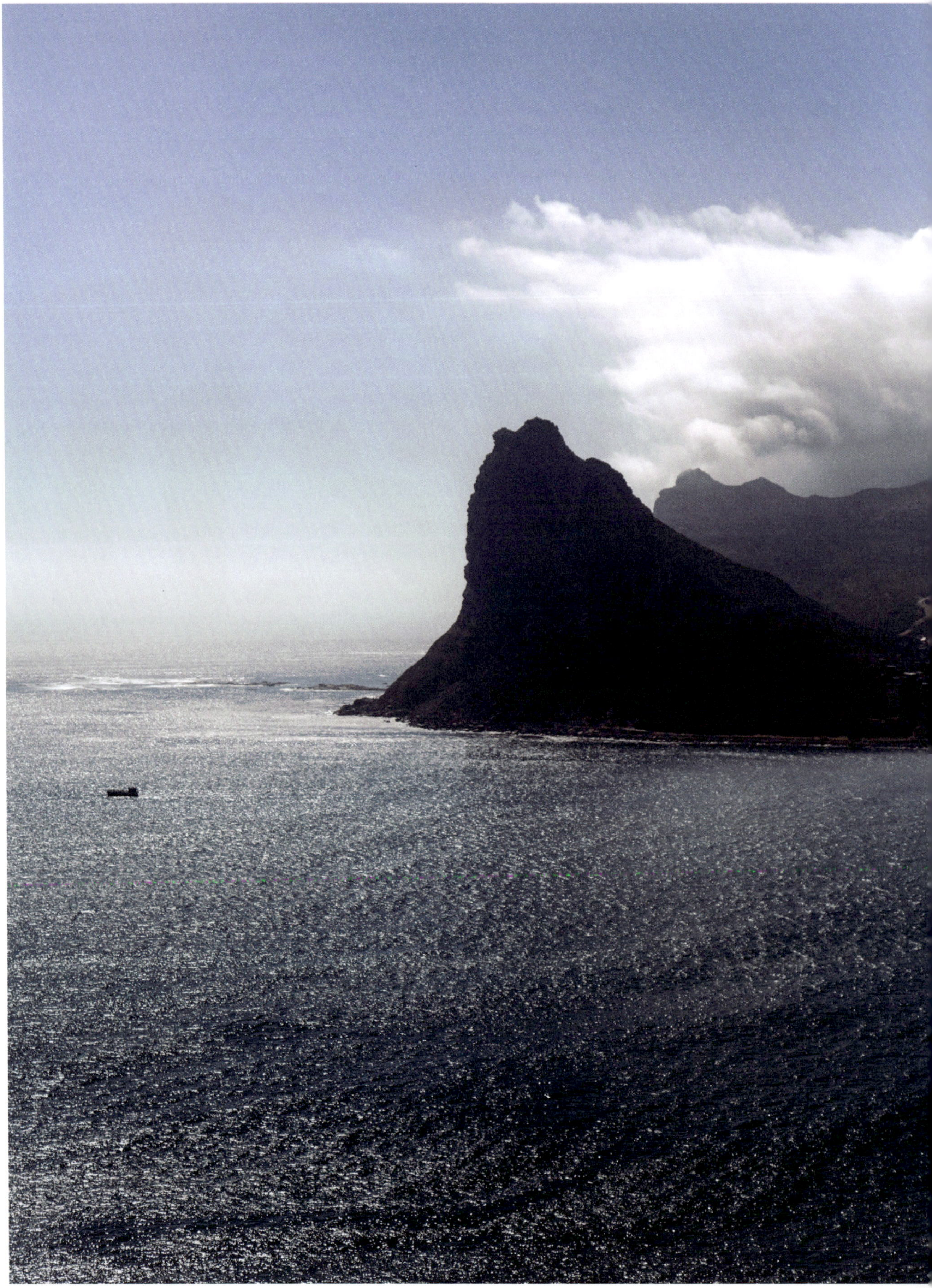

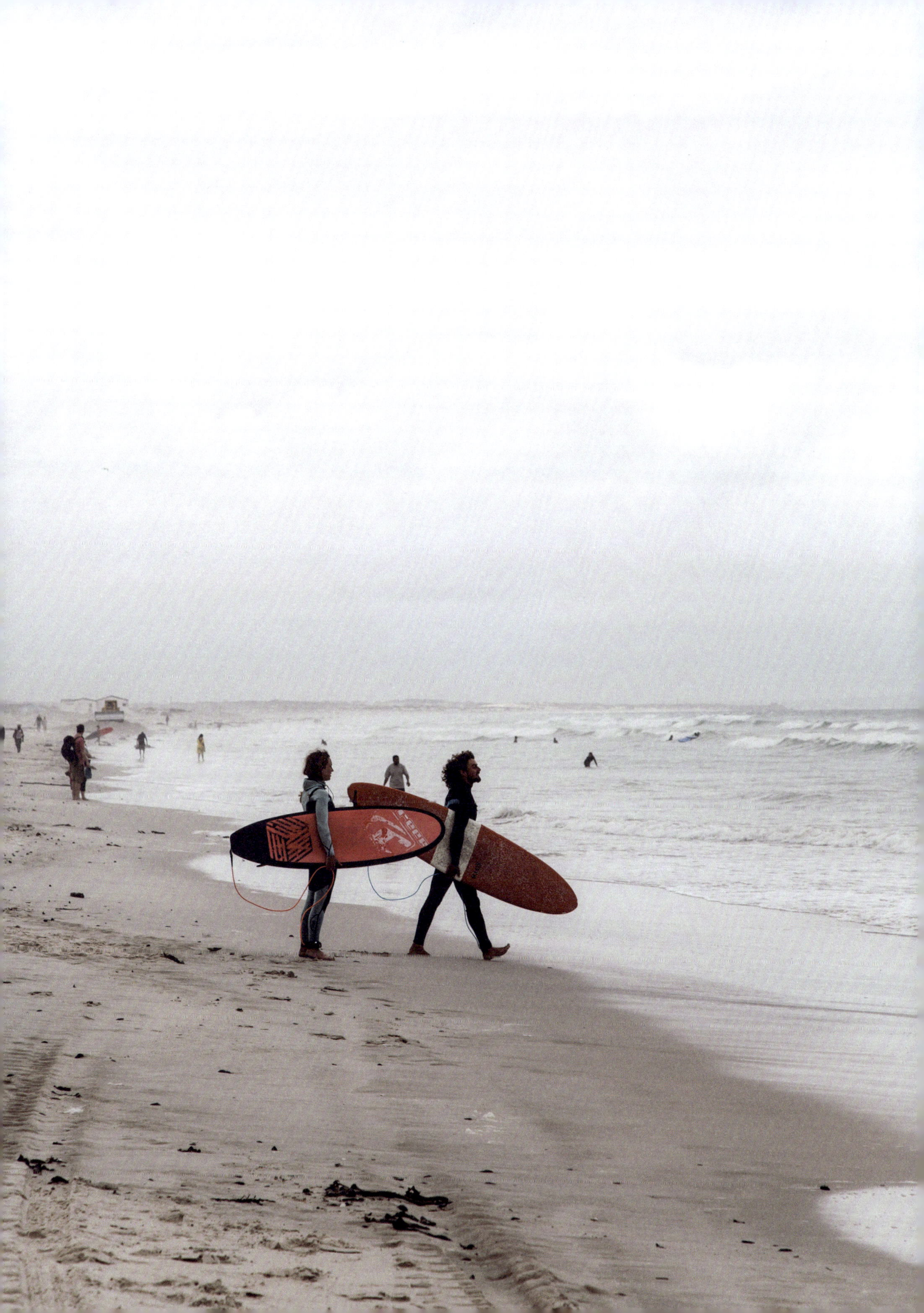

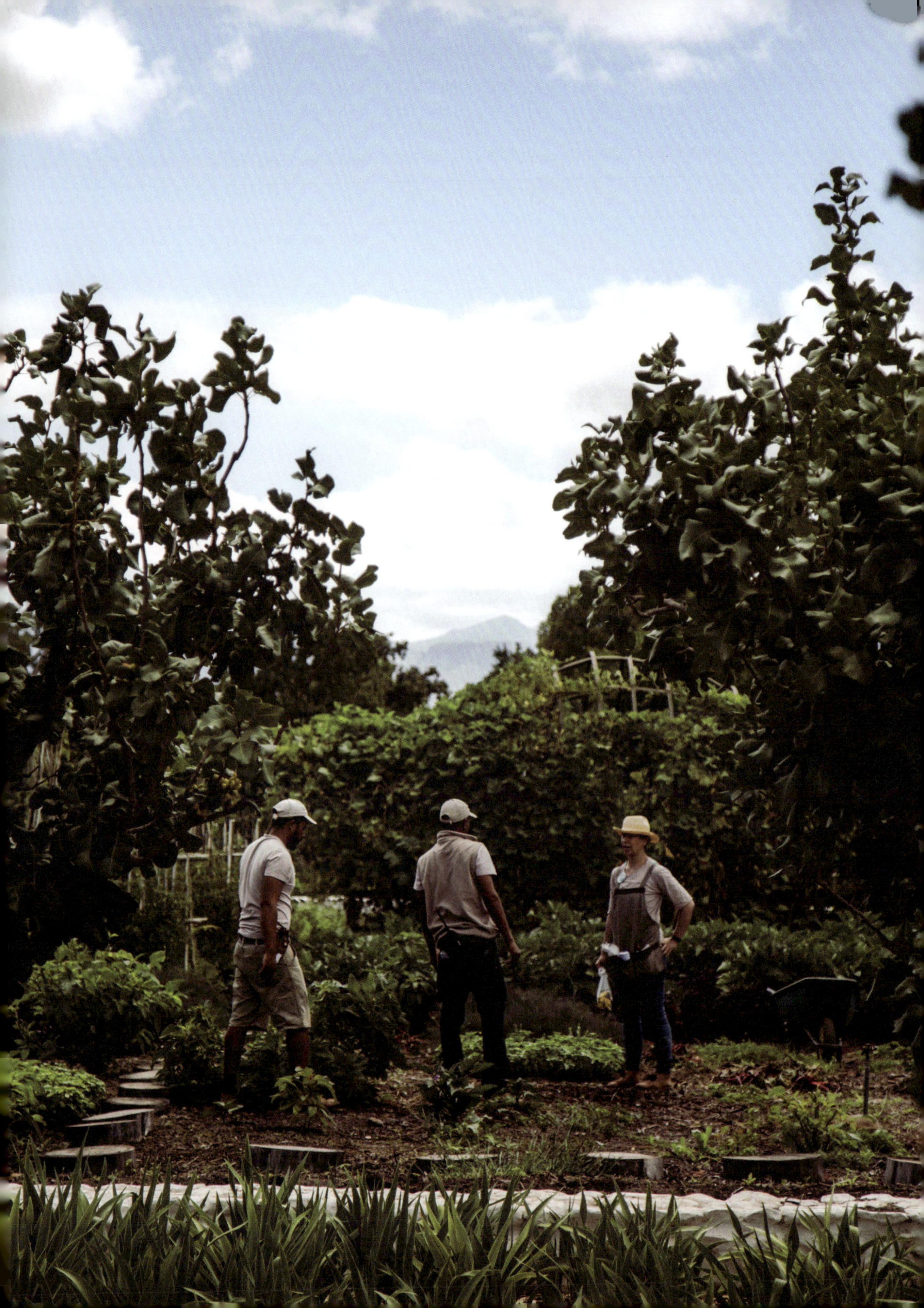

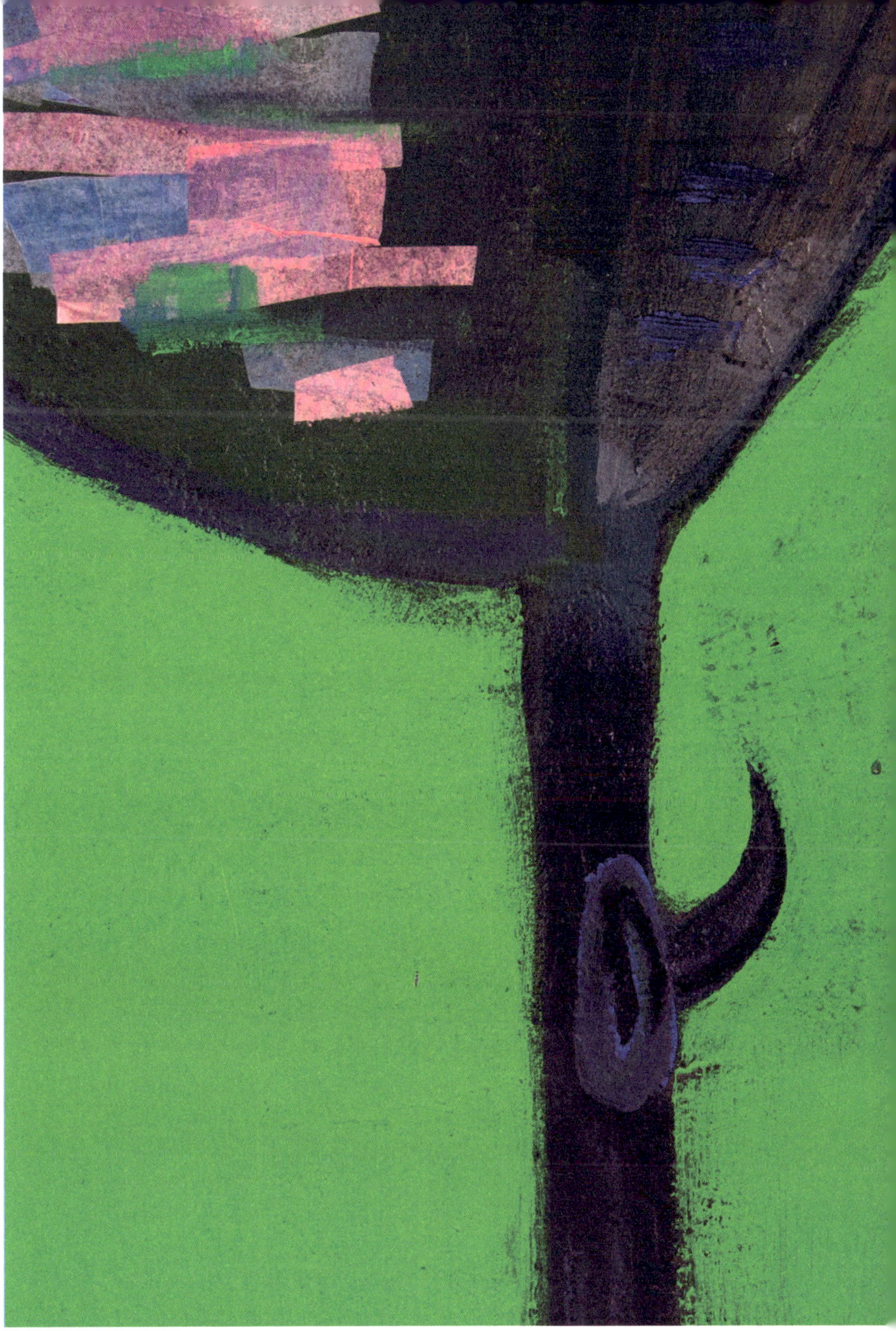

Babylonstoren

The land and the early 18th-century Cape Dutch farm buildings on the estate inspired Karen Roos to found her agricultural and culinary utopia. Explaining what Babylonstoren stands for in just a few words is complicated. It combines tradition with quality, it is both contemporary and earthy, idealistic and a business. When you roam around the estate, you realise how much passion and hard work it takes to grow all this beauty and deliciousness.

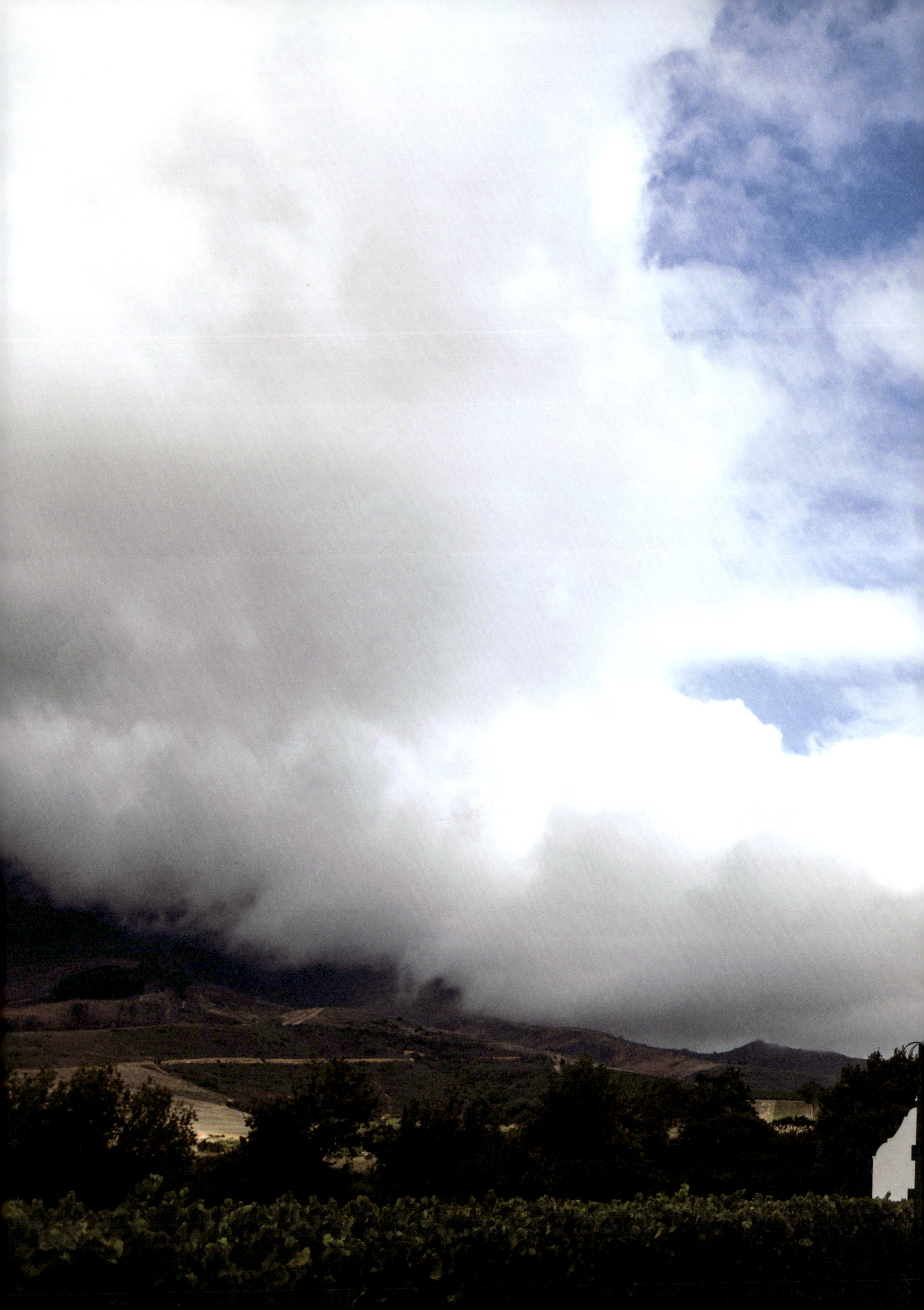

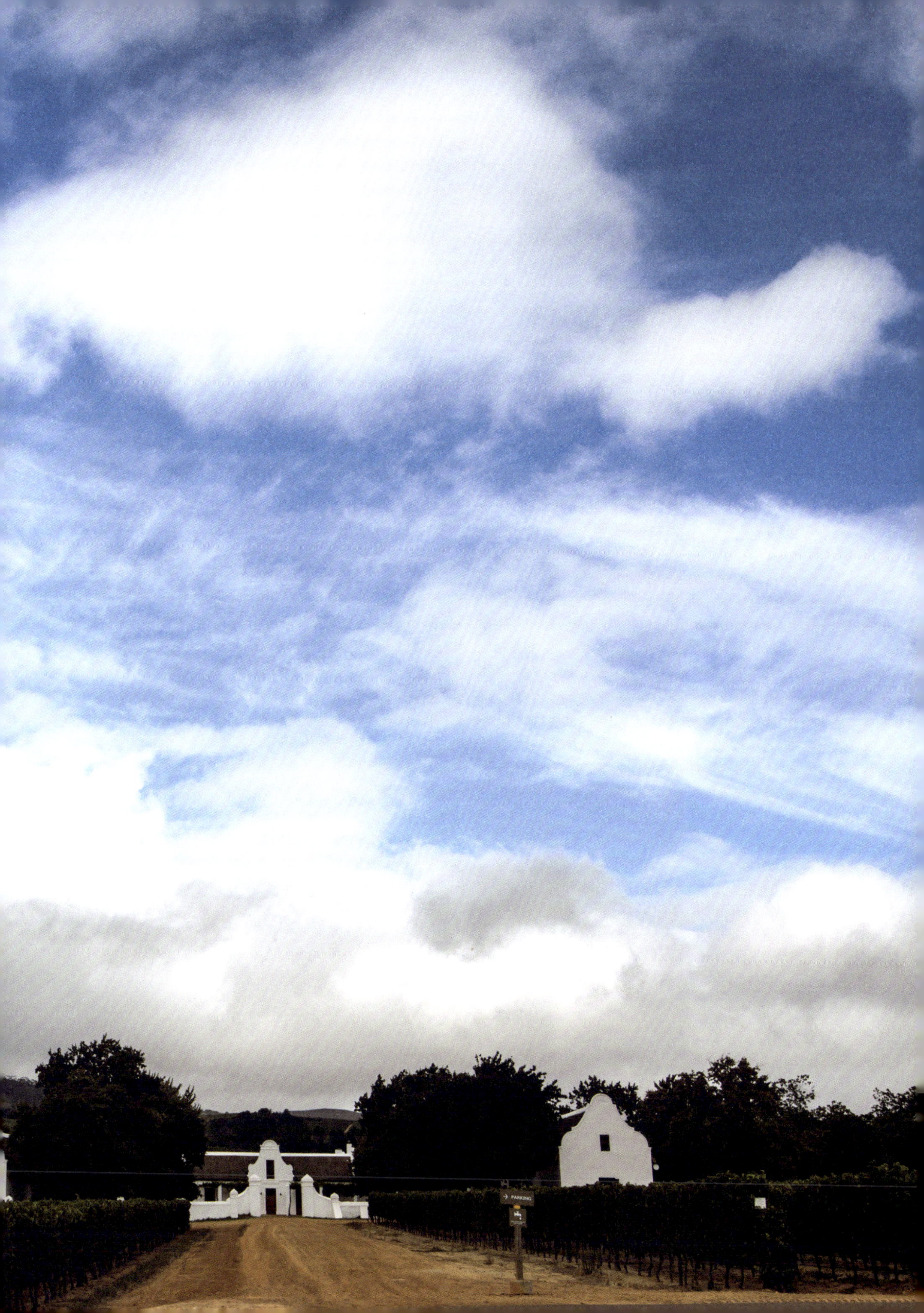
PARKING

2

Weskus

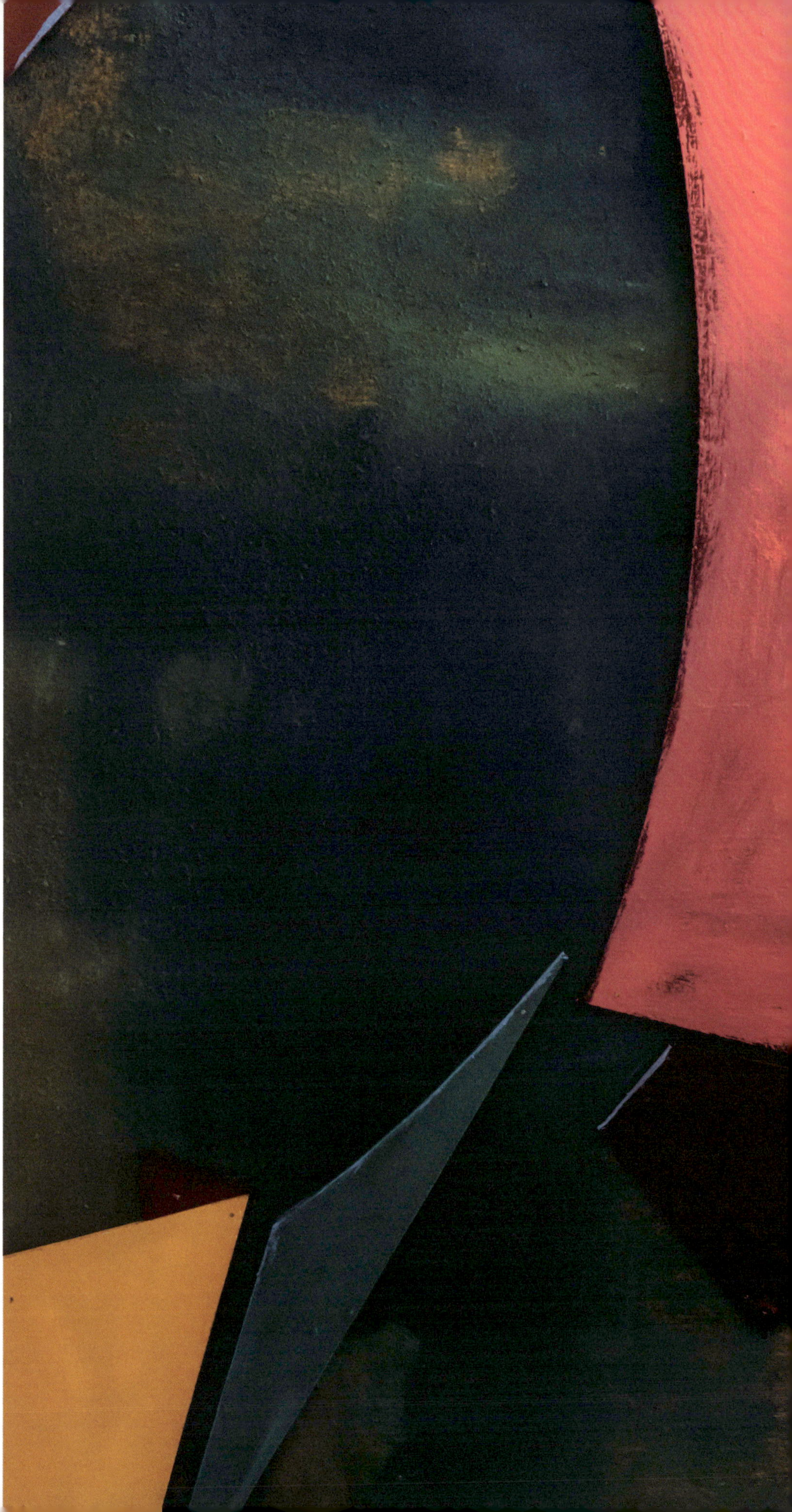

40

From Cape Town we drove north along the coast to the old fishing village of Paternoster, with its characteristic whitewashed houses.

Our first stop was Langebaan Lagoon, where the funnel-shaped bay provides world-class conditions for kitesurfers. The brightly coloured kites create quite the visual spectacle as the surfers glide across the lagoon at great speed. The nearby national park is a tranquil and cool spot. The many unique bird species are the main attraction, producing the only sound you will hear besides your own footsteps.

The West Coast offers a more varied scenery. Dunes and long sandy beaches alternate with sections where large boulders seem to have been cast into the sea. Large, dark brown, angry-looking rocks, on which the incoming waves break, transforming them into a white foaming swirling body of water that works its way through and around the smaller rocks. An almost hypnotic scene that never ceases to fascinate.

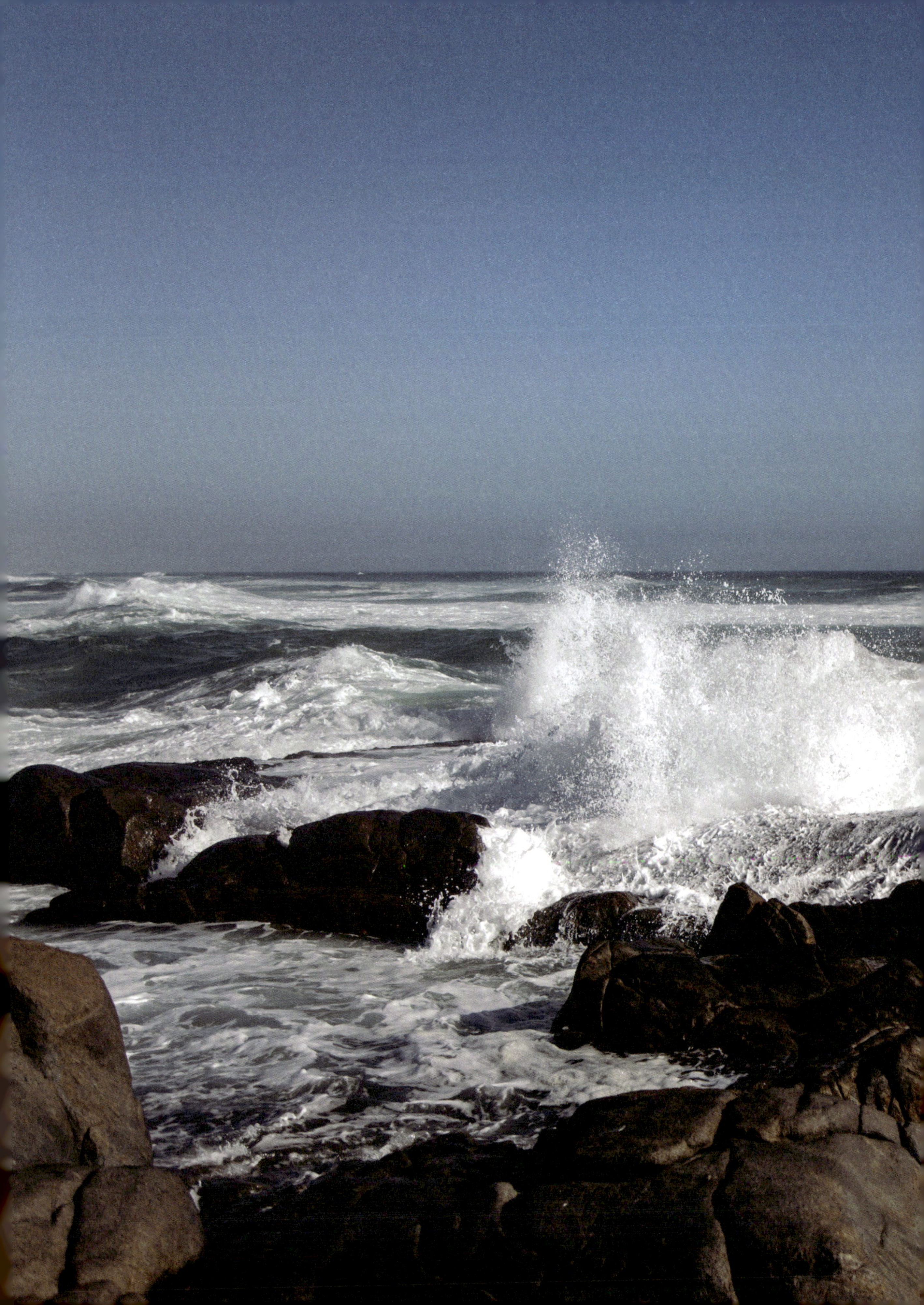

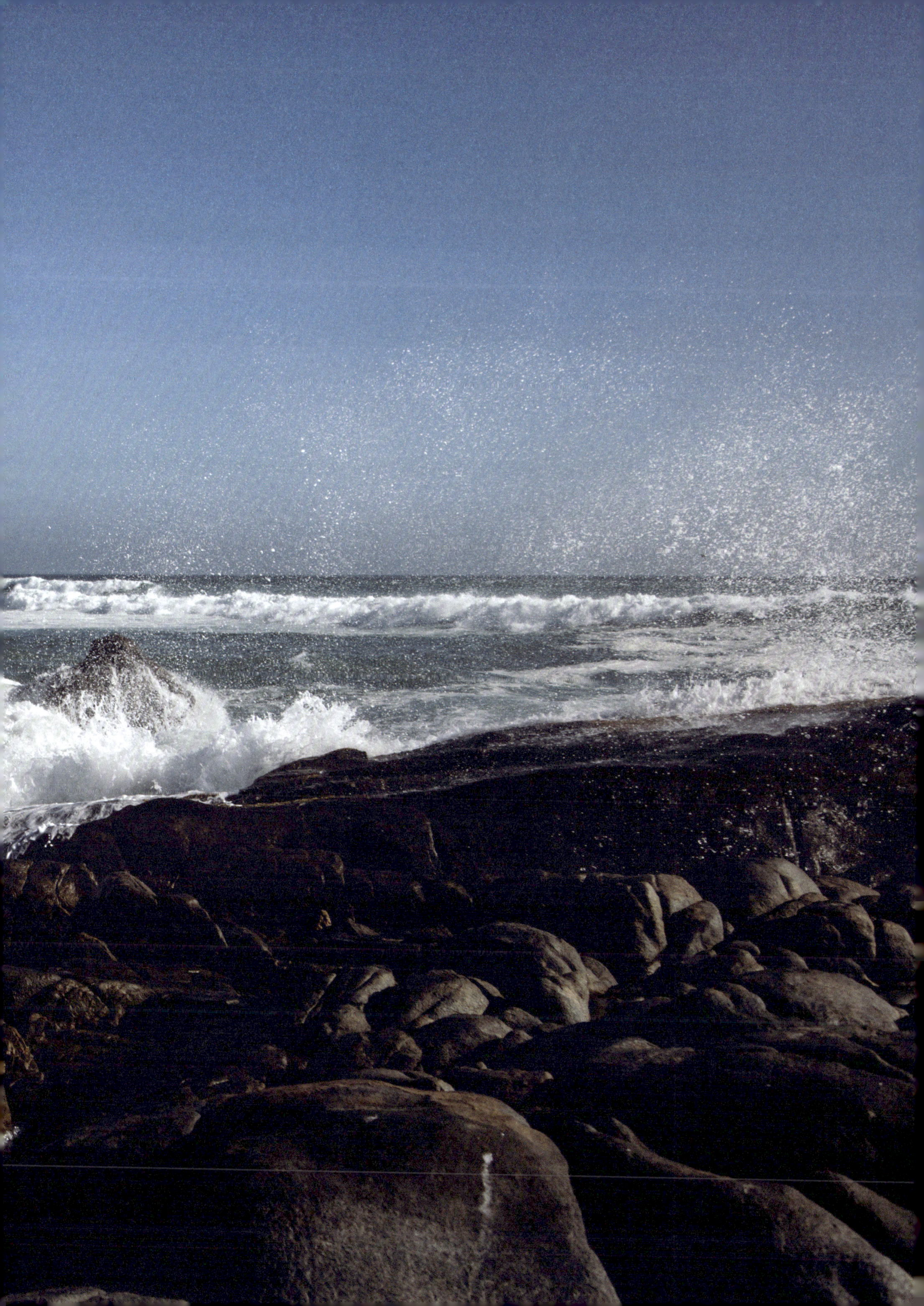

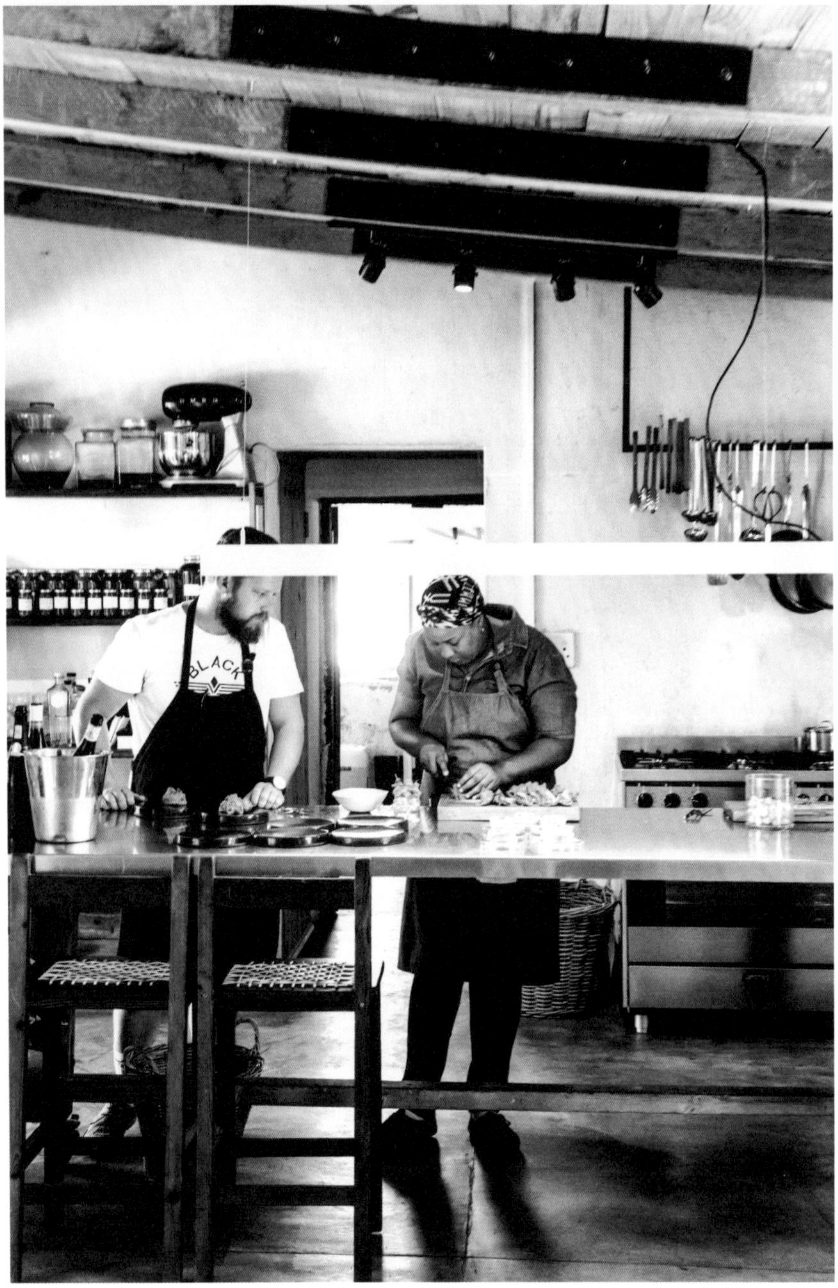

Wolfgat

Kobus van der Merwe opened his restaurant in the fishing village of Paternoster just a few years ago. It is an unassuming place with just 20 seats that overlooks the ocean and is only open for lunch. The restaurant soon started making waves in the area, and the rest of the country. In 2019 it was named the world's best restaurant. Kobus and his small team prepare the most refined dishes with ingredients they forage for every day in the surrounding dunes, combining them with what the ocean has to offer.

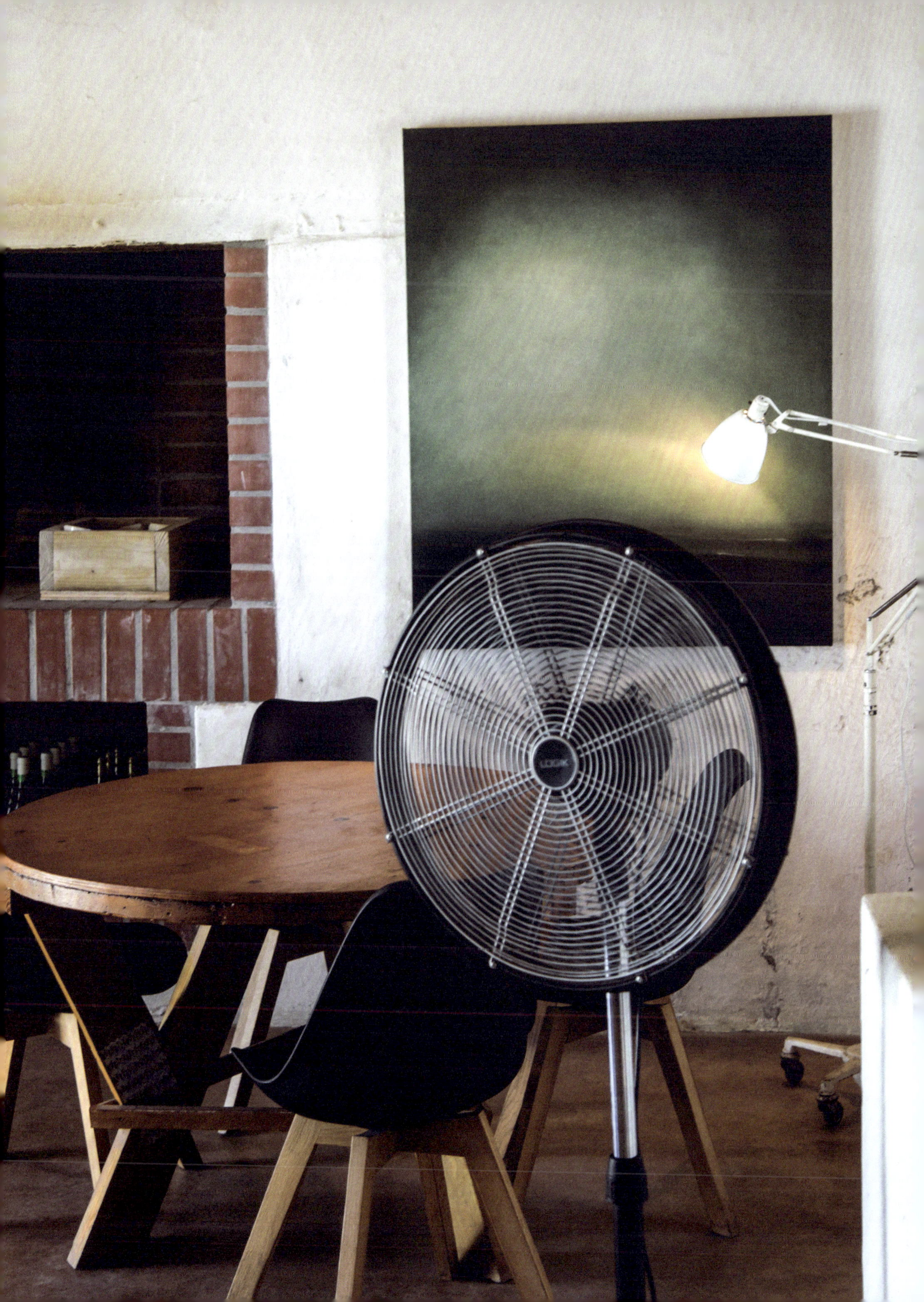

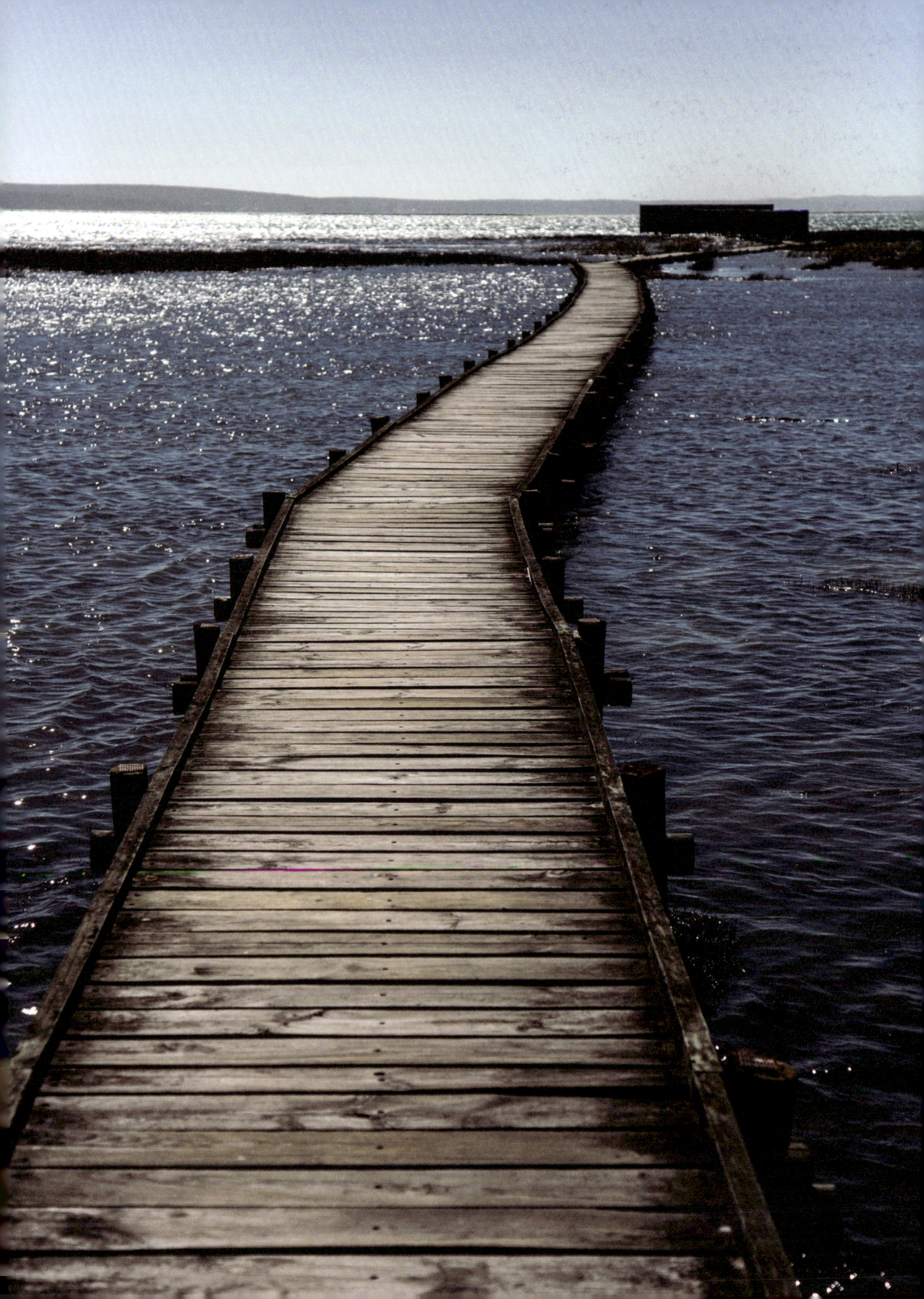

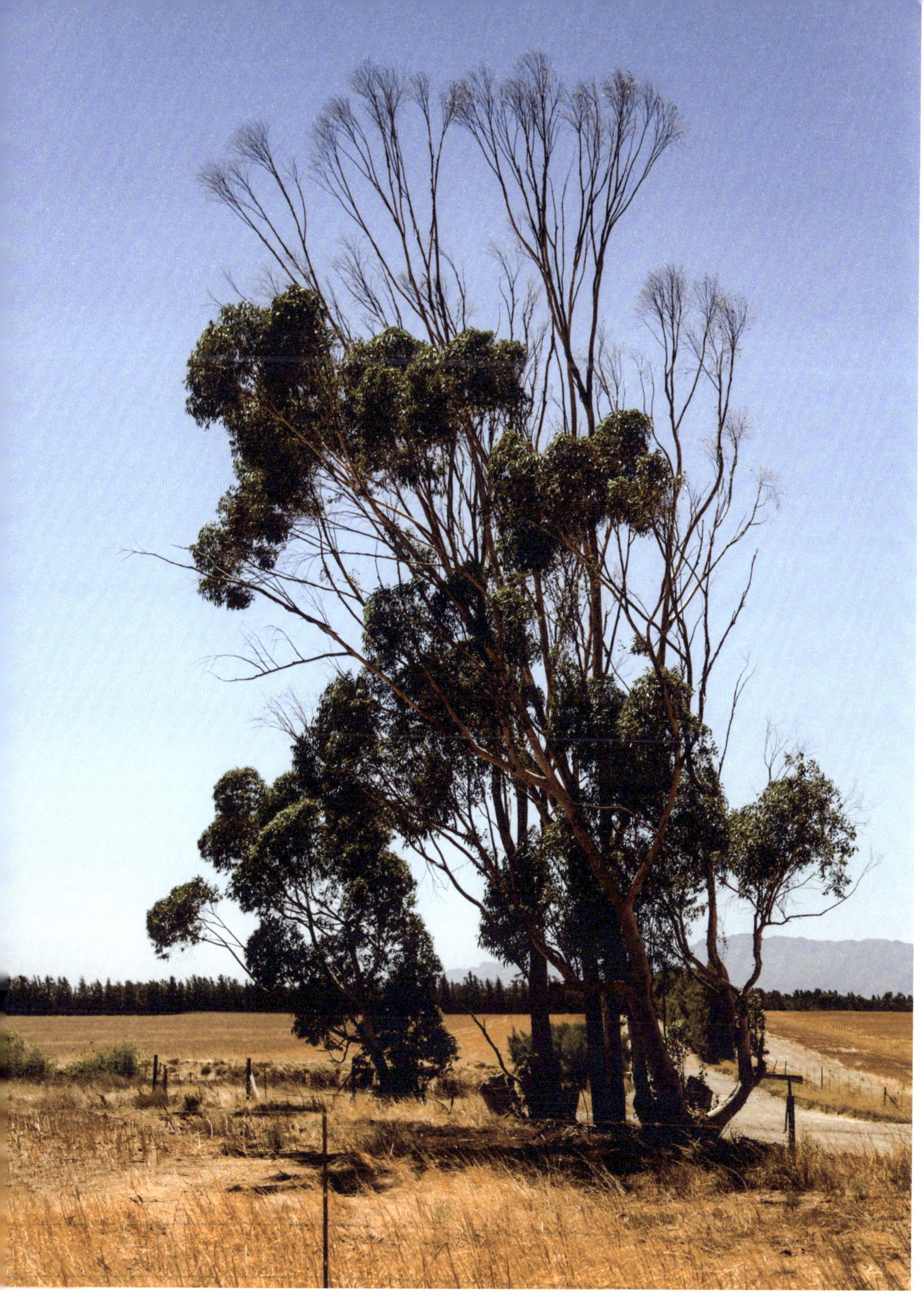

Walking on water

You feel like Jesus as you walk along this wooden jetty in Langebaan Lagoon, leading to a wooden cabin. Sit on the bench in the bird hide and gaze out through the elongated windows. A birdwatcher's idea of heaven.

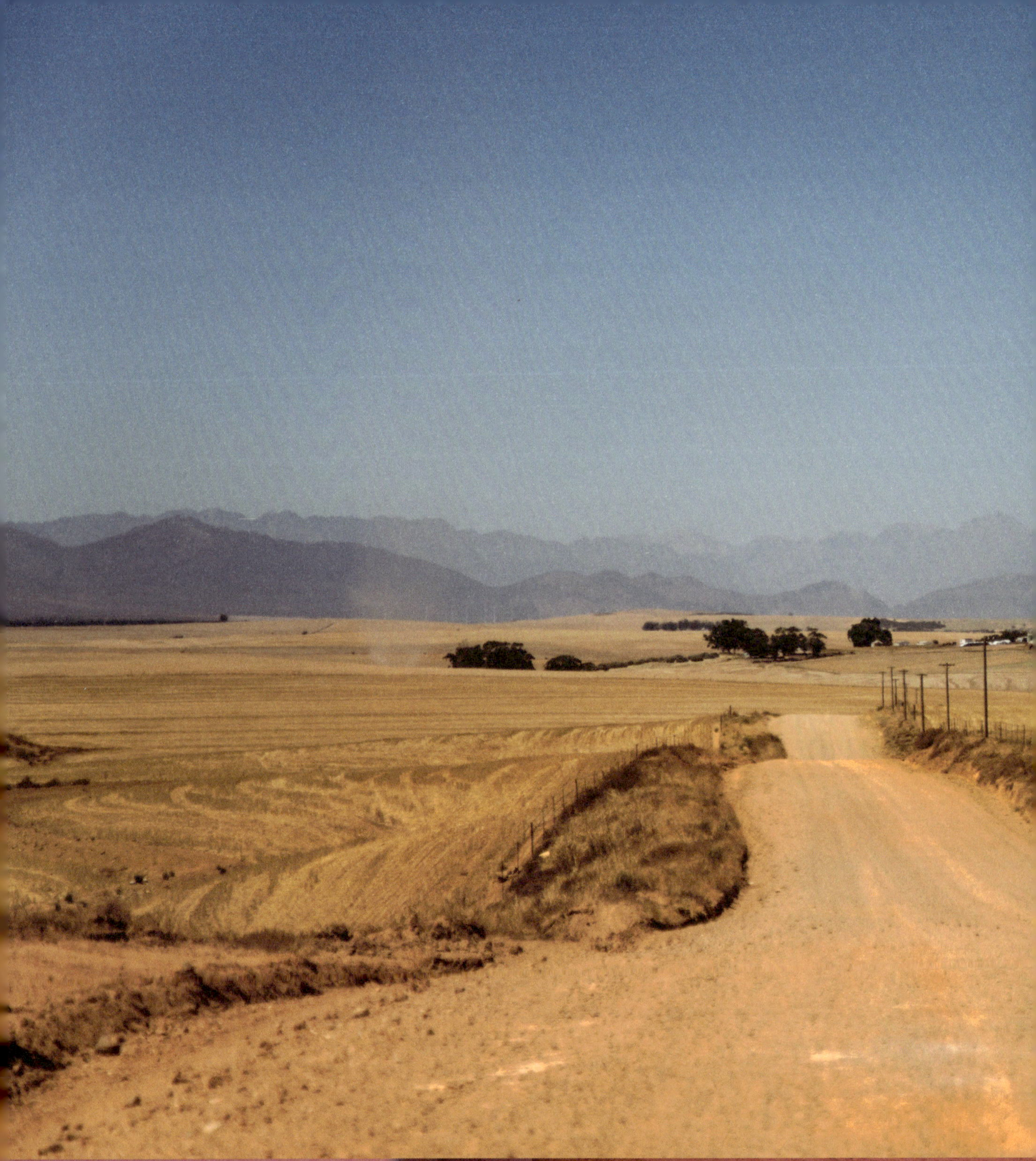

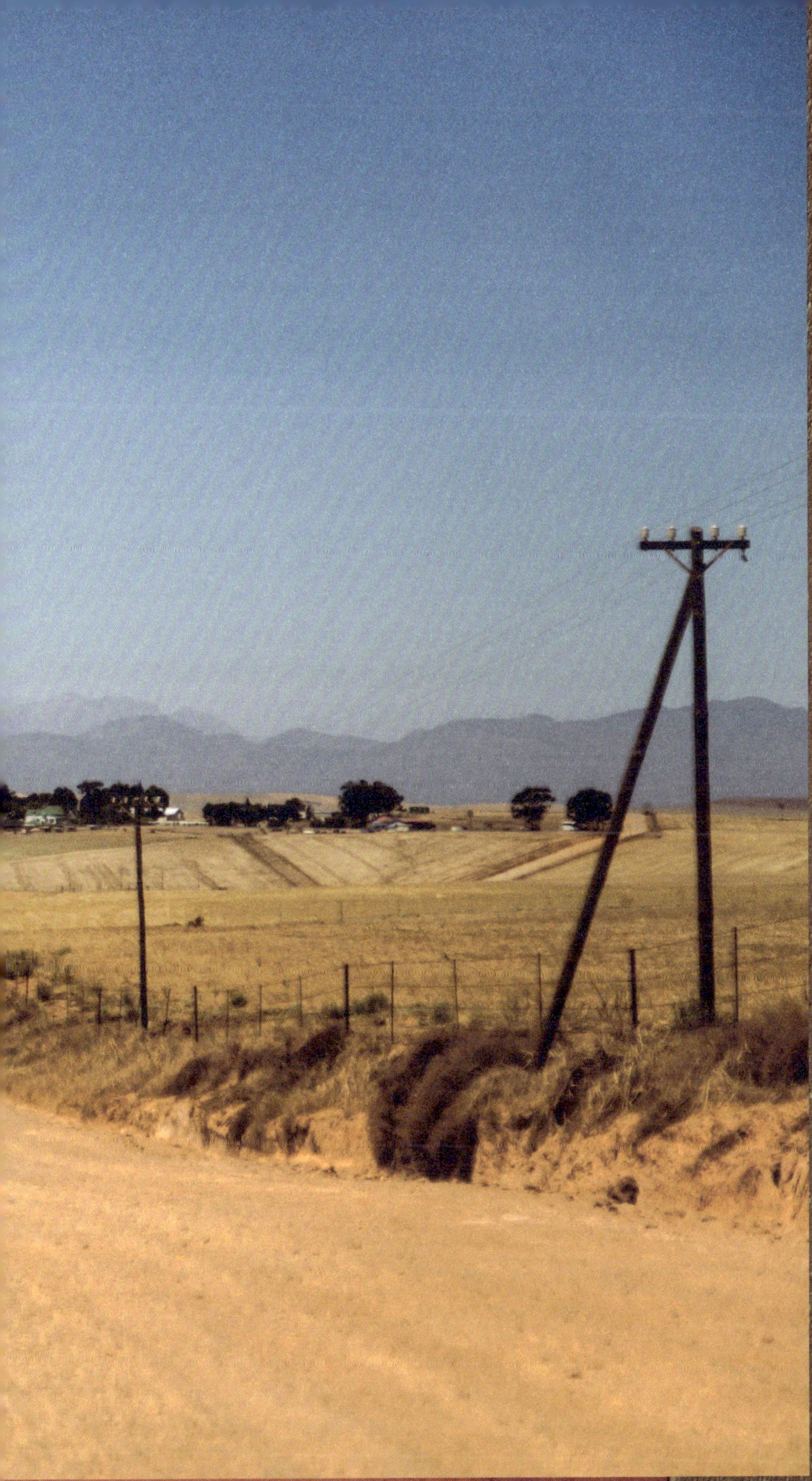

Dusty highways

Endless unsealed roads are a common sight in South Africa. They are actually highways where you can easily hit speeds of more than 100 km per hour, as you watch the dust kick up in your rear-view mirror and bear down on you as if to devour you. But even in your small rental car, you are just fast enough to avoid getting caught. The roads are mostly empty, the dust clouds on the horizon being the only indication that there are more motorists ahead of you.

Couvaloup, the wolf den. That's what Laurent Bayard named his house, after the town in southern France where he spent so many summers with his grandparents, who were antique dealers. They taught him to appreciate beautiful things, and encouraged his love of nature and animals.

Laurent left his parental home at a young age for Paris, where he worked for a famous shoe designer. Some years later he moved to London where he continued to work in fashion. He started travelling for his job, buying jewellery and other accessories. His life was hectic, exciting and wild. A bit too wild even, at one point. He realised that he needed a way out. Almost 15 years ago he made the switch to another lifestyle, after a friend recommended Cape Town as a place to escape. There he would be able to restore some semblance of balance to his life.

After a few years of working with antiques in Cape Town, his continuing desire for change led him to Hopefield, where he ended up by coincidence. In this village of little significance, he stumbled upon a dilapidated house with a for sale sign. Laurent immediately spotted its charm and potential. In less than a year's time, he succeeded in transforming the house and garden into the welcoming, arty and lavish place that Couvaloup is today.

Laurent knows no limits, and sometimes his obsessions send him down the wrong path. But most of the time, his boundless energy and talent help him accomplish what other people take years to complete or never even bother to start with in the first place.

Couvaloup is Laurent's home and also a B & B, where he and his five dogs personally welcome his guests. There are eight rooms, all of which have been decorated in Laurent's own style. Antique, modern and handmade items are arranged alongside each other. Large photographs, works of art, and funny gadgets seamlessly blend together in a playful and eclectic mix: Laurent's style in a nutshell.

Transforming the garden into the verdant space it is today was a huge feat. Laurent loves to work in the garden. It 'grounds' him.

Laurent Bayard

A Frenchman in Hopefield

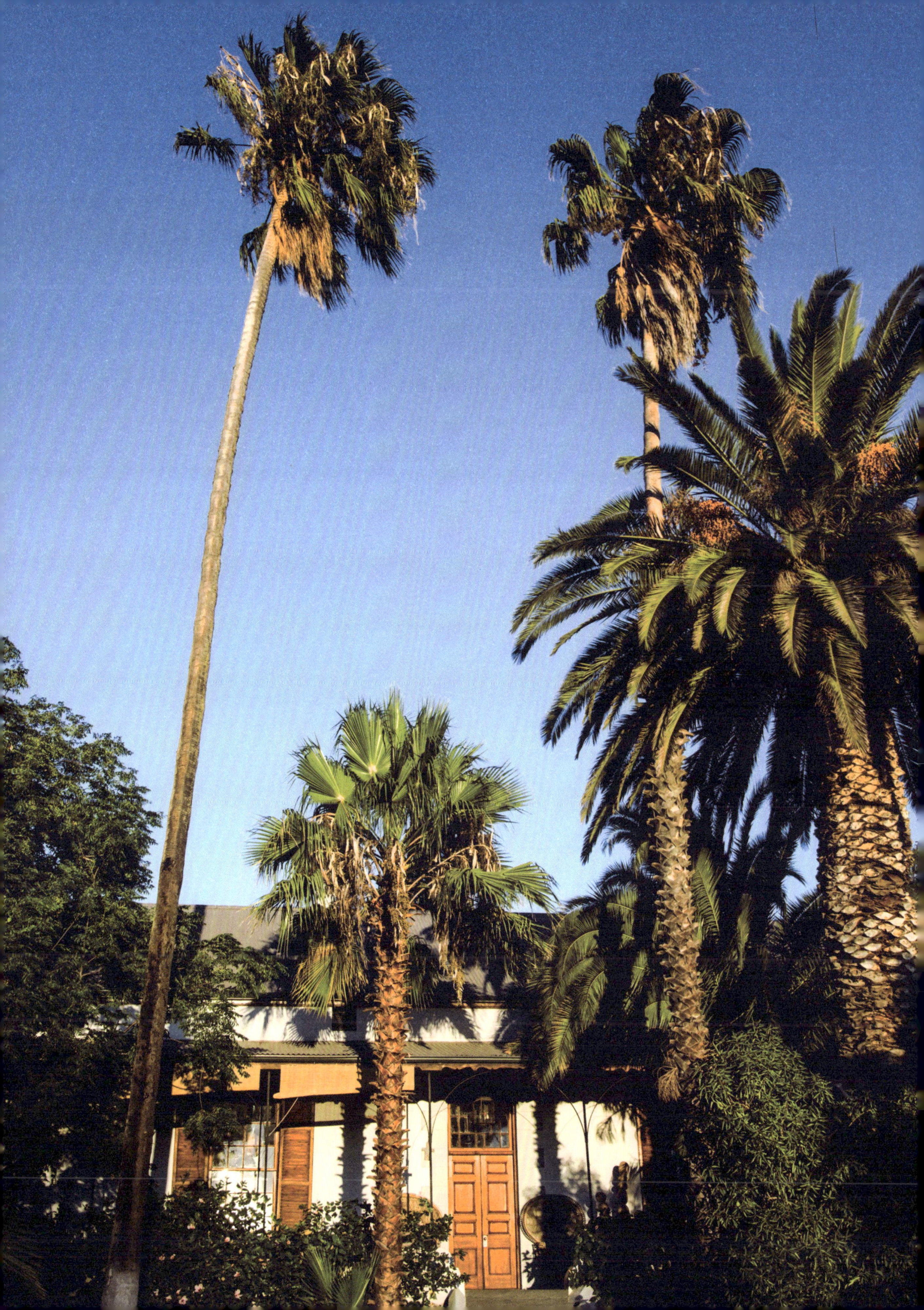

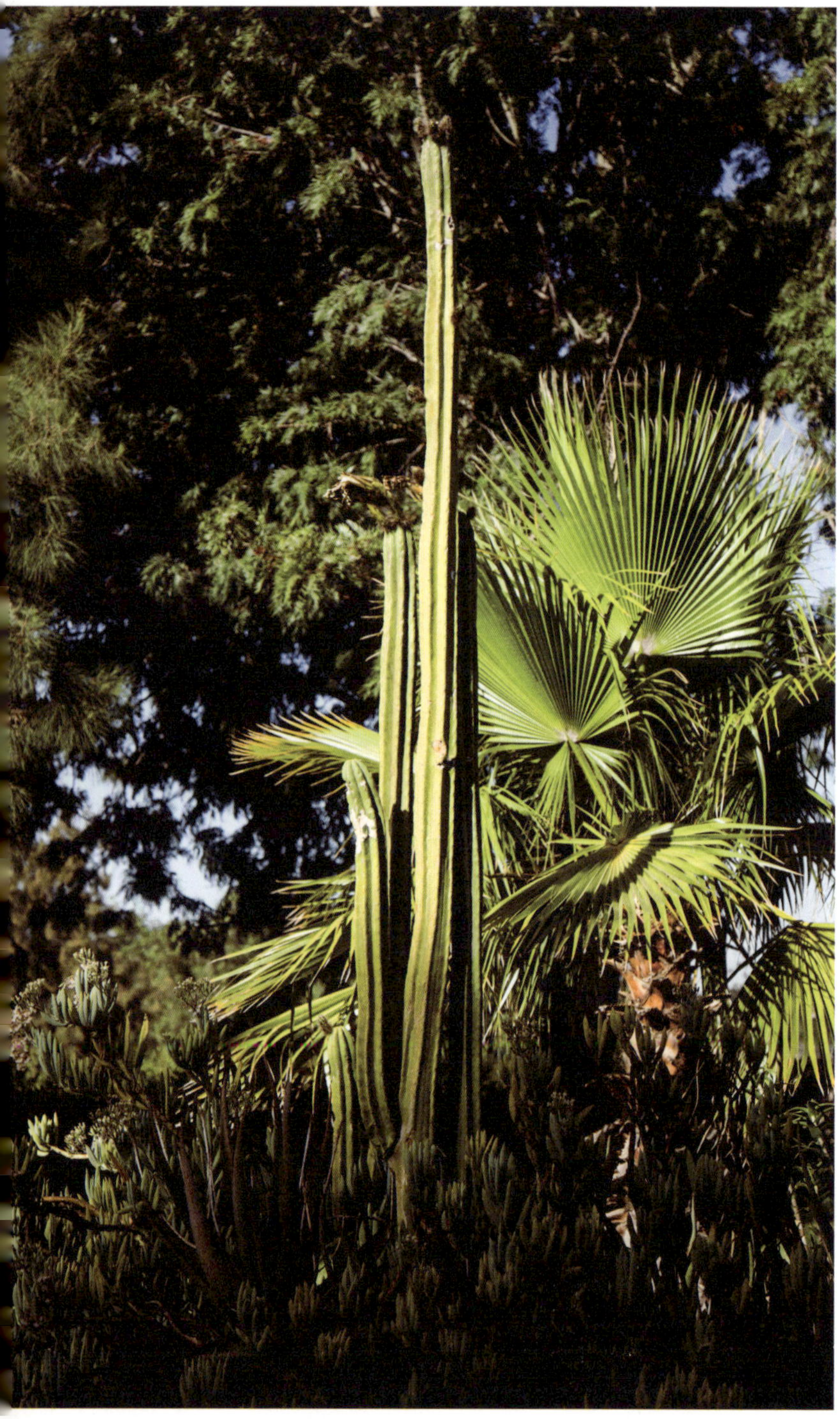

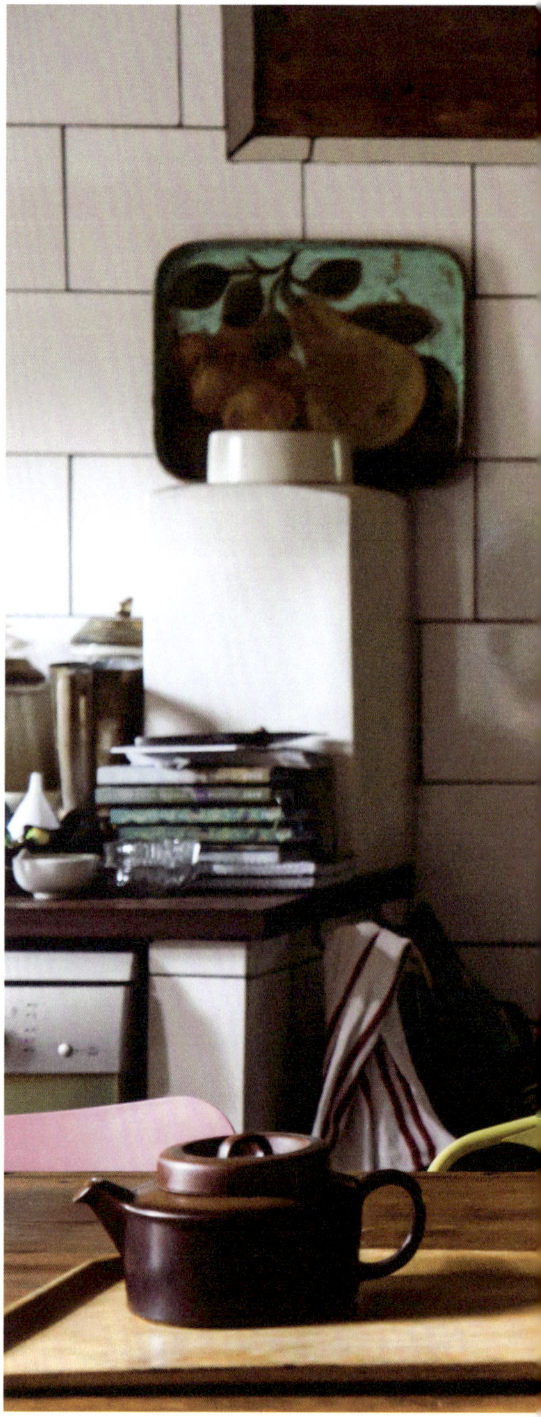

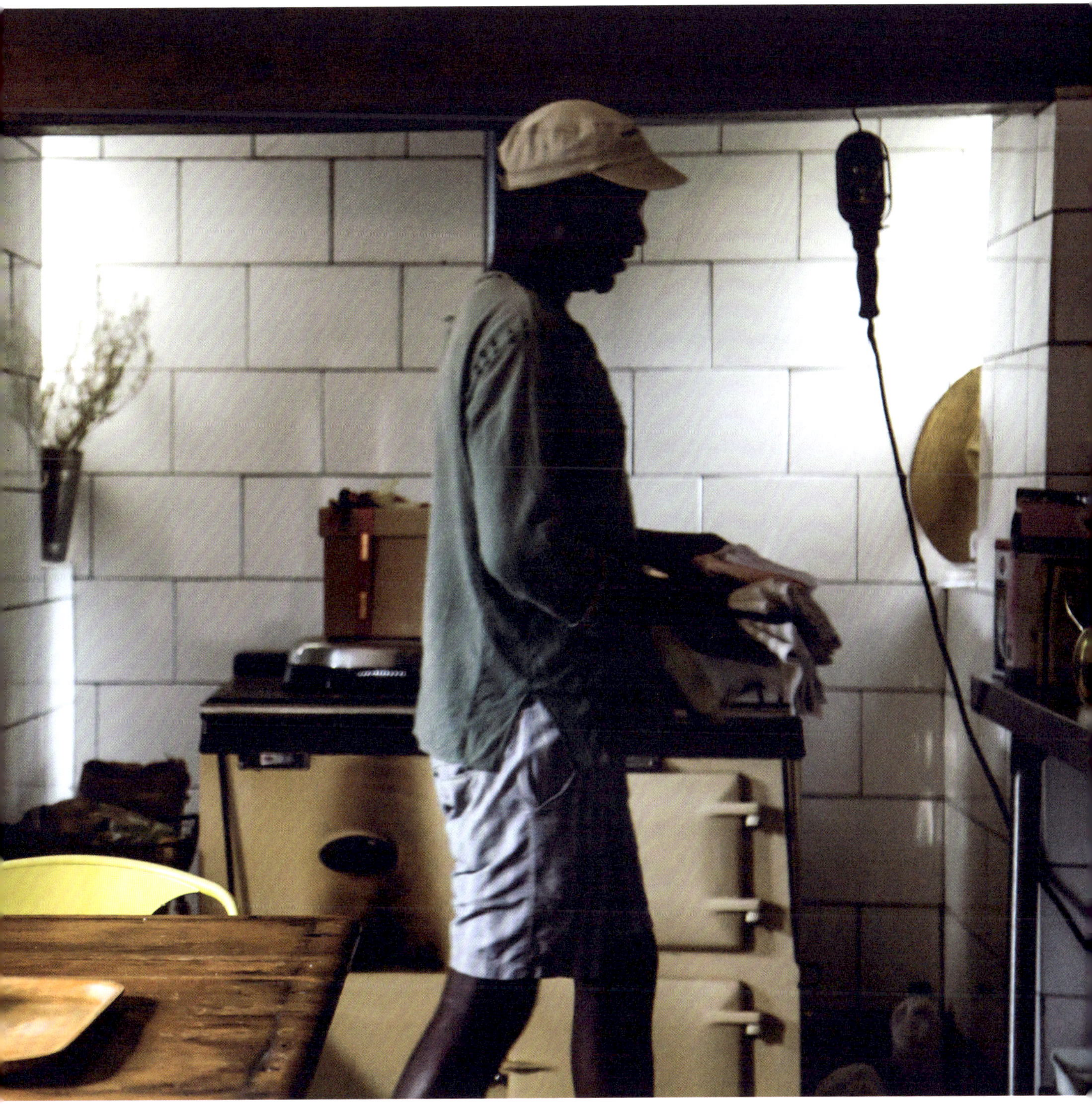

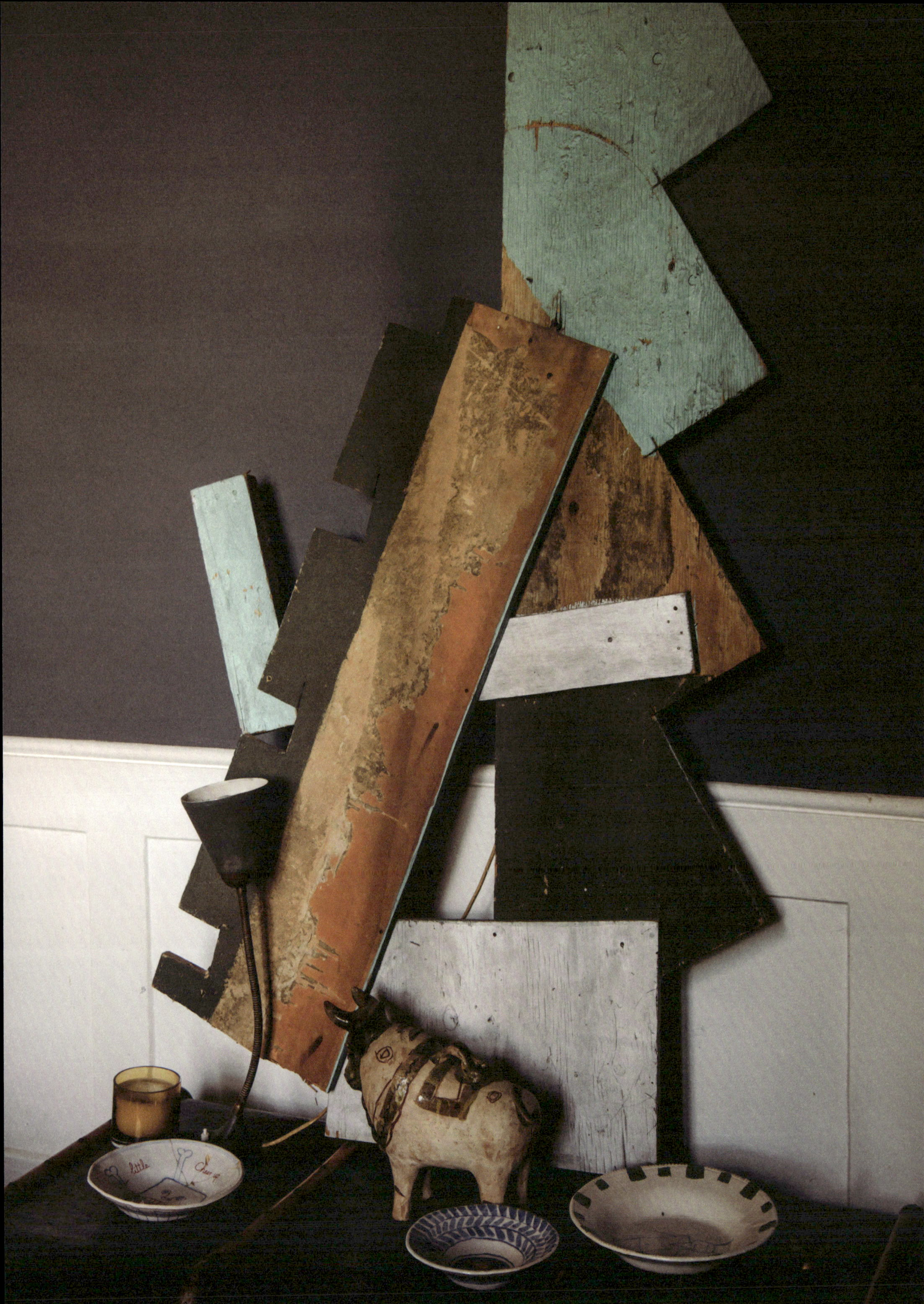

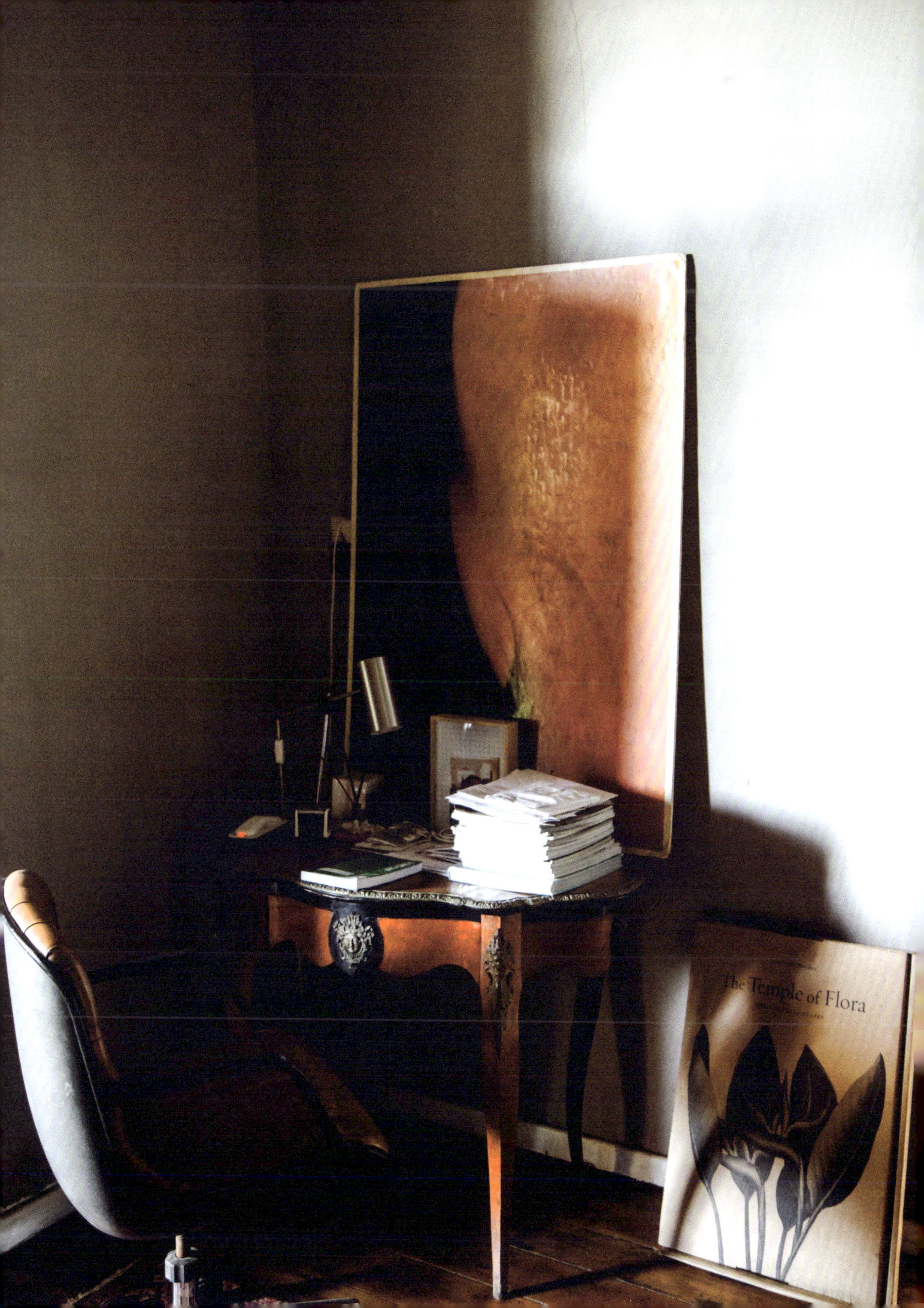
The Temple of Flora

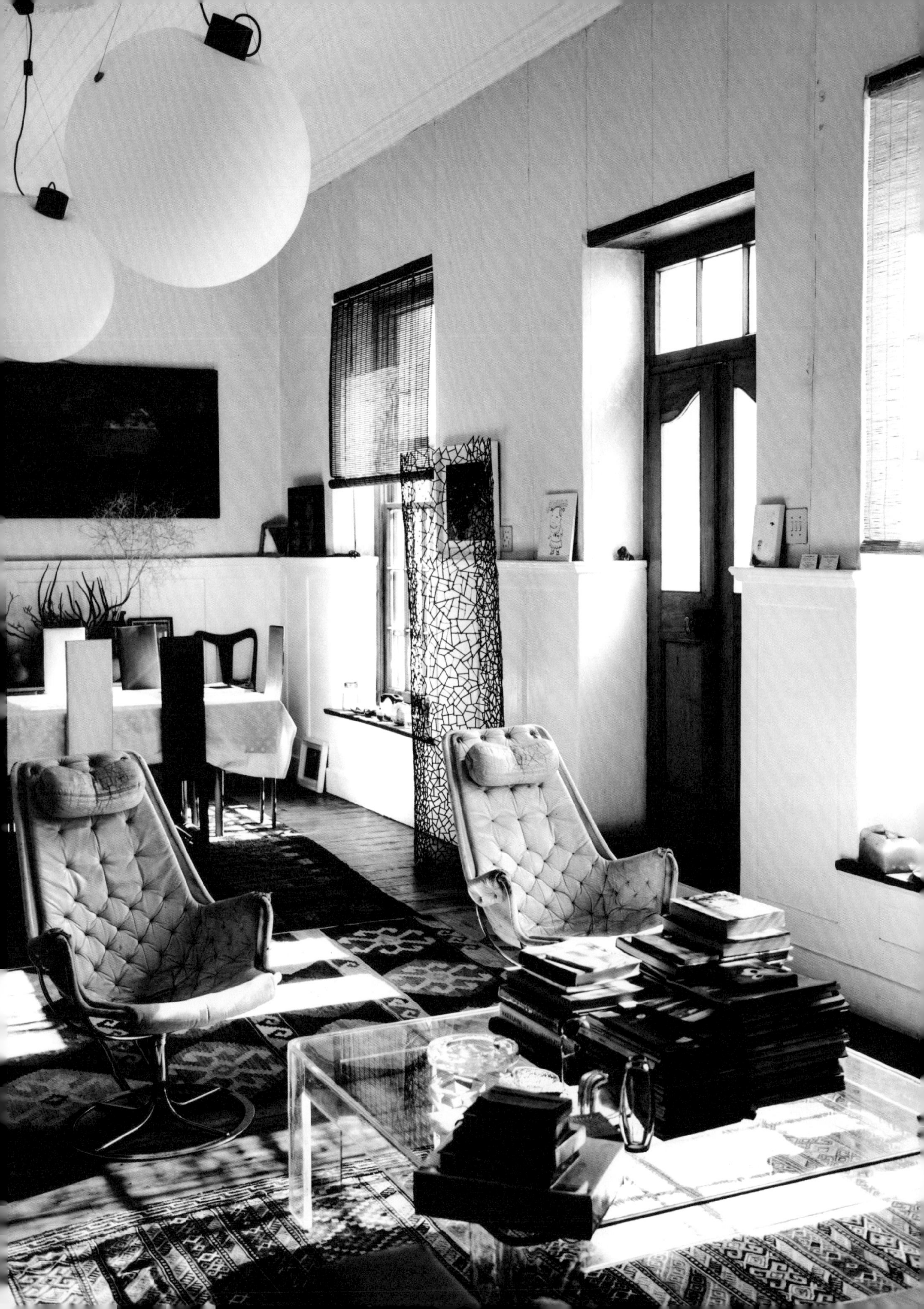

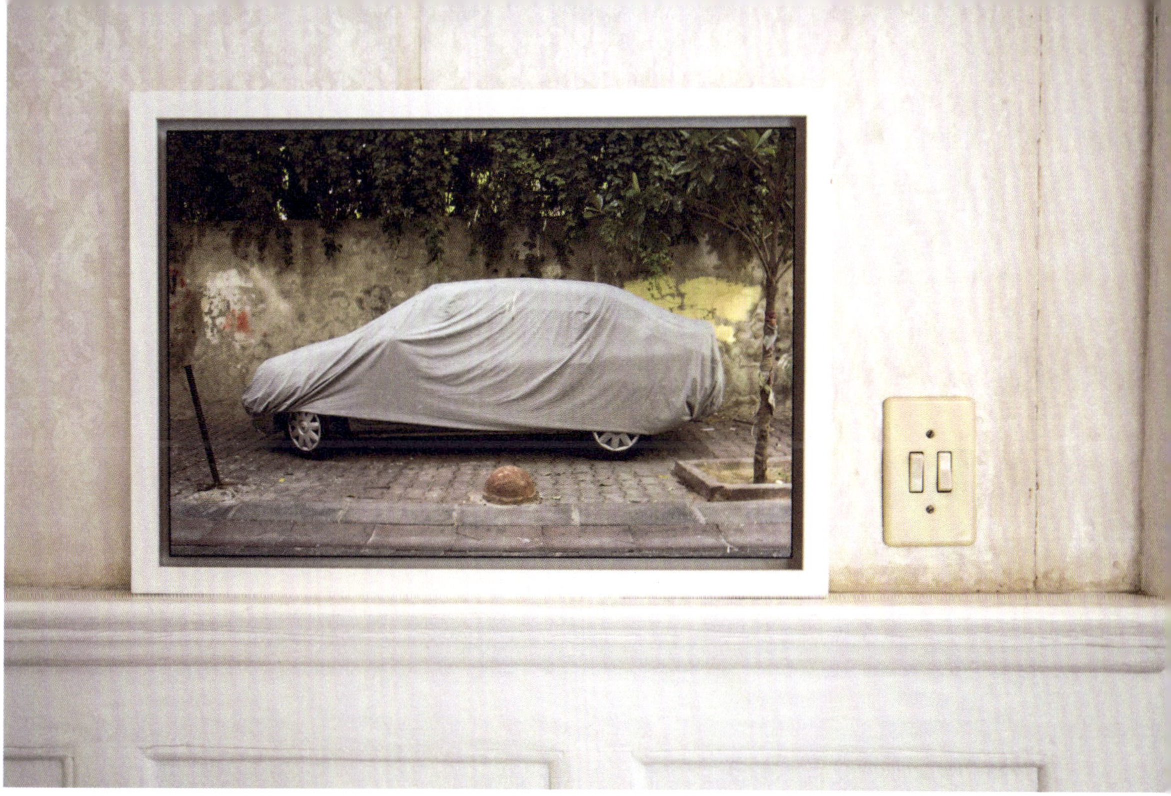

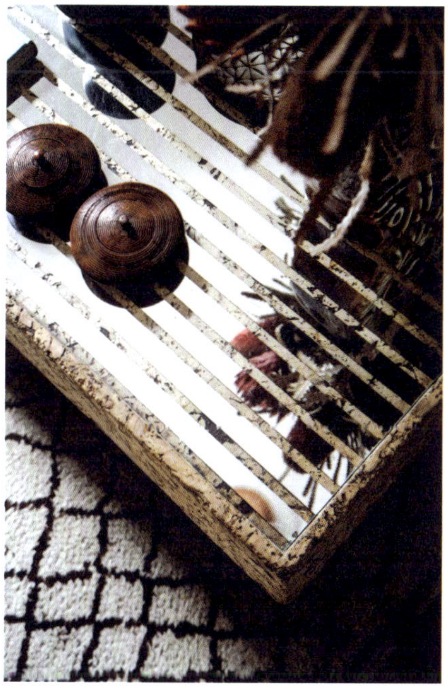

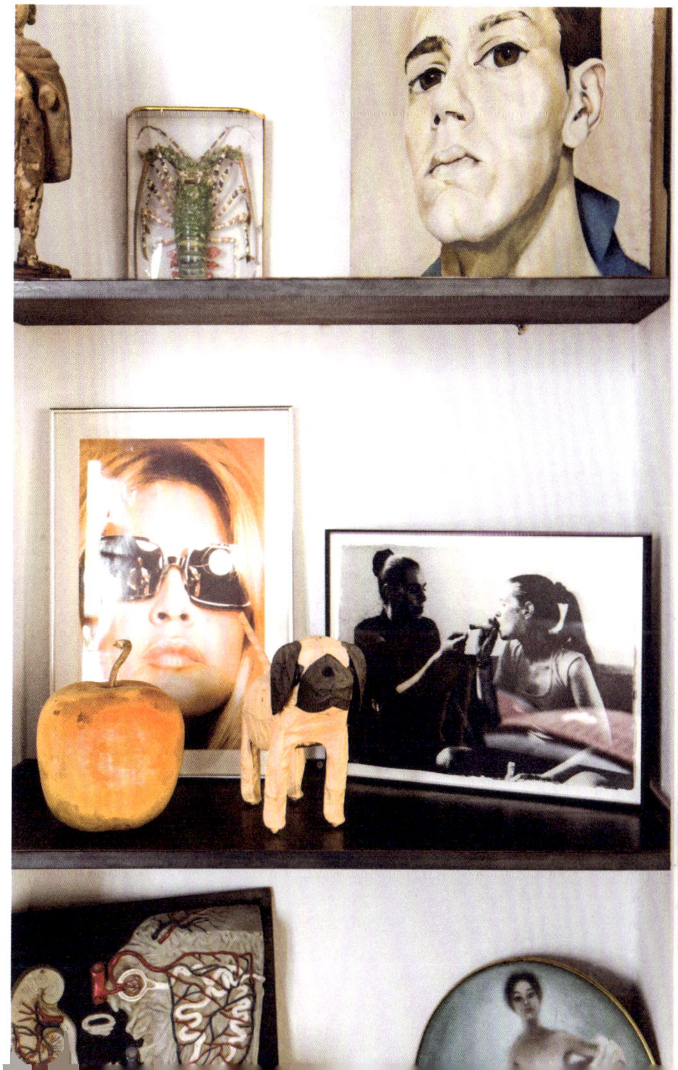

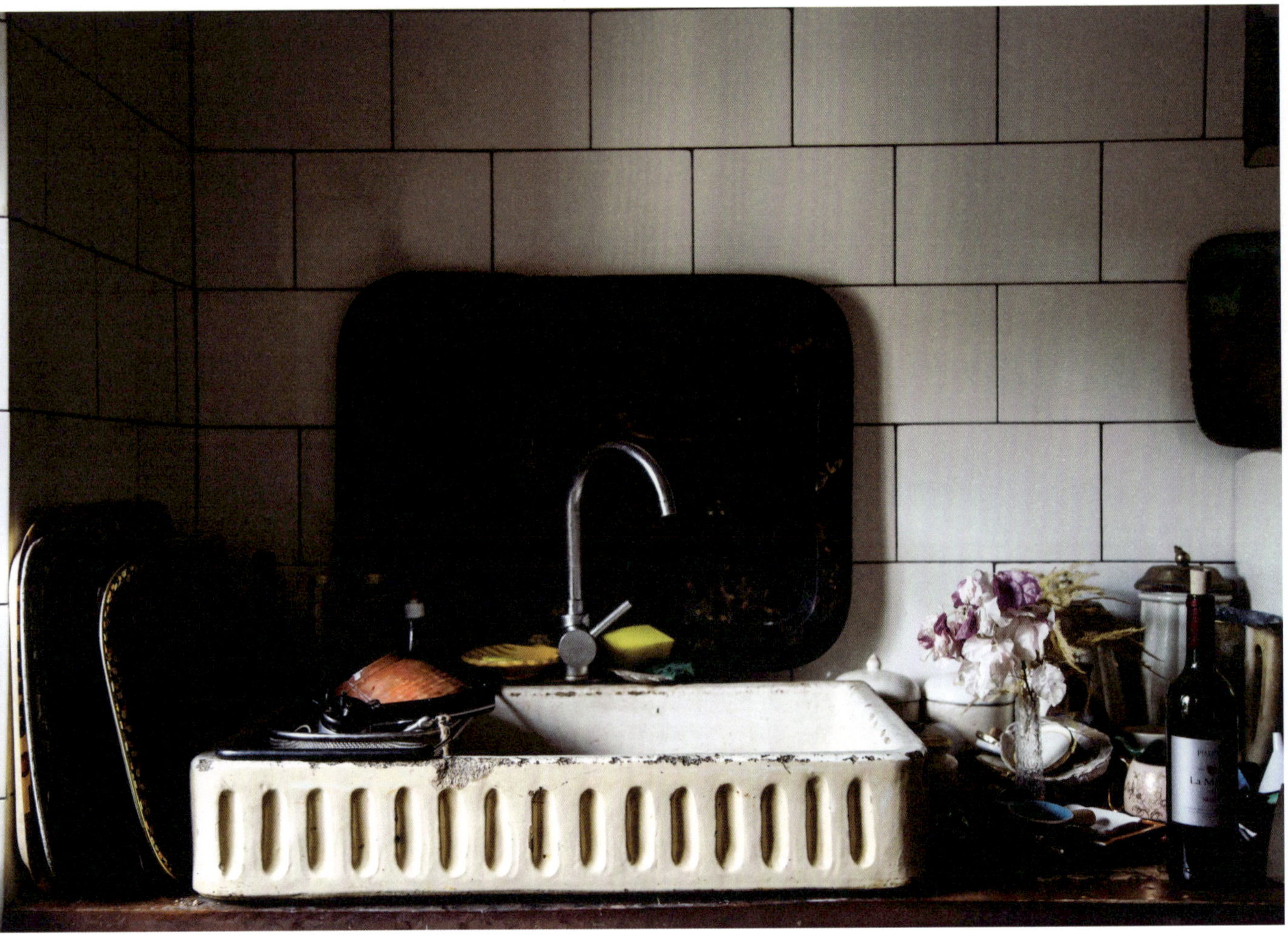

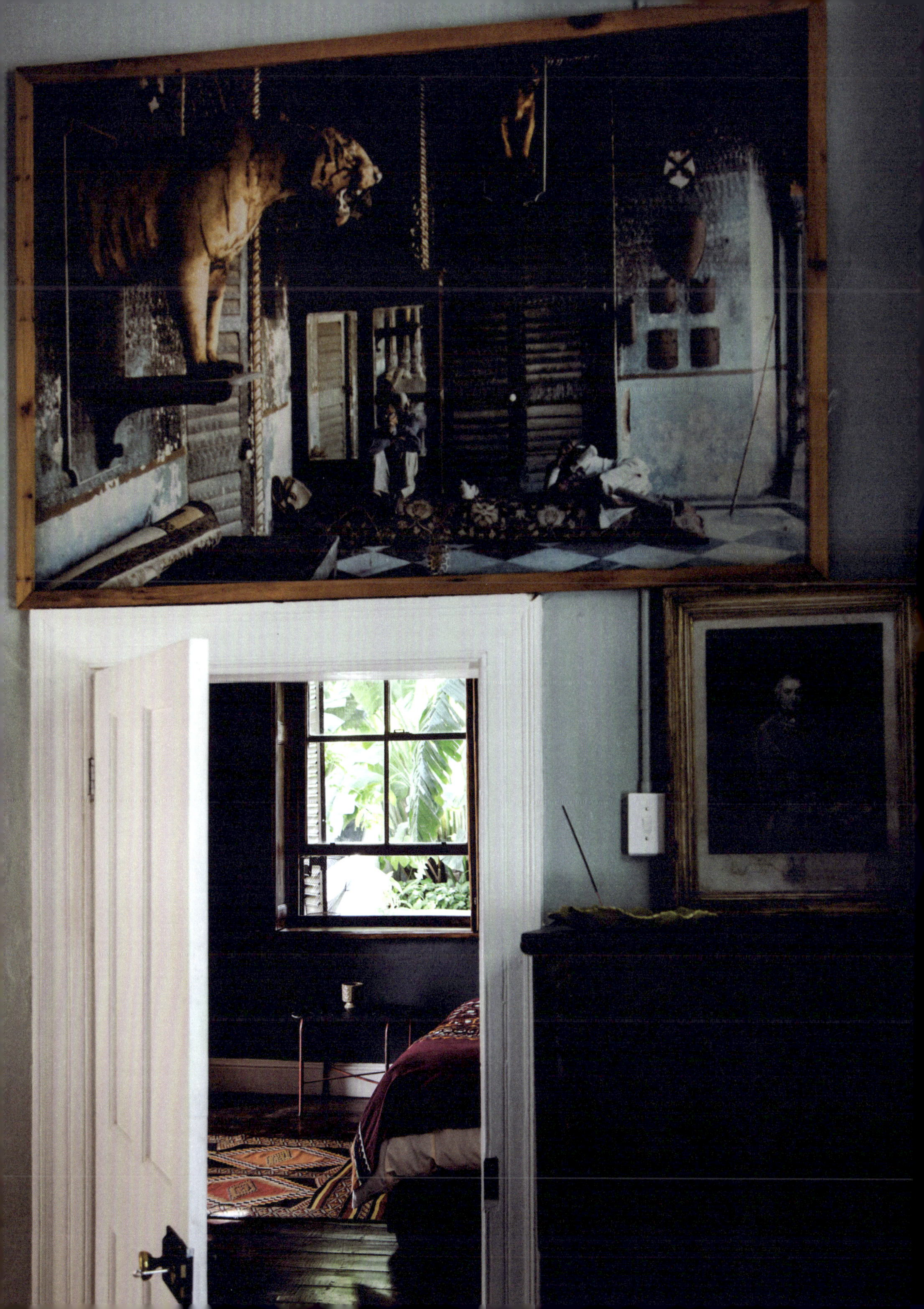

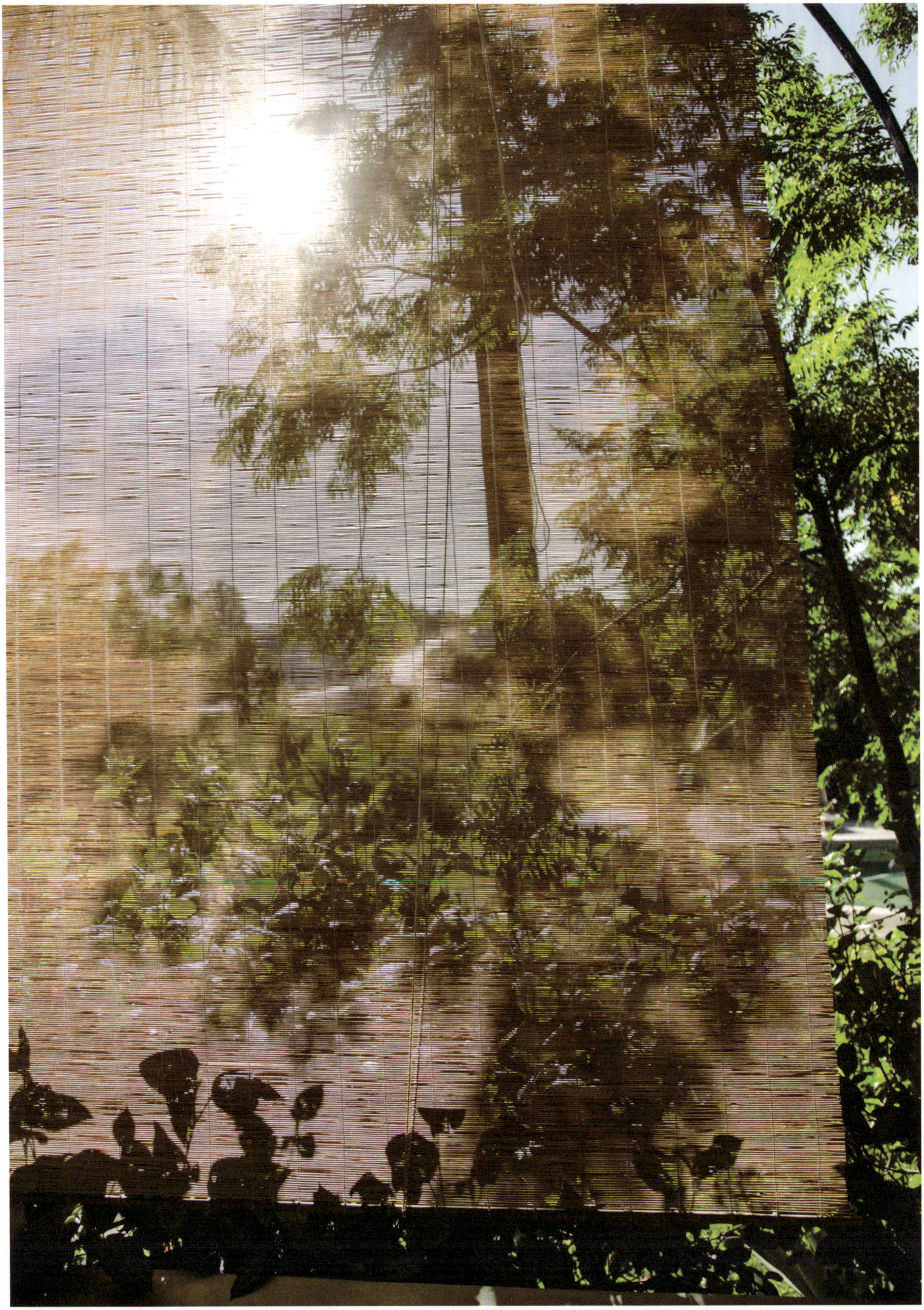

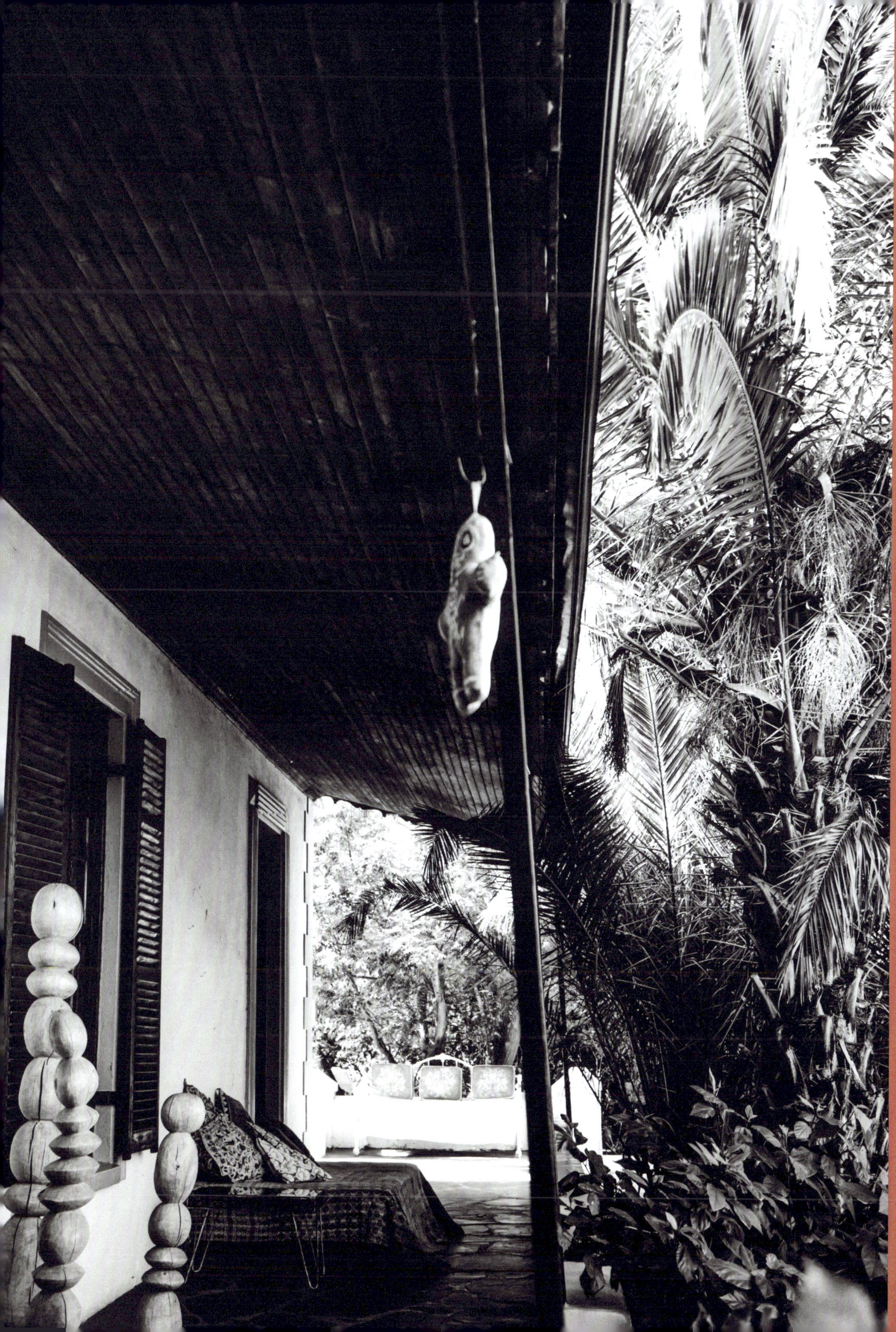

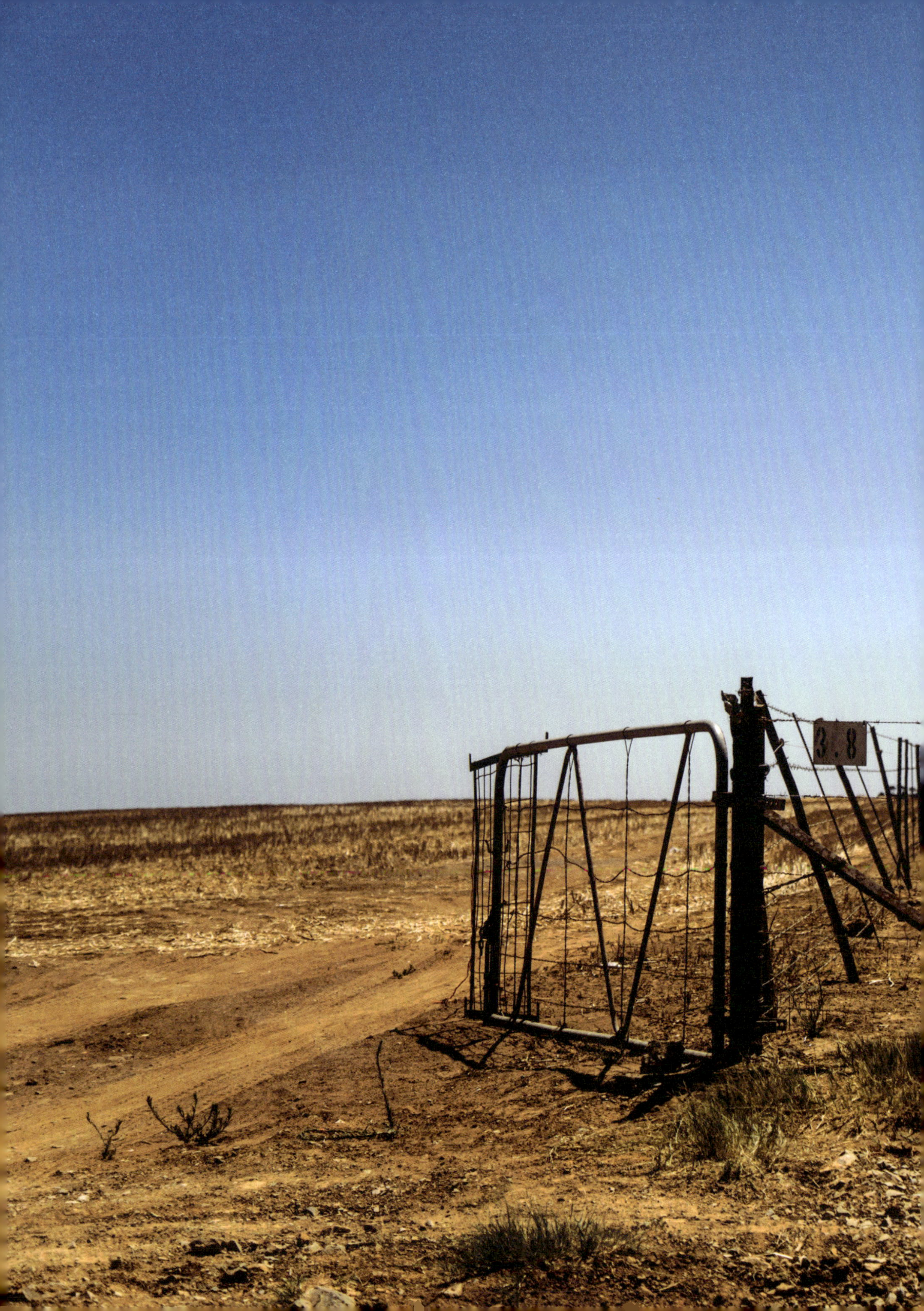
3.8

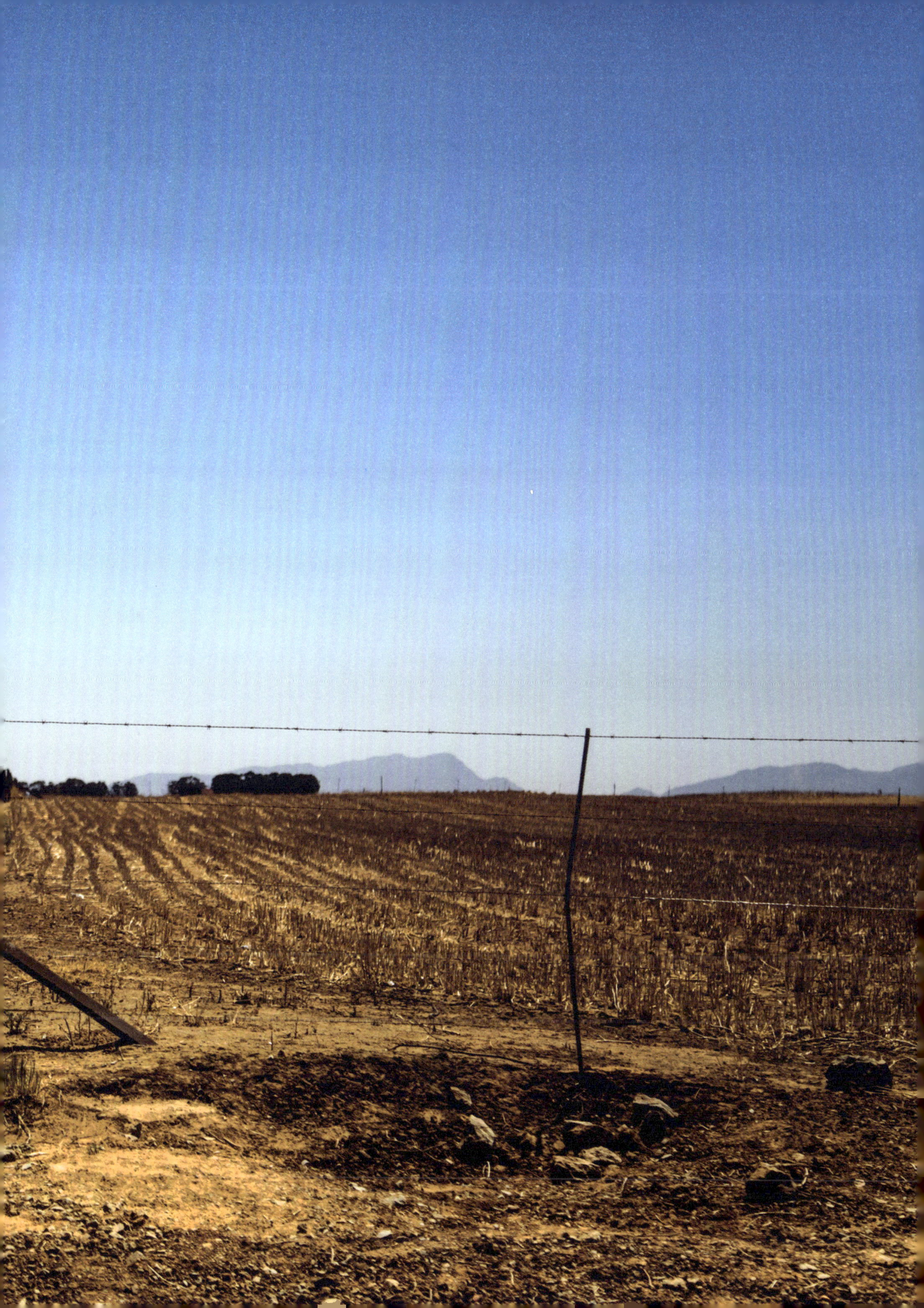

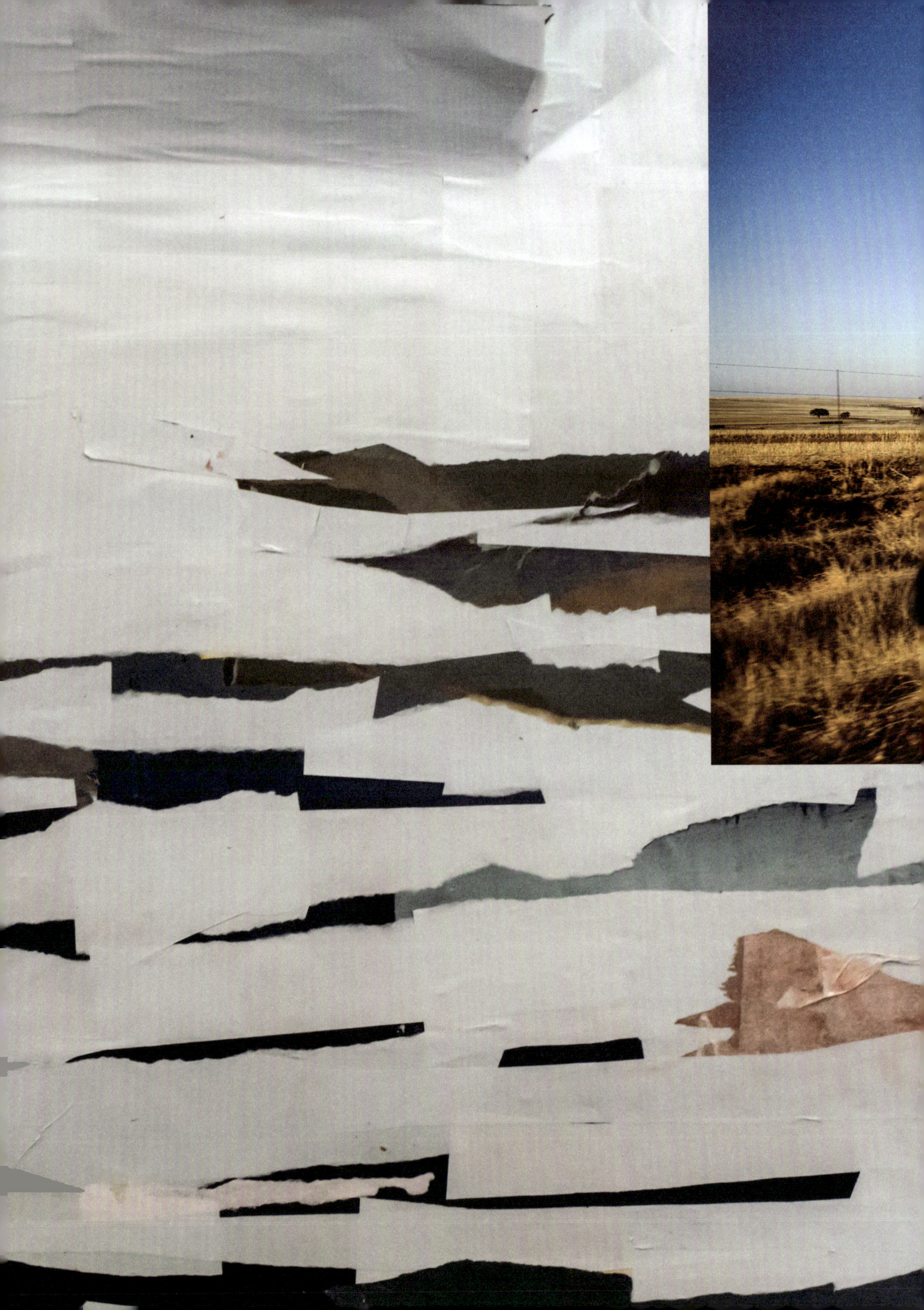

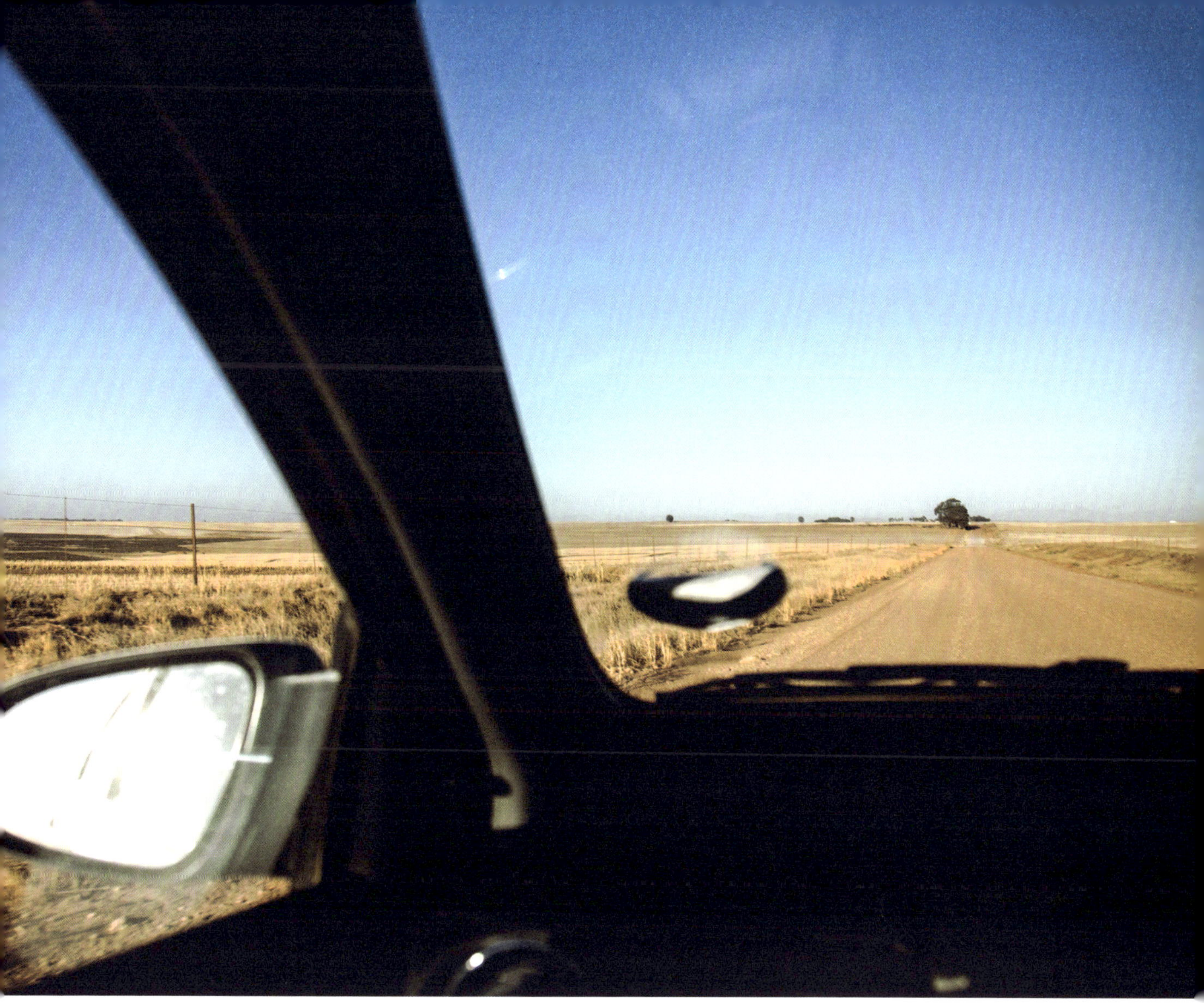

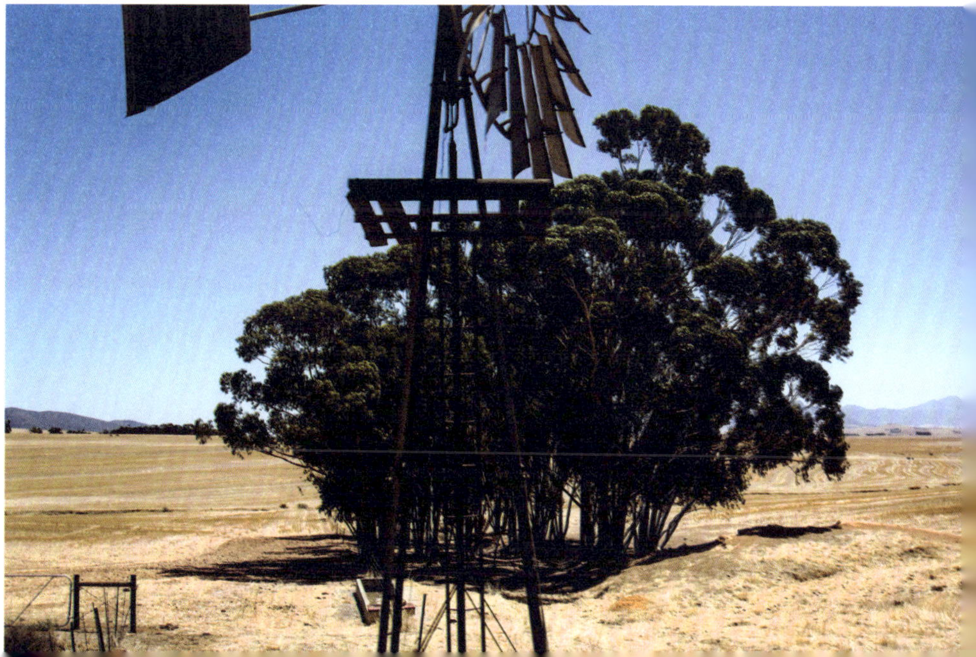

3

Little Karoo

66

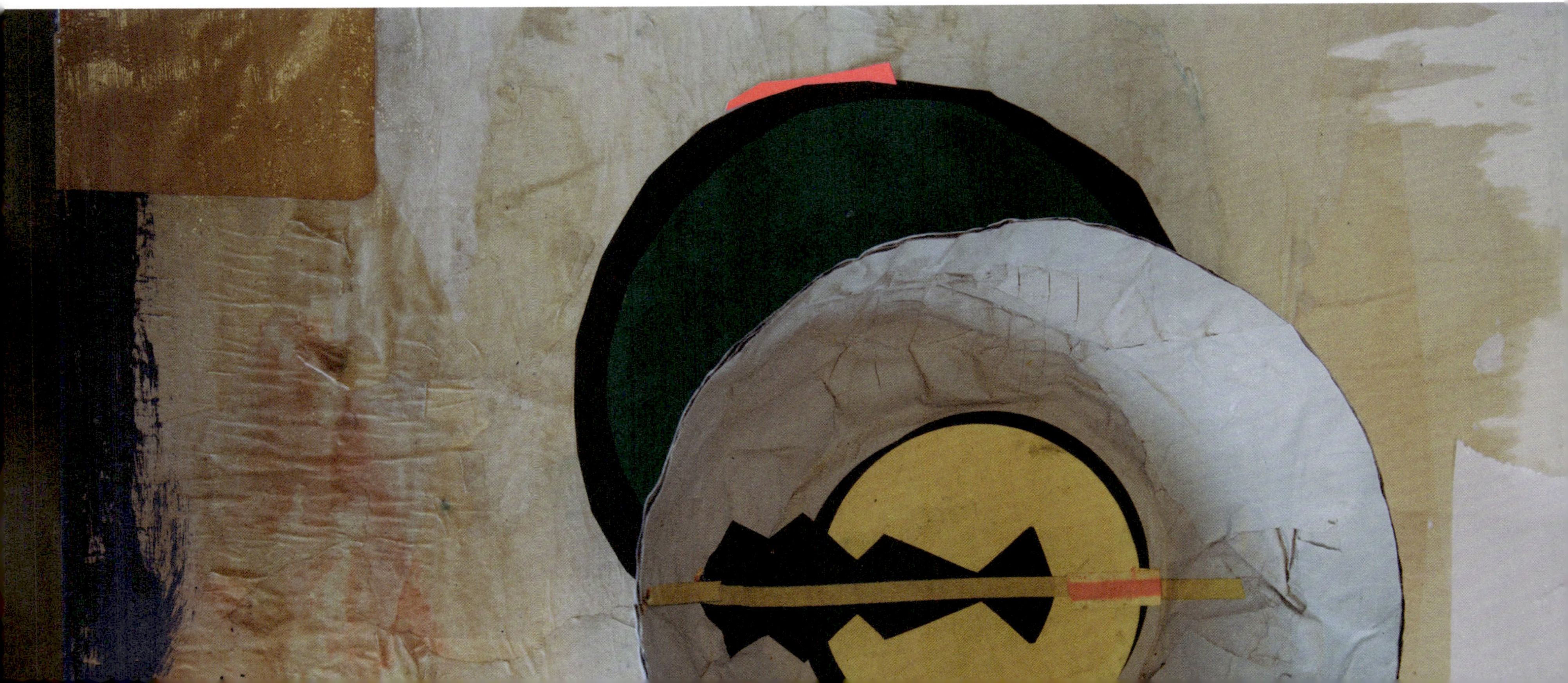

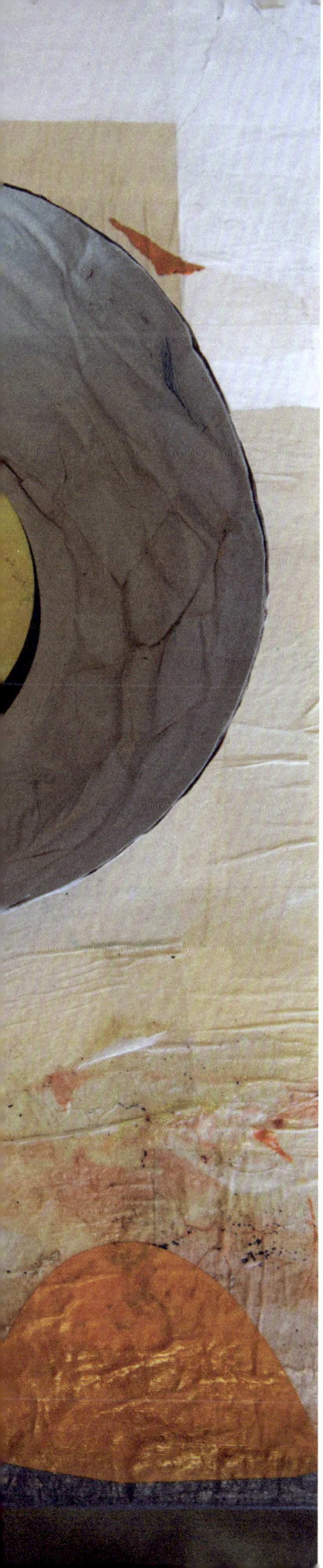

The Klein Karoo, the small southern part of the Karoo, is surrounded by majestic mountains to the south and north, and borders on the Garden Route in the Western Cape. Cape Route 62 from Barrydale in the west to Oudtshoorn in the east meanders along this long, rather narrow valley. As we made our way through it, we passed through fruit growing, wine producing and ostrich farming towns.

The mountain ranges that enclose the valley offer a constantly changing spectacle. The sky cracks open in a wide palette of stunning pinks and blues, which seem to be vying with each other to be the most beautiful.

The Klein Karoo is also one of the most diverse wine regions in South Africa. In this dry climate, the vines grow in the fertile soil along the river. There are plenty of wineries along the way where you are welcome for a wine tasting experience.

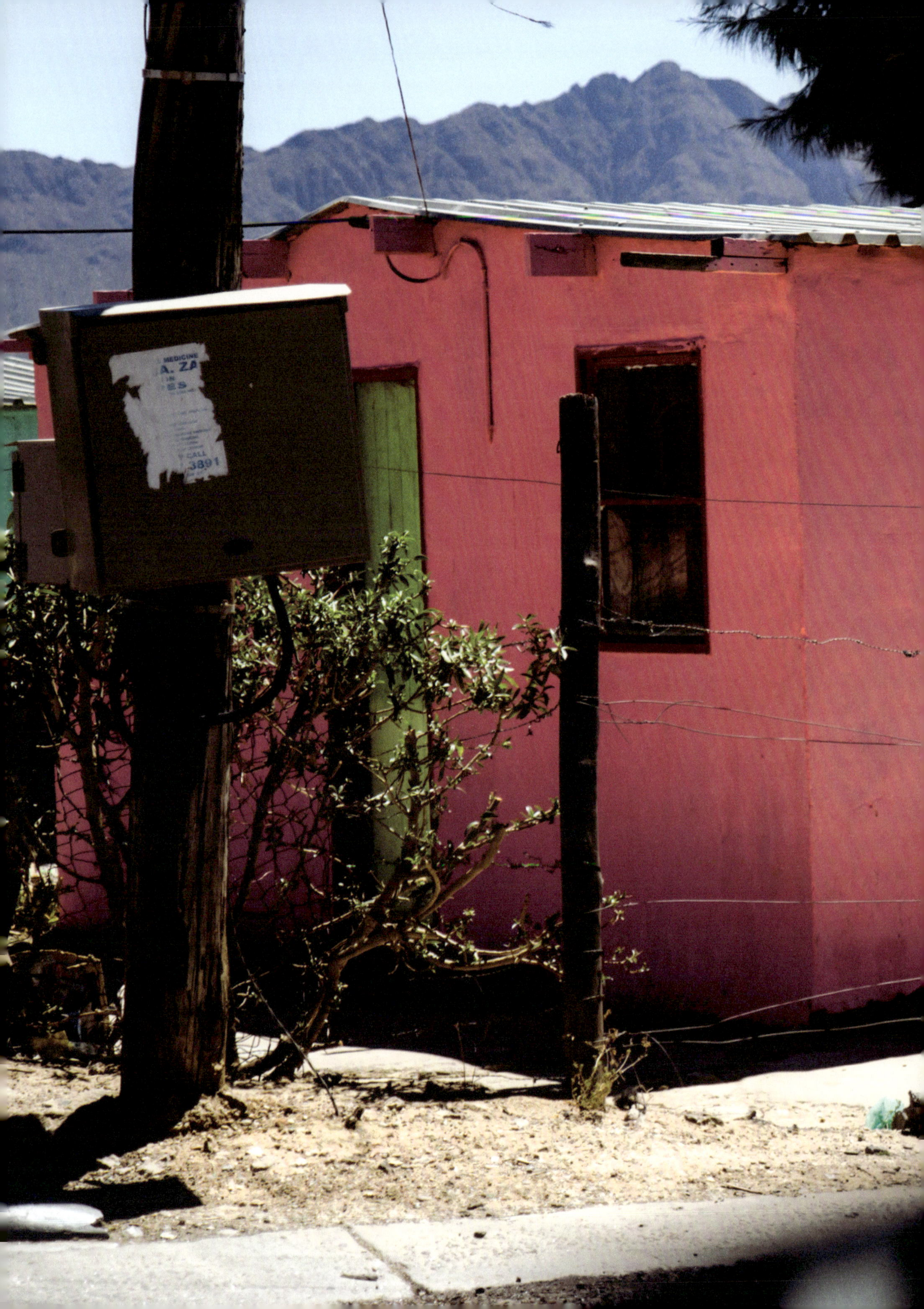
MEDICINE
CALL
3891

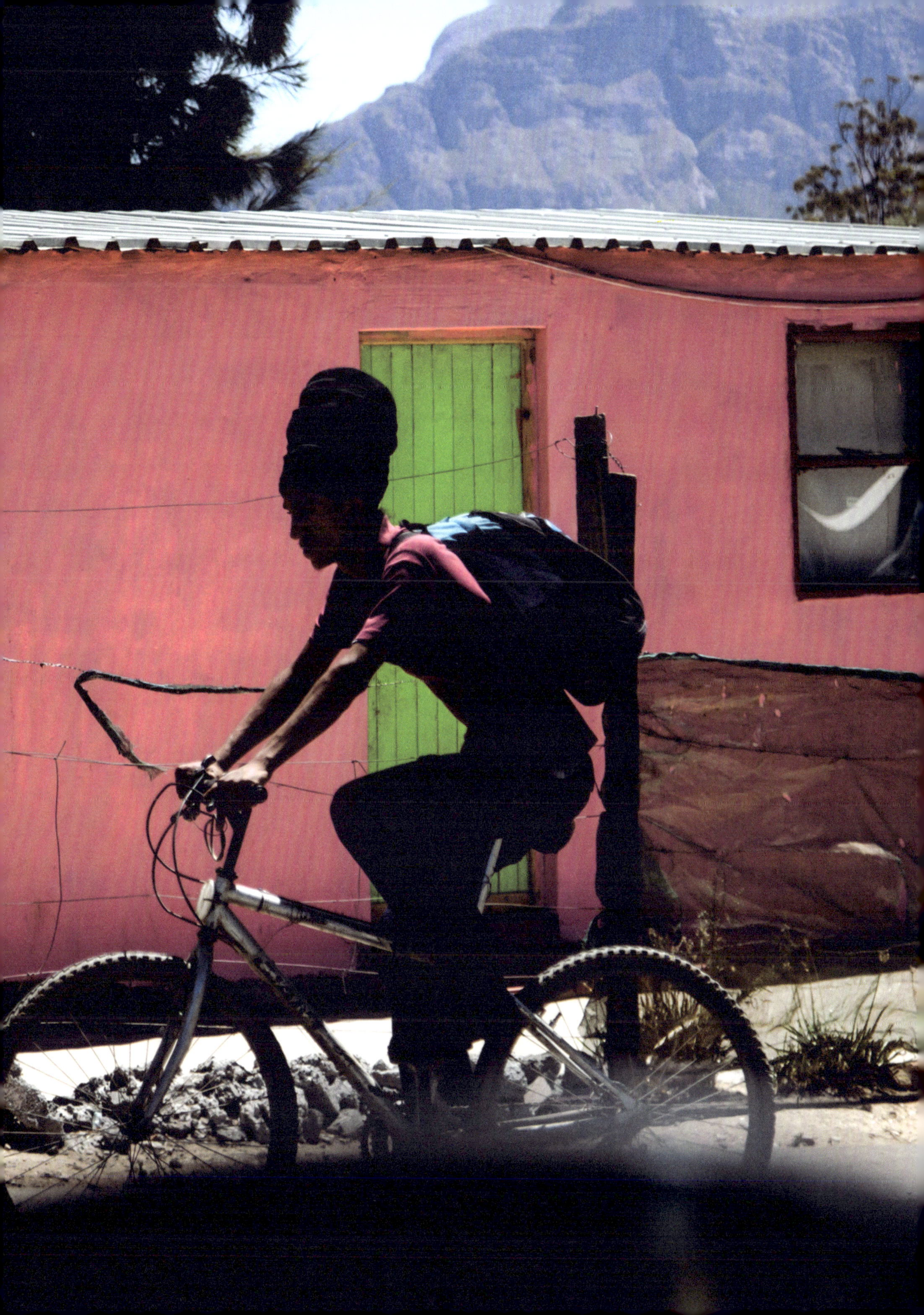

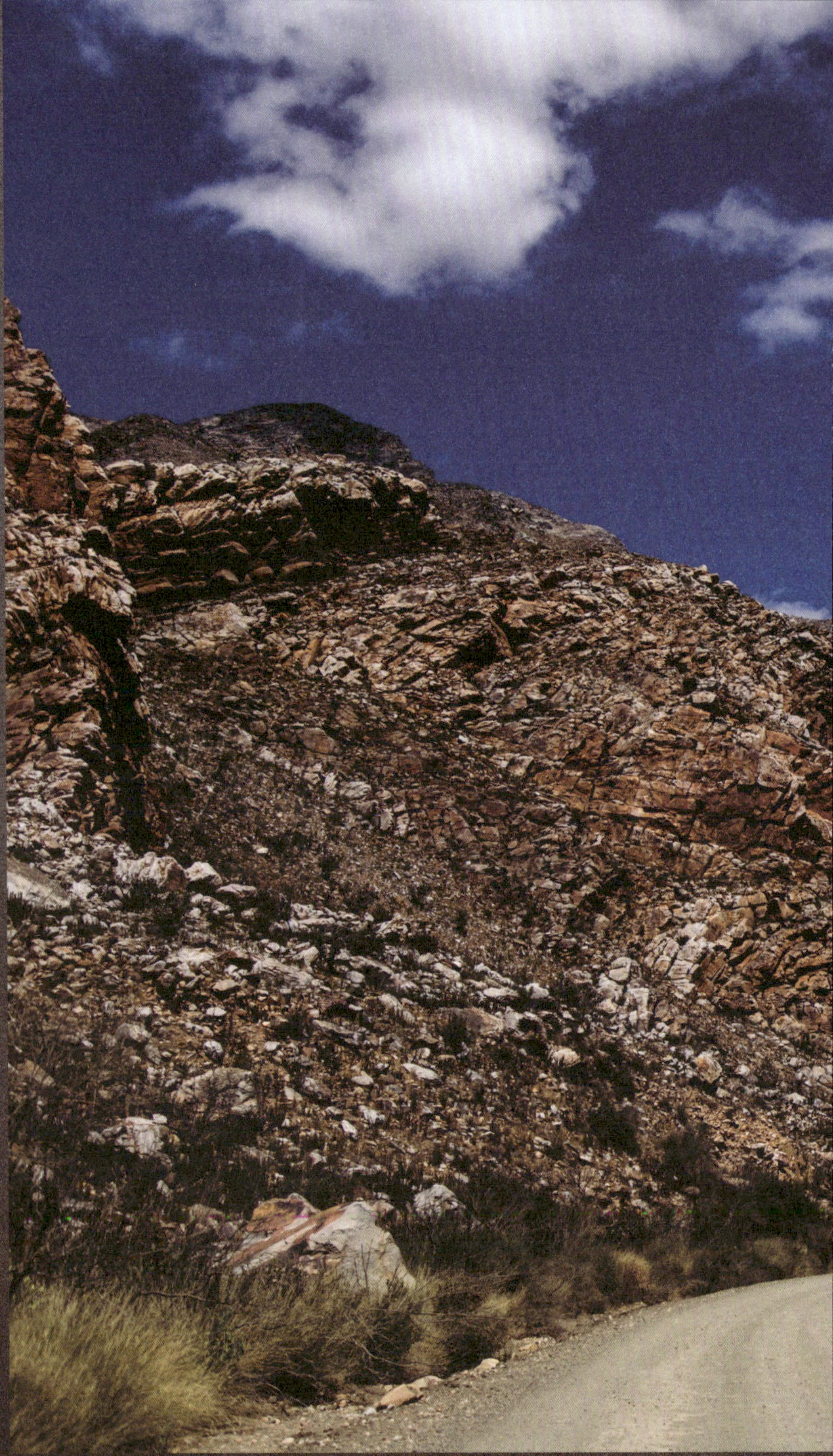

Rocky ride

Is driving through endless stretches of dry landscape monotonous? Most certainly not. Rocks in extraordinary hues rise up straight ahead of you, standing out against the blue sky with its beautifully shaped clouds. The scarce water gives the few plants that grow here an opportunity to showcase their strange beauty.

The road seems to guide us into a funnel of rocks. Soon we realise it's not a dead-end road, but an unexpected, extremely narrow passage leading us down a winding road, along a stream to another fairy-tale landscape on the other side of the huge rock formations. Our journey continues...

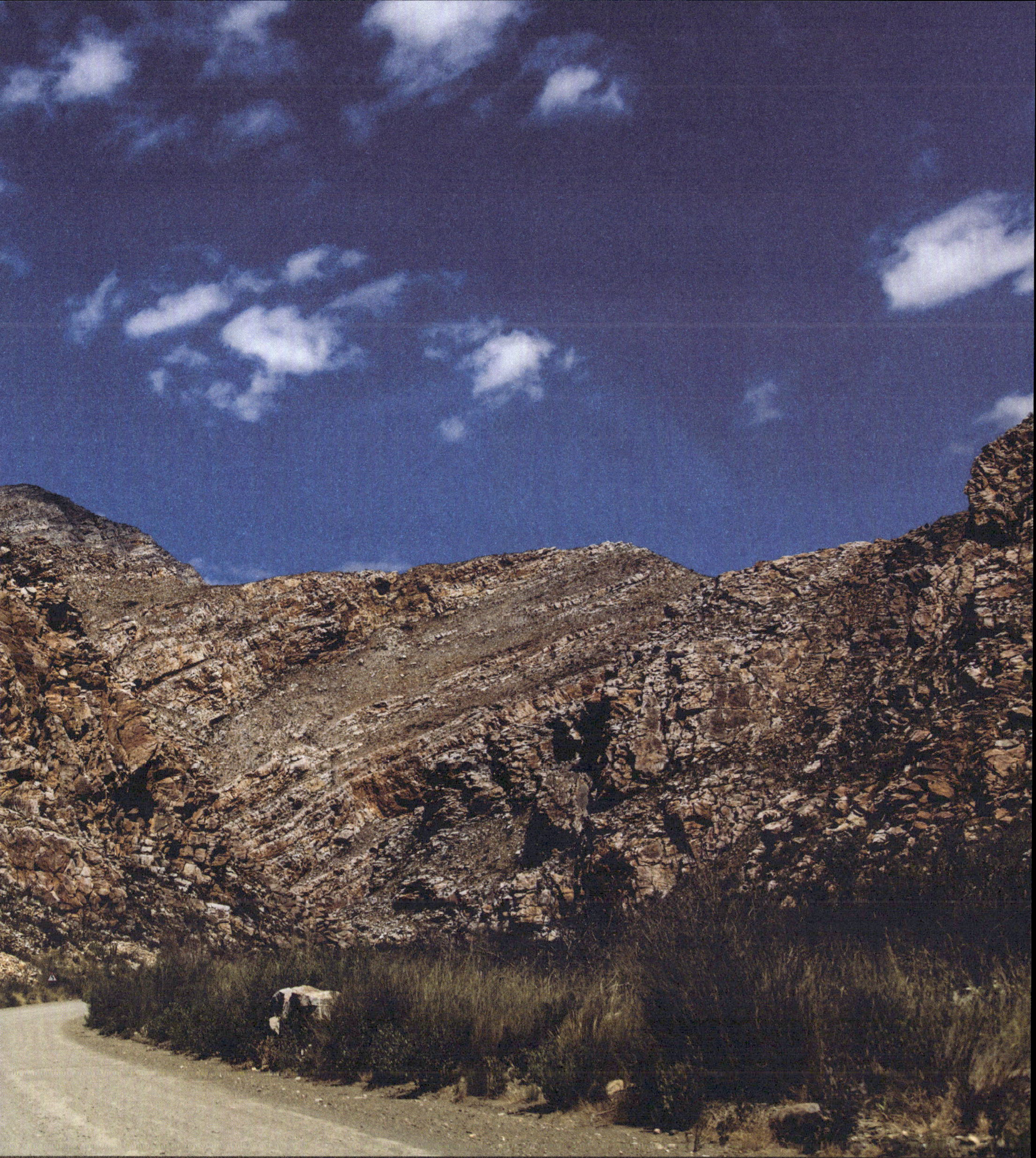

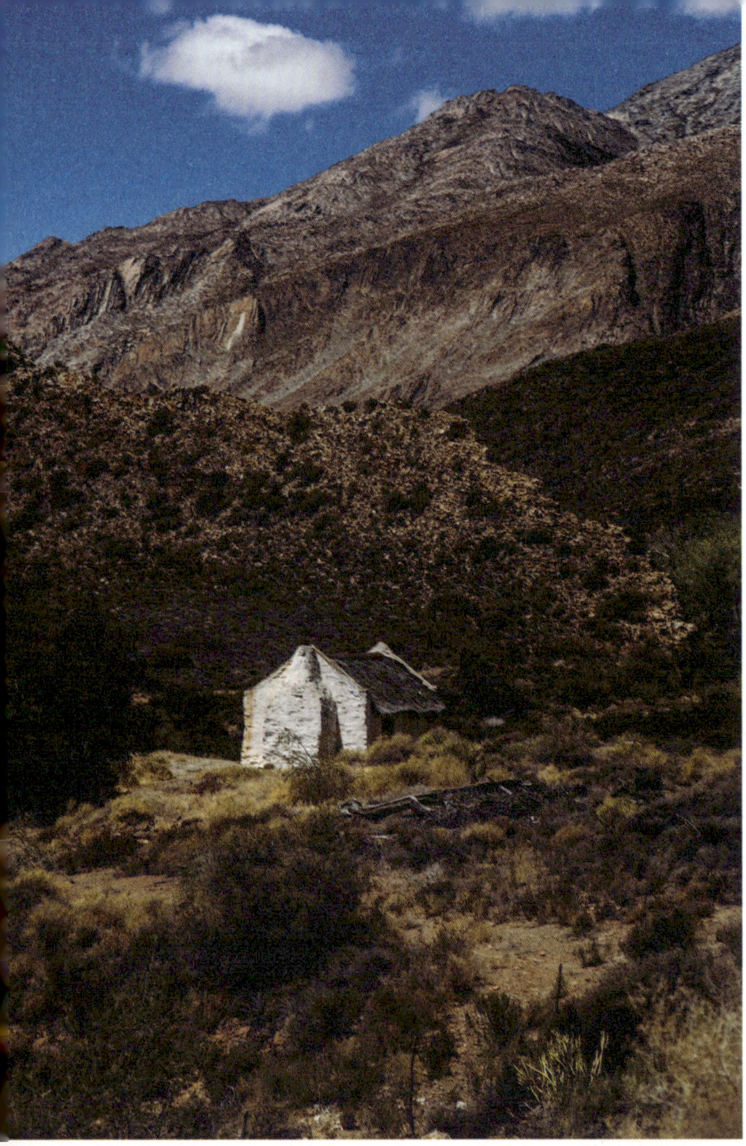

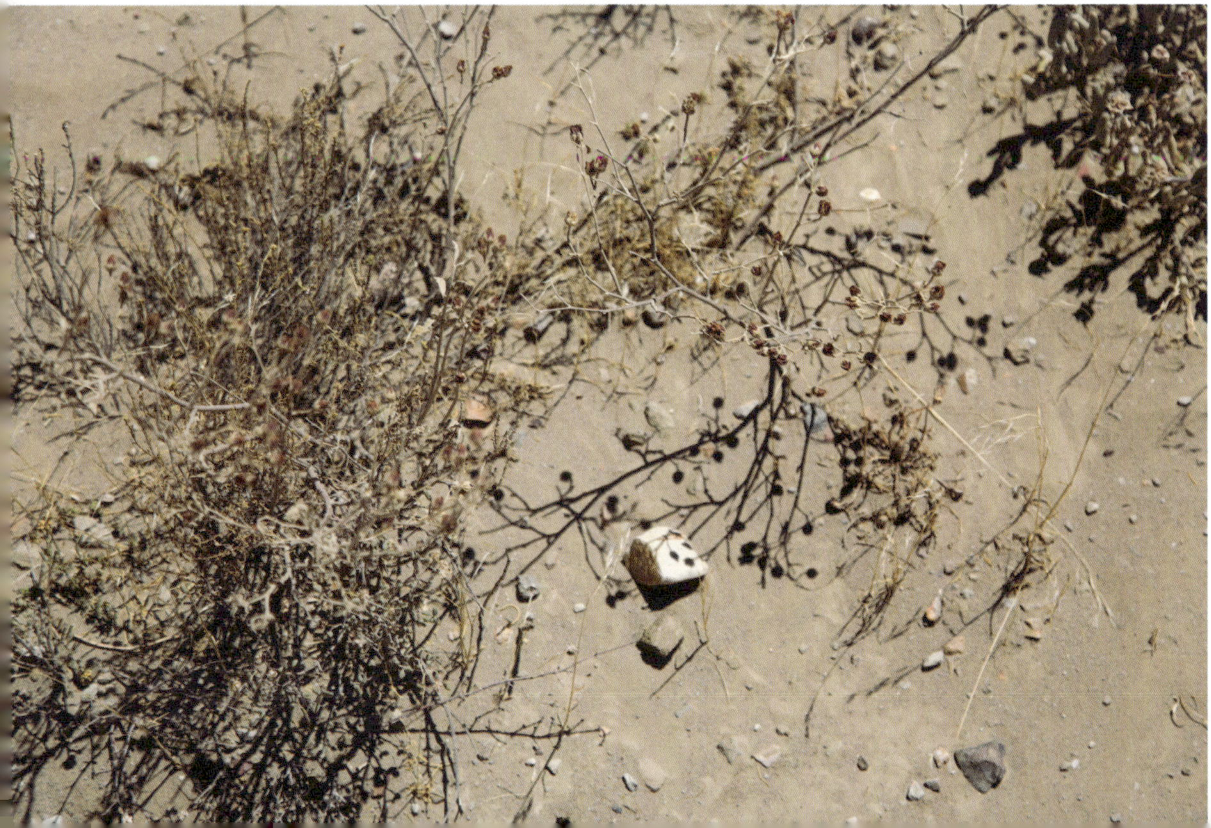

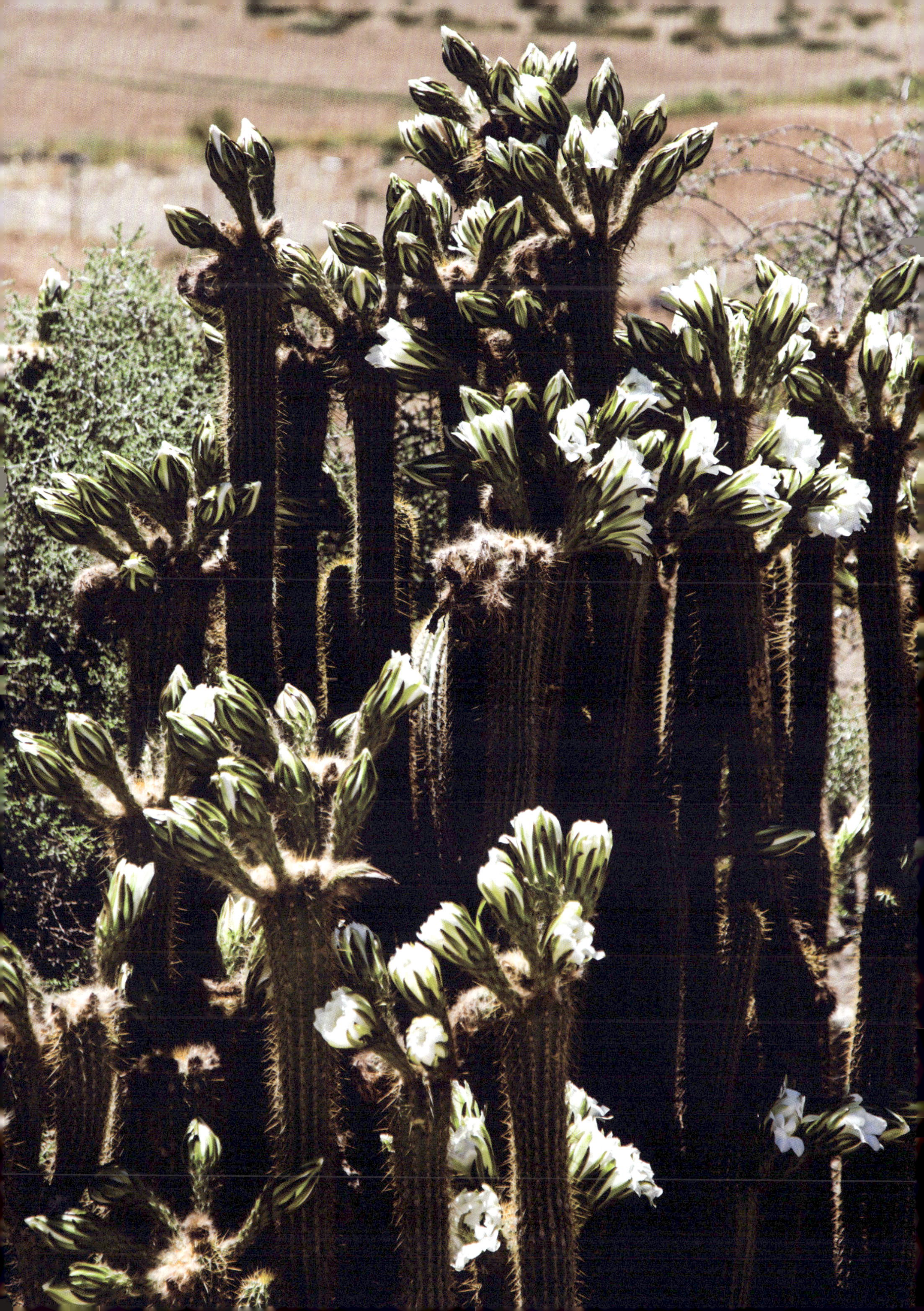

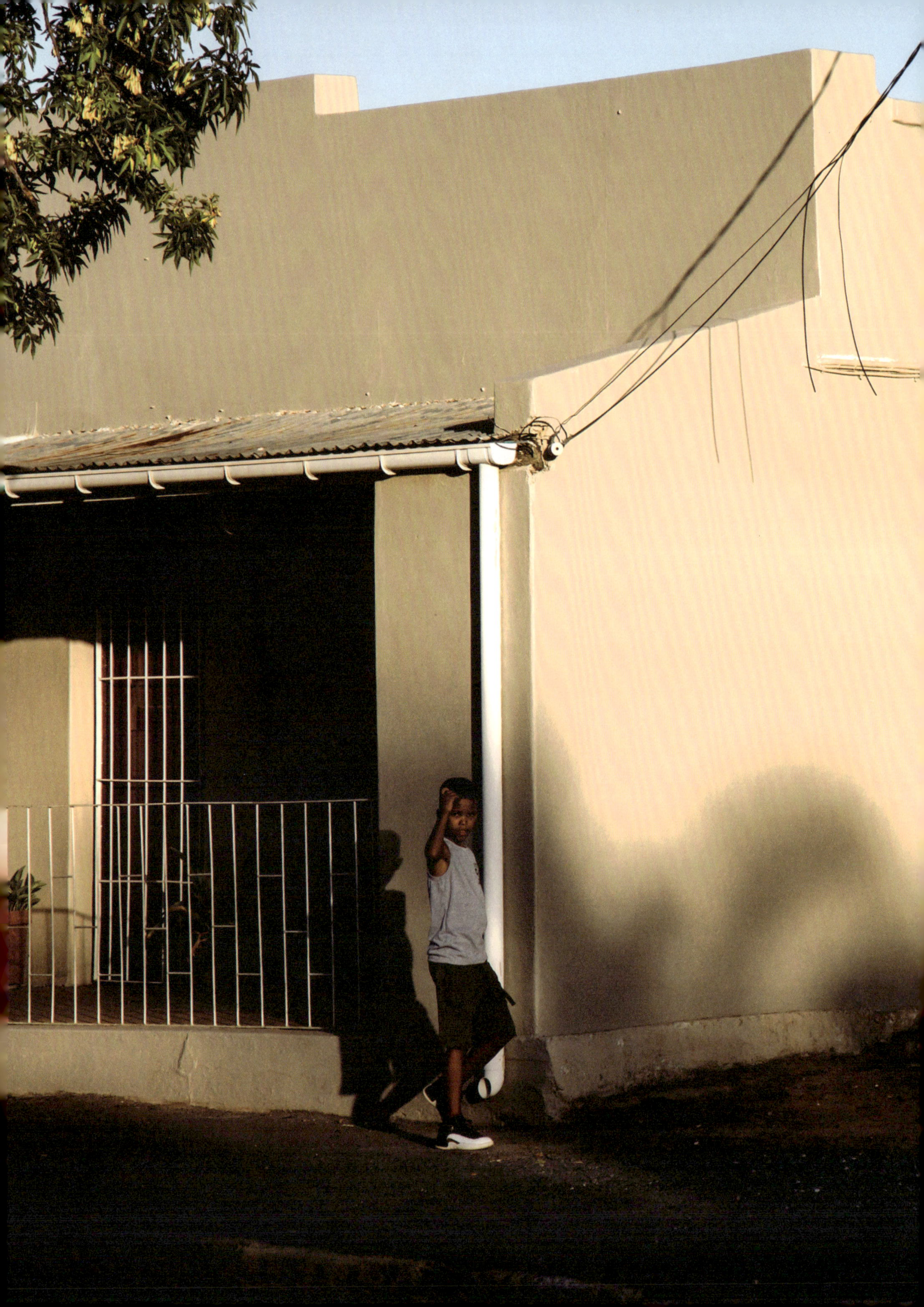

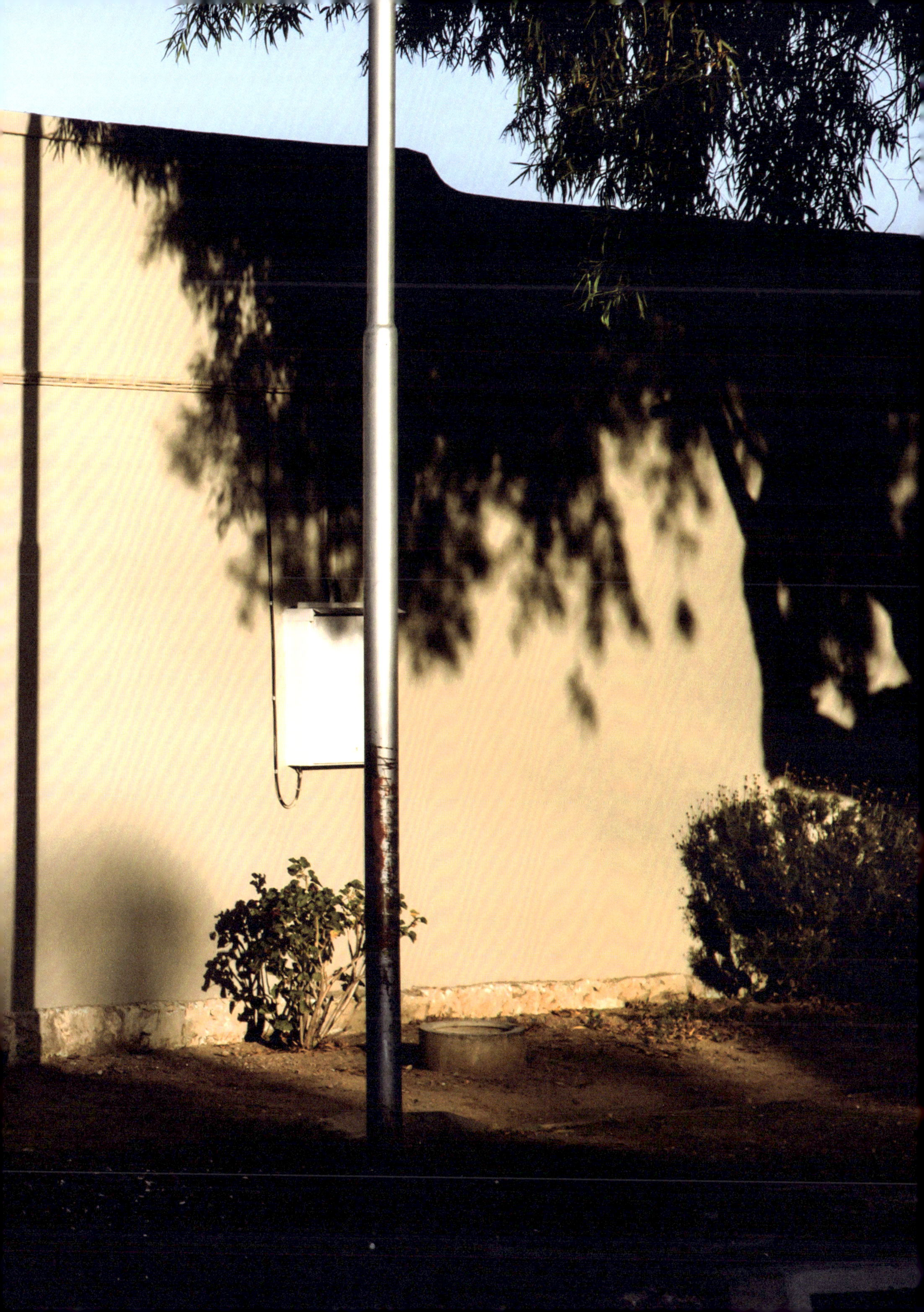

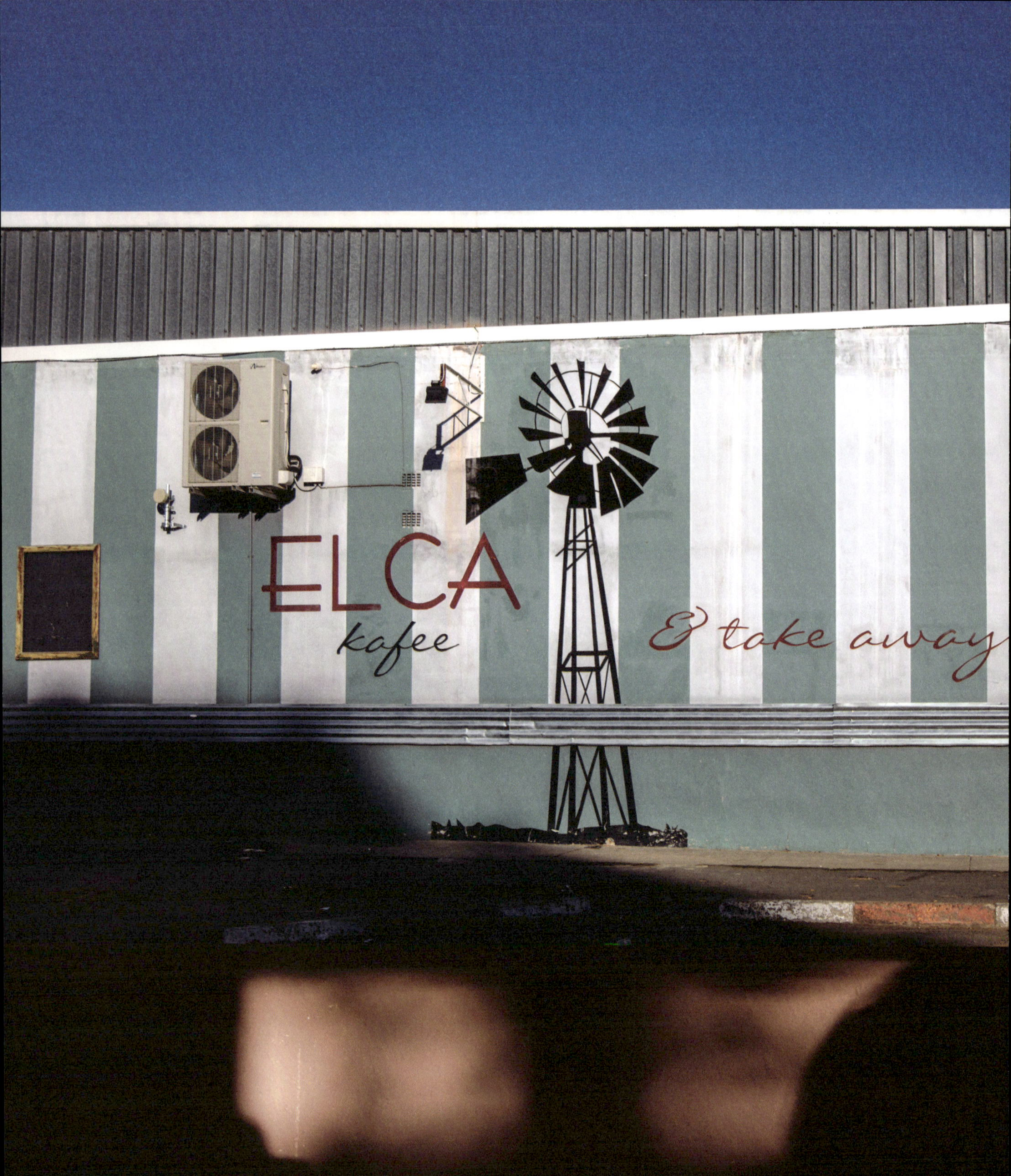
ELCA
kafee
& take away

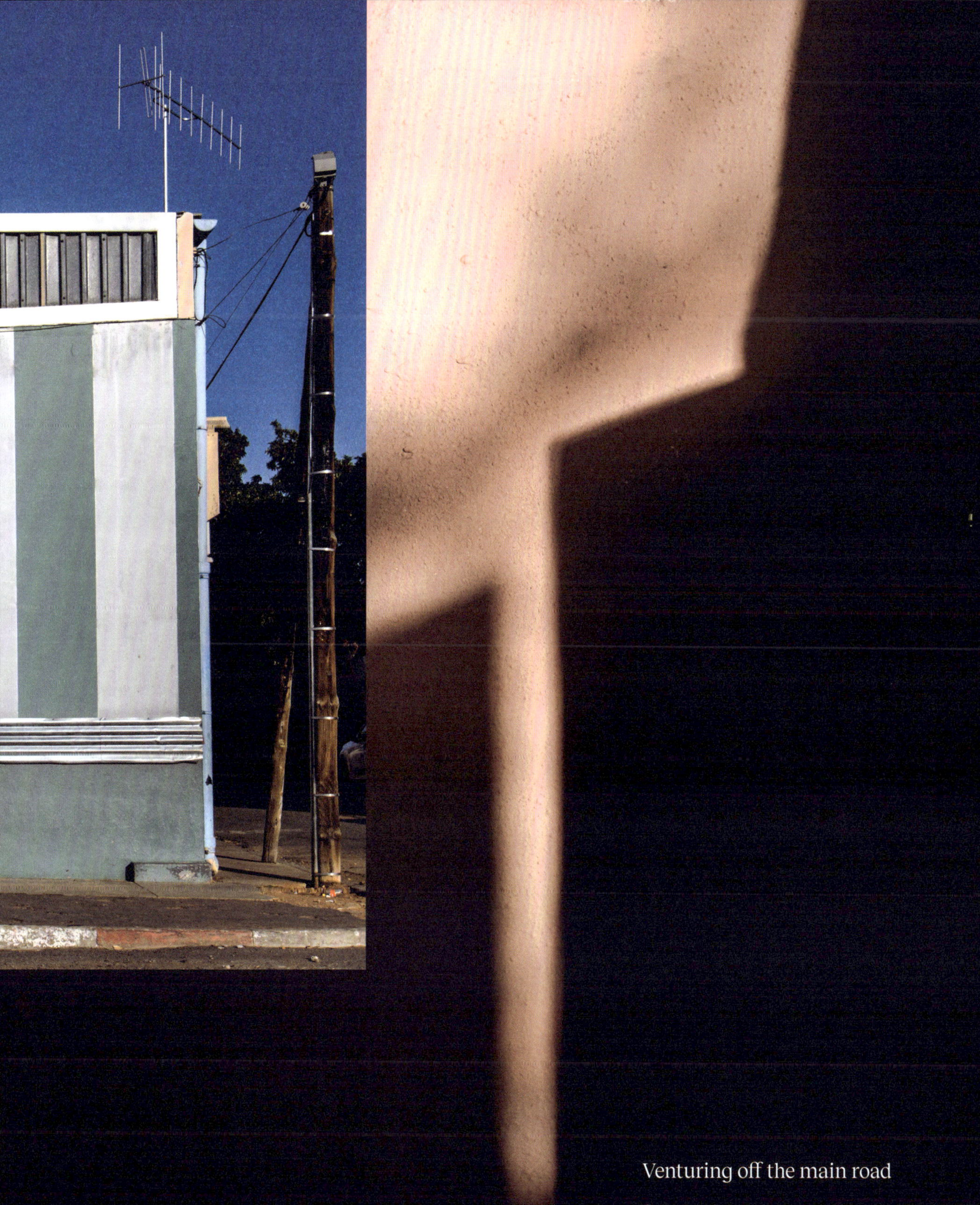

Venturing off the main road

If the three little pigs from the fairy tale had joined forces, instead of each building their own house, then this would be the cottage they built. It is named Strooi Kooi, Afrikaans for straw bed. But it is not just made of straw. This rustic cabin is far more ingeniously built. The double frame structure of long poles has been stuffed with straw bales, and clad with clay. The adobe technique makes this a solid and environmentally friendly place to stay. The small complex has two rooms, both with a kitchenette. Zelma Kriek built it at the rear of her garden. Zelma is originally from Johannesburg, where she owned an interior design shop. Her professional background is apparent in the many thoughtful details in the simple interior of this cabin. She is one of the 'city refugees' who discovered the village and gave it a fresh momentum.

It can get hot here in summer, so the outside shower is a real treat. Showering at night is also a special experience, when the many stars above you blend in with the waterdrops that fall softly on your head. After a deep sleep, the early morning sun awakens you. From your bed, you look straight onto the vineyard.

If the Three Little Pigs had joined forces, they would have built this humble masterpiece.

Zelma Kriek

Earthy comfort

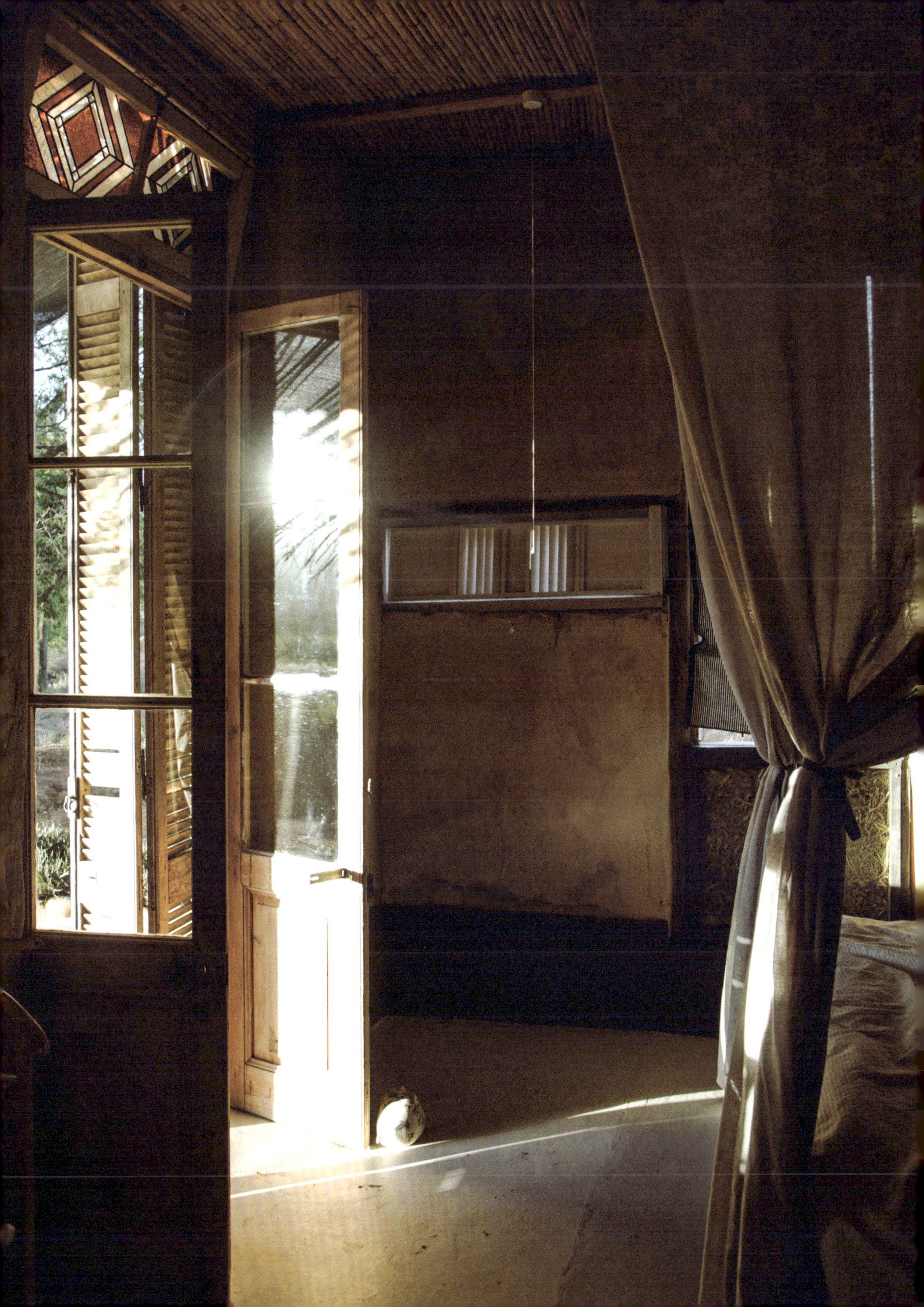

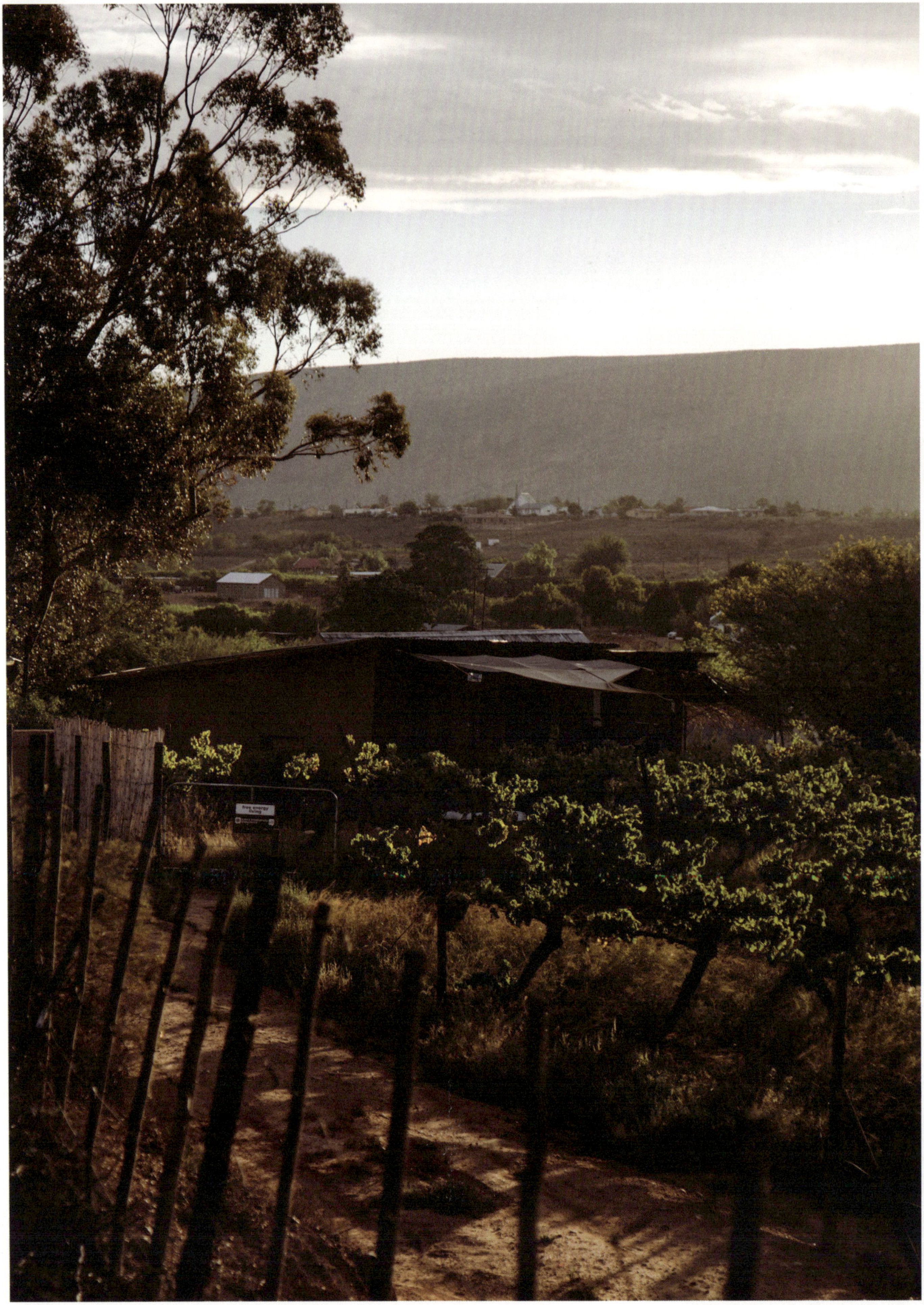
free energy
living

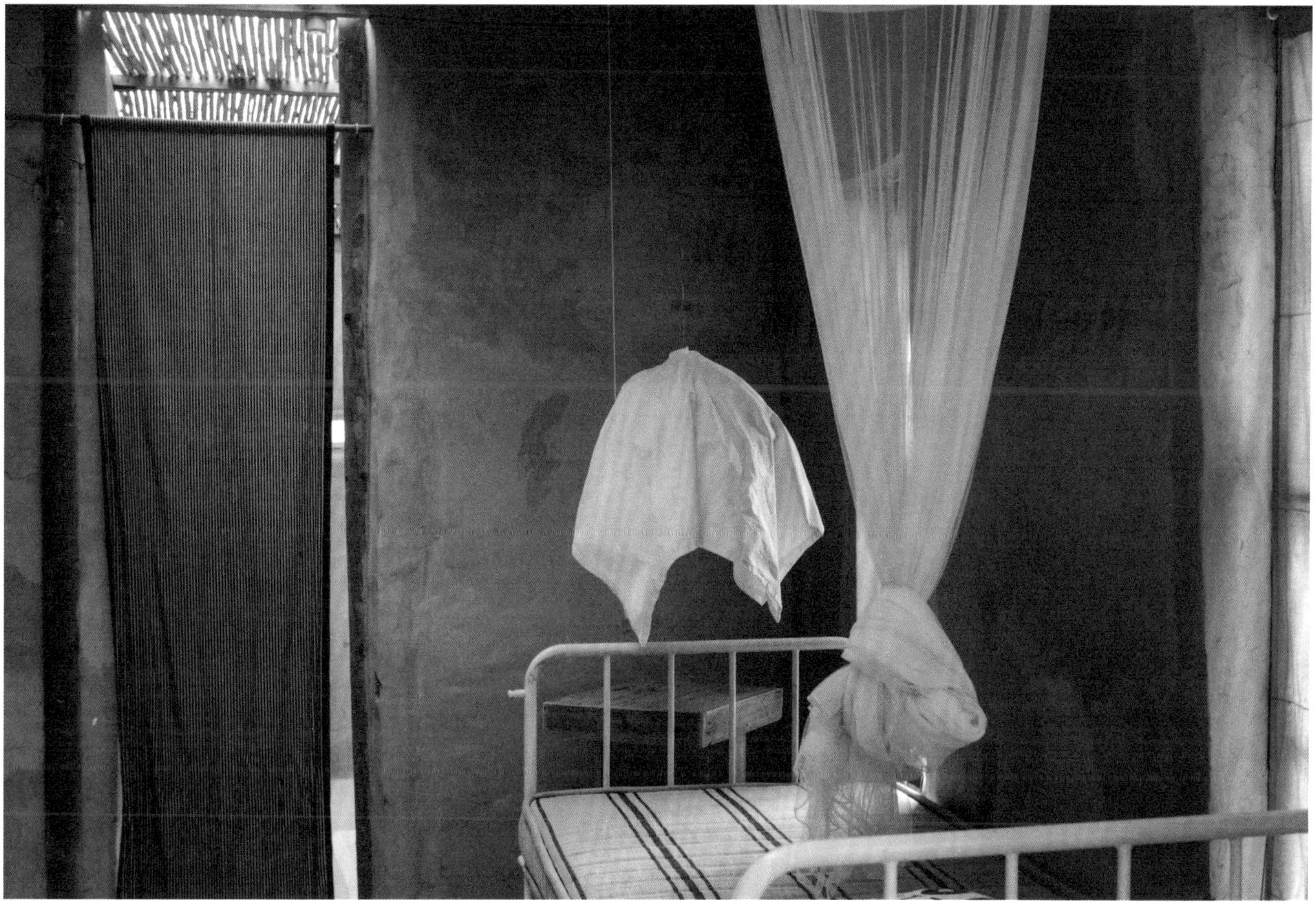
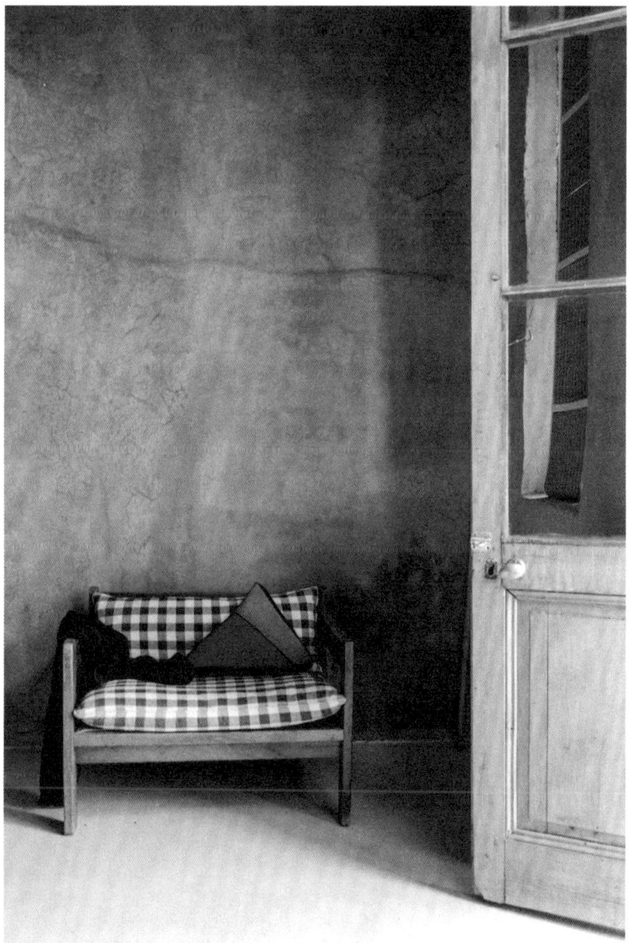
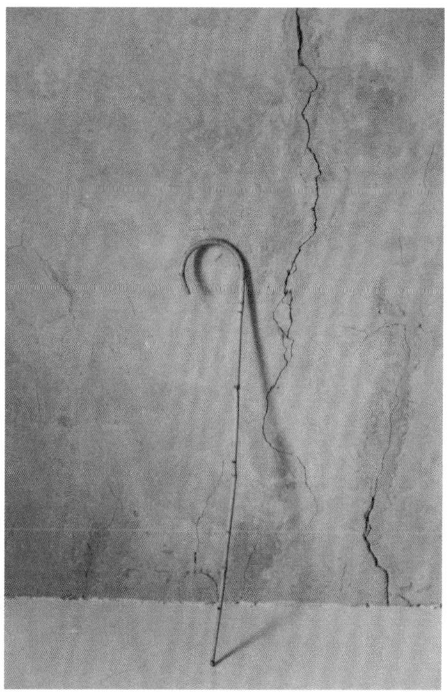

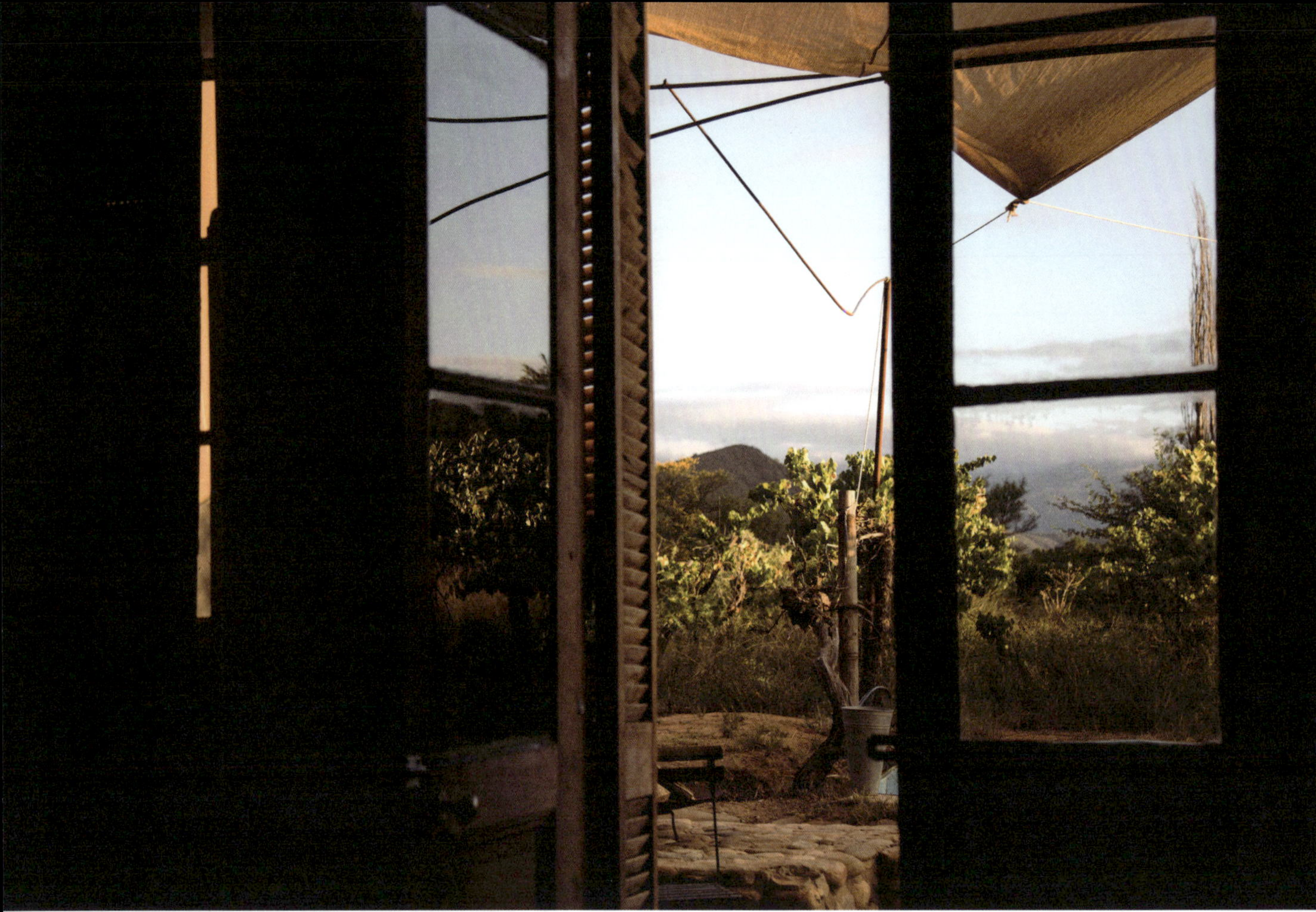

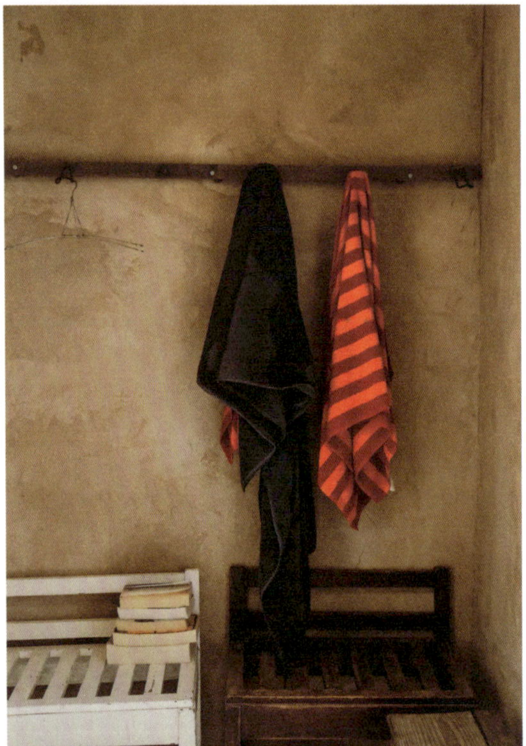

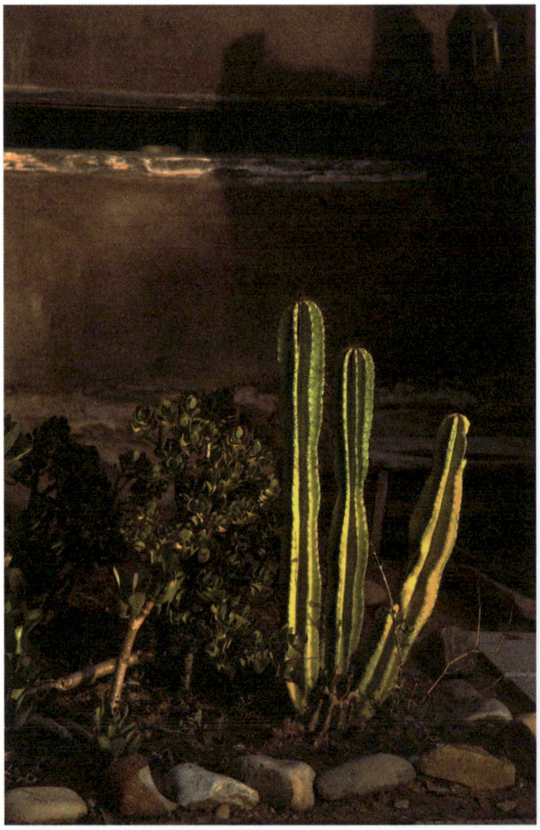

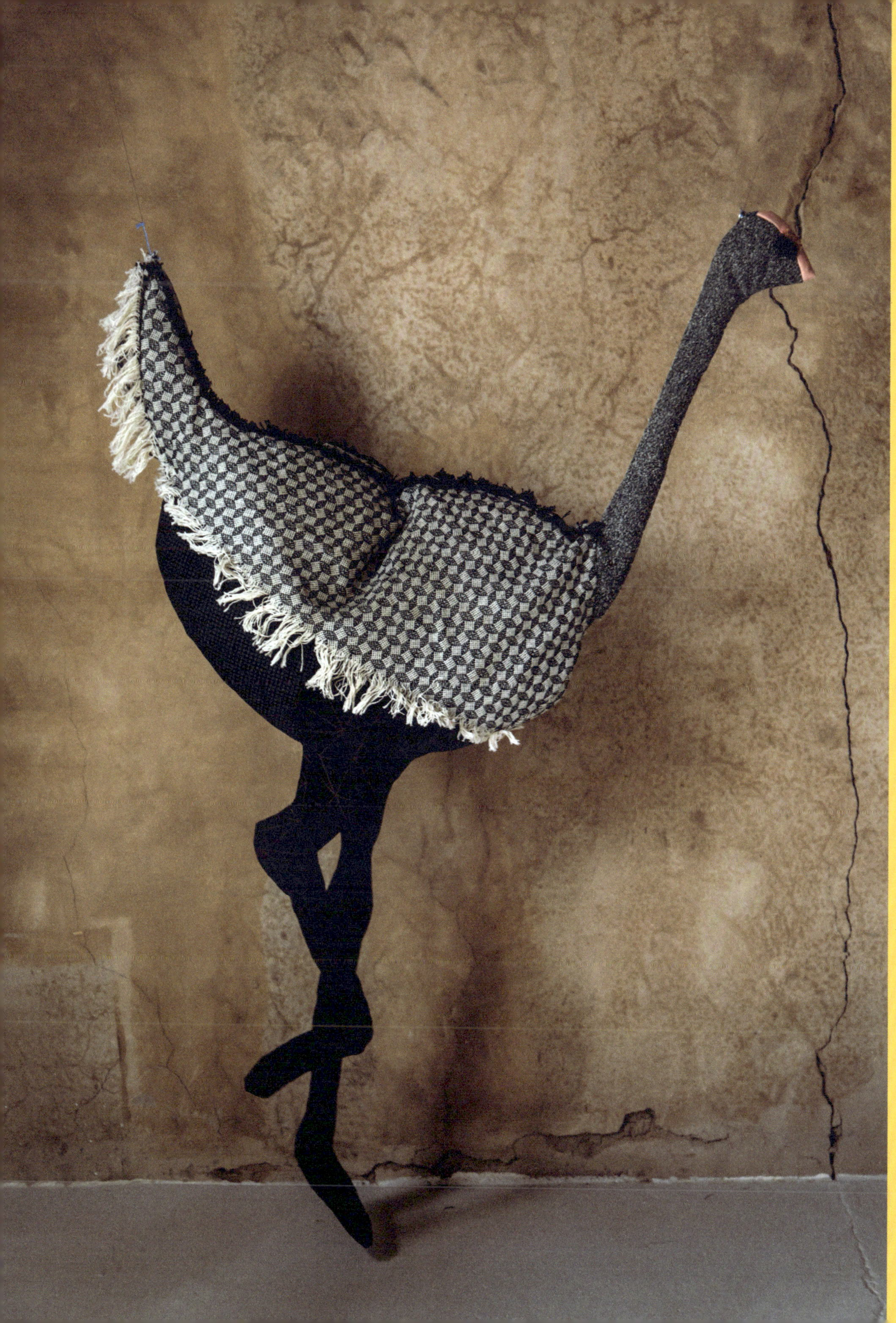

Off track

Occasionally straying off the beaten path can be tempting and often necessary to find accommodation for the night. We drive through a ramshackle gate, up a very bumpy path with loose rocks that hit the bottom of the car with a lot of noise. Driving carefully in order not to get stuck, or on the contrary, accelerating and using the various gears, we make it up the steep slope. It's all part of the adventure.

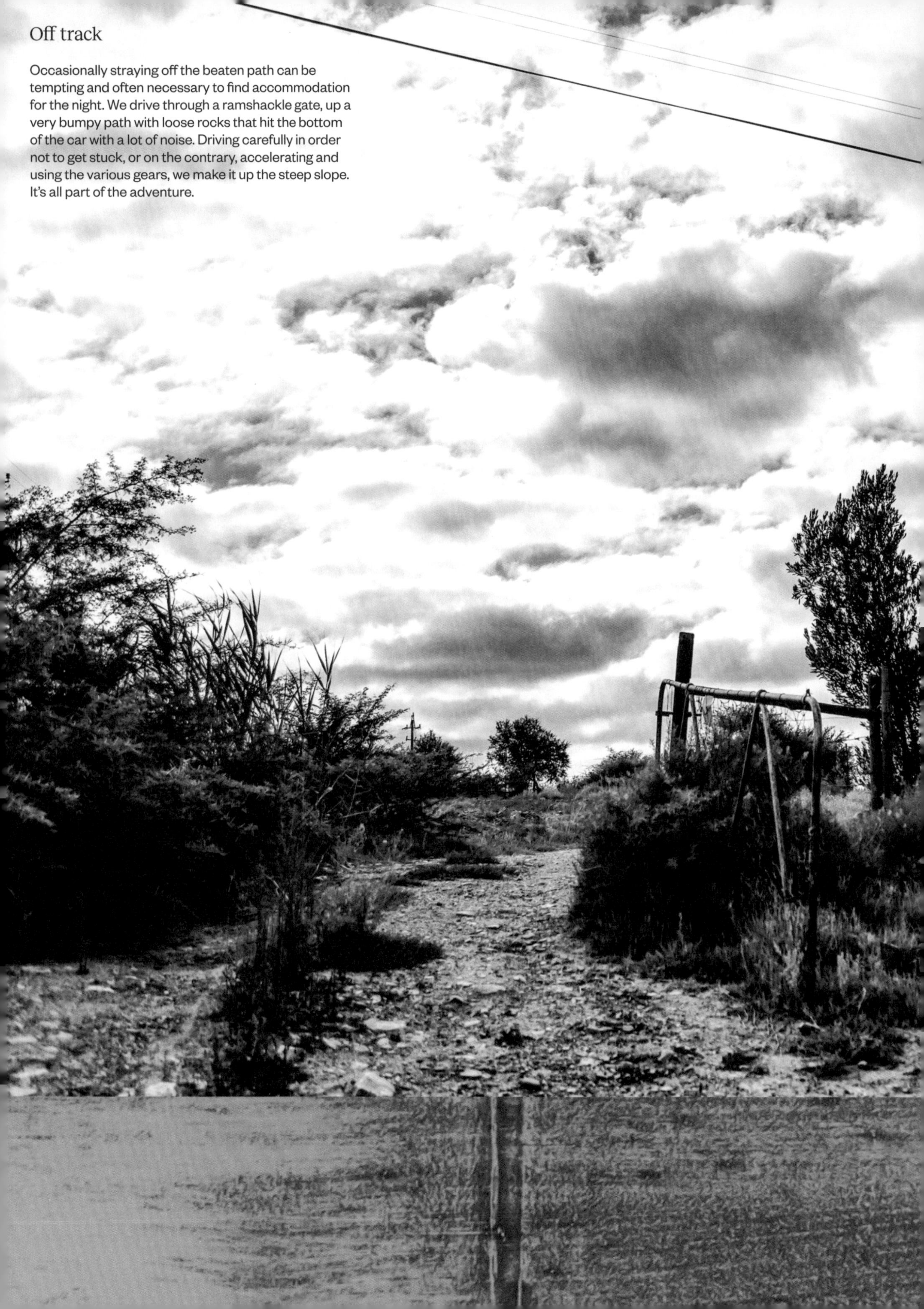

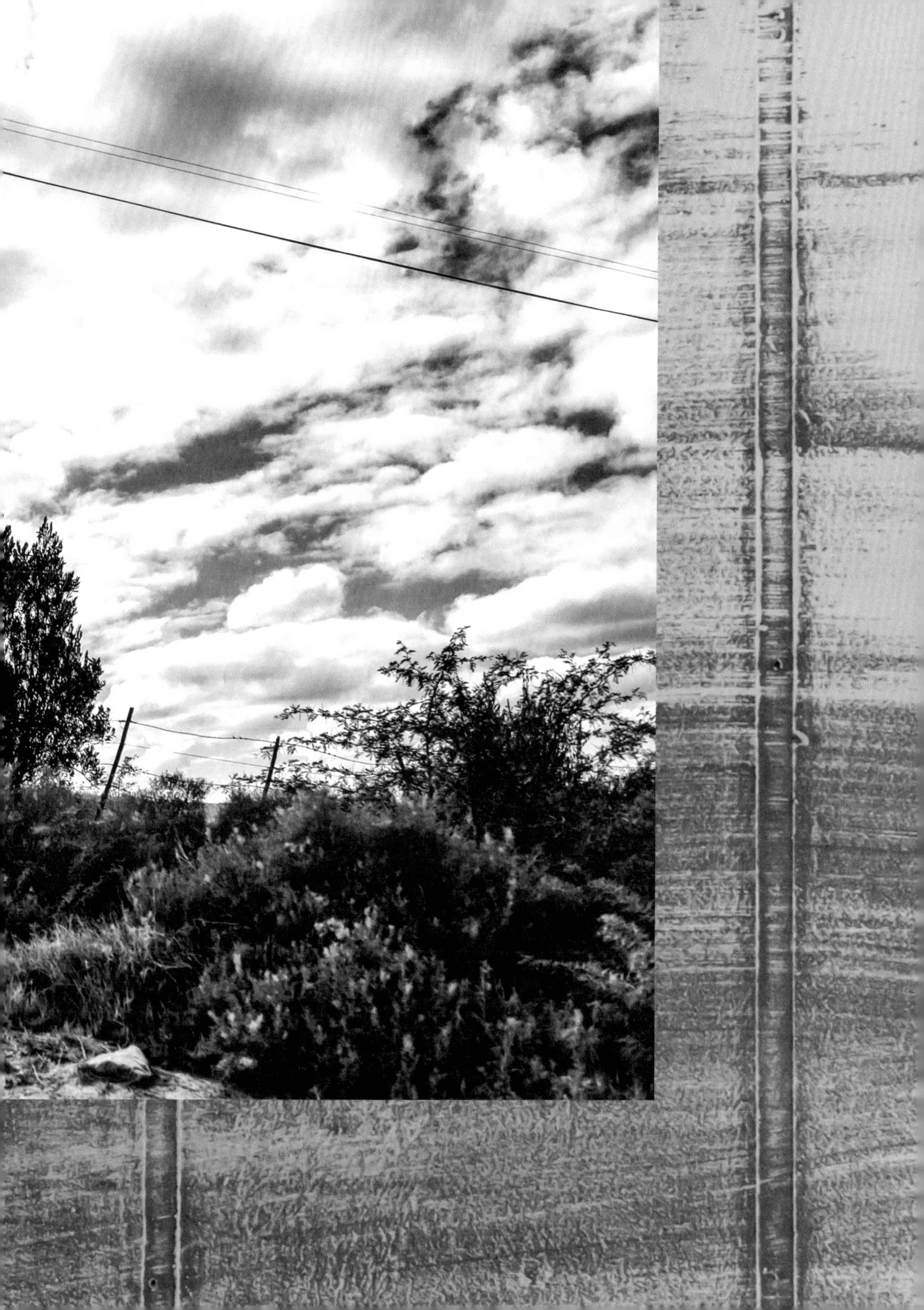

Hylton Nel has enjoyed a long career as a successful ceramic artist and has been living and working in Calitzdorp for several years. His elaborately decorated house is just as colourful as his work and his personality. The different rooms in the house are still used intensively. There are cupboards full of books and trinkets everywhere, and all the walls are covered with paintings and ceramics.

The house is elaborately decorated and colourful. It is charming and teeming with stories, much like Hylton's personality.

In the old barn across the street Hylton has his studio. His ceramic artwork - plates and other objects - is displayed on shelves and hangs on the wall in orderly chaos. The intense South African sunlight shines in through some tiny windows. The dust that gets blown in from the road is caught in the light, adding another dimension to this magical world.

Hylton is represented by the famous Stevenson gallery in Johannesburg. His work was recently shown in London and almost all of the exhibited works were sold. "Now I have my gallery pay it out on a monthly basis. It's my pension", he says with a smile.

The artist lives a simple, old-fashioned lifestyle. He owns neither a computer, nor a car. He has no social media accounts, but he does have a social life. Friends drop in and enjoy a drink on the veranda with him, where they talk and listen to his many stories about the years he spent in Europe and his daily life here. He is a man with a keen interest and considerable knowledge of the world, politics and art.

The neighbourhood children come to watch the football match on his television. Hylton's house is always full of life and open to everyone. Until 6 p.m., he says, because that is when he closes the gate to enjoy some private time, in the company of his dogs.

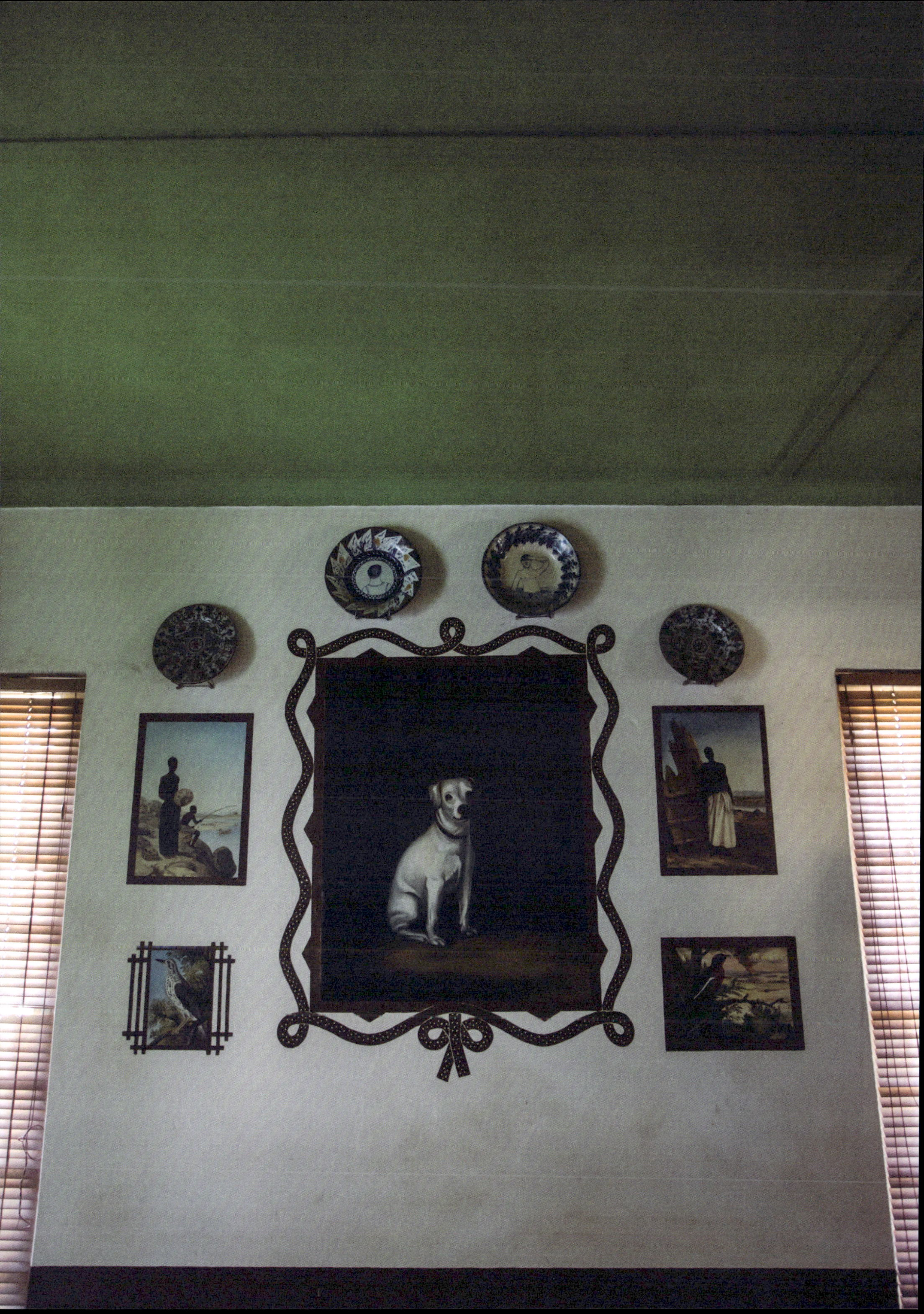

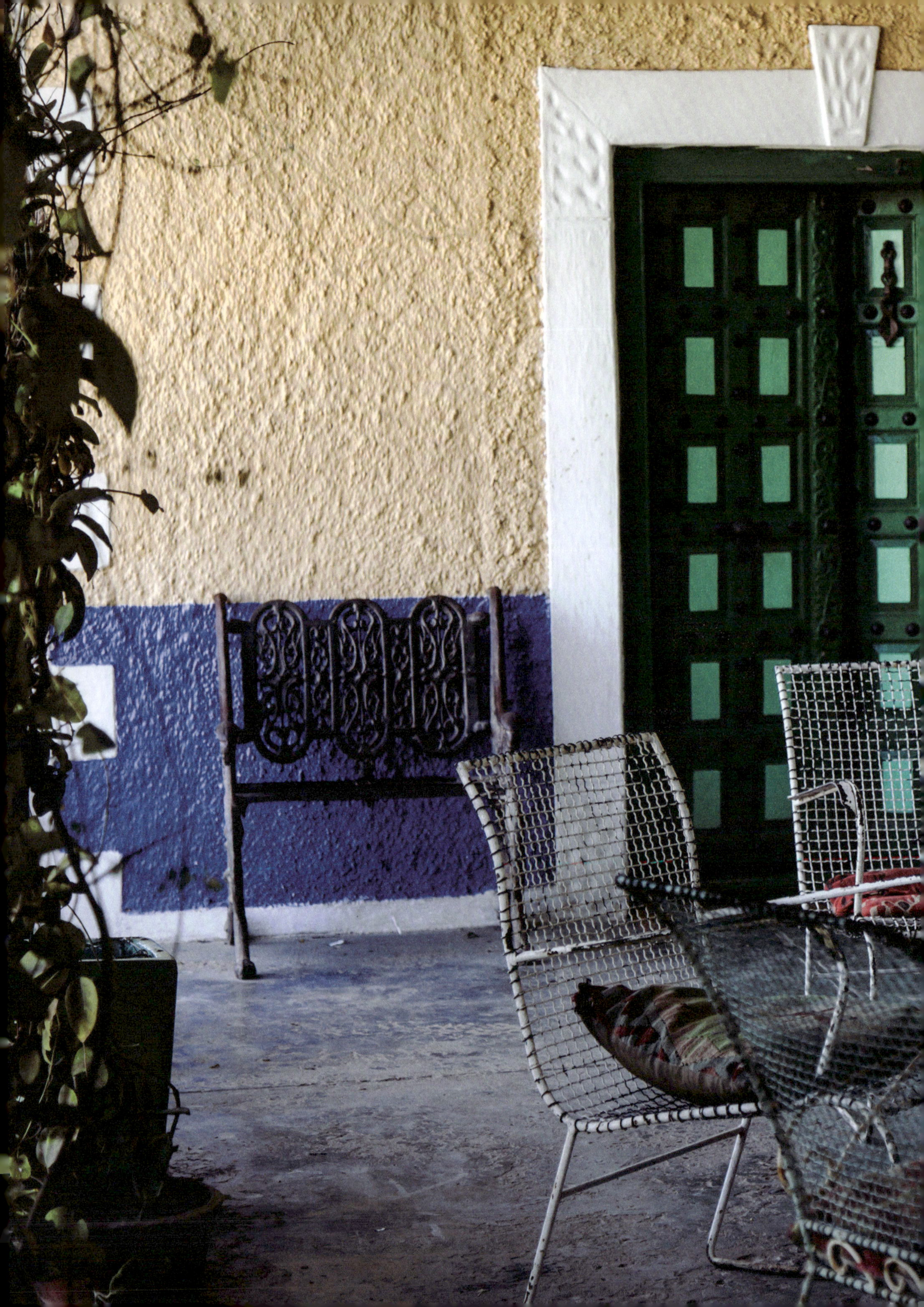

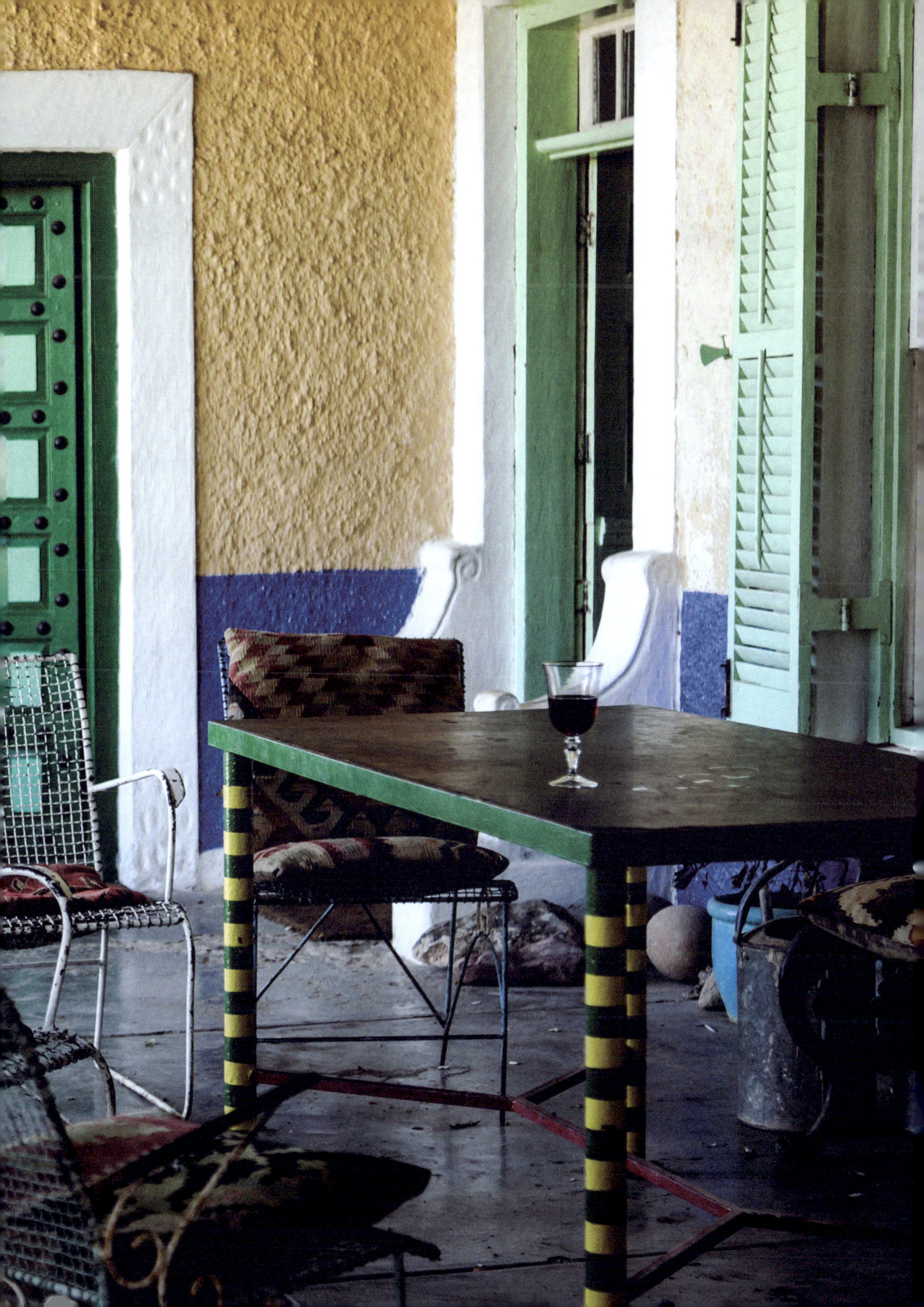

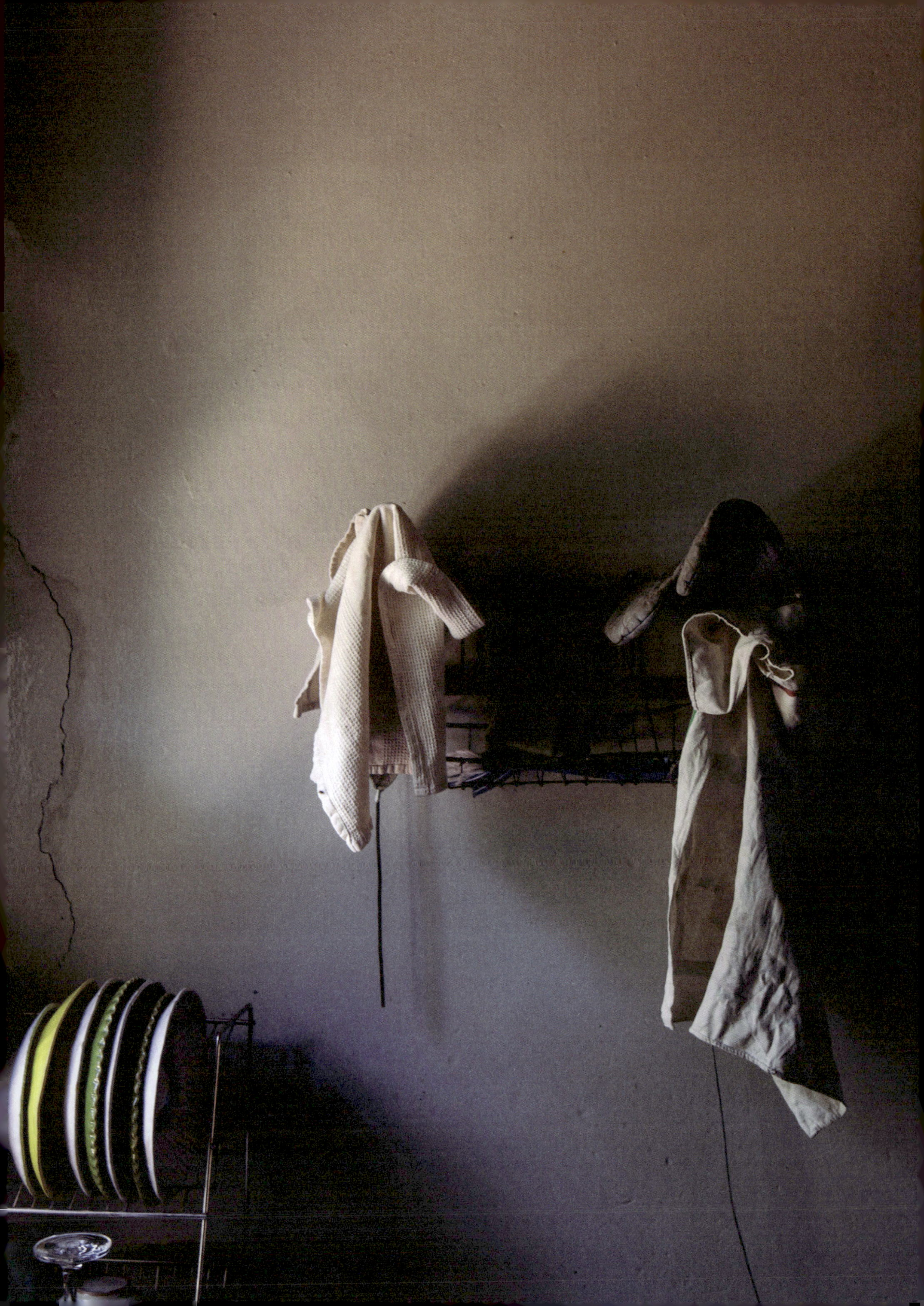

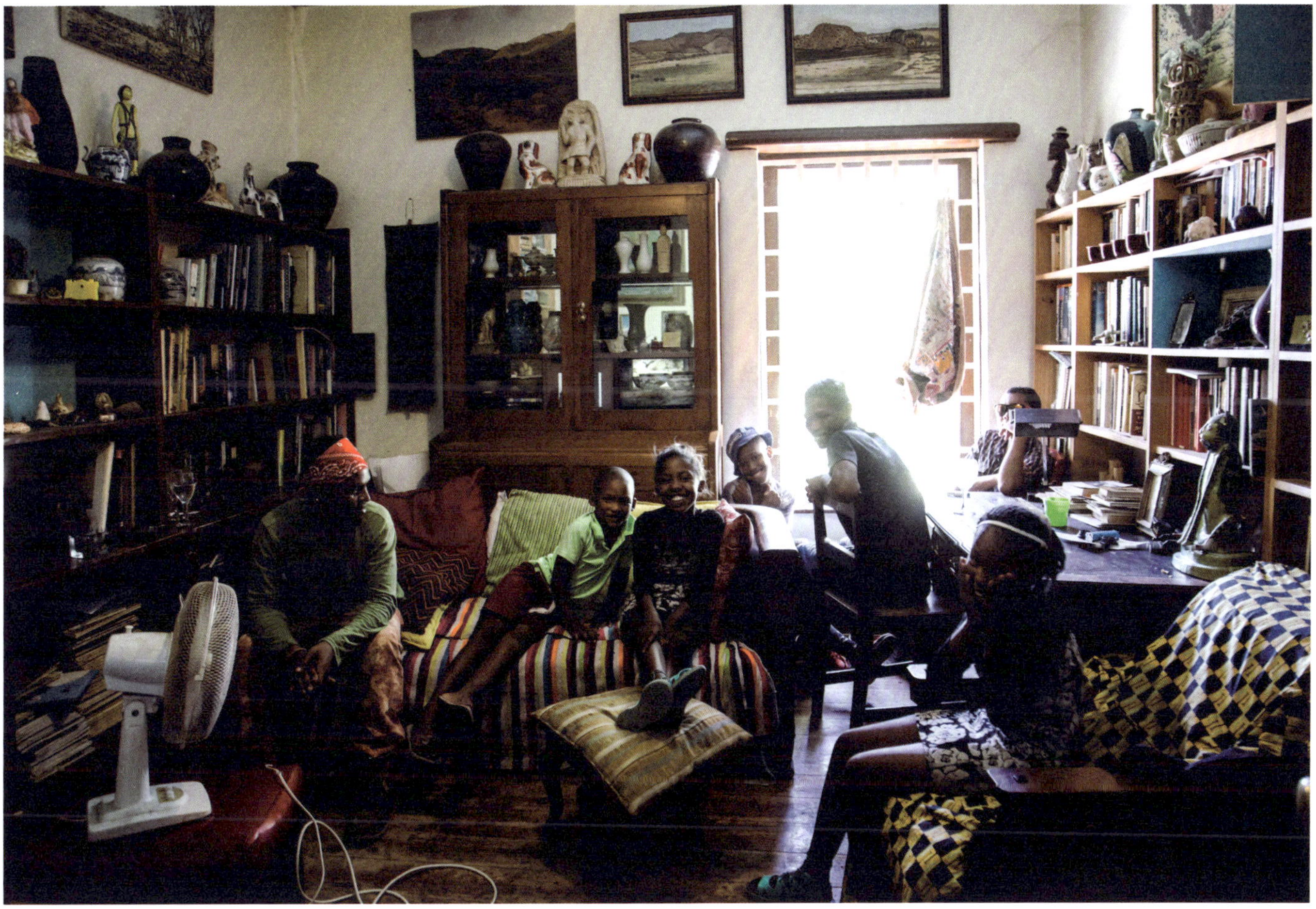

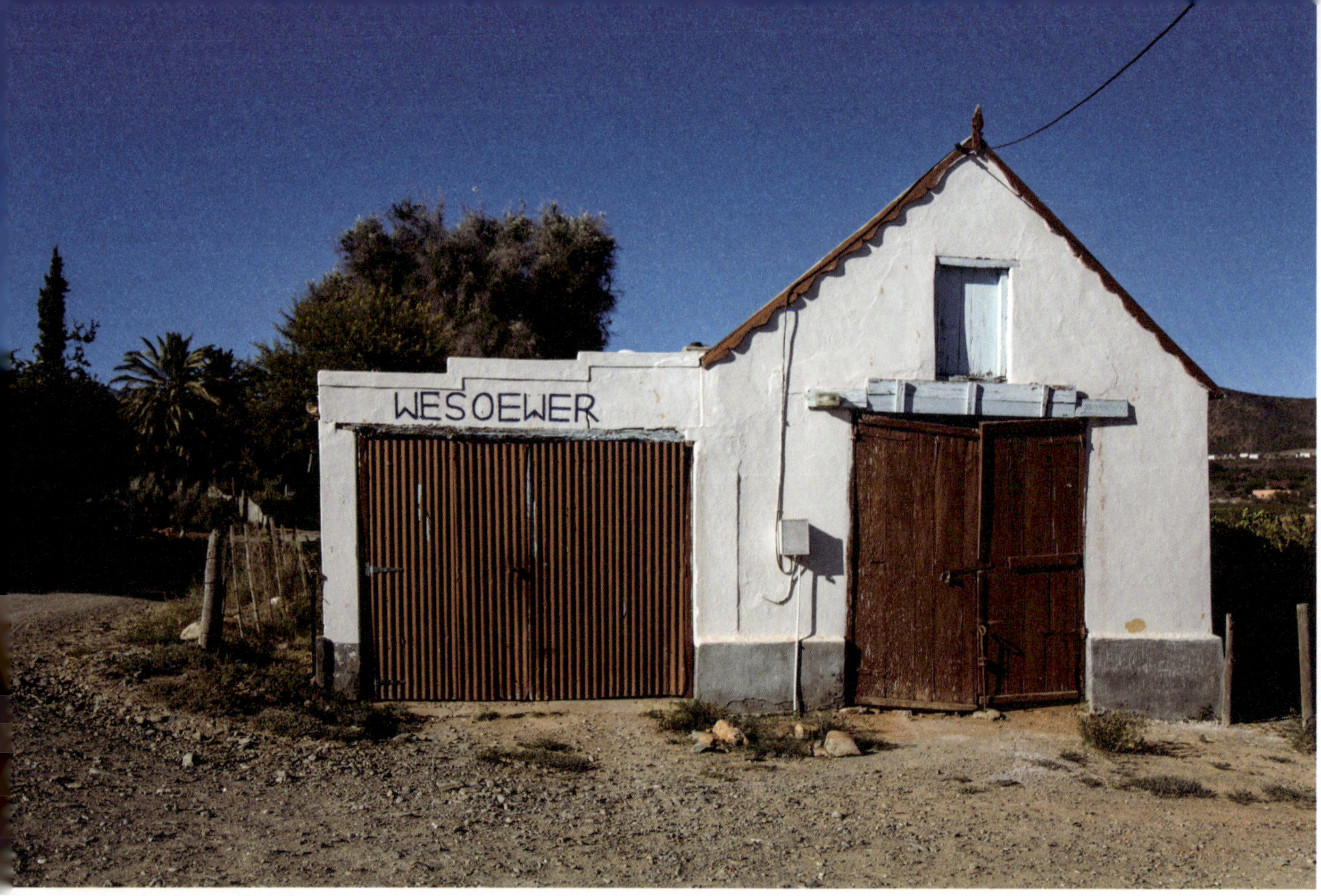
WESOEWER

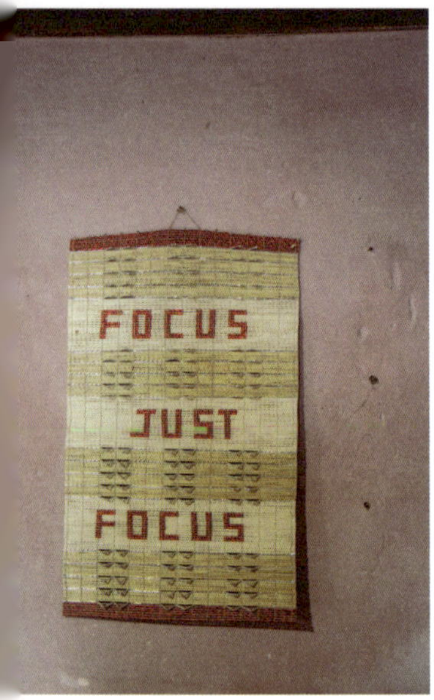
FOCUS
JUST
FOCUS

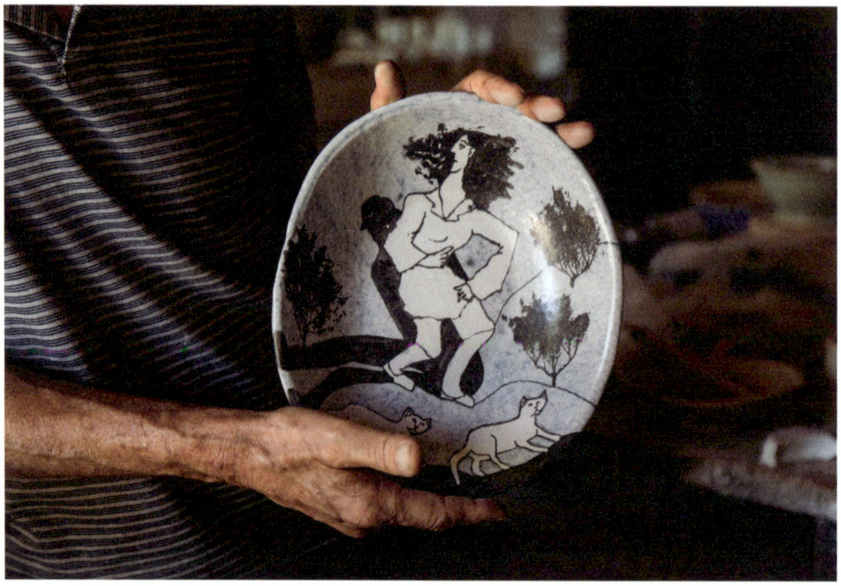

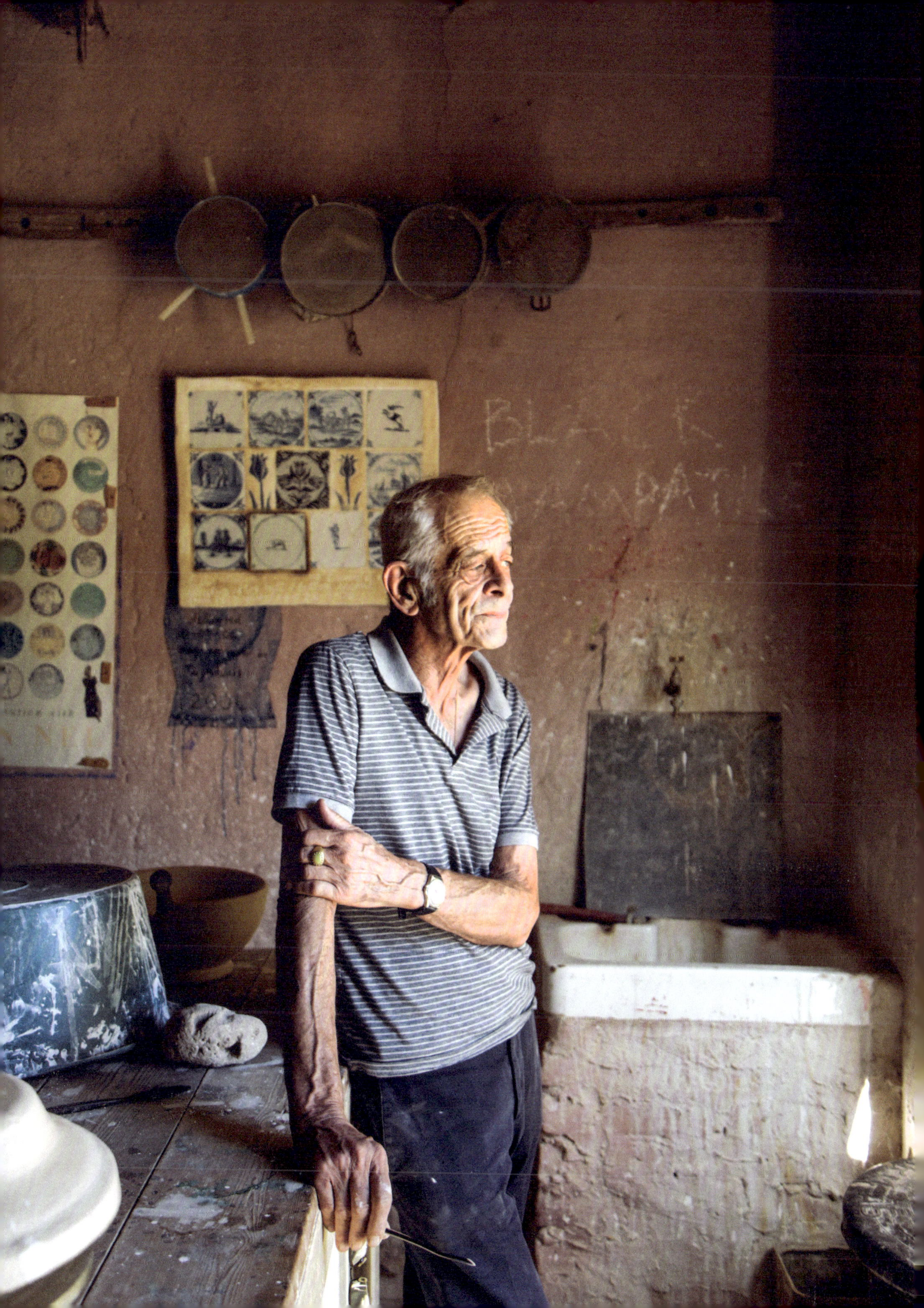

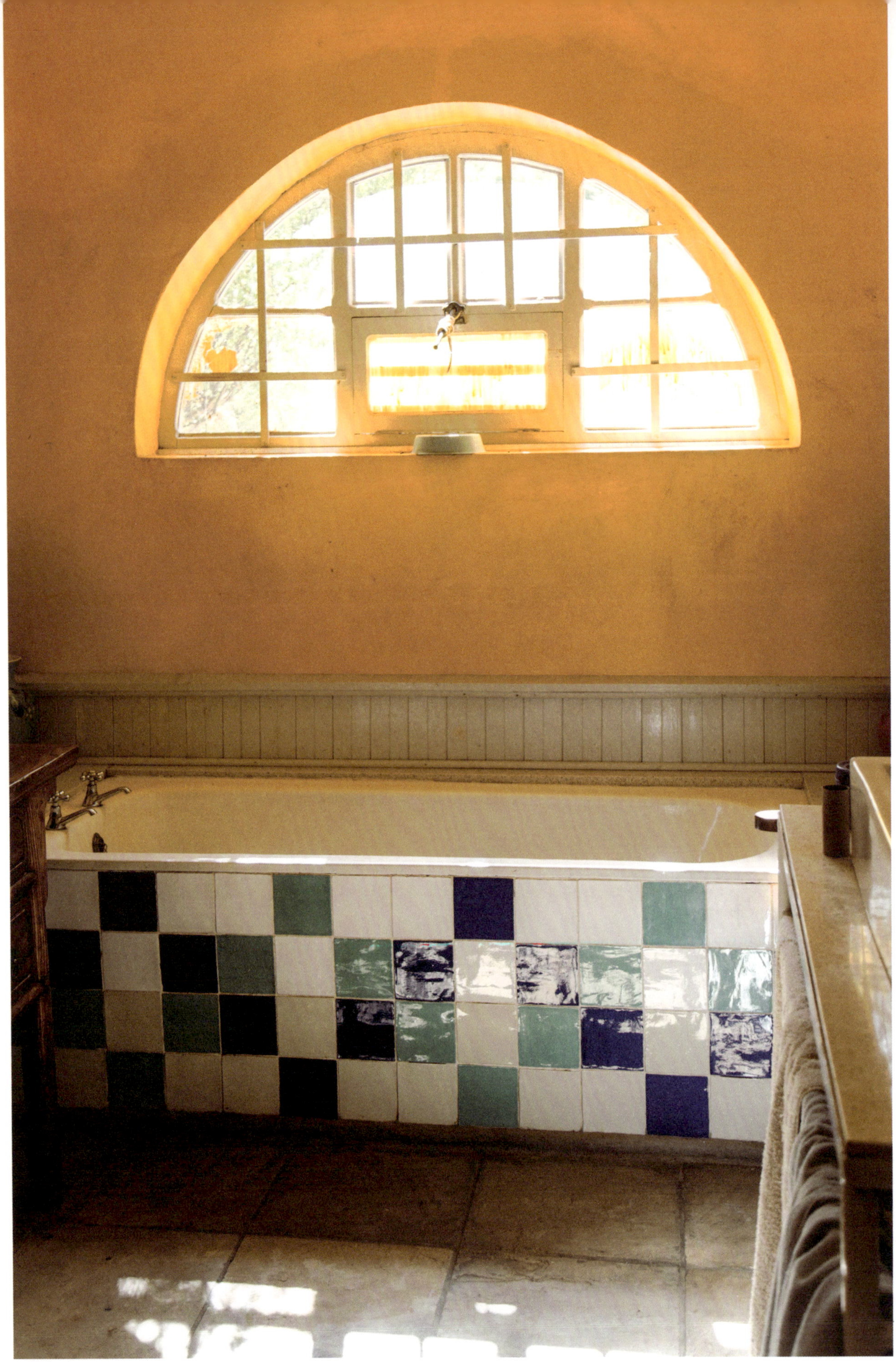

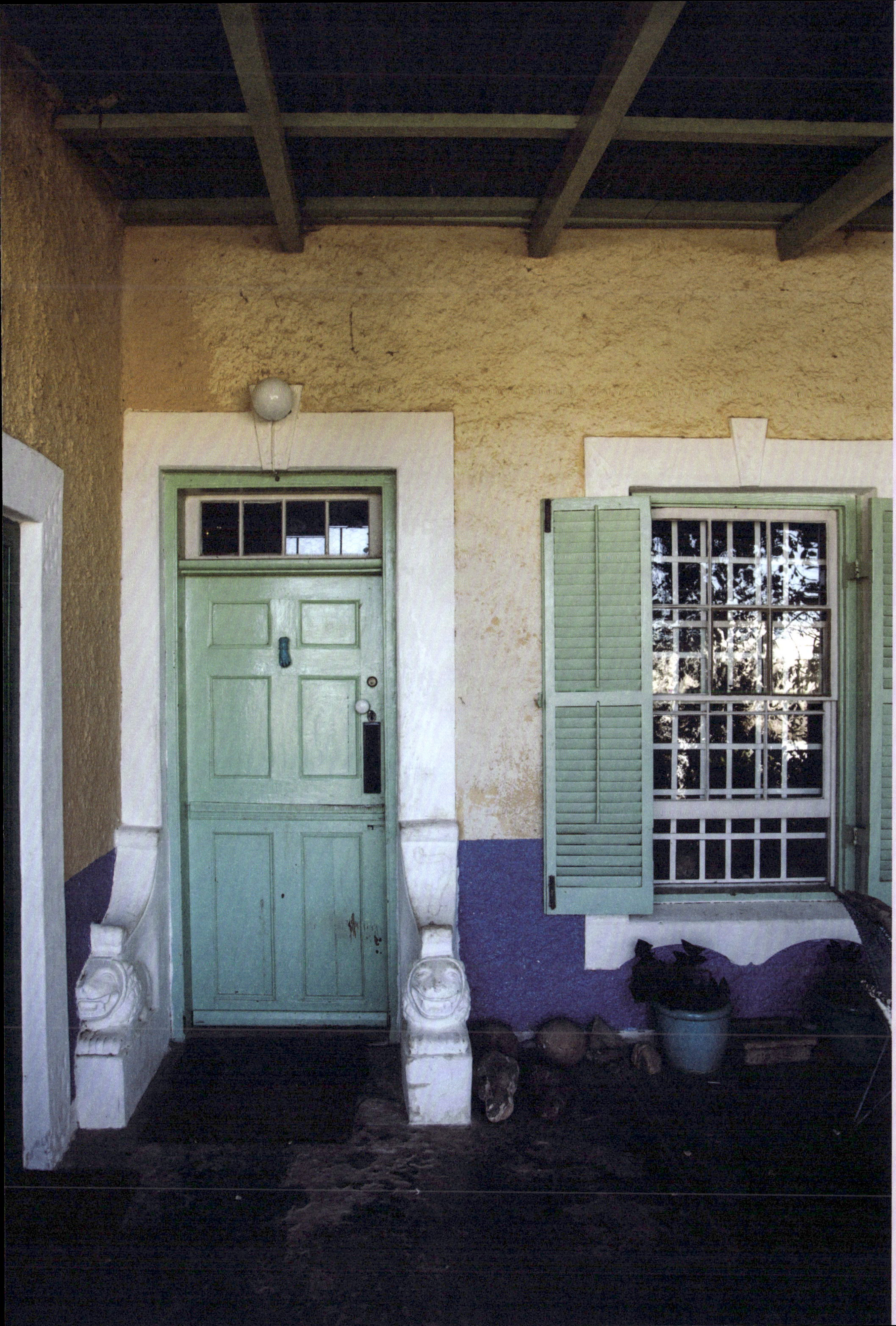

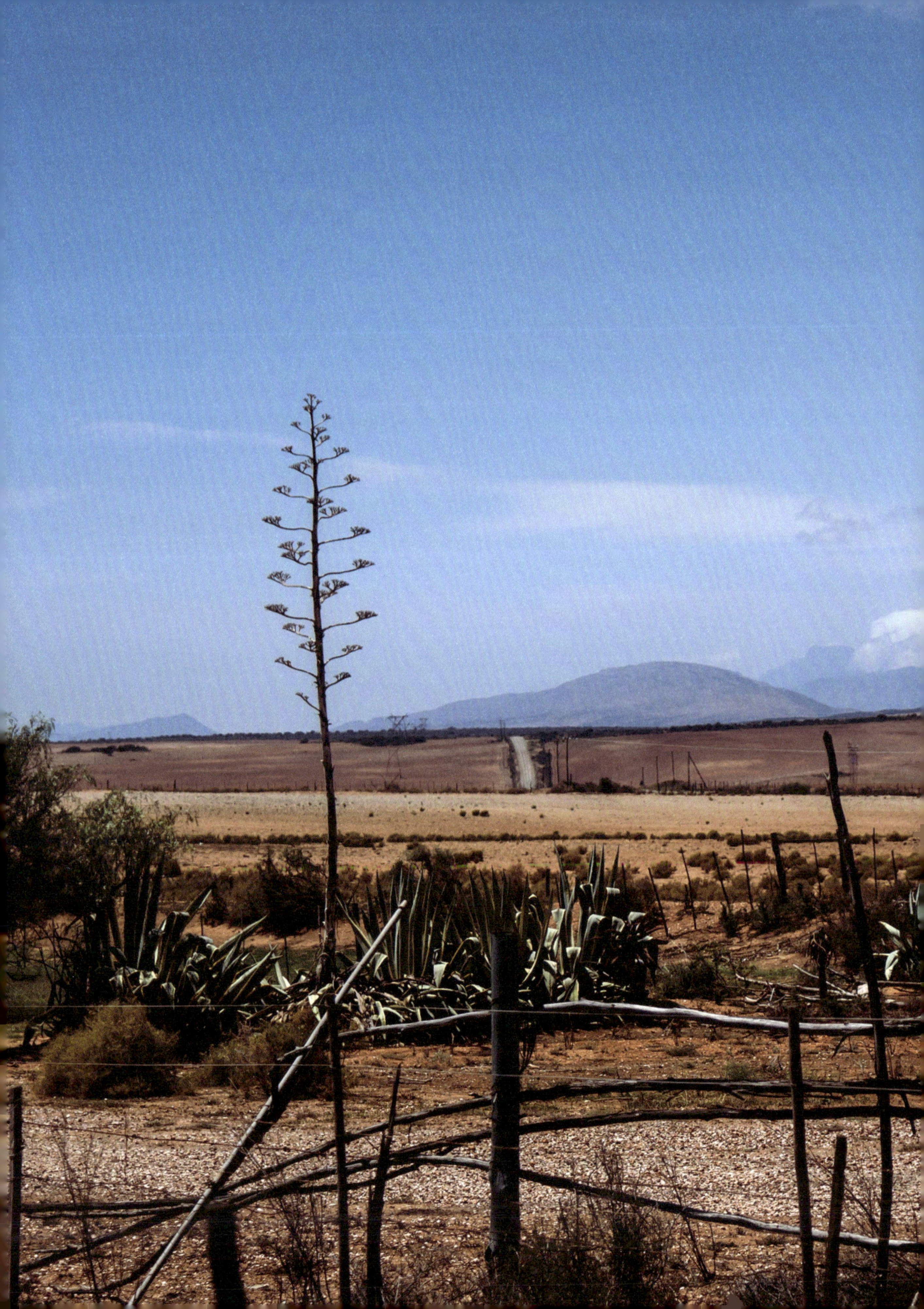

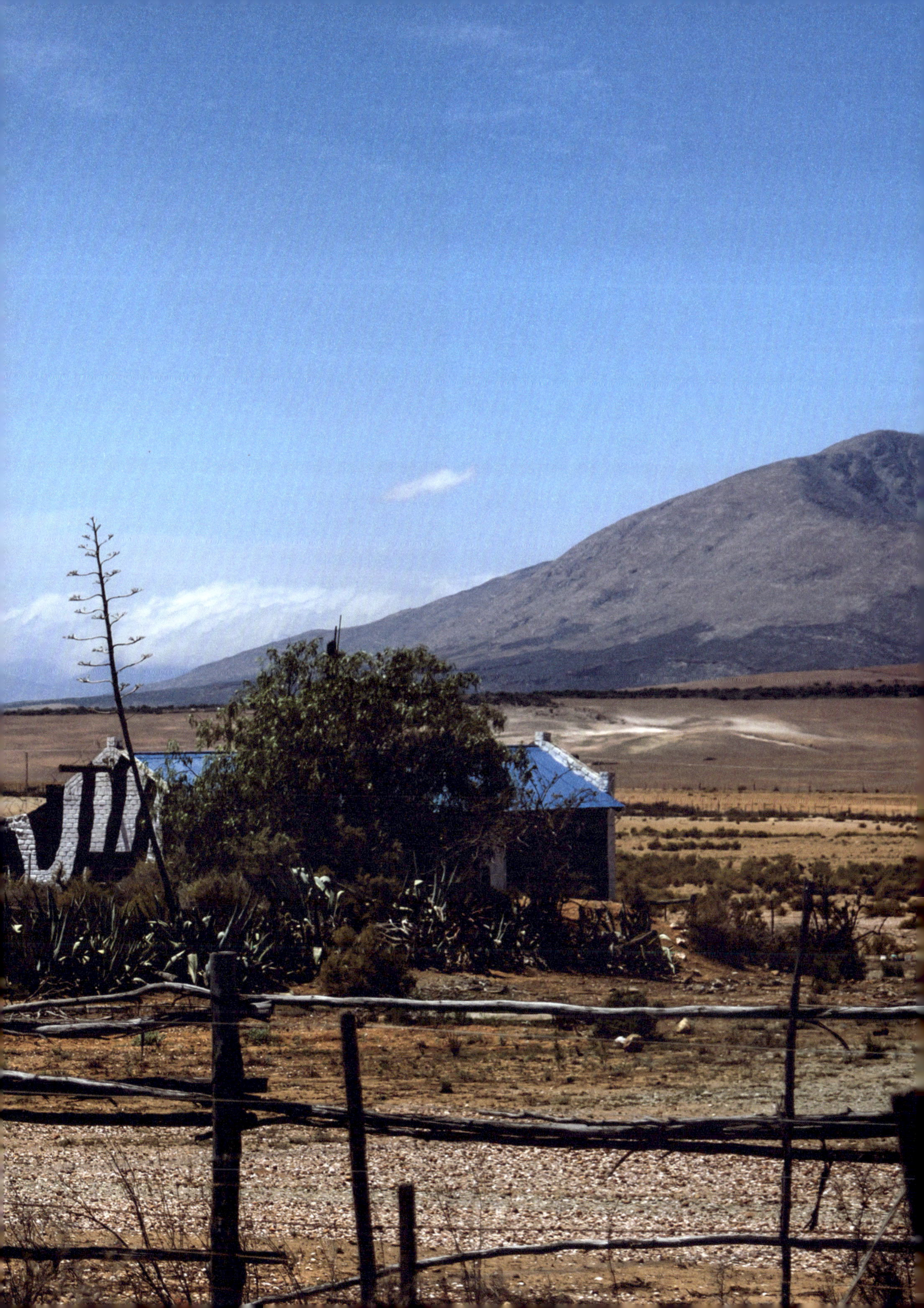

4

Garden Route

98

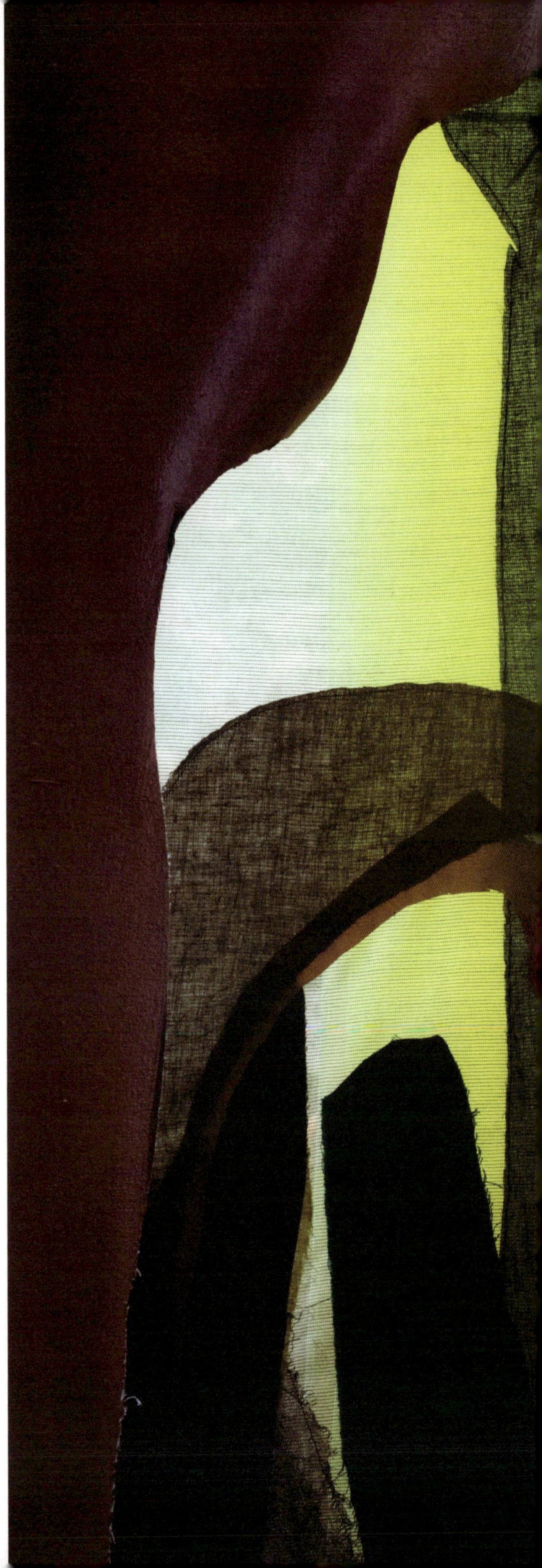

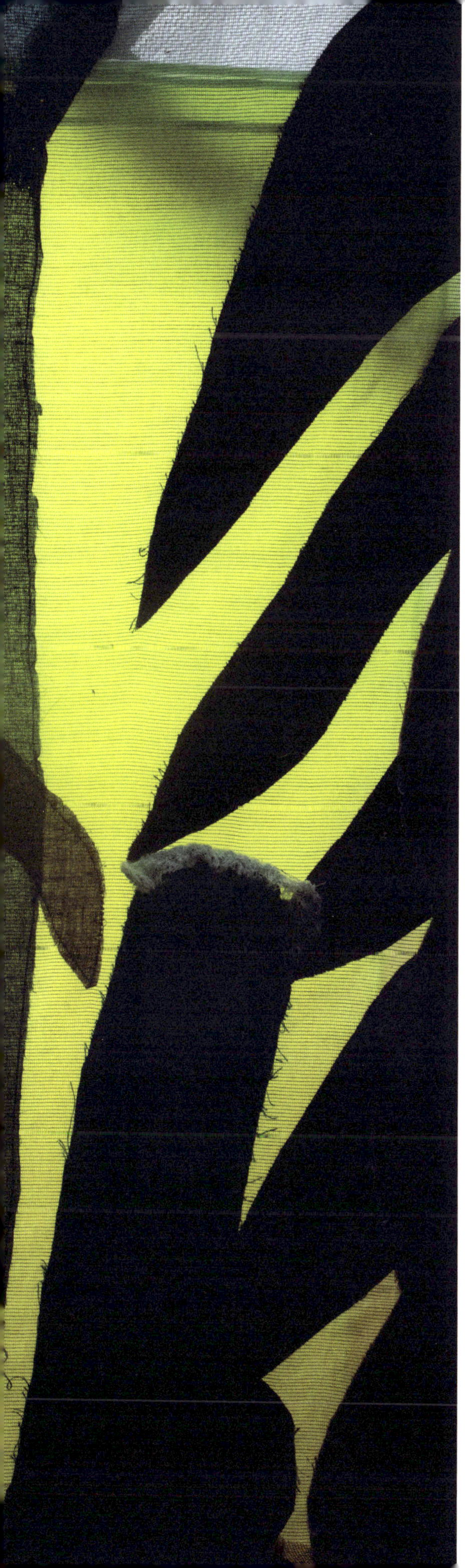

It is not entirely clear where the Garden Route starts and where it ends. But who cares? This itinerary takes you past some of the most beautiful places in the country.

When most people hear 'garden route', they envisage a short Sunday ride, past lovely little gardens that are contenders in the competition for the best-cut hedge or the best-kept rose bed. But this route has none of that. No pristine, manicured gardens here. Instead, the Garden Route winds its way along the wild coastline, through mountain ranges and game reserves.

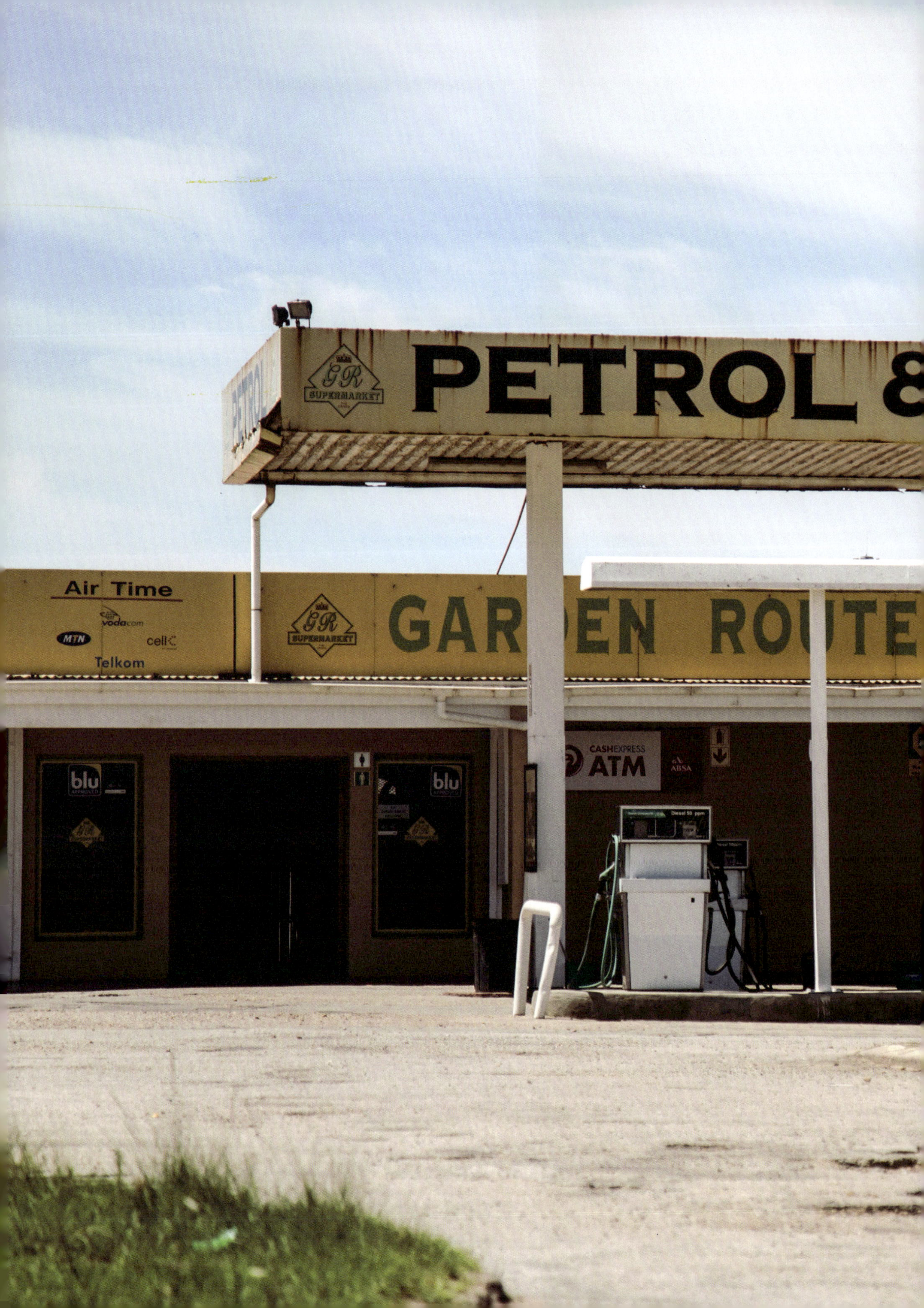
PETROL
GR SUPERMARKET
Air Time
vodacom
MTN
cell C
Telkom
GAR EN ROUTE
CASHEXPRESS ATM
ABSA
blu
Diesel 50 ppm

A road movie set

The seemingly abandoned petrol station is still very much in operation. The lettering on the building, the layer of dust on everything you see and touch, and the harsh light make us feel as if we have accidentally stumbled onto the set of an American road movie.

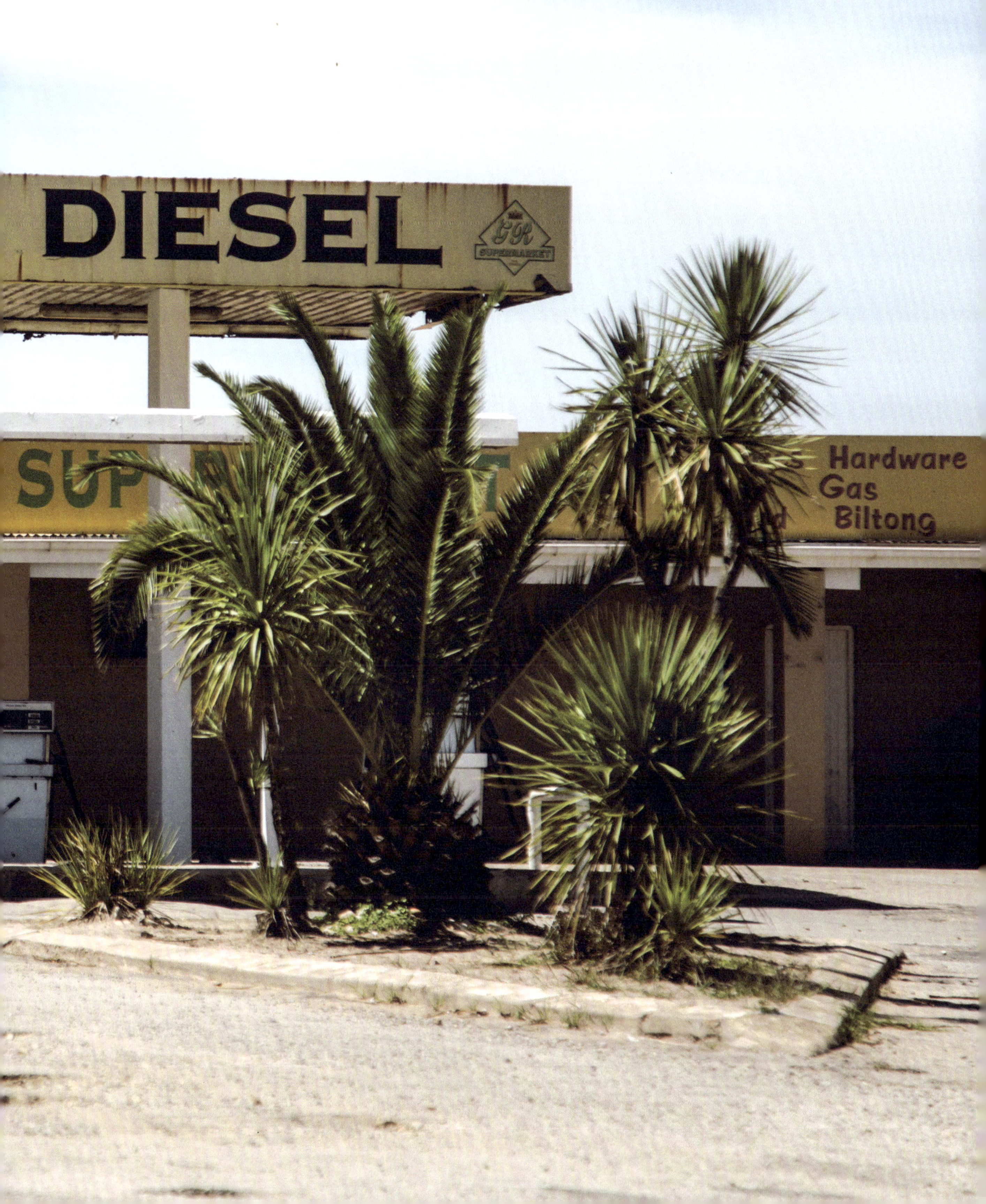

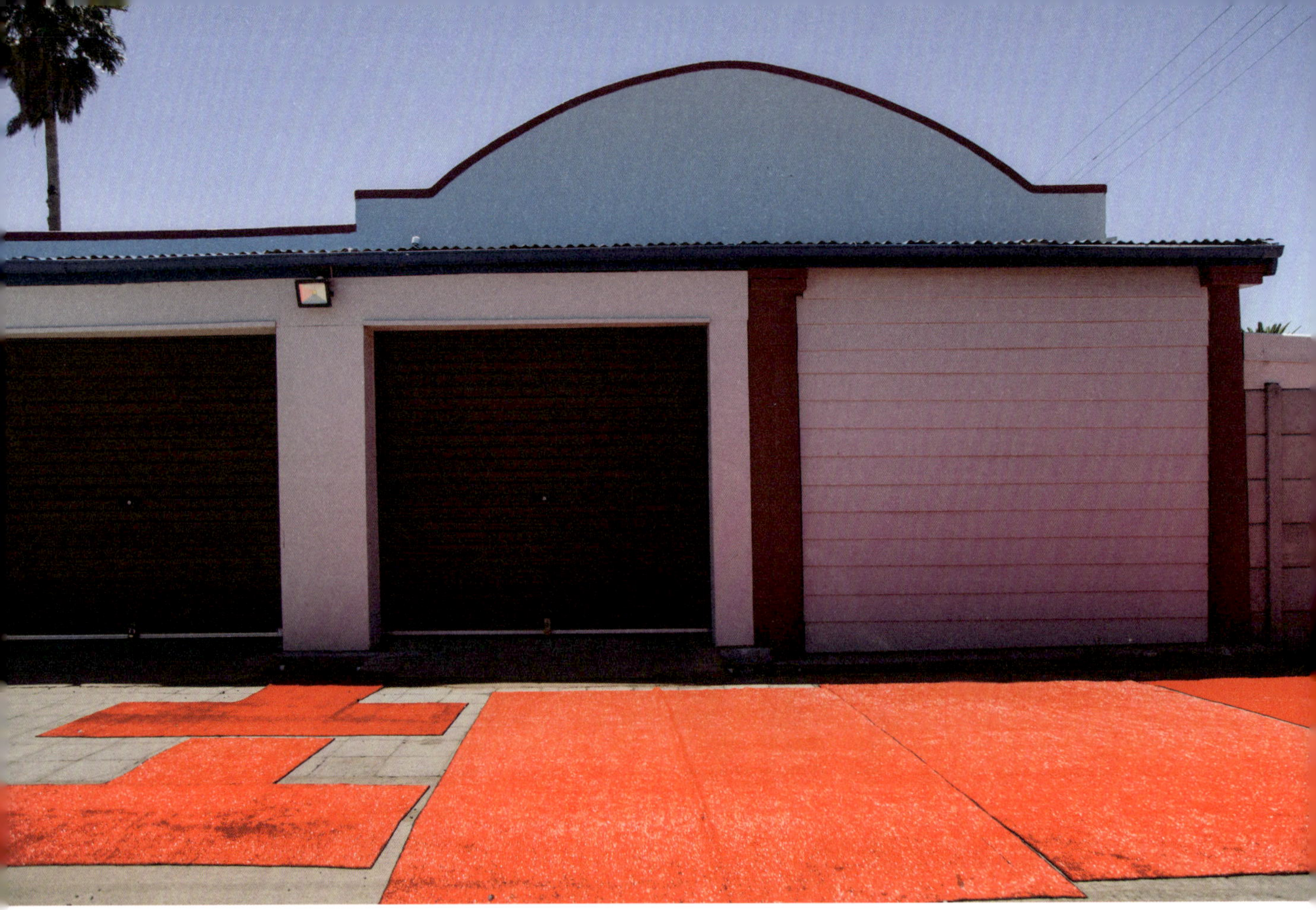

Heading back to the coast

Leaving the arid landscape behind, we make our way to Mossel Bay. Along the way, we come to realise that the trip is not just unforgettable because of the great views or the stunning sunsets. The unusual beauty of a number of brightly coloured rugs that have been laid to dry outside in the sun, is even more memorable.

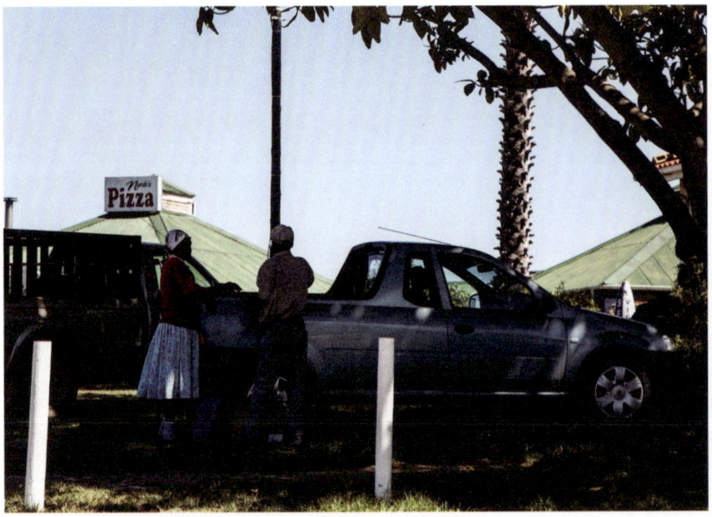

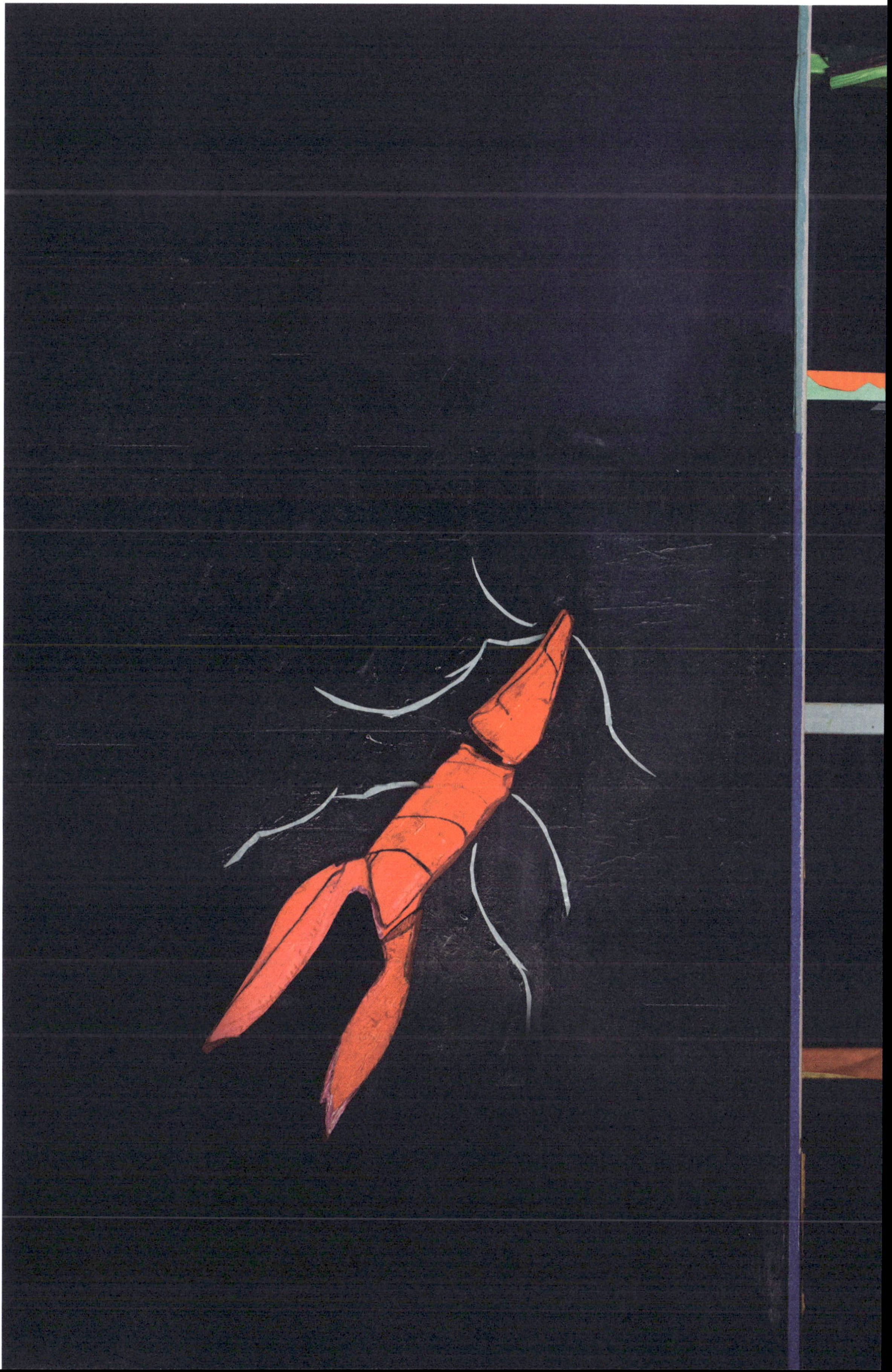

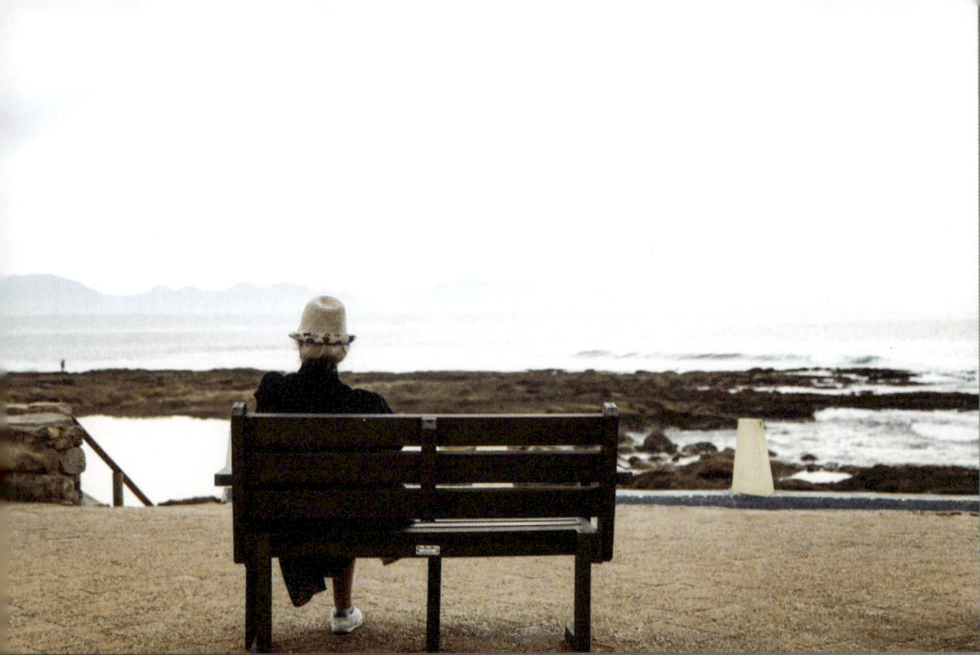

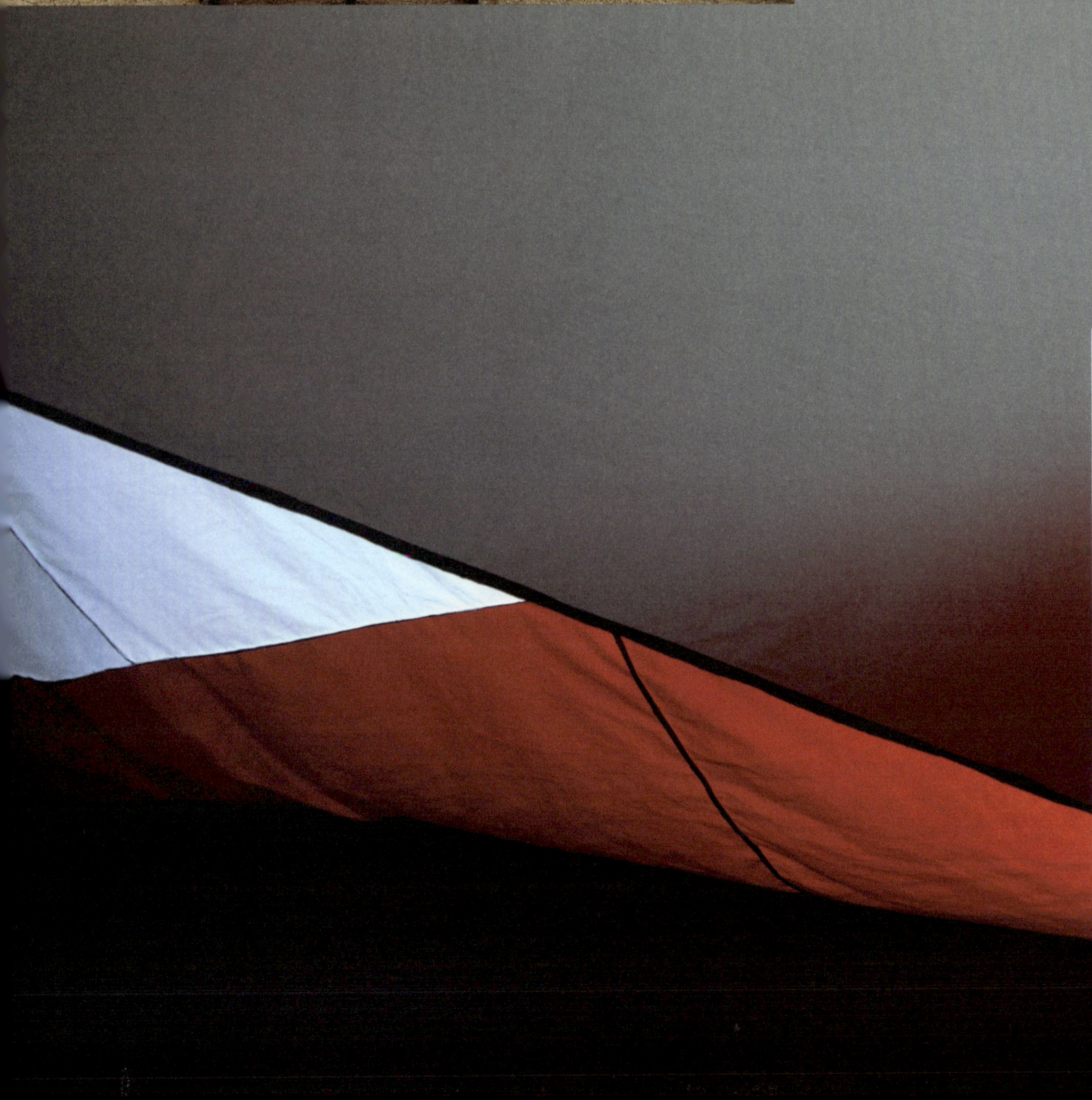

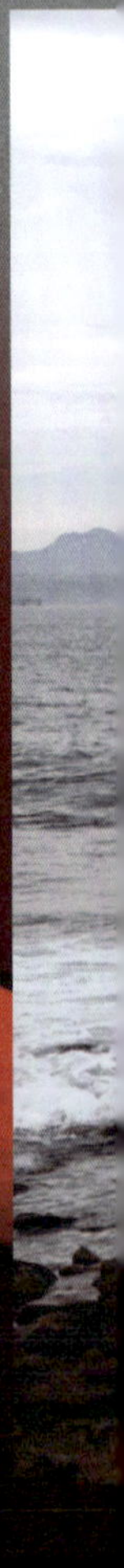

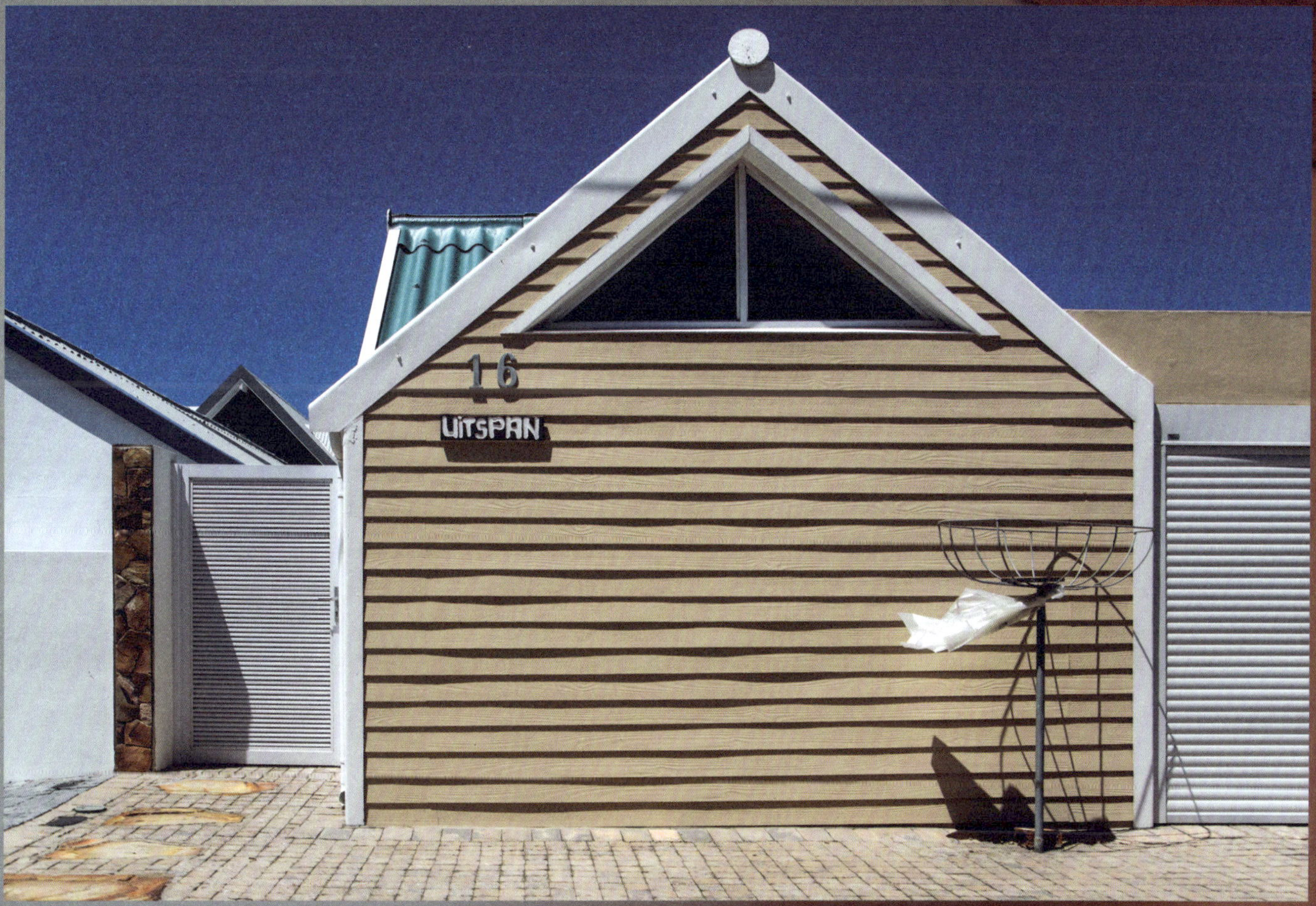
16
UITSPAN

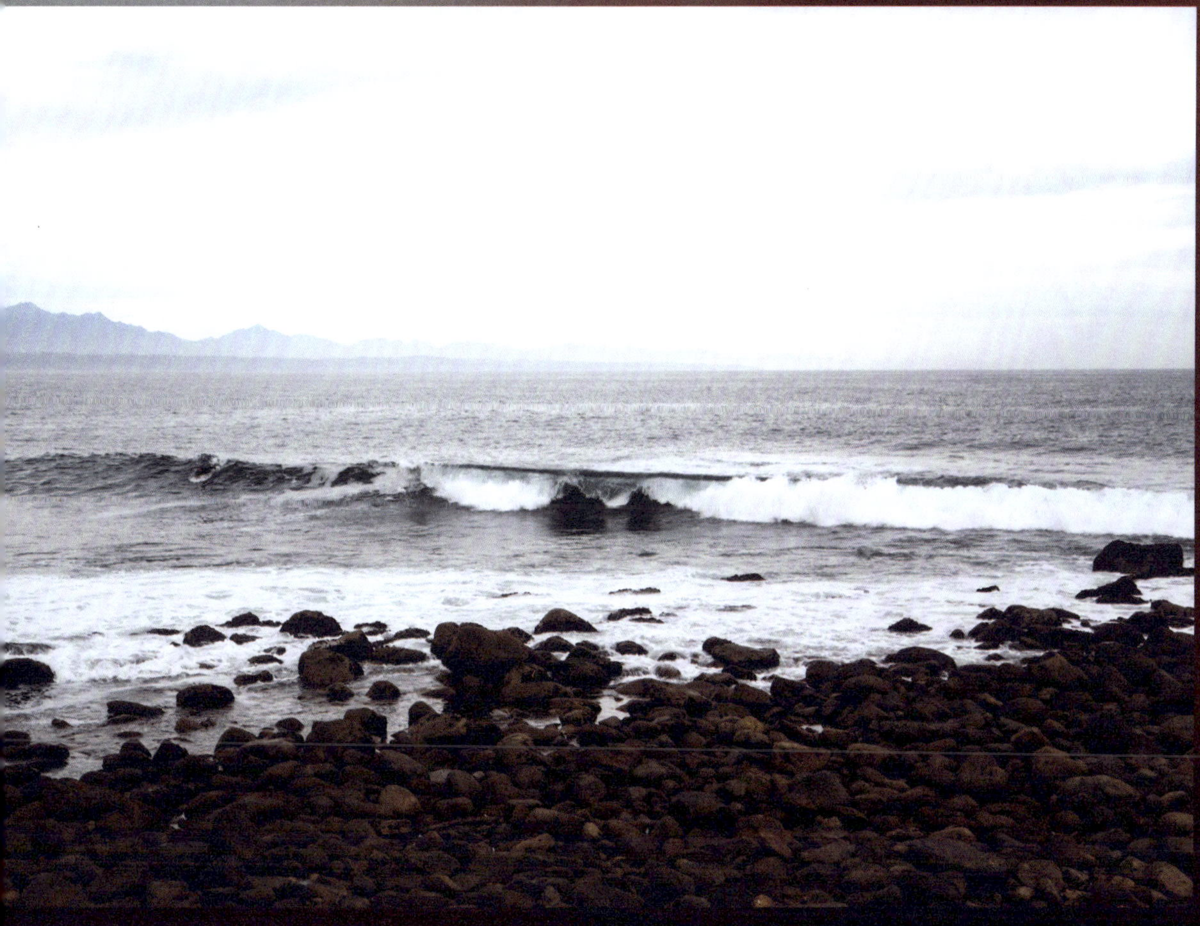

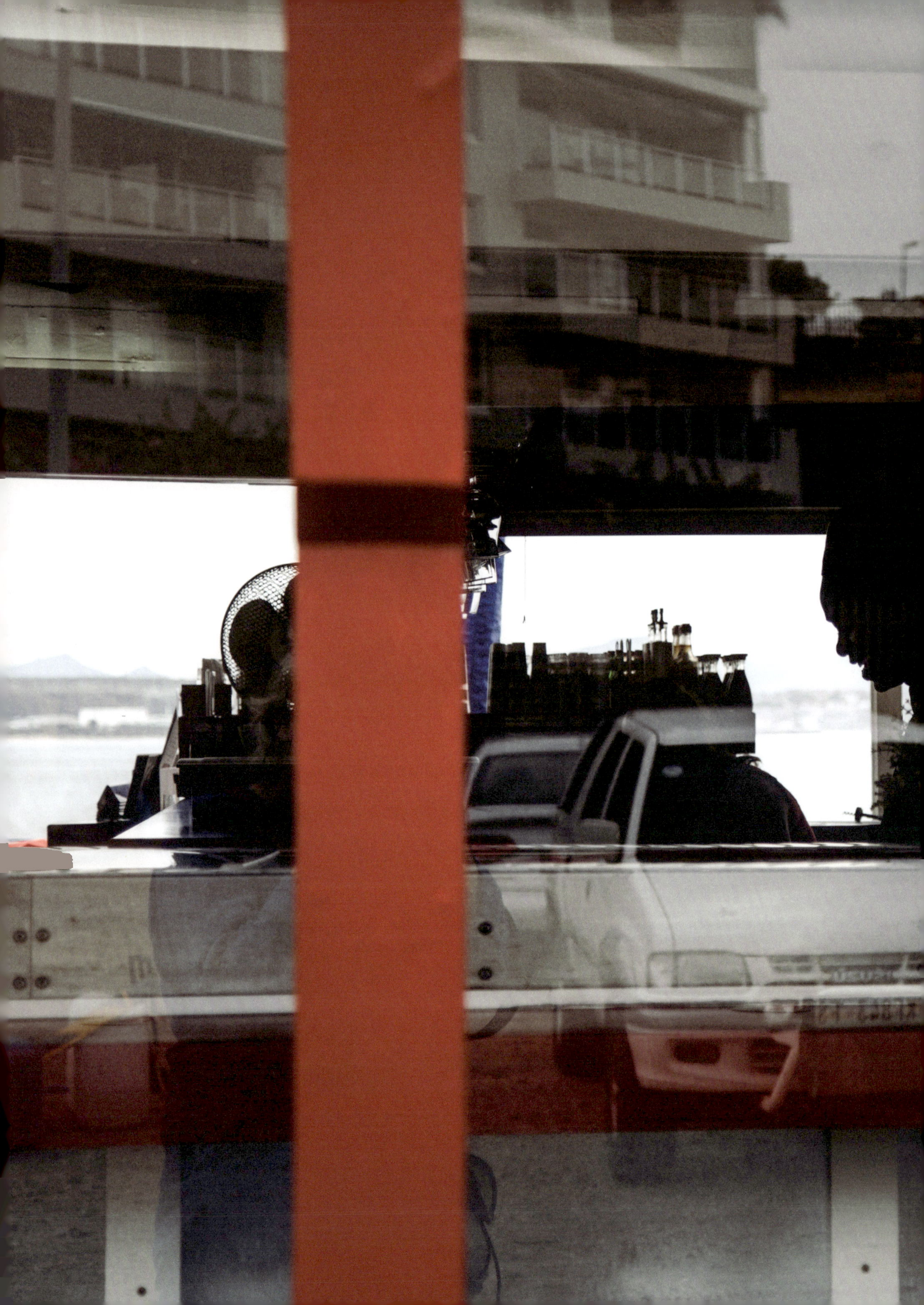

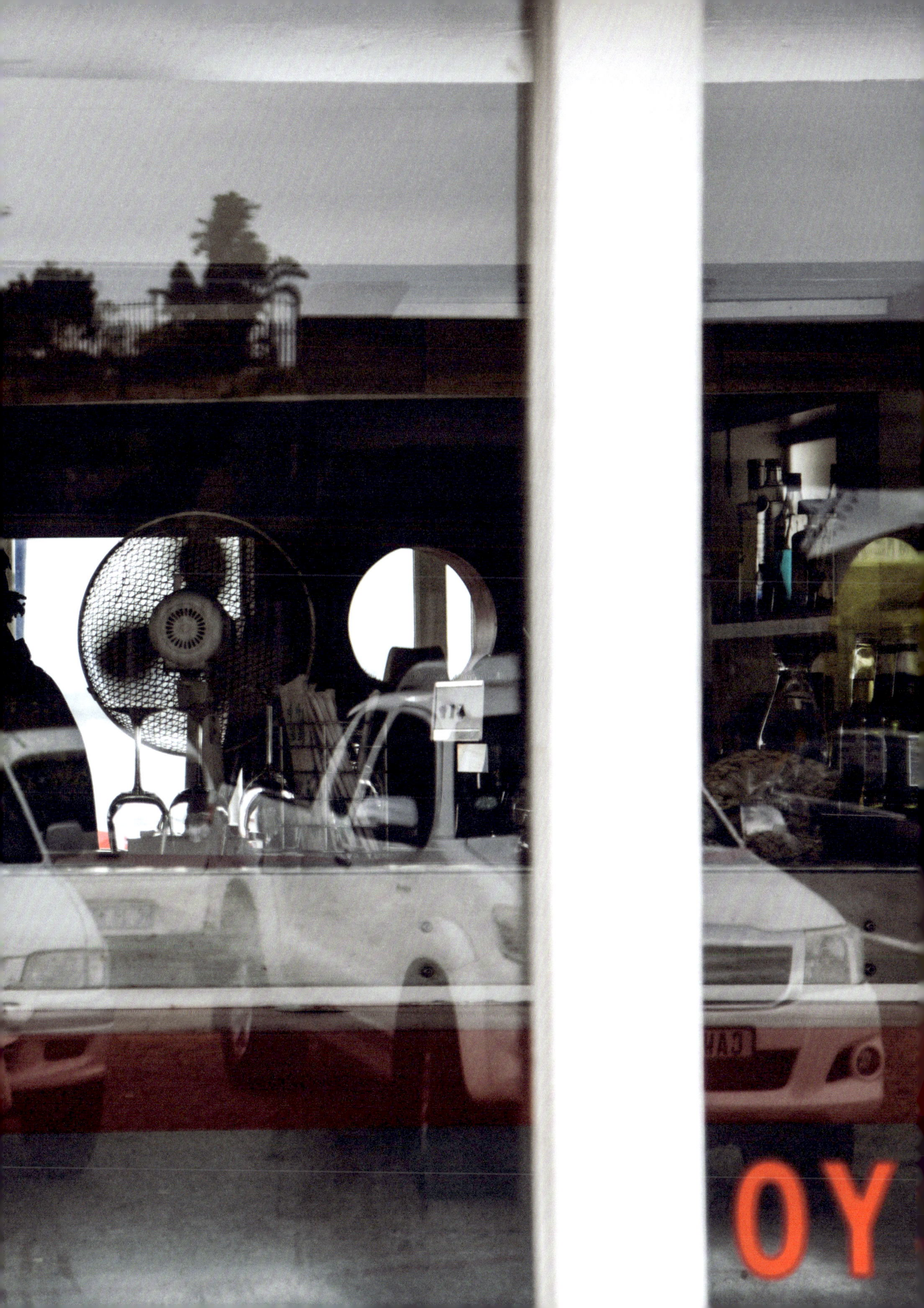
OY

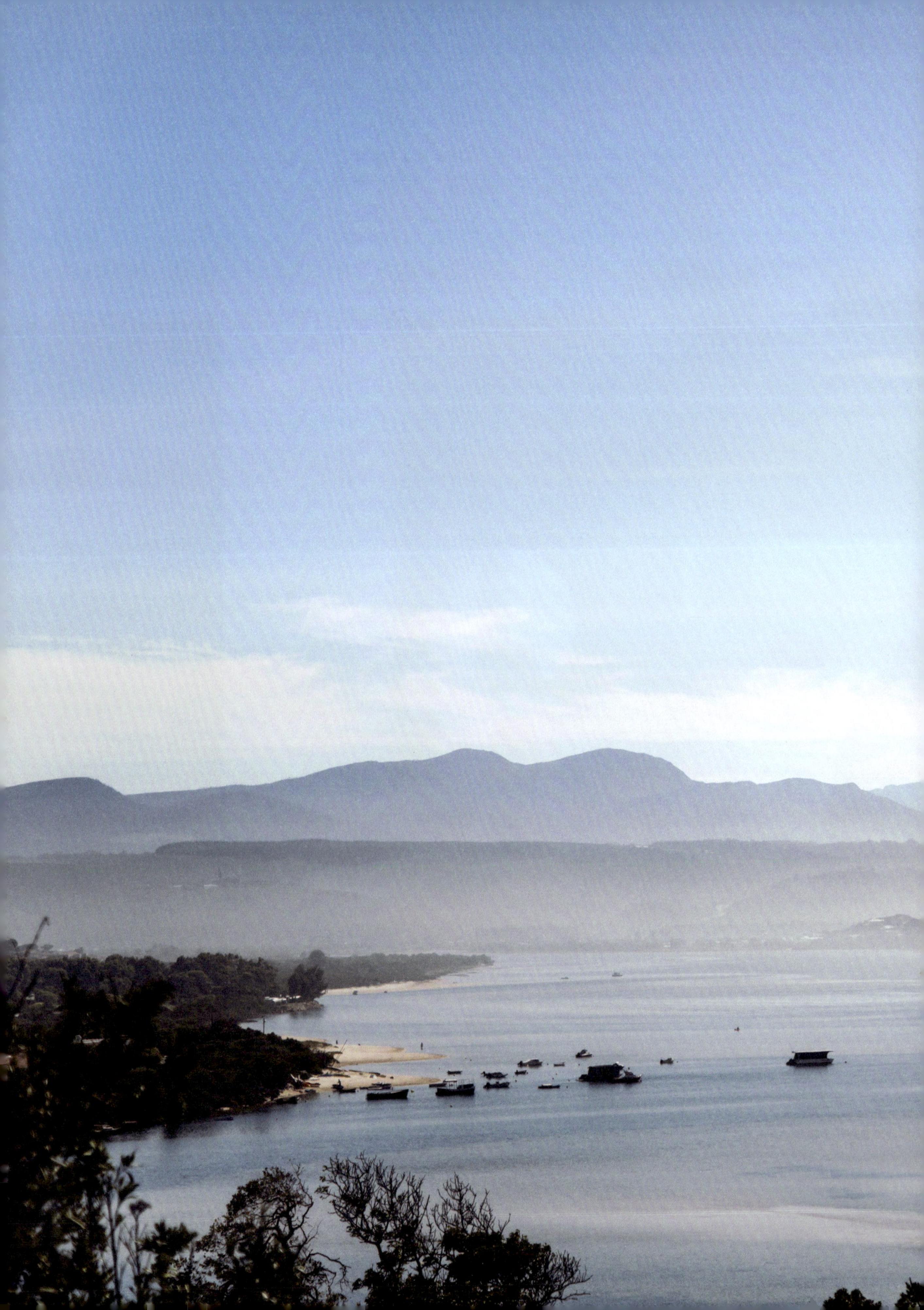

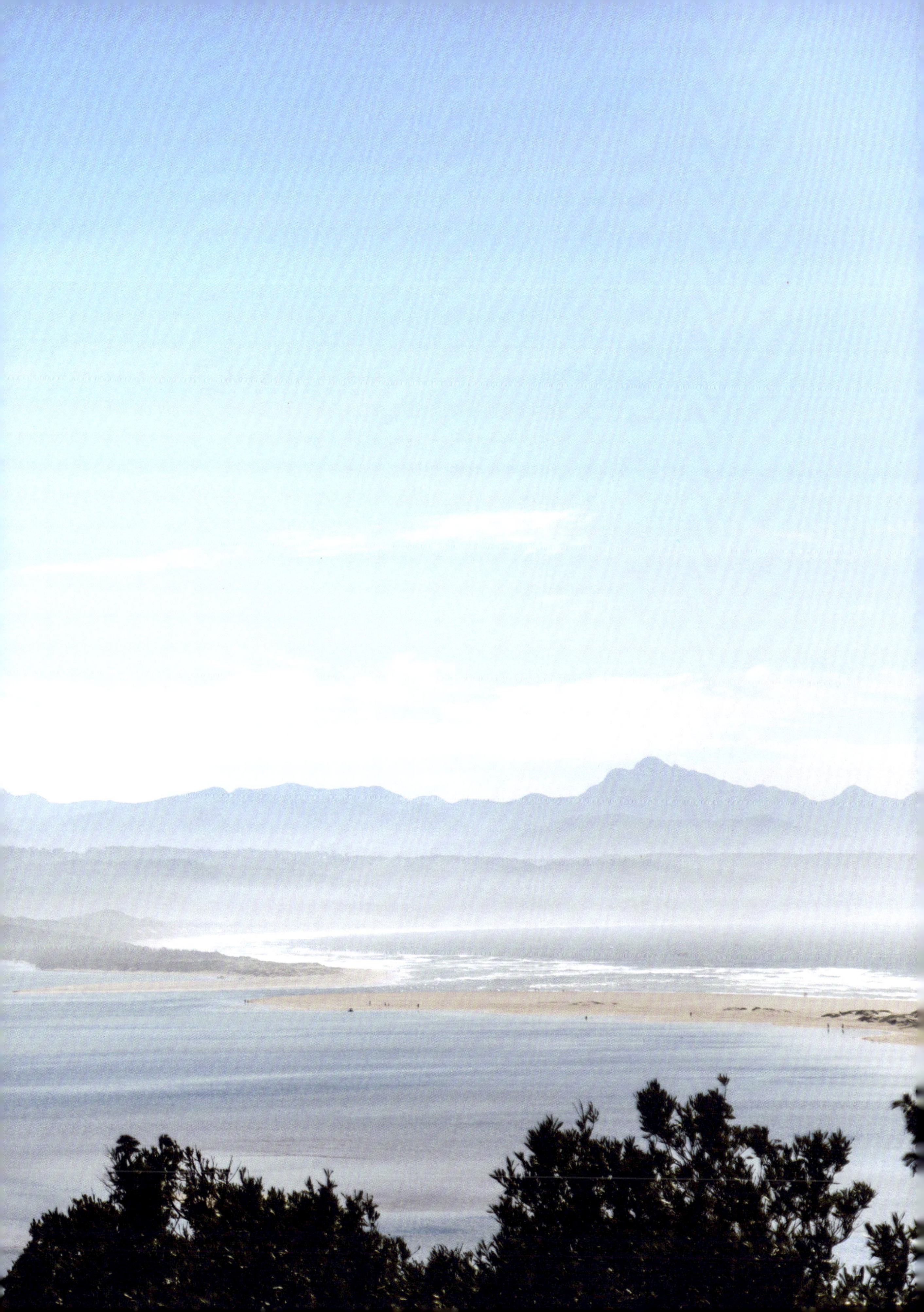

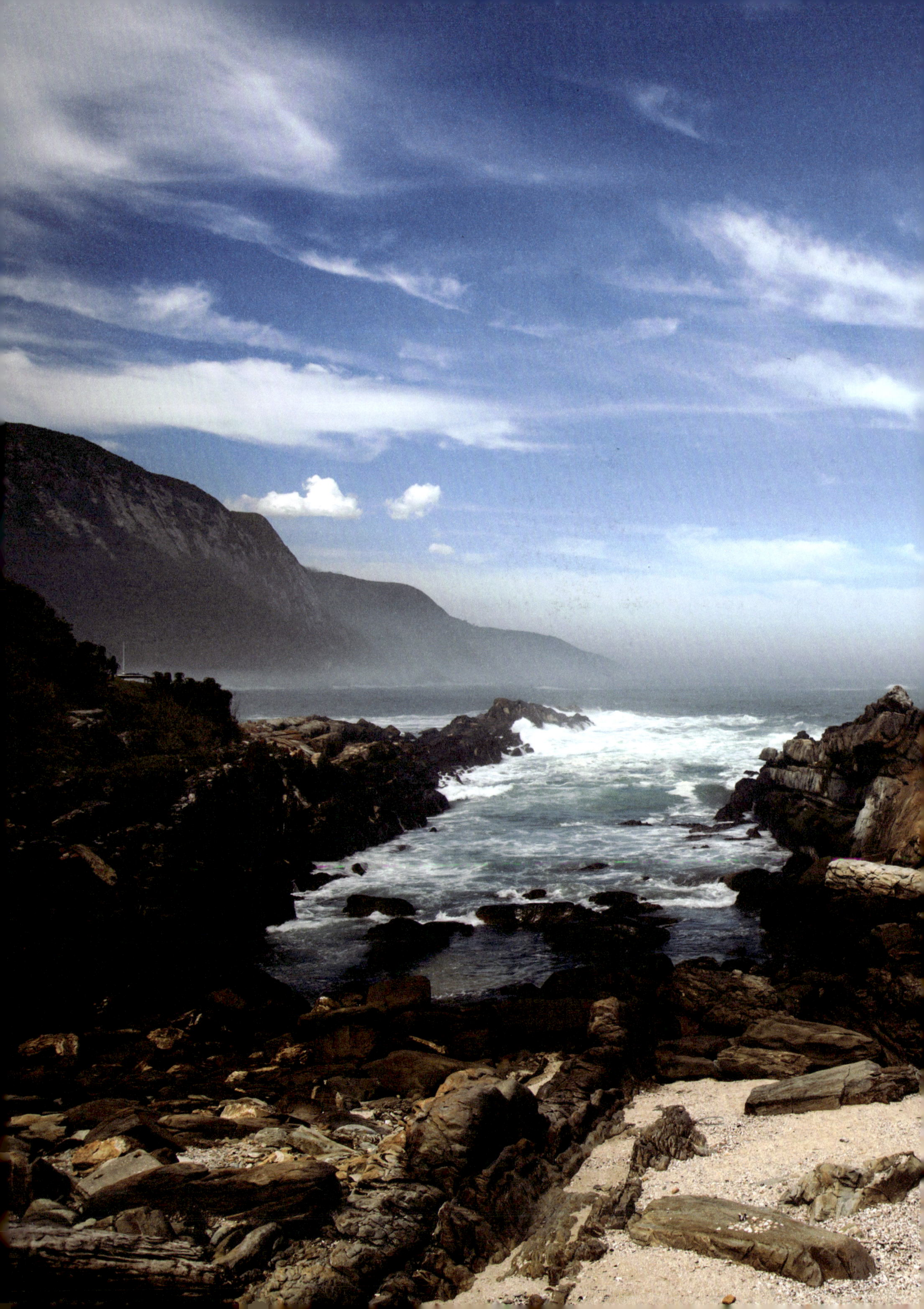

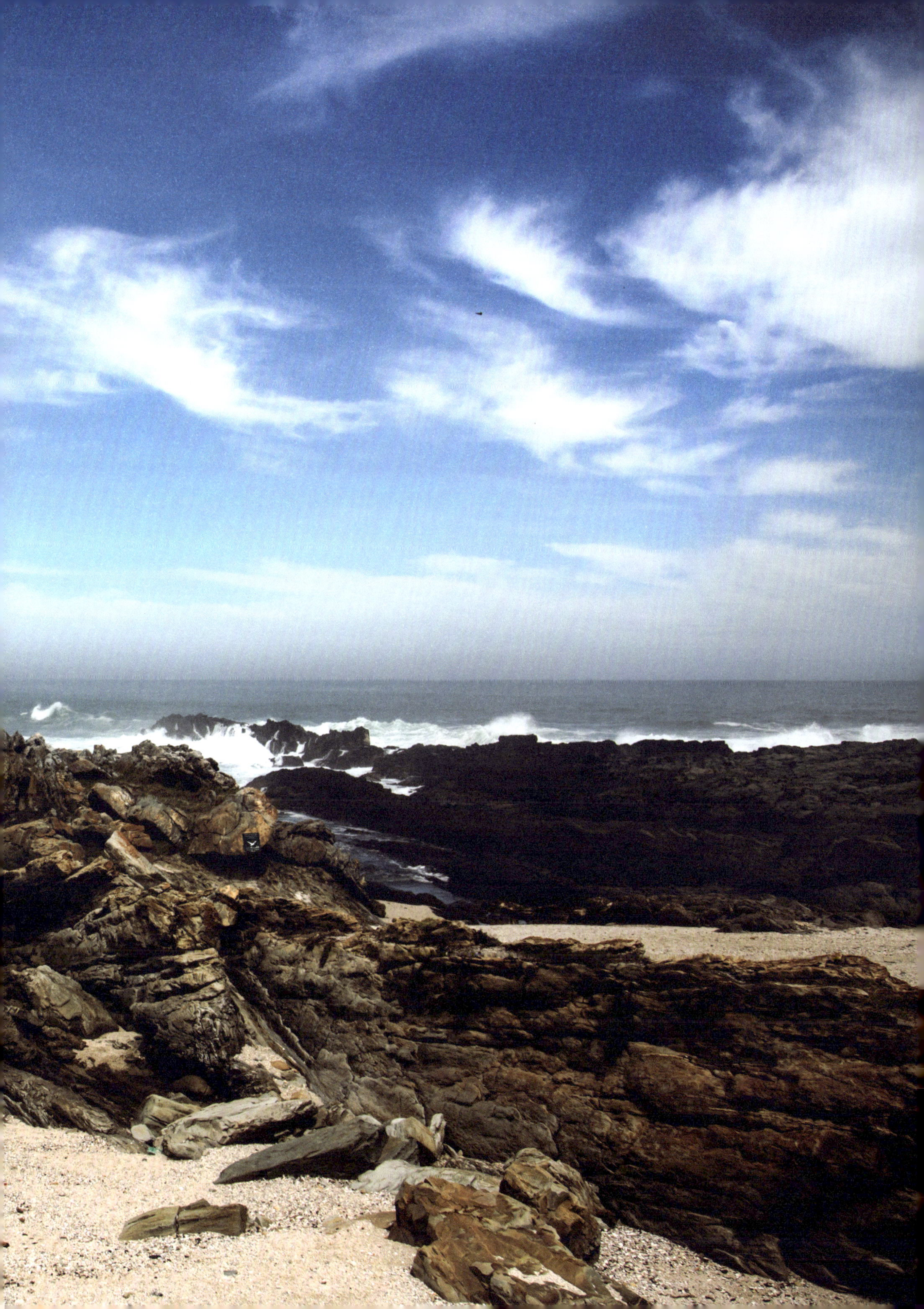

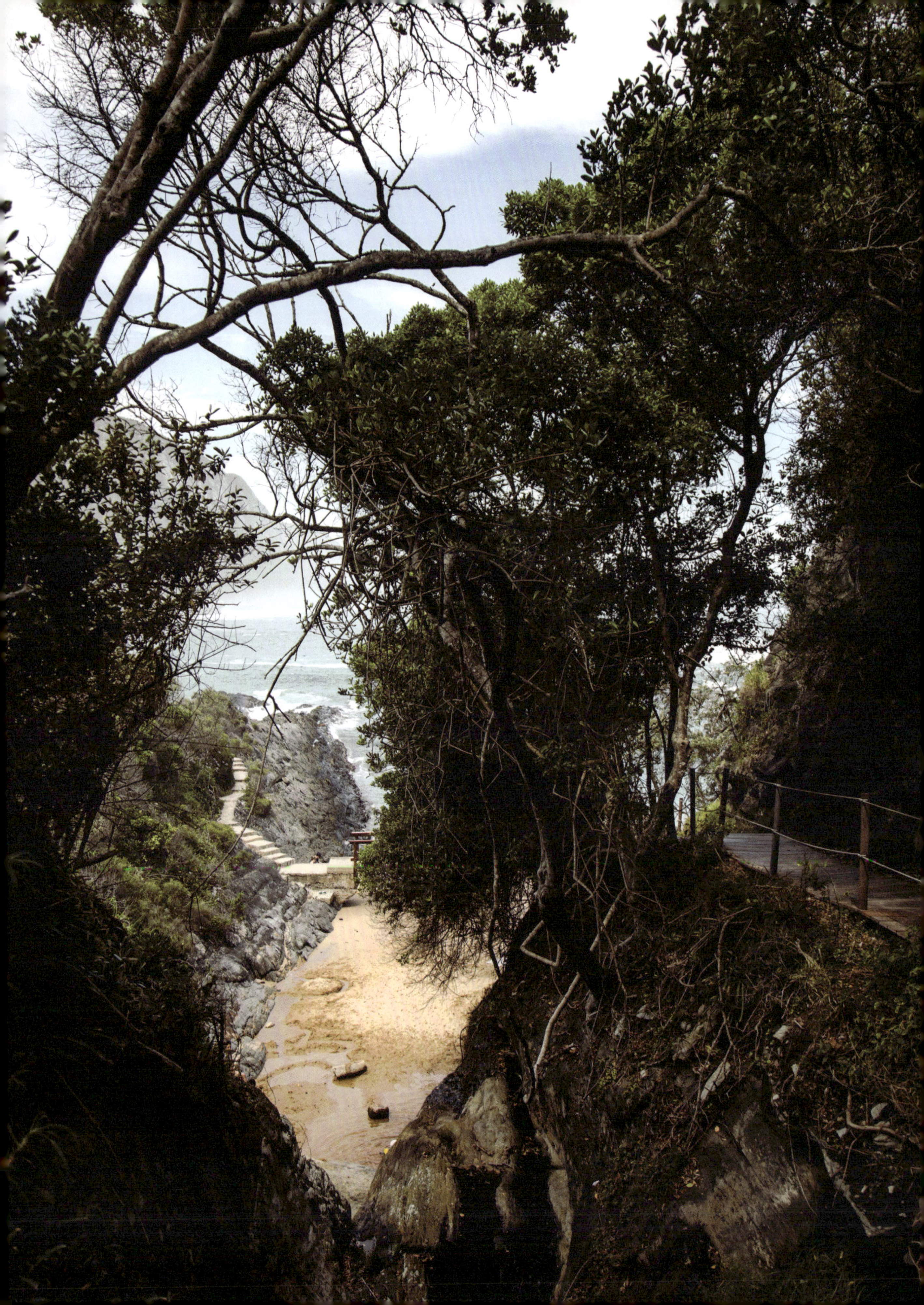

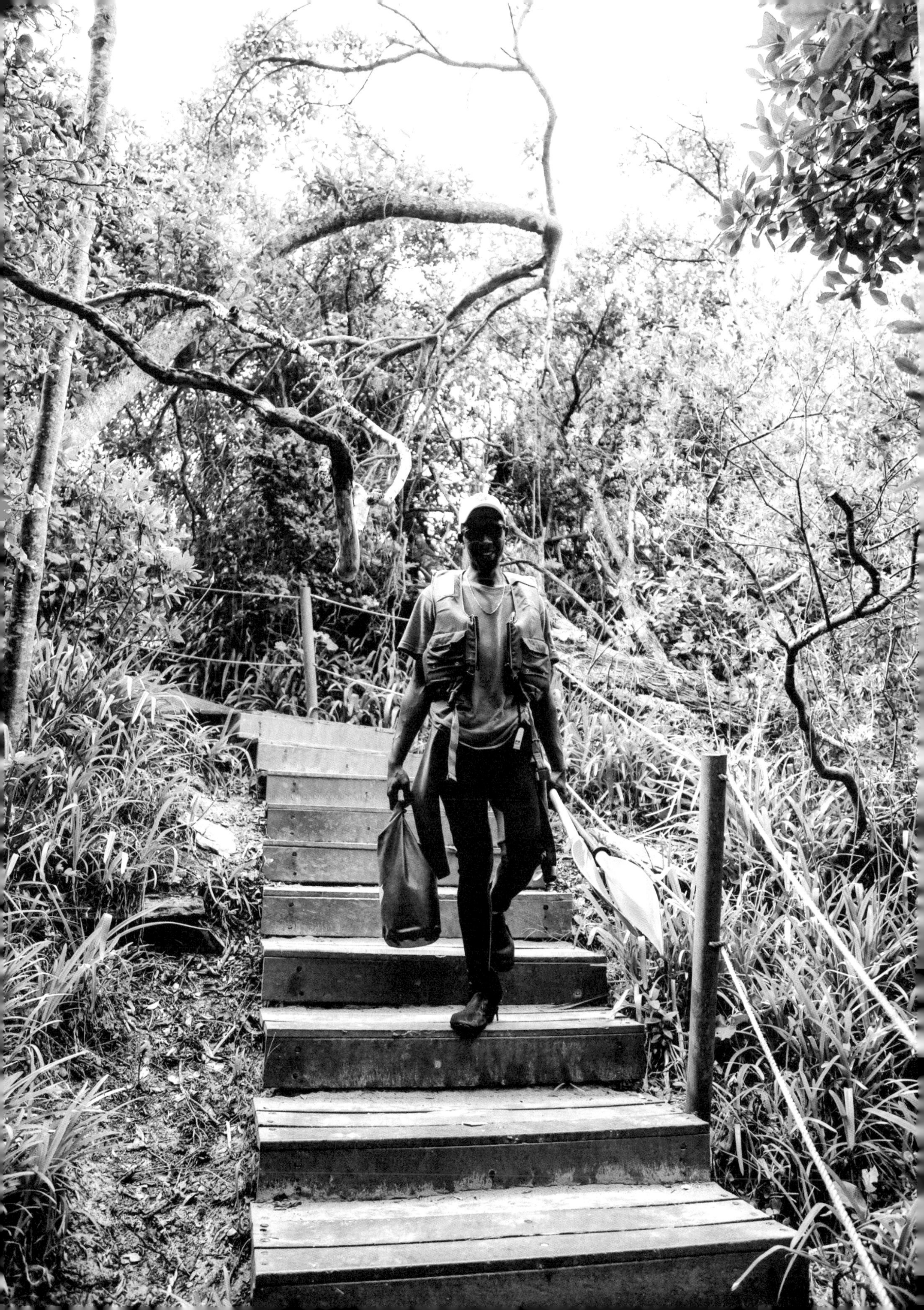

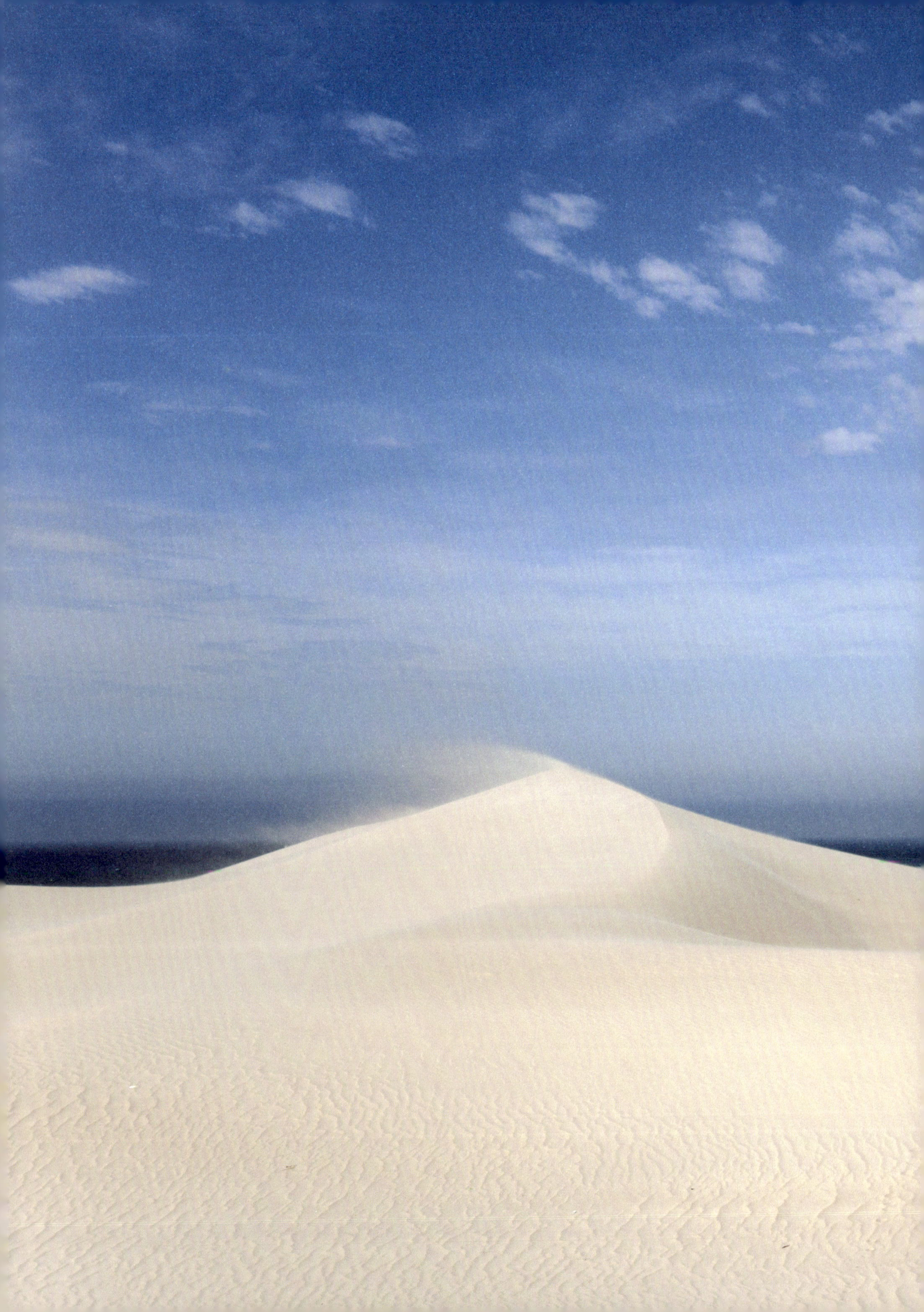

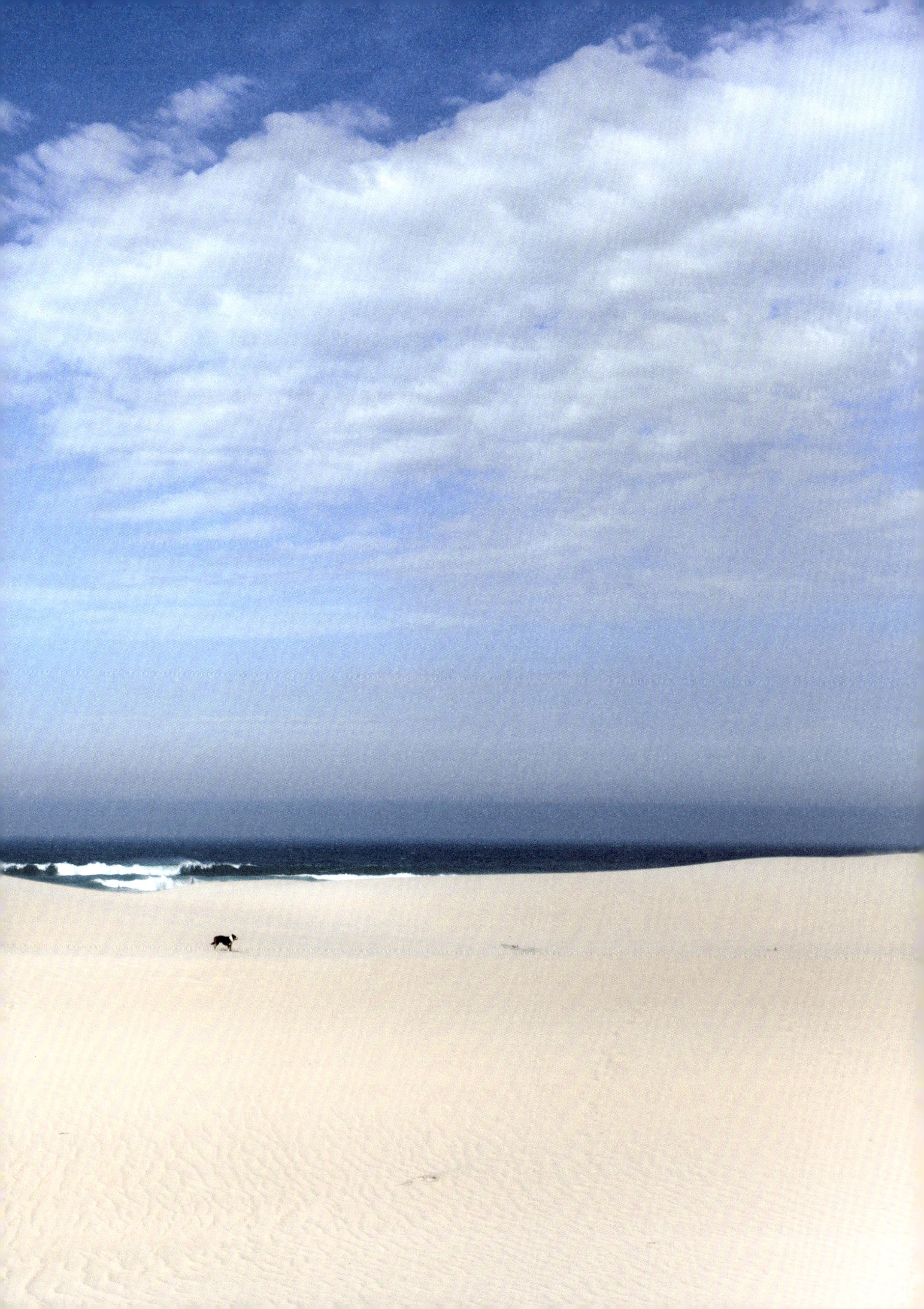

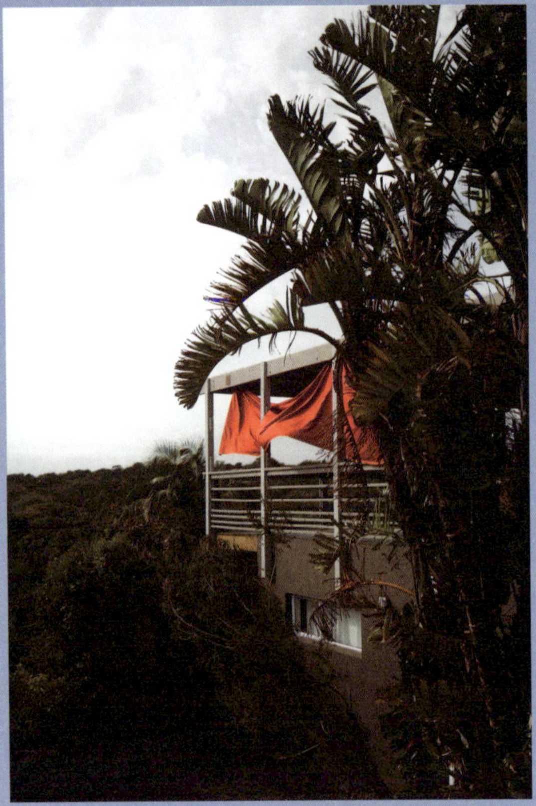

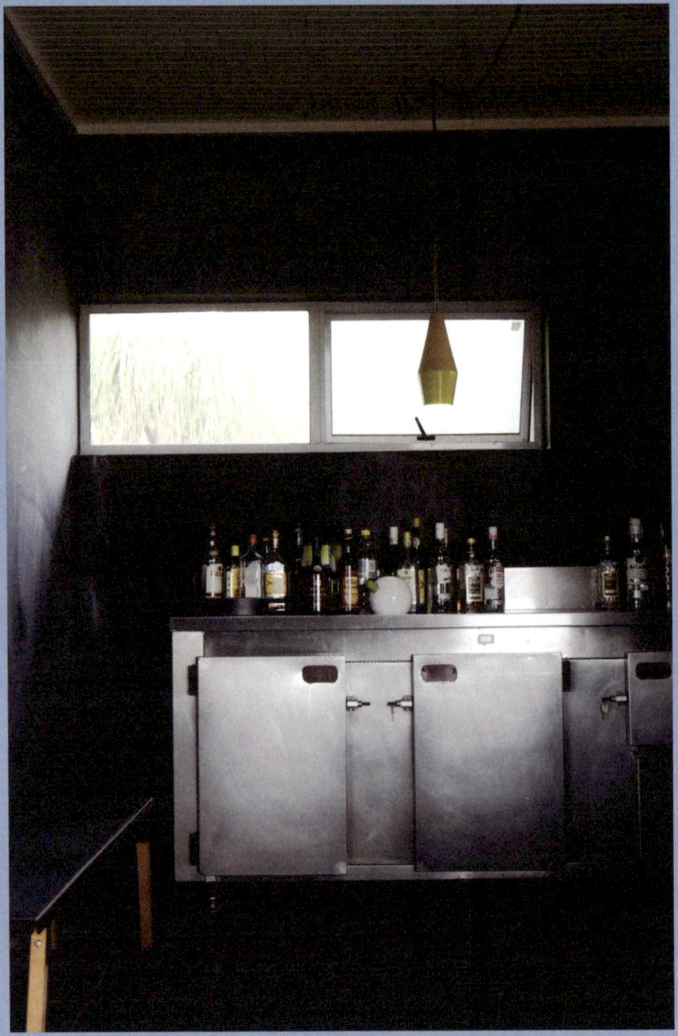

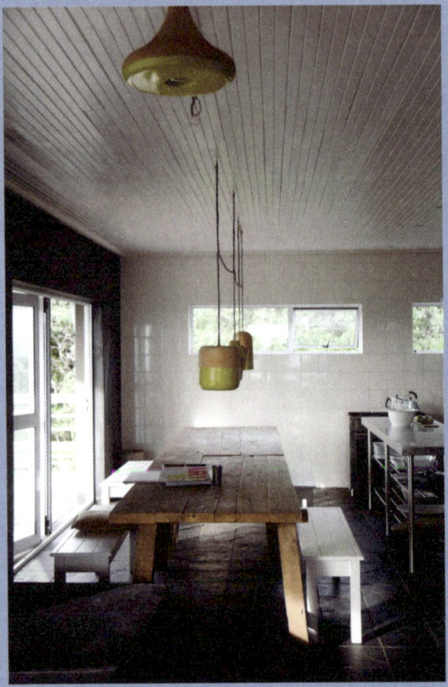

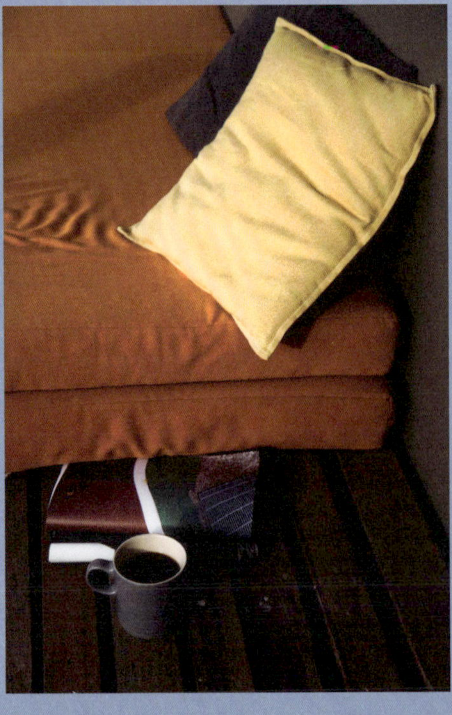

Sand between our toes

We were invited by a friend to pause our trip for a few days to stay with him at his vacation house in Oyster Bay, a tiny coastal town which is not on the tourist route. Famous, as far as people know it, for its dazzling white and high dunes.

Our early morning barefoot walk over the loose sand of the high dunes was a pleasant challenge.

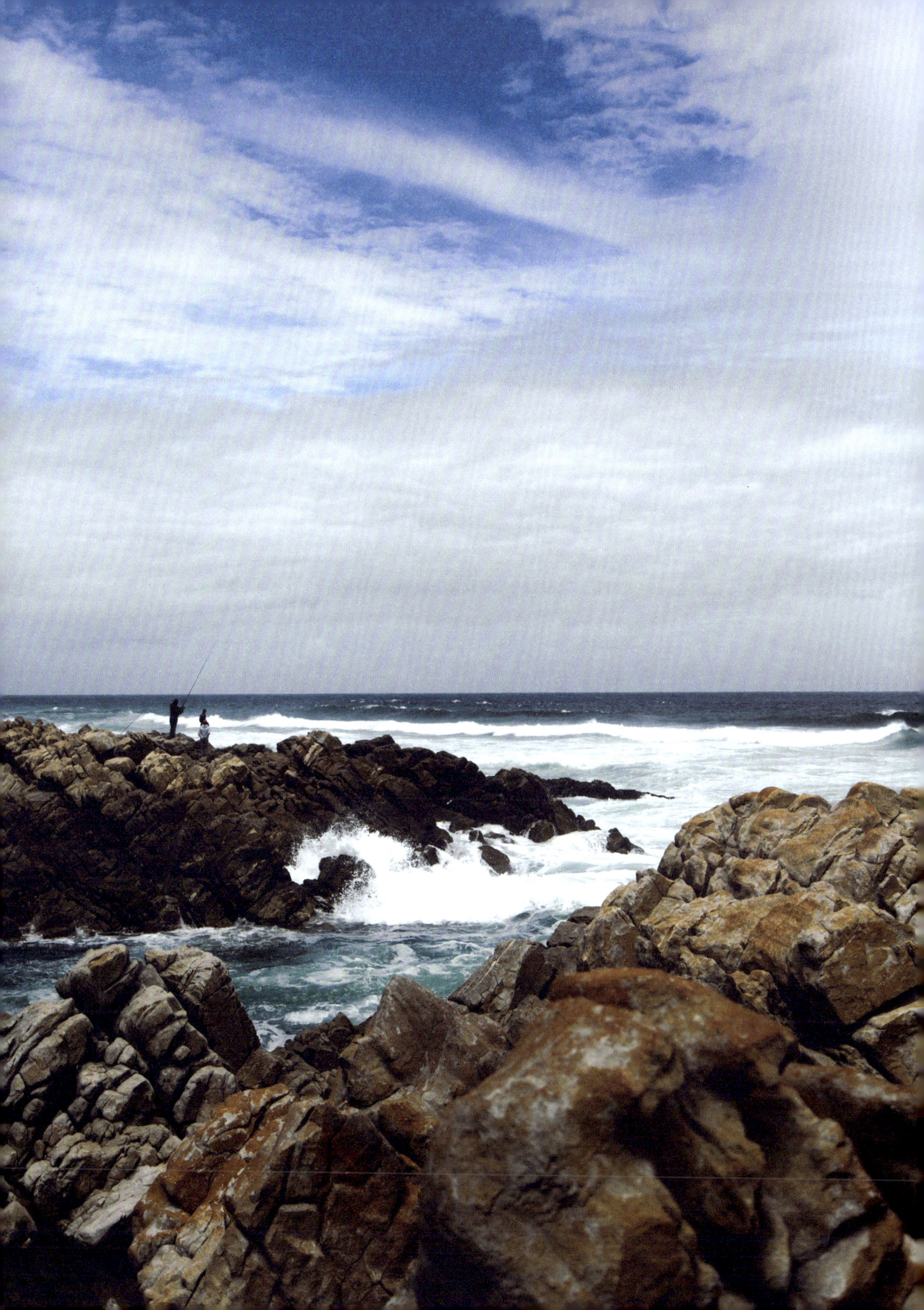

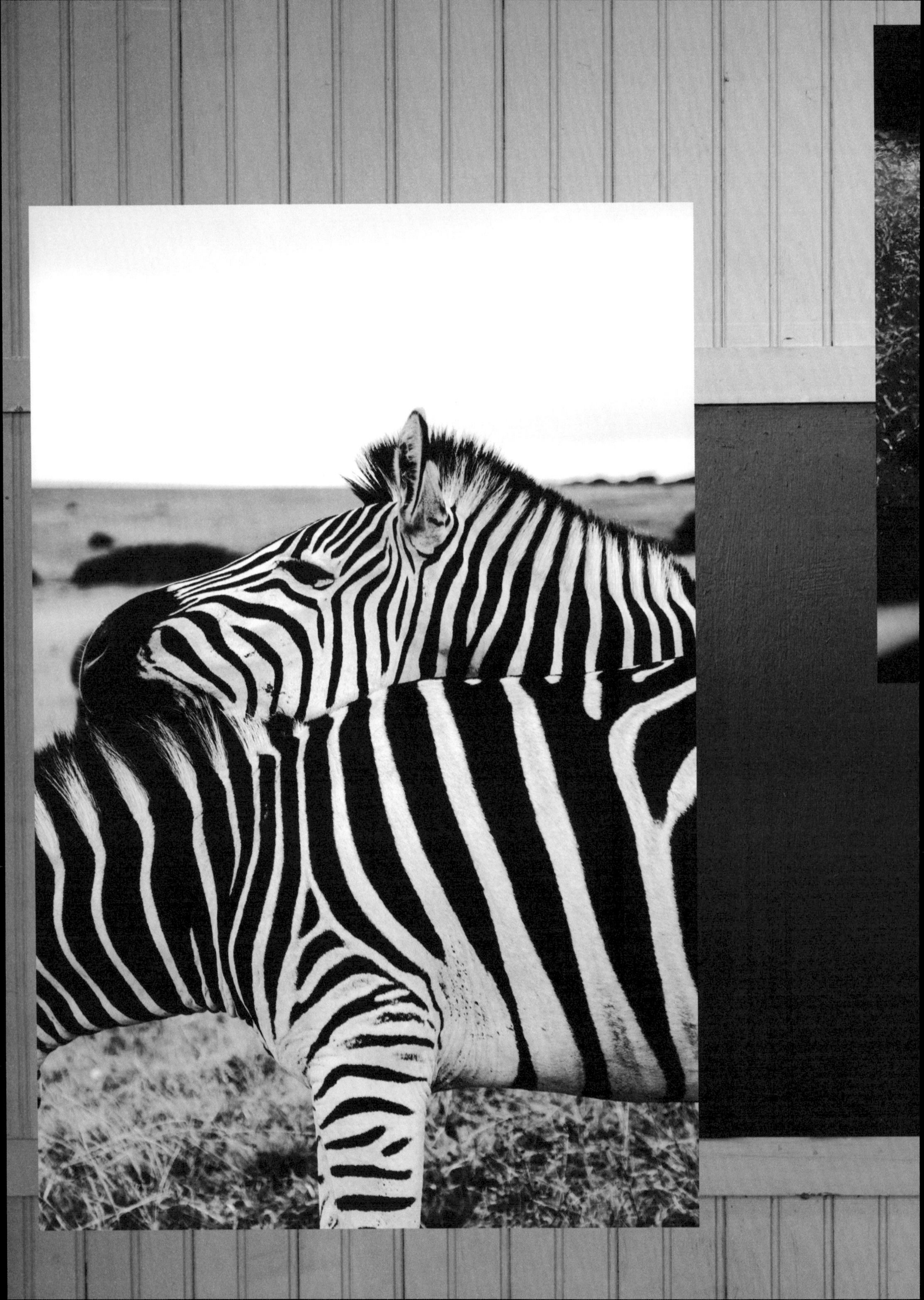

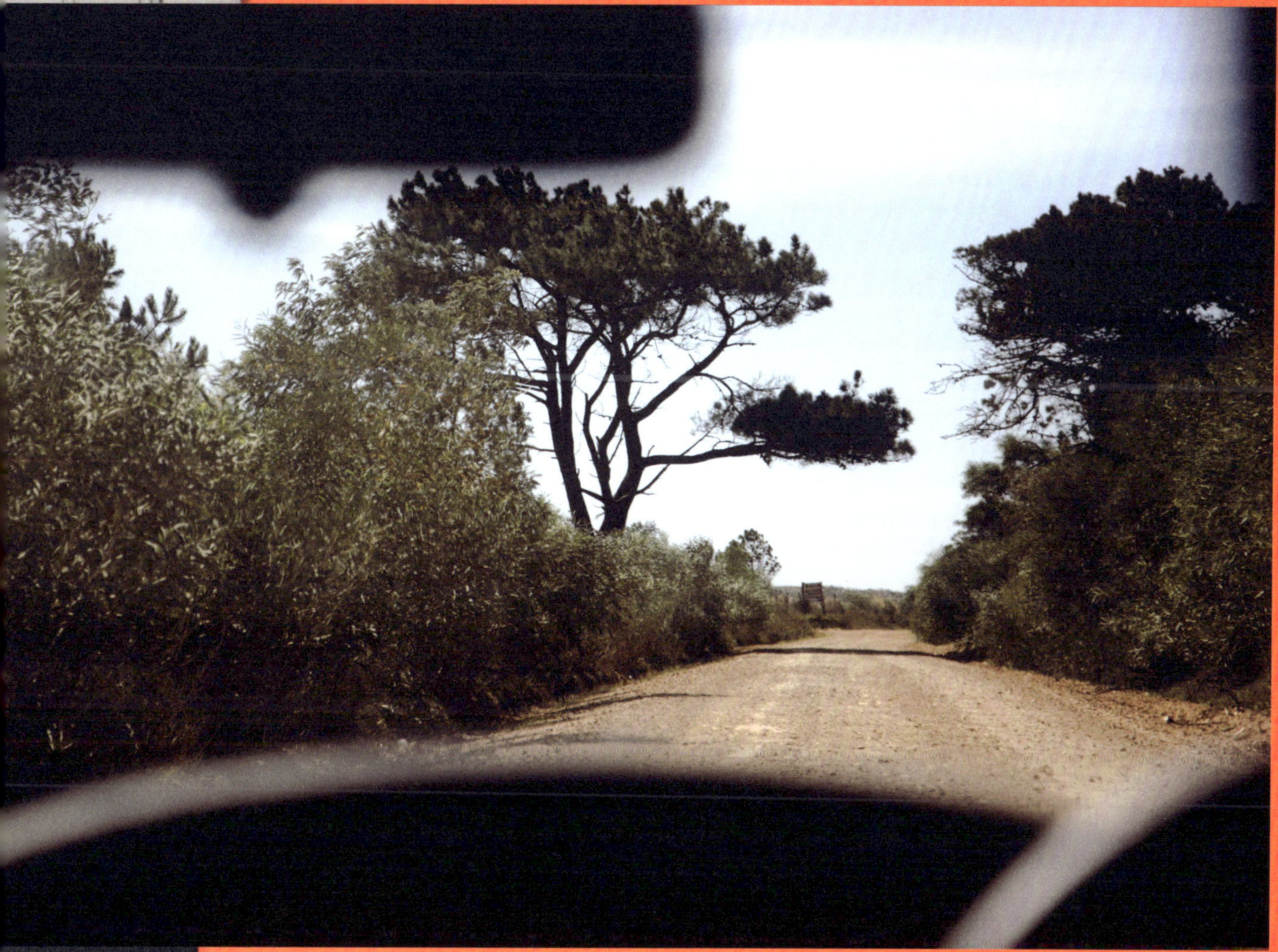

Among the wild beasts

An entire elephant family seems to be walking straight into our car, but they are really only interested in the juicy bushes across the road, which they devour in one piece.

Although exploring Addo Elephant Park by car is the most common way to see the animals, it is quite a strange feeling to stand between the zebra and other wild animals with a group of cars, like a herd in its own right. Not much is happening, but it is fascinating to watch the animals for a while and take in the experience.

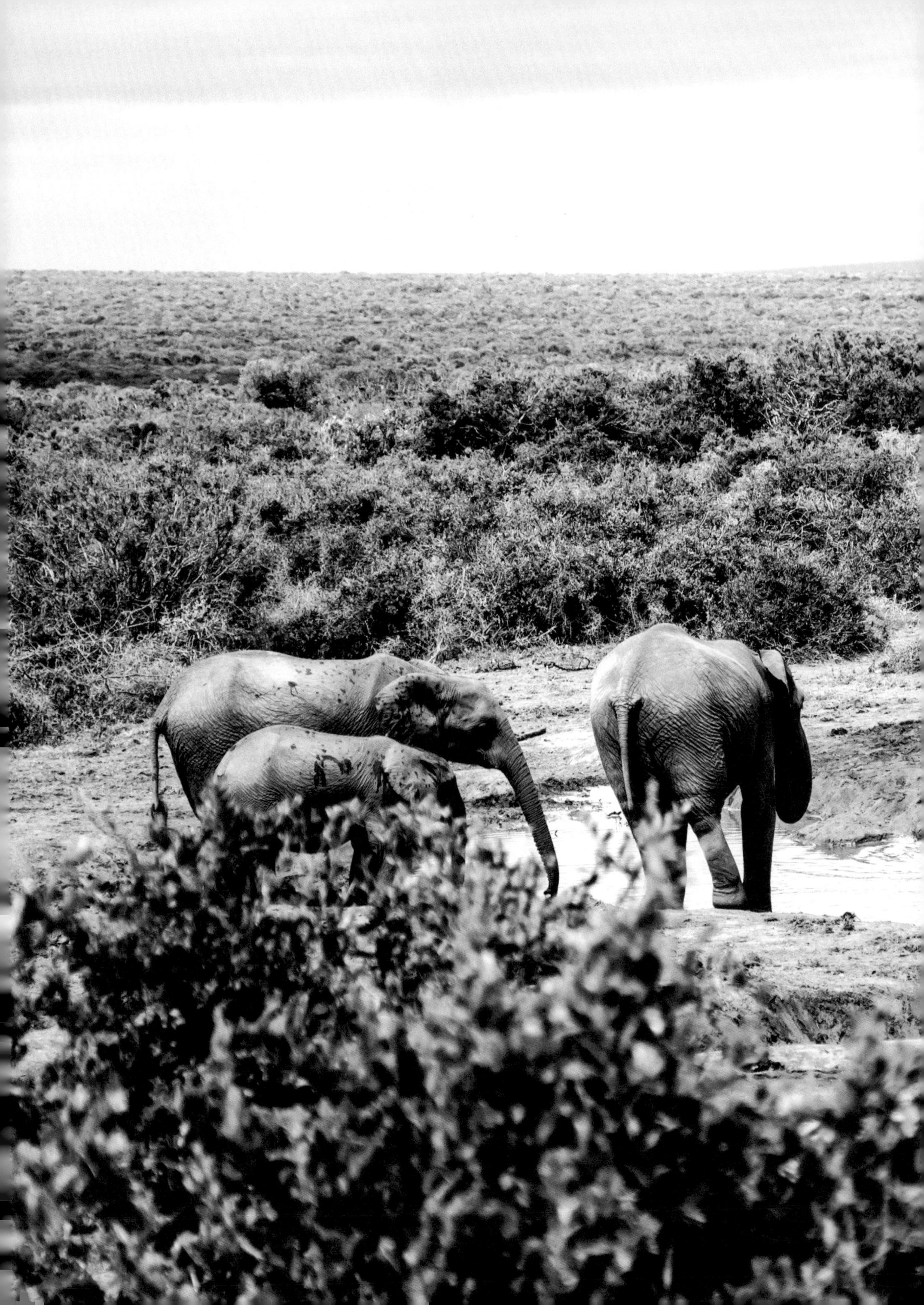

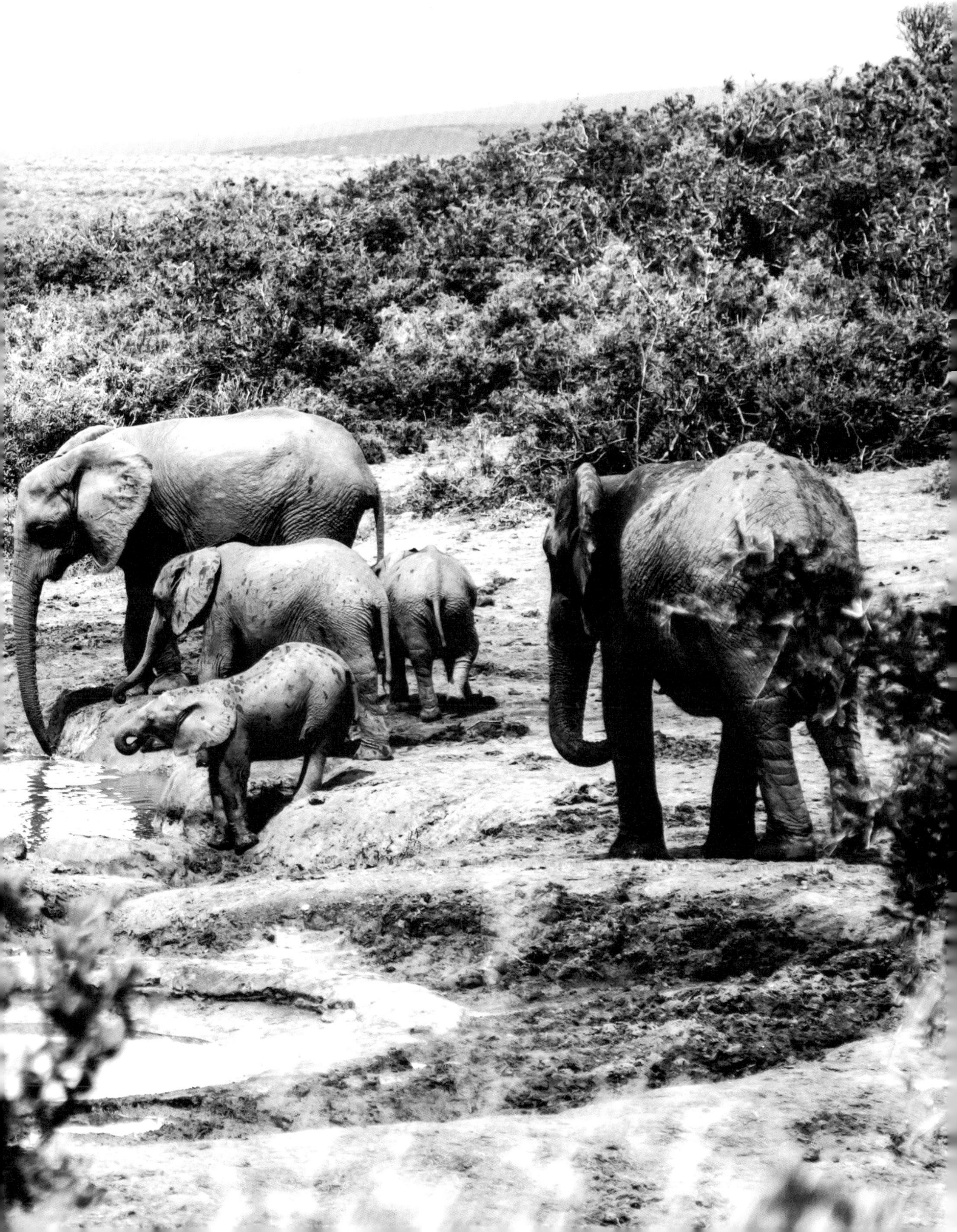

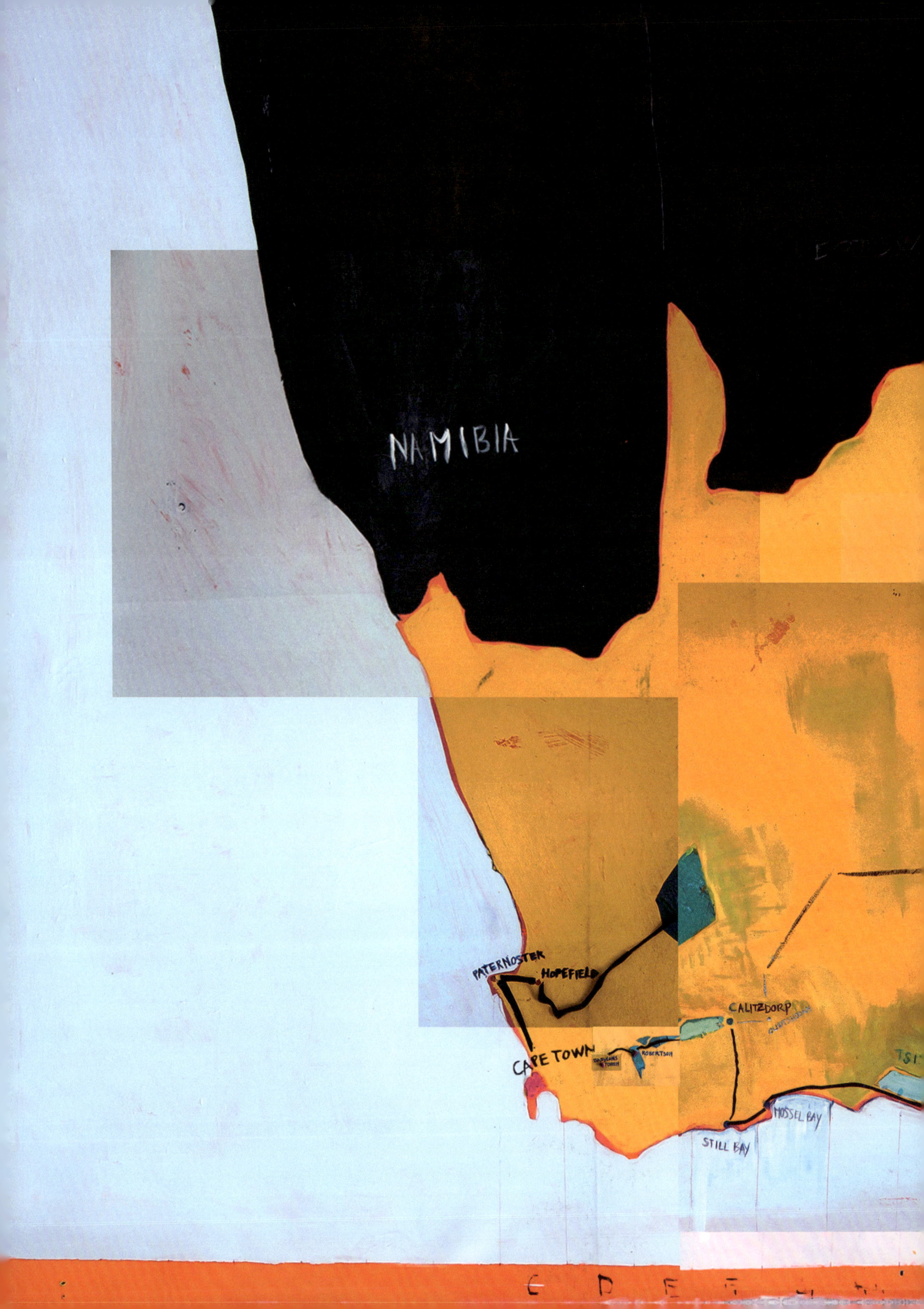
NAMIBIA
PATERNOSTER
HOPEFIELD
CAPE TOWN
ROBERTSON
CALITZDORP
MOSSEL BAY
STILL BAY

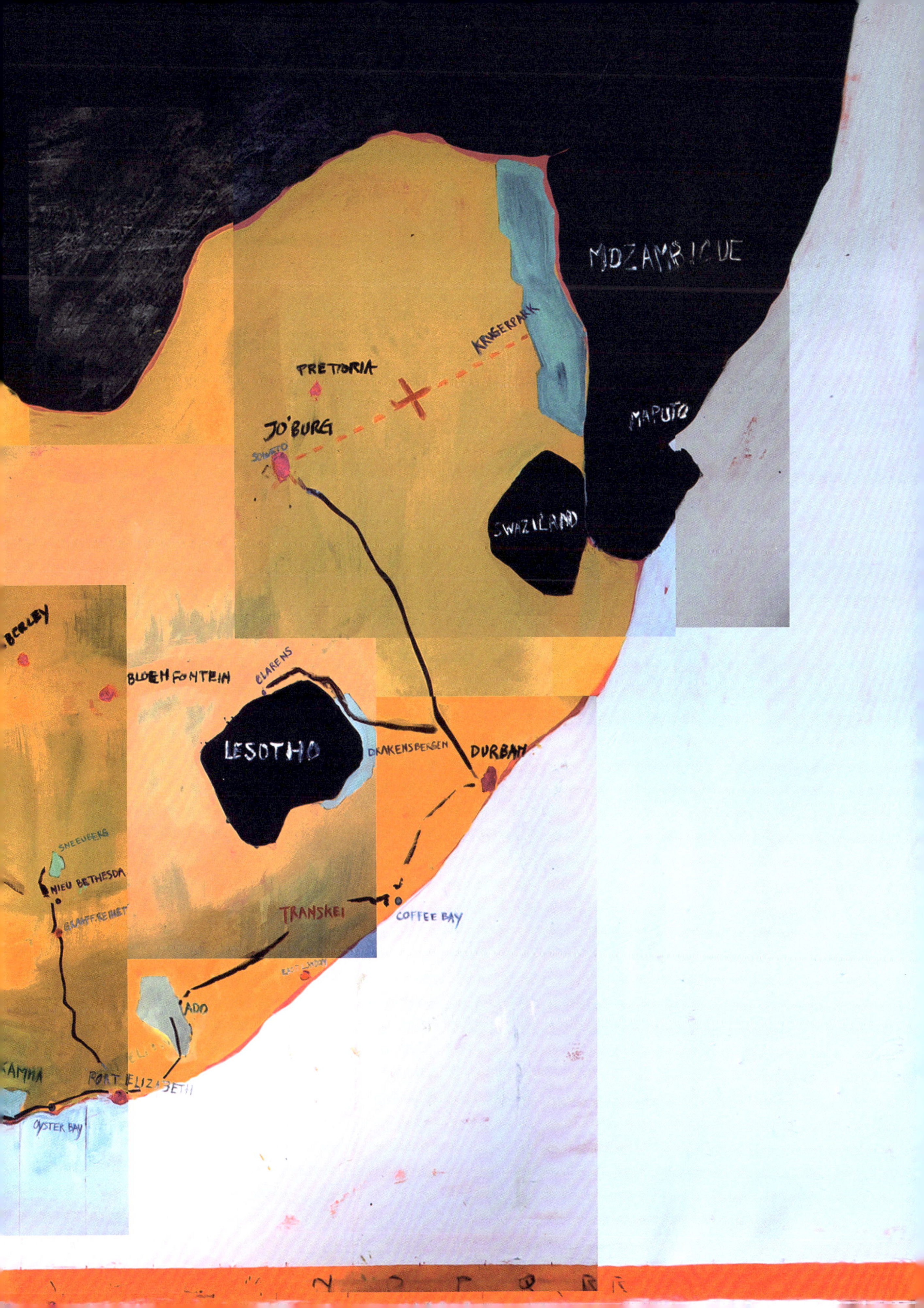
MOZAMBIQUE
KRUGERPARK
PRETORIA
JO'BURG
SOWETO
MAPUTO
SWAZILAND
BLOEMFONTEIN
CLARENS
LESOTHO
DRAKENSBERGEN
DURBAN
TRANSKEI
COFFEE BAY
NIEU BETHESDA
ADO
PORT ELIZABETH
OYSTER BAY

5

Great Karoo

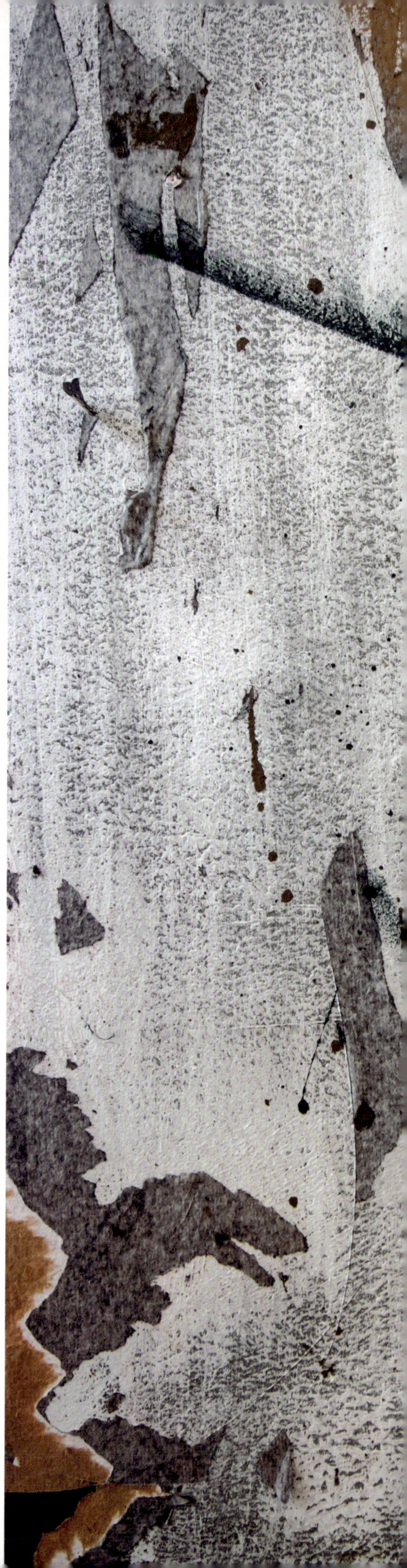

124

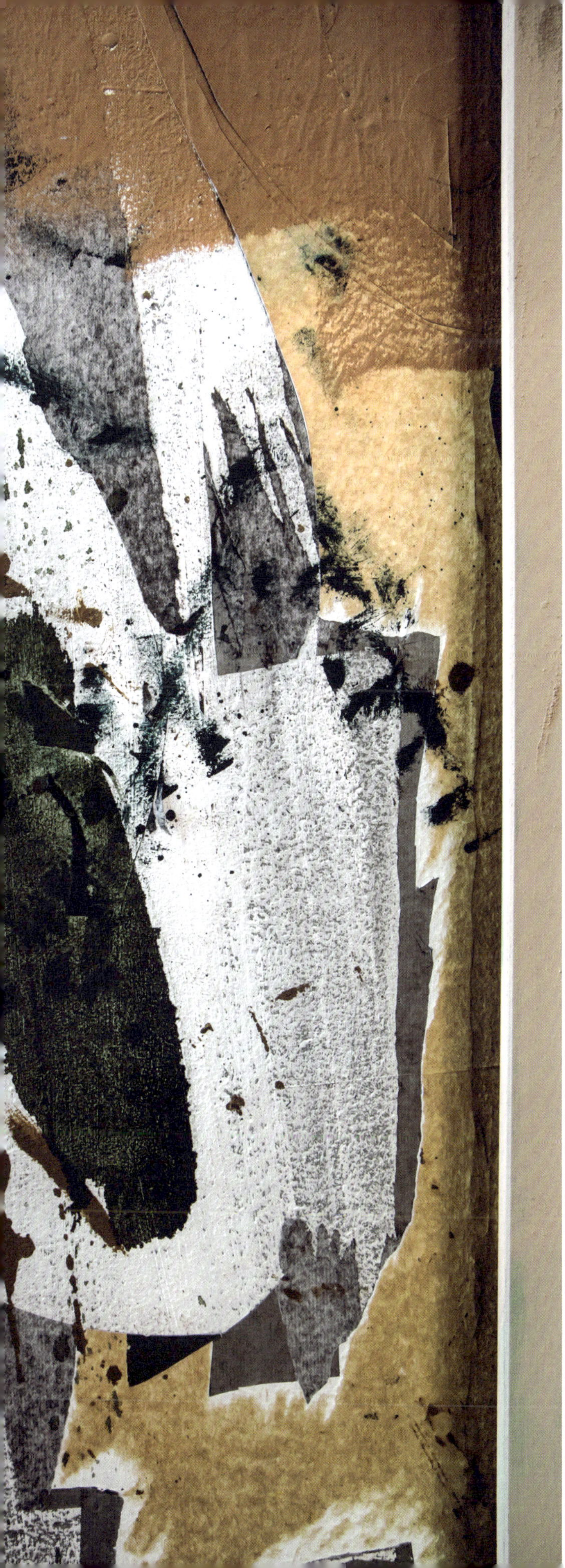

This vast area's thirsty soil couldn't welcome its first permanent settlers until the mid 1800s, when the multi-bladed wind pump was invented in America. Now water could be pumped up from deep down to make the dusty land fertile and green.

These clever and simple wind pumps are still in full use and have become as iconic of the Great Karoo landscape as the flat-topped mountains in the hazy blue distance. Apart from that, not much has changed in over 150 years. Crossing this land by car, the majestic scenery is powerful and overwhelming.

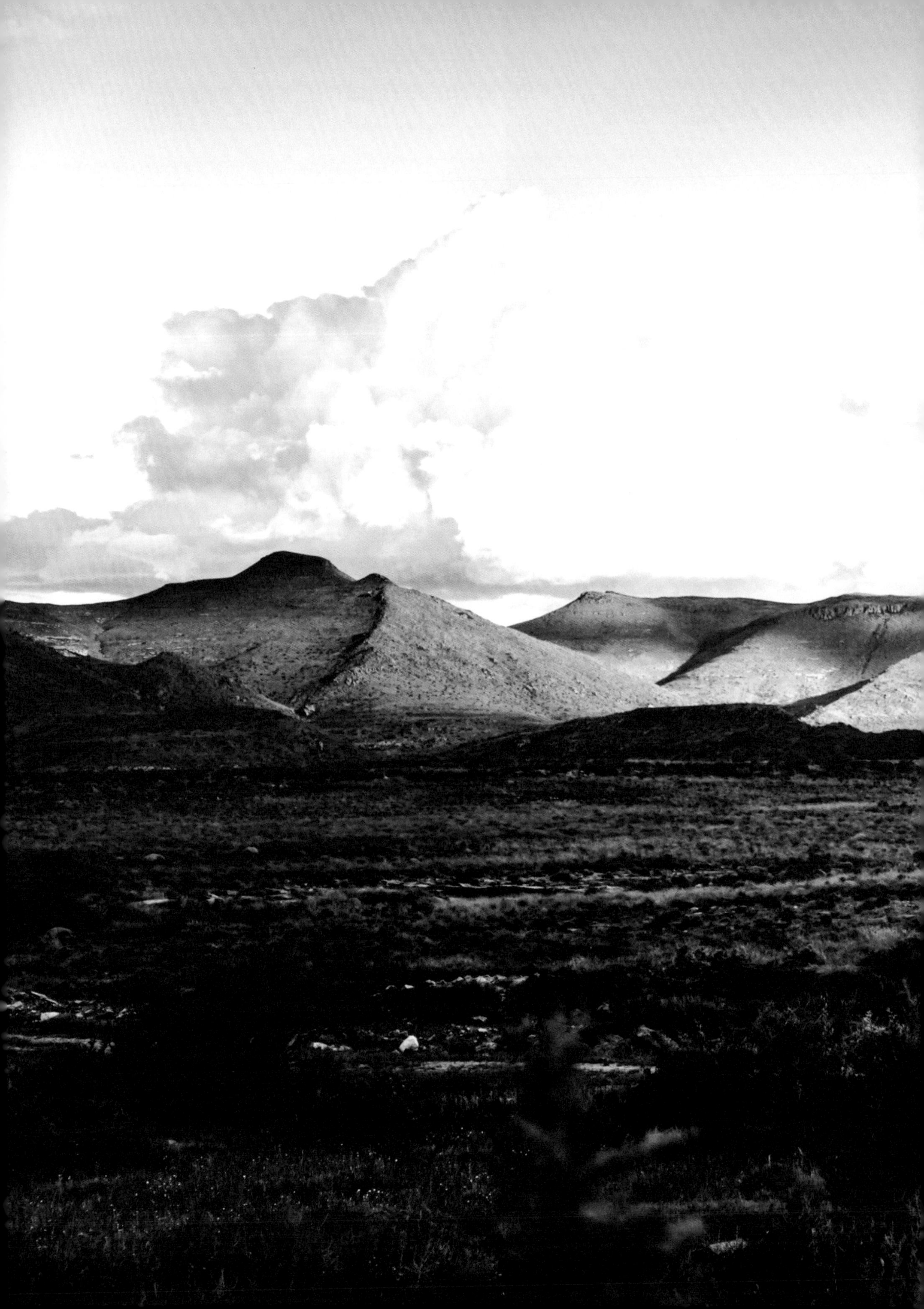

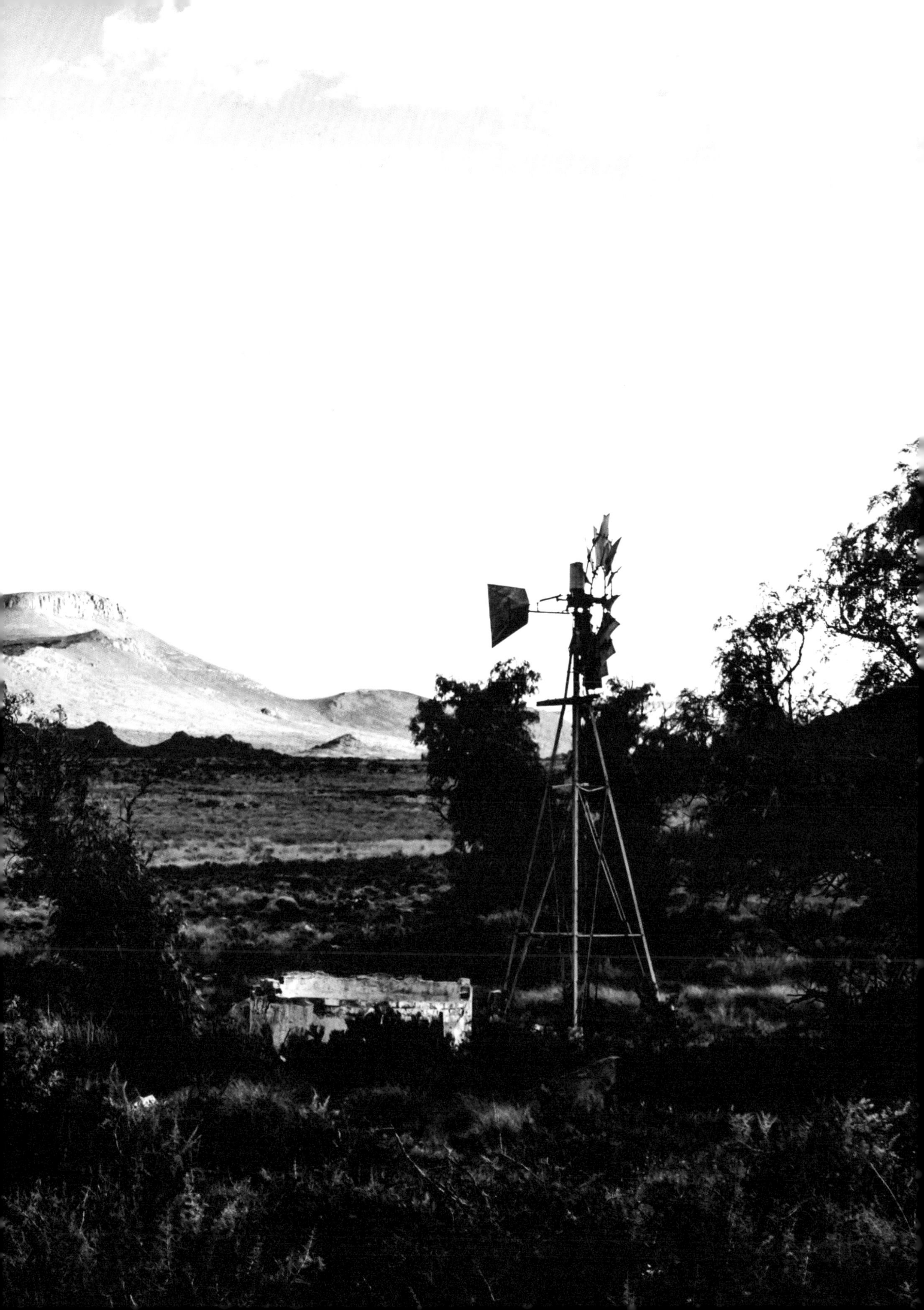

Having lived abroad for many years, Charlotte Daneel returned to South Africa with her Dutch partner, introducing him to her homeland. She was very lucky to be able to acquire the Sneeuberg estate, where she spent many childhood holidays. The renovation of the stone ruin next to the well in a remote part of the estate was a special project. Here, Charlotte decided to build a completely new house.

It was a very personal project where everything - from how the fireplace is built to the unique way in which the walls have been clad with sand and concrete - has been done with great precision. Most of the materials were sourced on the property itself. Local builders who are expert stoneworkers went out into the fields to collect the materials they needed for the stone walls and floors. Old fencing posts were used to build shelving and lintels. Poplar trees that grow in the area provided the beams for the roof. Charlotte also personally selected the finishing touches for the house, including the bathroom taps and the soft linen sheets on the beds.

Charlotte's bold use of materials and her good taste make the house special in itself. Everything was done in a very clever way, with the utmost respect for this unique location. The transformation from a bunch of walls providing shelter for sheep into this elegant hideaway, is stunning. It is grand yet intimate, and for a place in the middle of nowhere it is surprisingly luxurious, albeit in an understated, subtle manner. Easy chic best sums up the style.

Charlotte rediscovered the Karoo, and realised that once this arid land gets under your skin, there really is no way back.

Charlotte
Daneel

Luxury in the middle
of nowhere

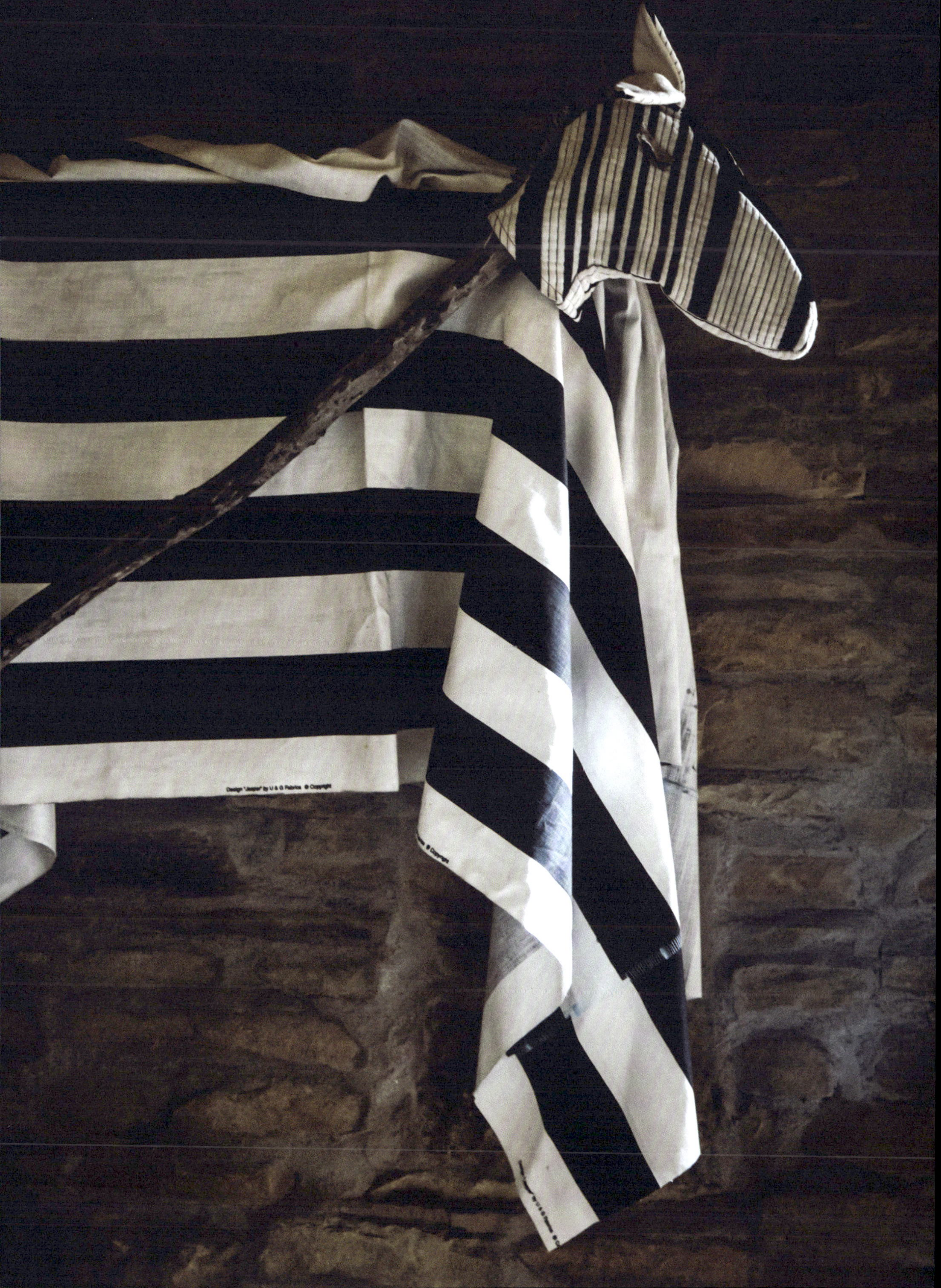
Design "Jasper" by U & G Fabrics © Copyright

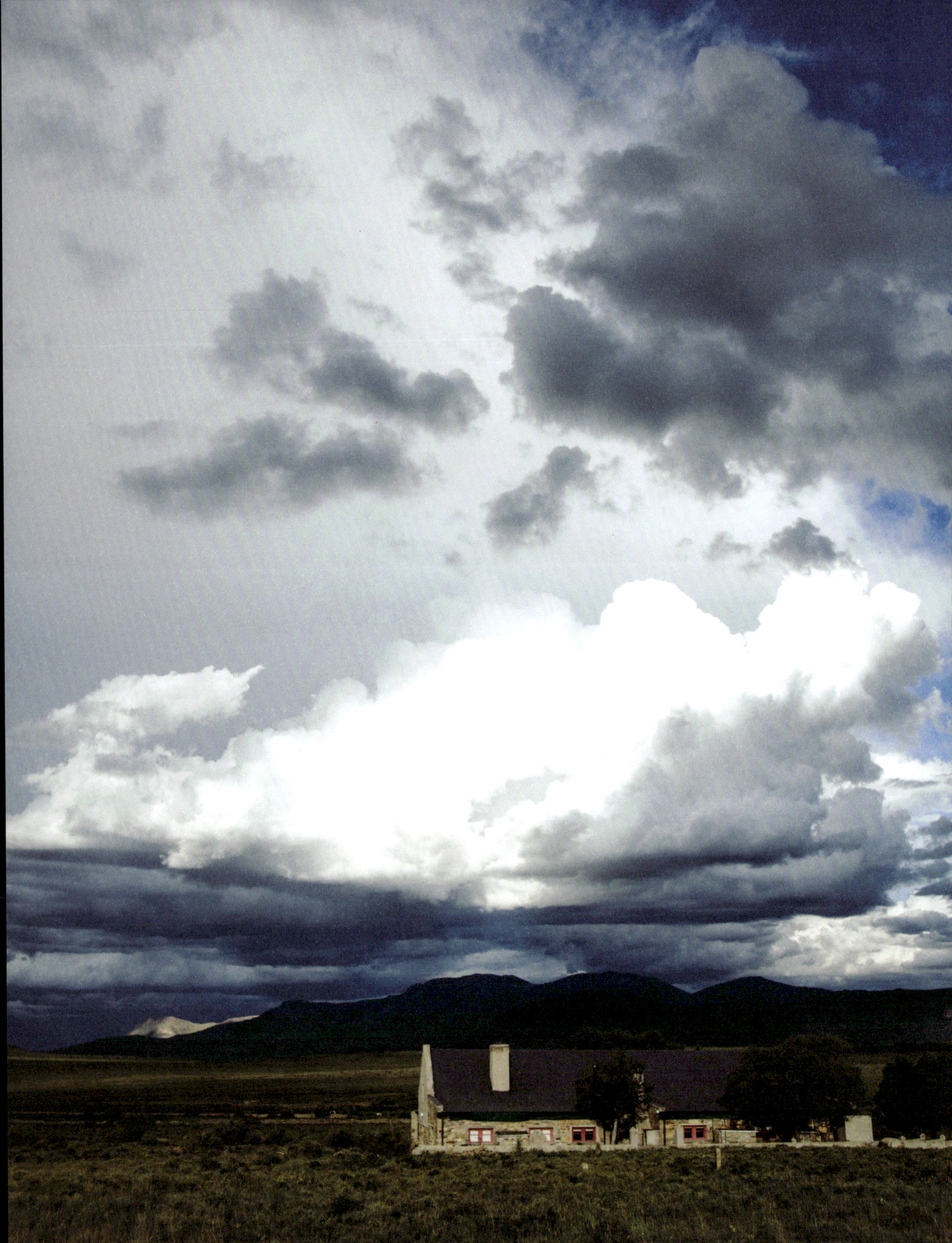

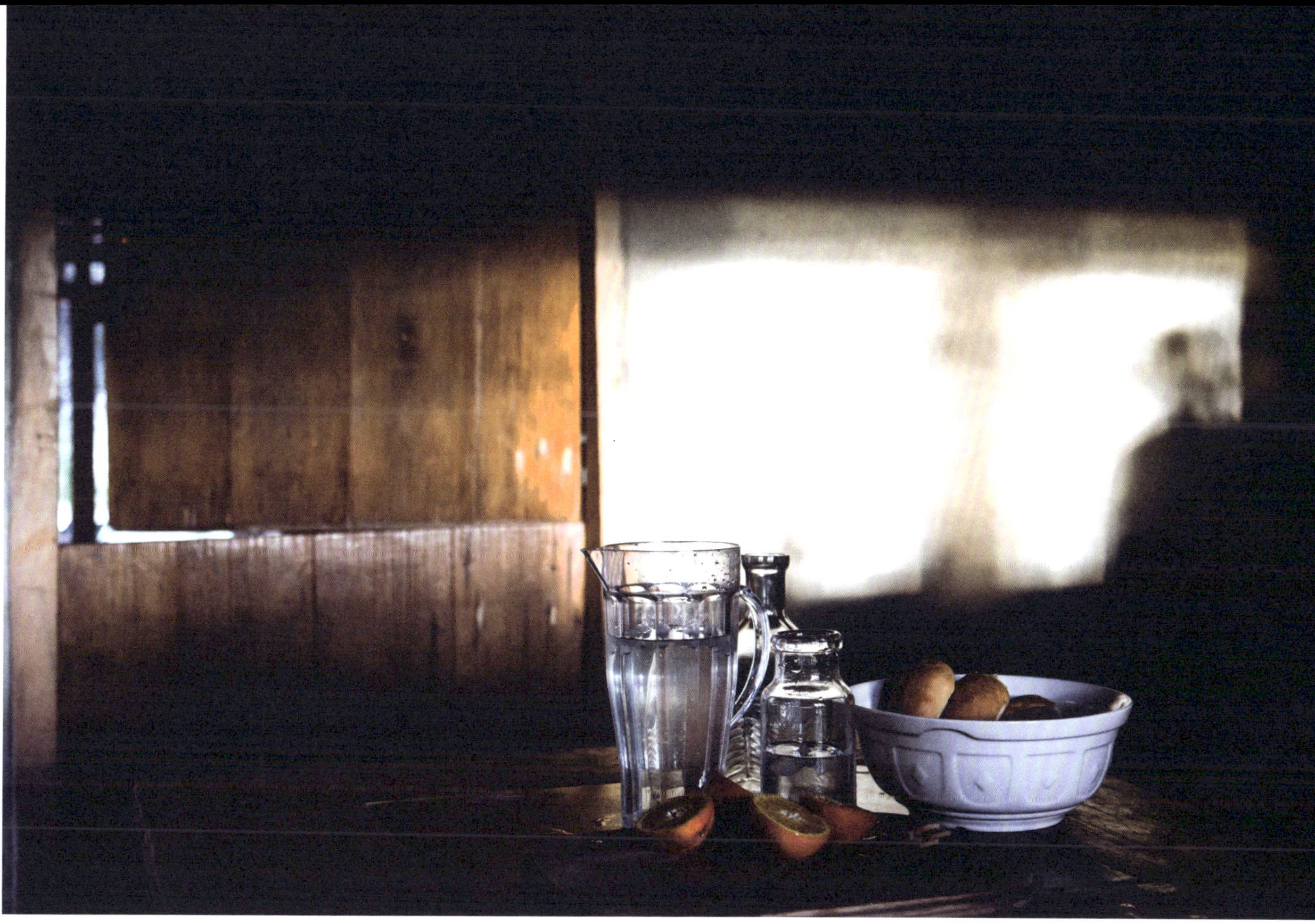

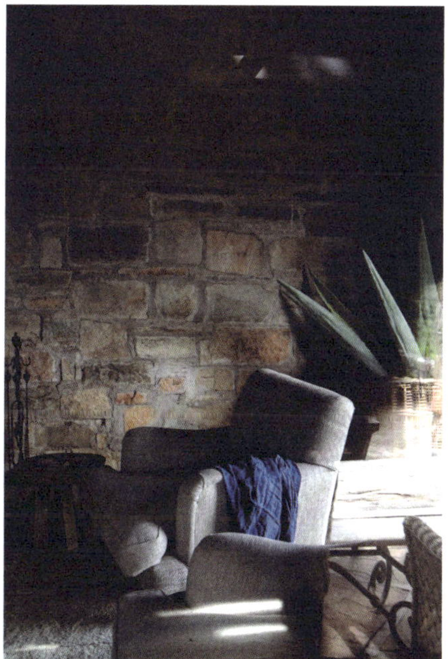

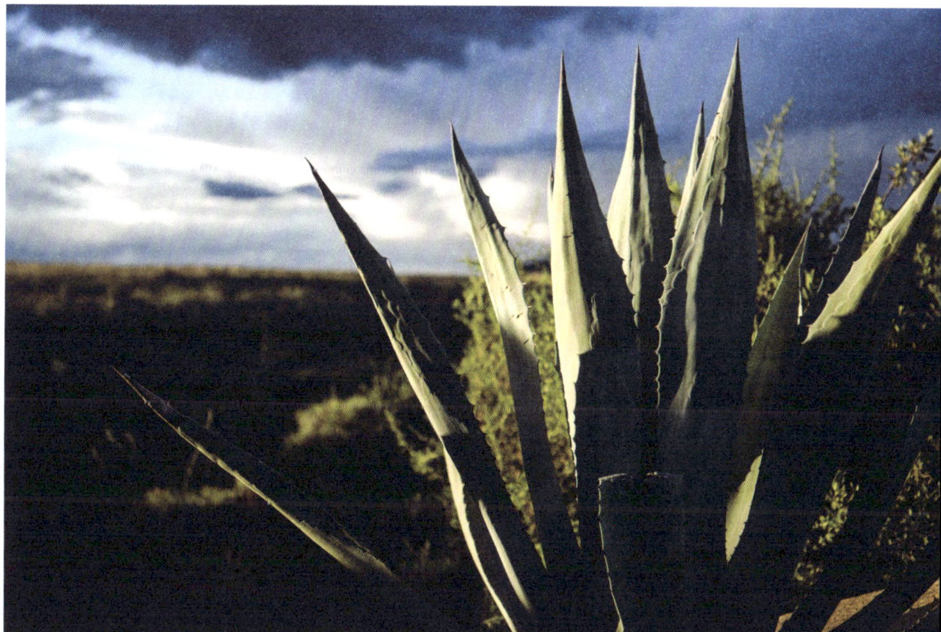

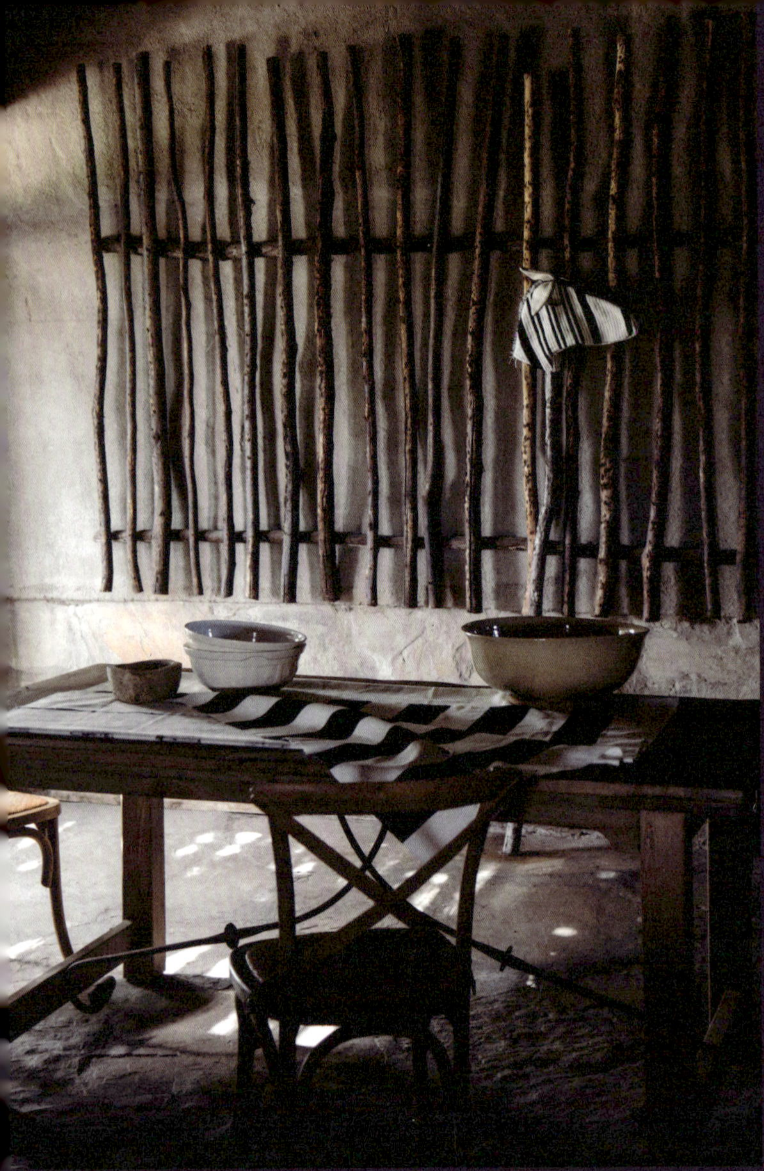

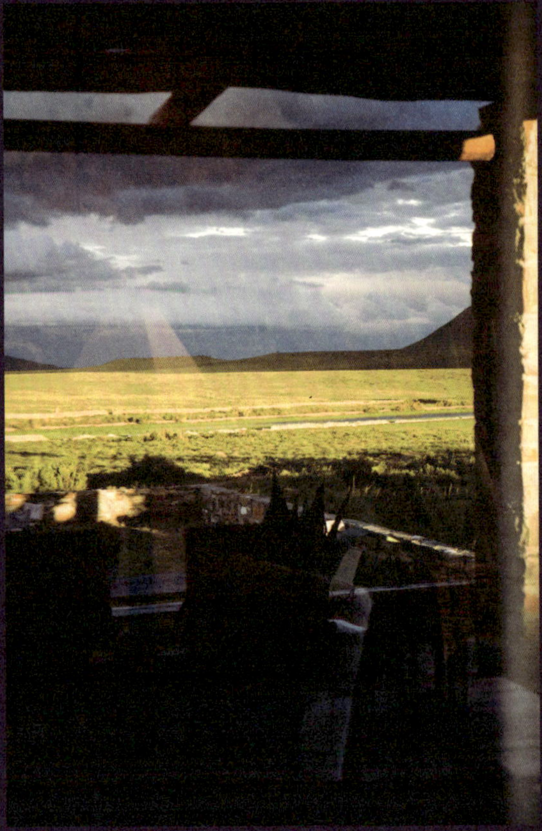

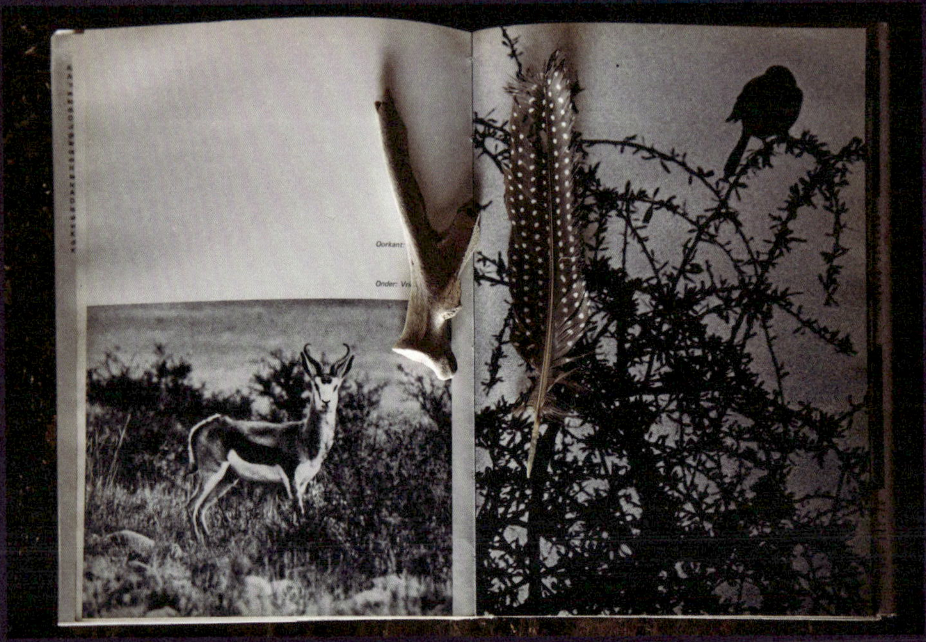

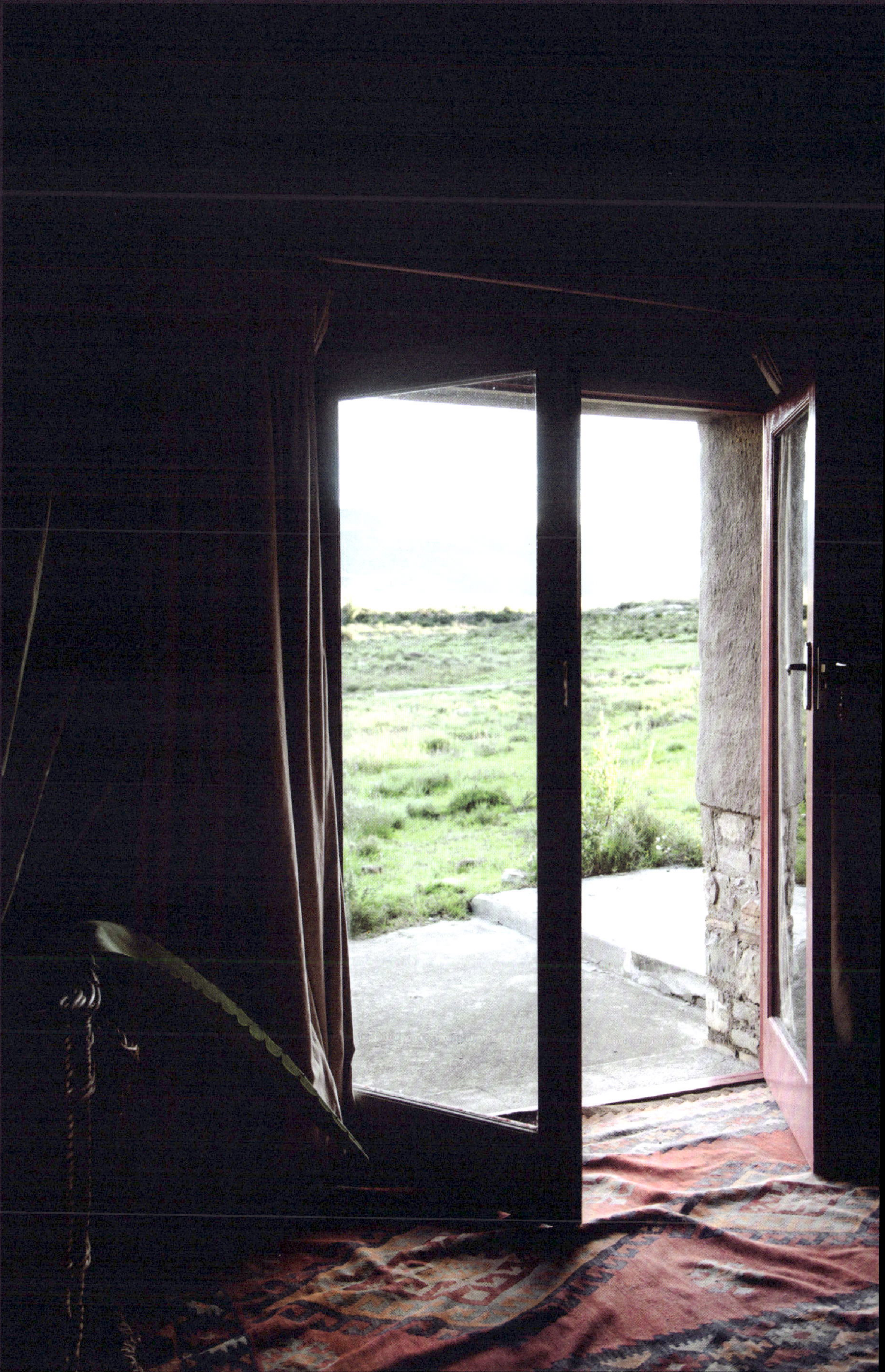

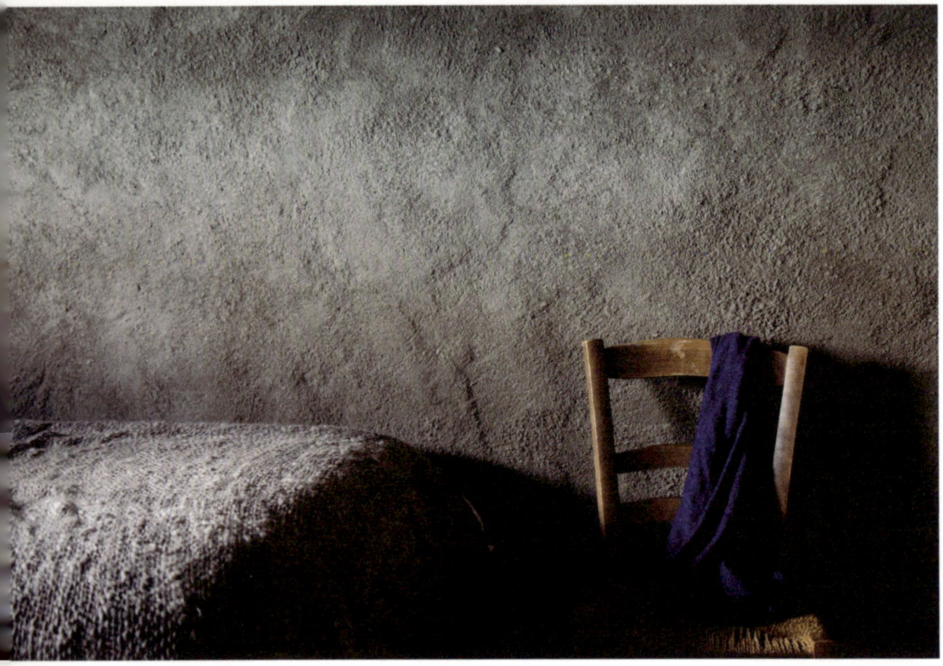

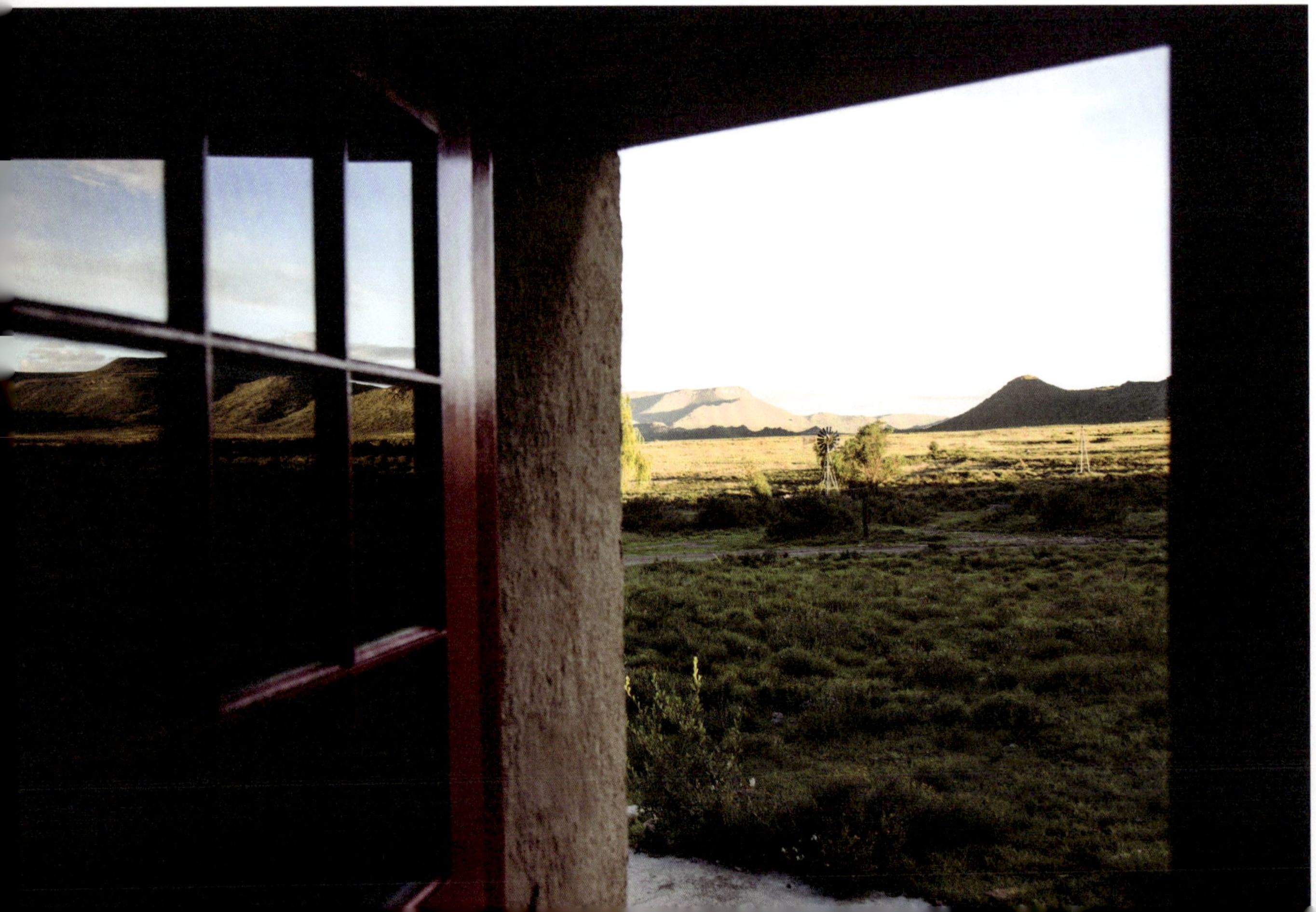

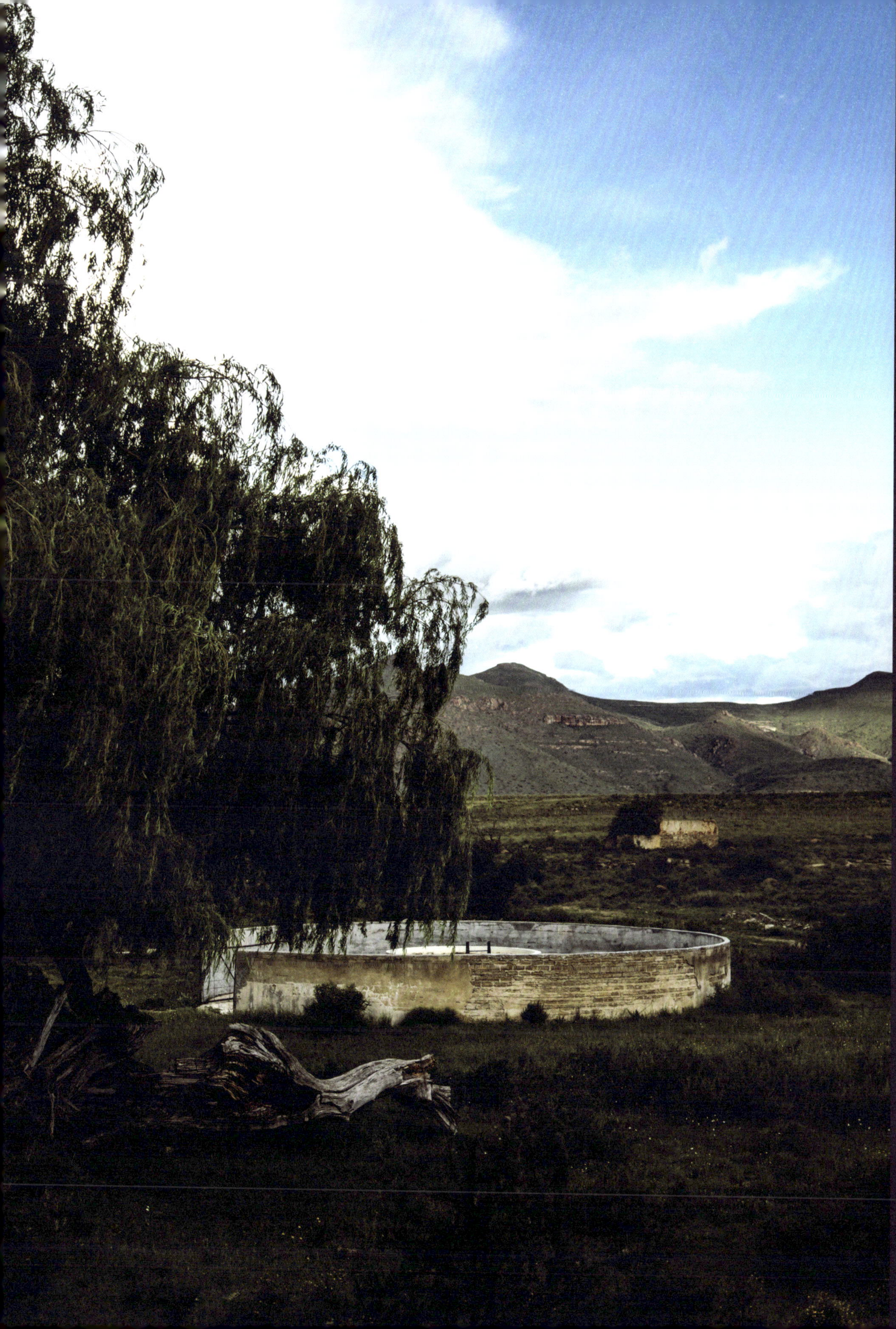

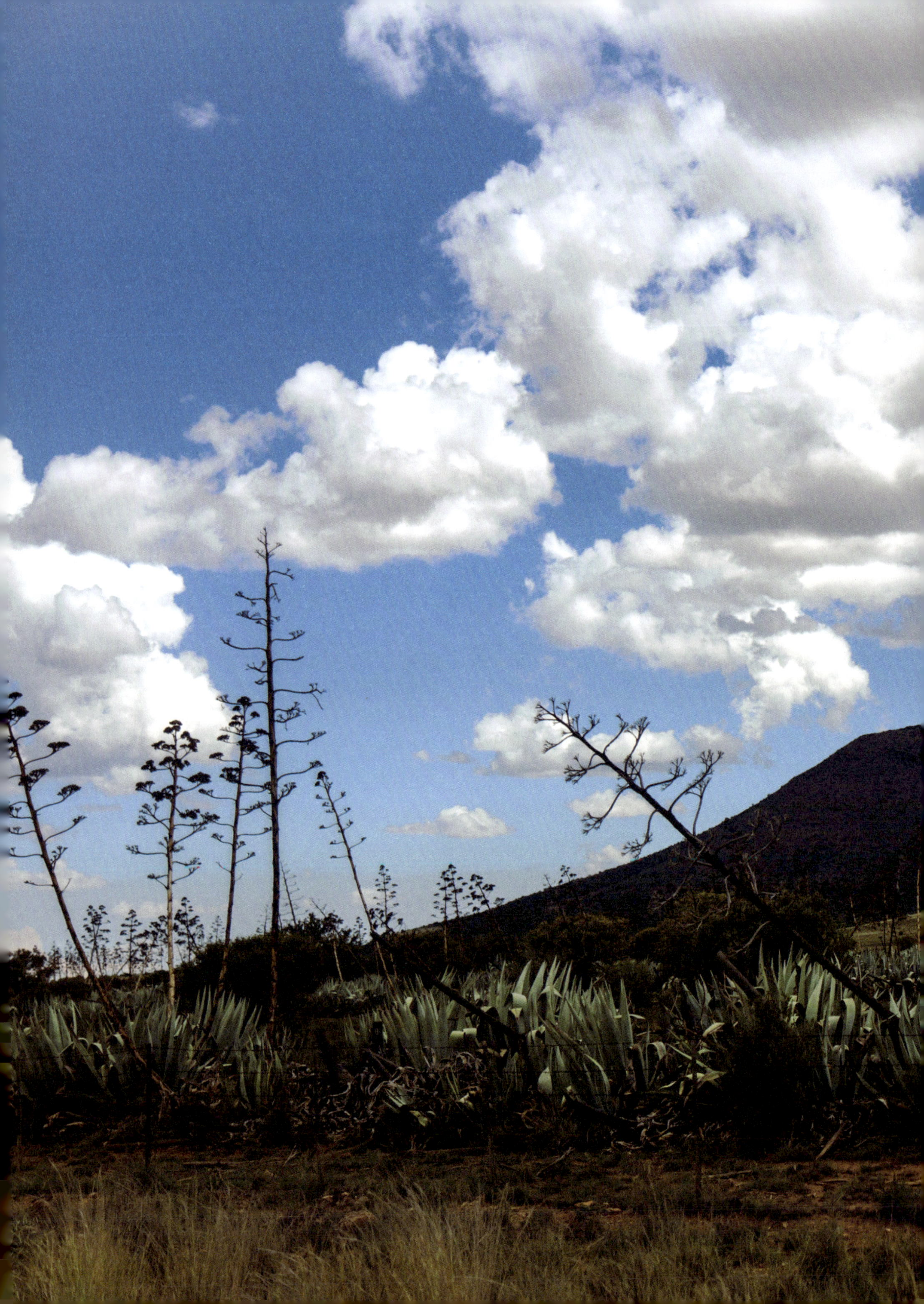

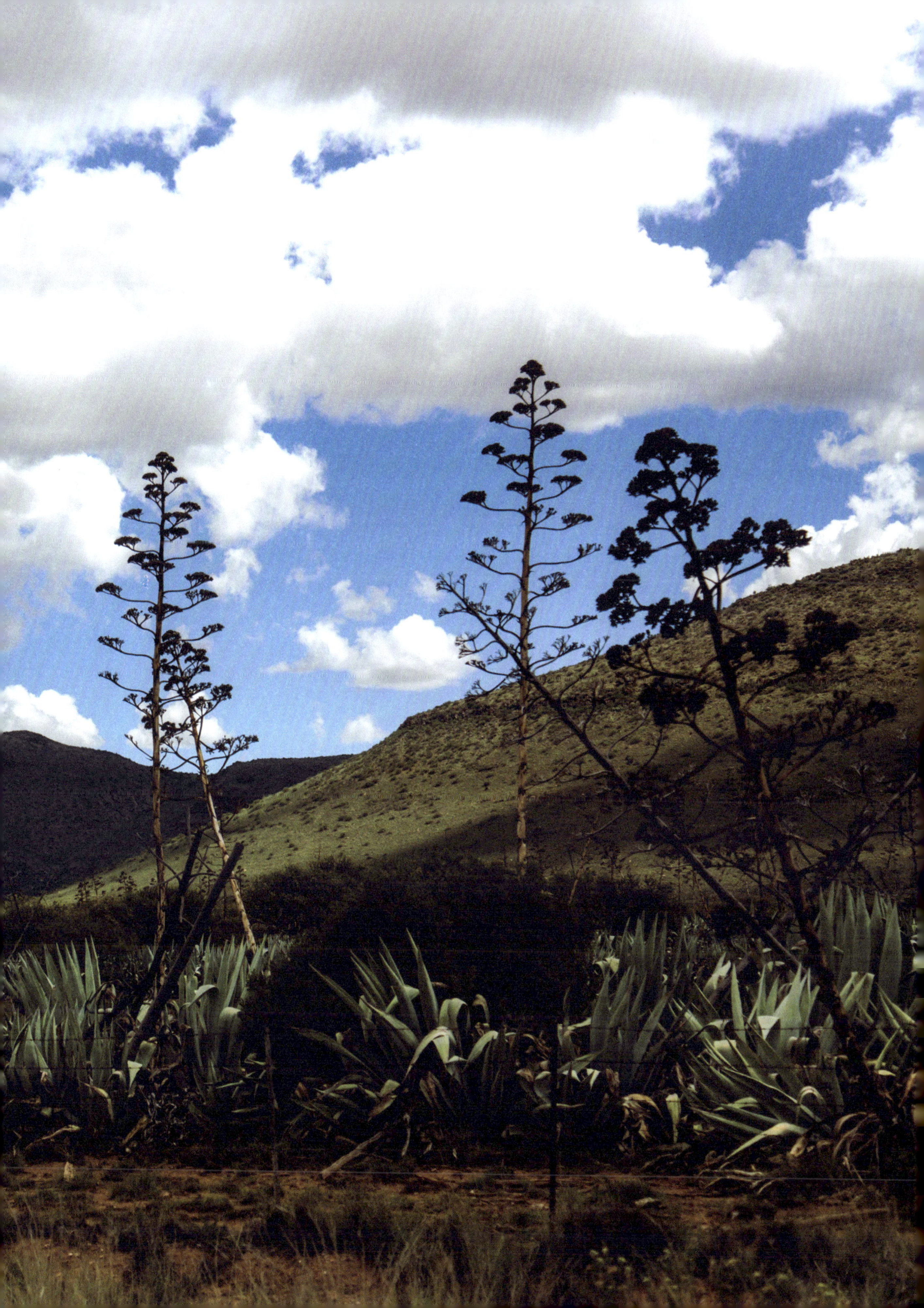

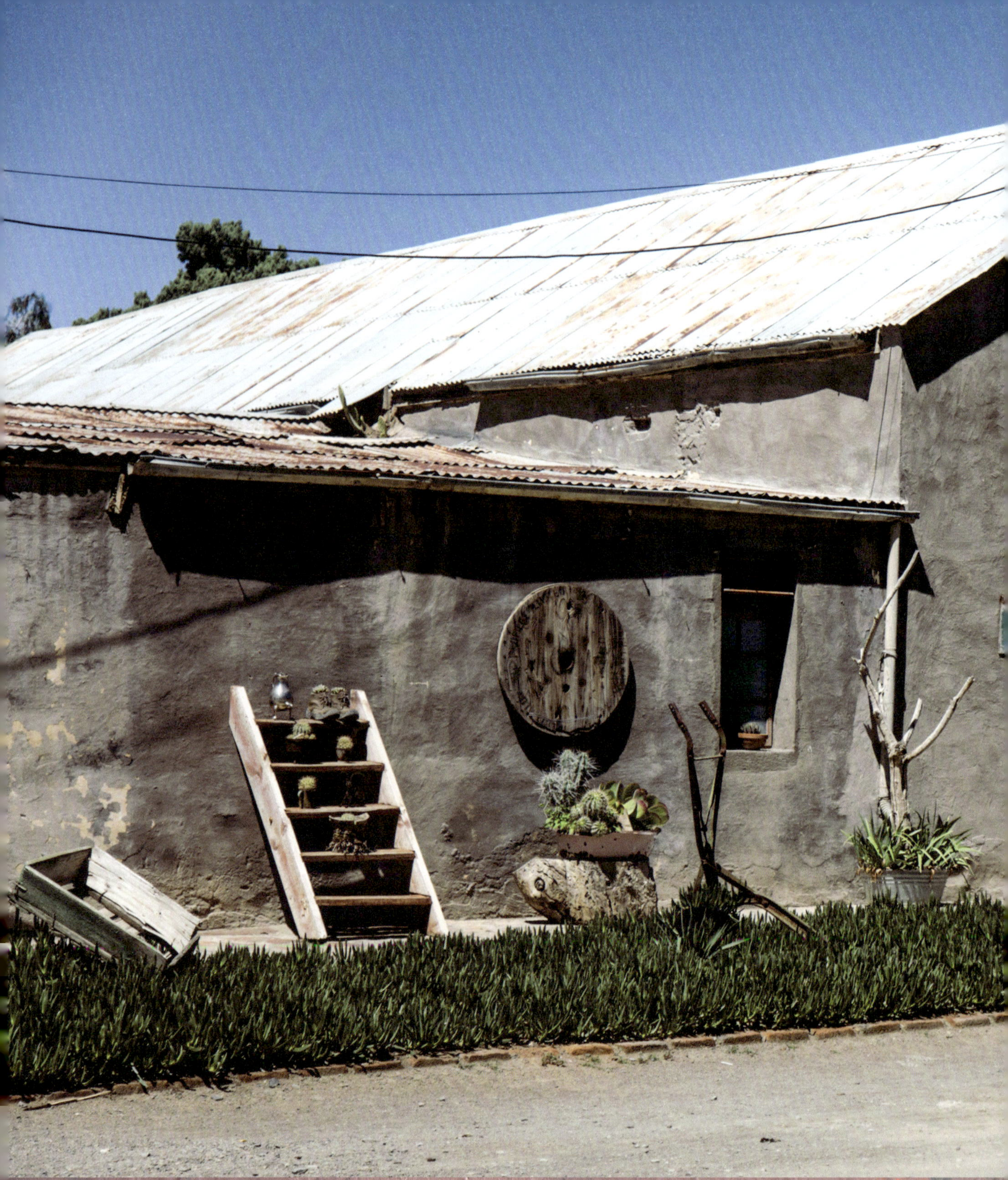

Gardens in the dust

Nieu Bethesda lies at the foot of the Compassberg, one of the highest mountains in the Karoo. Because of the eternal spring higher up, it lies in a fertile valley. In this small village, time seems to have stood still, or never really matters. The streets remain unsealed. The dust drifting in the wind contrasts beautifully with the green leaves of the tall trees along the lanes and the flowers in the well-kept gardens.

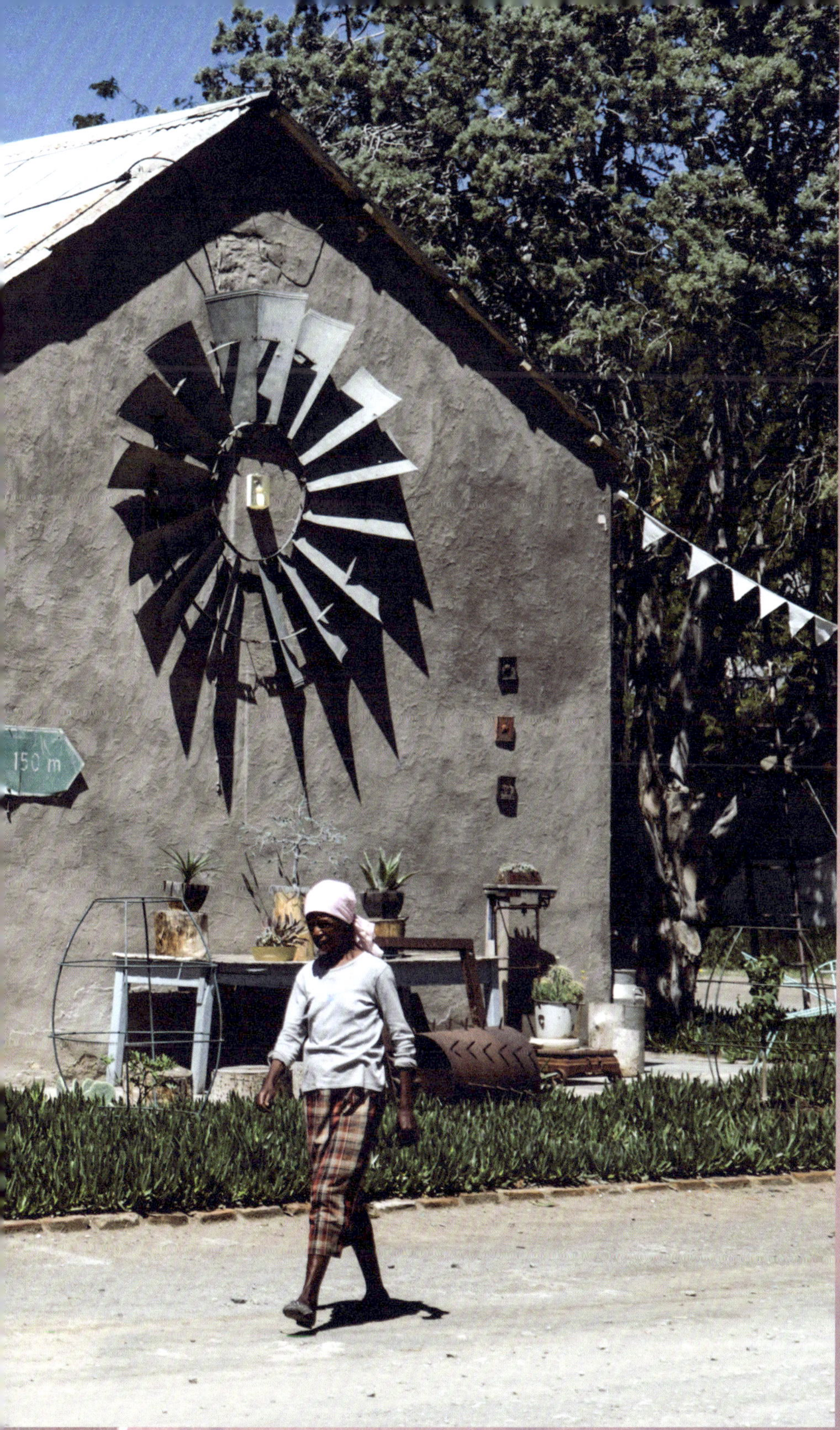
150 m

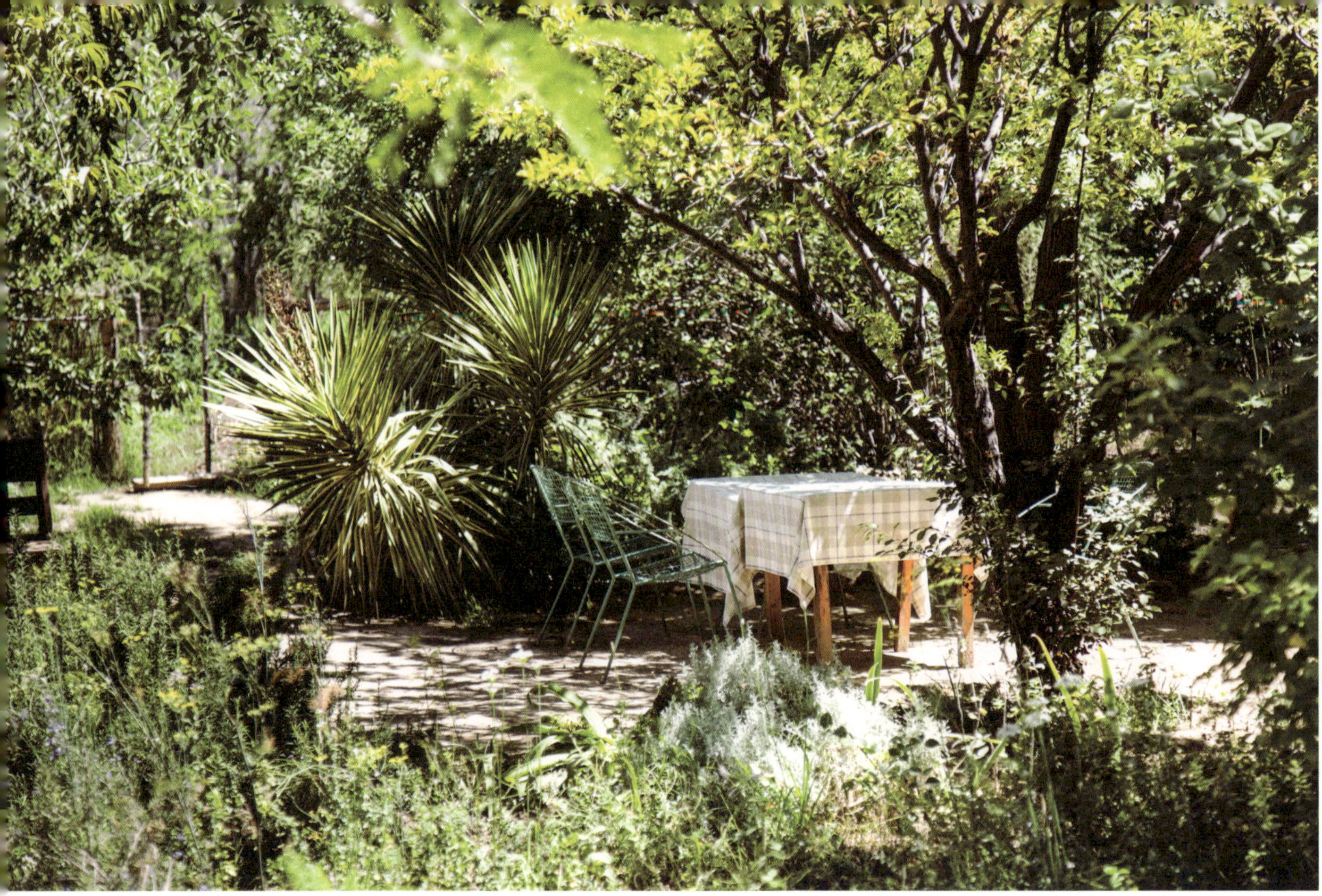

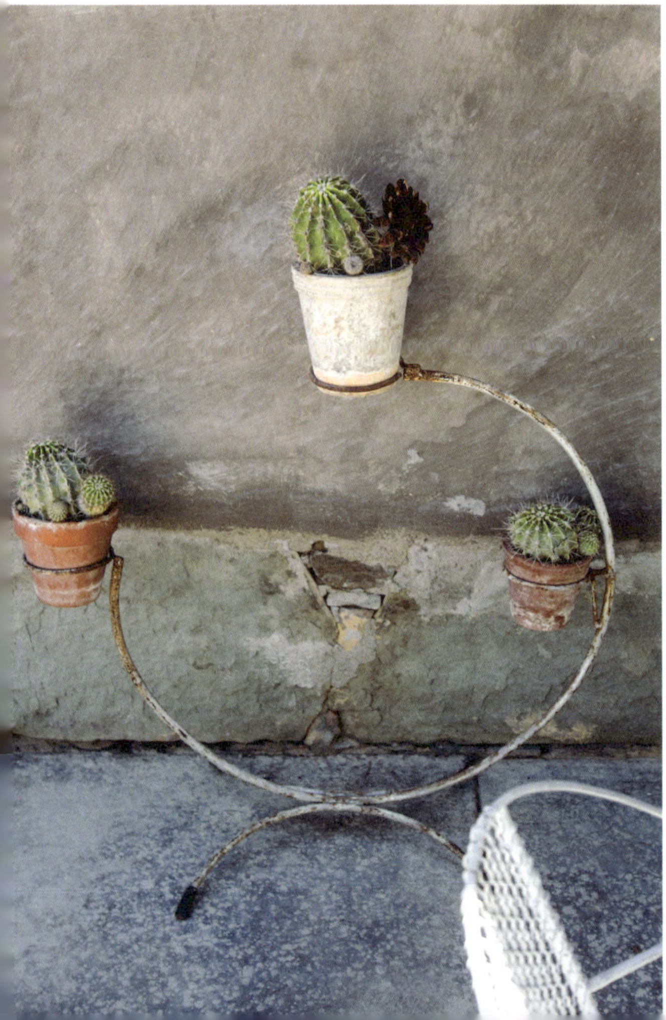

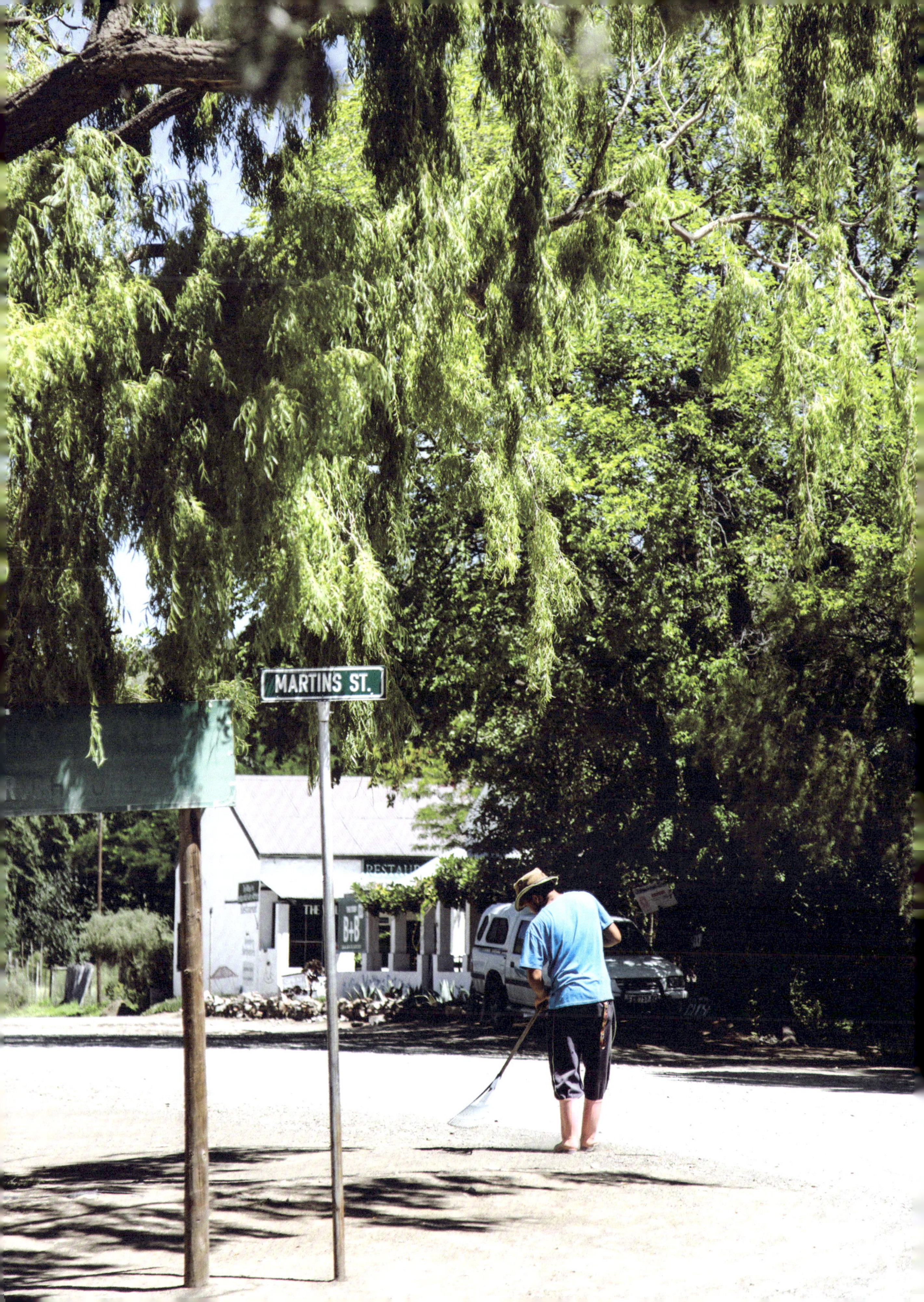
MARTINS ST.

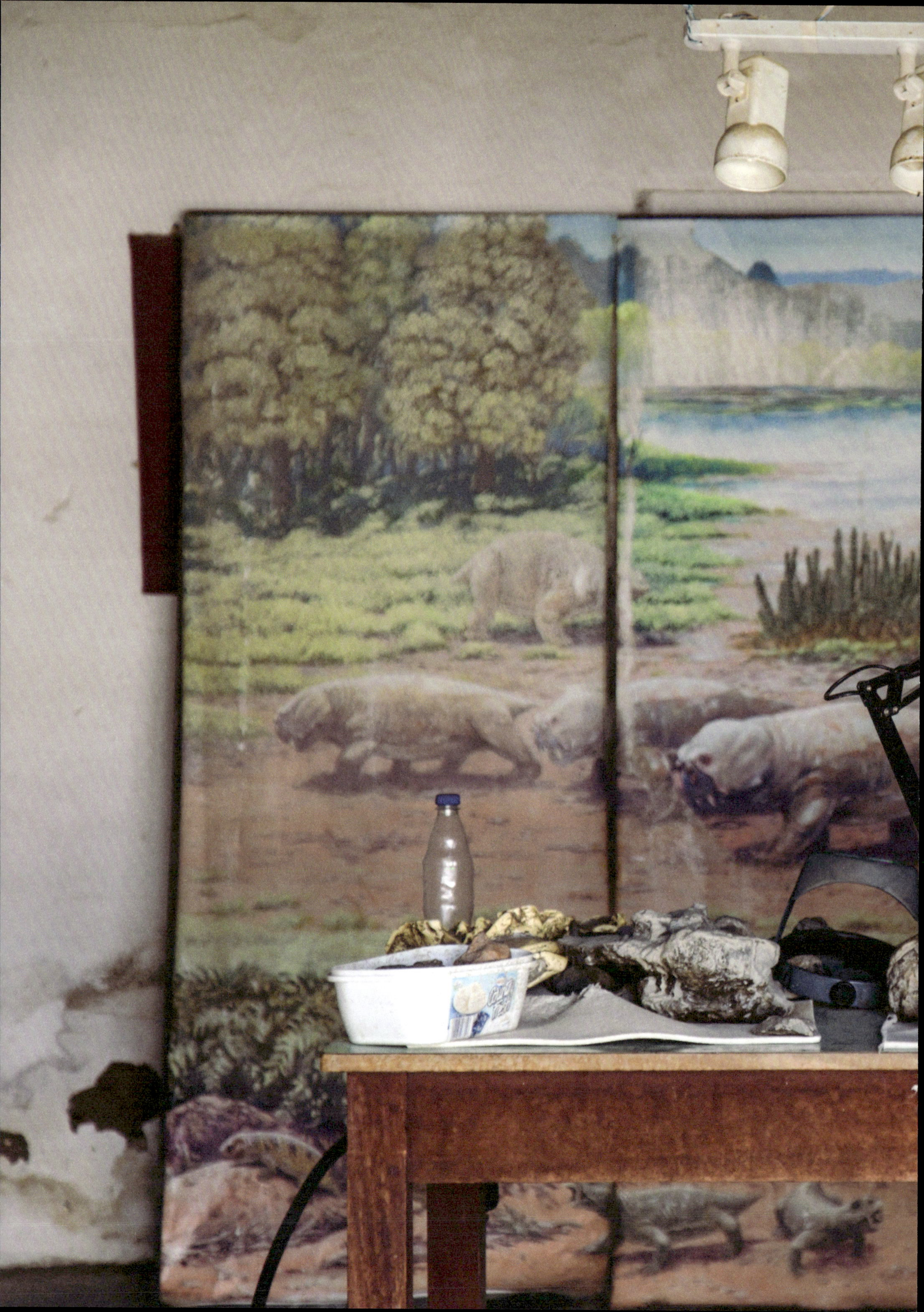

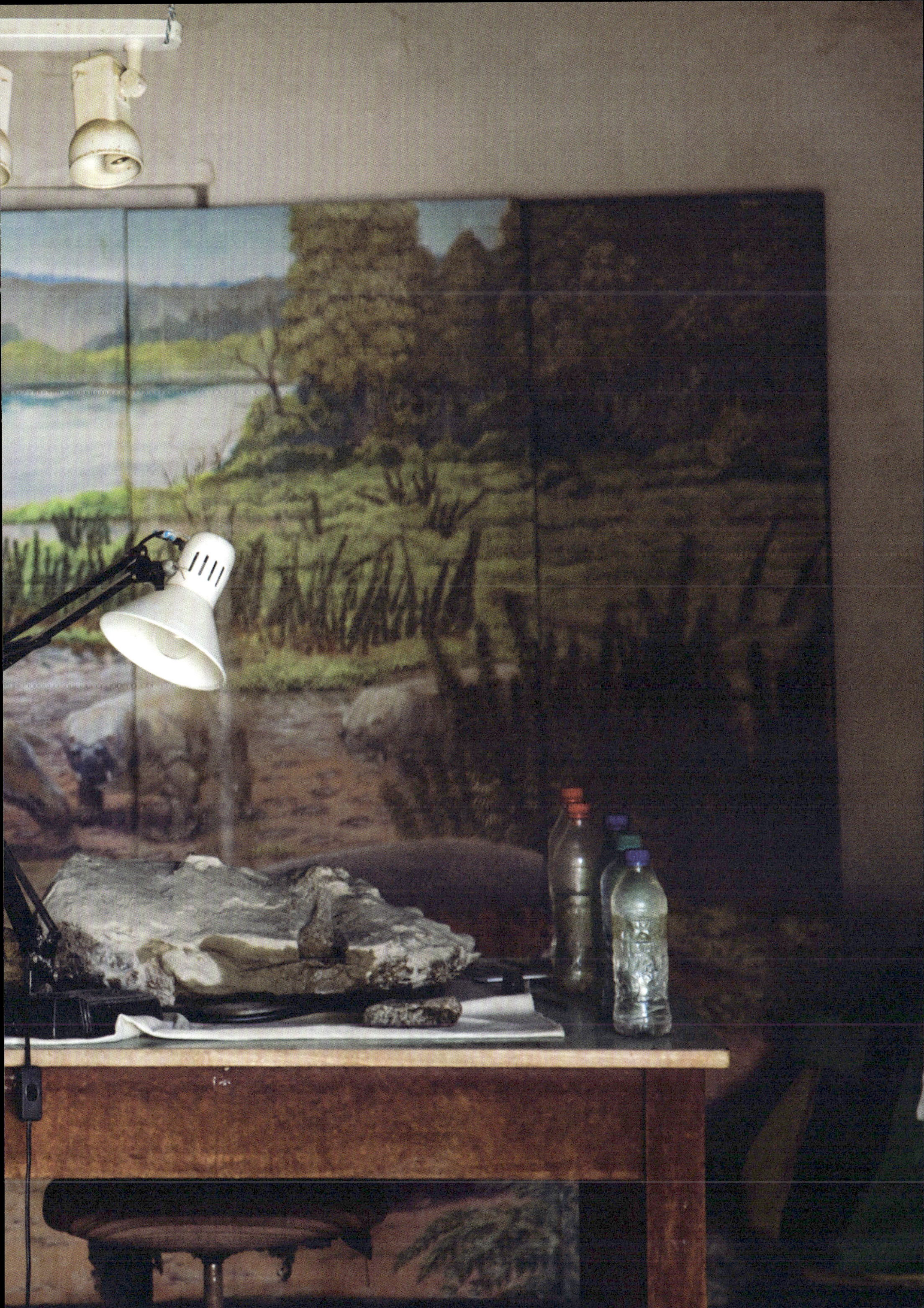

The Owl House was once the home of Helen Martins, an eccentric lady who lived from 1897 to 1976. After being away from her hometown for many years, Helen returned to Nieu Bethesda, where she spent the rest of her life. When both her parents passed away in the early 1940s, she started turning her parental home into a unique fantasy world.

To her, this mission was a remedy for the emotional instability she suffered from her whole life. In the following decades she managed to transform the entire house and garden into a beautiful work of art. Together with Koos Malgas, a fellow villager, she began working on a sculpture garden. A visual tale inspired by her own imagination, biblical figures and the poetry of Omar Khayyam, culminating in a colourful procession of human figures and animals. All of them are looking east or appearing to travel in that direction.

Many of the statues depict a biblical or mythological story, but just as often they tell funny tales of mischievous figures who seem to be lazing around with a small glass of wine.

Inside the house, all the walls and ceilings are covered with glass grit. Coloured glass bottles were collected and ground to an almost powder-like substance. The different shades were applied to the surfaces in large geometric shapes. The combination of these special shades of ground glass and the many differently shaped mirrors throughout the house creates an atmosphere that contrasts sharply with the dusty world outside.

The house and garden are modest in size, but nevertheless our visit had us wandering around for hours and hours, admiring all the great details that revealed themselves more and more with each look. It was a special experience being the only visitors there, which kept the tranquillity and extraordinary beauty of the house intact.

Once the home of an eccentric lady, the house and garden are now a museum that is the highlight of a visit to the small town.

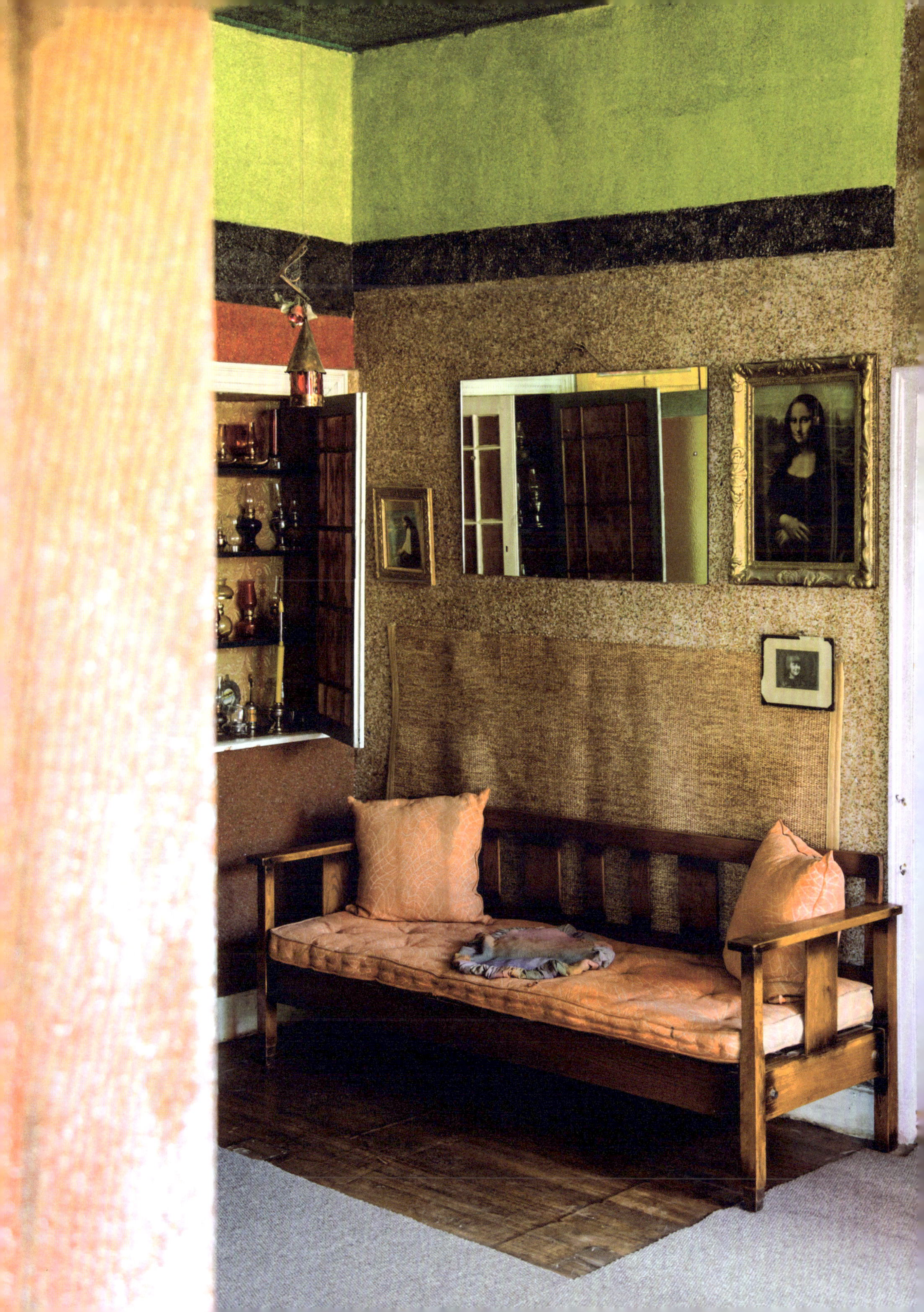

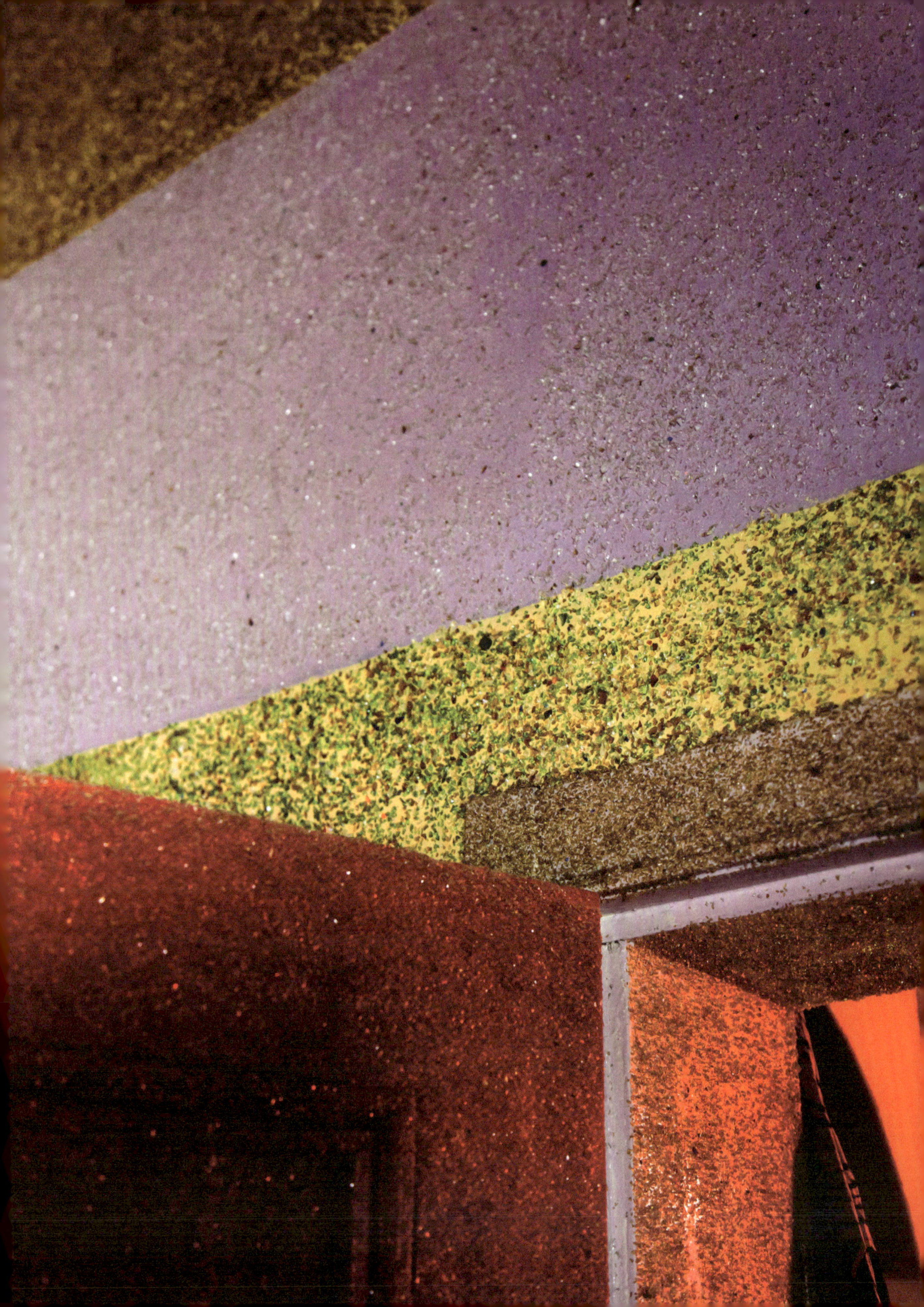

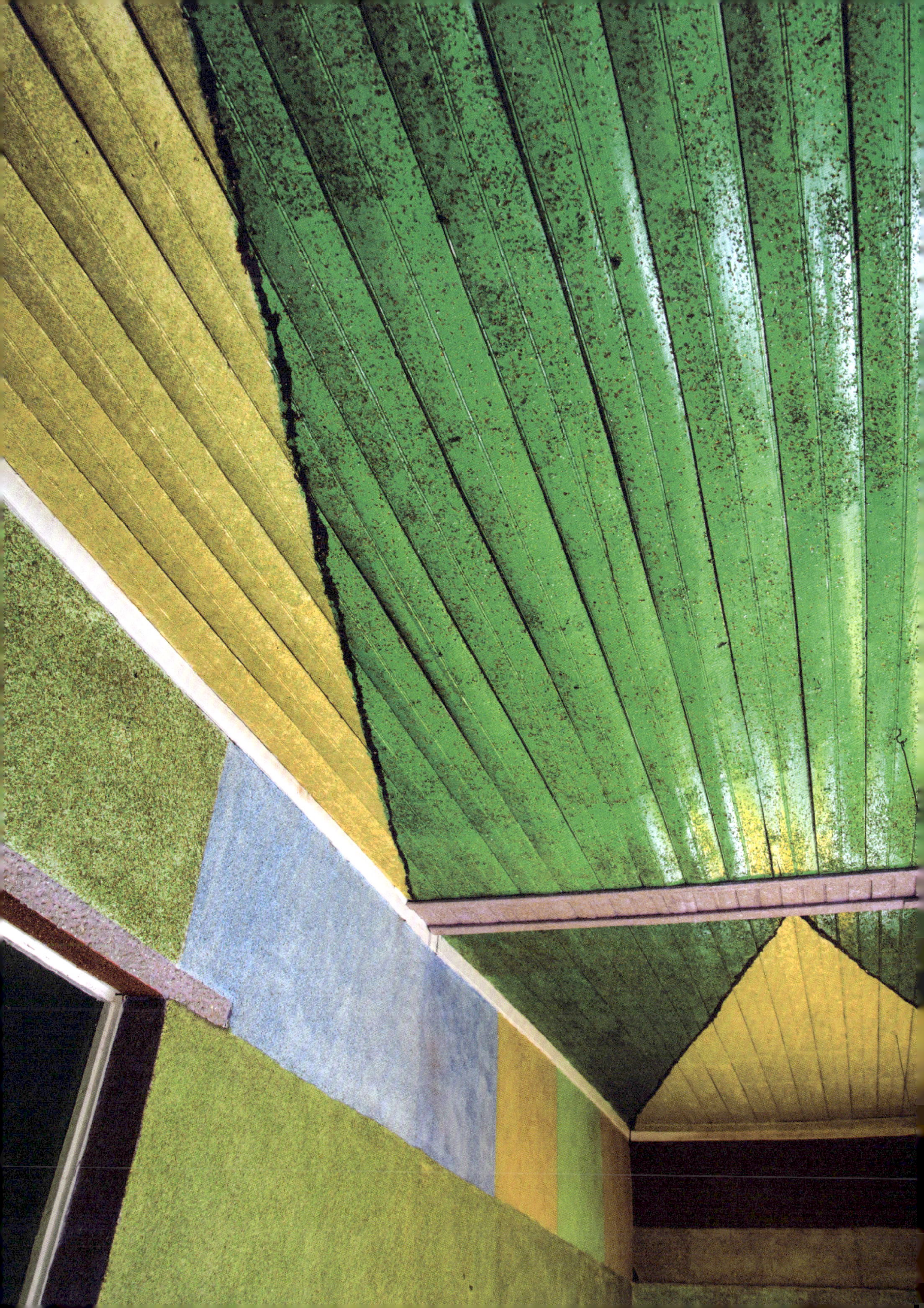

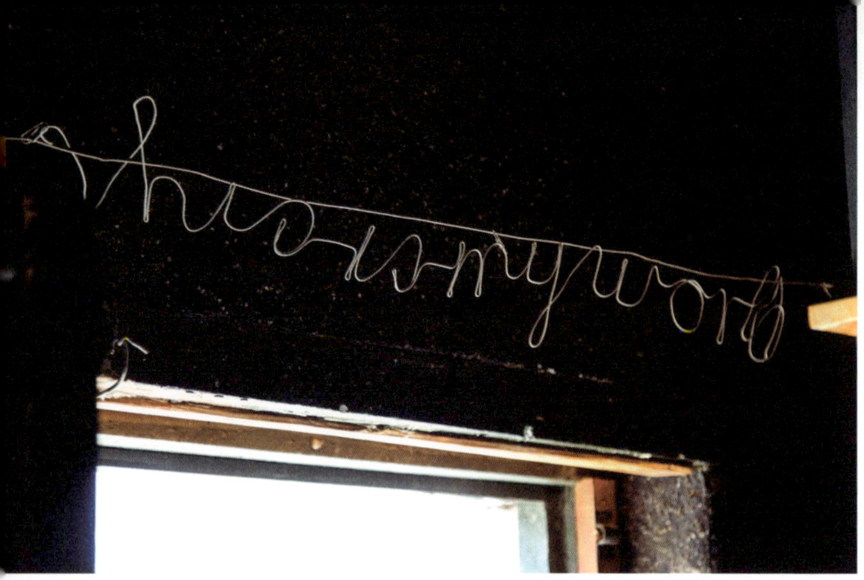
this is my world

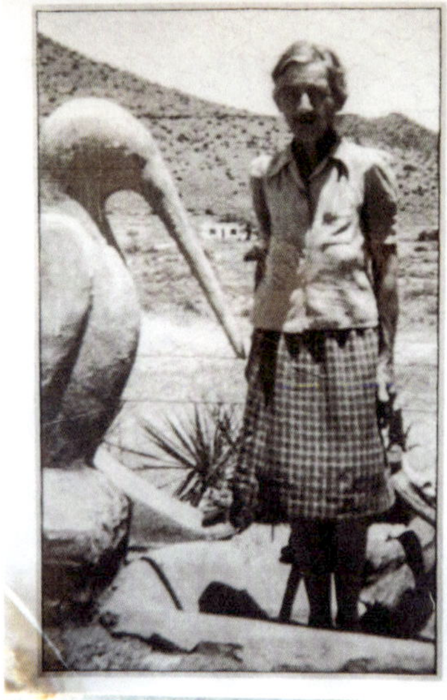

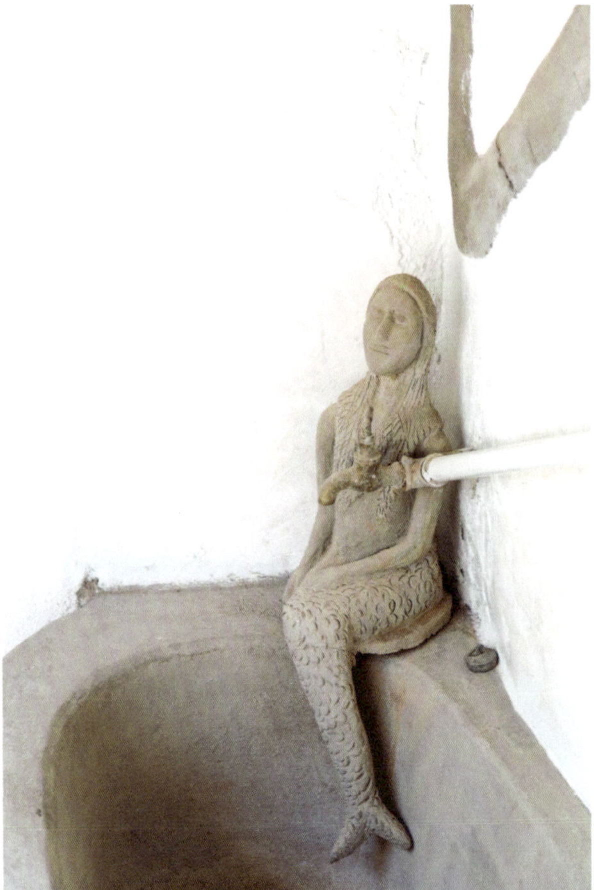

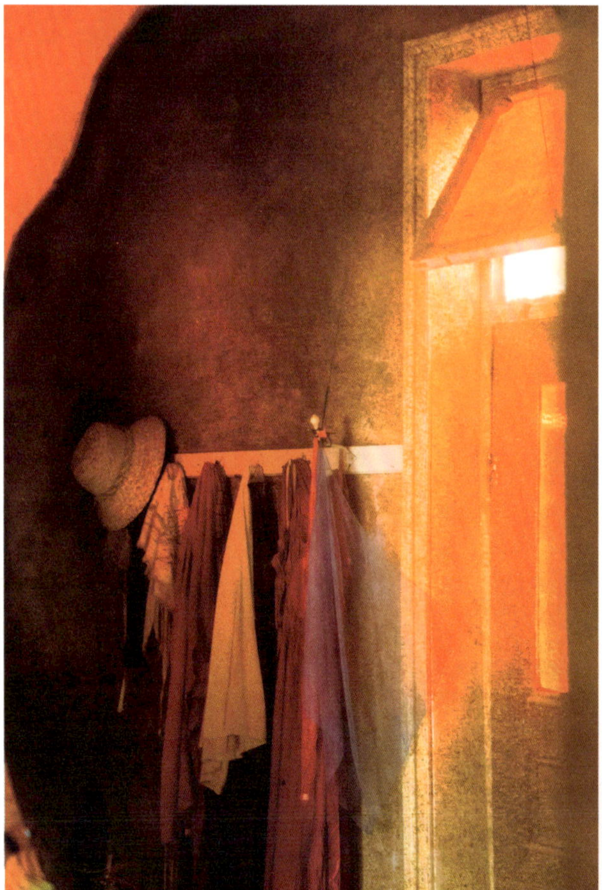

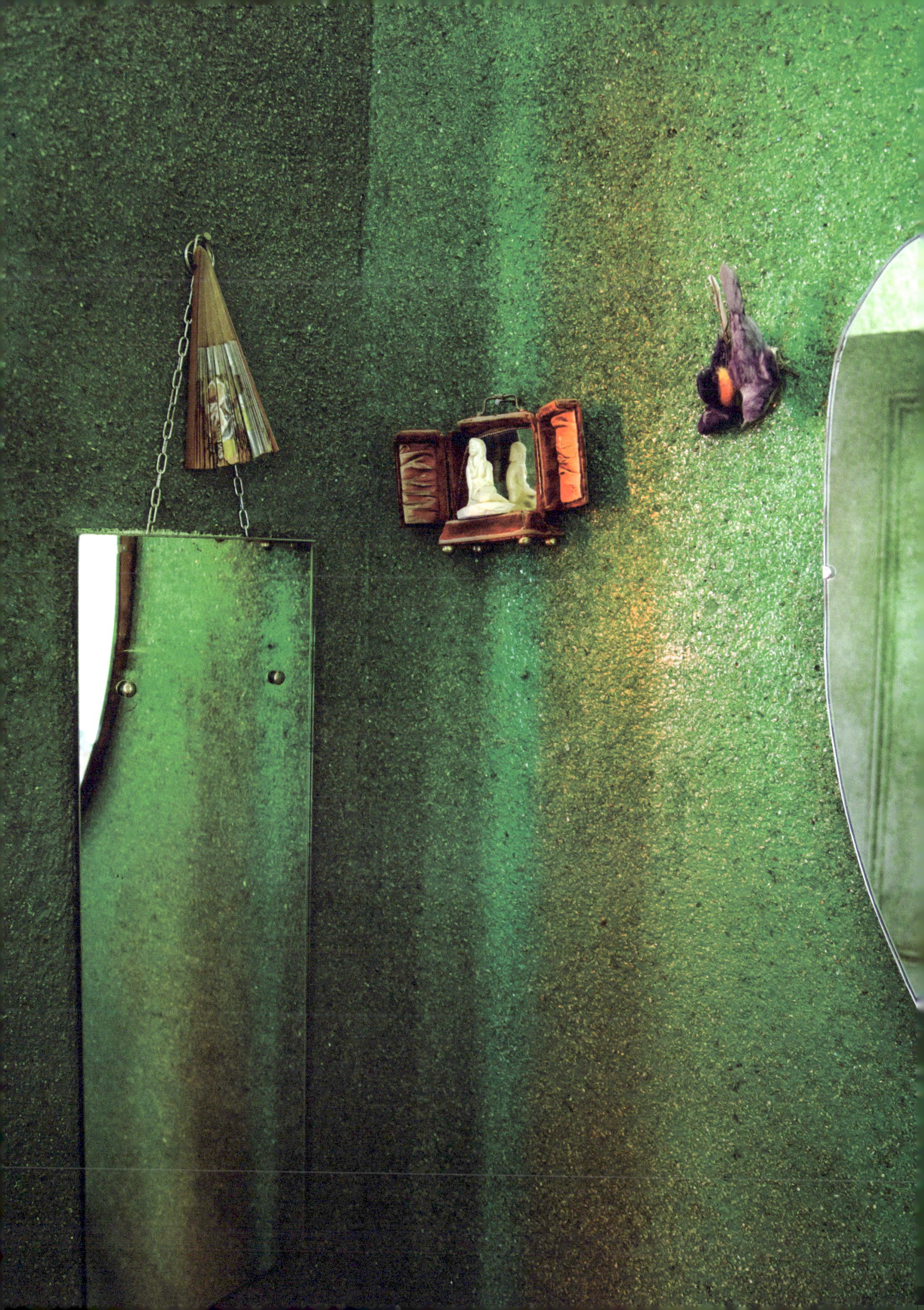

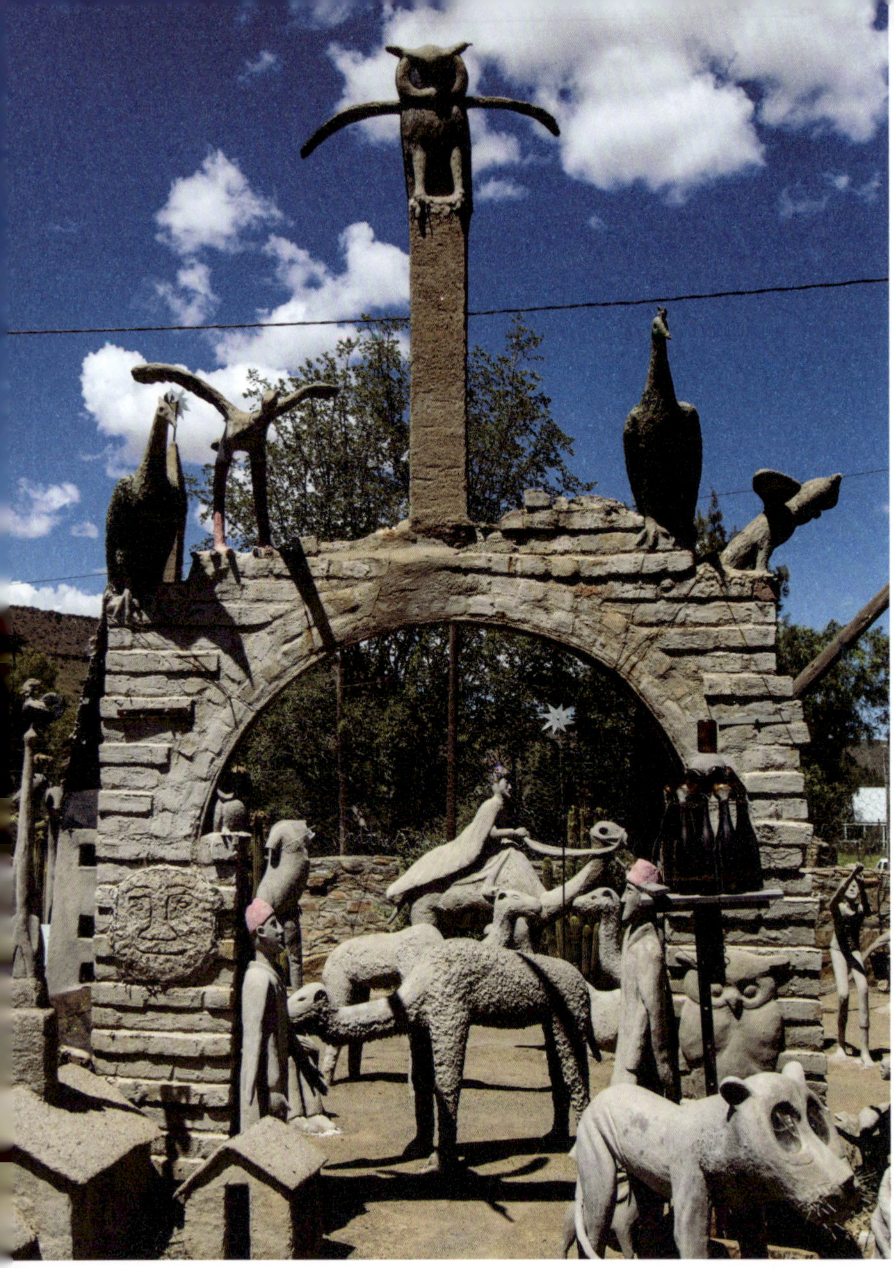

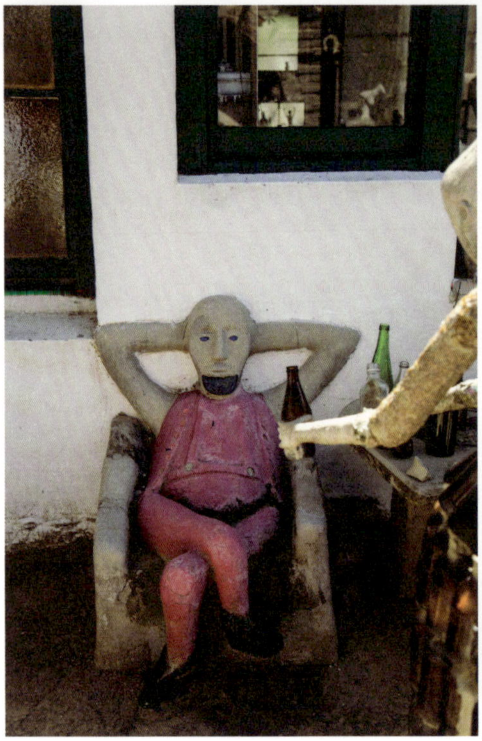

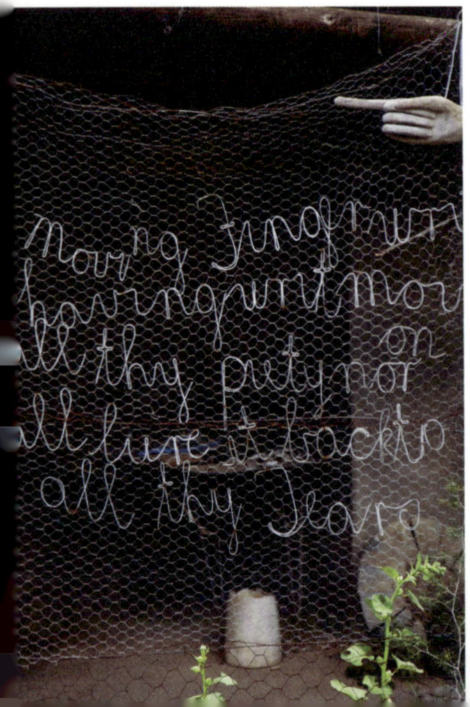
all thy piety nor
all thy Tears

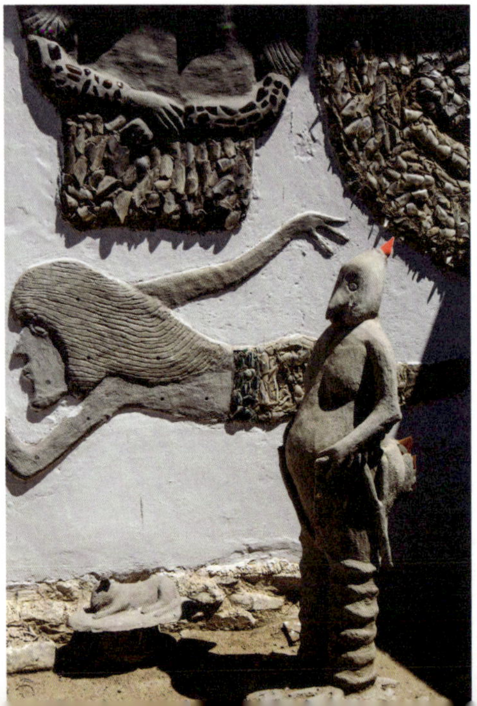

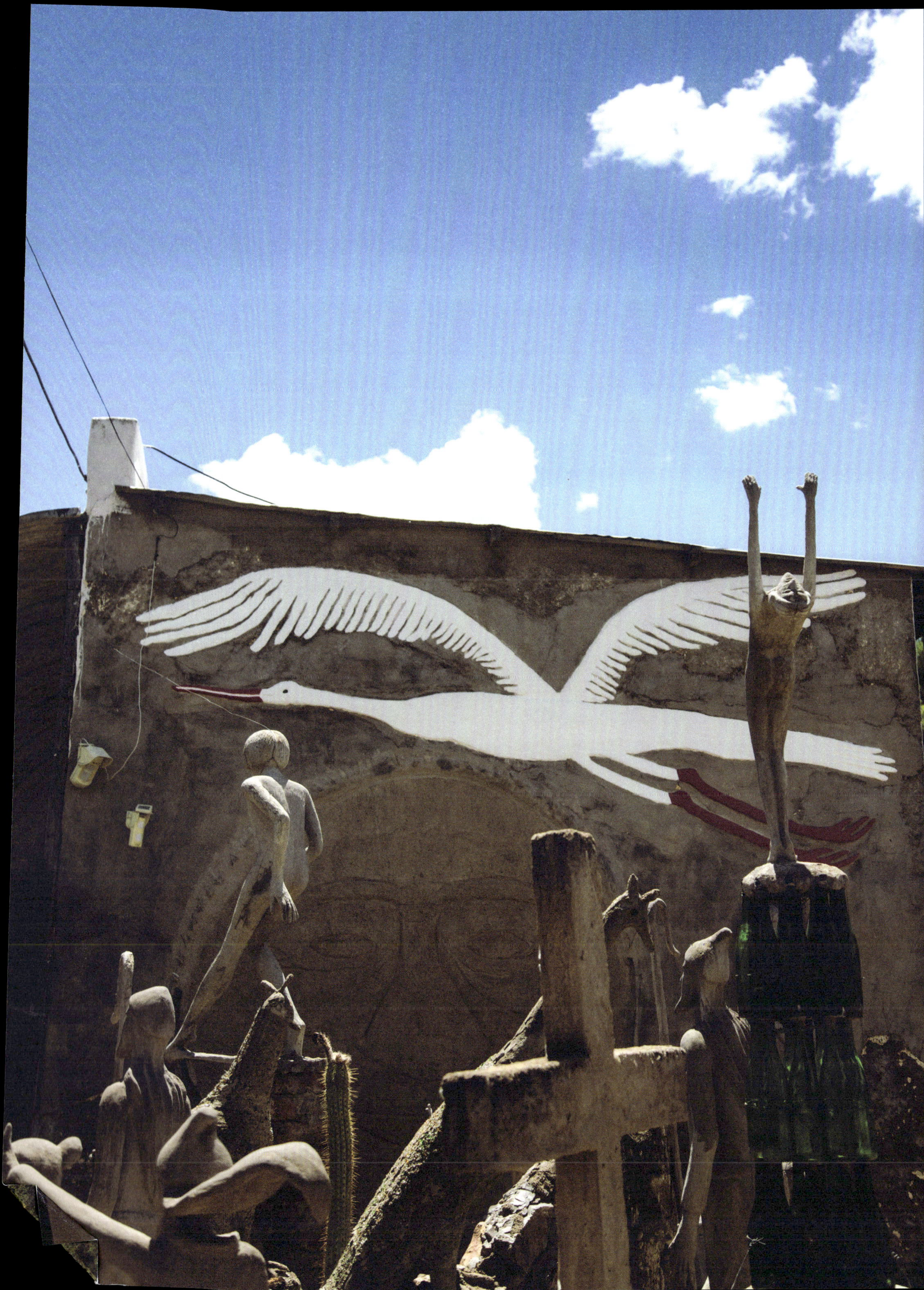

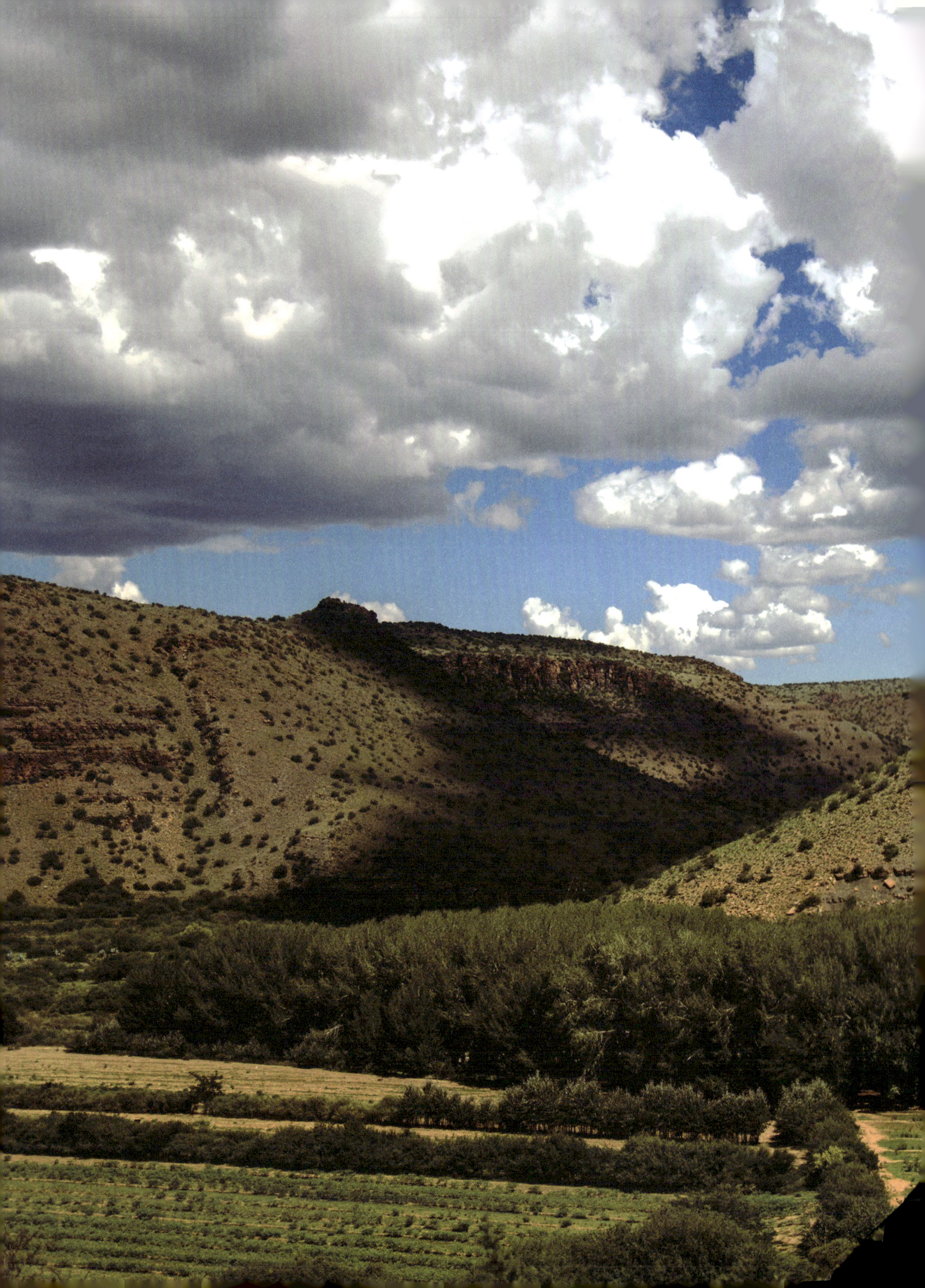

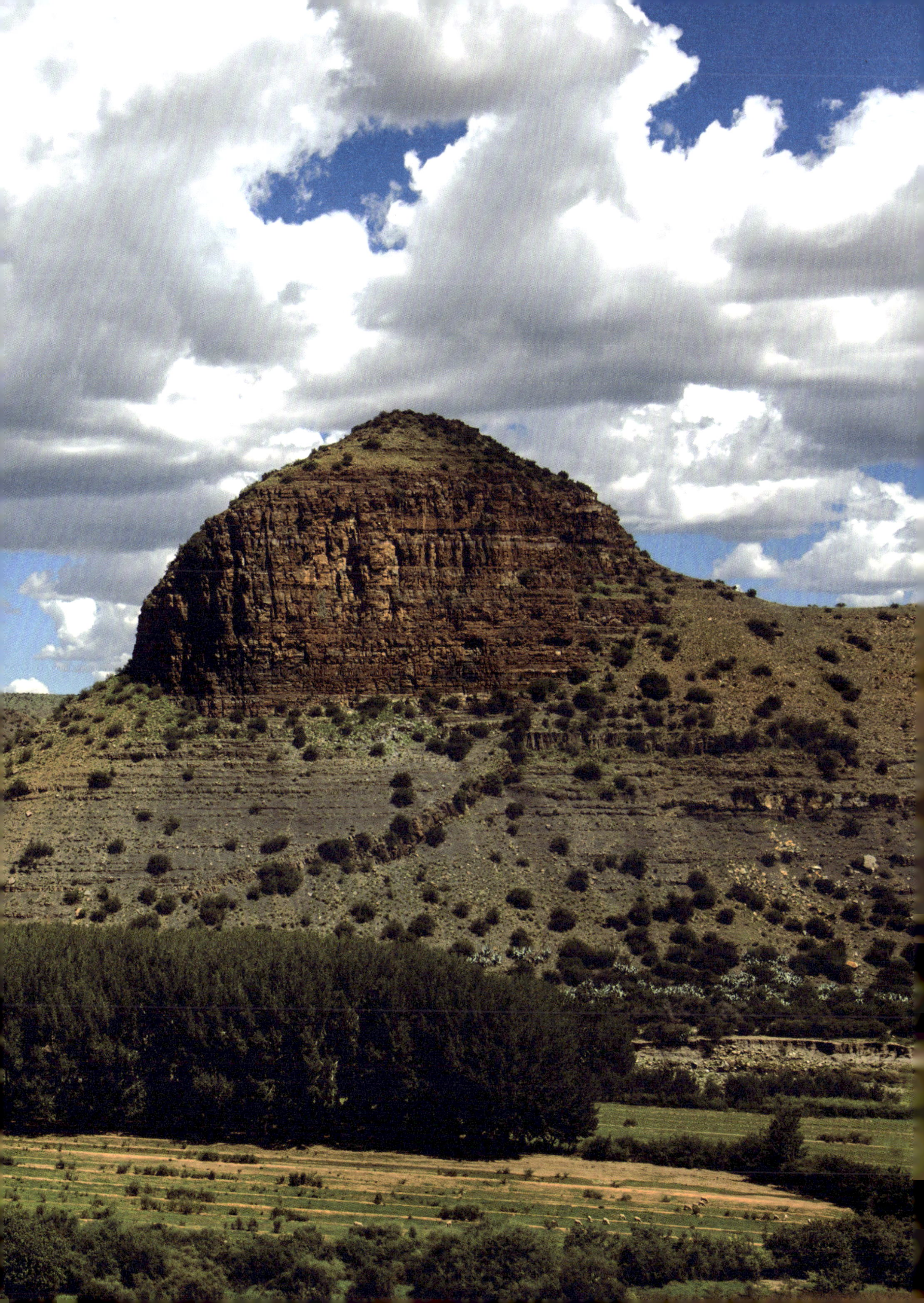

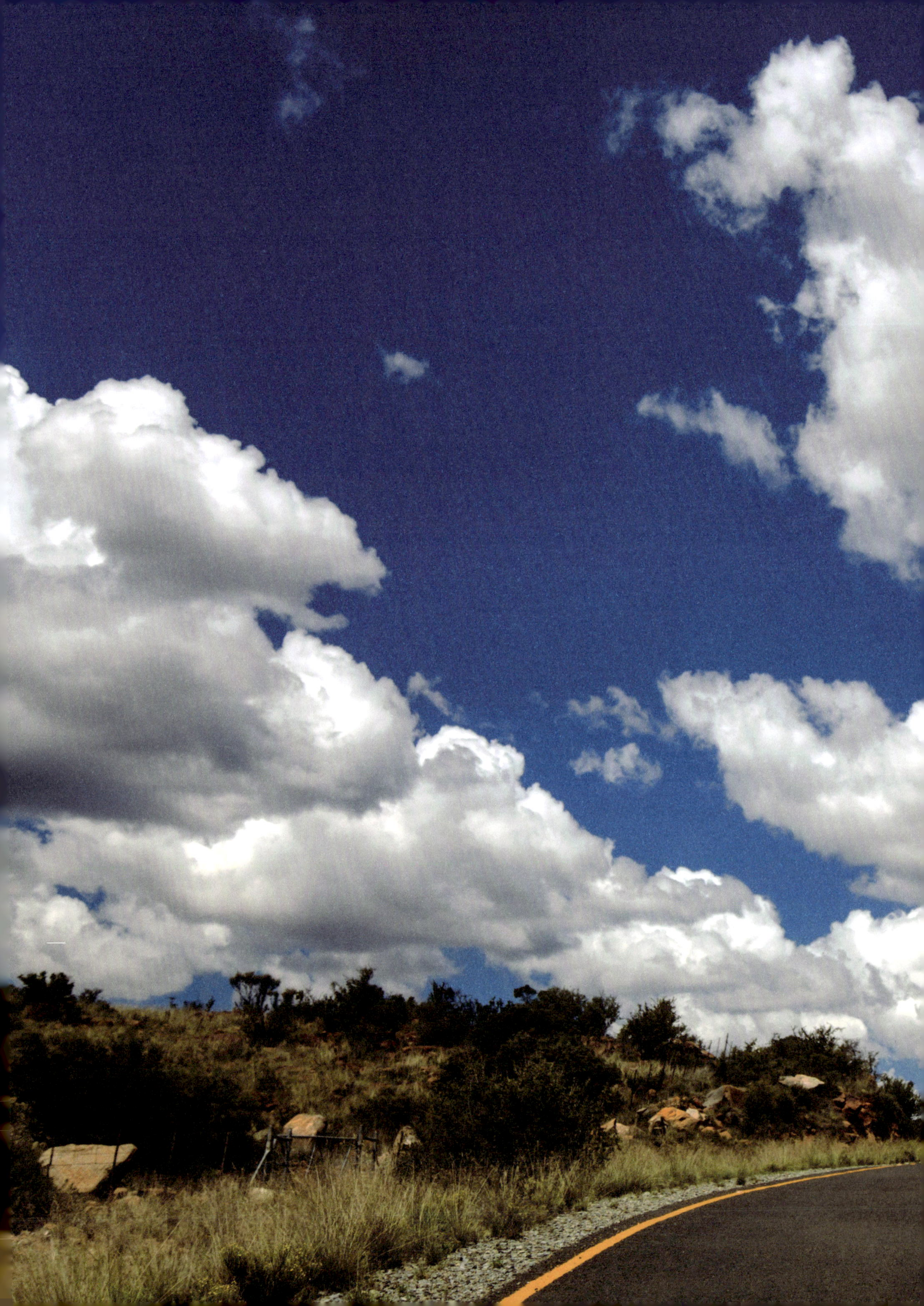

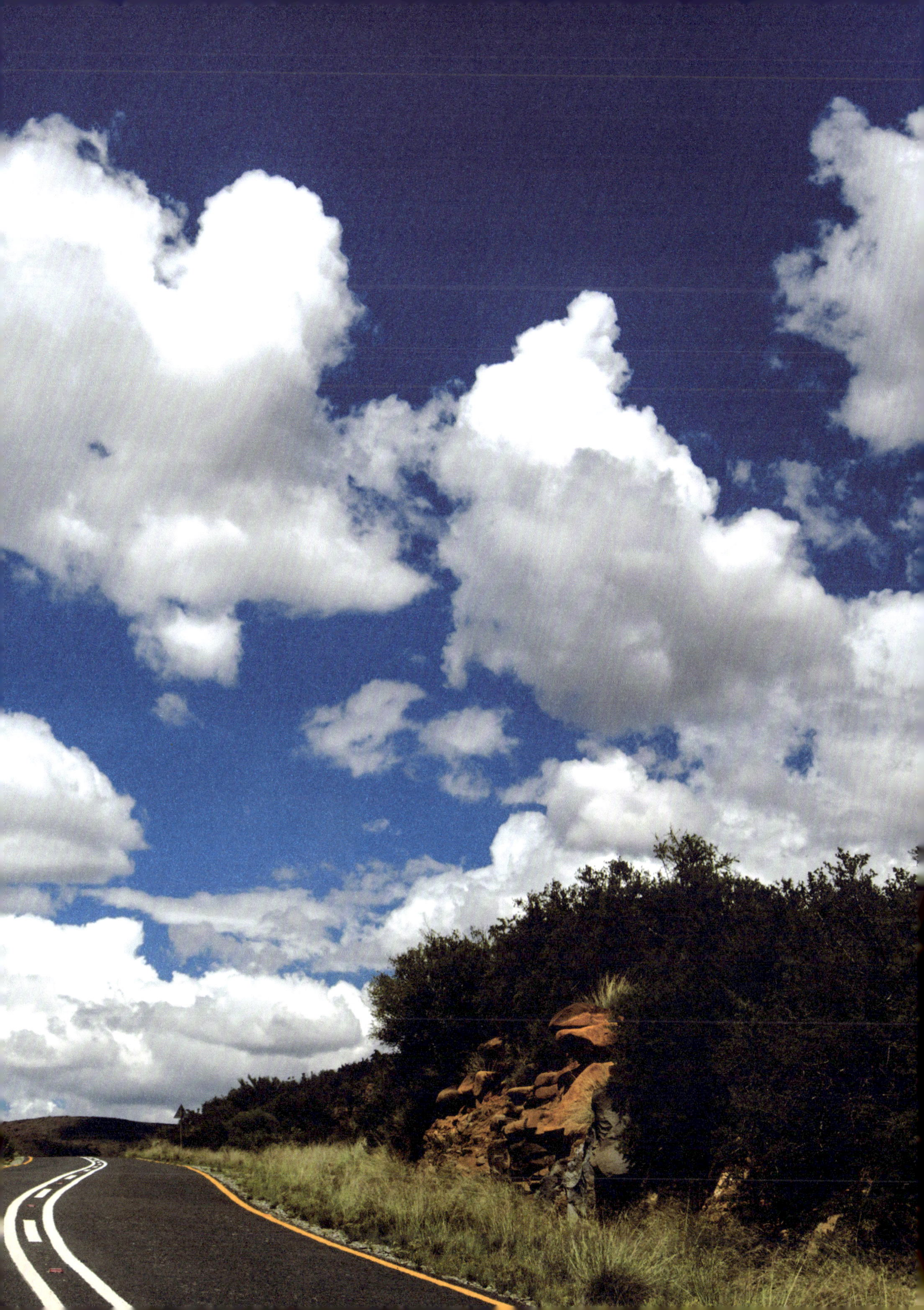

Transkei is a former homeland: officially an independent country reserved for the black population of South Africa, established by the apartheid regime as part of their malicious segregation politics. However, in the harsh political reality of that time, it was actually a country held hostage by that same regime. It is now part of South Africa, but it has managed to retain its own identity and unique atmosphere. The Xhosa make up a large part of the population.

The road to the coast meanders through the hilly landscape; green 'bumps' with brightly coloured houses on top. People walk along the road, beautifully dressed in their characteristic dress style: brightly coloured layers, woollen hats and blankets printed with geometric patterns wrapped around them like coats. The scenery and the people create such a beautifully harmonious visual narrative, that you have to be careful not to get too distracted from the narrow winding roads.

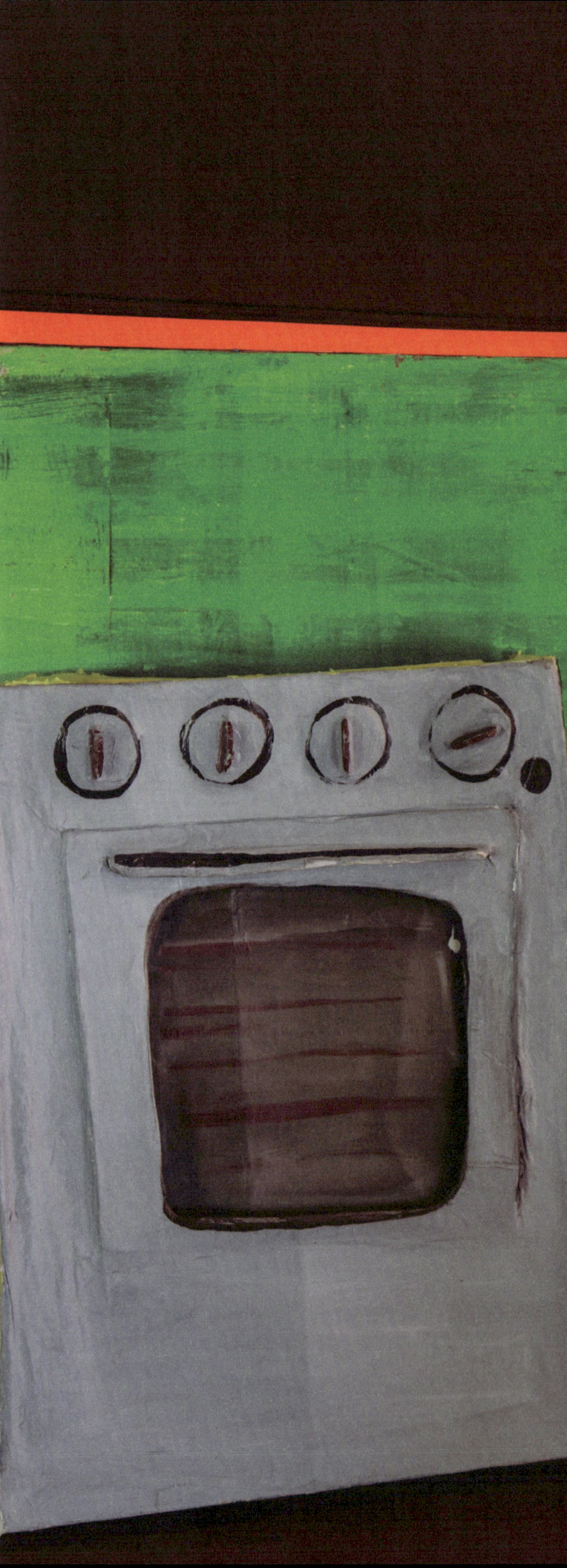

6

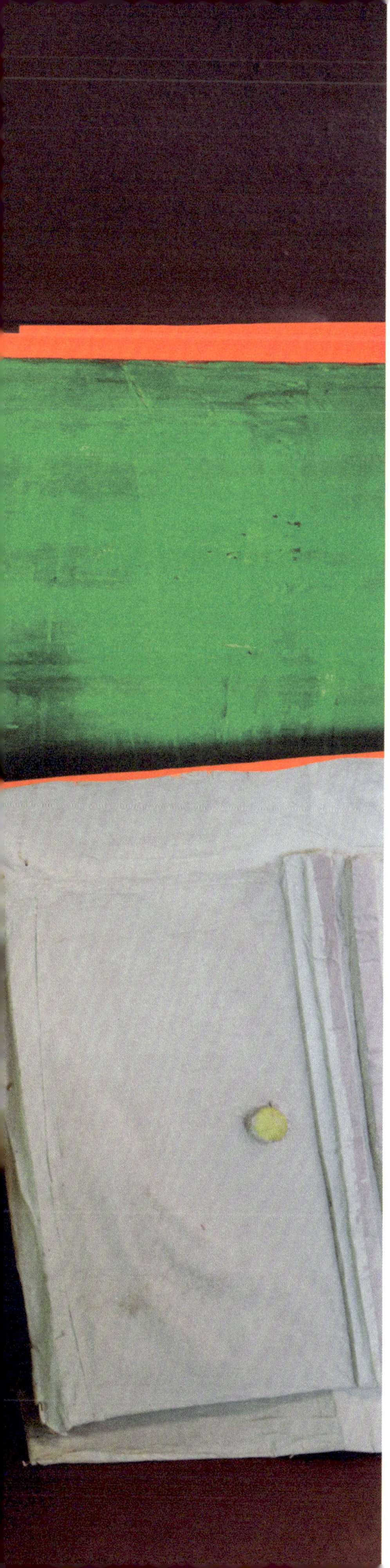

Transkei

157

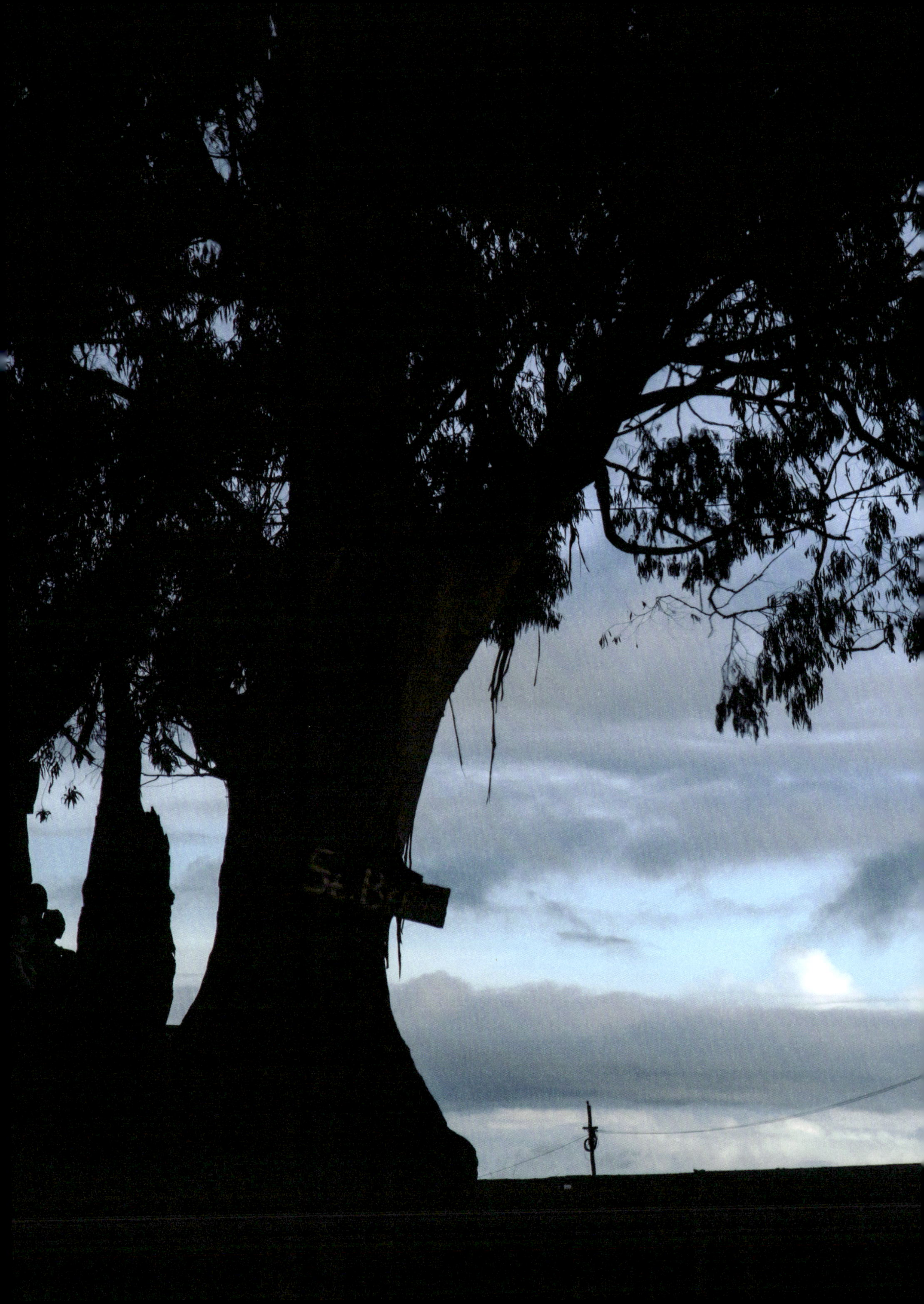

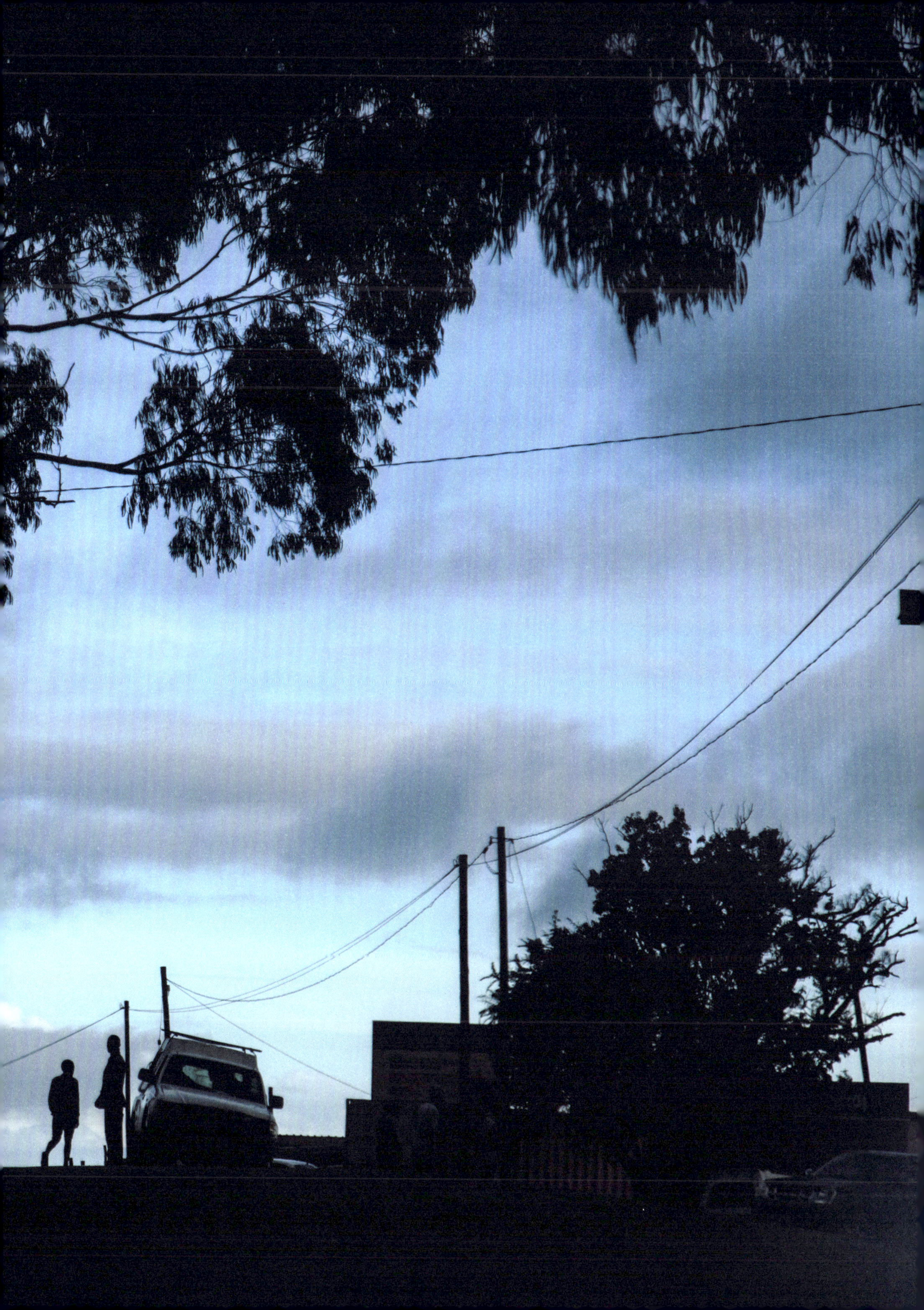

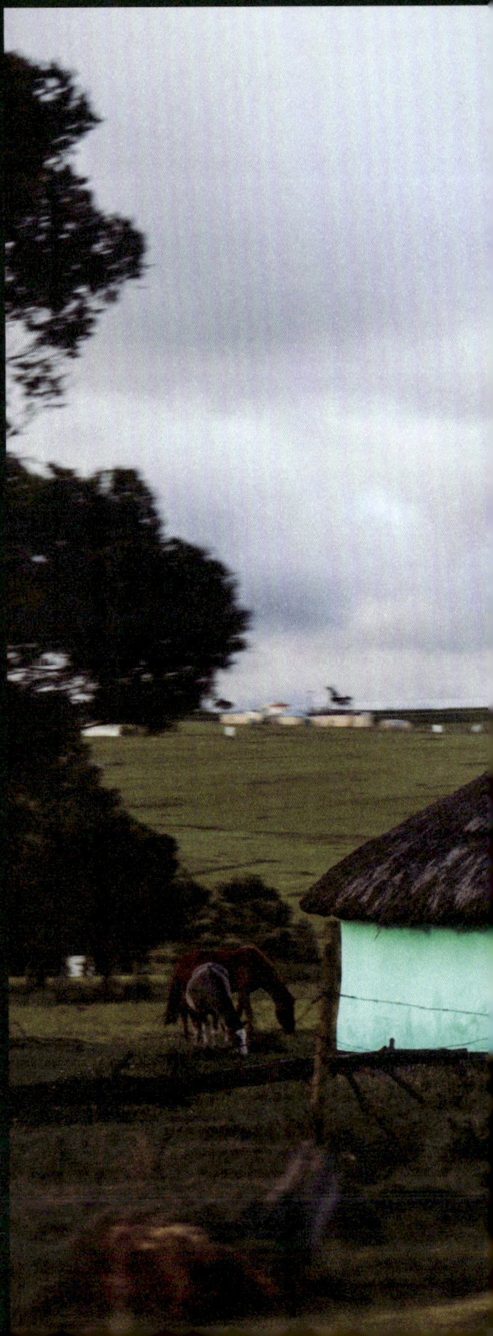

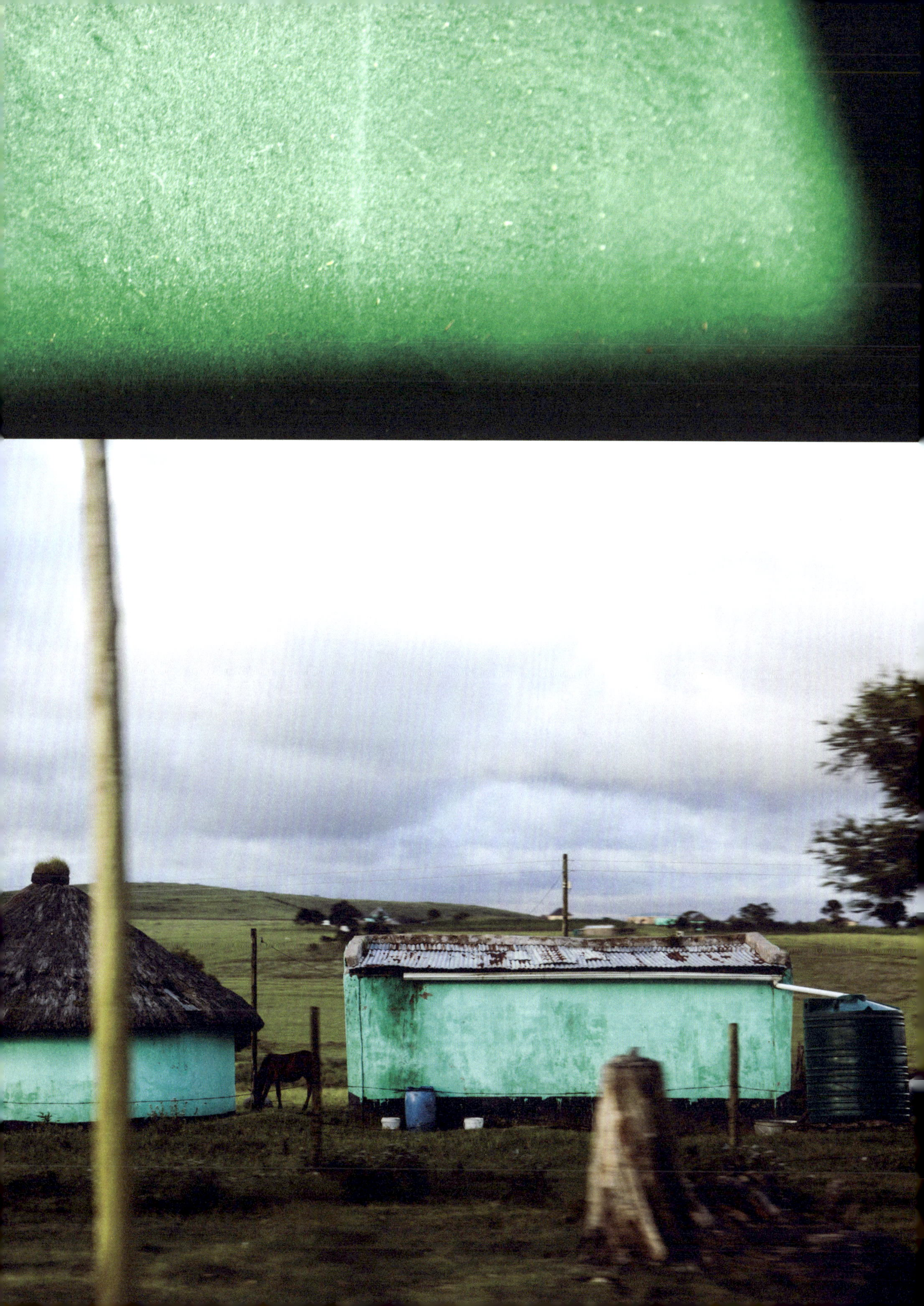

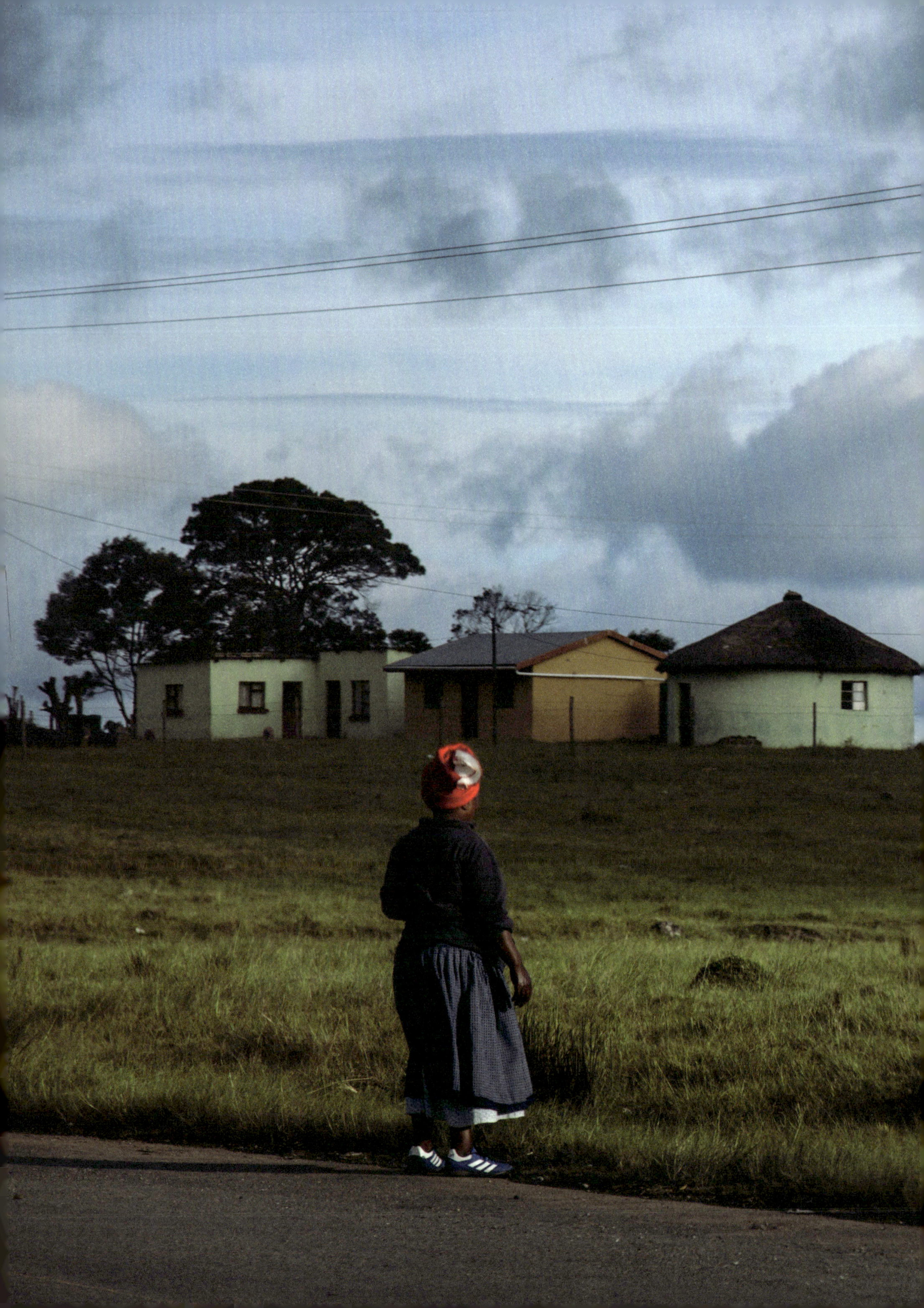

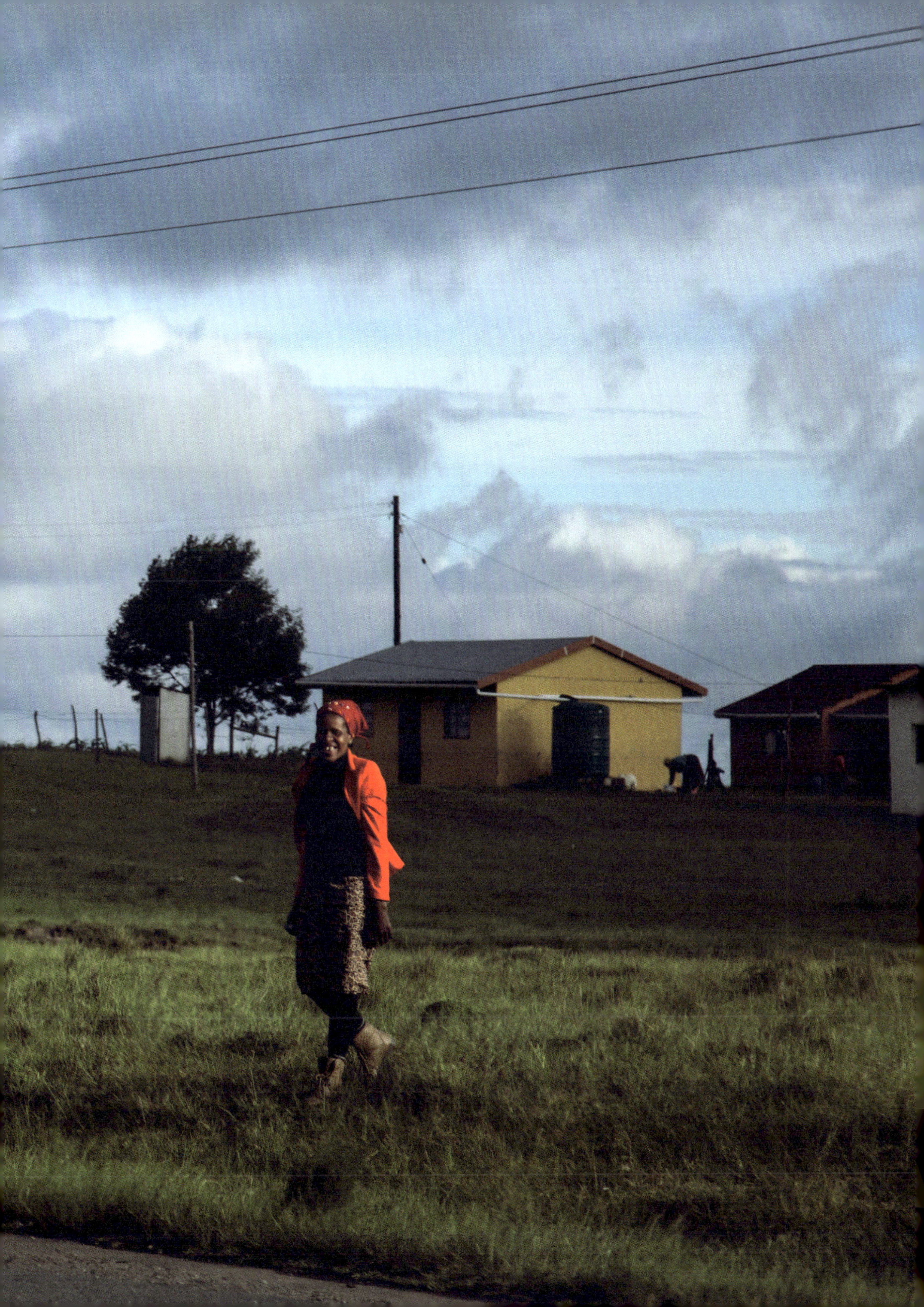

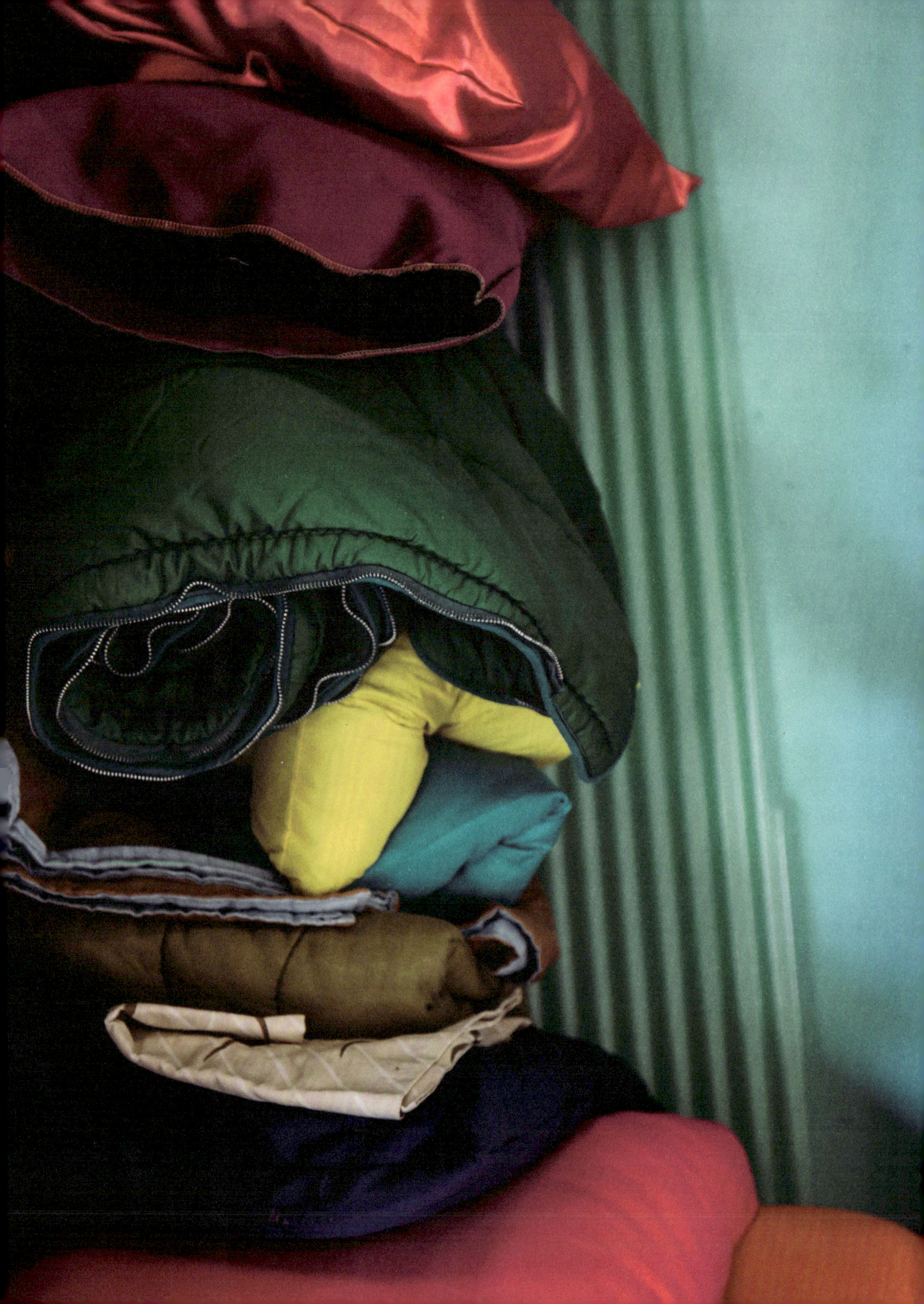

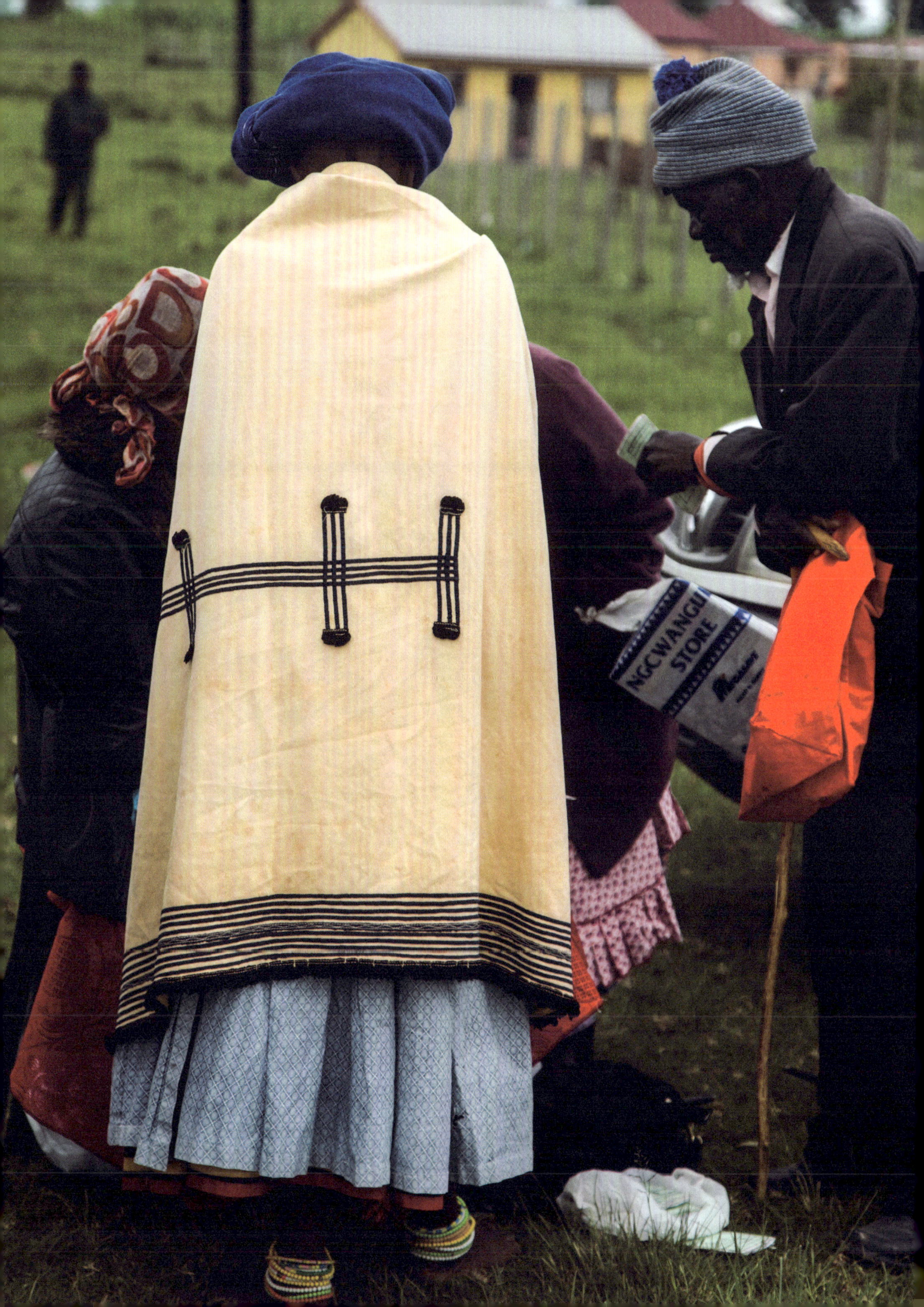
NGCWANGU
STORE

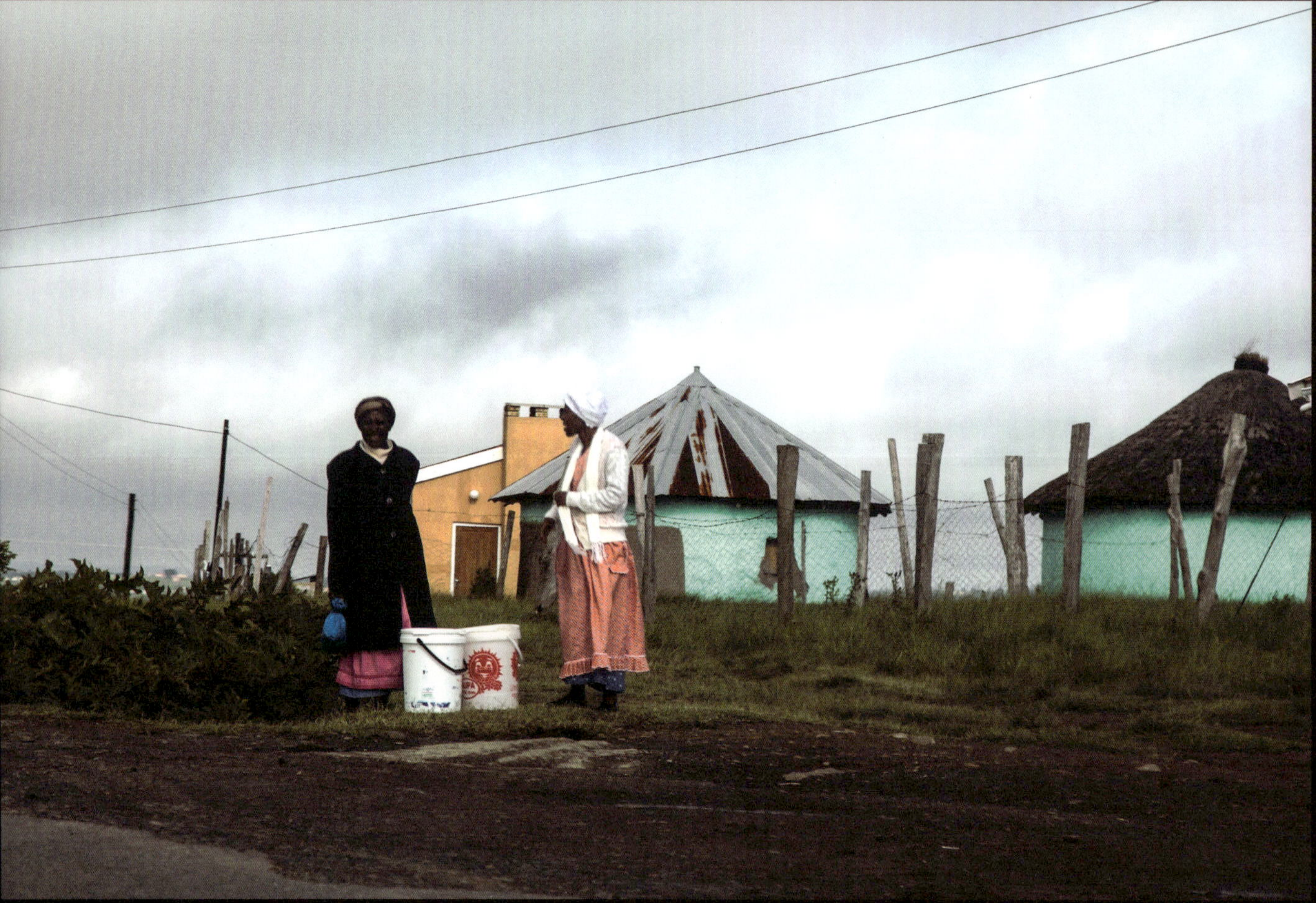
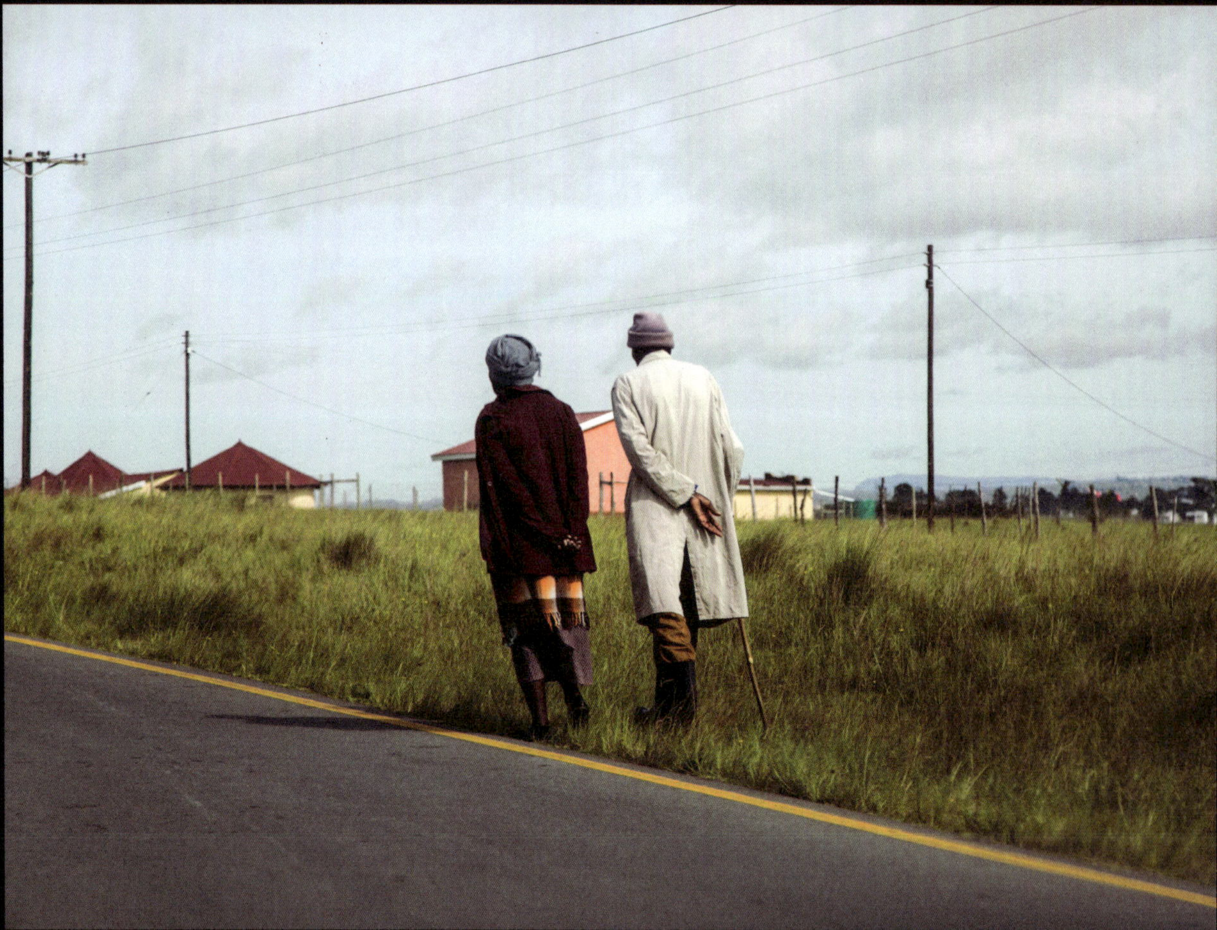

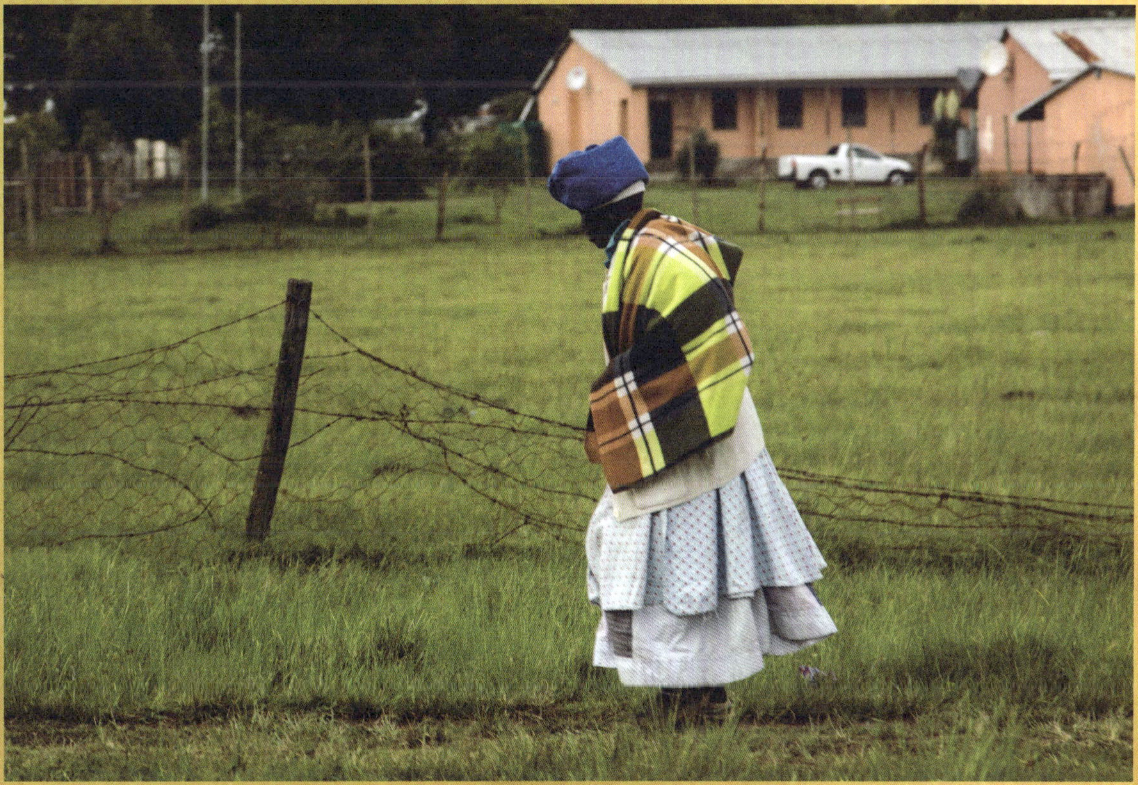

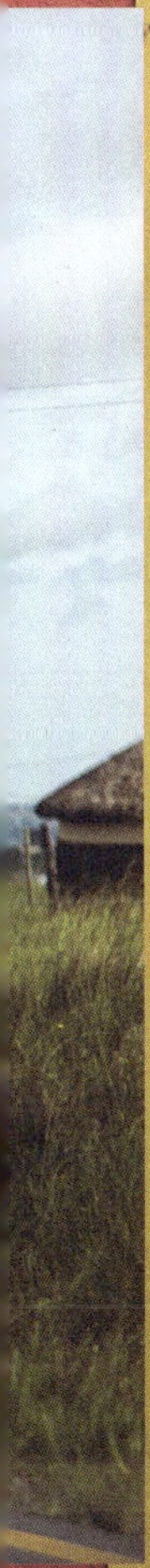

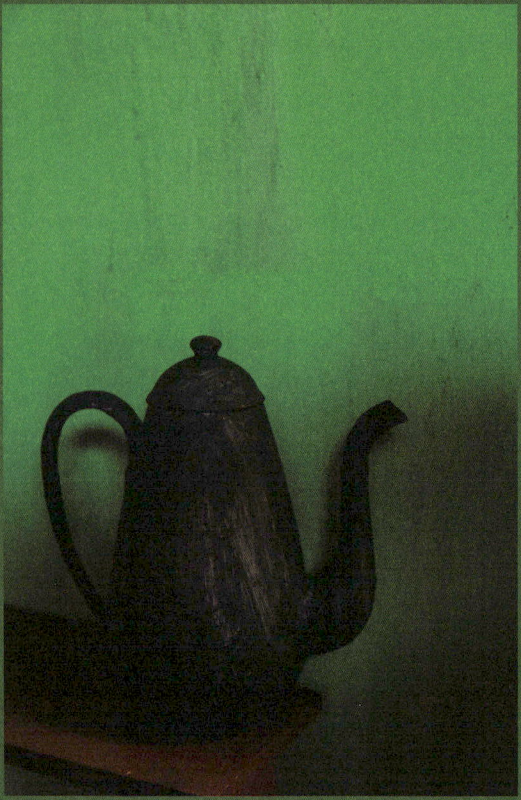

Walking along the edge

Coffee Bay got its name after a shipment of coffee beans was thrown overboard during a severe storm and washed ashore in the bay.

From our hotel we took a long walk to another seaside village to admire the famous 'Hole in the Wall'. The path along the coast is narrow and the cliffs are steep. The sea below is wild, and the wind fierce. The surrounding hills are green and juicy. It is a poetic setting, with a rough edge. Booking a guide to get you on the right track is wise, and it is also quite enjoyable to hear their curious stories.

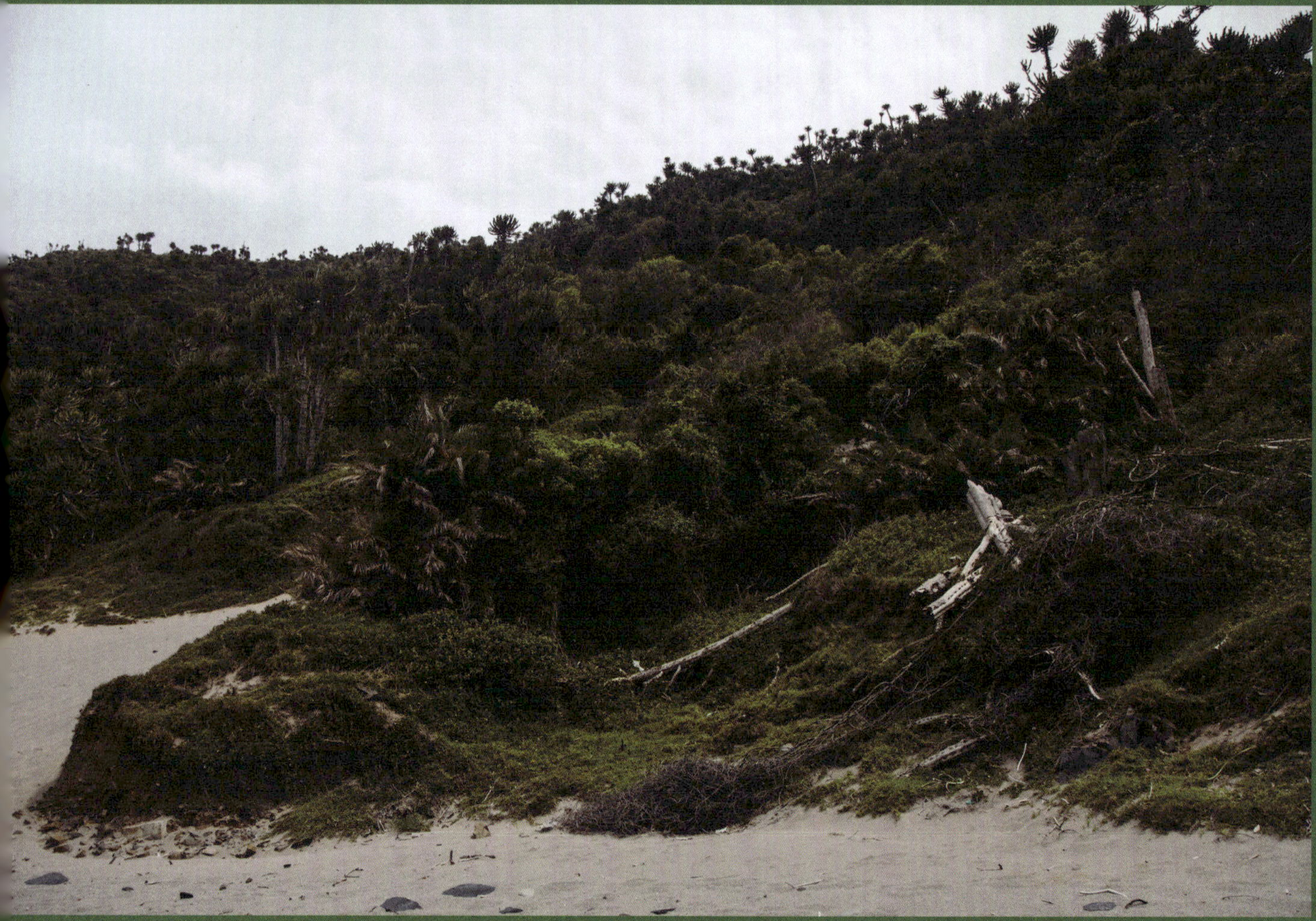

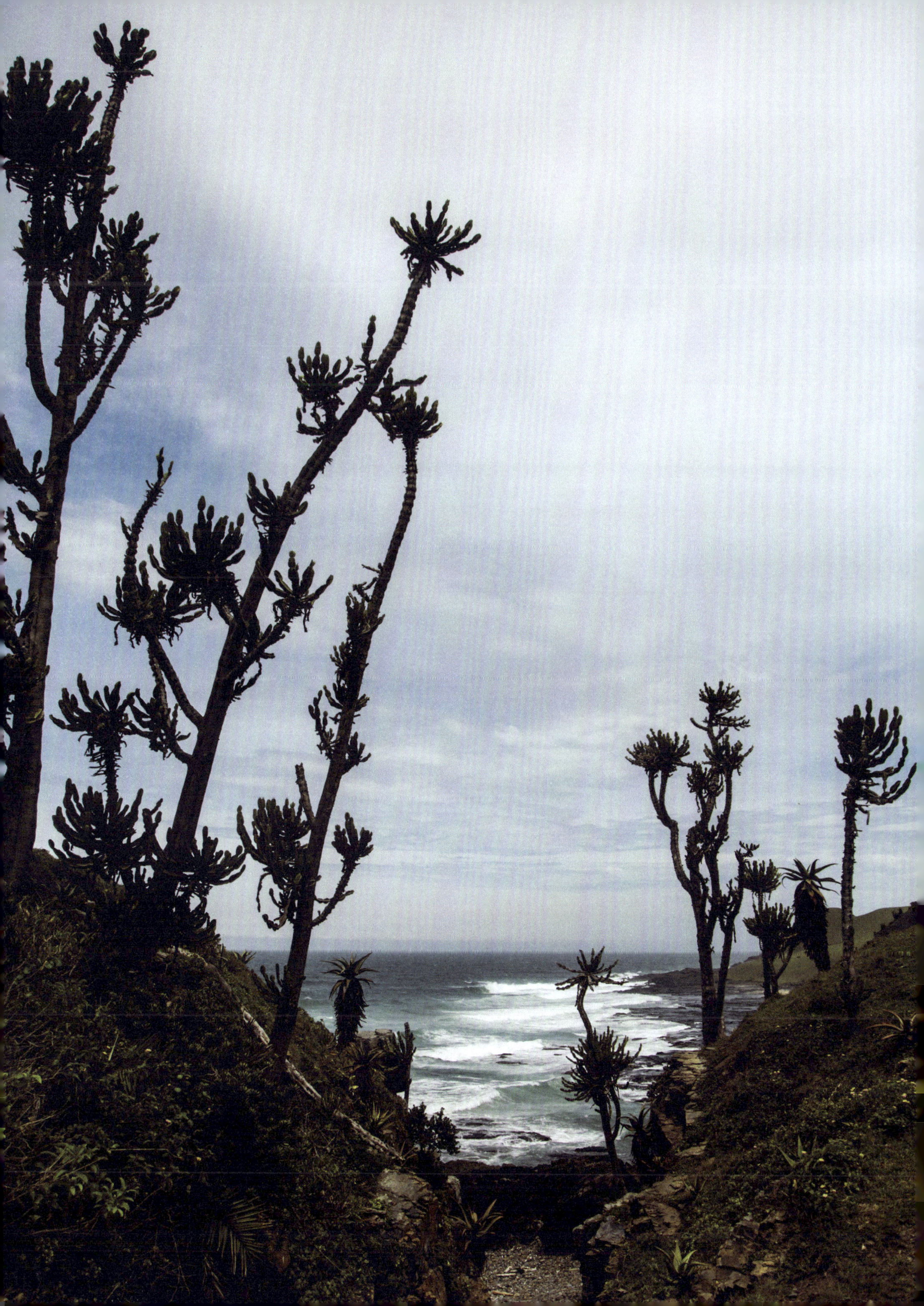

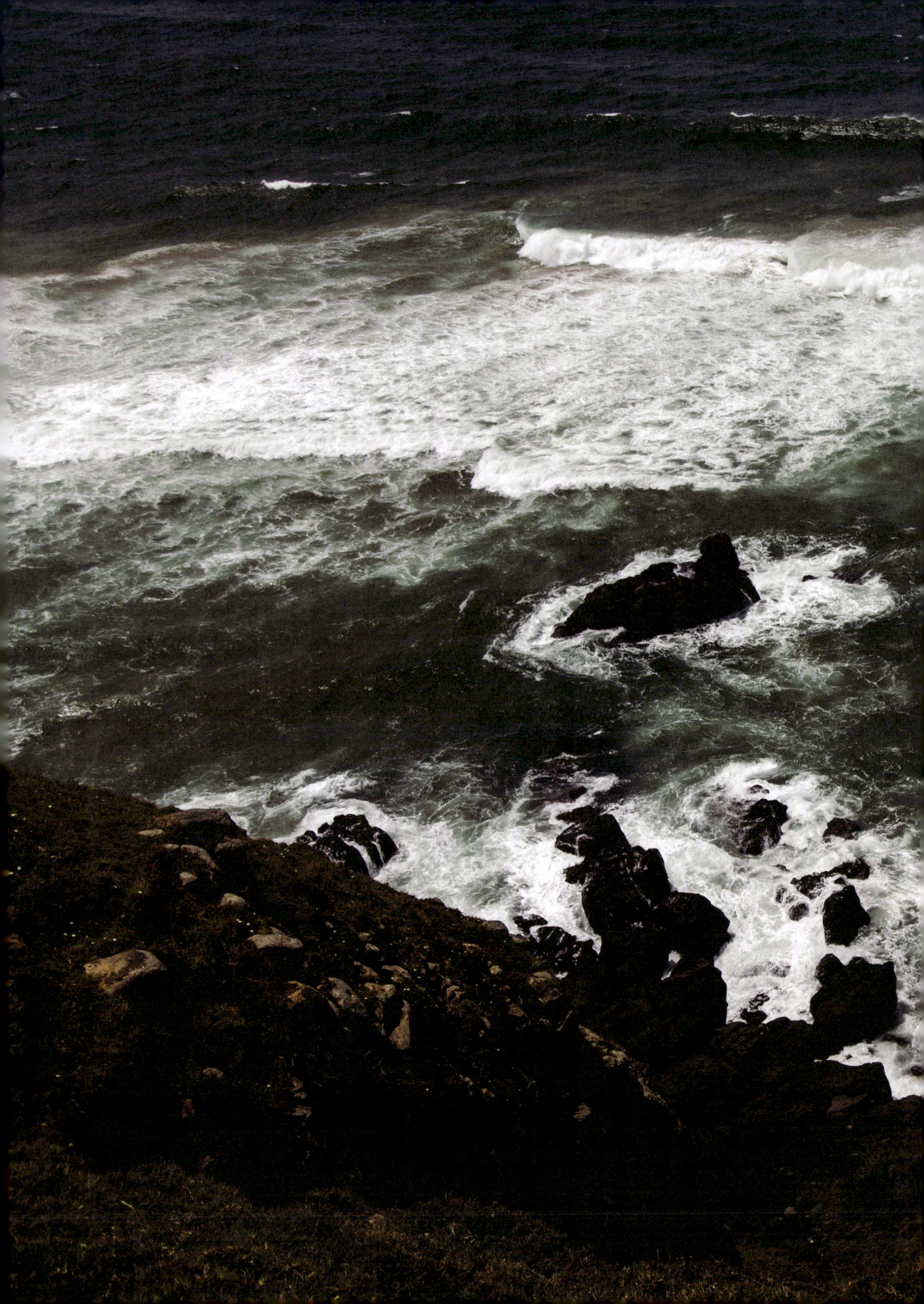

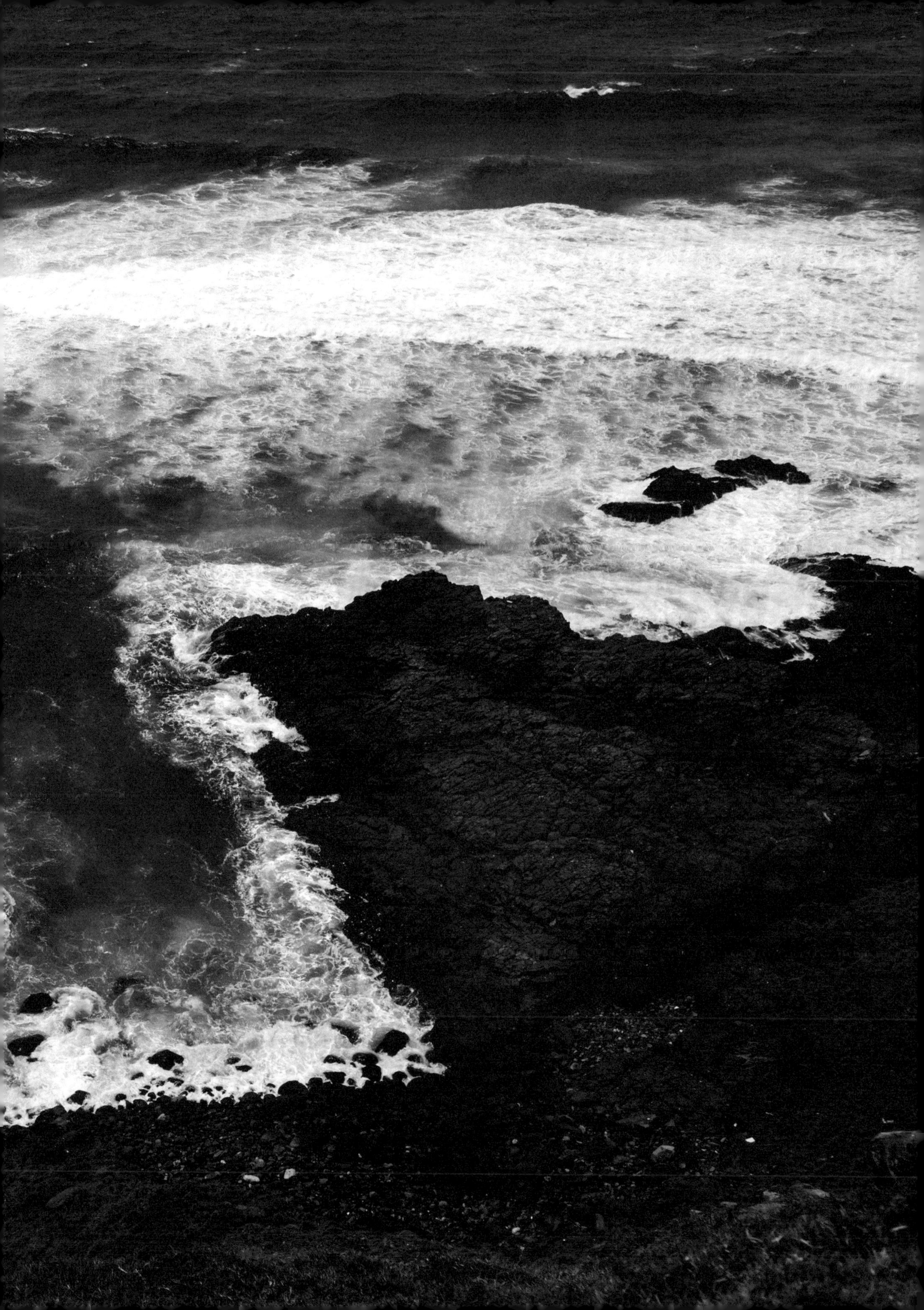

Durban is the third biggest city in the country and lies in the KwaZulu-Natal region. It is a city by the sea, but due to its geographical location it has a very different vibe from Cape Town.

With its subtropical climate, the ocean is warmer and friendlier in Durban, which affected how the city was built. Wide boulevards run along the city beach. Tall palm trees and water playgrounds complete it. For a long time, Durban has been the perfect beach holiday destination for locals and foreigners alike.

The city centre is one big market. Barbers have built simple tent-like constructions to give customers a shave or a haircut on the street. Opposite the chaos of the main bus station, you will find a long line of stalls in all shapes and sizes where special Zulu relics and attributes are sold. On the busy street a little further down, Indian entrepreneurs have their traditional textile and modern electronics shops.

In Durban, all roads lead to the sea. So any random exploration on foot will take you to the beach in the end.

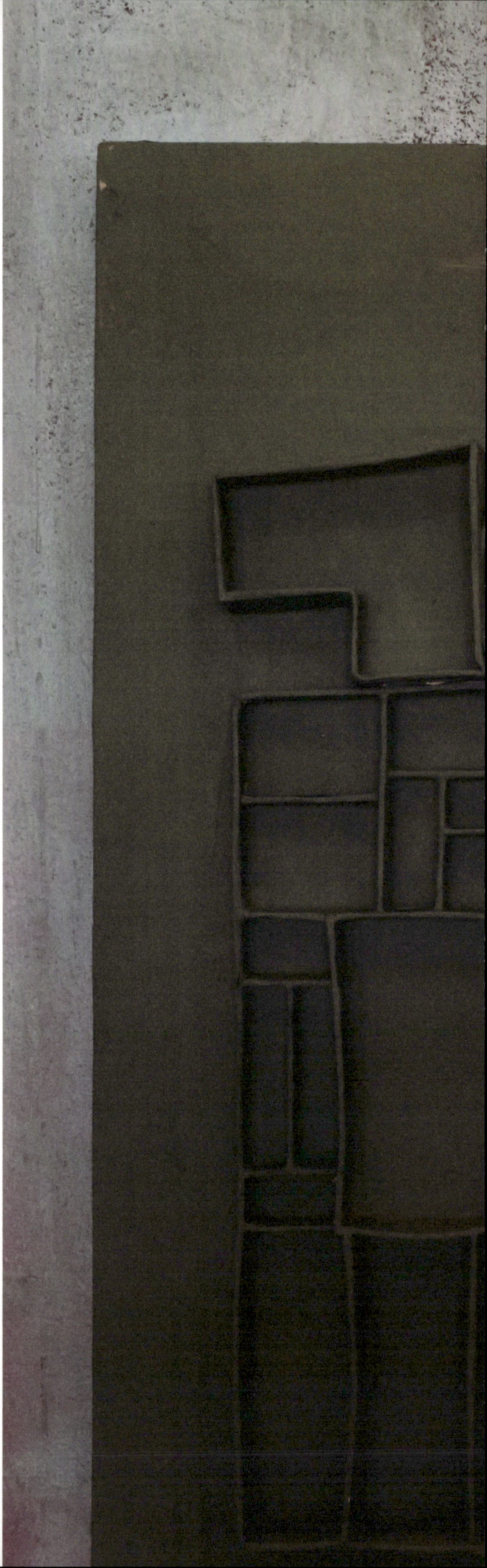

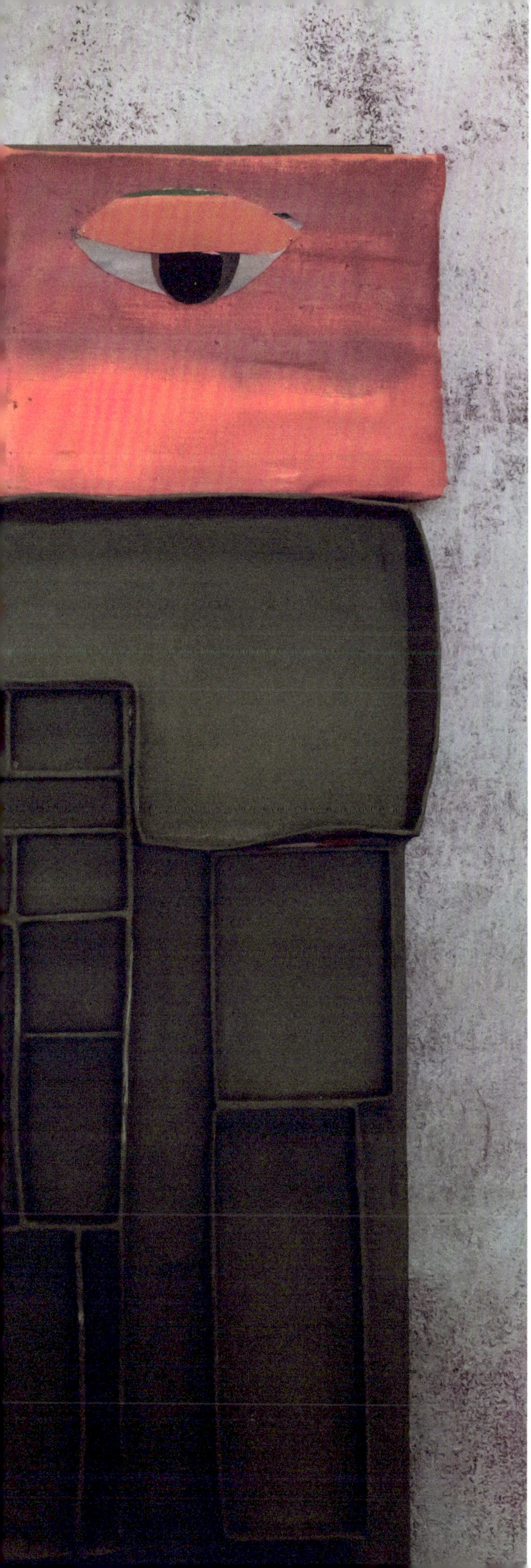

7

Durban

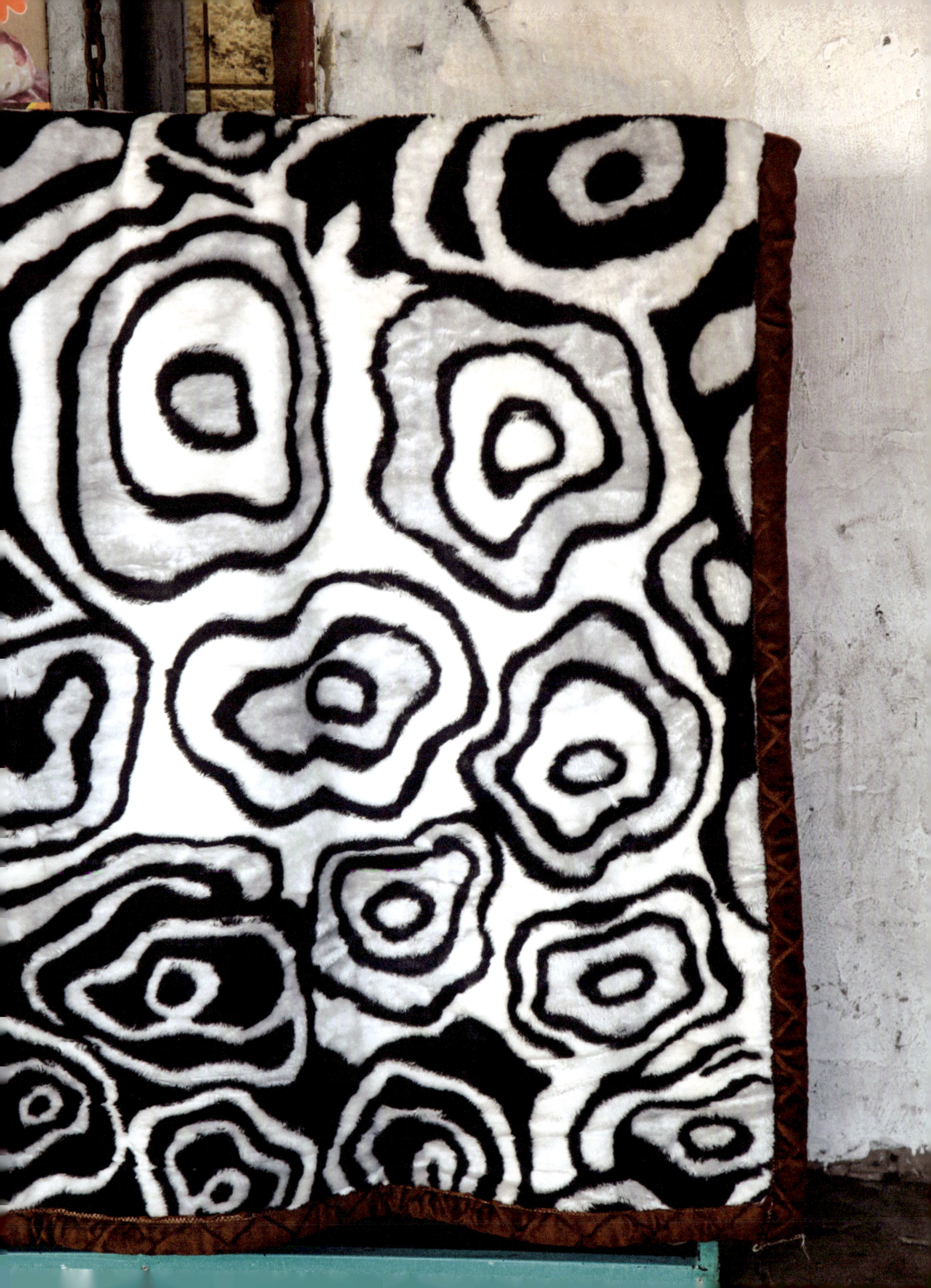

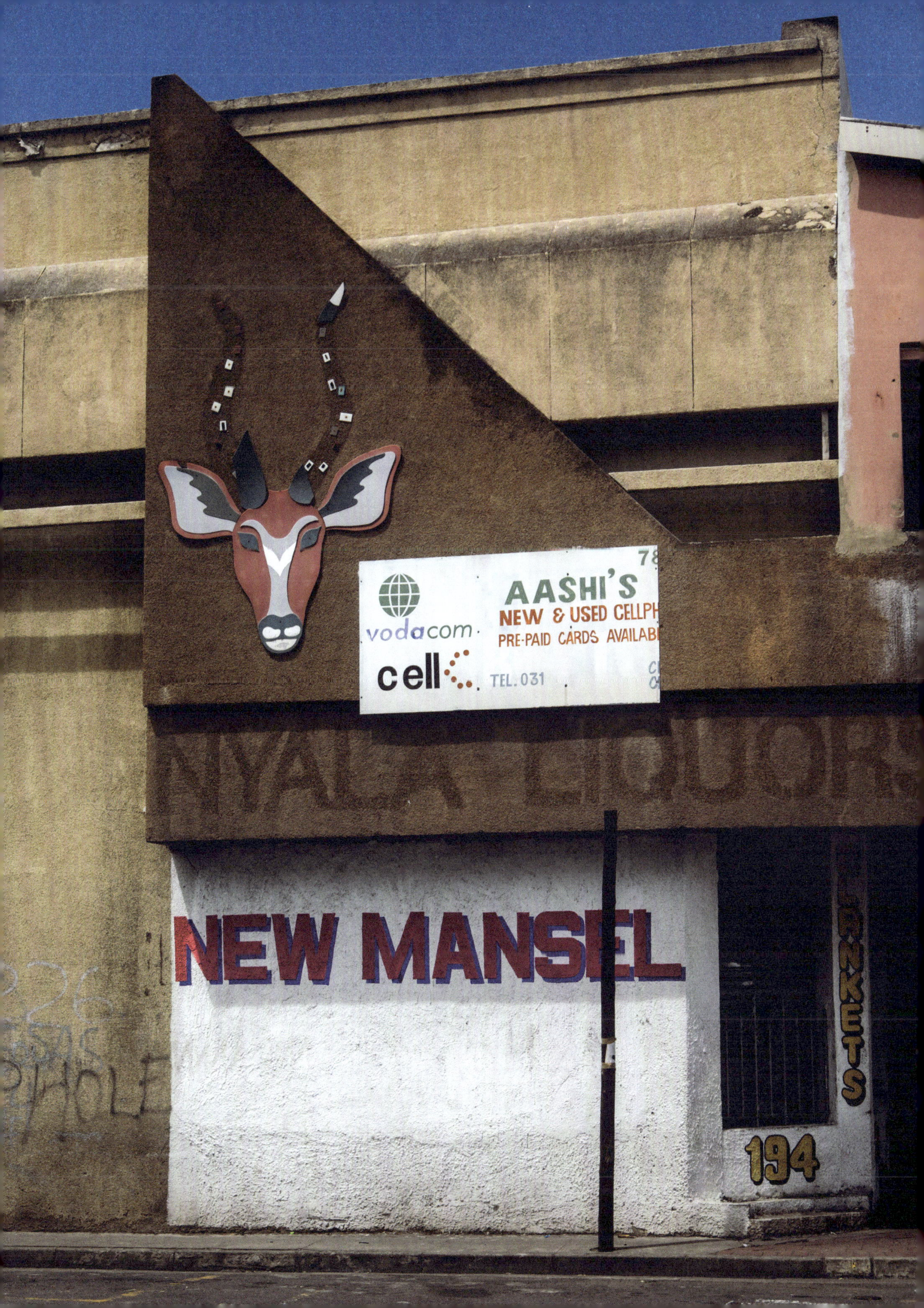

78
AASHI'S
NEW & USED CELLPH
PRE-PAID CARDS AVAILAB
vodacom
cell C
TEL. 031
NYALA LIQUORS
NEW MANSEL
RNKETS
194

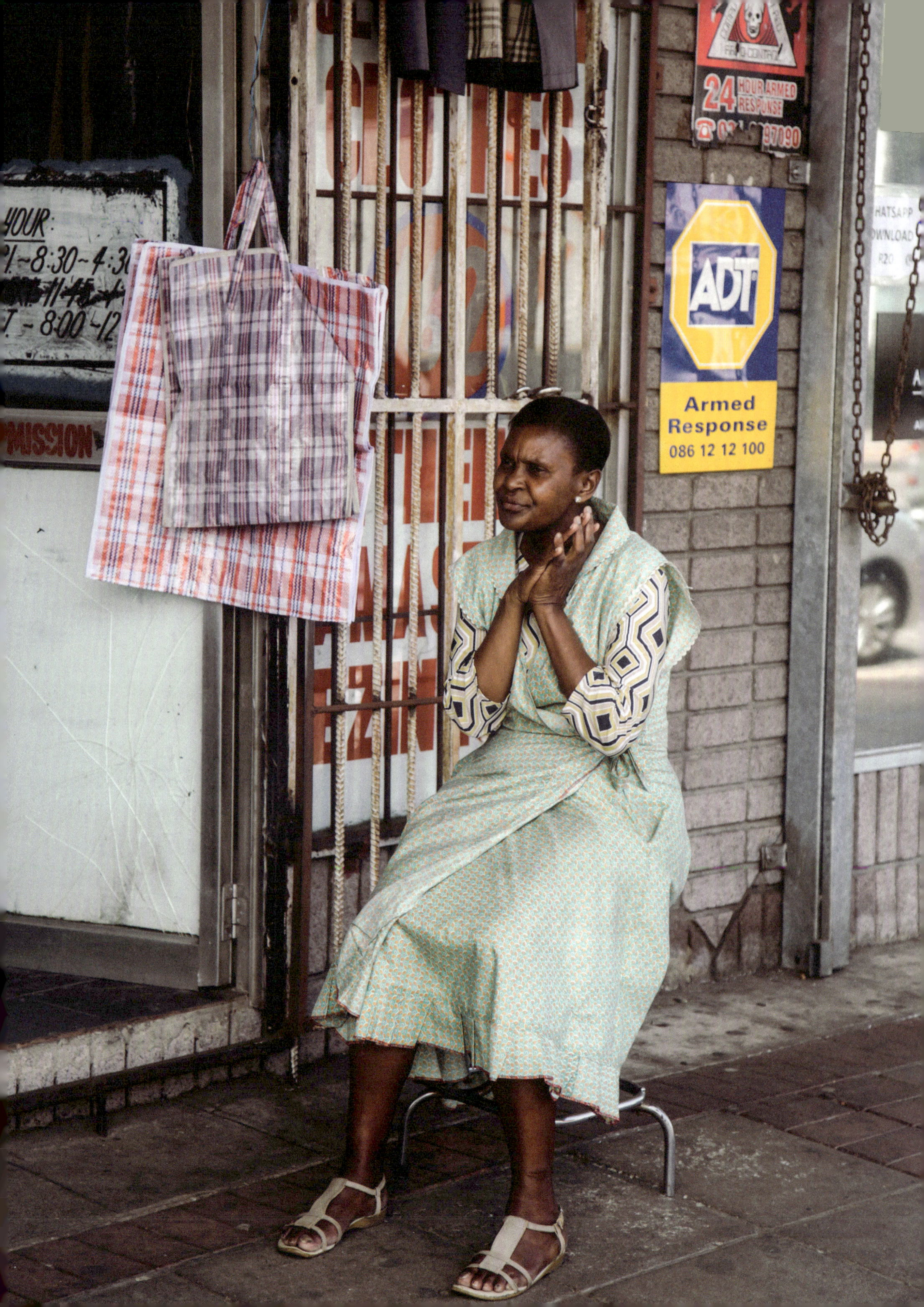

24 HOUR ARMED RESPONSE
ADT
Armed Response
086 12 12 100

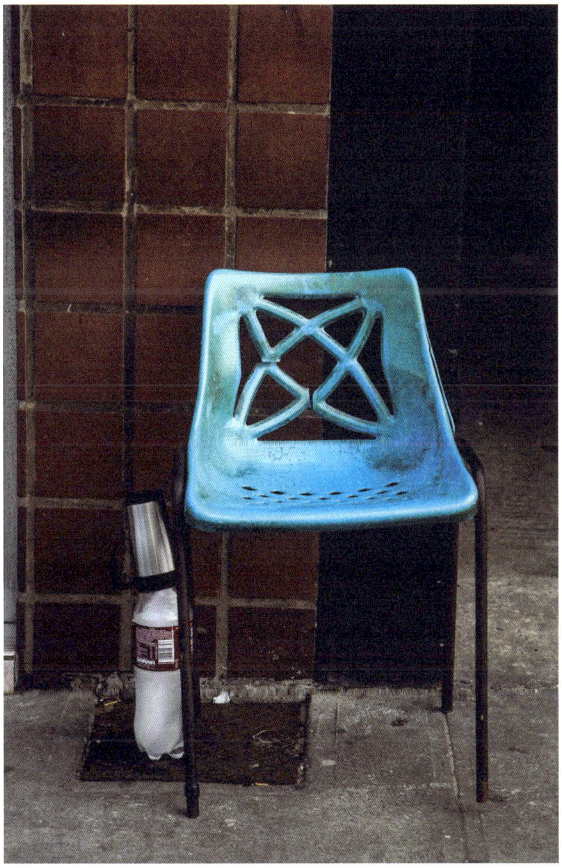

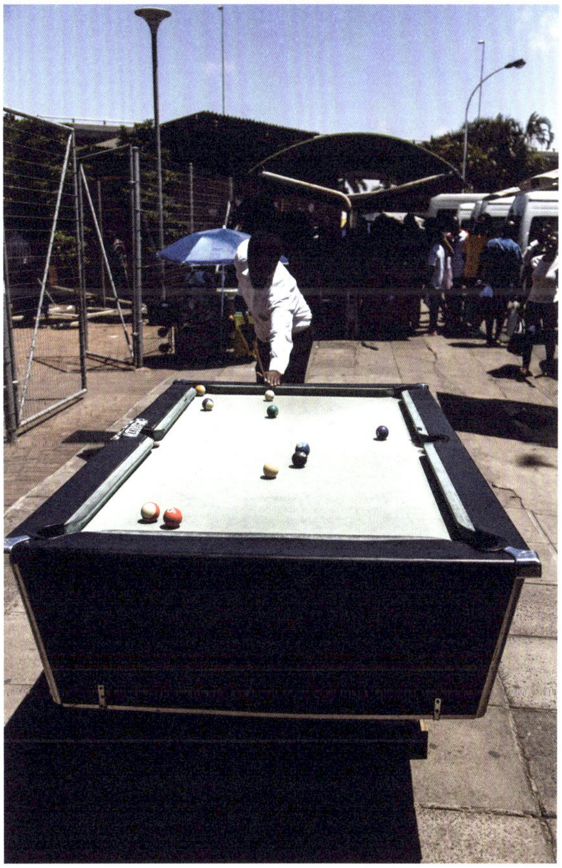

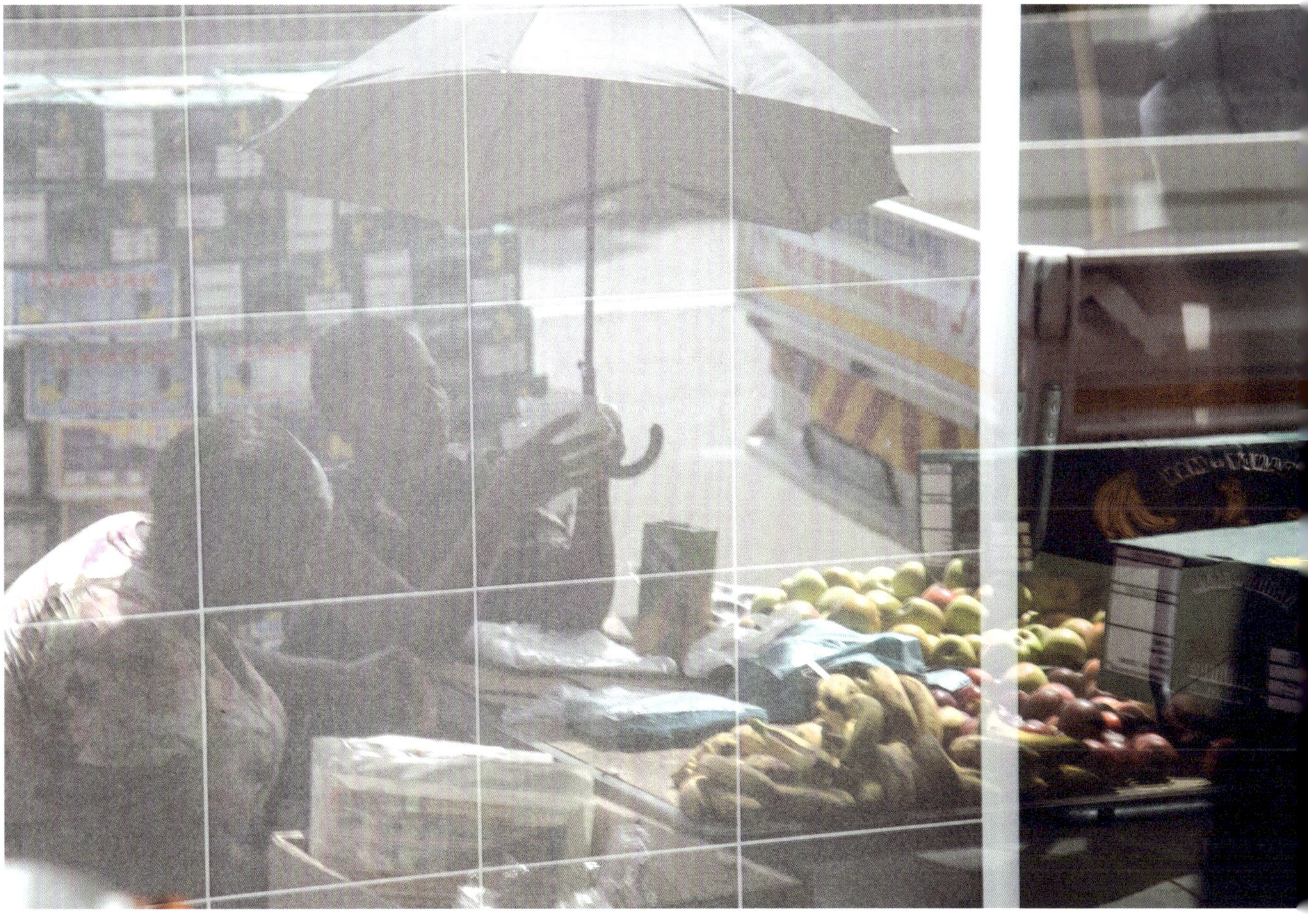

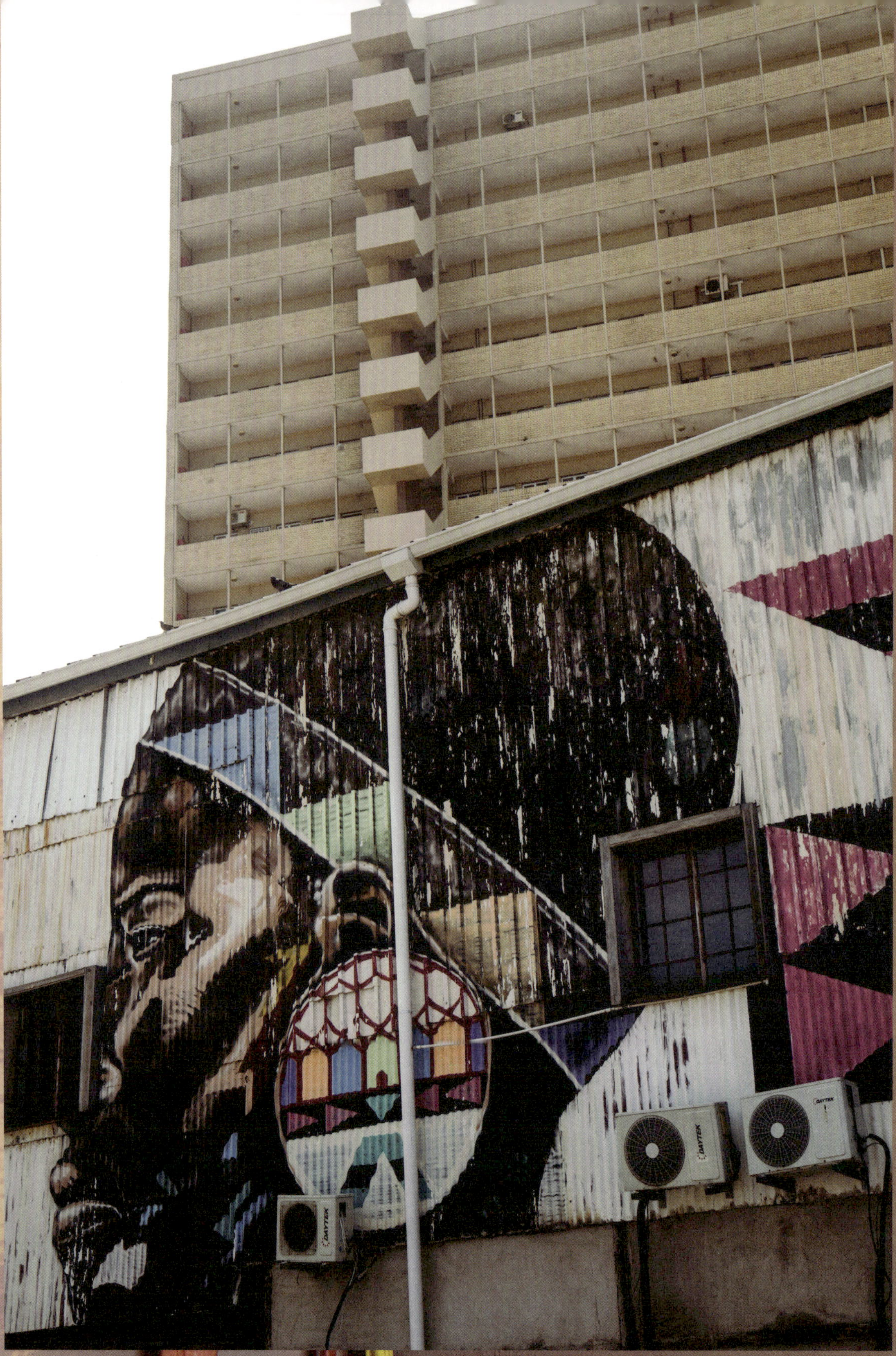
DAYTEK
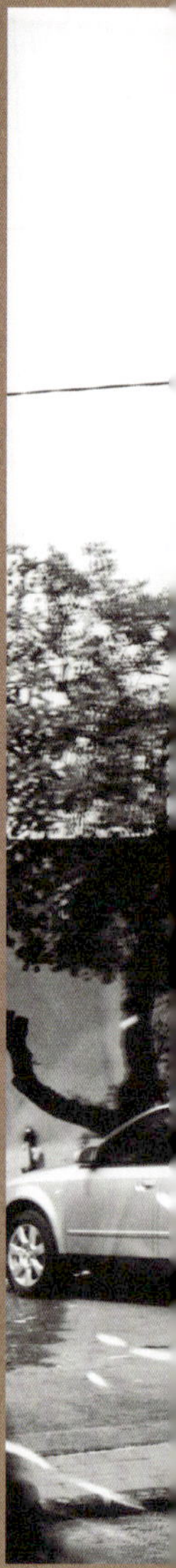

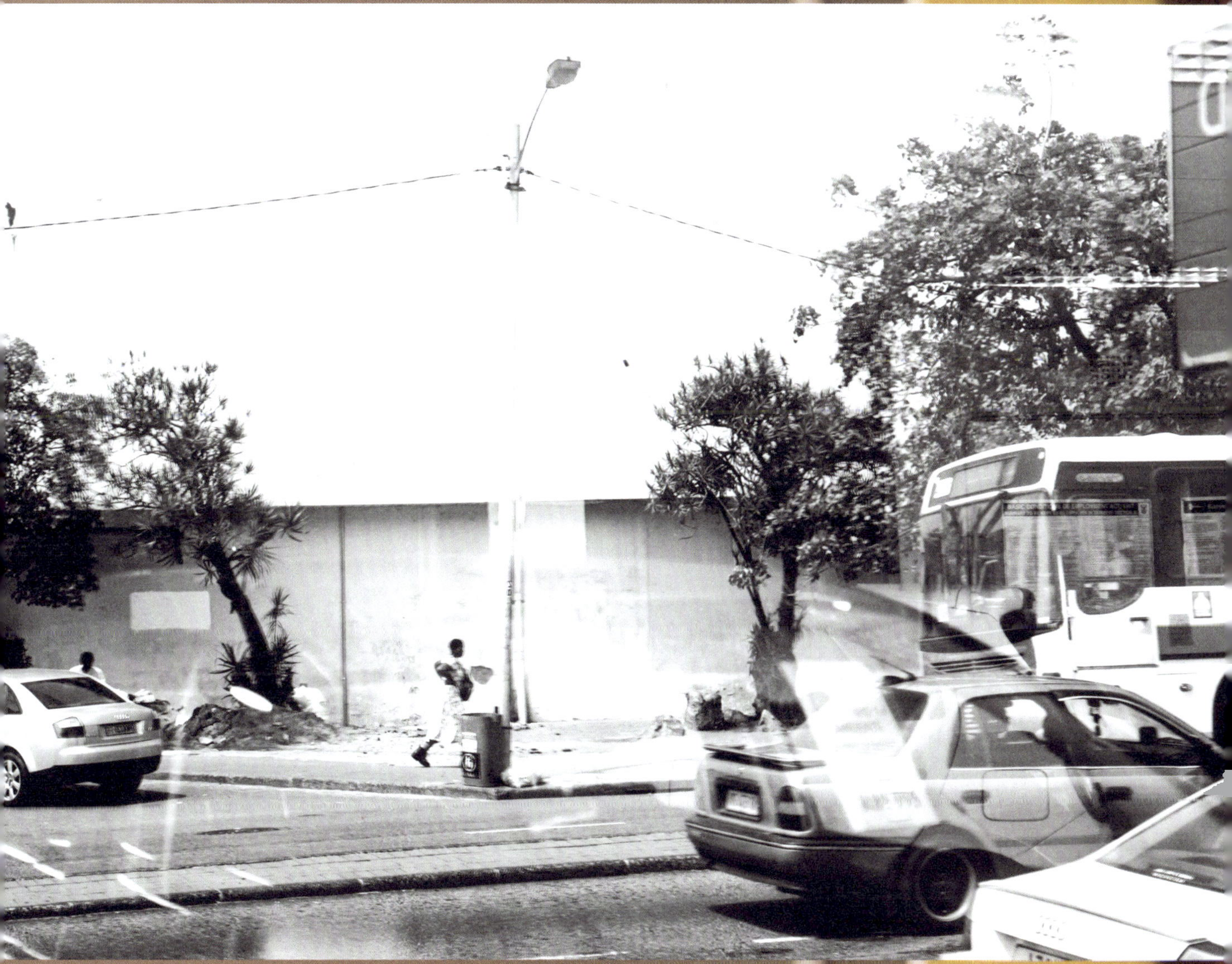

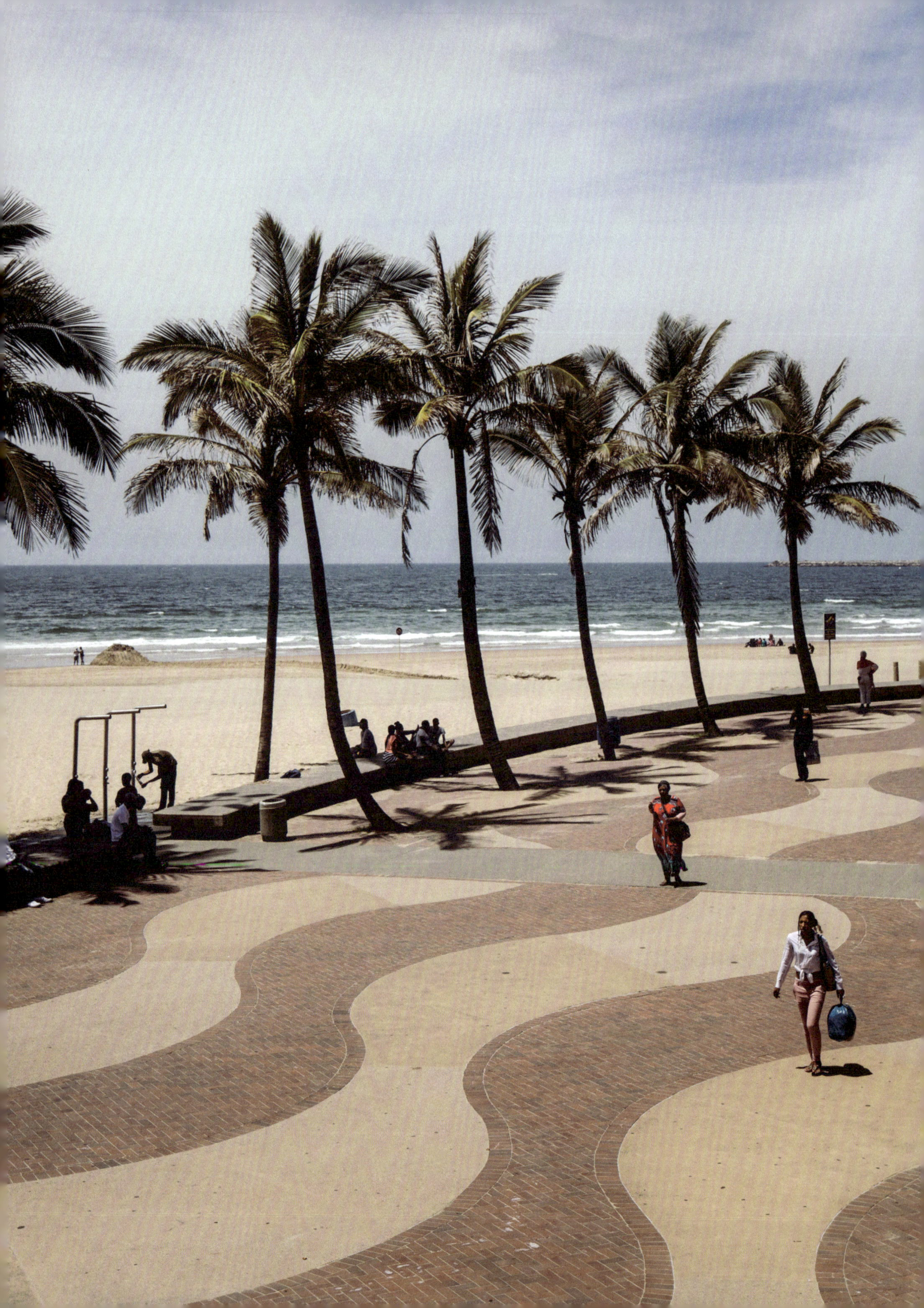

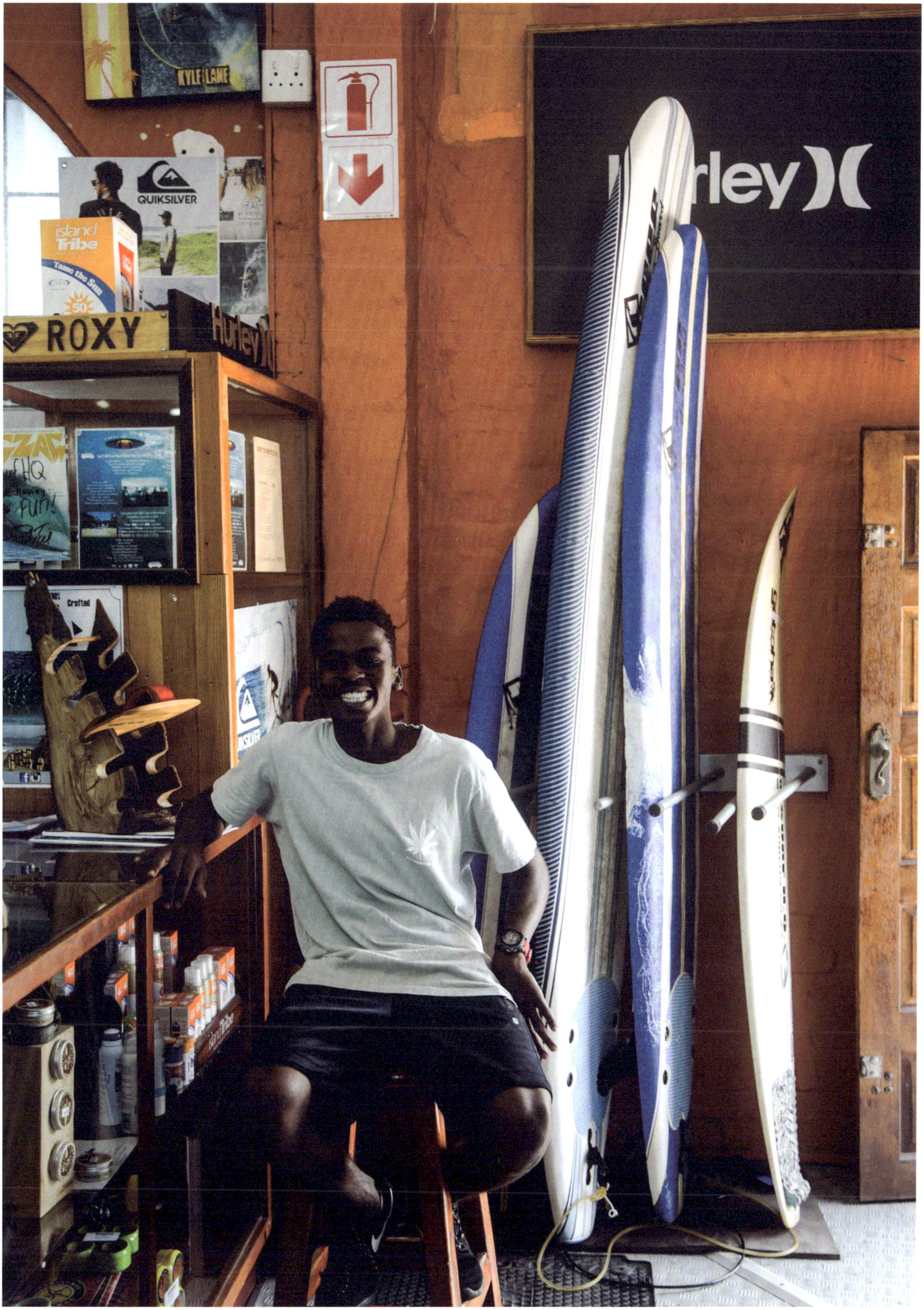
KYLE LANE
QUIKSILVER
island Tribe
ROXY
Hurley

The connecting traffic vein between the metropolis of Johannesburg and the port city of Durban is obviously a very busy one.

At some point you can leave the highway to take a quieter and more scenic route in the direction of the Drakensberg, the high mountain range which forms the border with Lesotho. The route goes through the Drakensberg National Park, crossing the beautiful highlands with their dragon-shaped peaks.

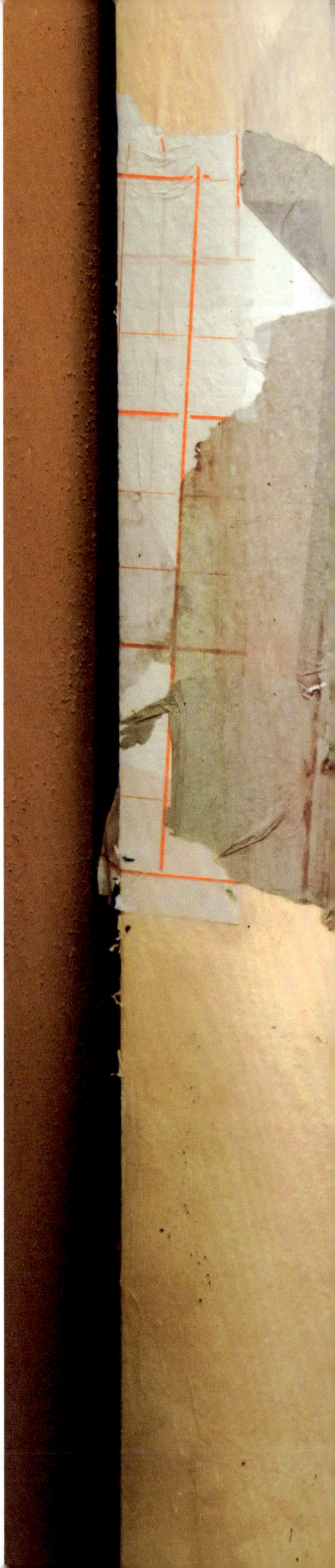

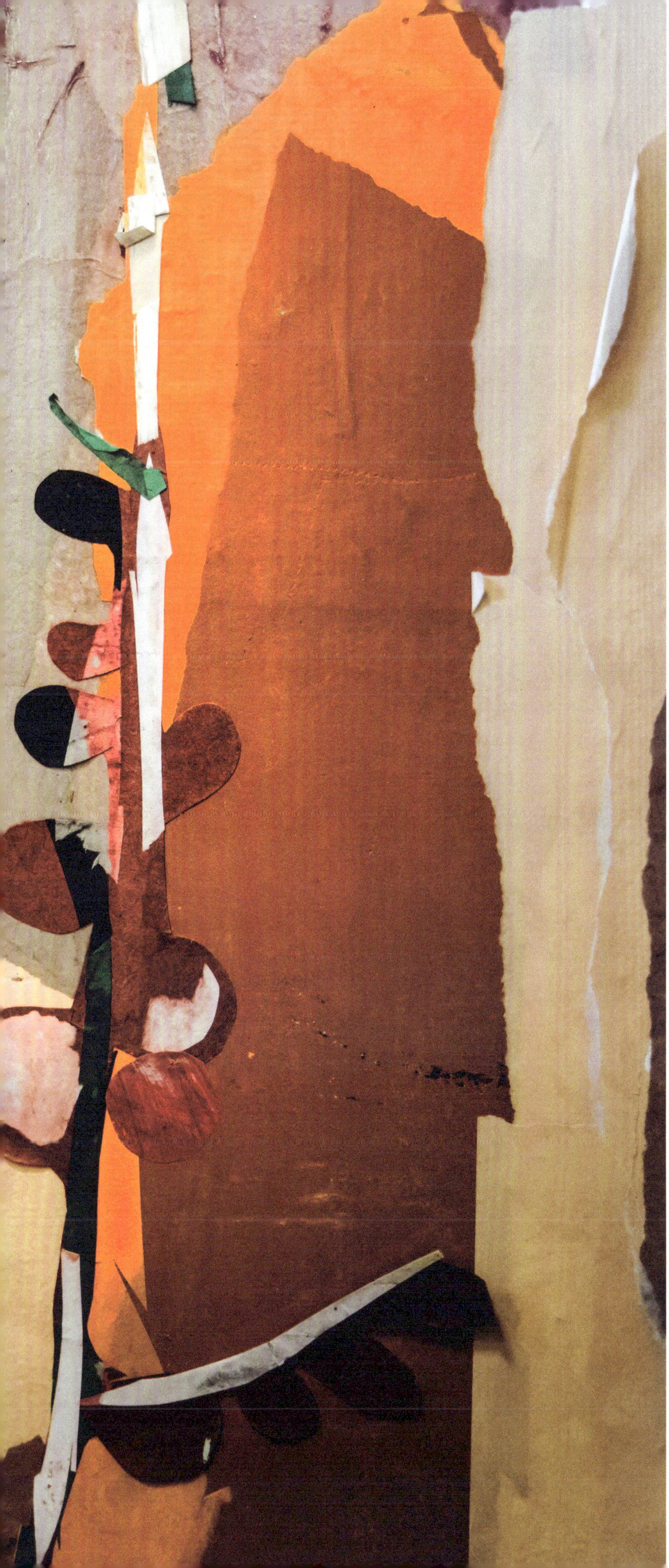

8

N3 Highway

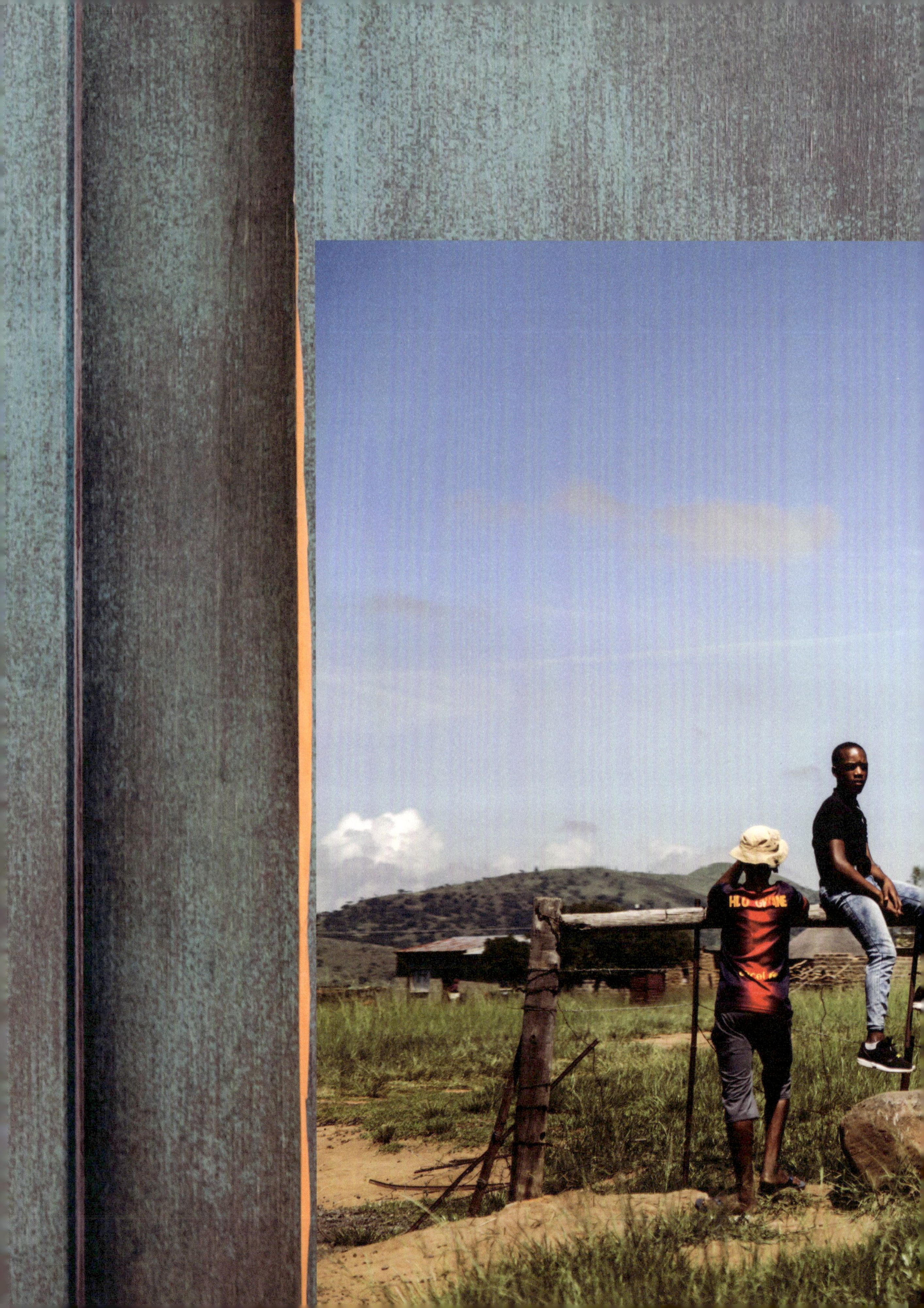

Waiting for the bus?

After hours of driving through an empty landscape we spot a group of young guys on a fence in the middle of nowhere. Are they waiting for something or is this just their local hangout?

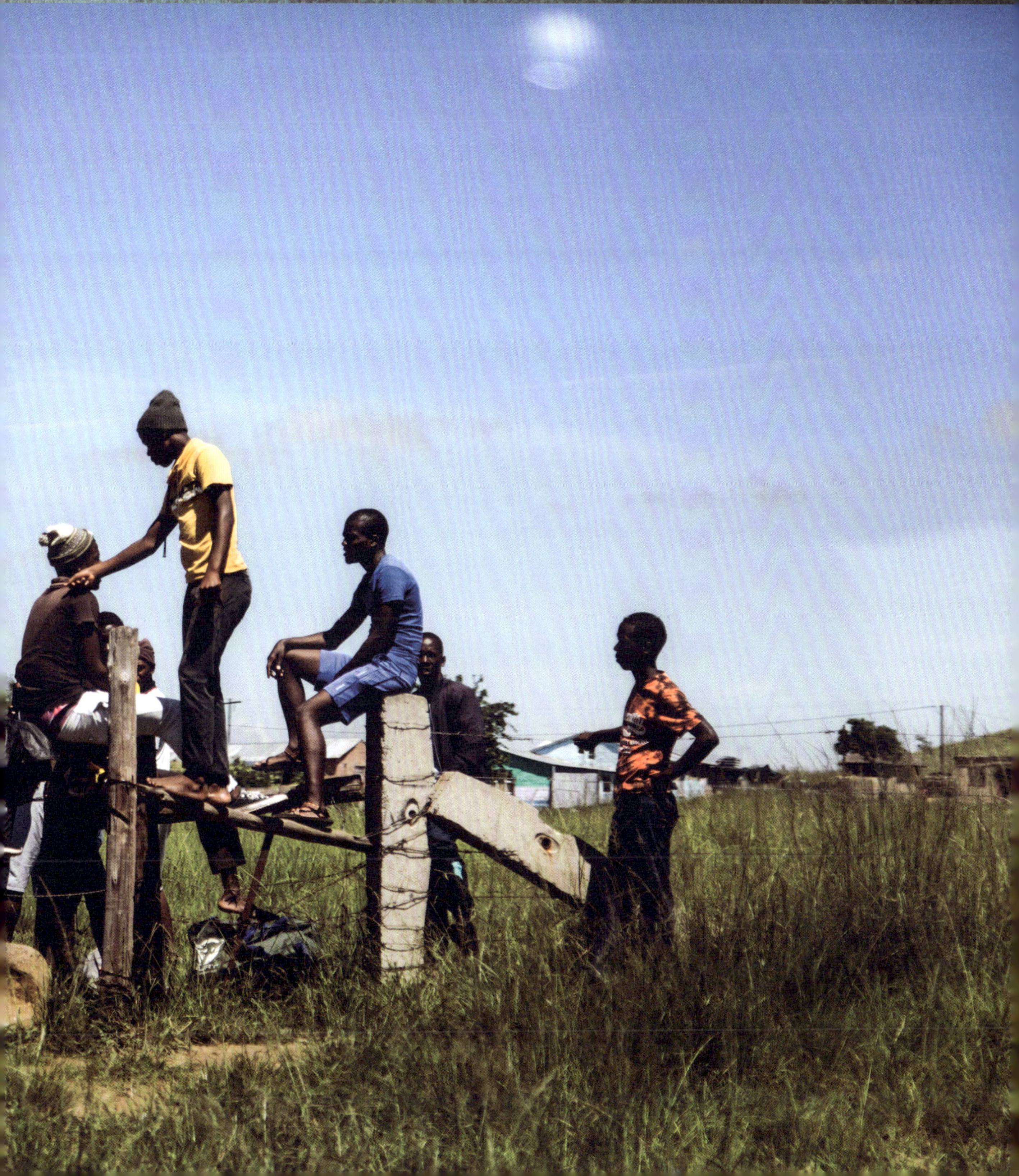

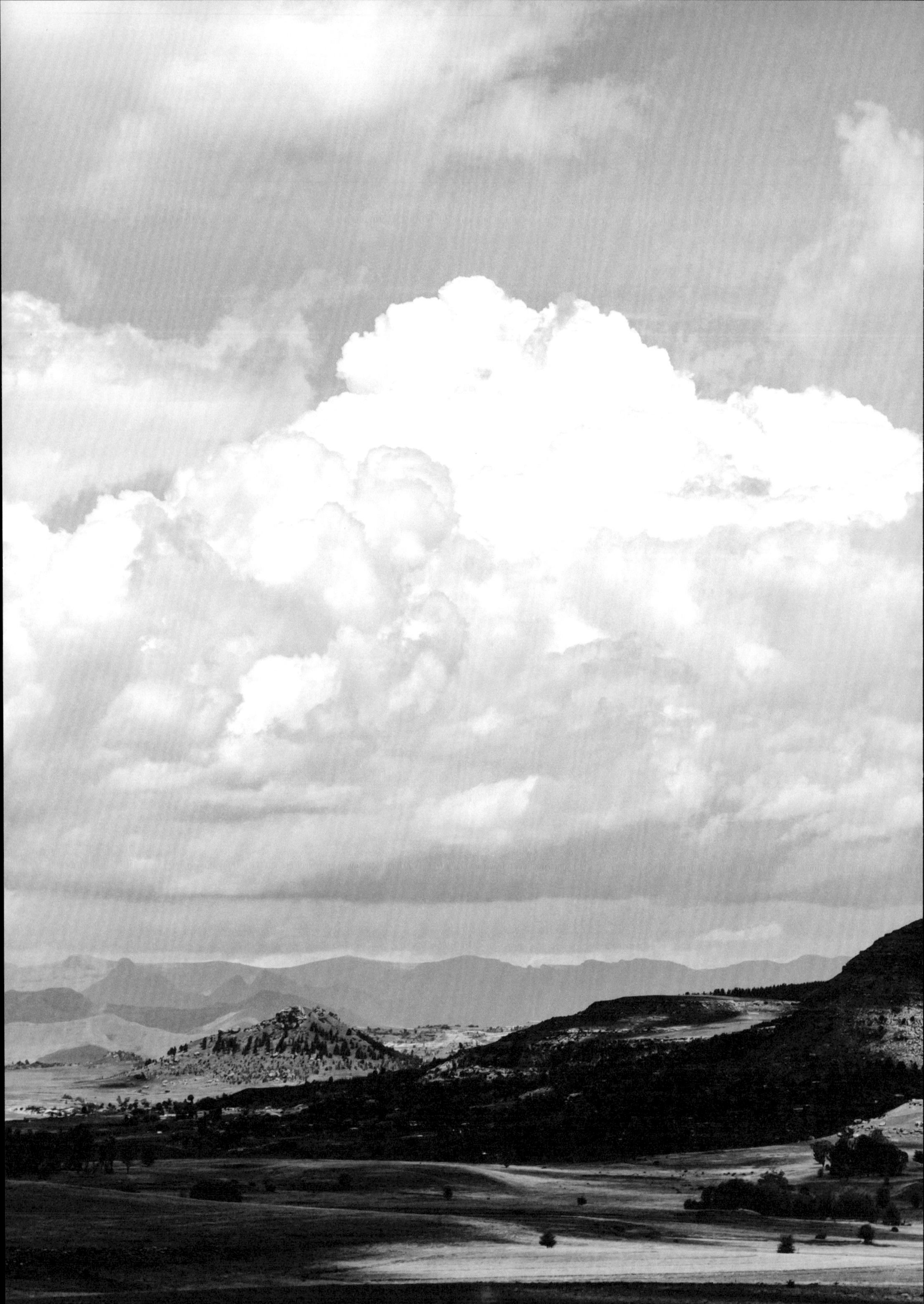

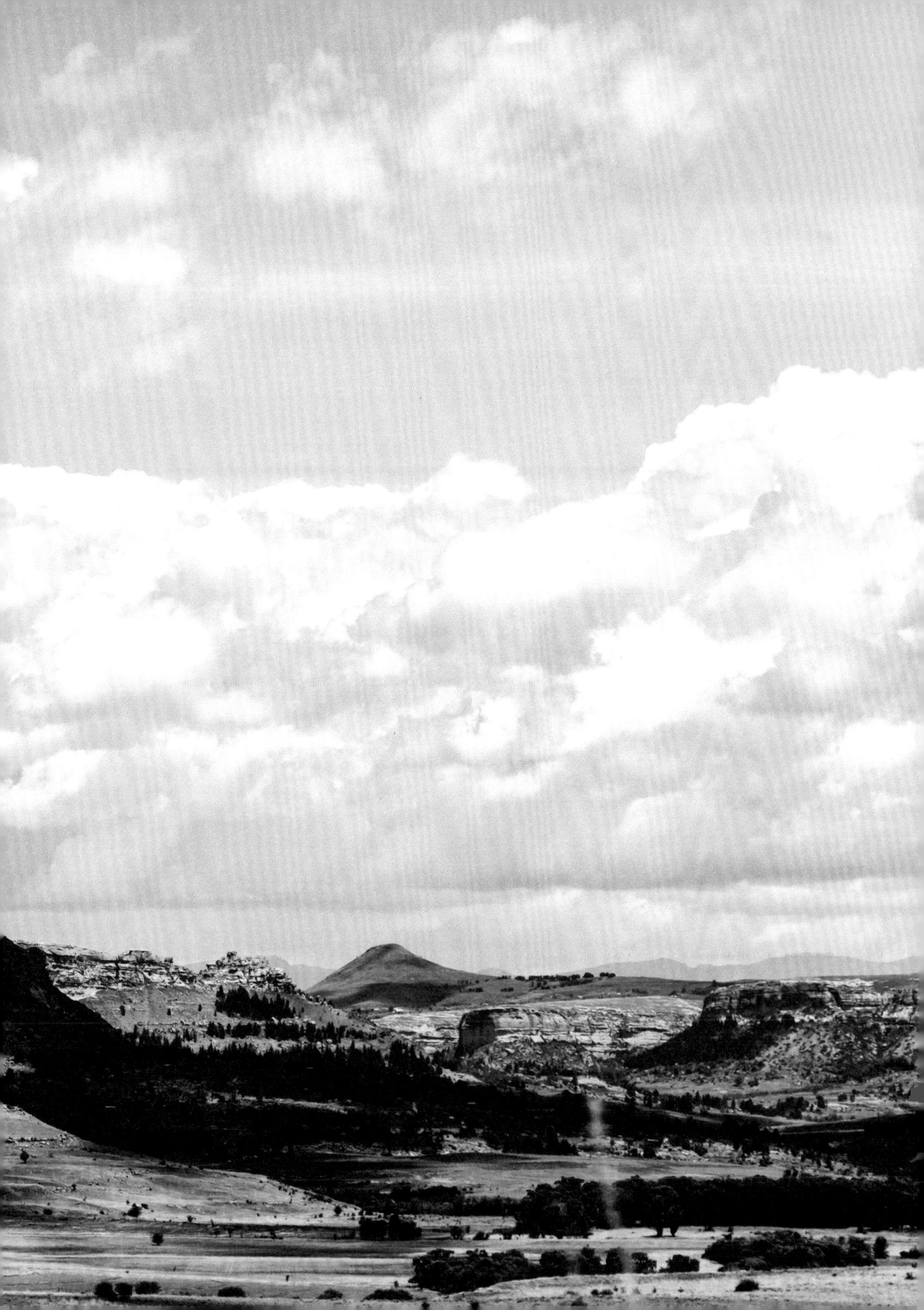

Prynnsberg Estate has a turbulent history. One that started somewhere at the end of the 19th century, when a poor immigrant from England who had become successful in the diamond industry, wanted to show off his newly acquired wealth and status by creating this grand estate. His hope of ensuring that the coming generations of his family would also live in luxury, turned out to be less realistic. Several big and small family tragedies one after the other caused the house and estate to fall into disrepair over the last century.

Until Rick and Sue Melville bought the estate. As people of the 'new South Africa', they brought fresh ideas to this seemingly doomed place. They made a plan for the main house, respecting its history and style but adding new elements. The land around the house had less historical baggage, making it much easier to work with totally new concepts for its renovation.

The estate is surrounded by round, bulky hills. One of these has an overhanging rock, forming a wide shallow cave, like a terrace overlooking the rest of the land. The perfect place to create an outdoor settlement.

Rick and Sue work in advertising and theatre respectively. Their communicative and theatrical way of thinking clearly shows in their approach of this project. It is not a cute little spot, but rather it has a certain grandeur: simple yet elaborate, with a humorous twist. It is a cool place.

Friends and family come here to enjoy each other's company, with good food and drinks. And to enjoy nature, of course. It is a modern variant on the way the cave dwellers lived together.

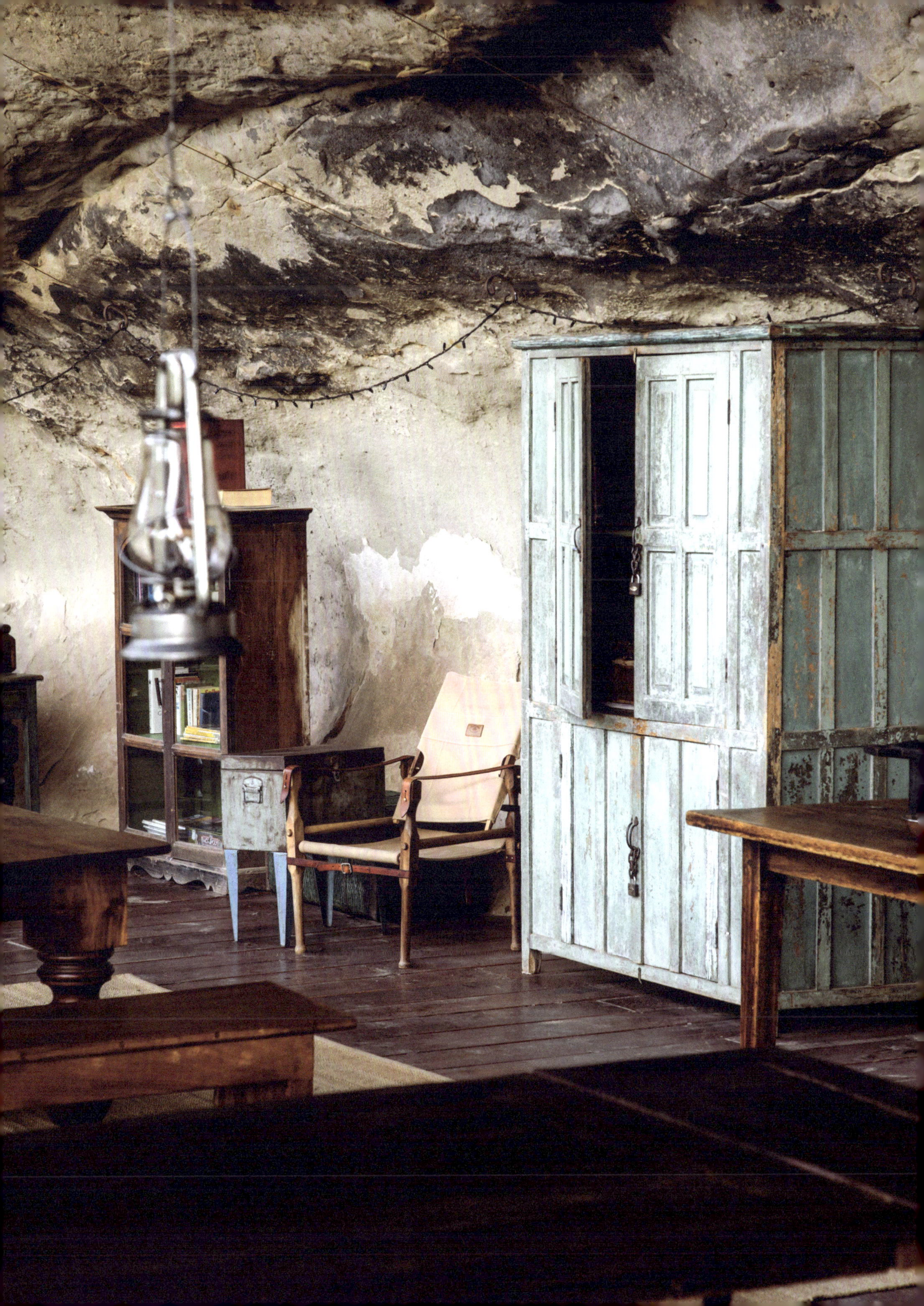

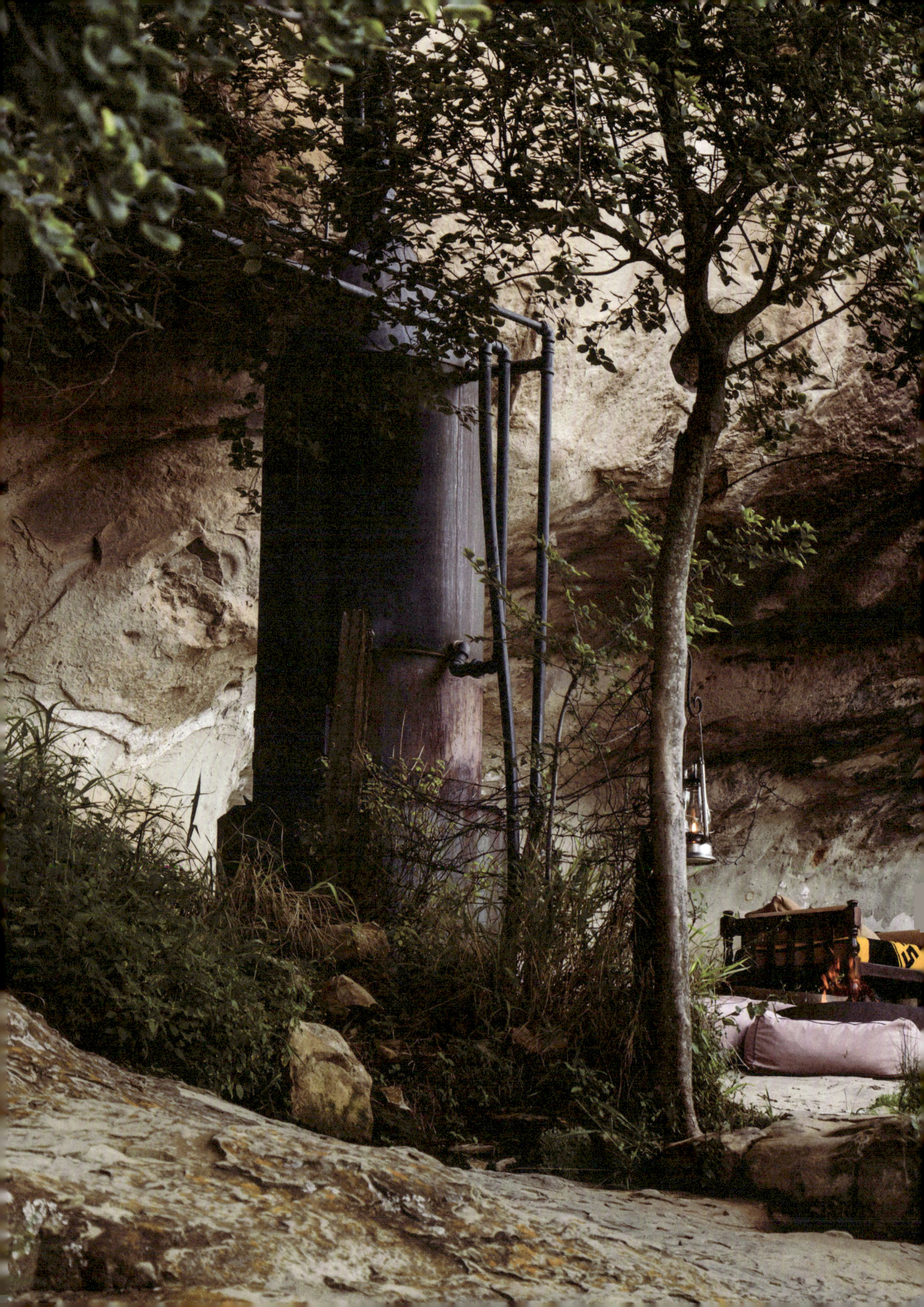

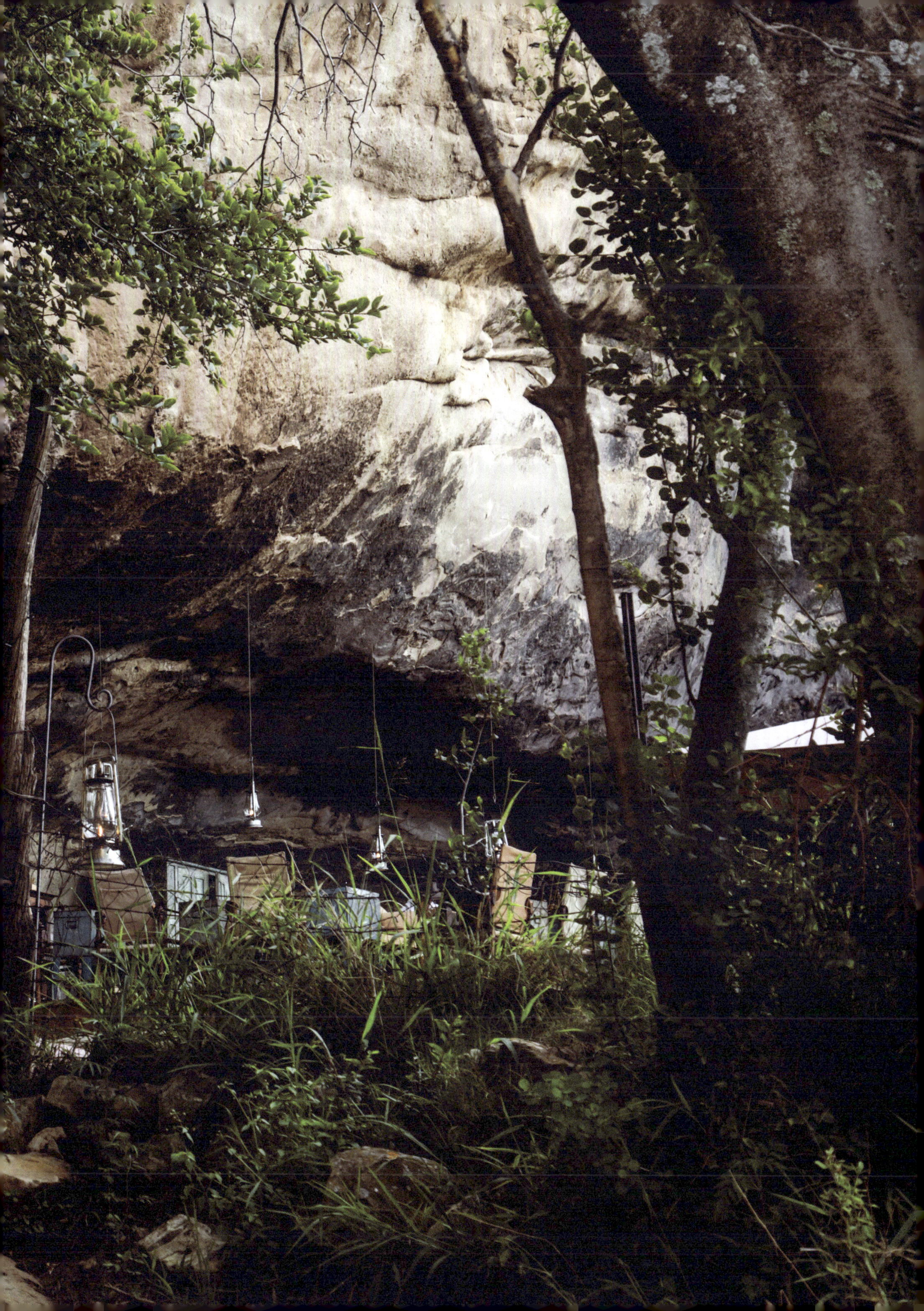

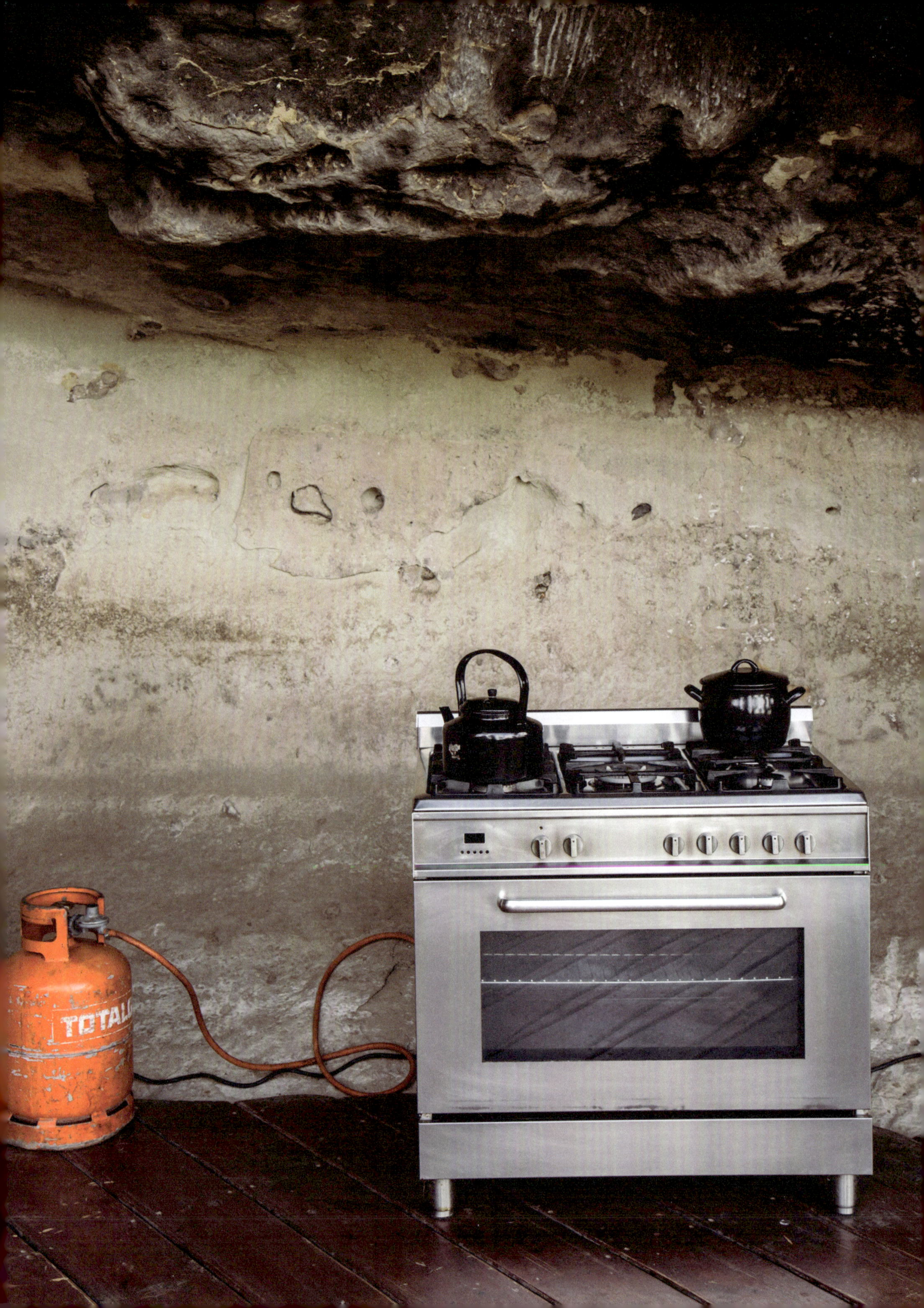

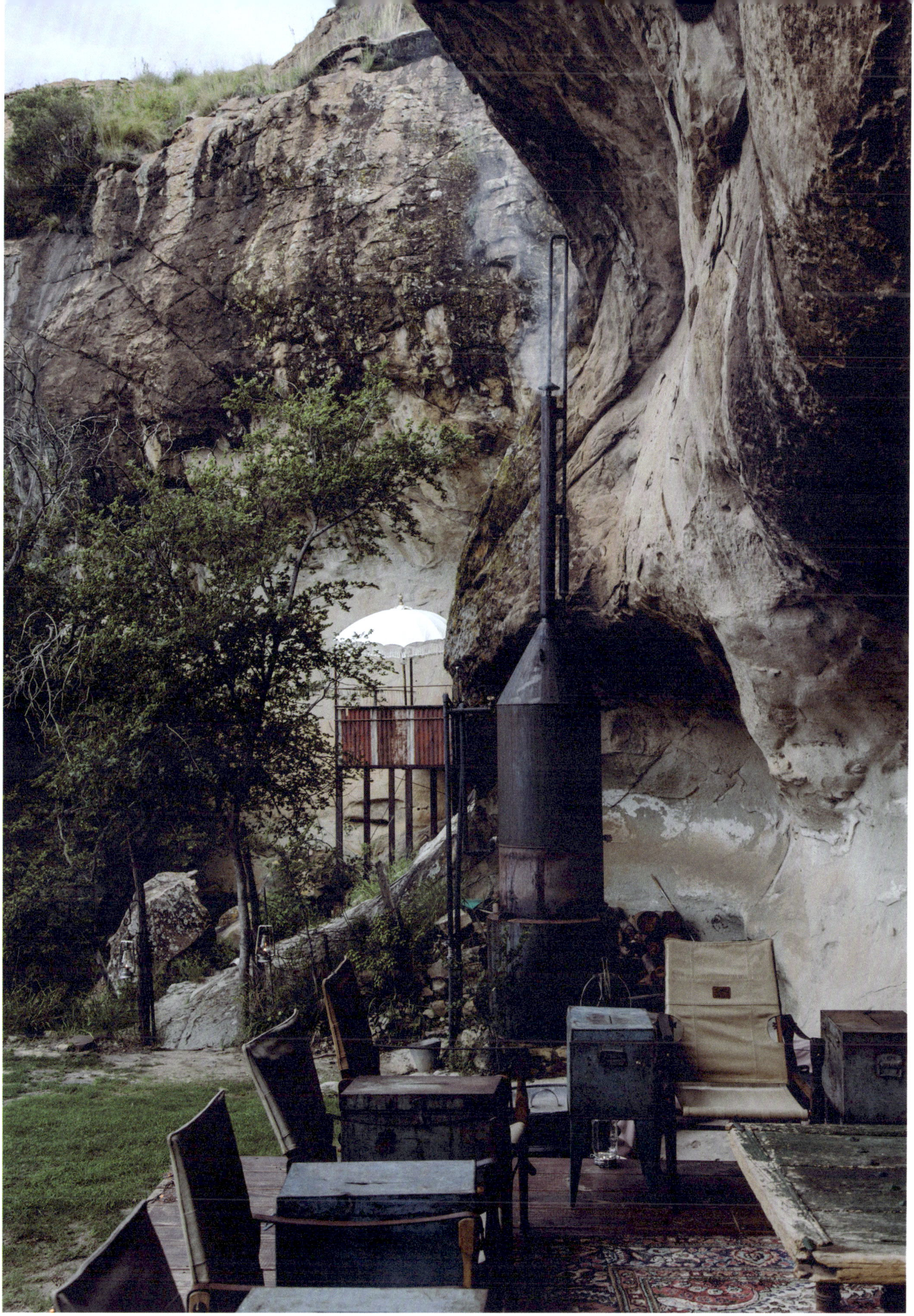

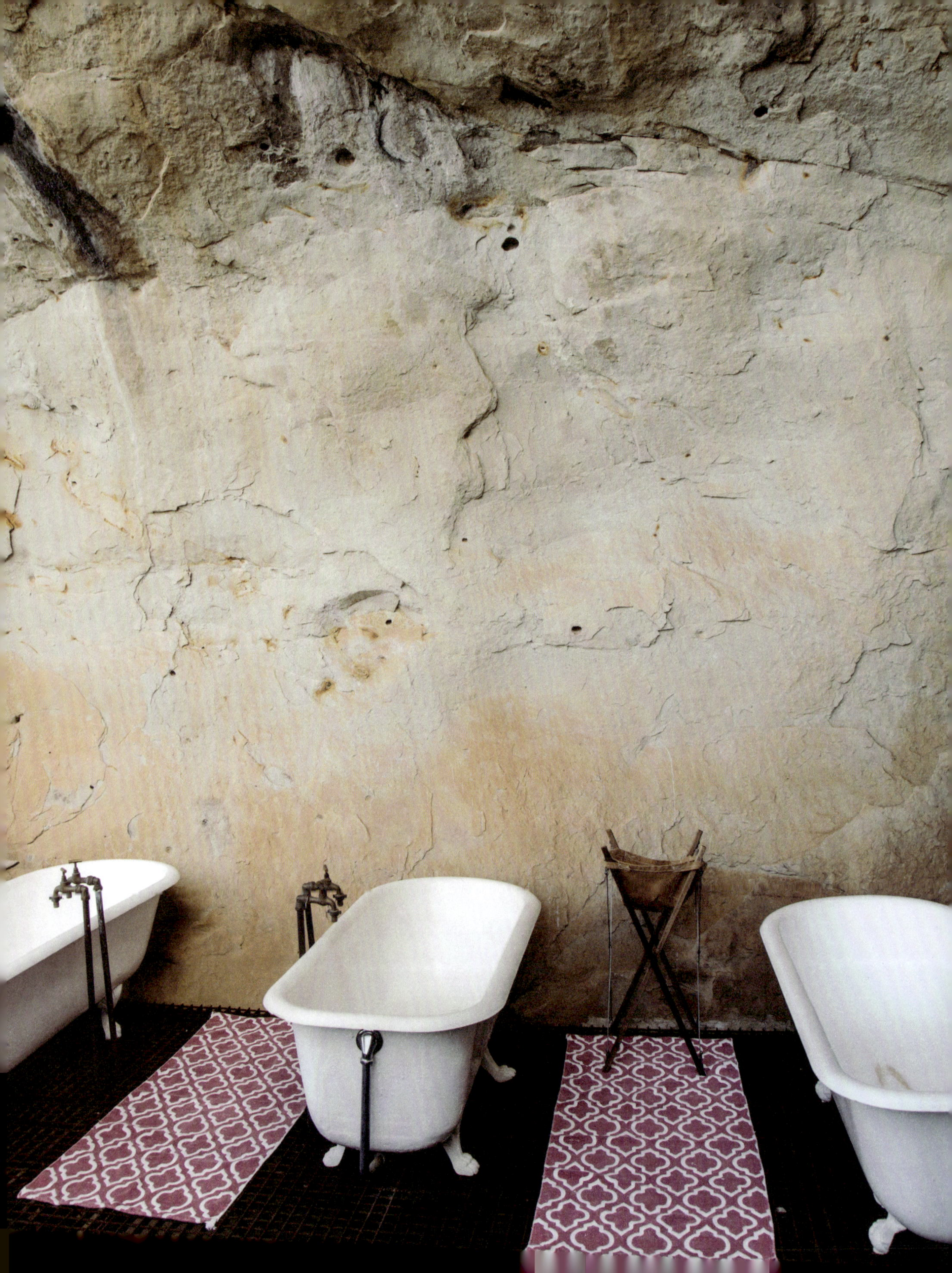

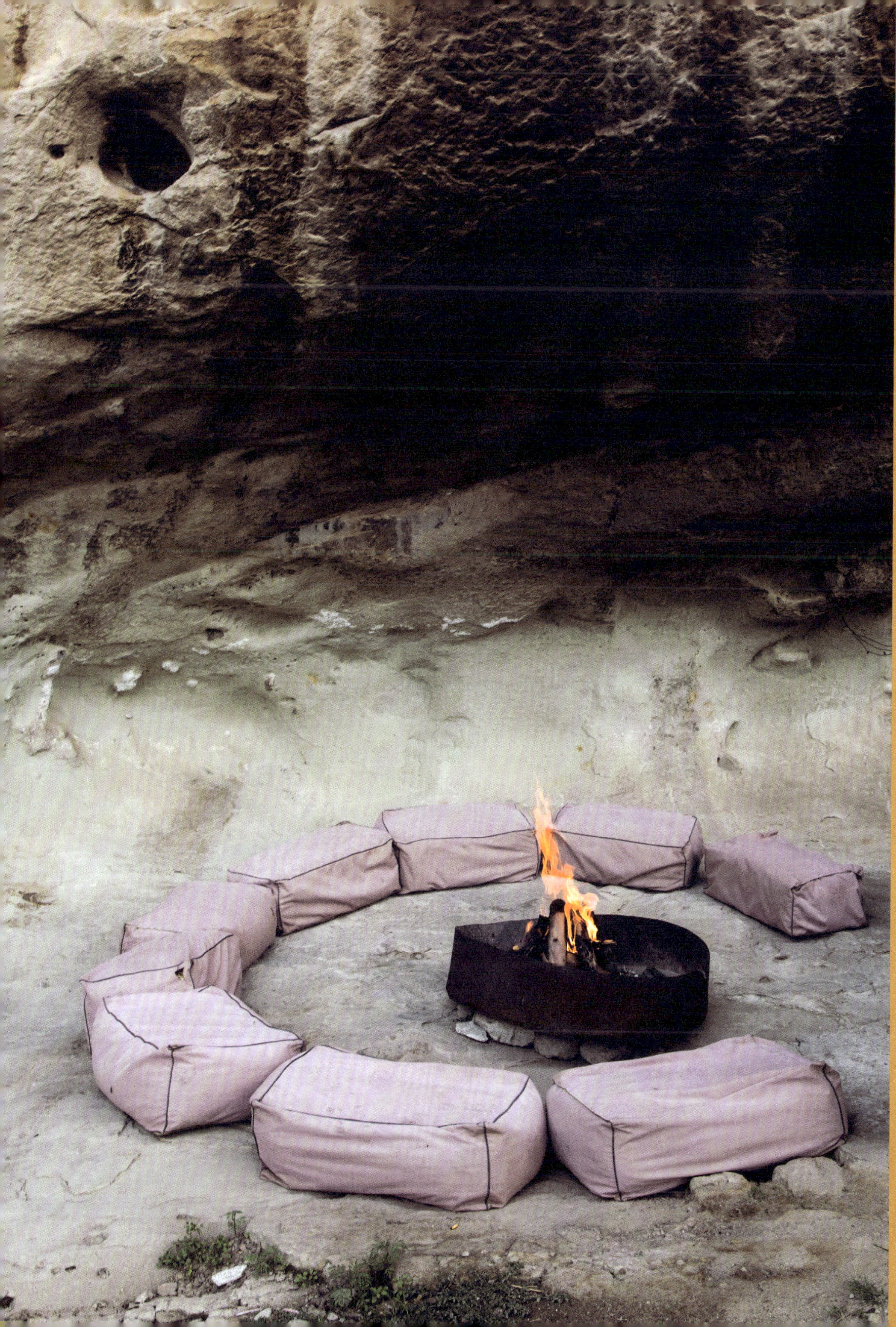

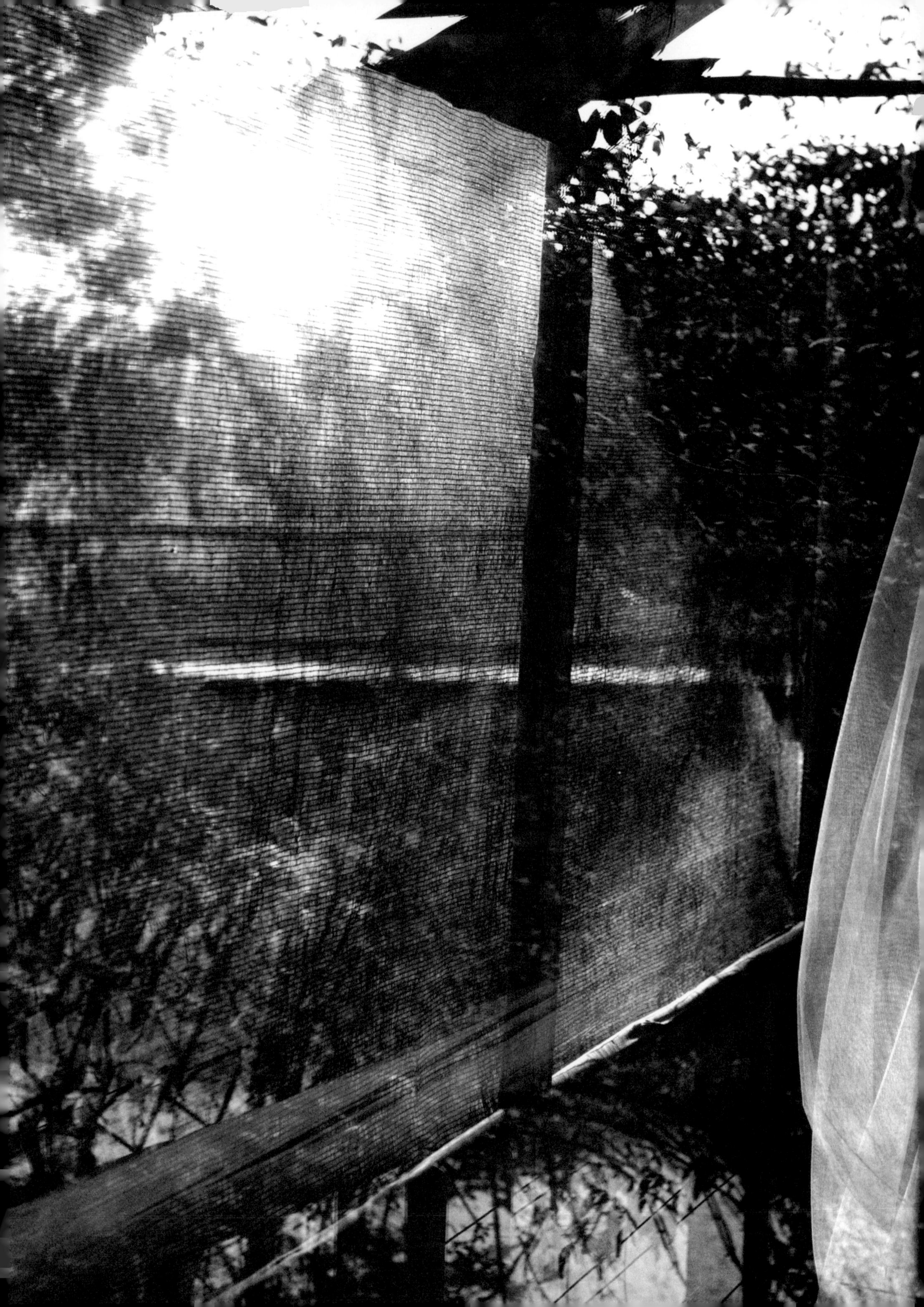

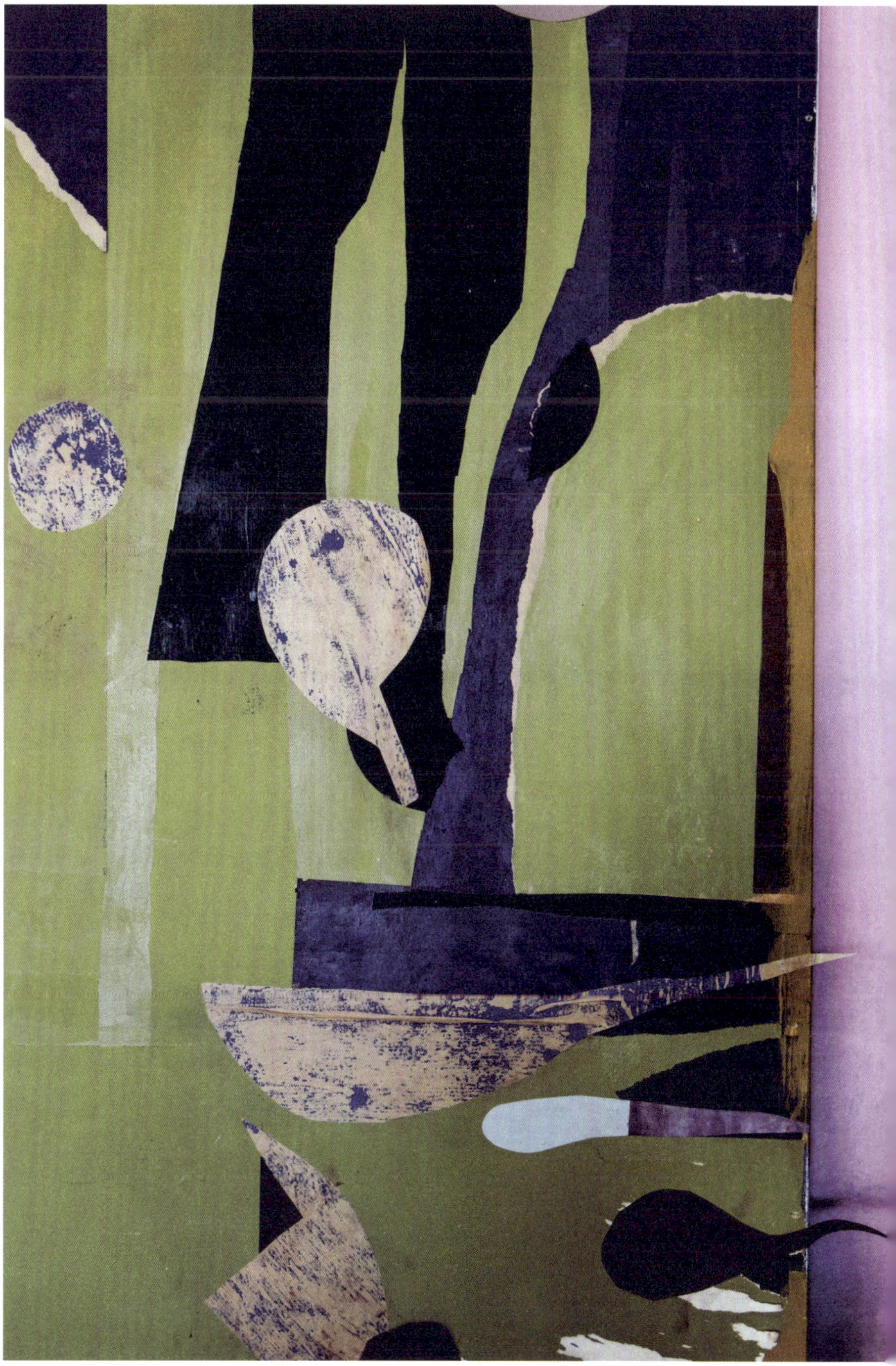

Without fences

The Kruger National Park in the far north-east of the country is one of the largest nature reserves in Africa. It is a long strip of land of more than 350 km in length and 60 km wide, bordering on nature reserves in Mozambique and Zimbabwe respectively. The fences between the parks in the different countries were removed a number of years back, creating one large so-called peace park. Now the animals can move freely from one country to another.

In addition to its size, the Kruger Park is also famous for its wide variety of animal species. You can spot all the animals in the Big Five here: lions, buffalo, leopards, rhinos and African elephants. Besides these big boys, many others including numerous special species of birds have found a safe habitat here.

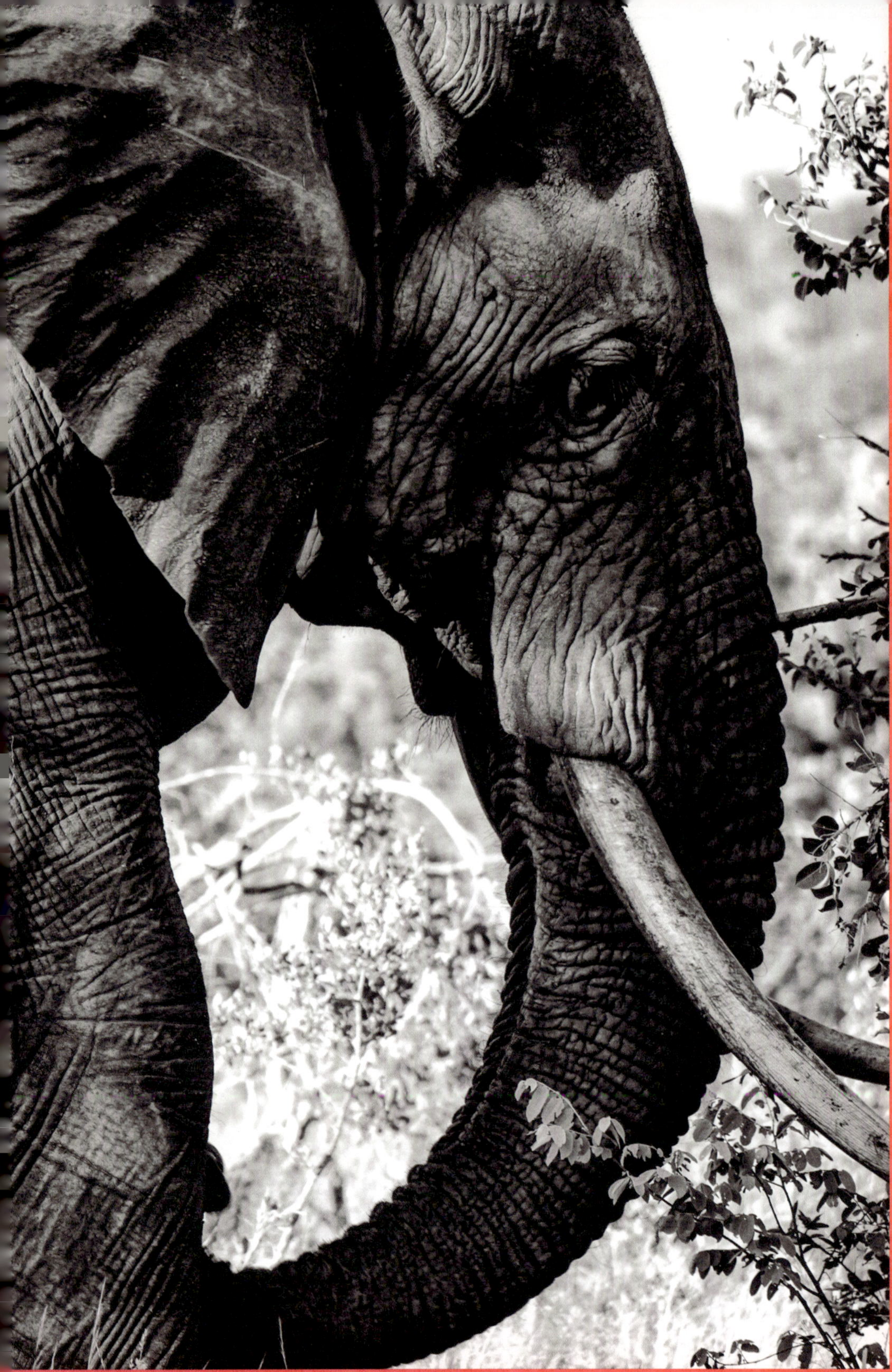

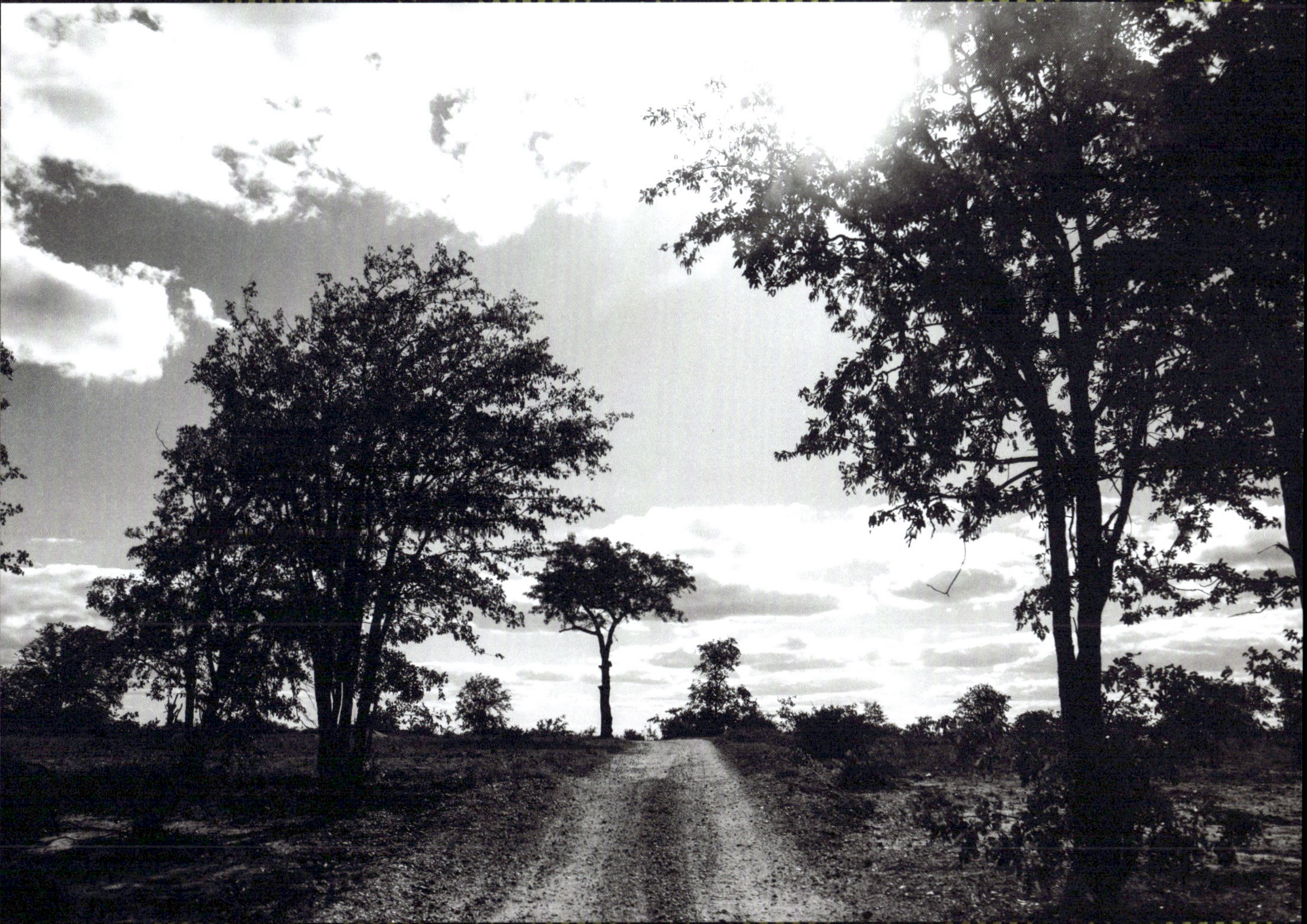

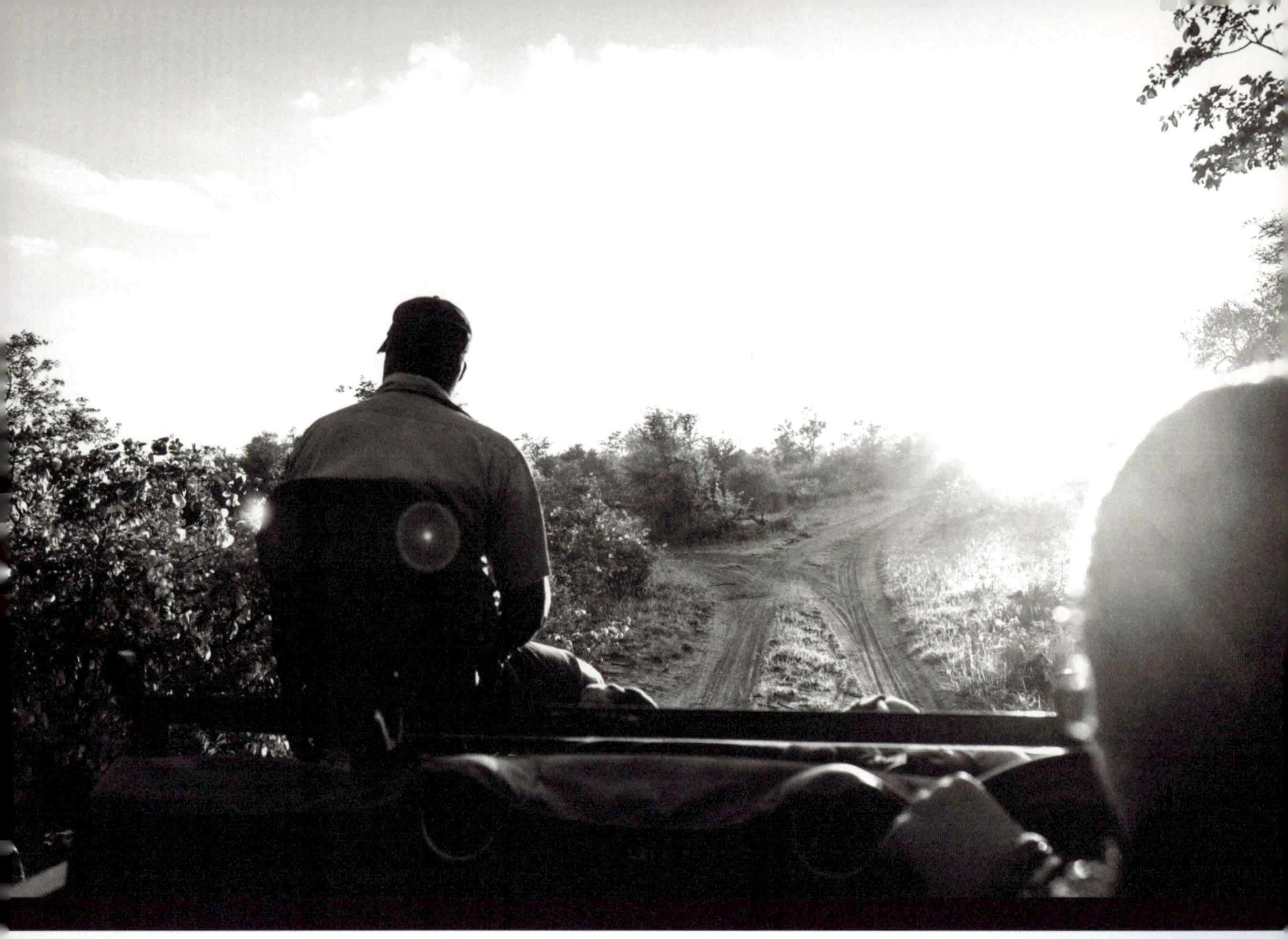

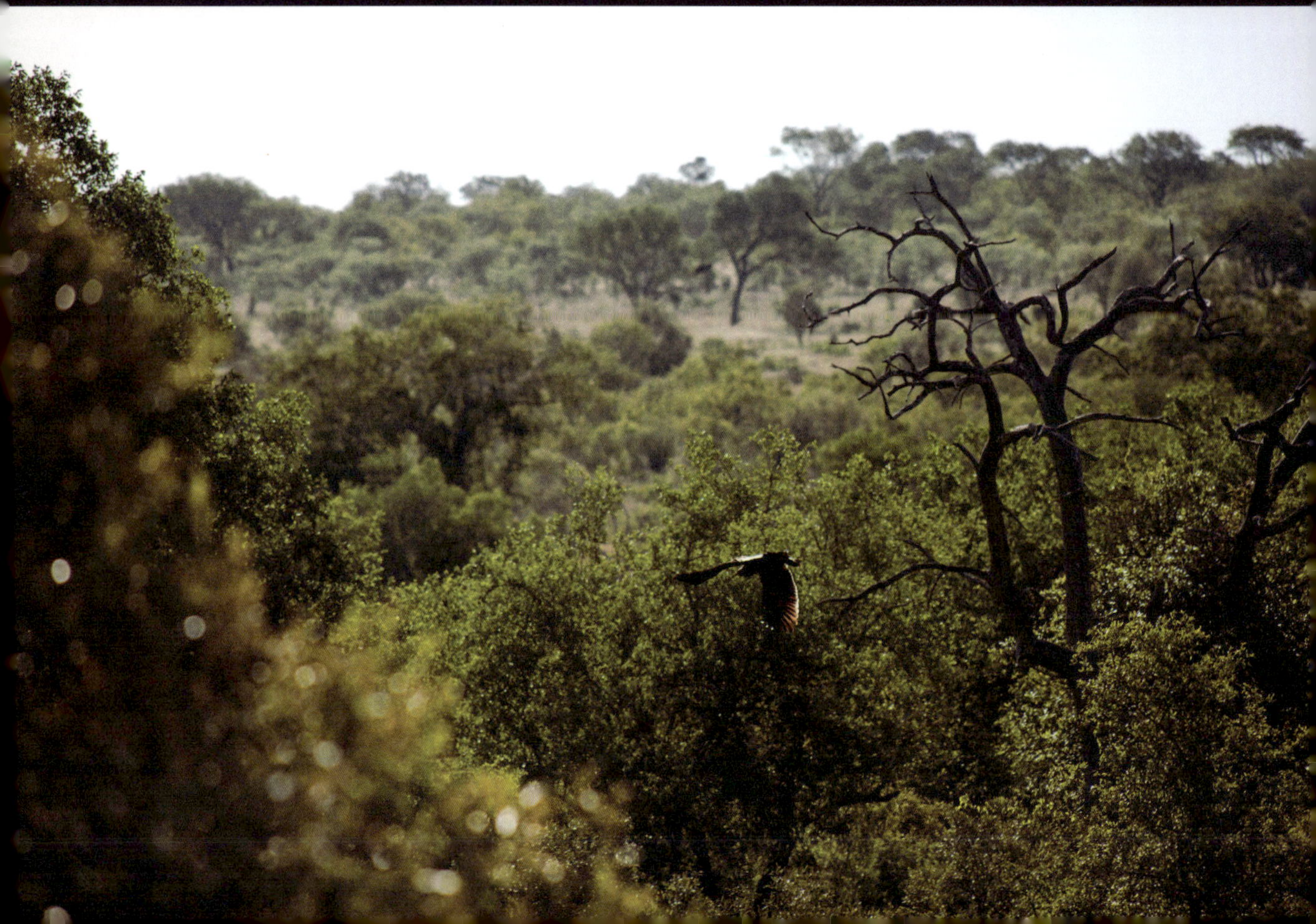

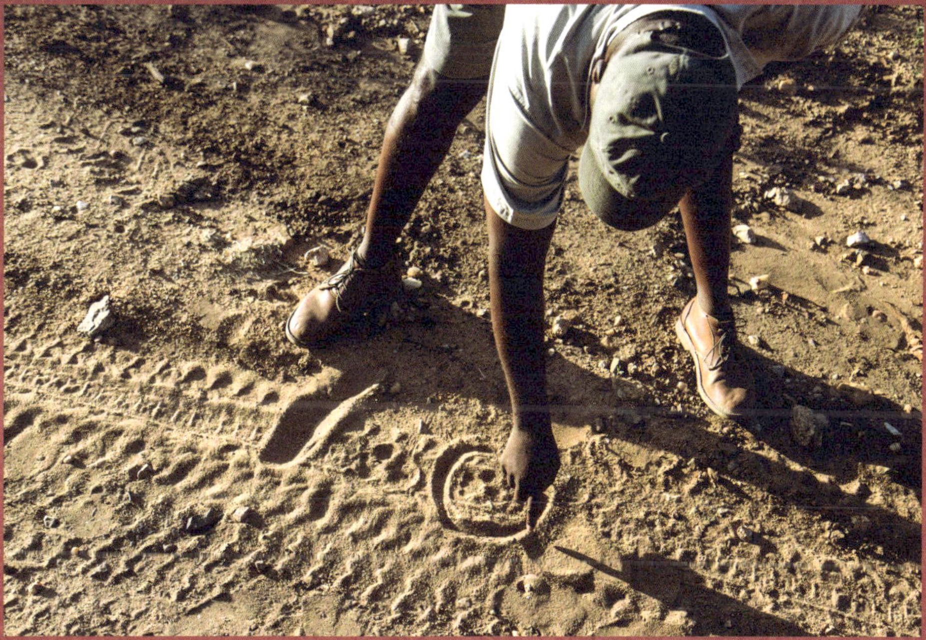

Reading tracks

Going on safari with a ranger makes your trip through nature even more special. The experienced rangers know so much about nature and animals, and are full of fascinating stories. They know how to interpret every track and sound and can tell exactly which animal can be found in a particular area. As they point out all kinds of interesting details to you, you will learn how everything in nature is connected and communicates with each other. Something that at first seems invisible, suddenly becomes clear.

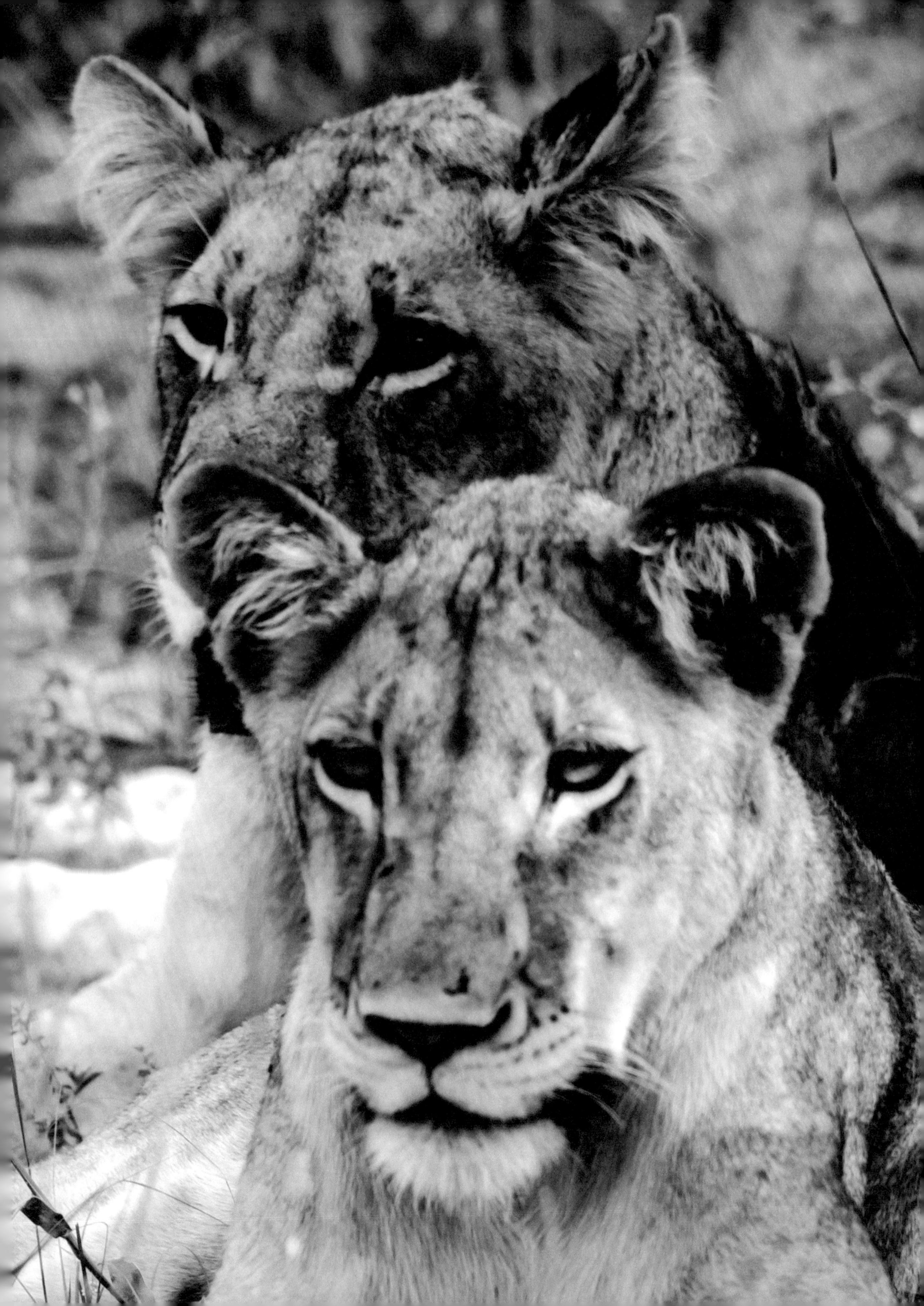

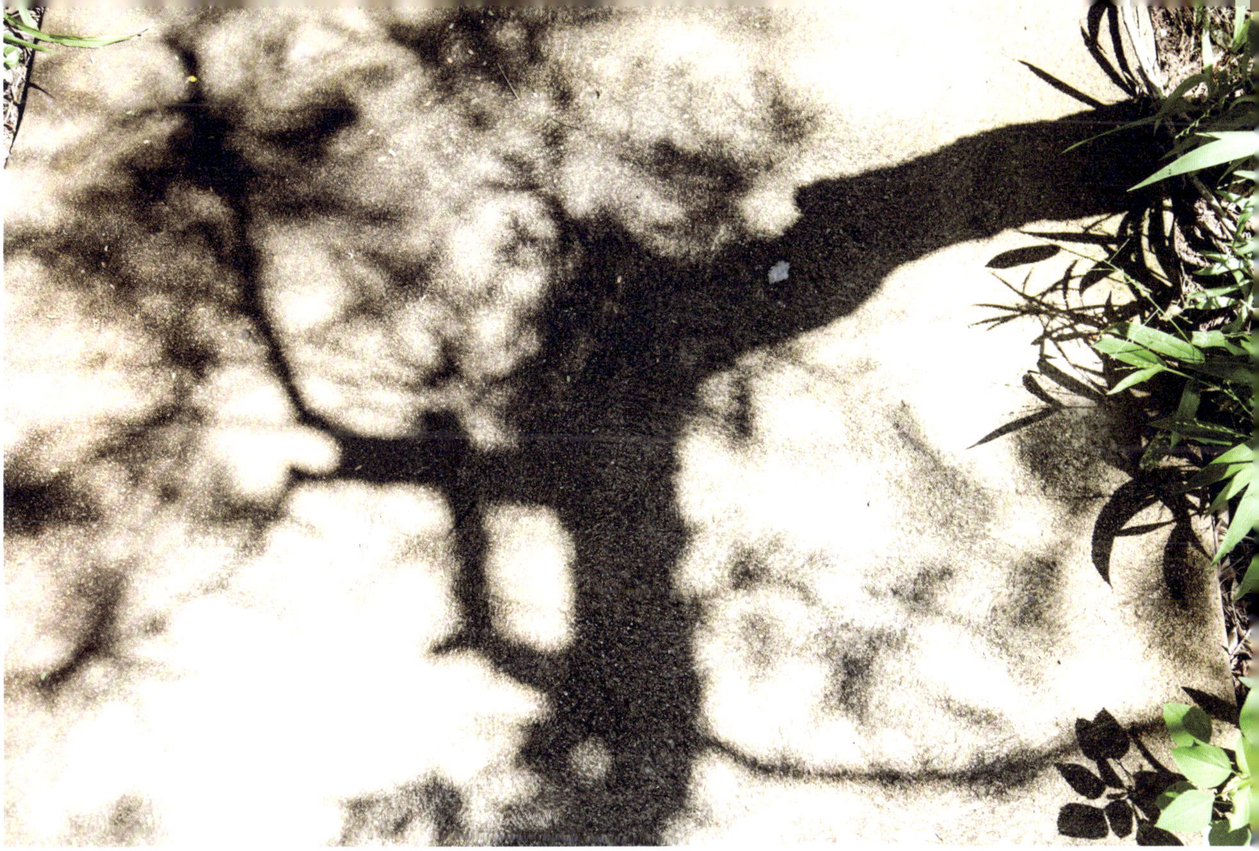

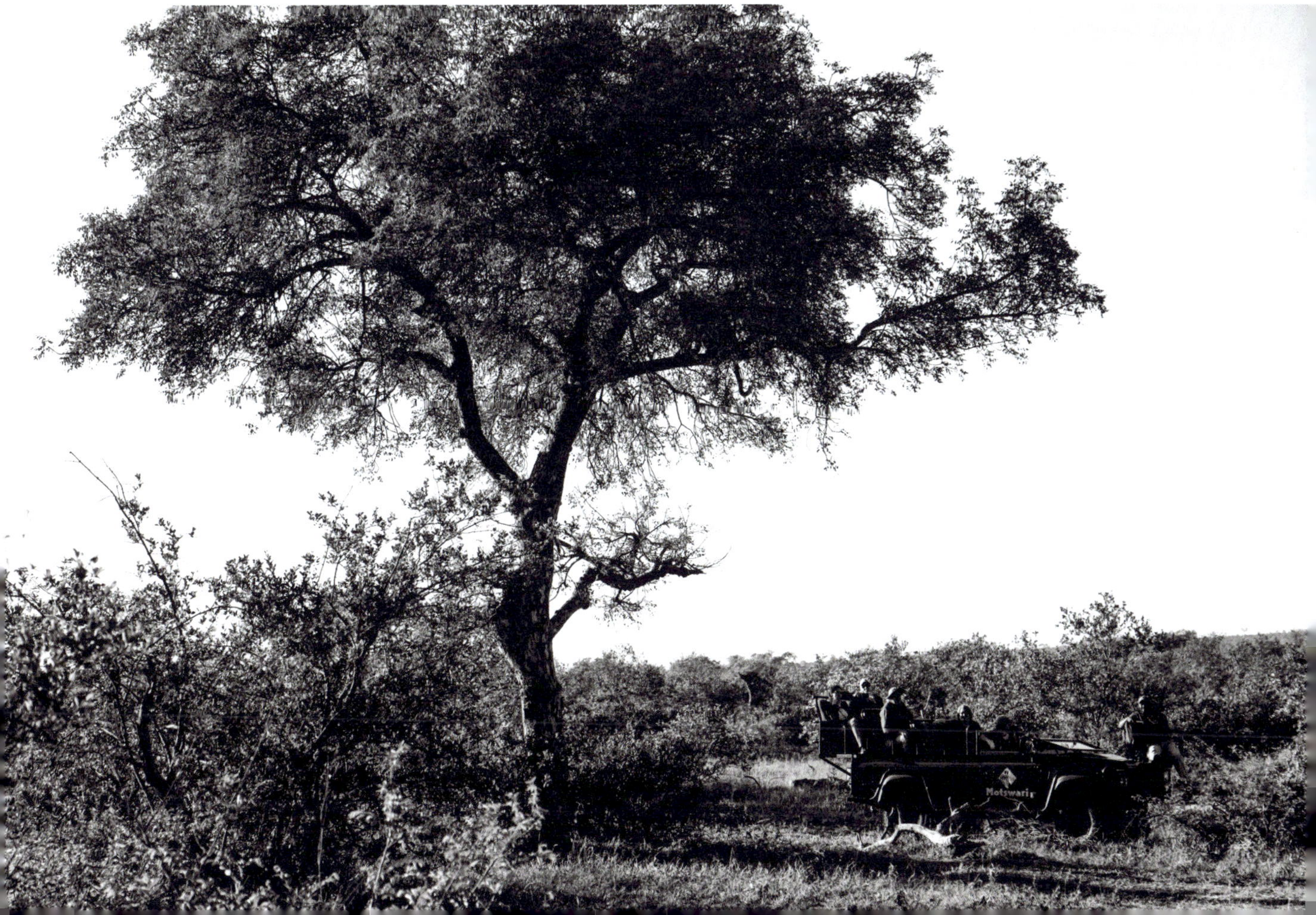
Motswari

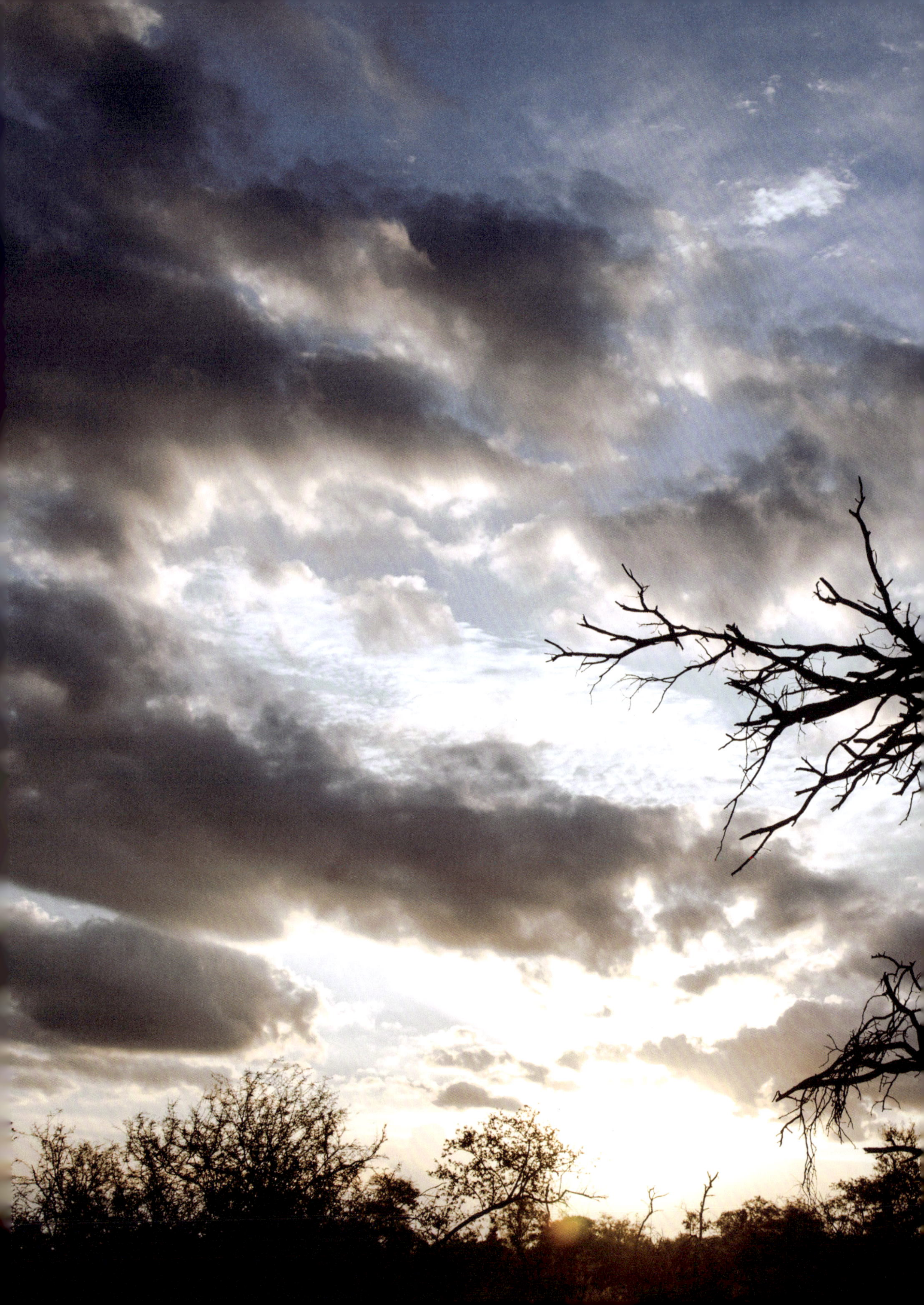

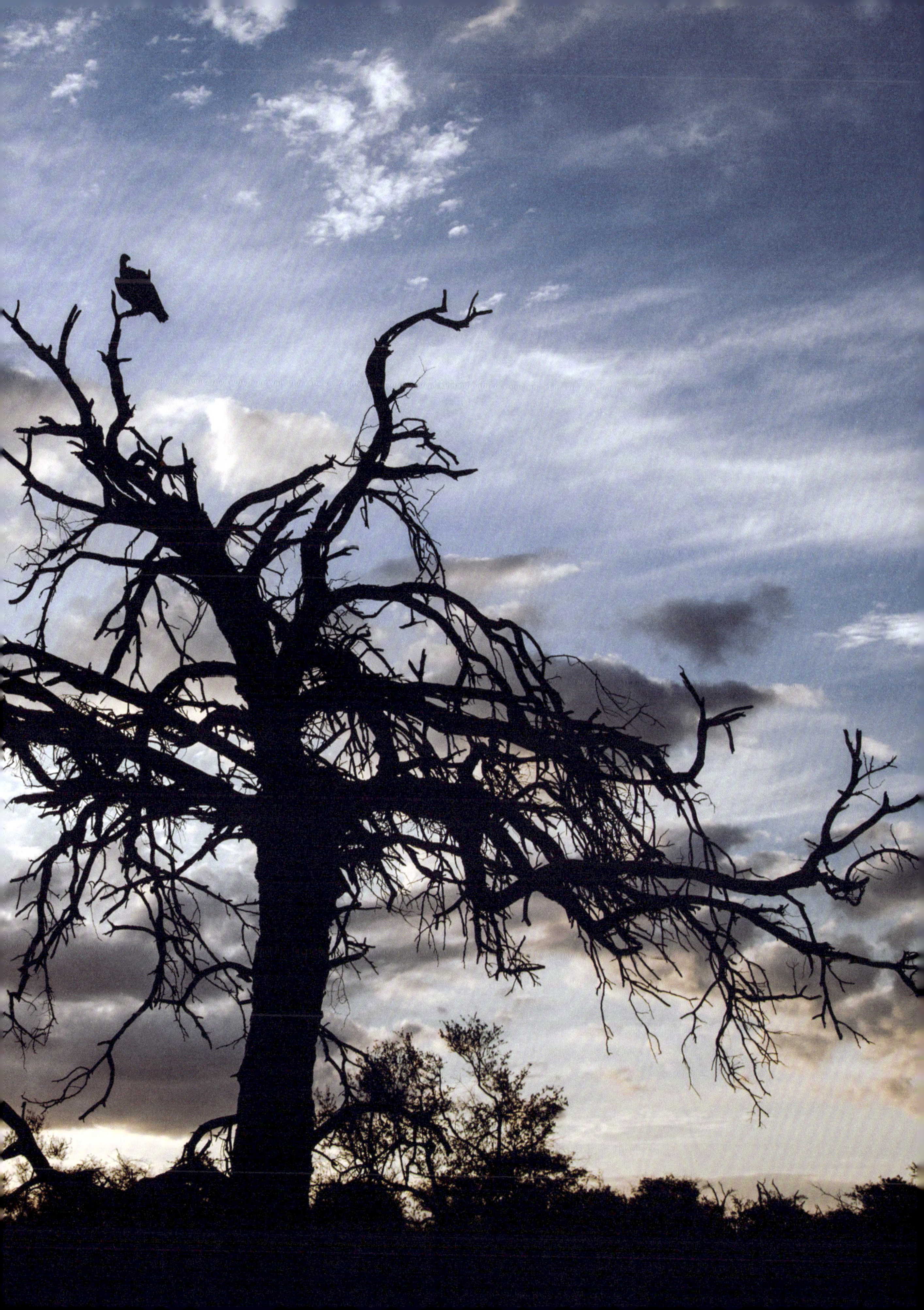

Johannesburg is a young city, compared with other major world cities. Gold was first discovered here at the end of the 19th century. From its modest beginnings as a mining town, it has since become Africa's richest and most developed metropolis.

A city of stark contrasts, with a turbulent history, where the struggle for freedom and democracy is fiercely fought among tall, gleaming buildings and in overpopulated townships. A place where crime was once rife in certain neighbourhoods, and where kindness and fun now have the upper hand in those very same neighbourhoods, thanks to the initiatives of a few visionaries who understand what the people of Jo'burg are longing for. While the bizarre and inhumane history of apartheid is still tangible, Johannesburg definitely feels more integrated today.

It is an attractive city, with plenty of character and a personality all its own. Not the easiest one perhaps, but an interesting one, where the optimism of the inhabitants is contagious.

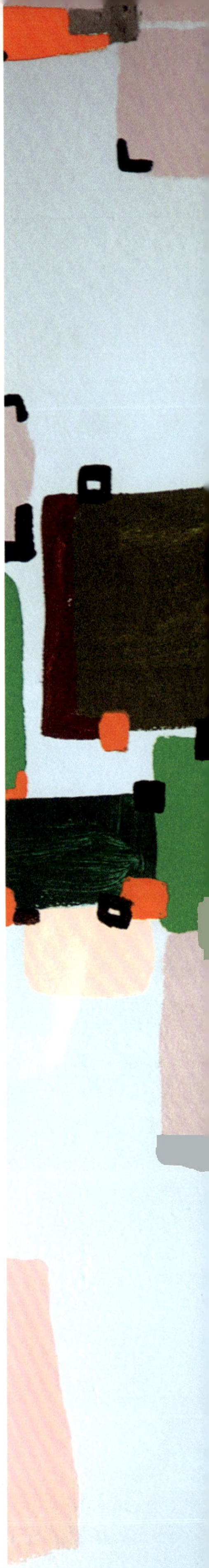

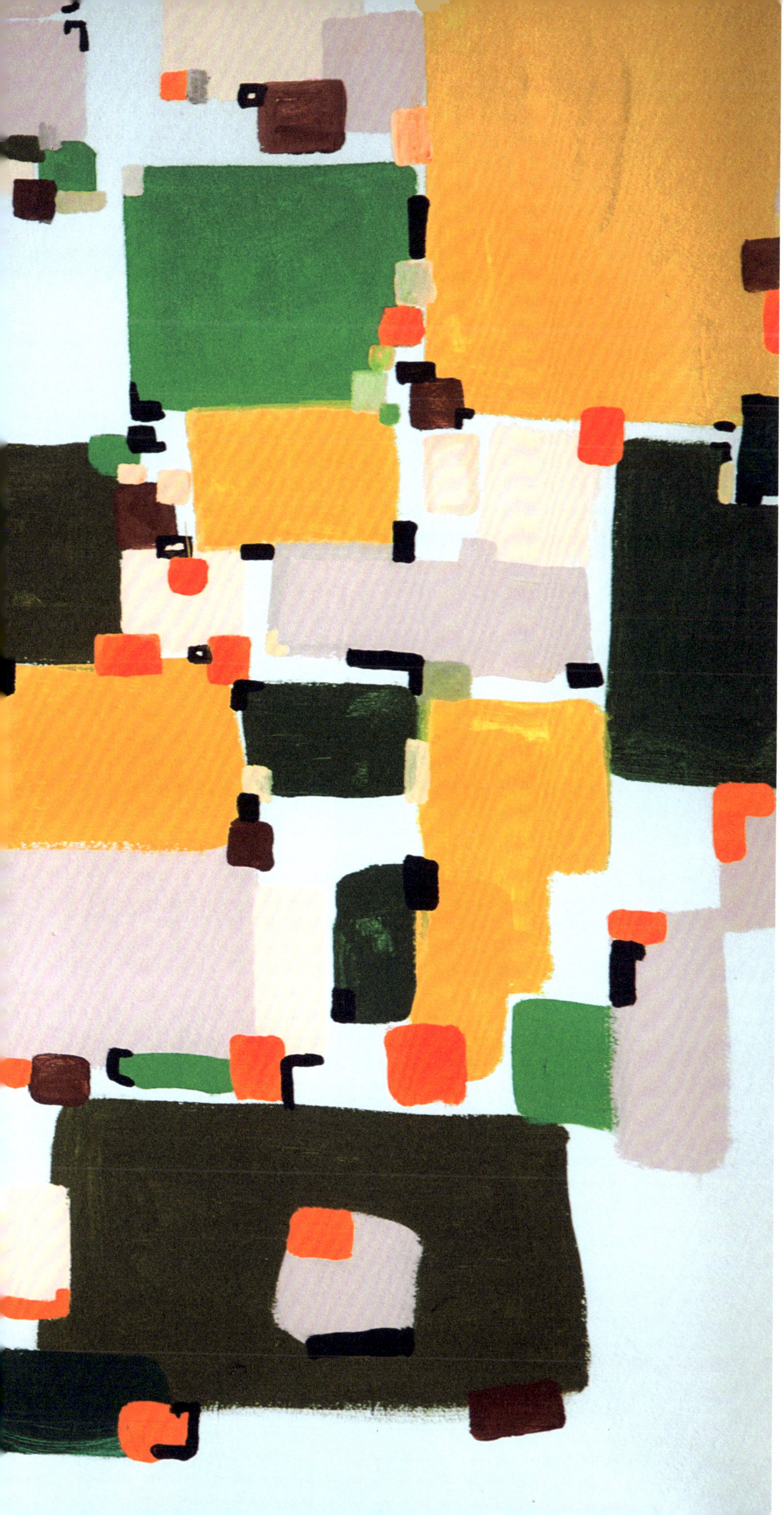

9

Johannesburg

207

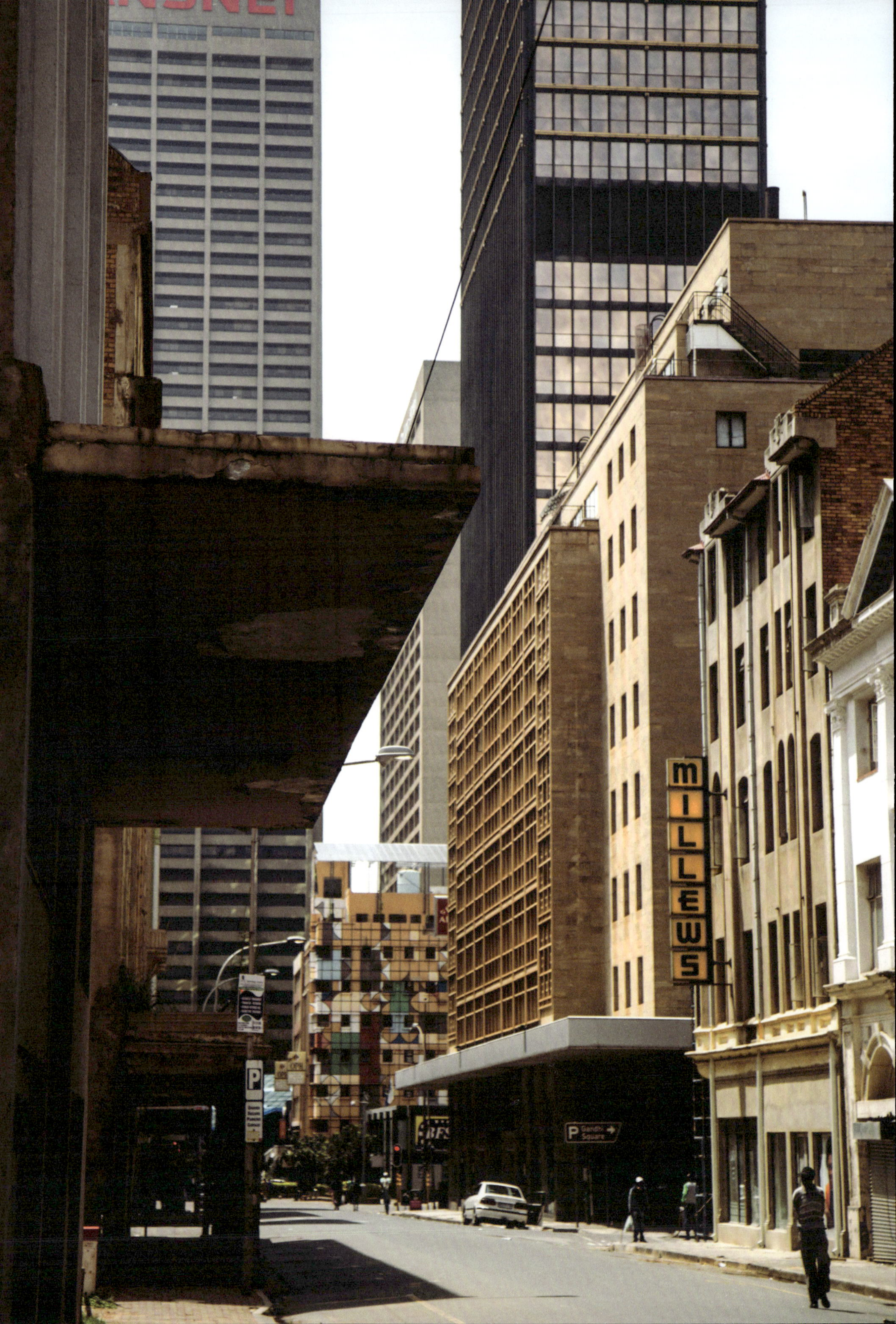
MILLEWS

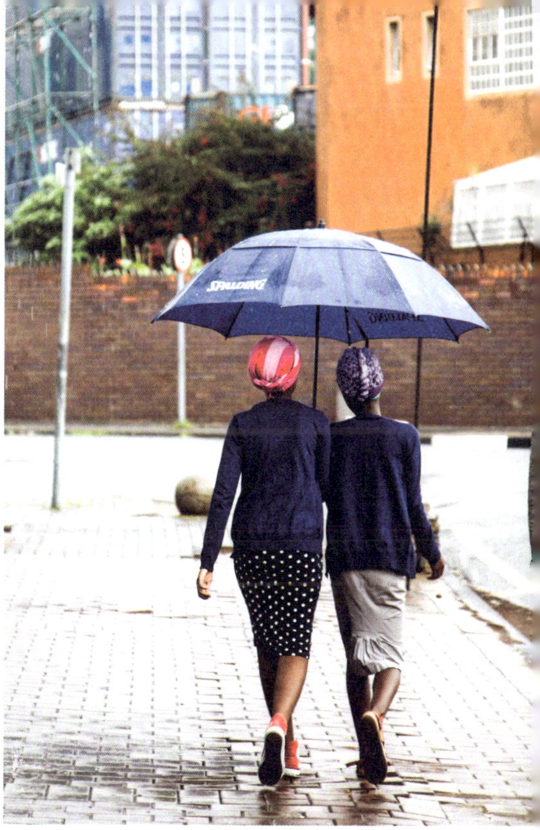
SPALDING

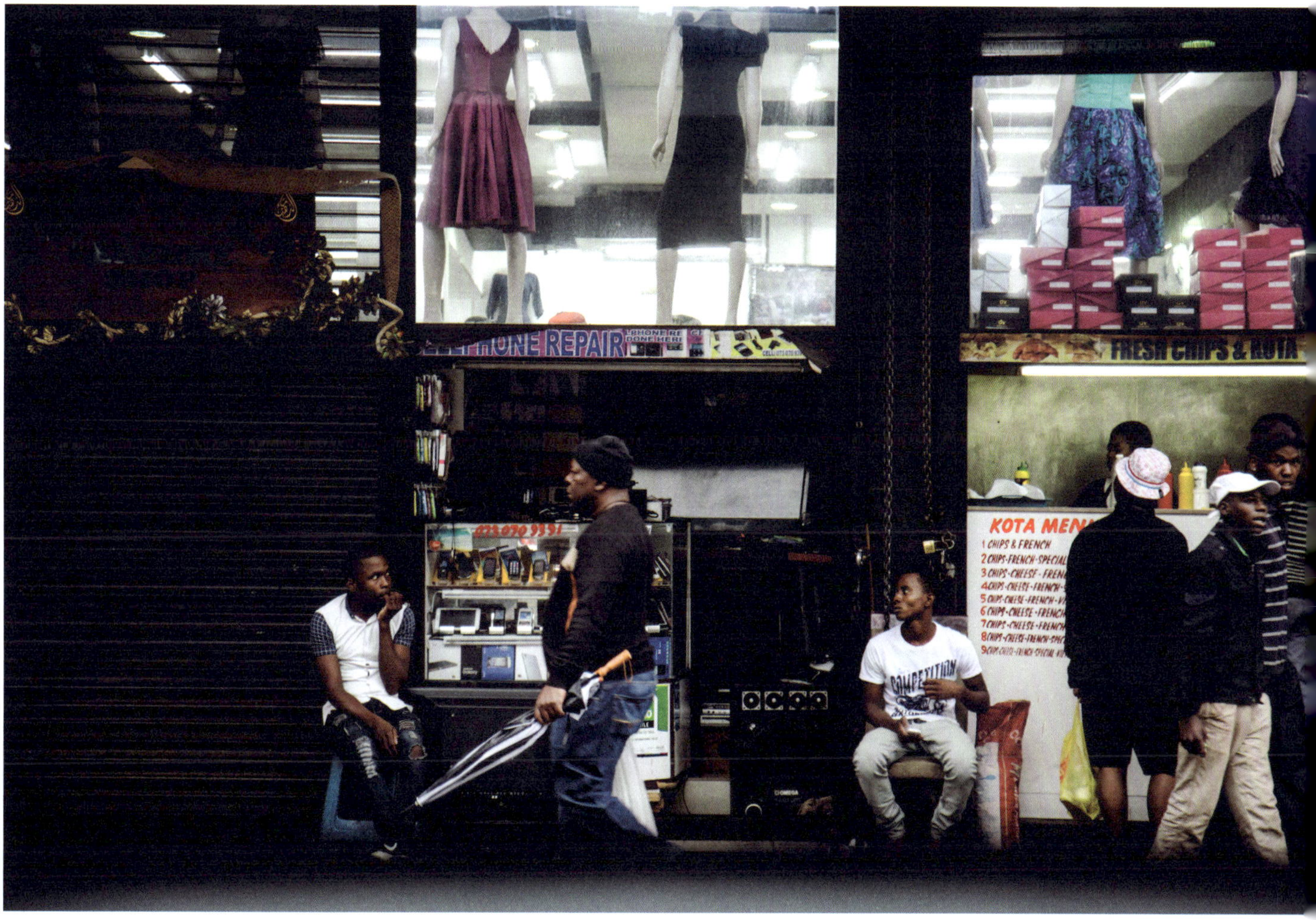
FRESH CHIPS & KOTA
1 CHIPS & FRENCH

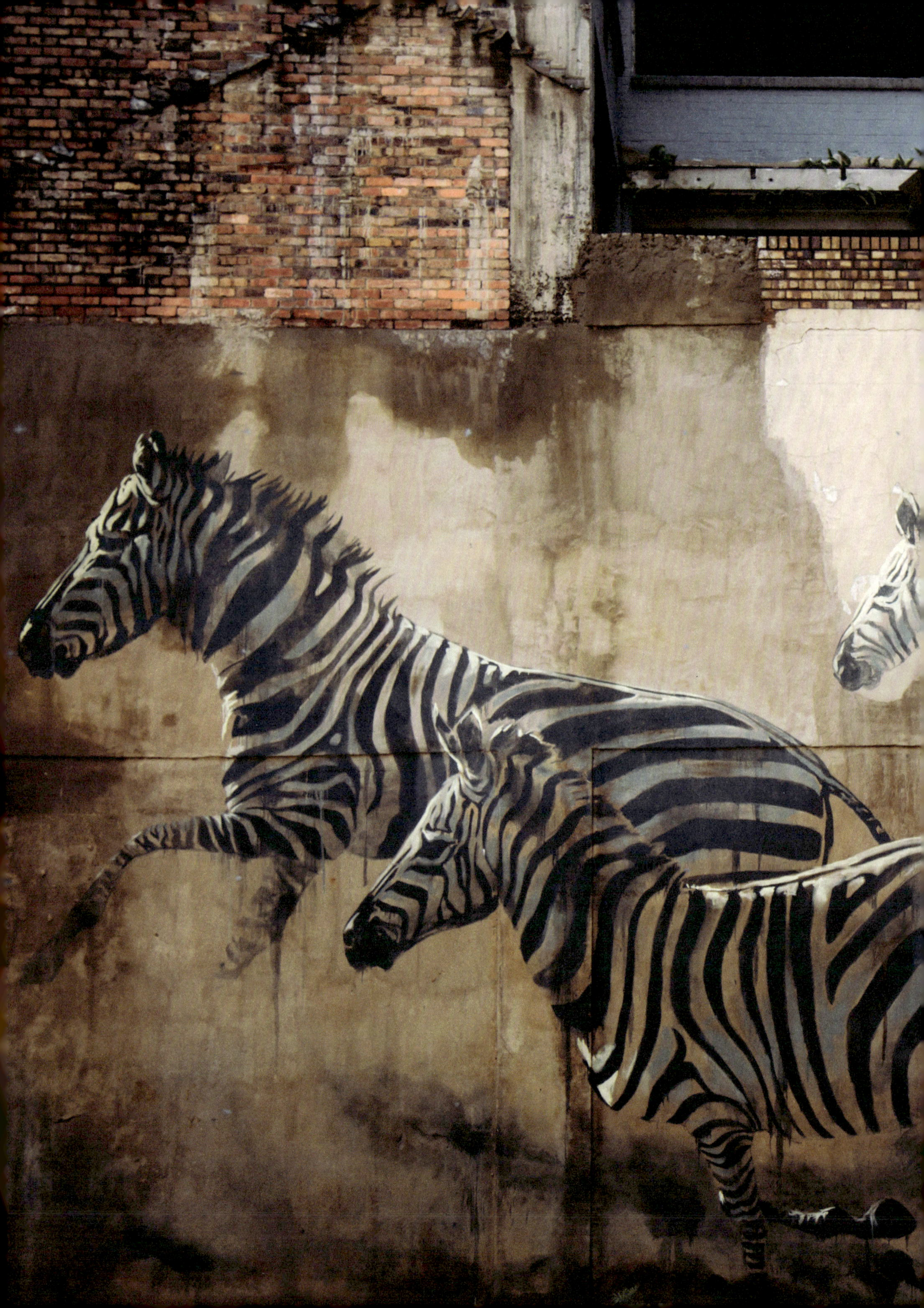

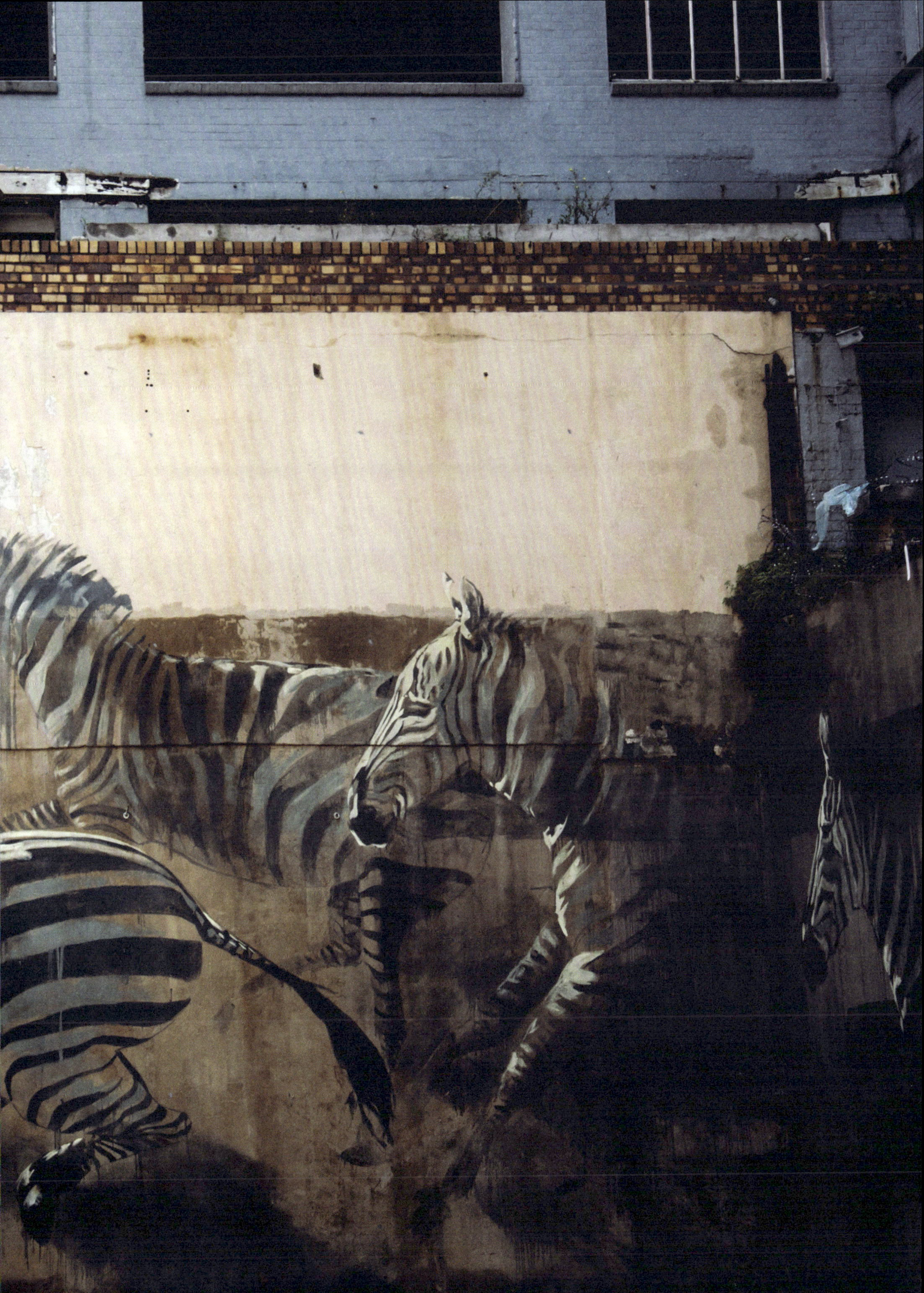

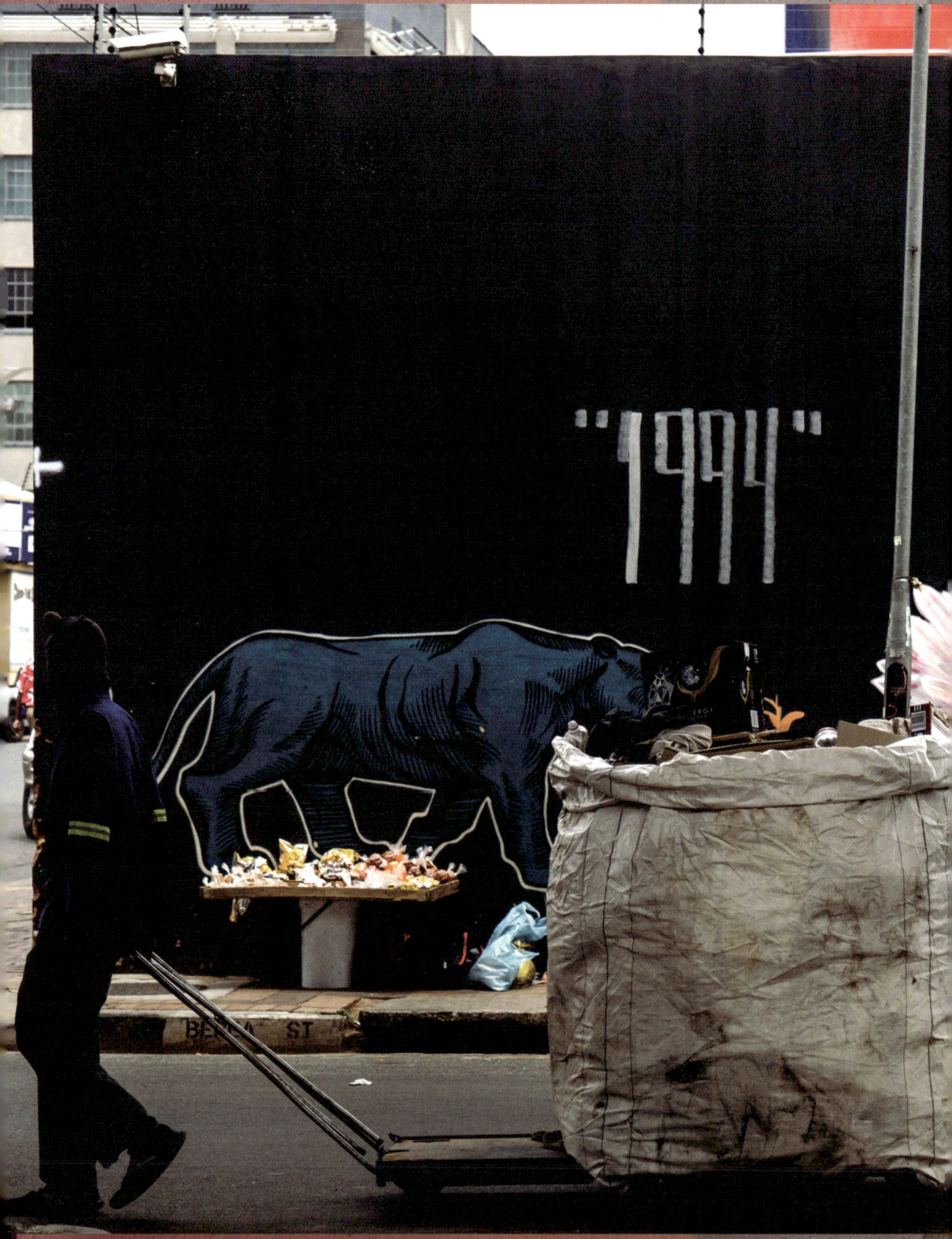
"1994"

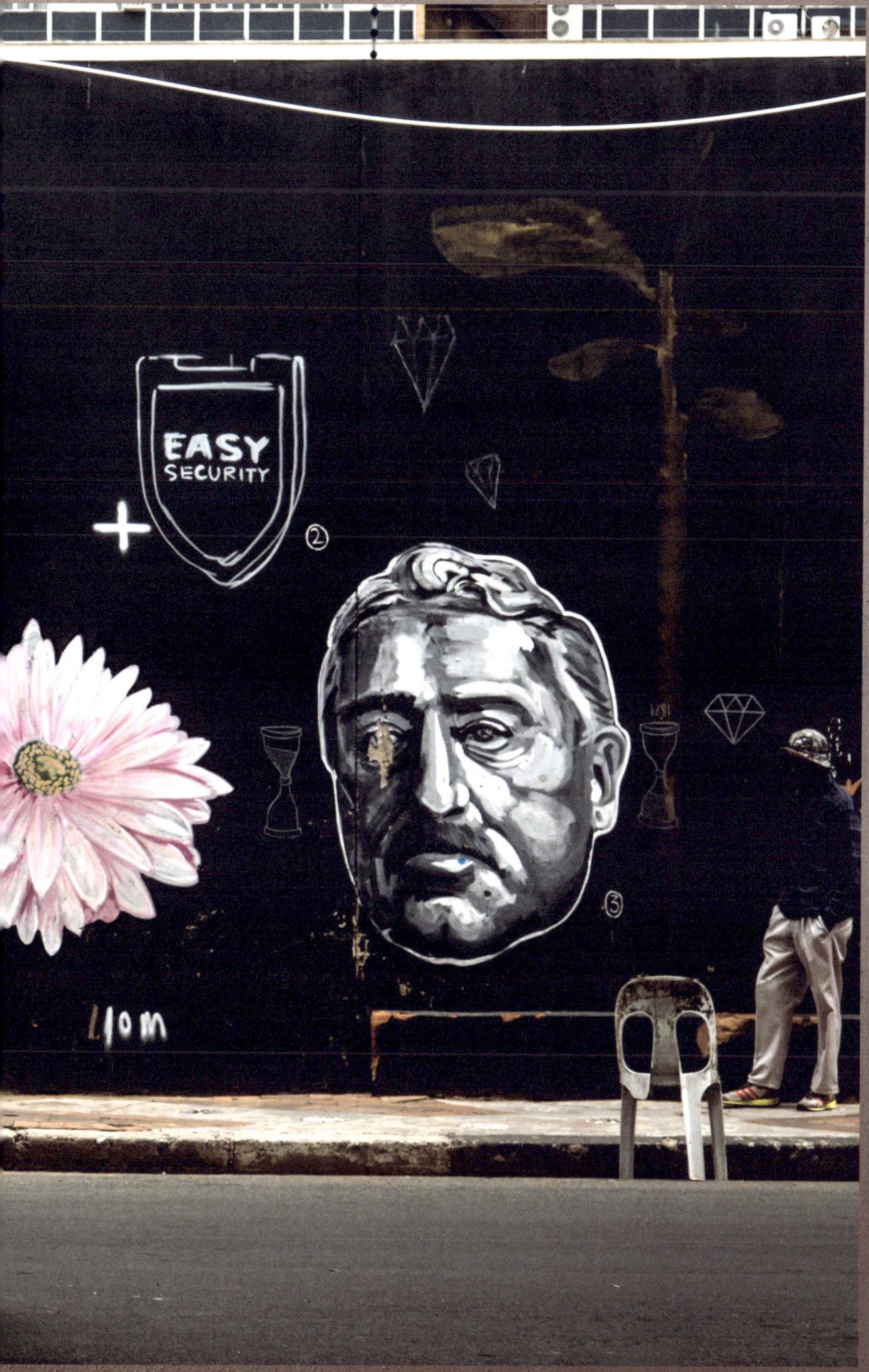
EASY
SECURITY

A large galvanised steel electricity pylon defines the somewhat messy view from the artist Roelof Petrus van Wyk's house, overlooking Johannesburg. The frame primarily consists of galvanised mild steel and glass. Raw stone masonry and piled stone structures provide an earthy match for the industrial aesthetic. Bright-coloured glass panels are a reference to De Stijl or Bauhaus, but also reflect the colourful sixties and seventies style high-rise buildings in Johannesburg's inner city.

Roelof originally trained as an architect. He embarked on this project together with his friend and fellow architect Karlien Thomashoff. As they come from the same cultural background the design process was a very smooth one. The biggest challenge was building the structure without using traditional brick and mortar and, in Roelof's words, 'unlearning to think traditionally'.

Ordinary materials, such as simple concrete slabs, are interpreted in a playful manner, acquiring a different aesthetic value in their new context. The long narrow building consists of one single, open-plan space that extends towards the view, with the kitchen at one end and the studio at the other. The living area, workspaces and bedroom are spread out across the rest of the building. There are hardly any walls. By making clever use of the different levels, Roelof has created spaces with some sense of privacy.

The furniture doesn't have a fixed place. Everything changes continuously, depending on Roelof's mood and functional needs. The same goes for the art that is very much present around the house. Art is Roelof's passion. Art objects are scattered throughout the house, propped up on a sideboard or simply placed on the floor. Although the house is large, Roelof's art collection is much larger. He only has room to showcase a small selection. The rest is stored in boxes or stacked against the walls, waiting for an opportunity to be displayed.

Roelof enjoys the openness and the great view of his home, which allows him to experience the different seasons in all their glory, including the majestic thunder- and rainstorms that occasionally tear through his beloved city.

Roelof is fascinated by Johannesburg. By its beauty, but also by its complexity and messiness. In fact, his house is in many ways inspired by this metropolis.

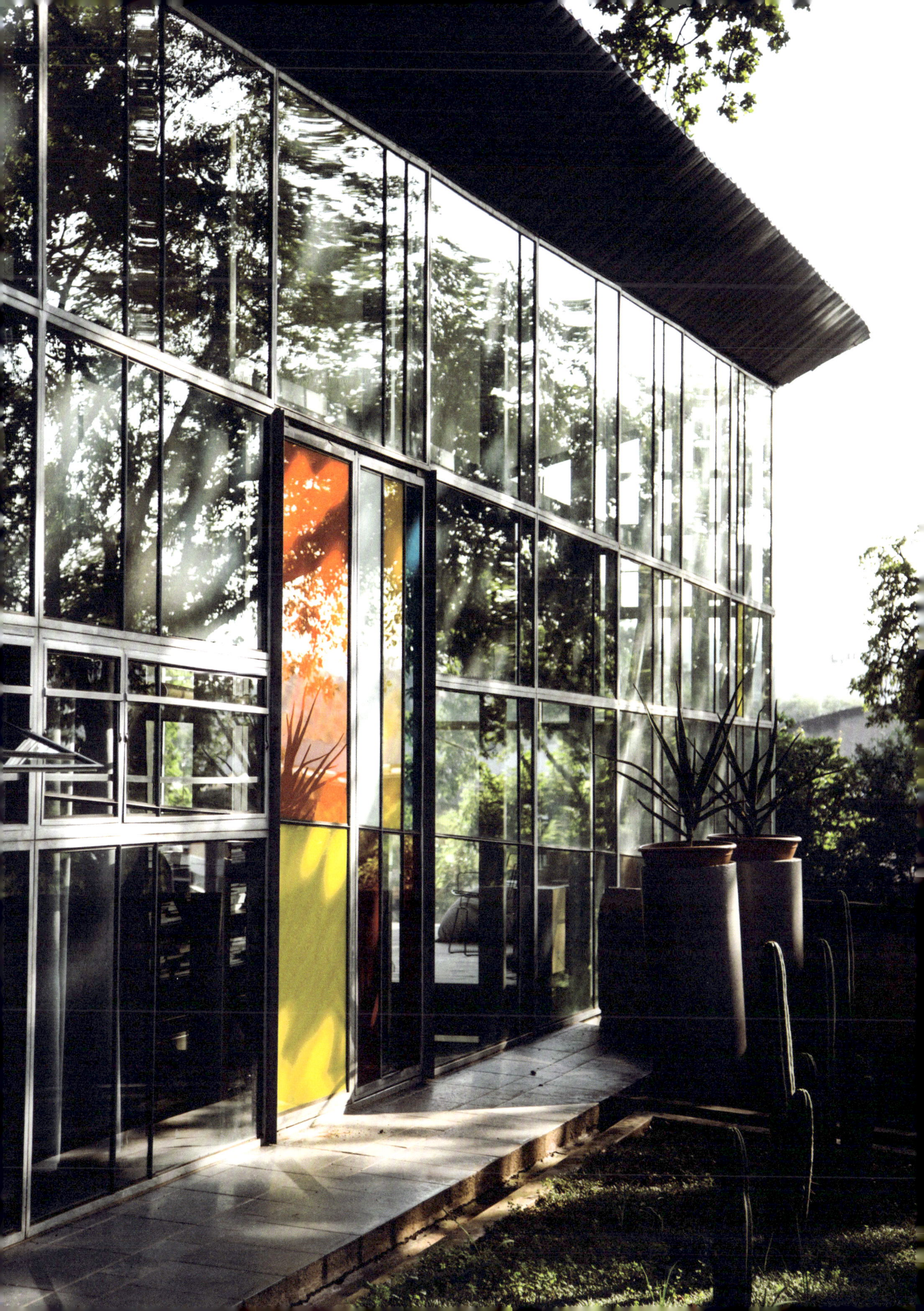

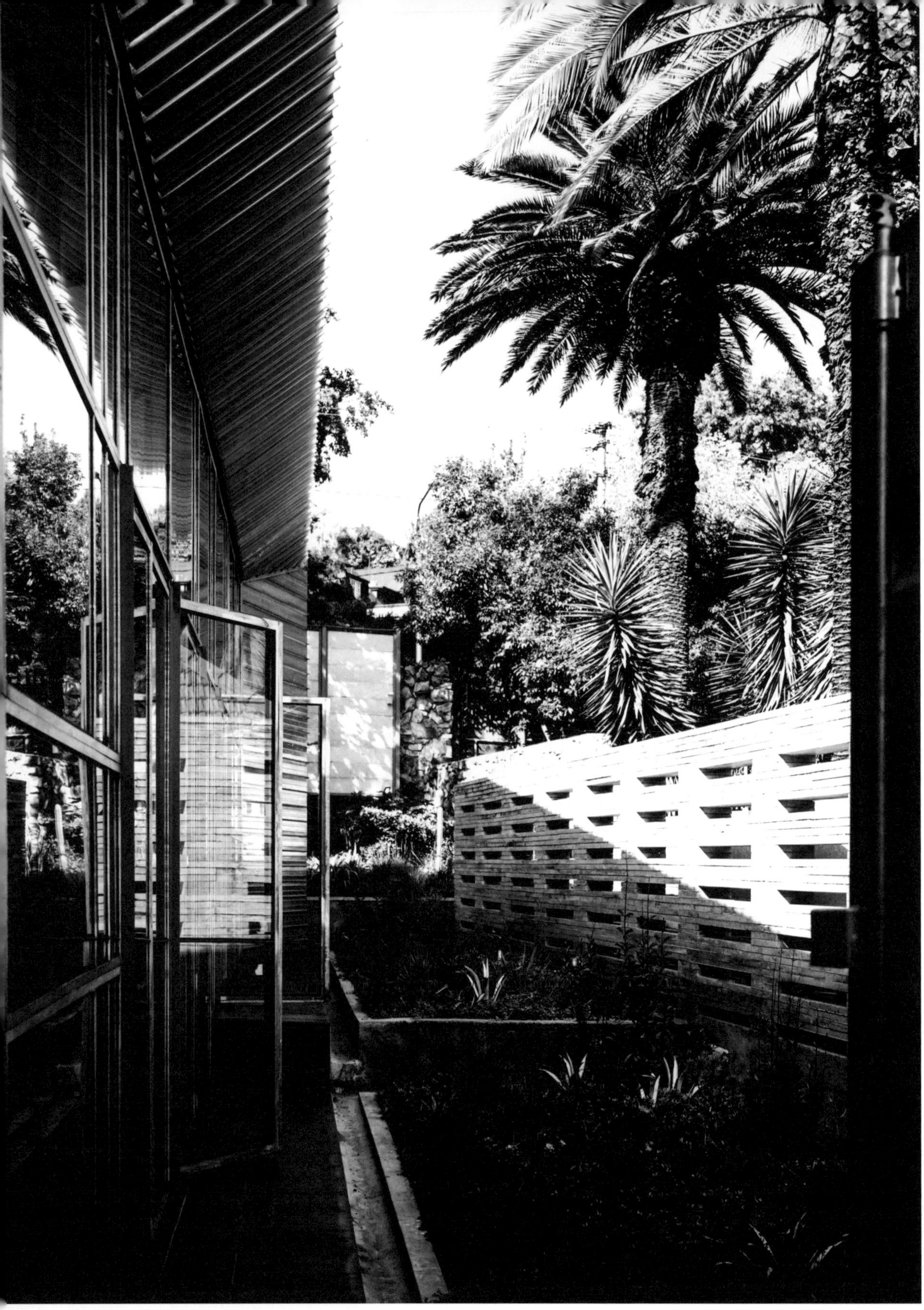

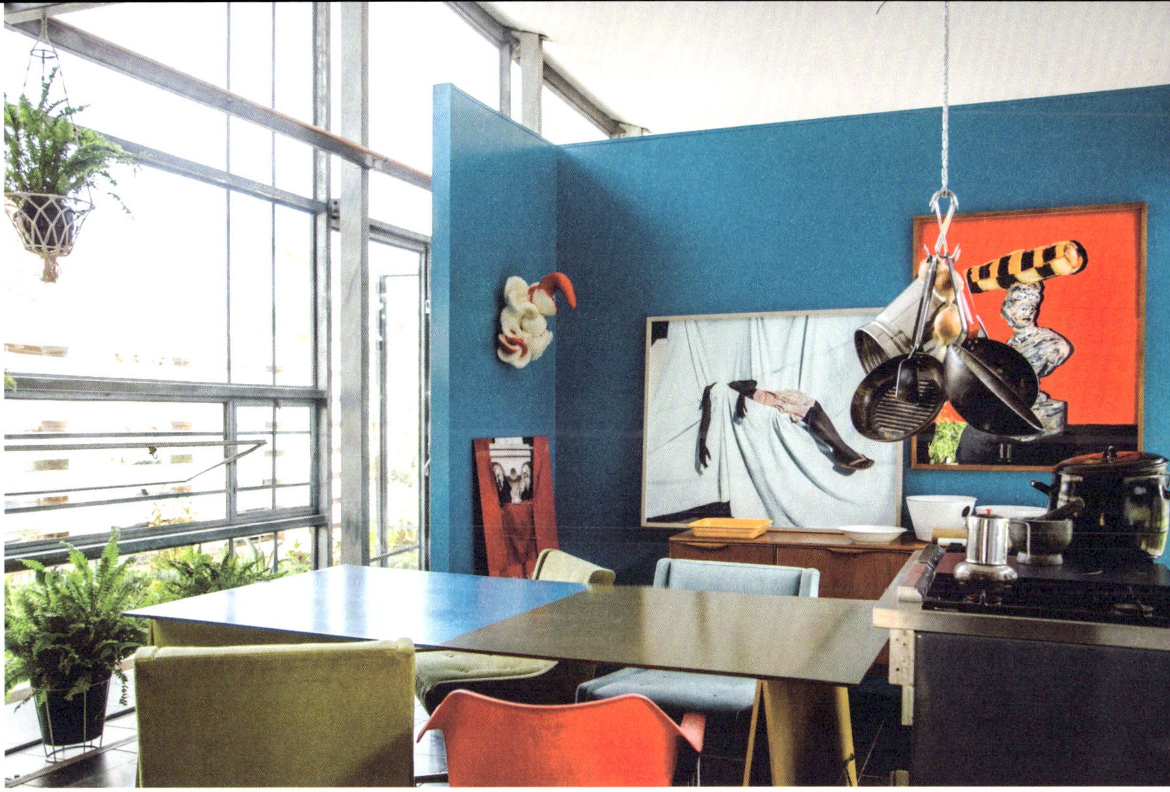

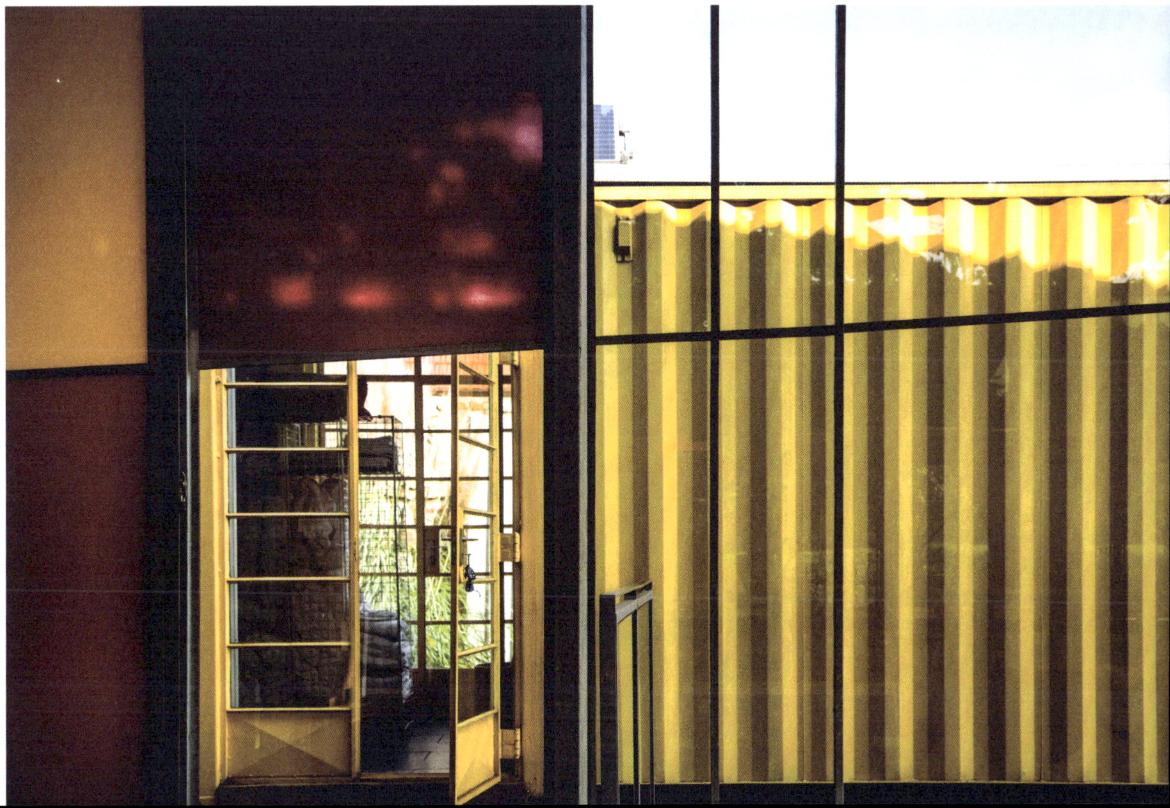

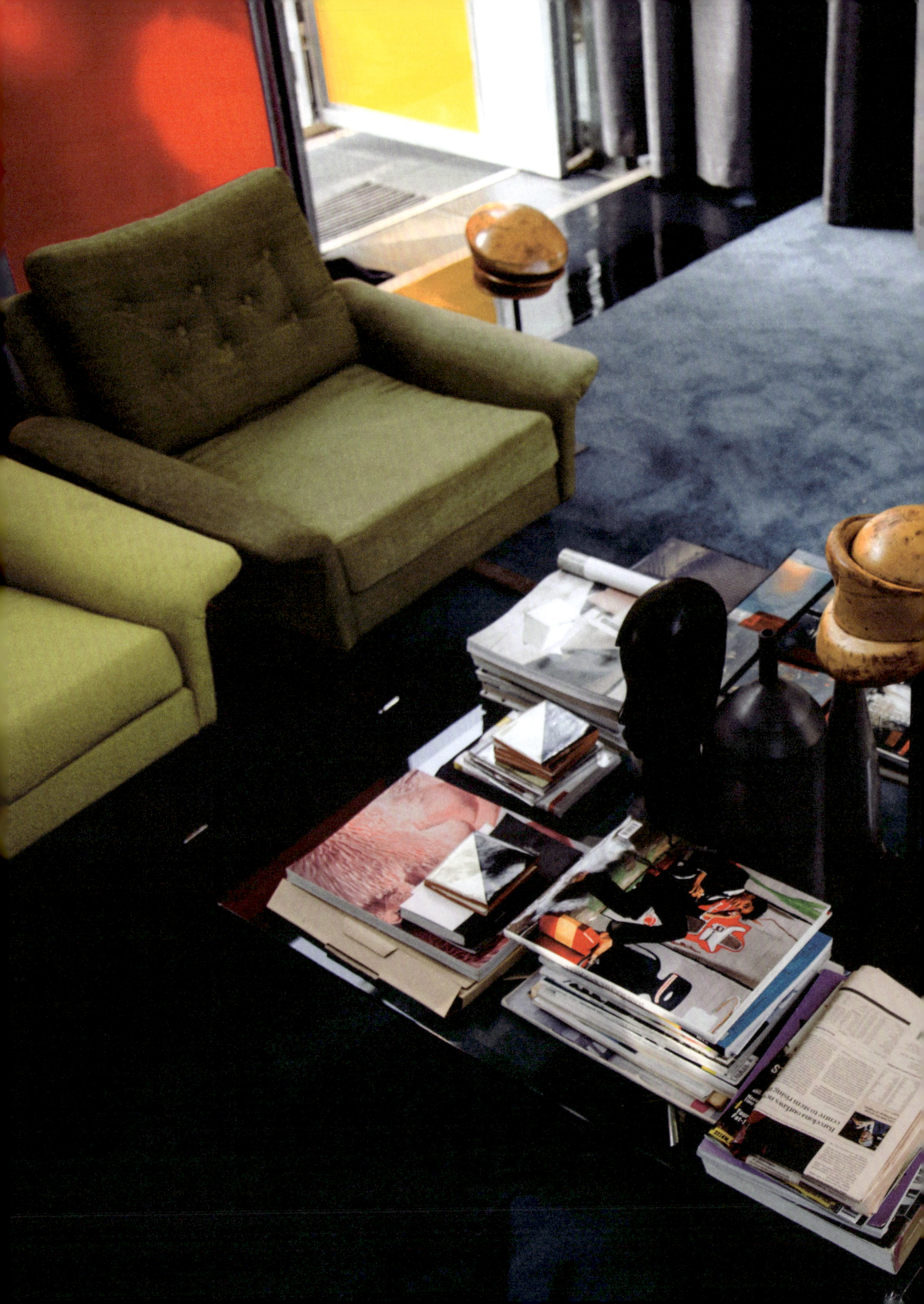

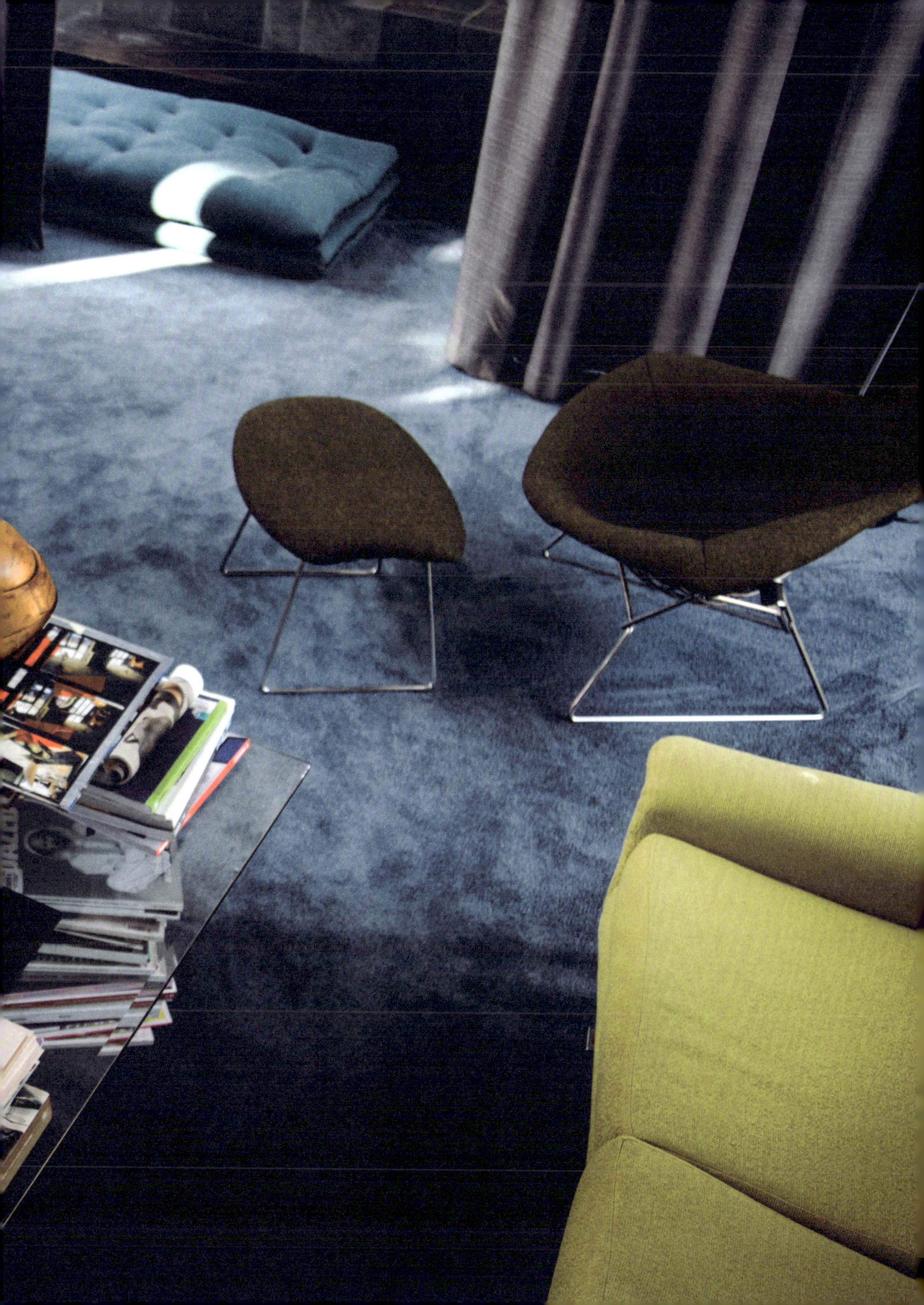

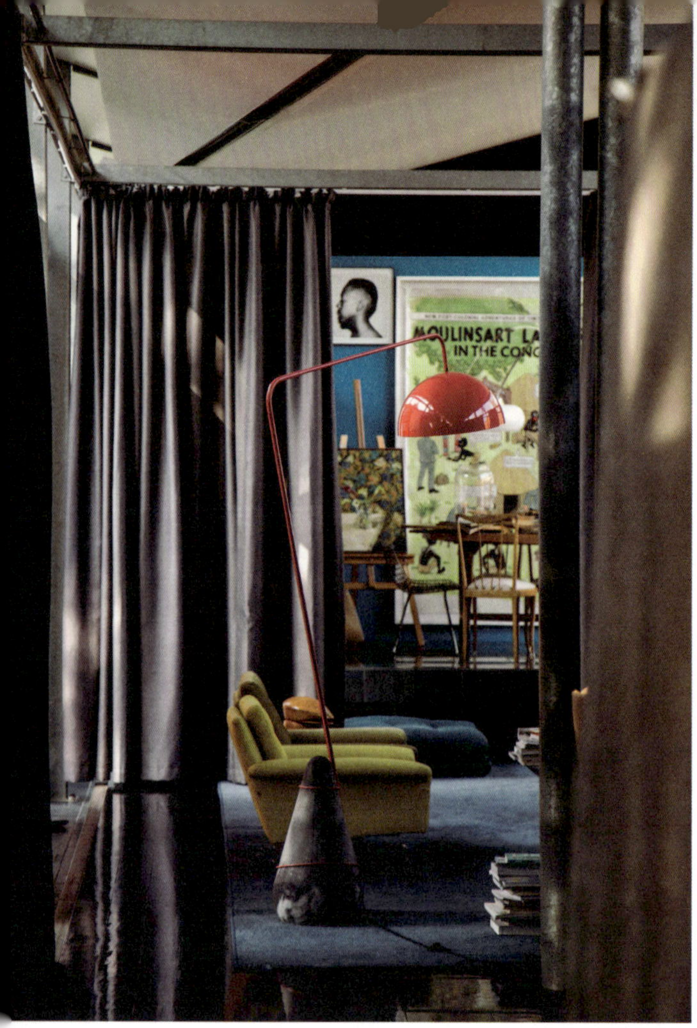
MOULINSART

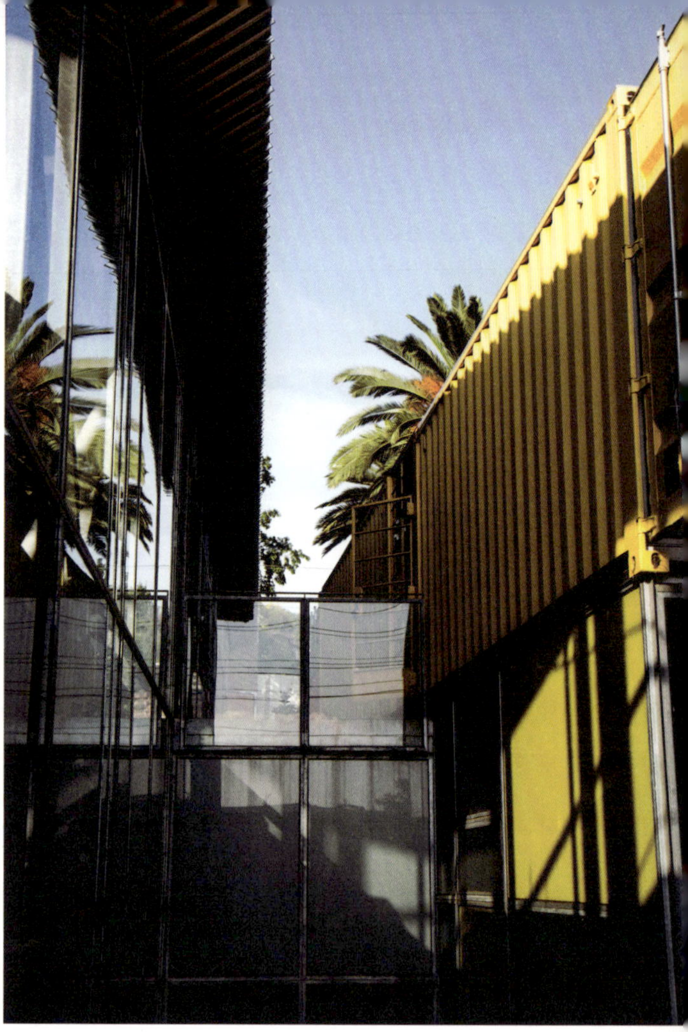

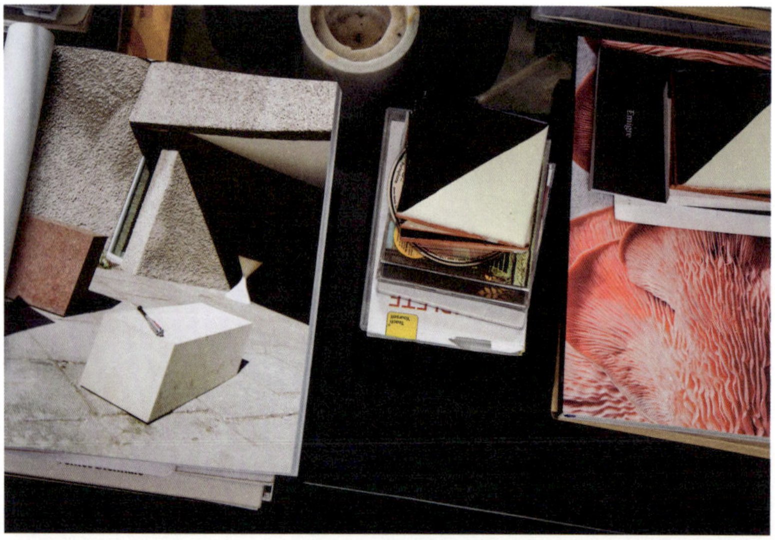

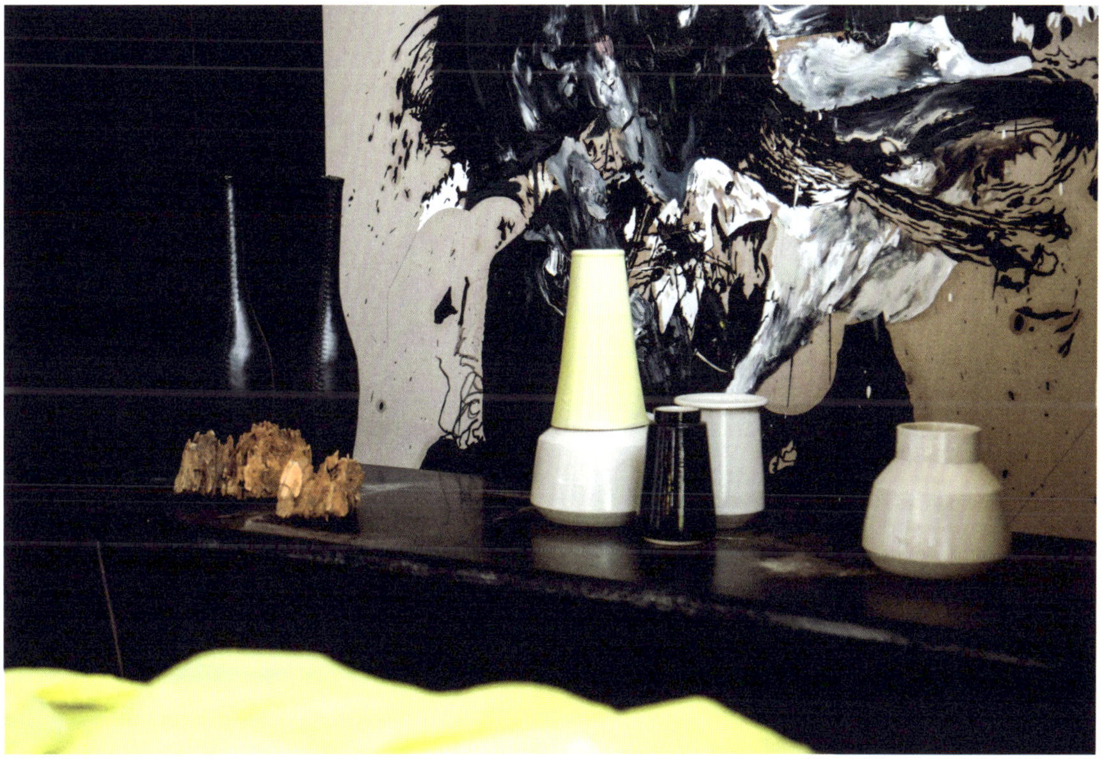

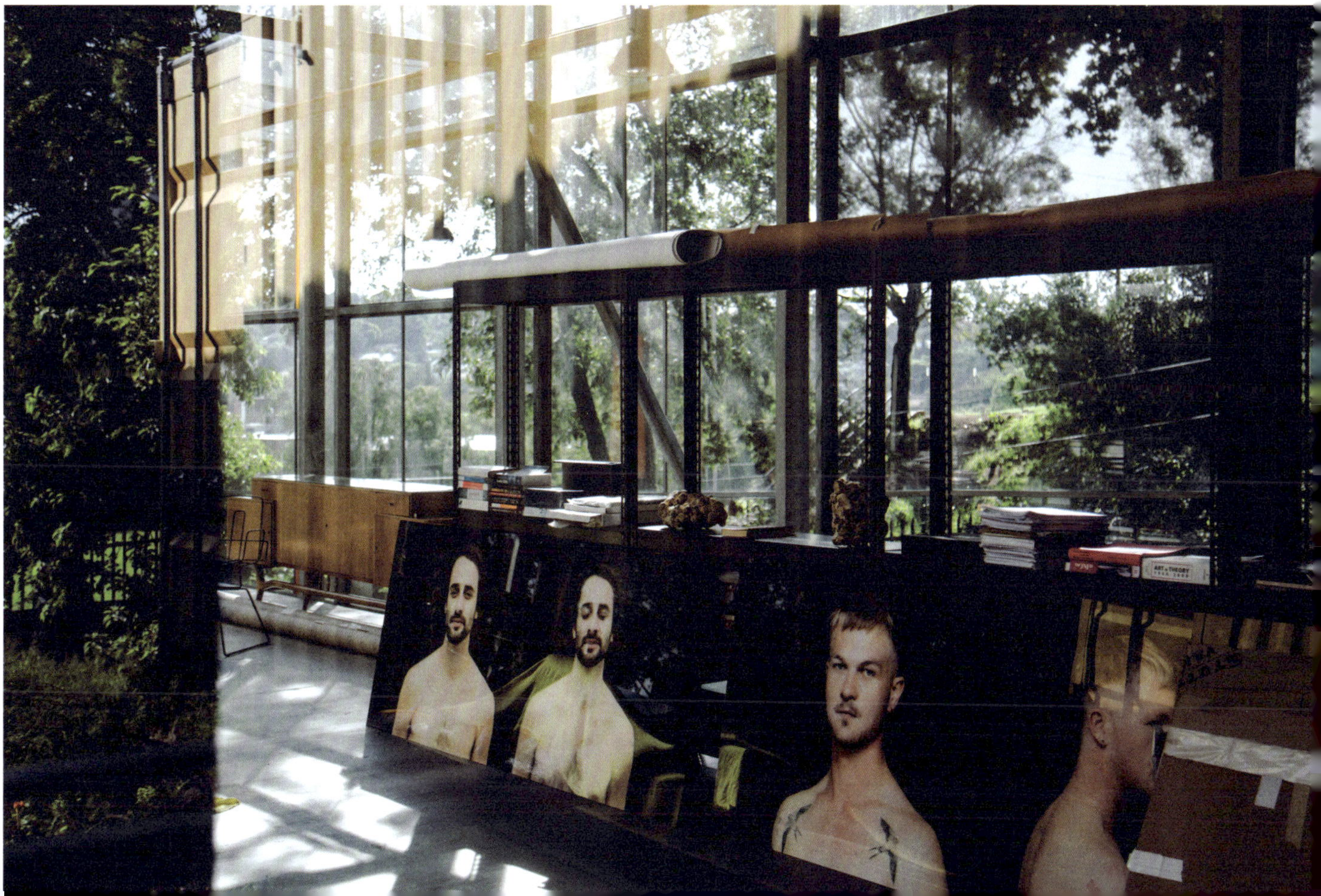
ART & THEORY

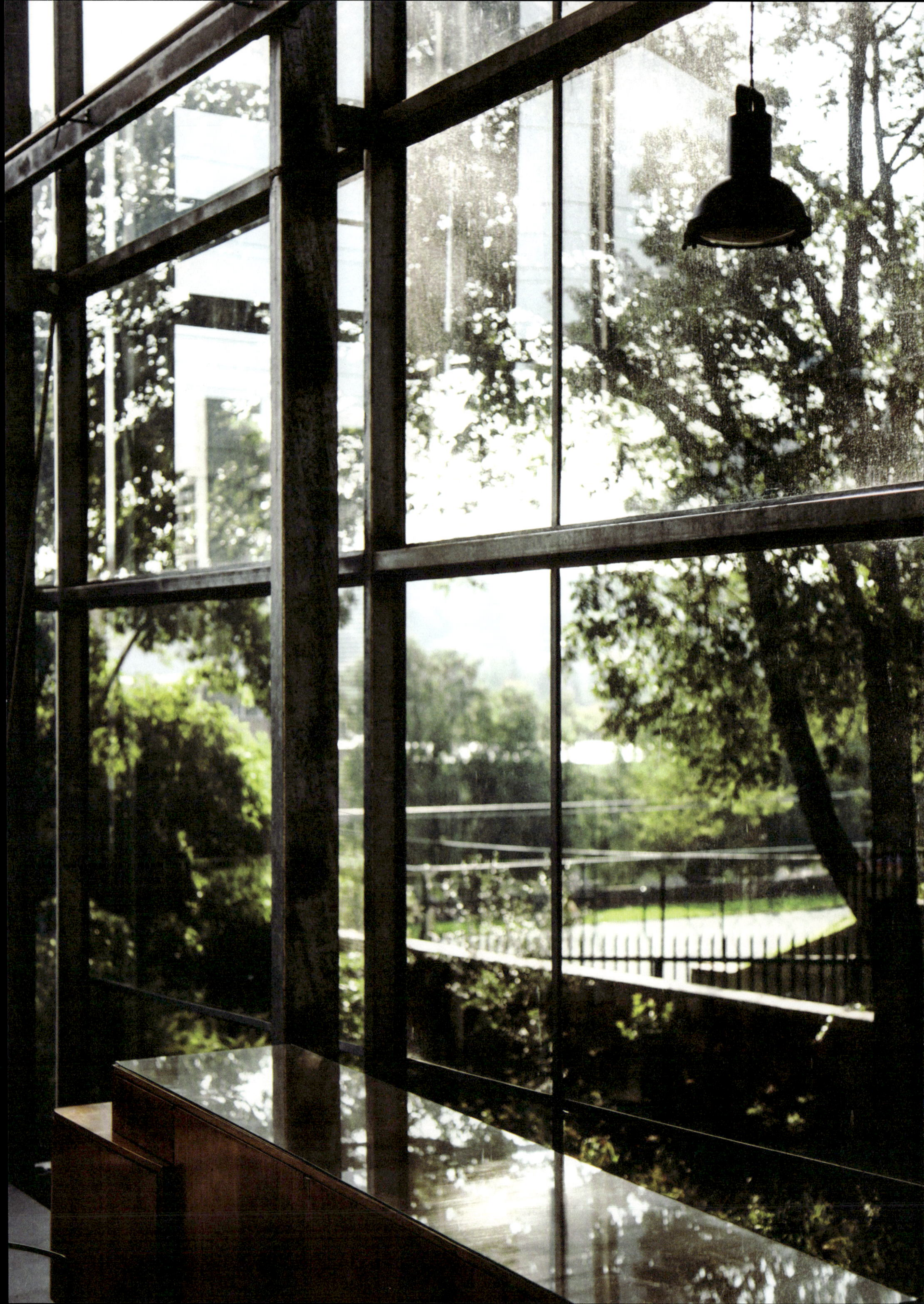

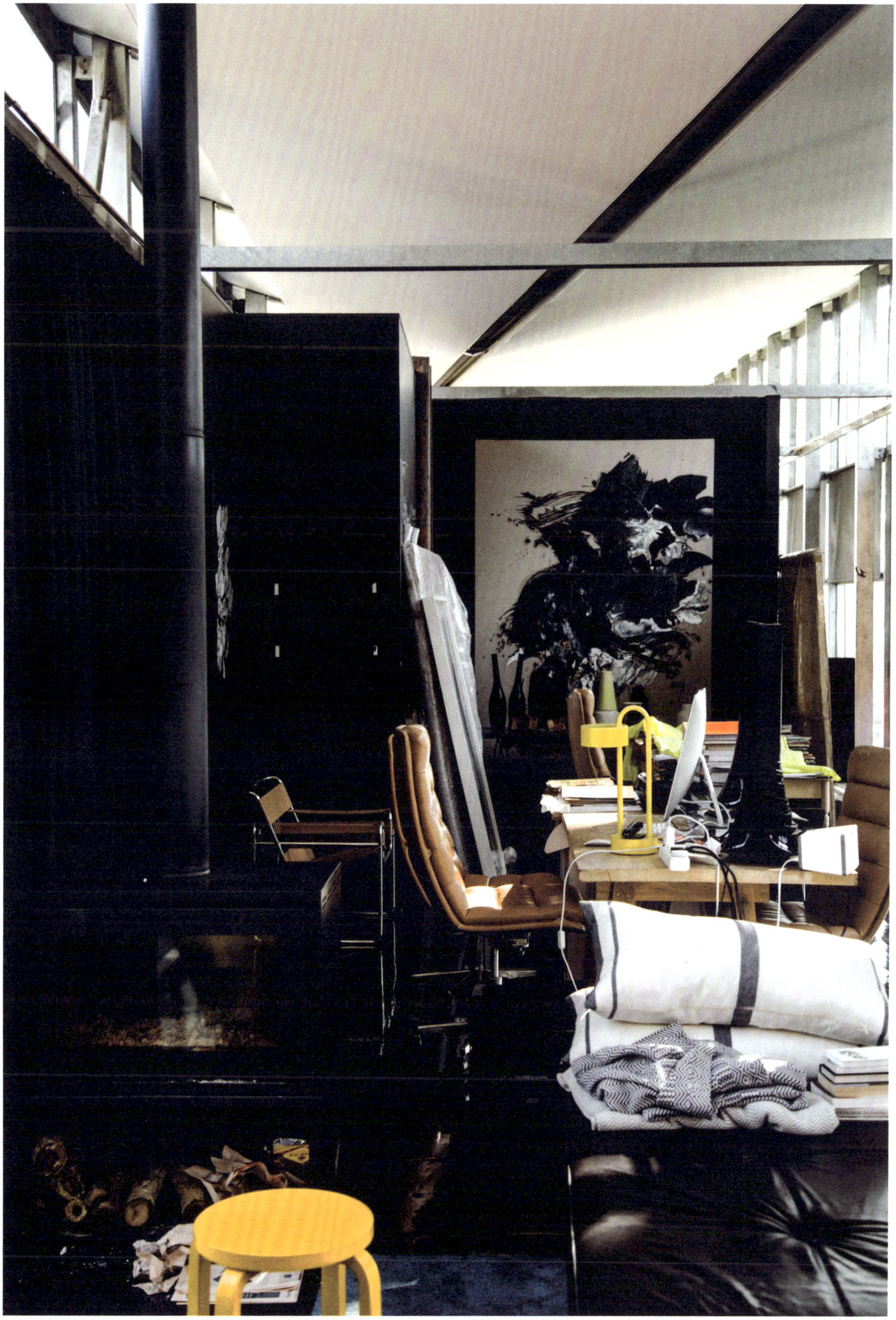

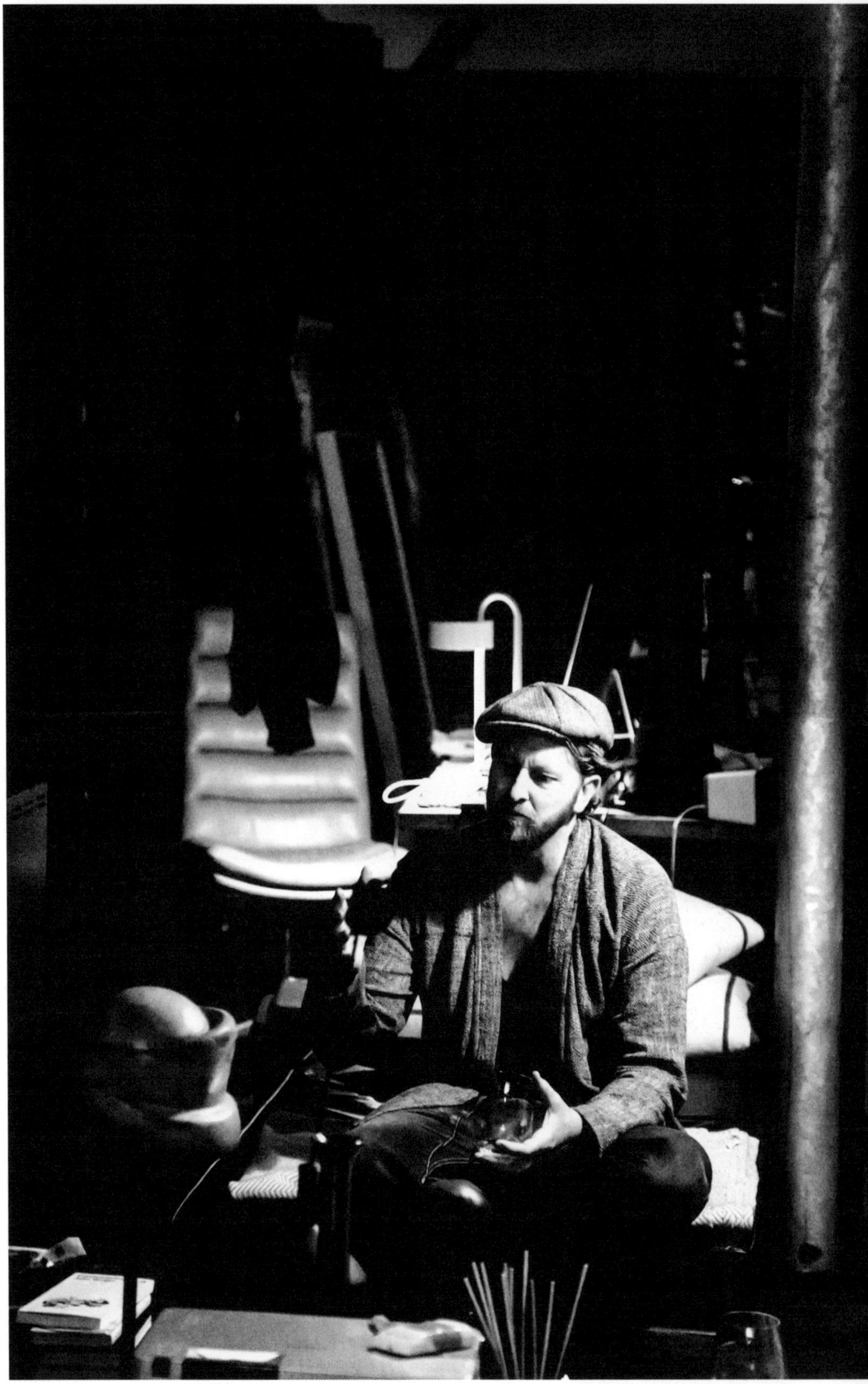

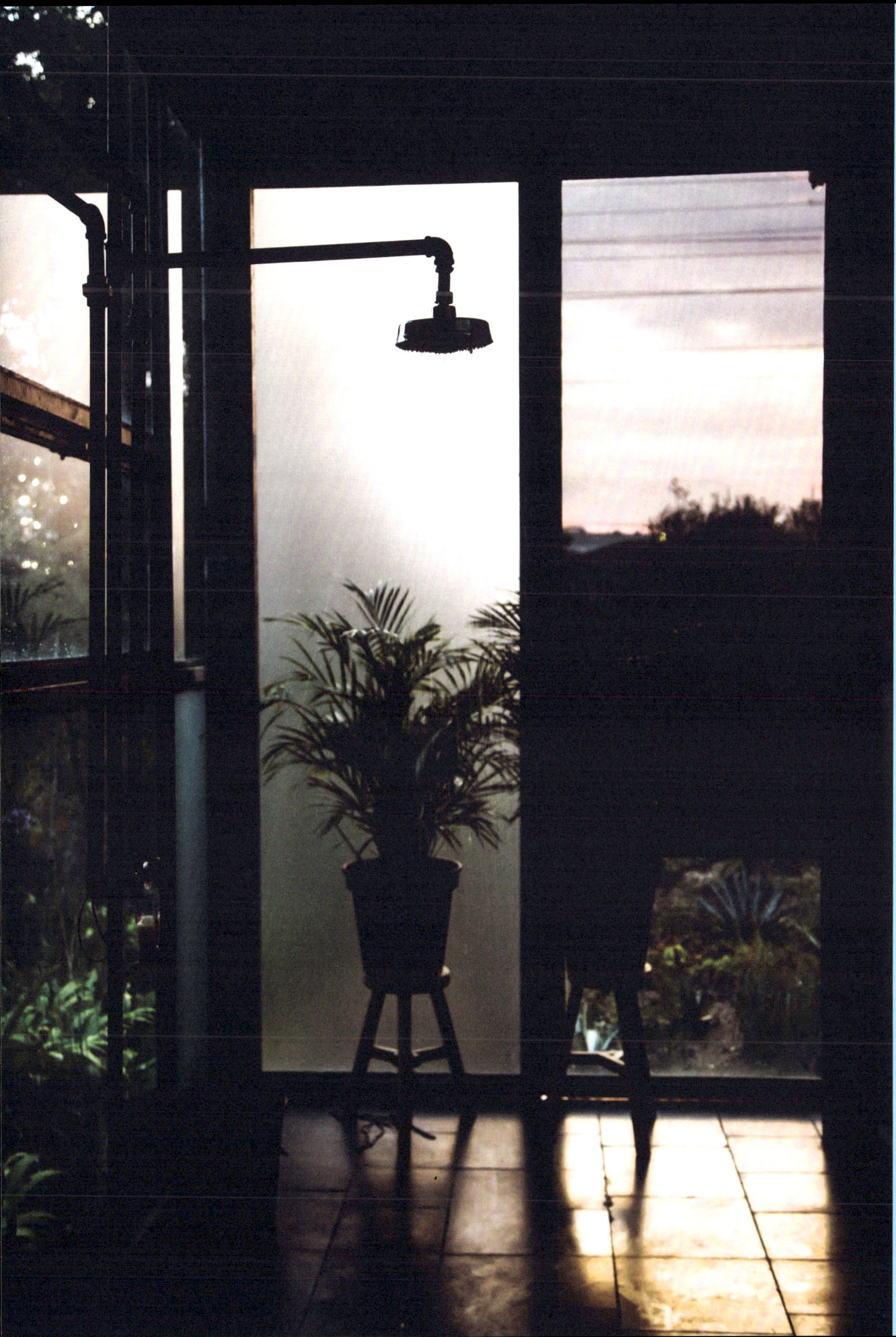

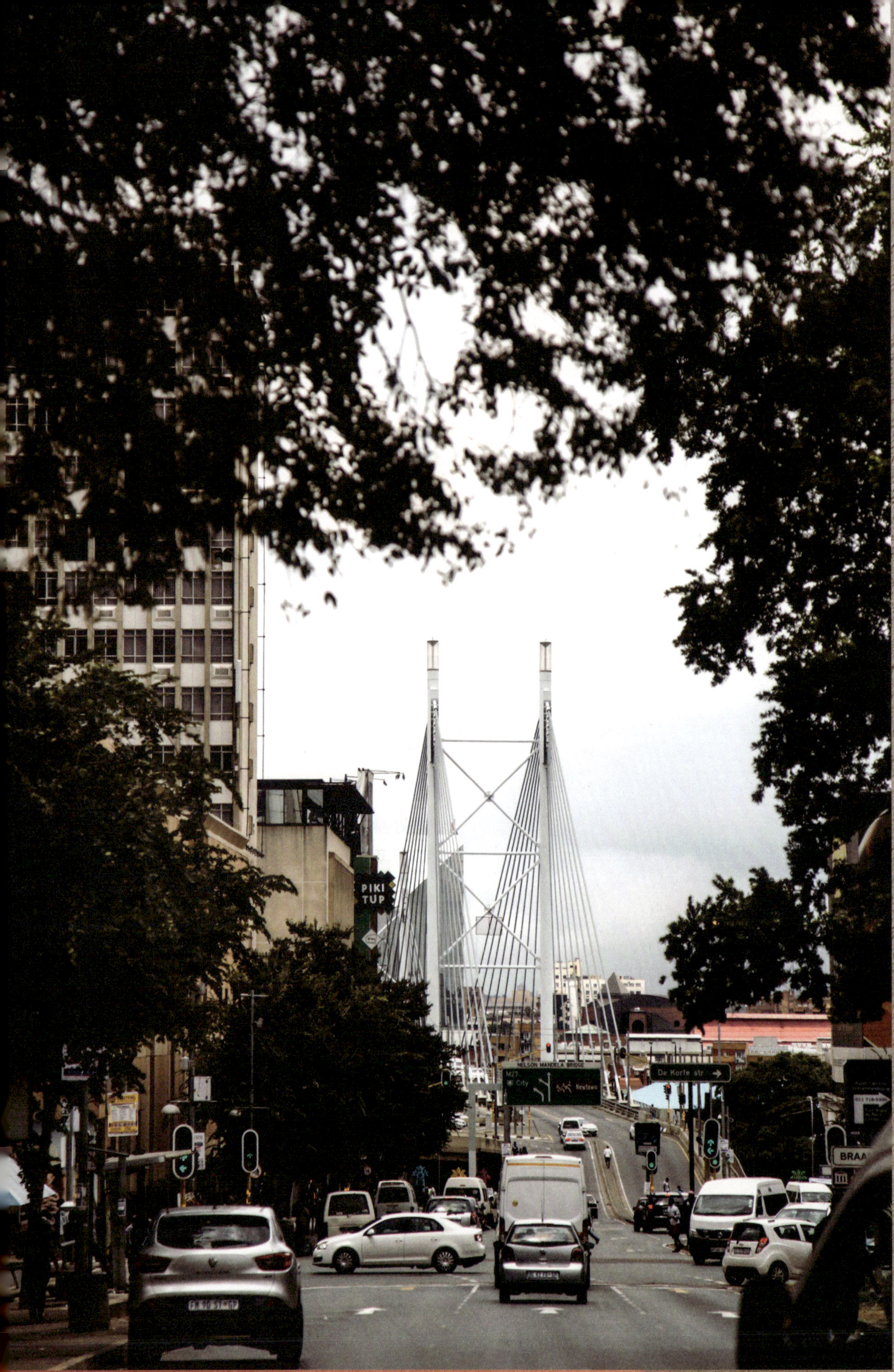
PIKI
TUP
NELSON MANDELA BRIDGE
M27
City
Newtown
De Korte str

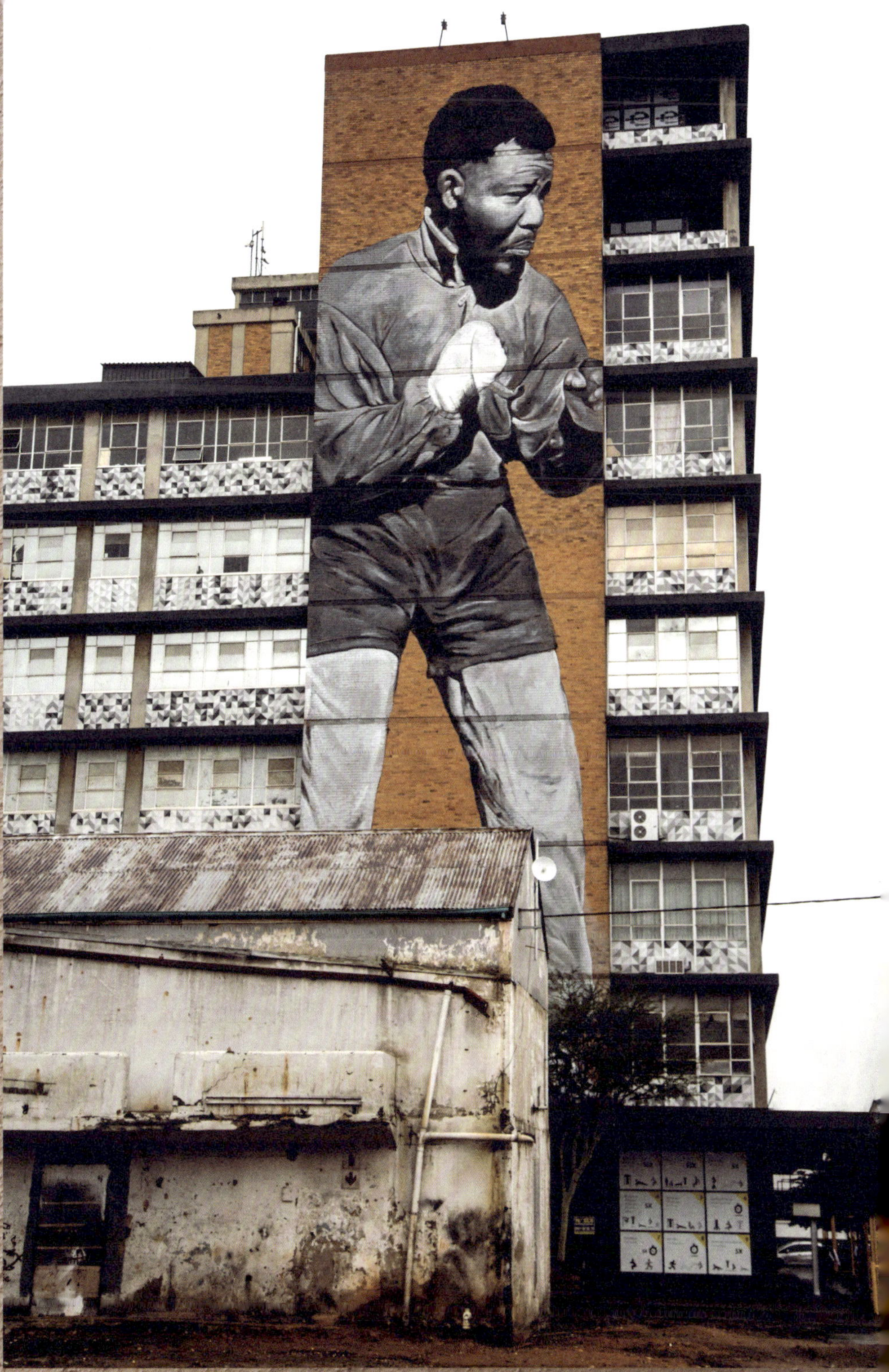

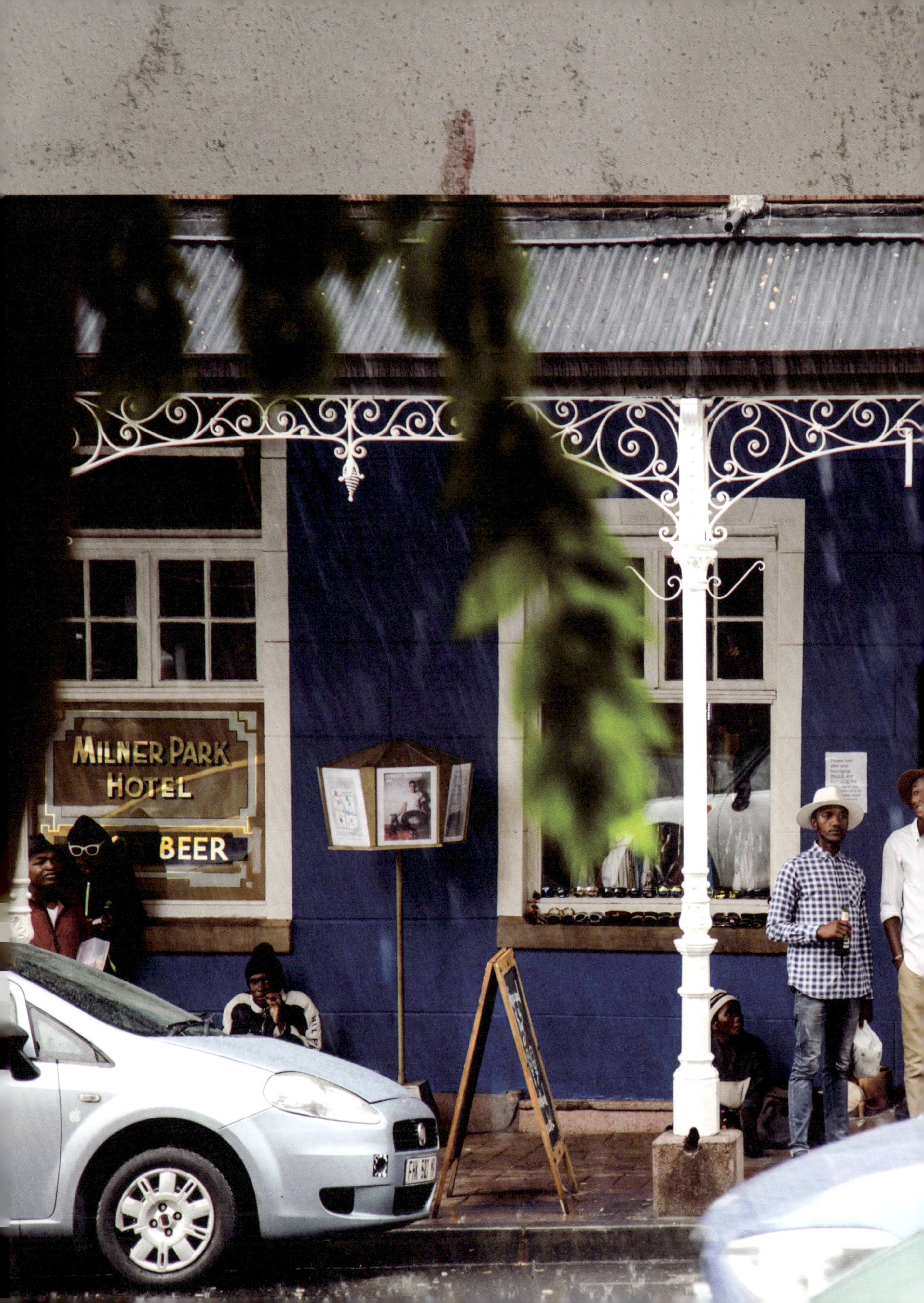
MILNER PARK
HOTEL
BEER

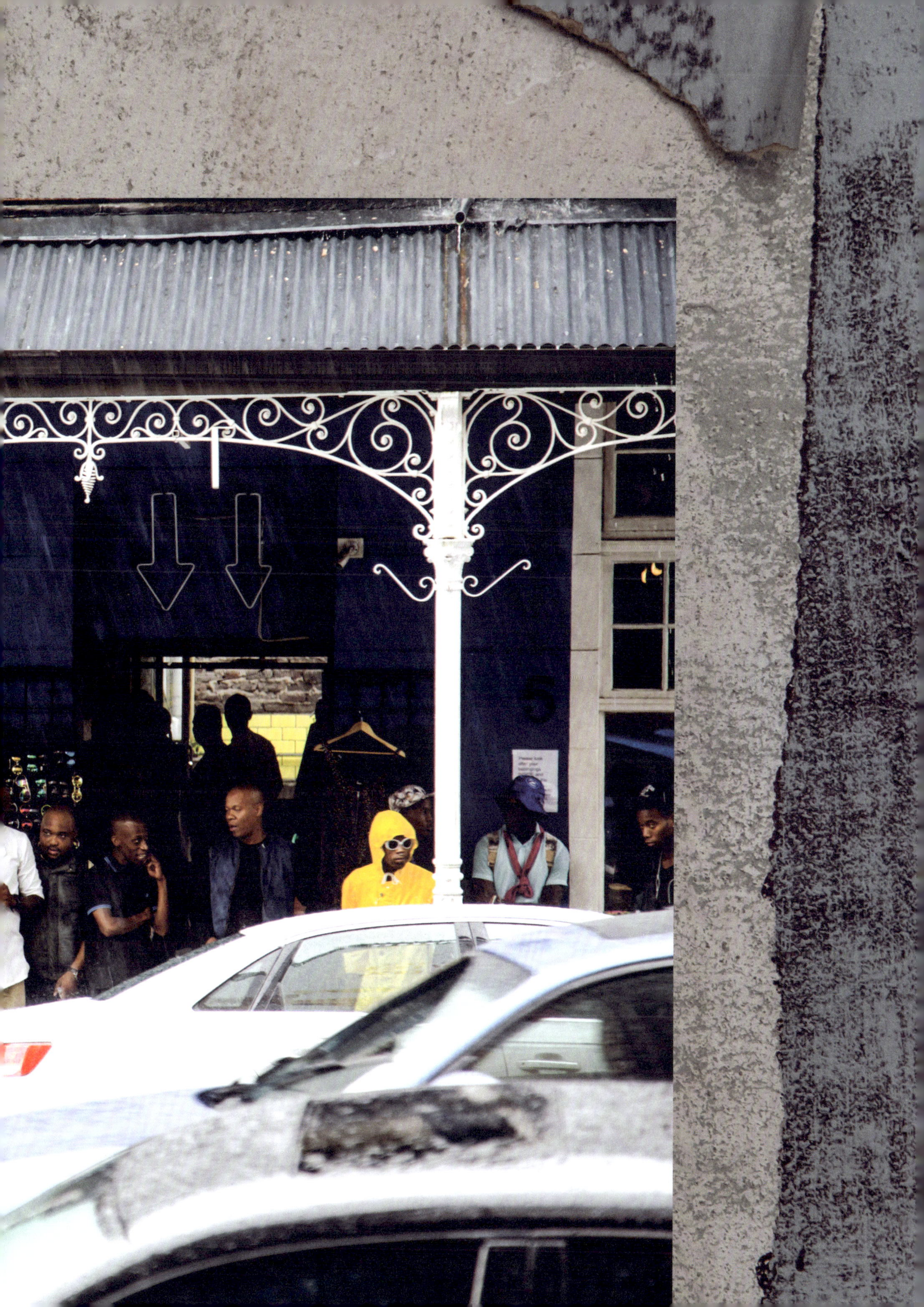

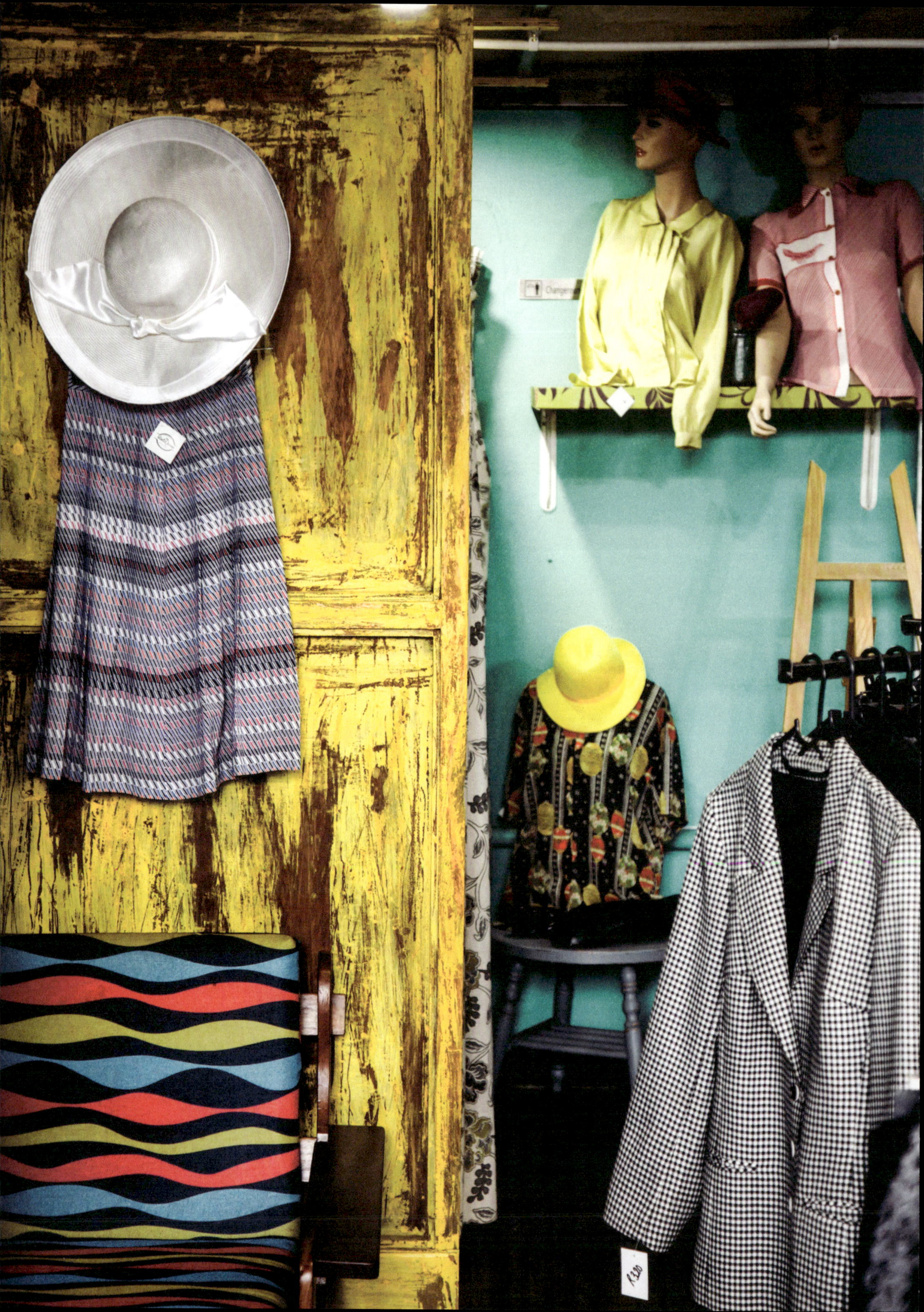

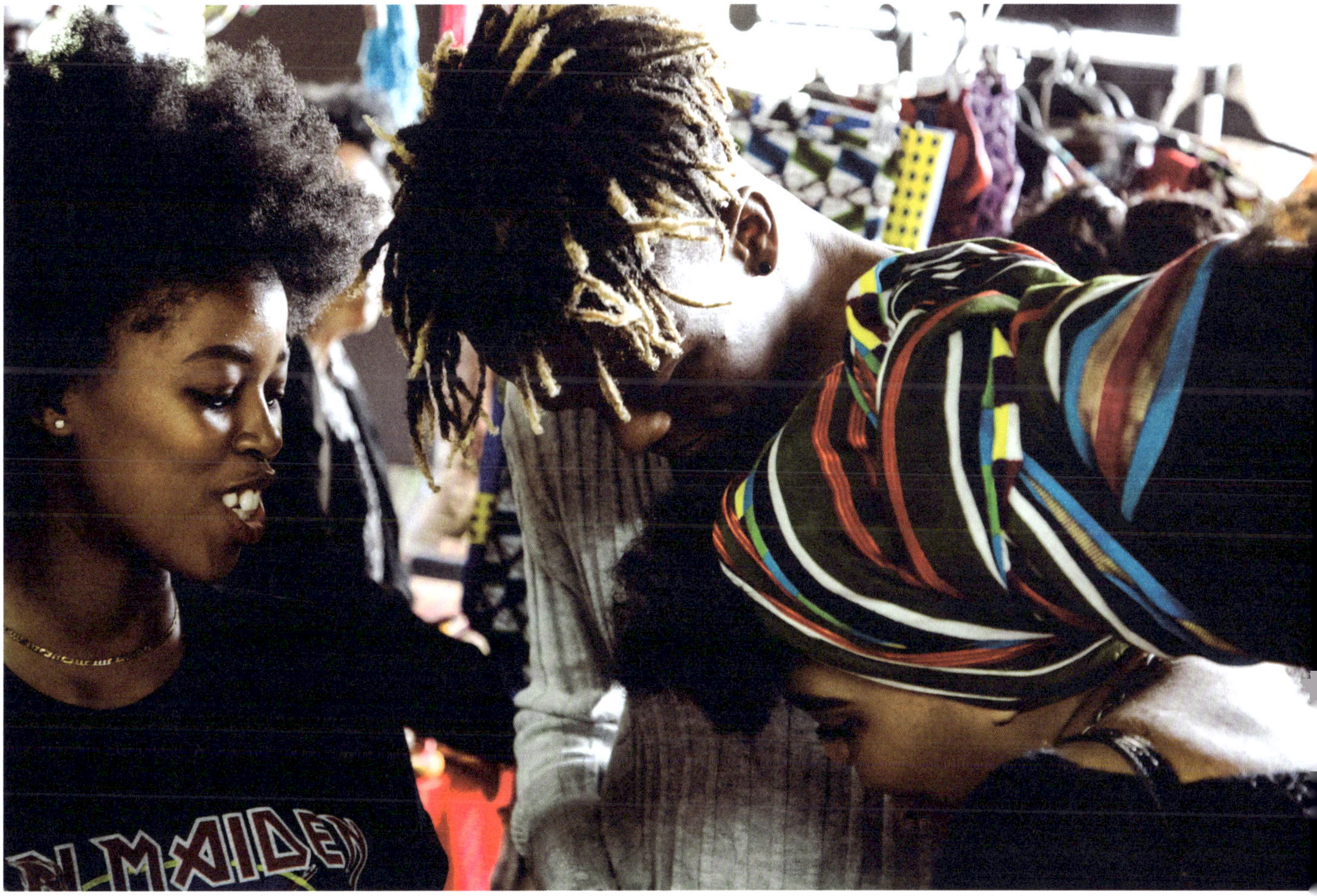

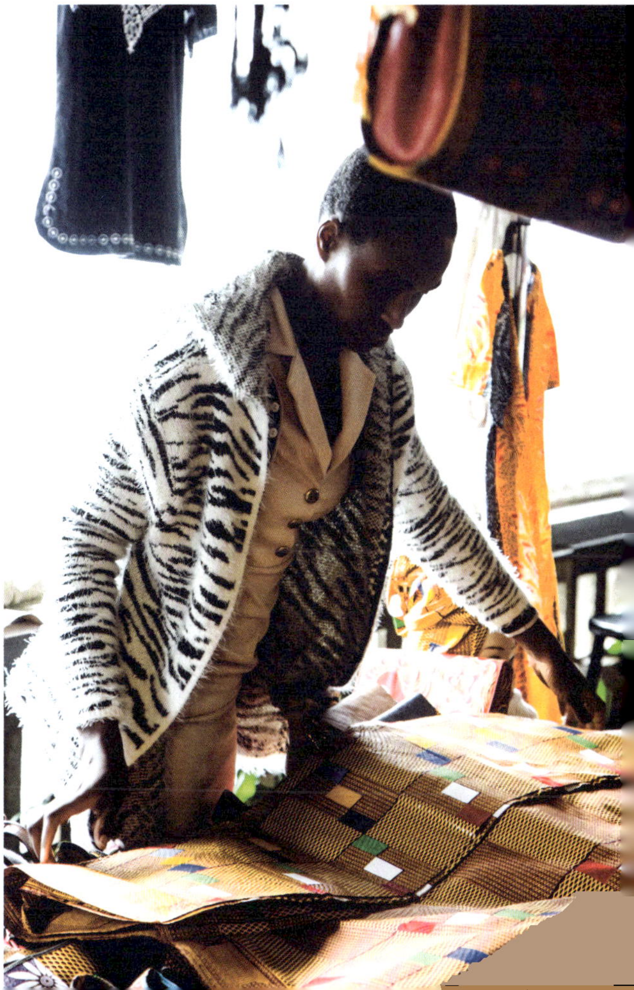

Daring style

The colourful dress styles you see everywhere on the streets of Johannesburg are a feast for the eyes. People dress according to the latest fashion trends, but style them in their own unique way. The African printed fabrics they integrate into their outfits make a daring fashion statement all on their own.

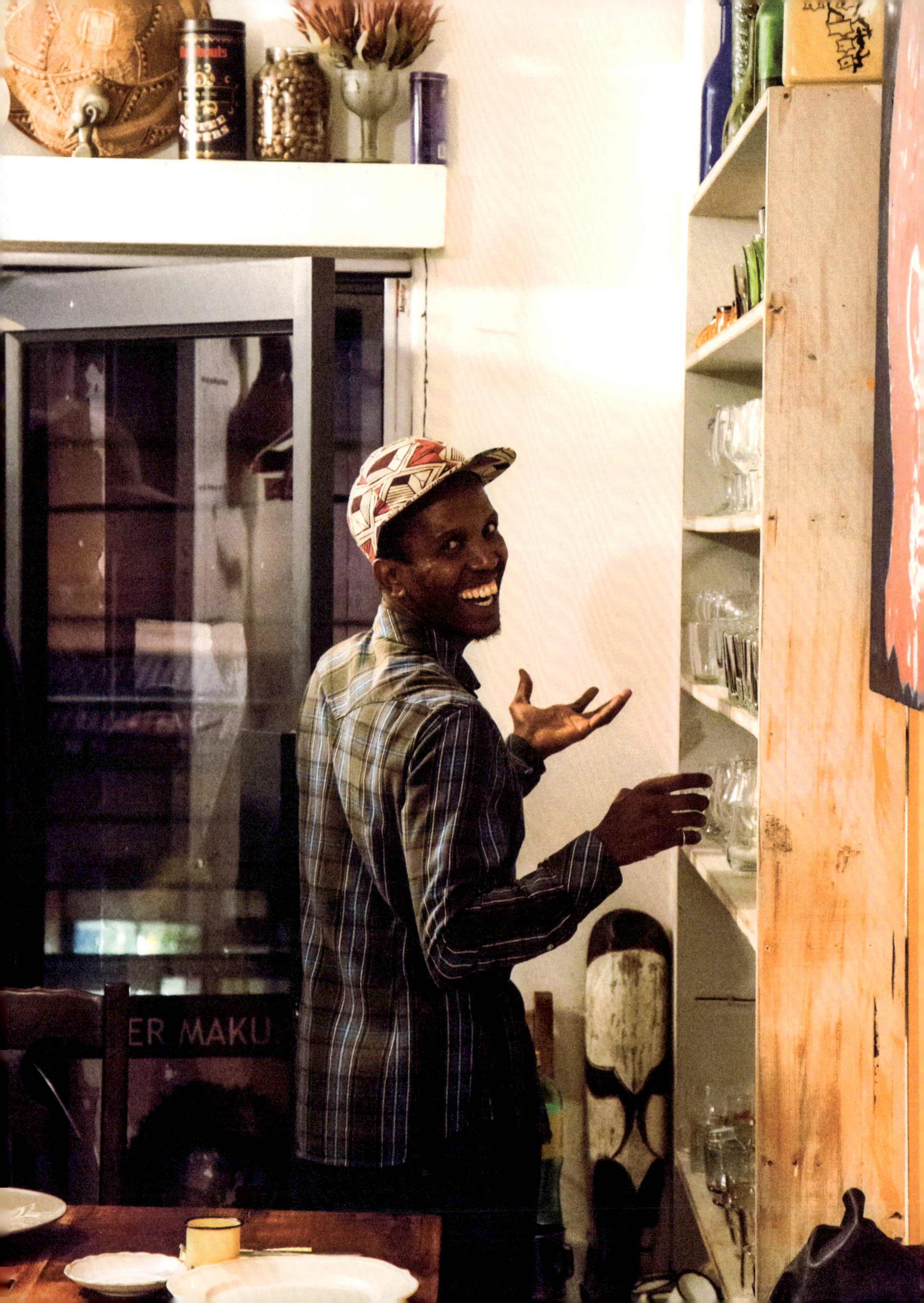
ER MAKU

Yeoville Dinner Club

Chef Sanza Sandile welcomes everyone at the long communal table in his restaurant. The compact place is on the first floor of a small business centre on Rockey Street. There is a balcony overlooking the lively street in this bustling neighbourhood. People from all over the continent have found a new home or business here. This 'pan-Africanism' is present in the various dishes that Sanza serves.

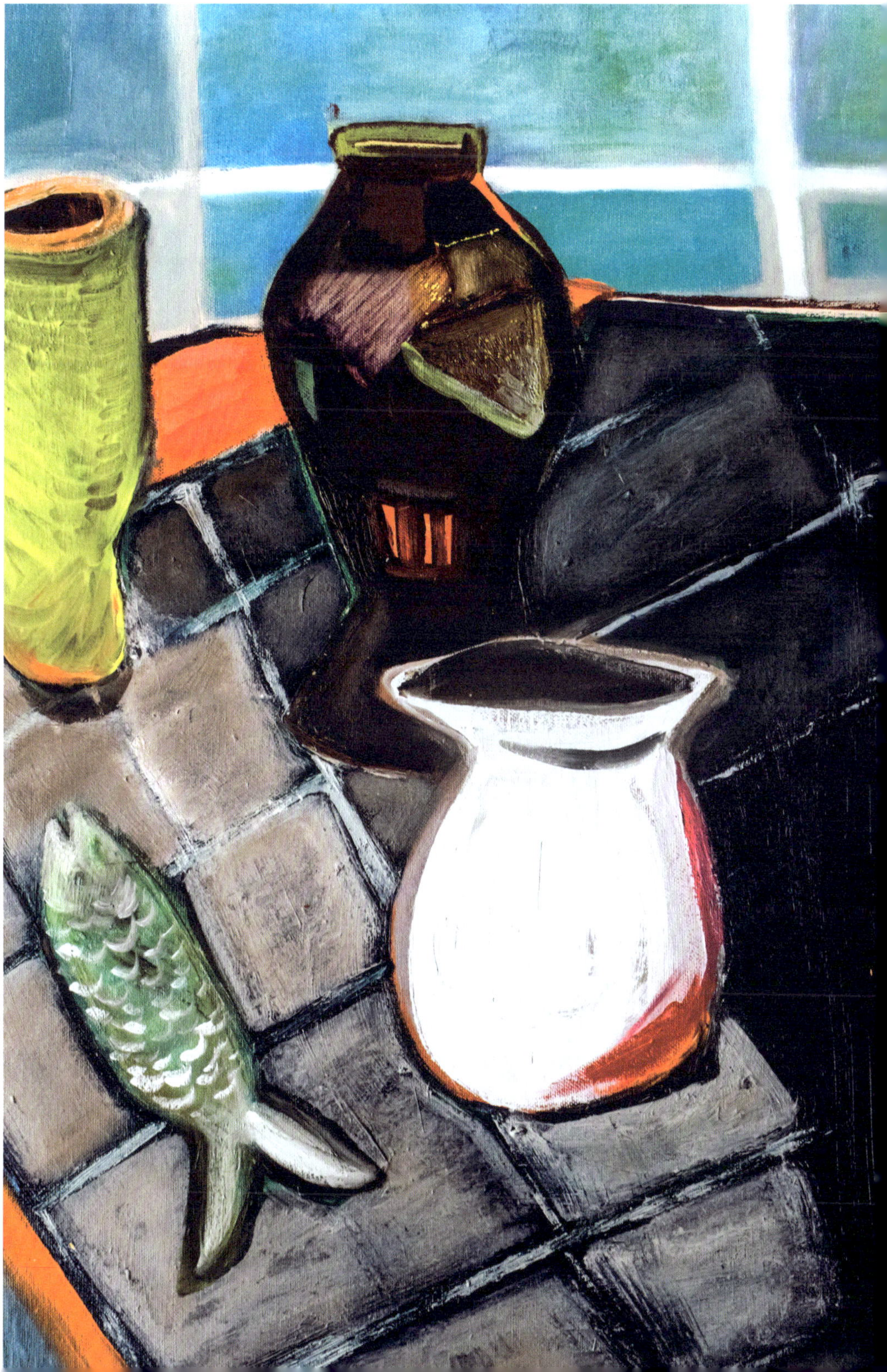

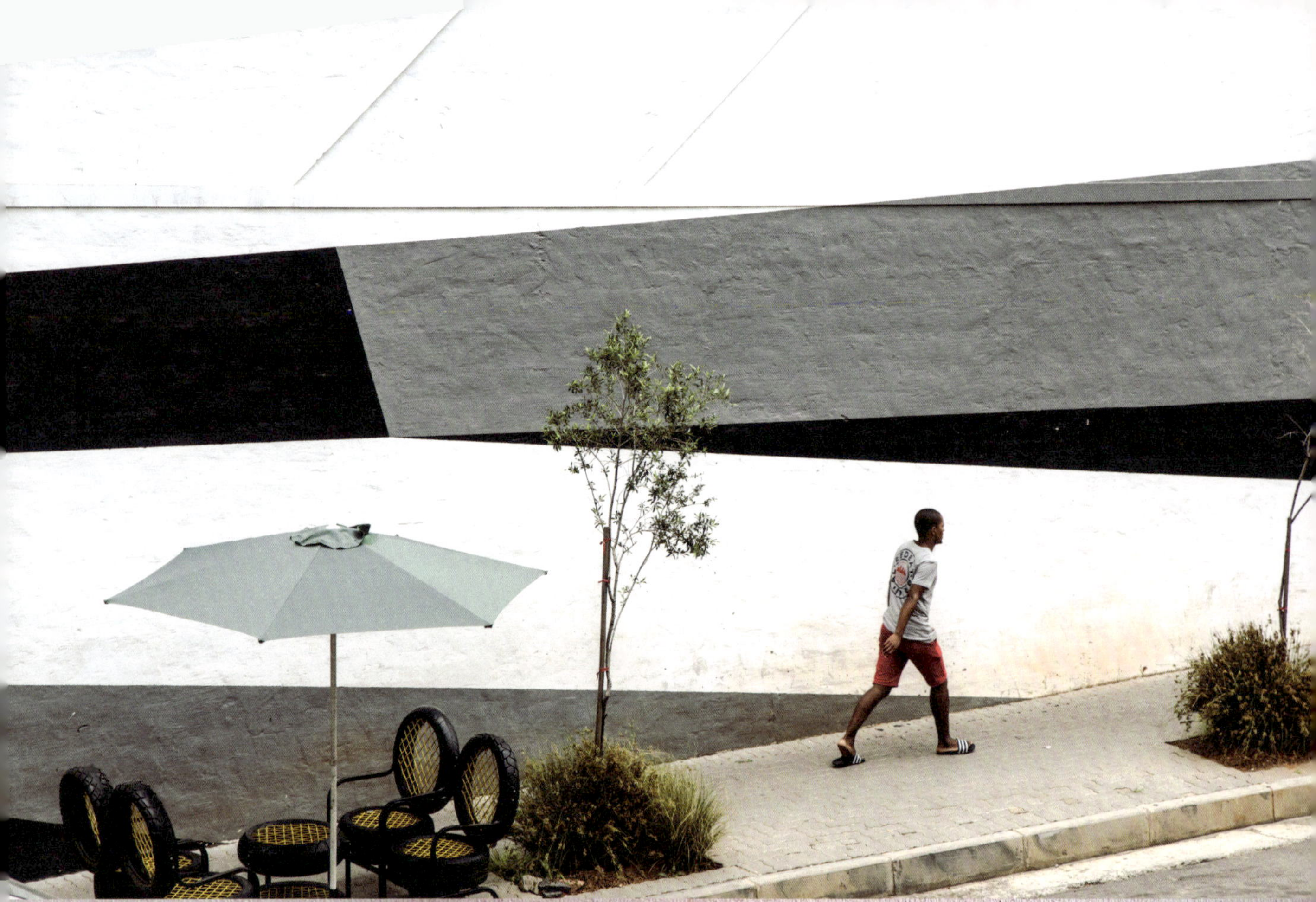

From no-go to must-go

Not long ago this area had a run-down vibe. Now, it has grown into a patchwork of creative companies and cosy cafes. Fortunately, Maboneng has also maintained its raw edge and is now a very popular hangout for visitors and locals alike.

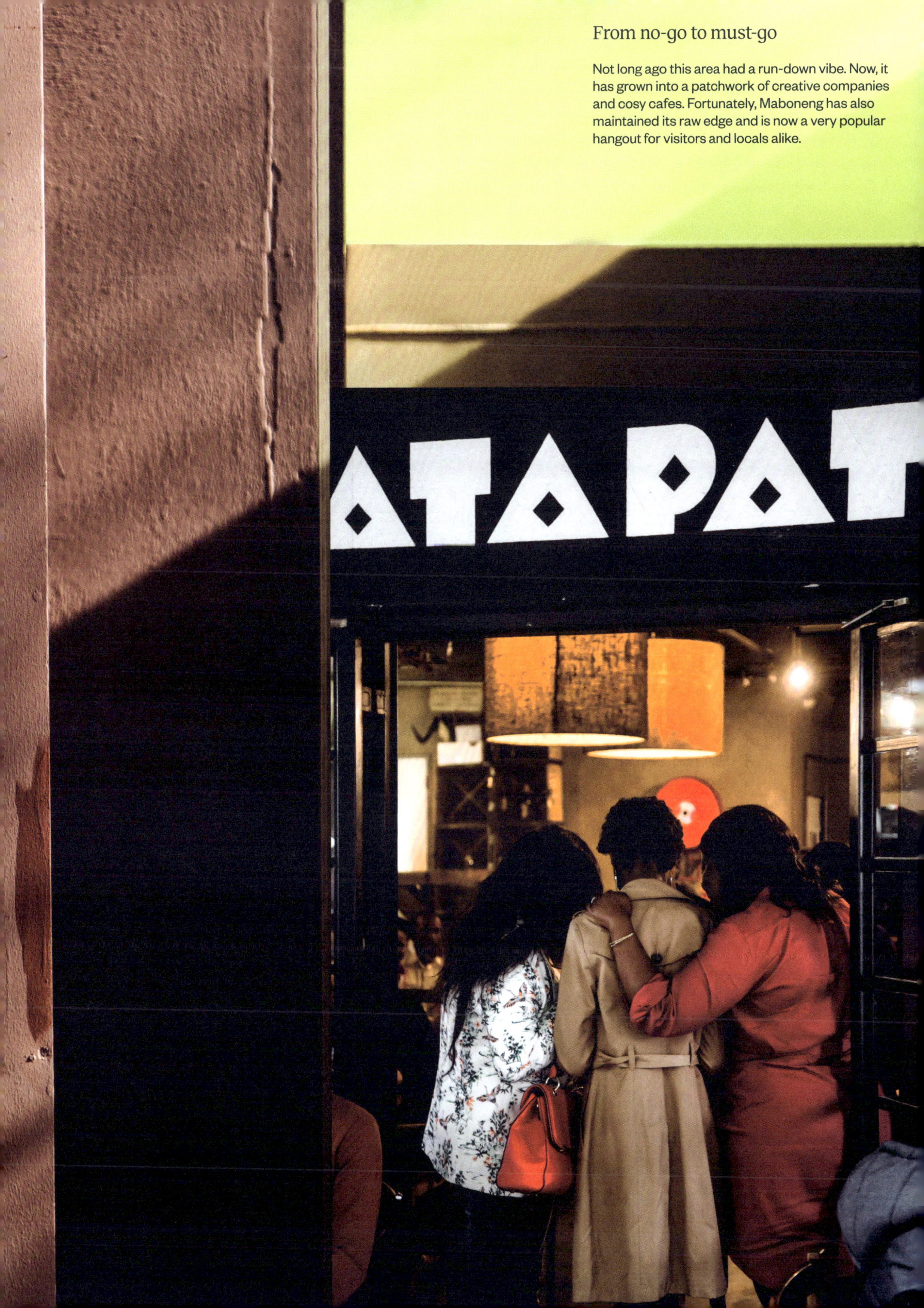

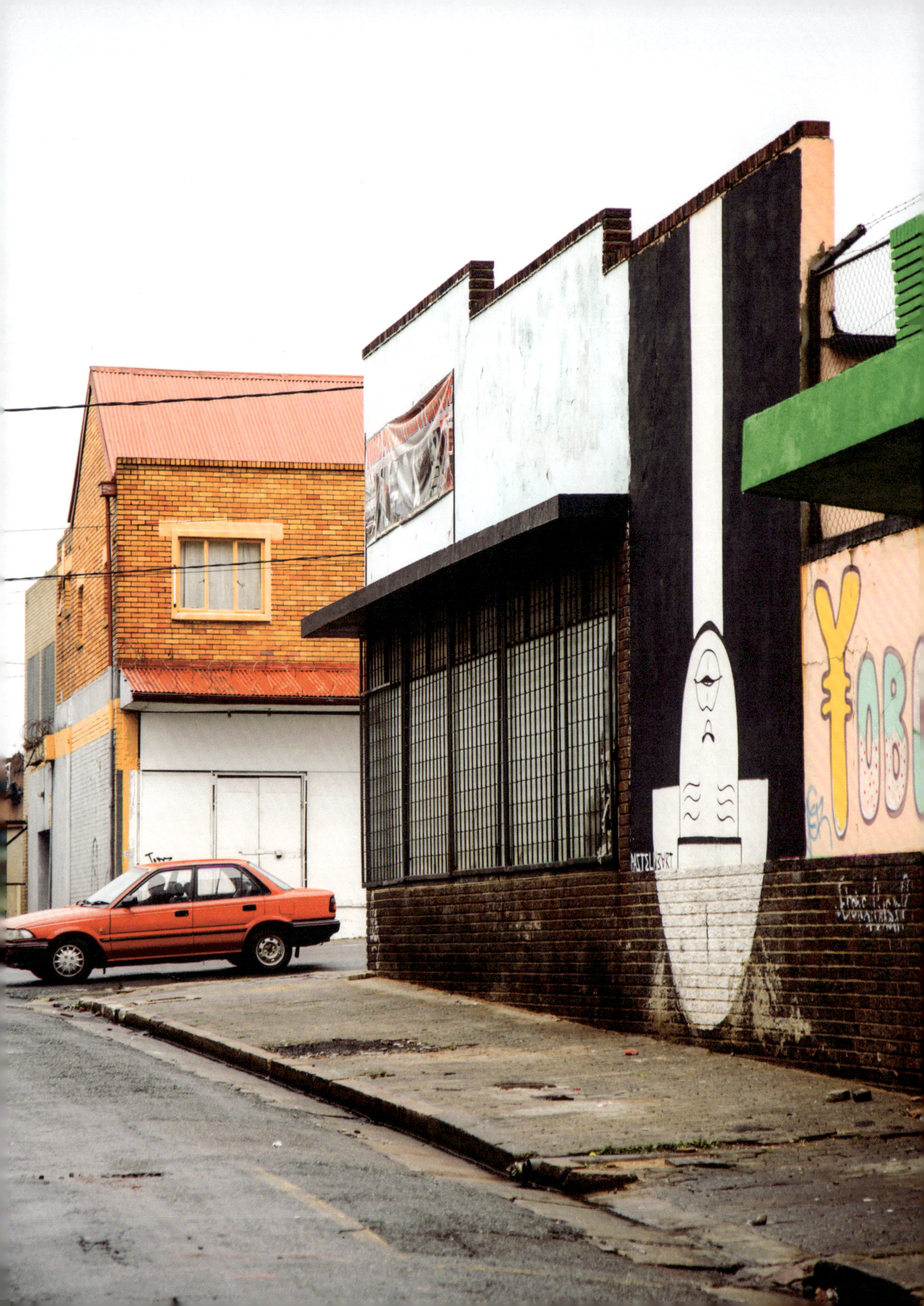

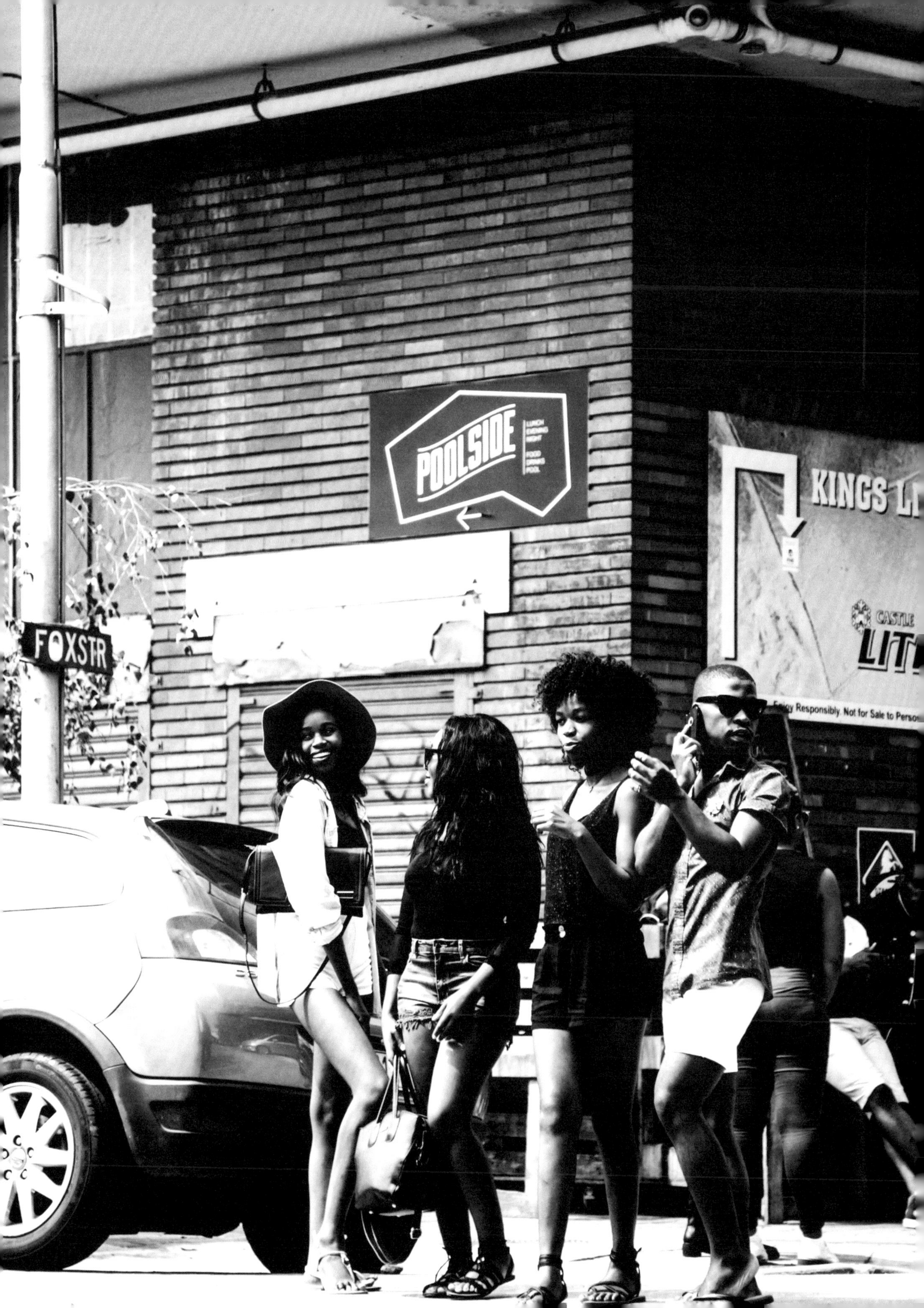
POOLSIDE
FOXSTR
KINGS
CASTLE

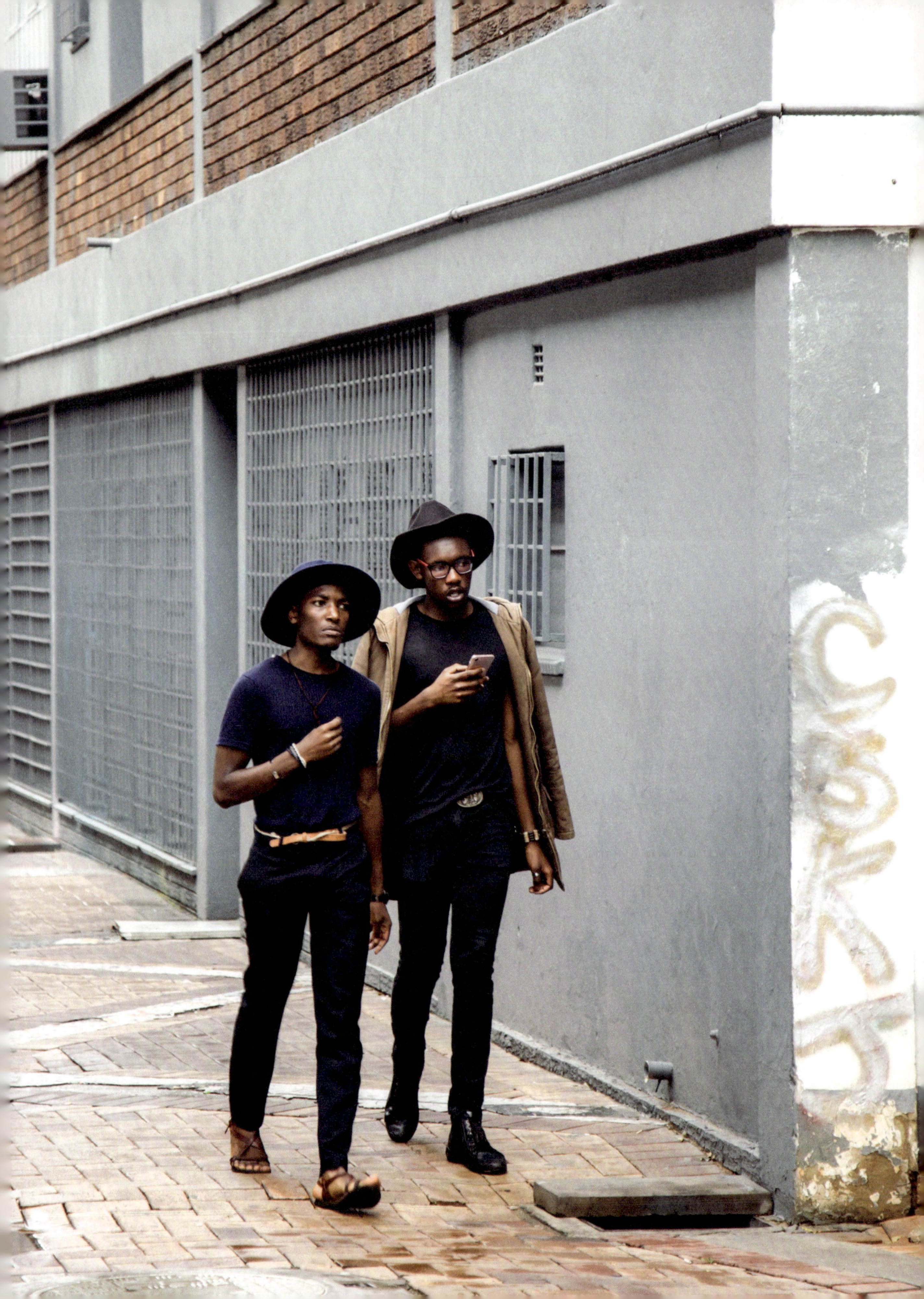

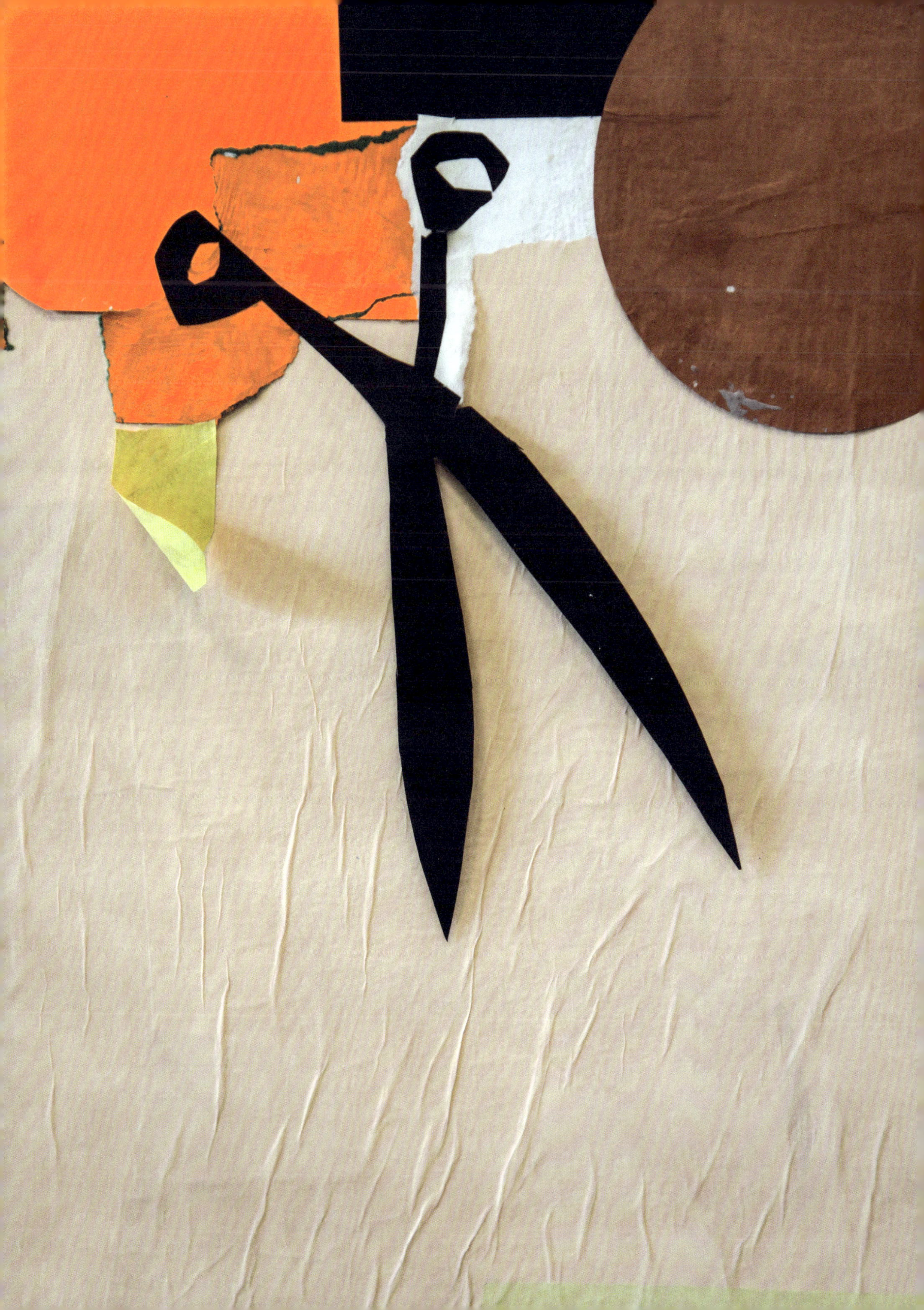

Marianne Fassler has been the grande dame of South African fashion for several decades. Her style is both rebellious and flamboyant, intellectual with a bit of hippy flair. A rich layering of materials, colours, prints and textures for an even stronger impact. This contradictory approach is also apparent in Marianne's house in one of the more chic neighbourhoods of Johannesburg.

Leopard Frock, Marianne's fashion label, also has its atelier here. Although she has chosen to keep her living quarters and work separated, her private and professional life are nonetheless intertwined. This makes the place feel ever so lively every day when her team of designers and tailors arrive to work. In addition to the prêt-à-porter collection, Fassler and her team also create unique outfits for special occasions. Clients come to the house to discuss and be fitted for their bespoke dresses.

Marianne's living quarters are at the front of the house. It is very likely that you will be overwhelmed when you enter the spacious living room. First by the colours, and then by the amount of furniture, paintings, art, textiles and the many artefacts on the walls and scattered throughout the room. After your eyes have recovered from the visual onslaught, you will start to notice more details and see a connection between the different materials and colours. The storytelling approach that Marianne applied to the interior design of her living area is consistently present in the other parts of the house and outside. The large swimming pool wouldn't look out of place in a 50s Hollywood movie.

The interior is populated with decorative figures and animals which, after you've spent a little time among them, seem to come alive and start to reveal their story.

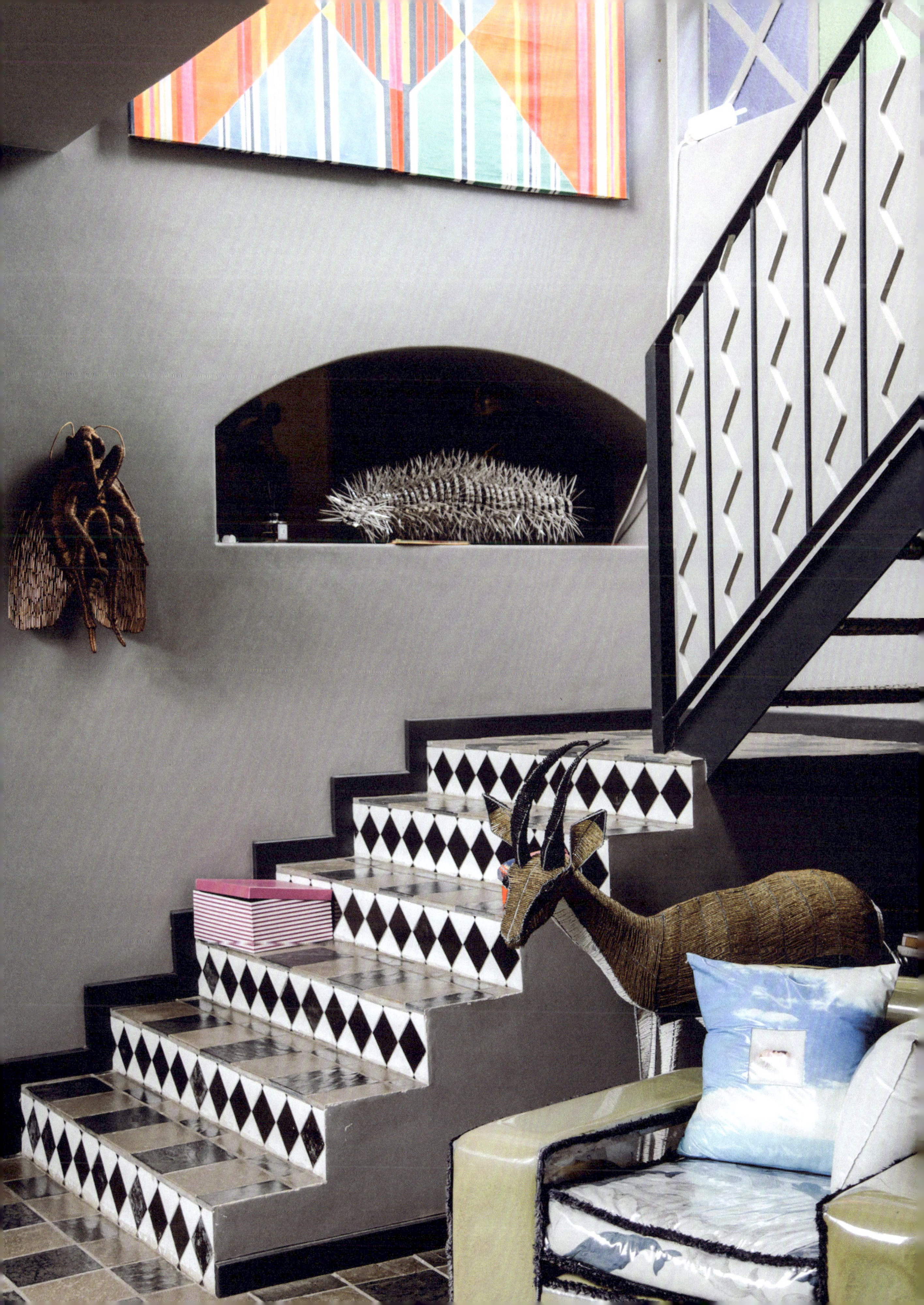

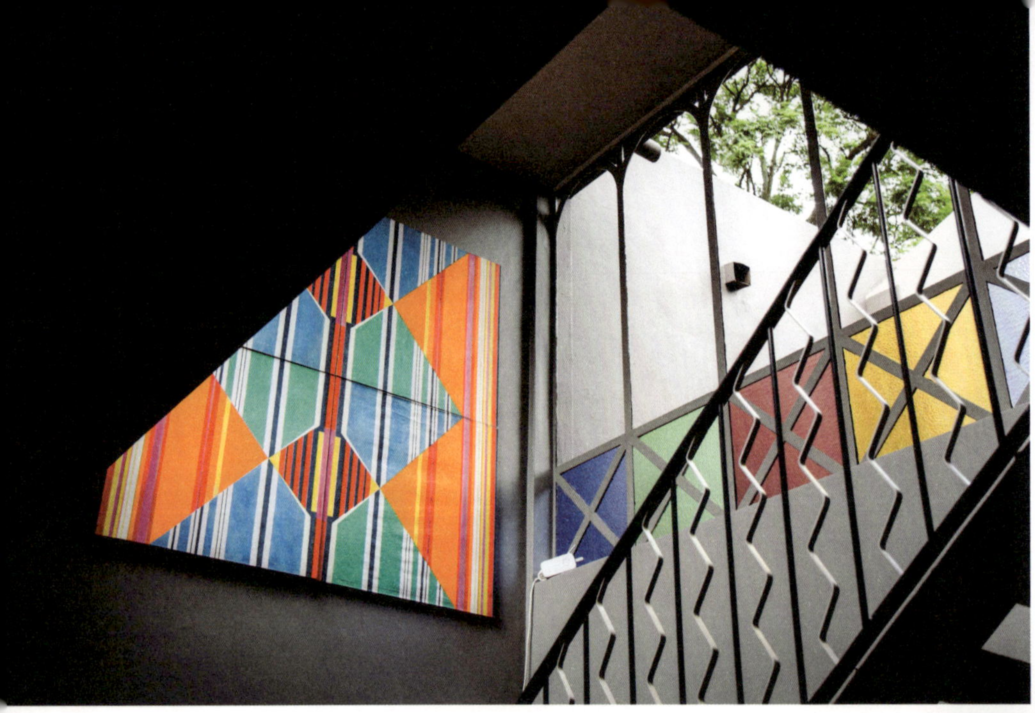

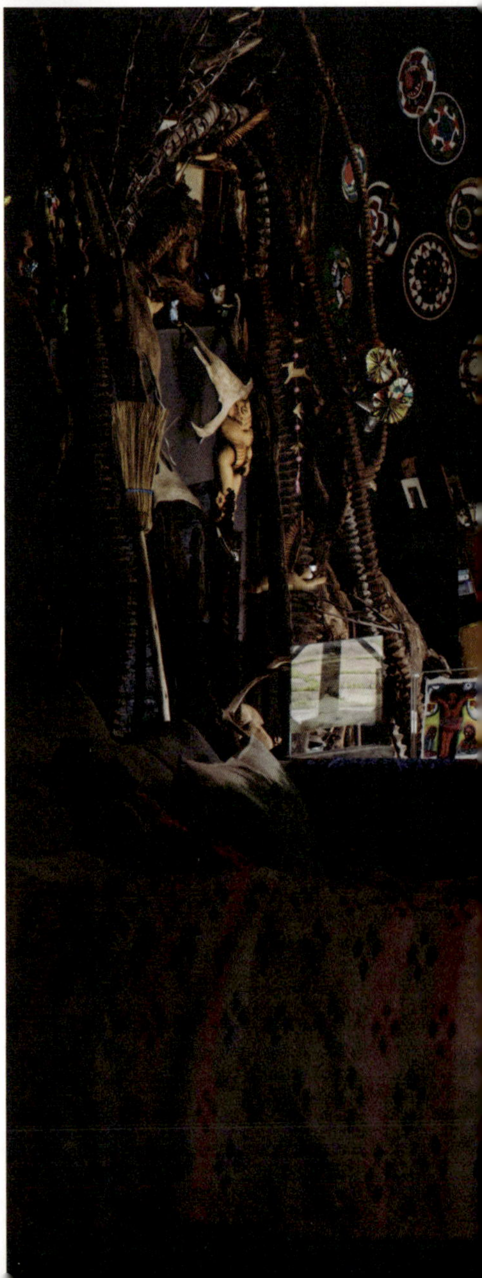

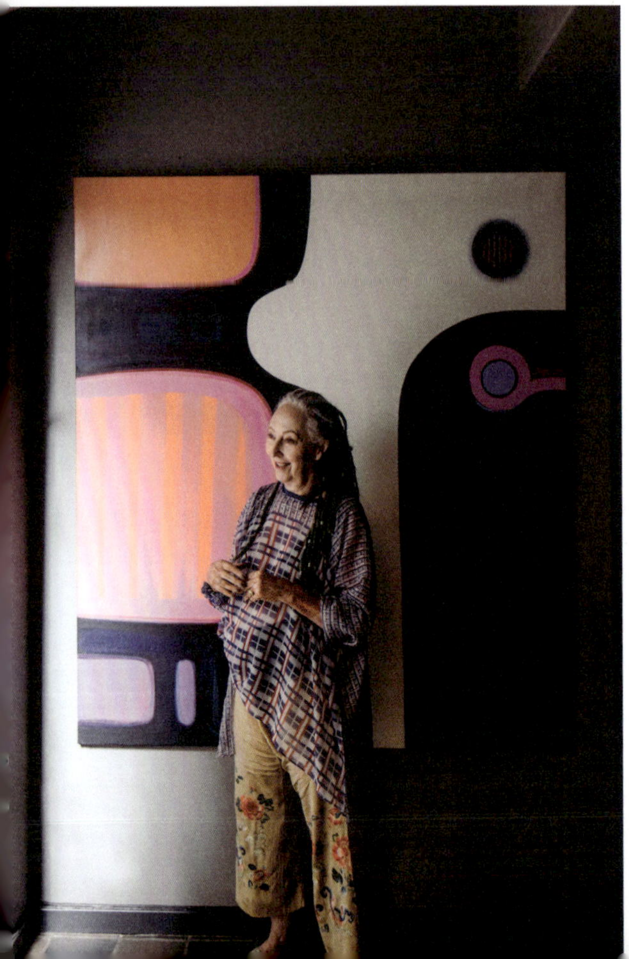

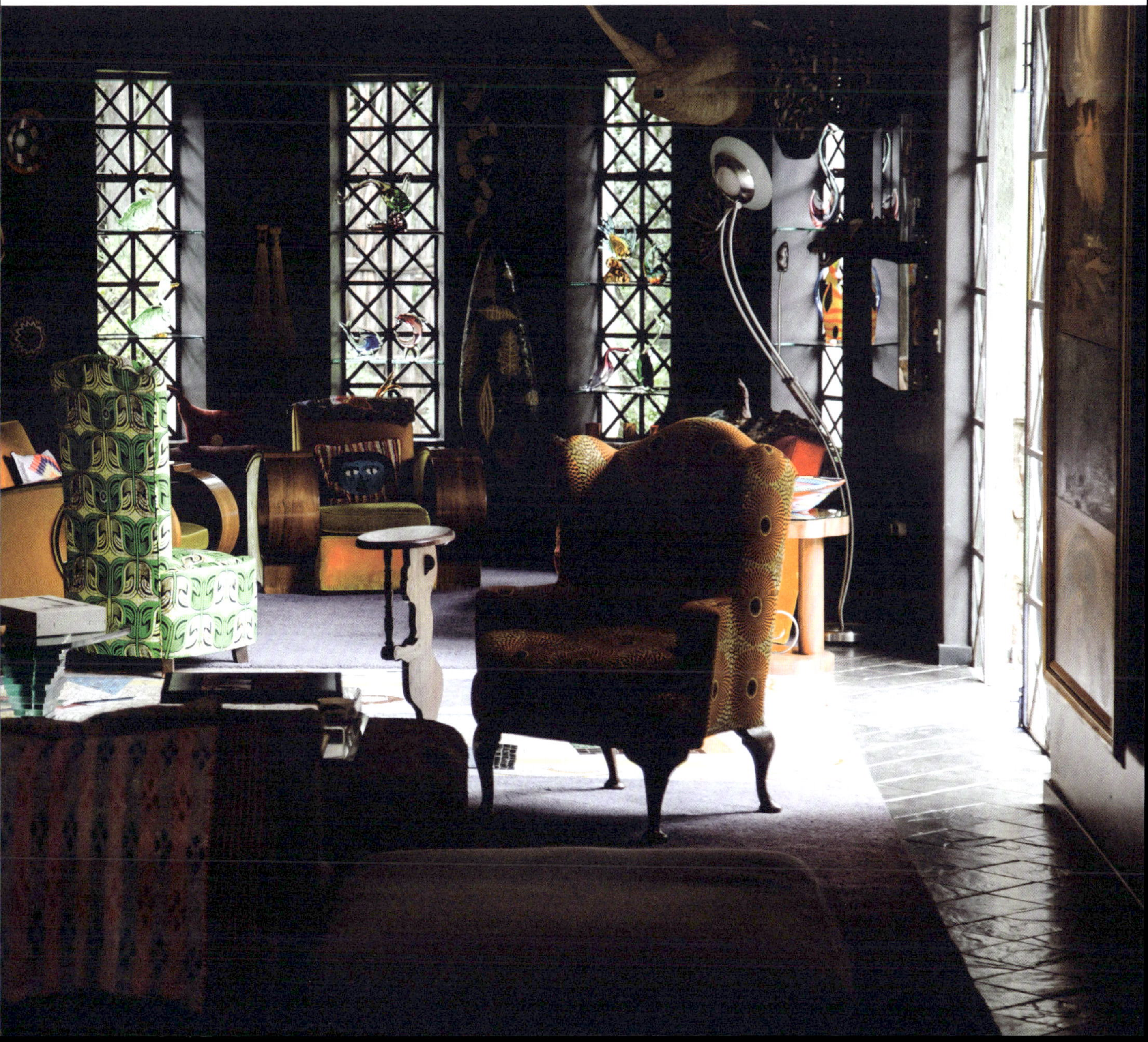

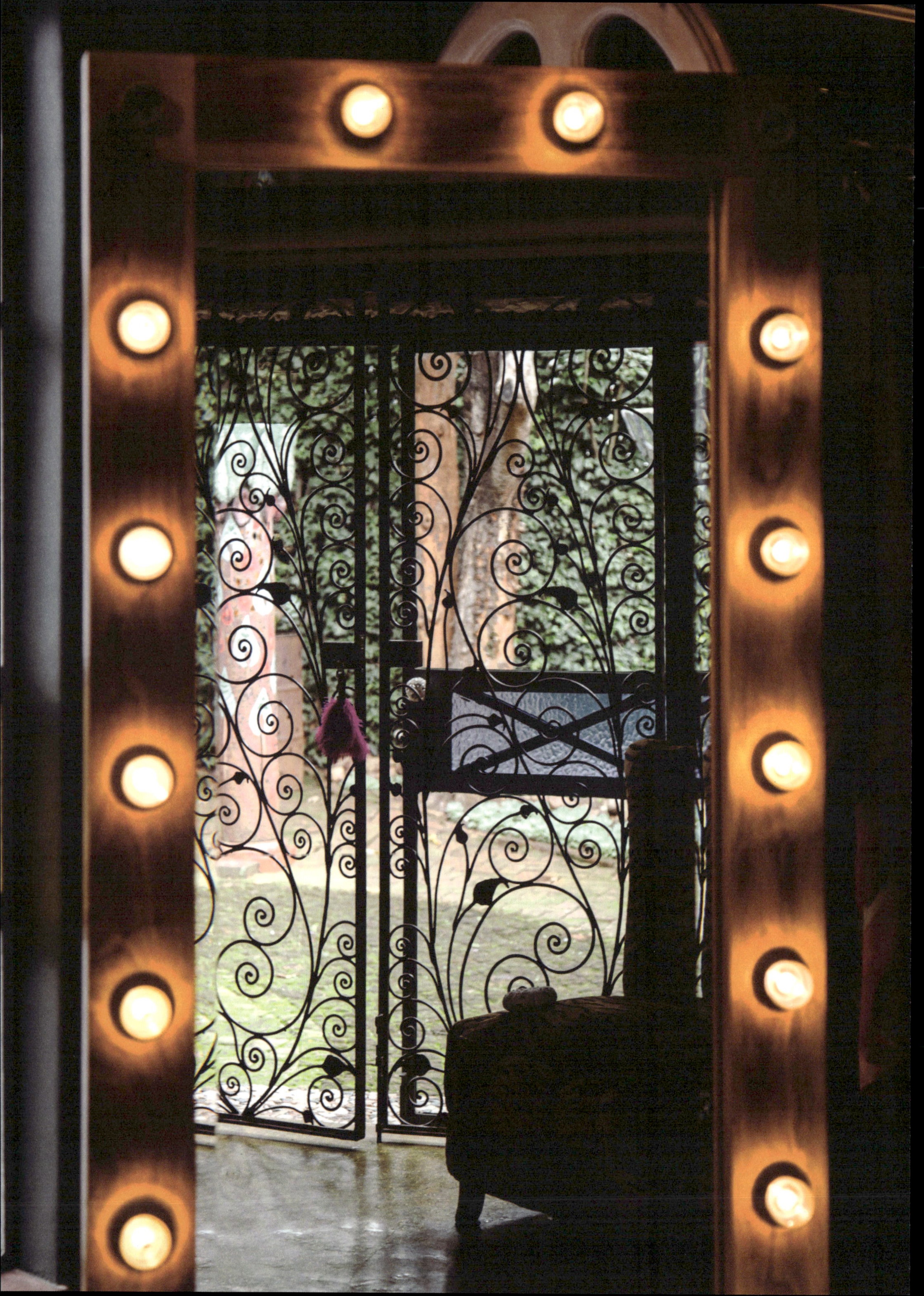

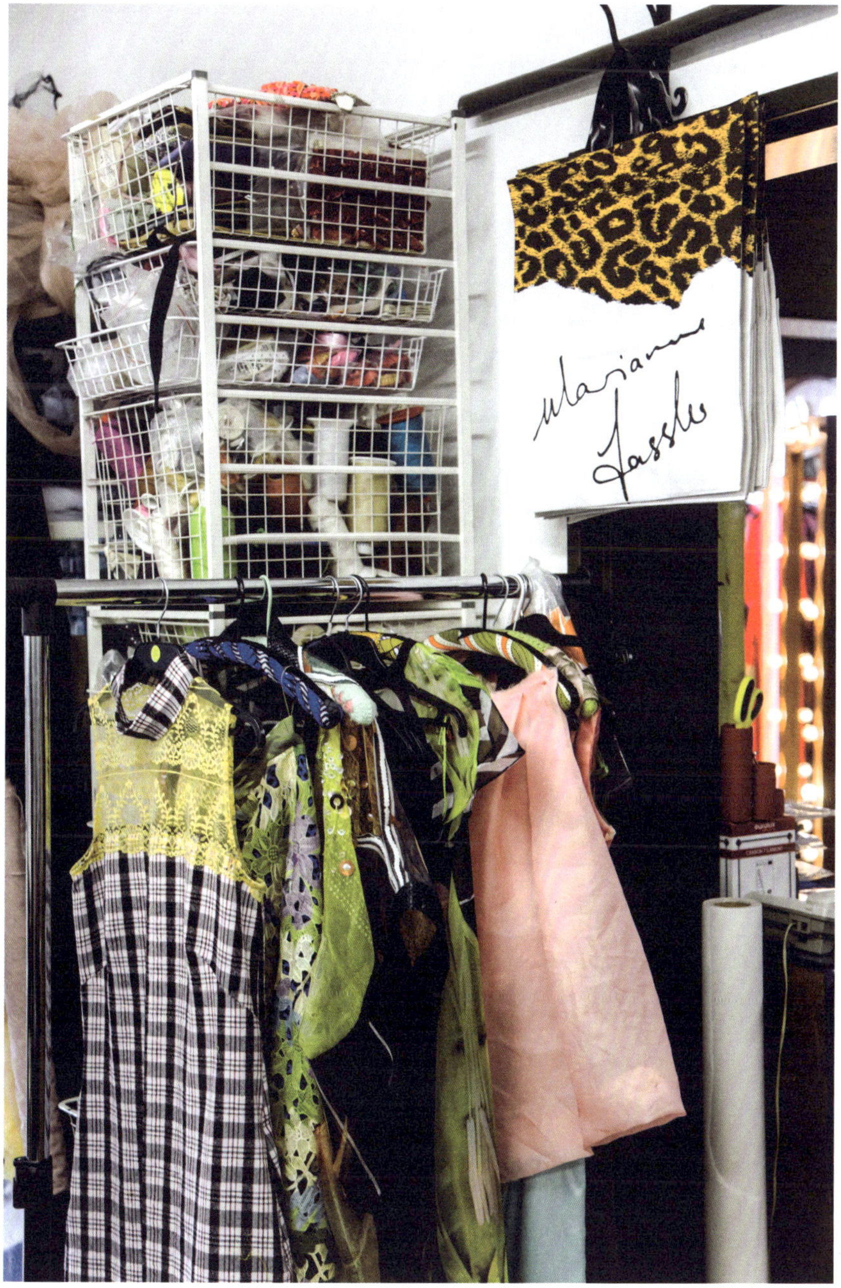
Marianne Fassler

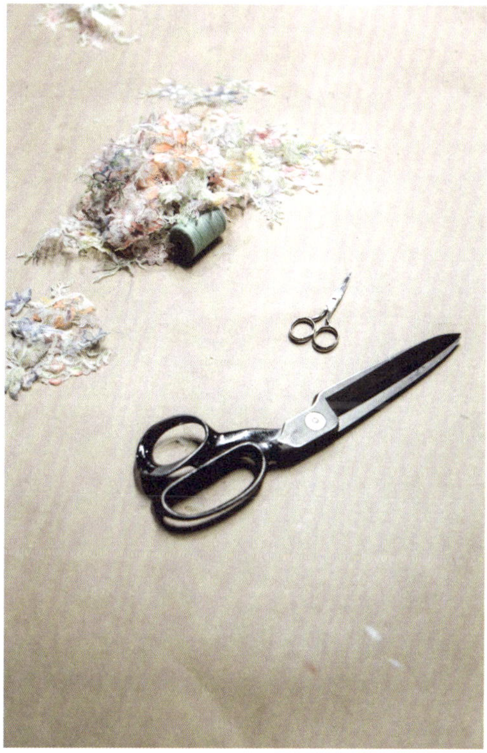

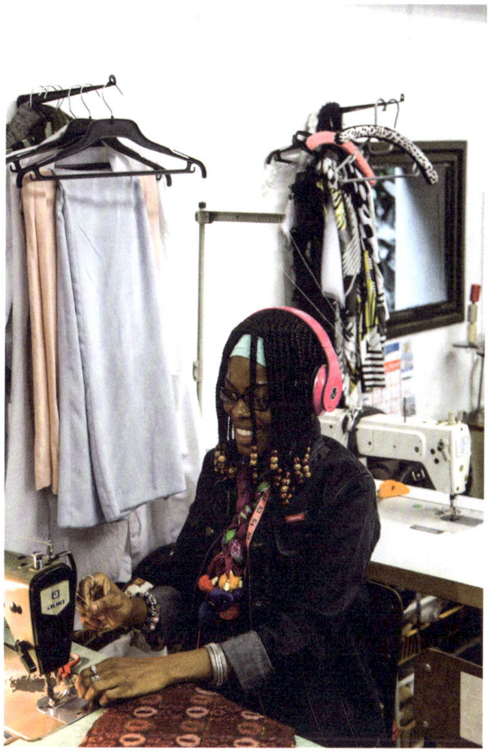

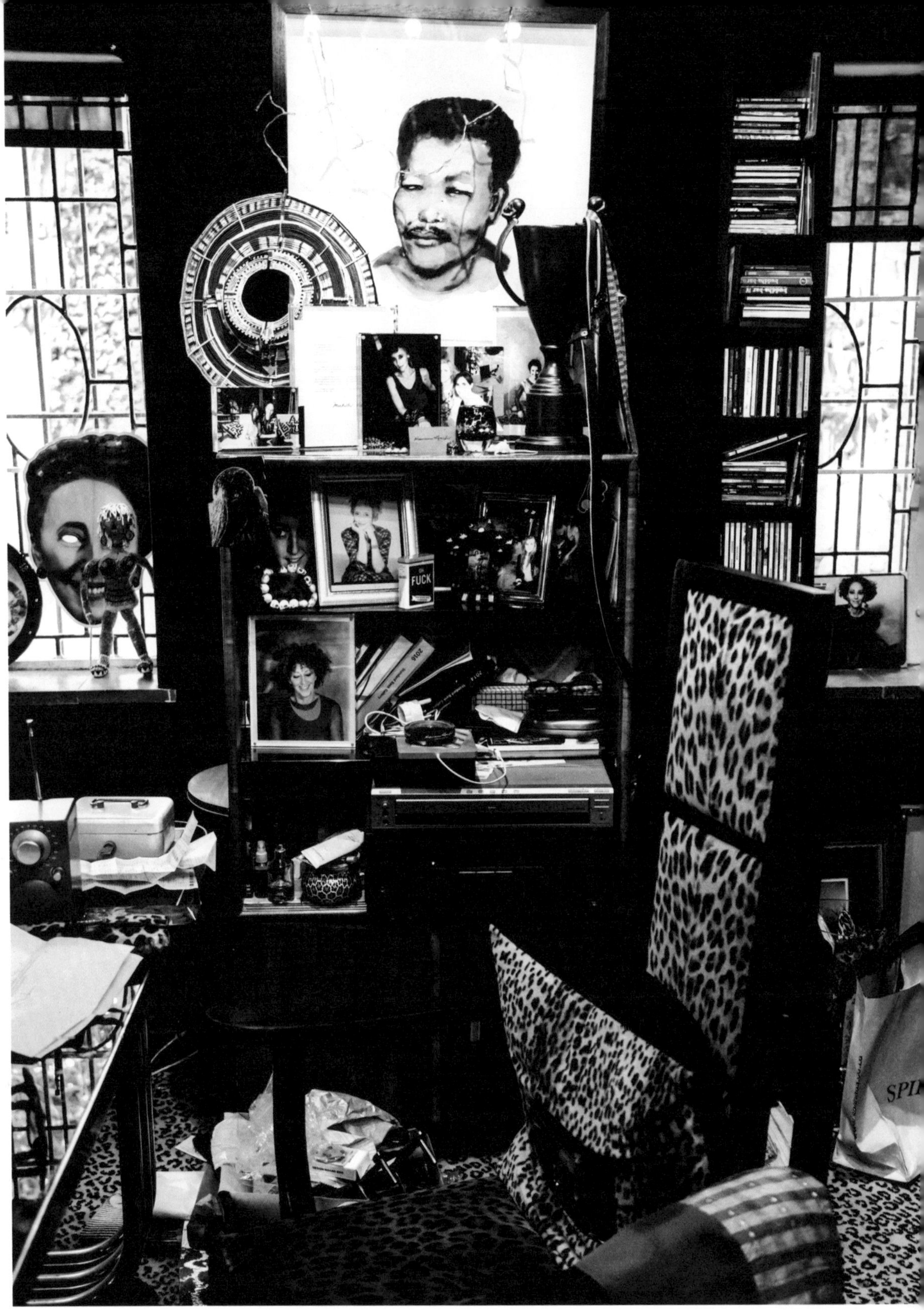
FUCK

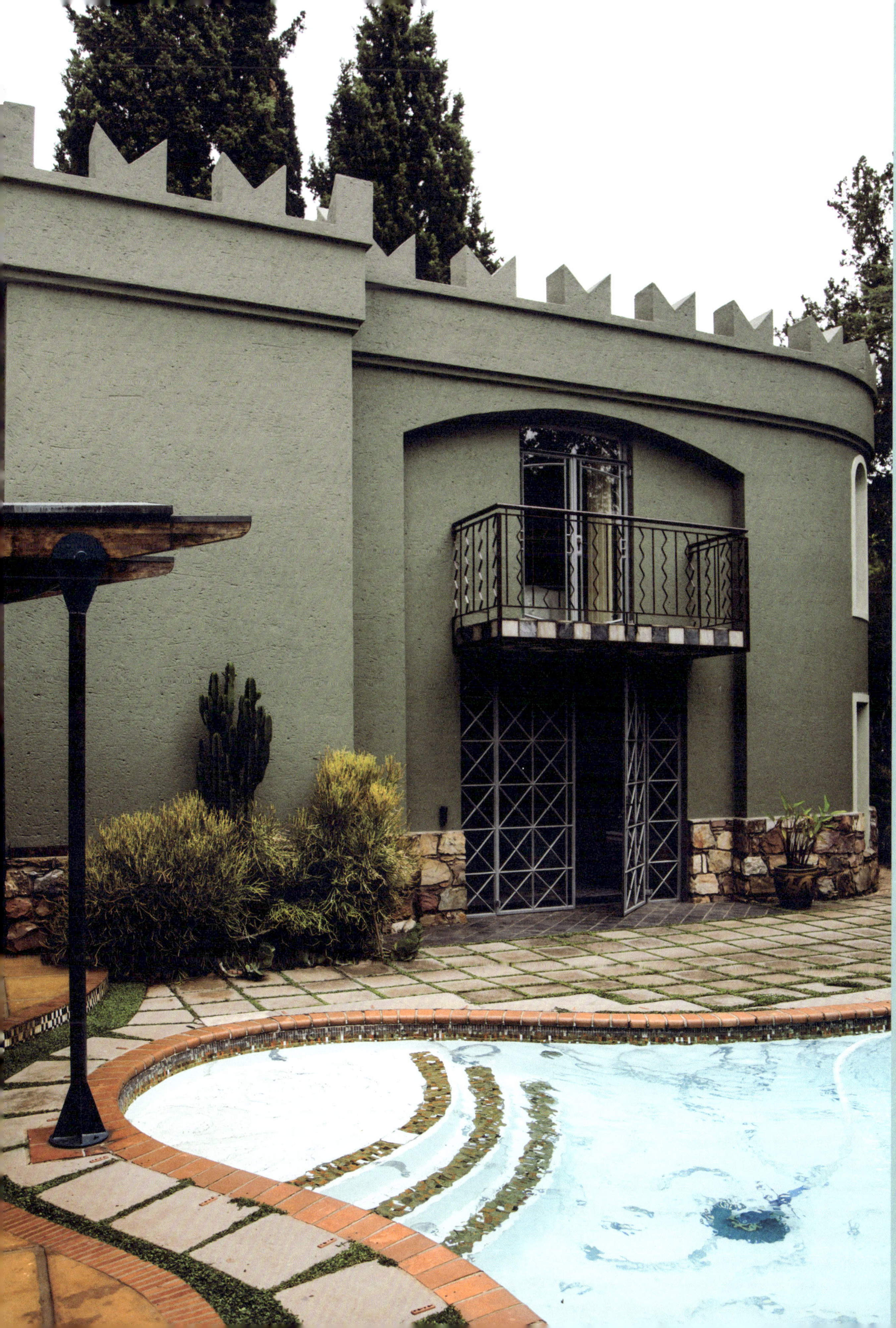

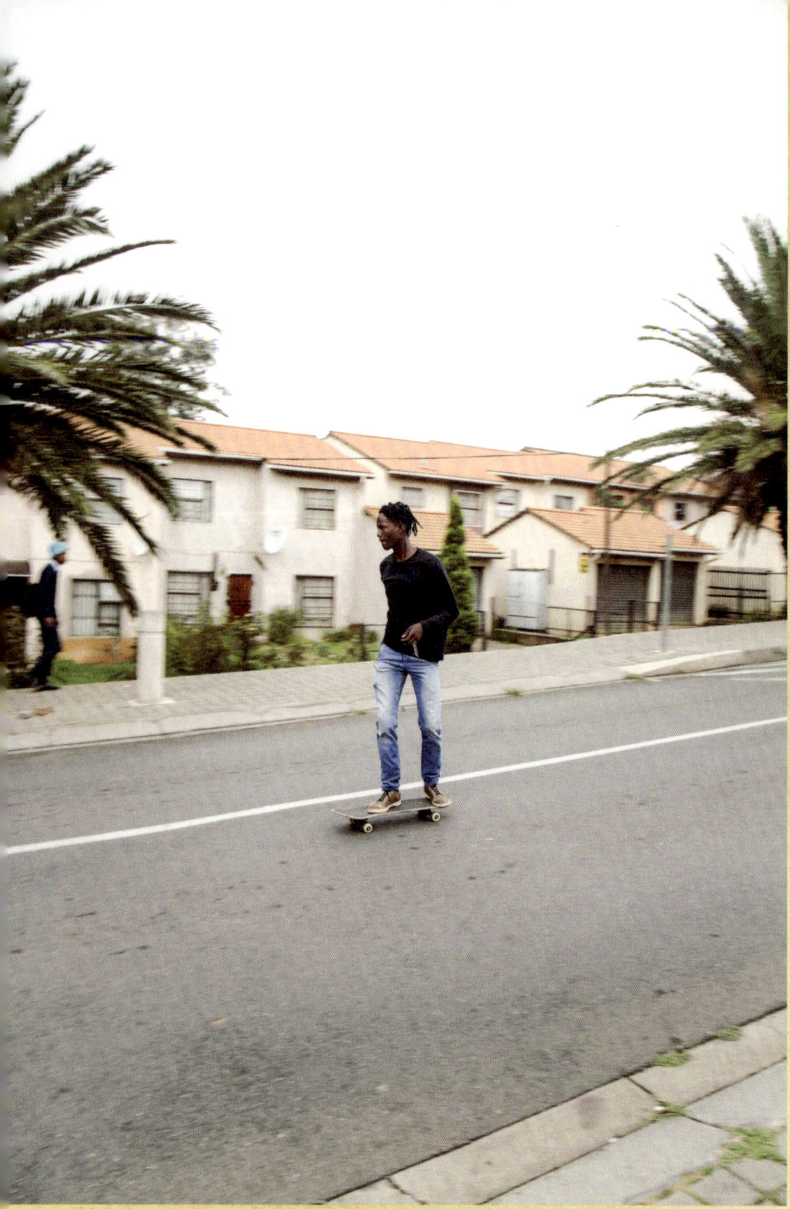

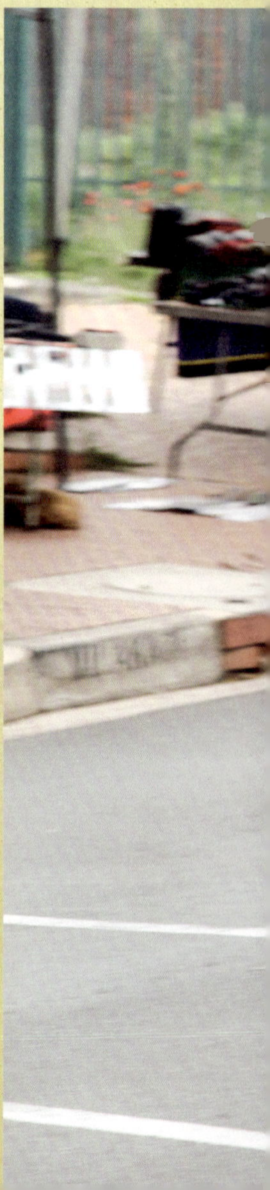

Soweto street style

Are long ties the latest fashion statement?
Schoolboys give their uniforms their own cool twist.

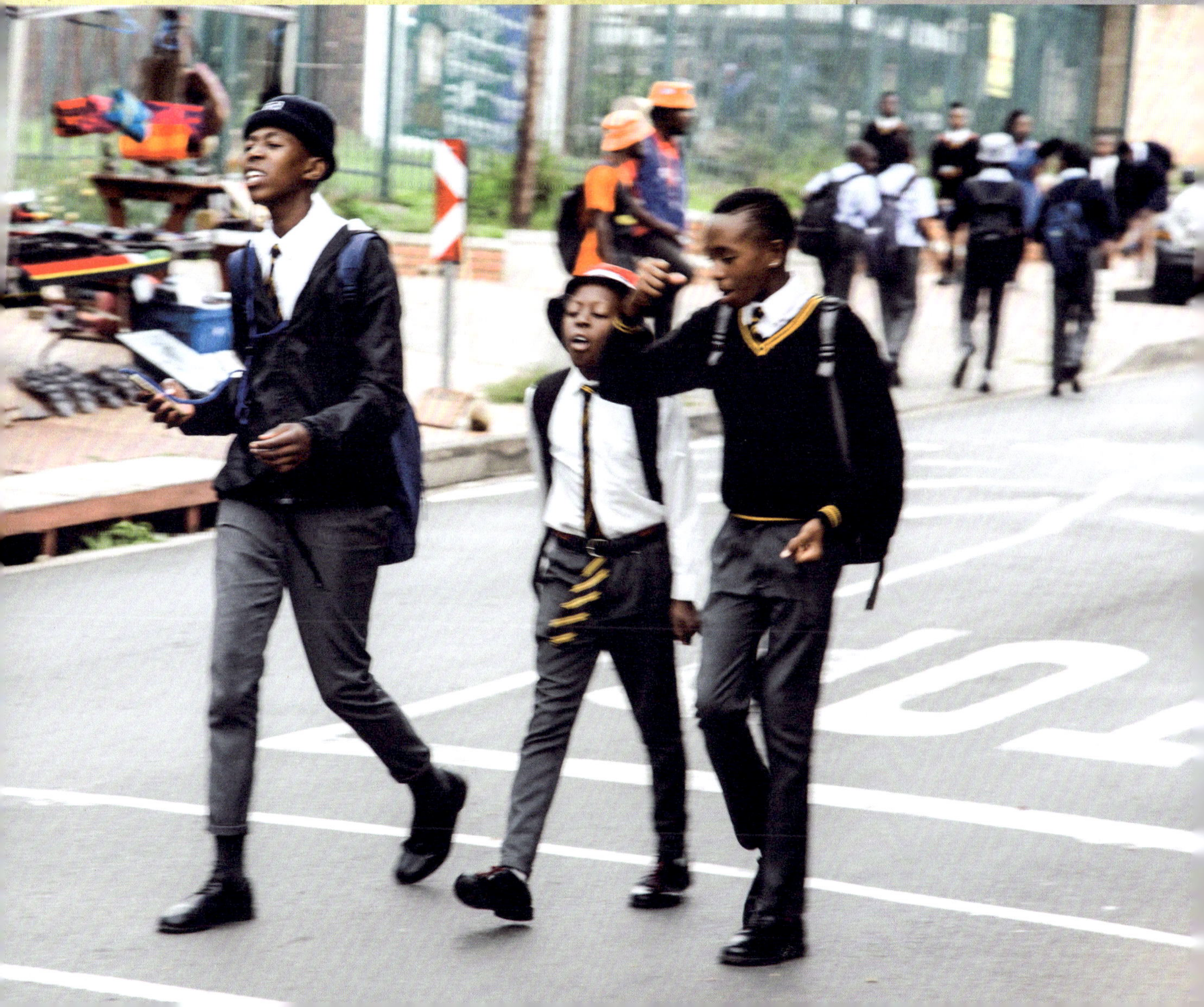

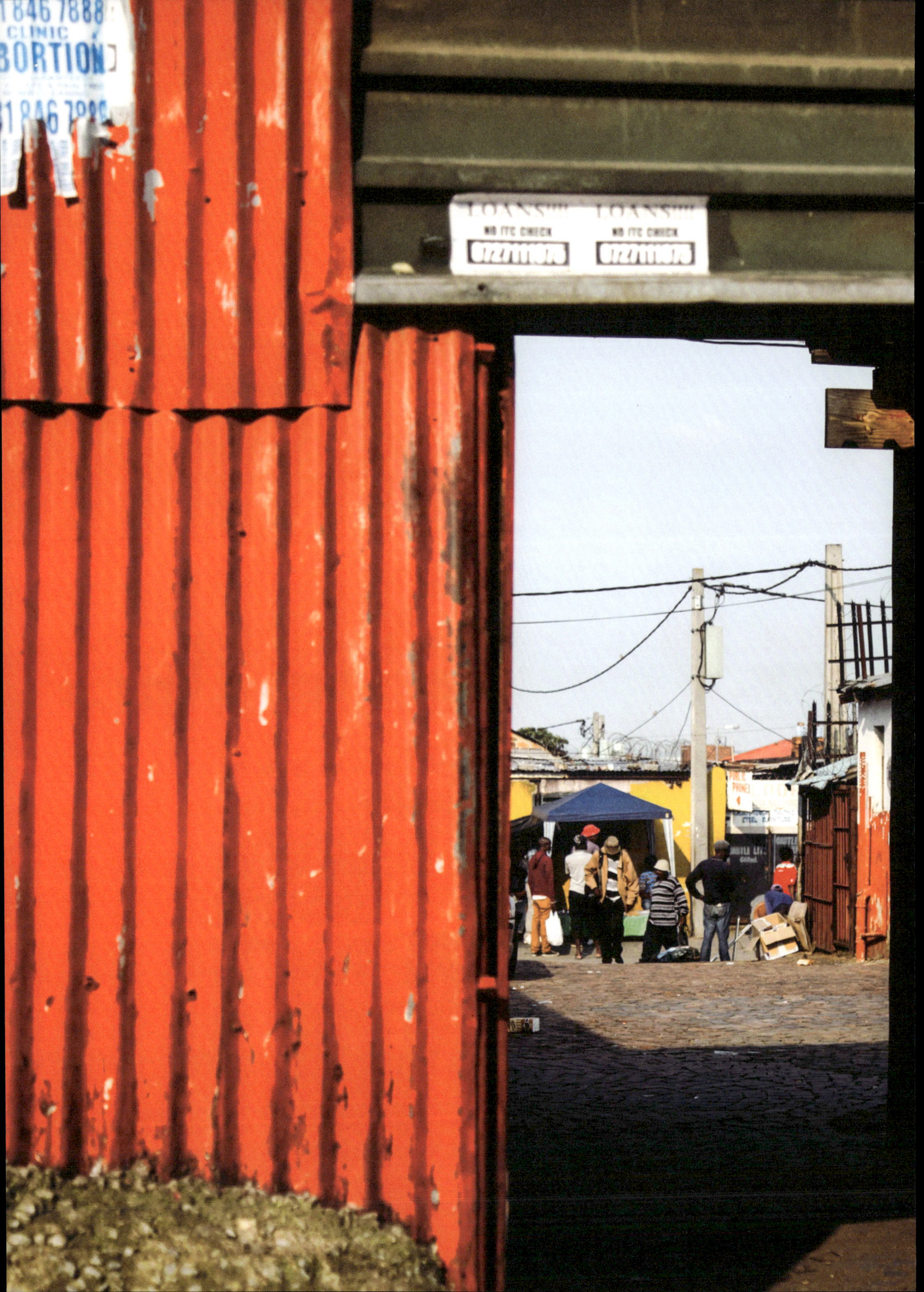
1846 7888
CLINIC
BORTION
LOANS!!!
NO ITC CHECK
LOANS!!!
NO ITC CHECK

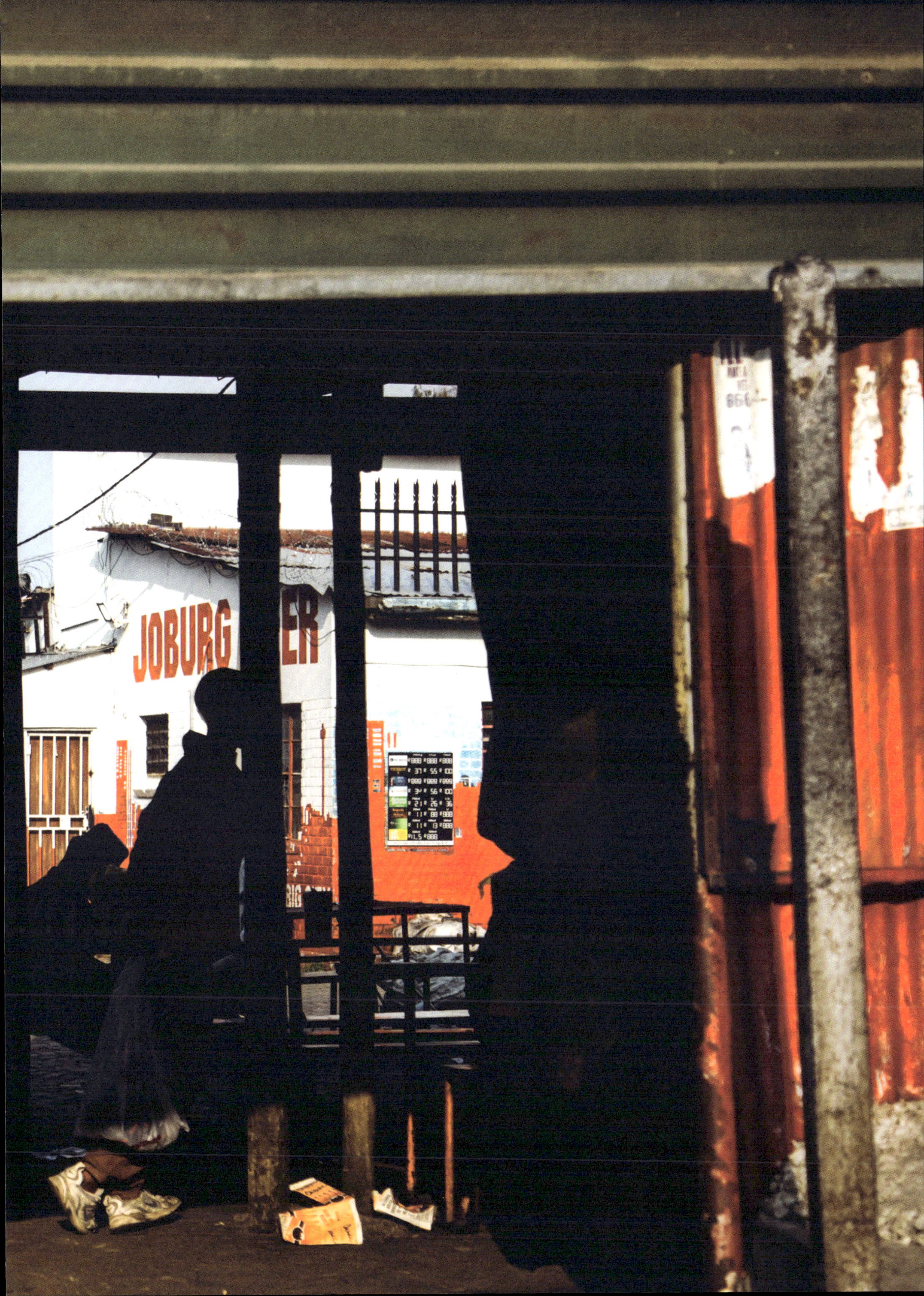
JOBURG

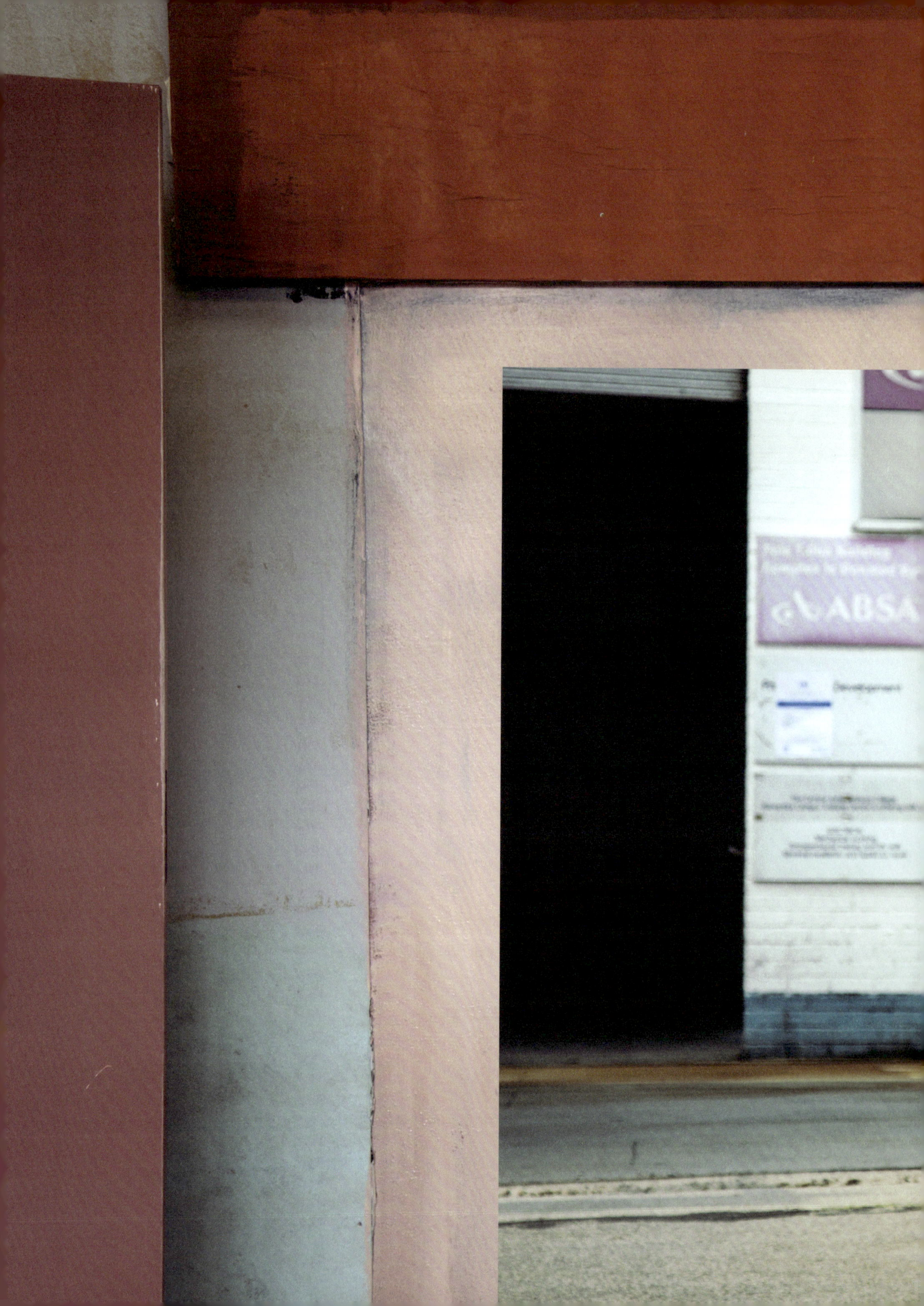
ABSA

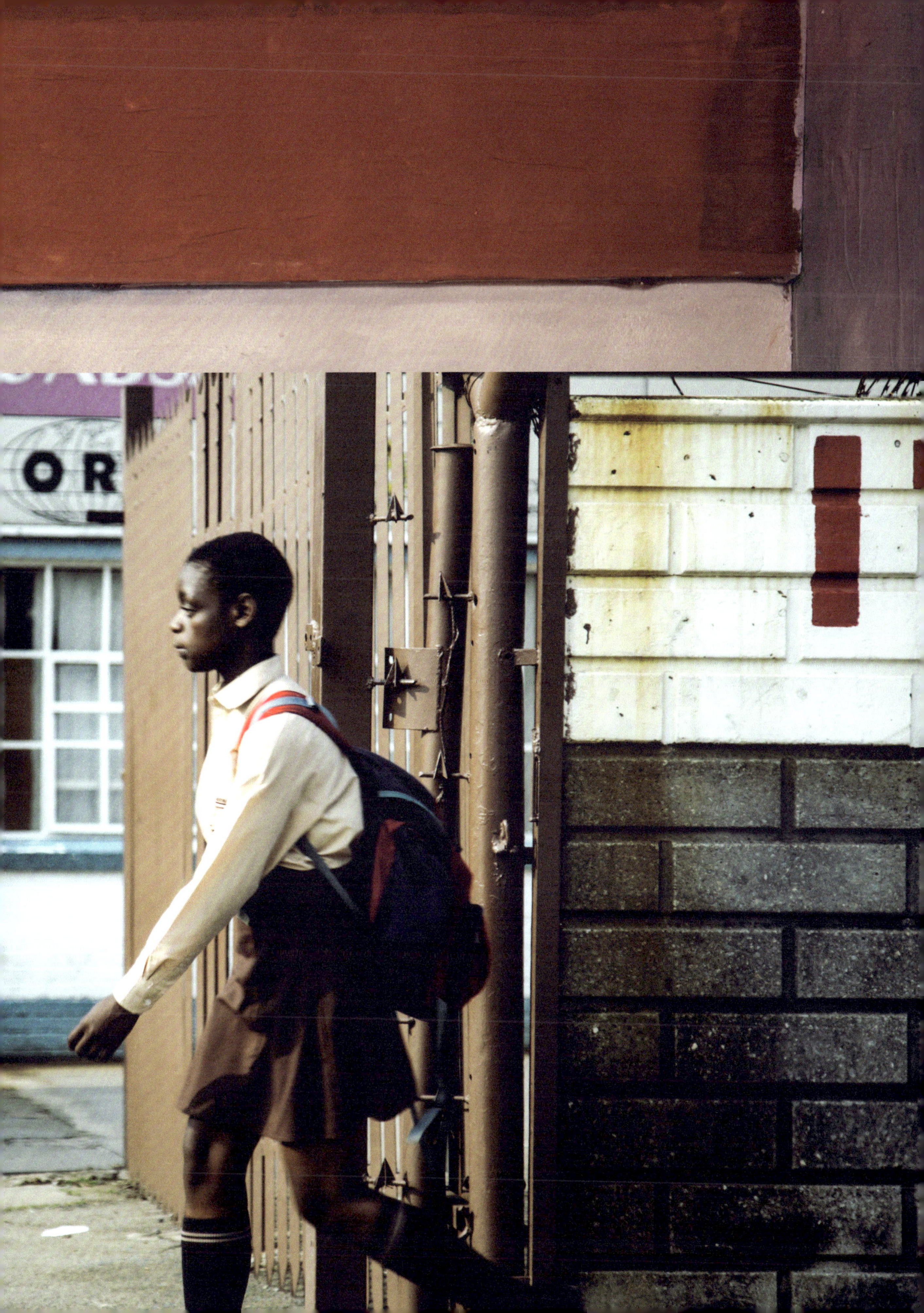
OR

We returned from our travels through South Africa with an enormous amount of images. Making a selection turned out to be a time-consuming, but very enjoyable process. Still immersed in the images of our trip, we started creating collages and illustrations in our studio. These collaborations were incorporated into the book as backgrounds and connecting images between the chapters.

We enjoyed compiling the book in a small team together with our publisher, editor and designer.

We also want to thank all the people we met during our trip, who opened their homes to us and helped us find inspiration for other fascinating people to meet and places to visit that might be interesting for our book.

Mirjam & Frank

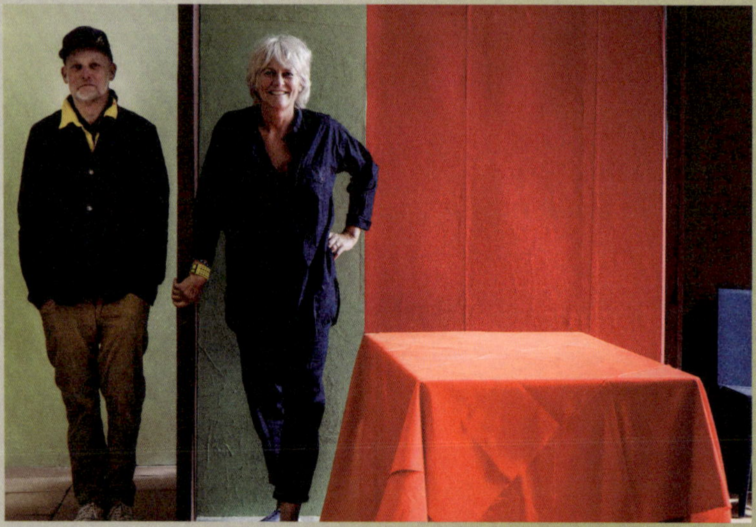

10

Back Home

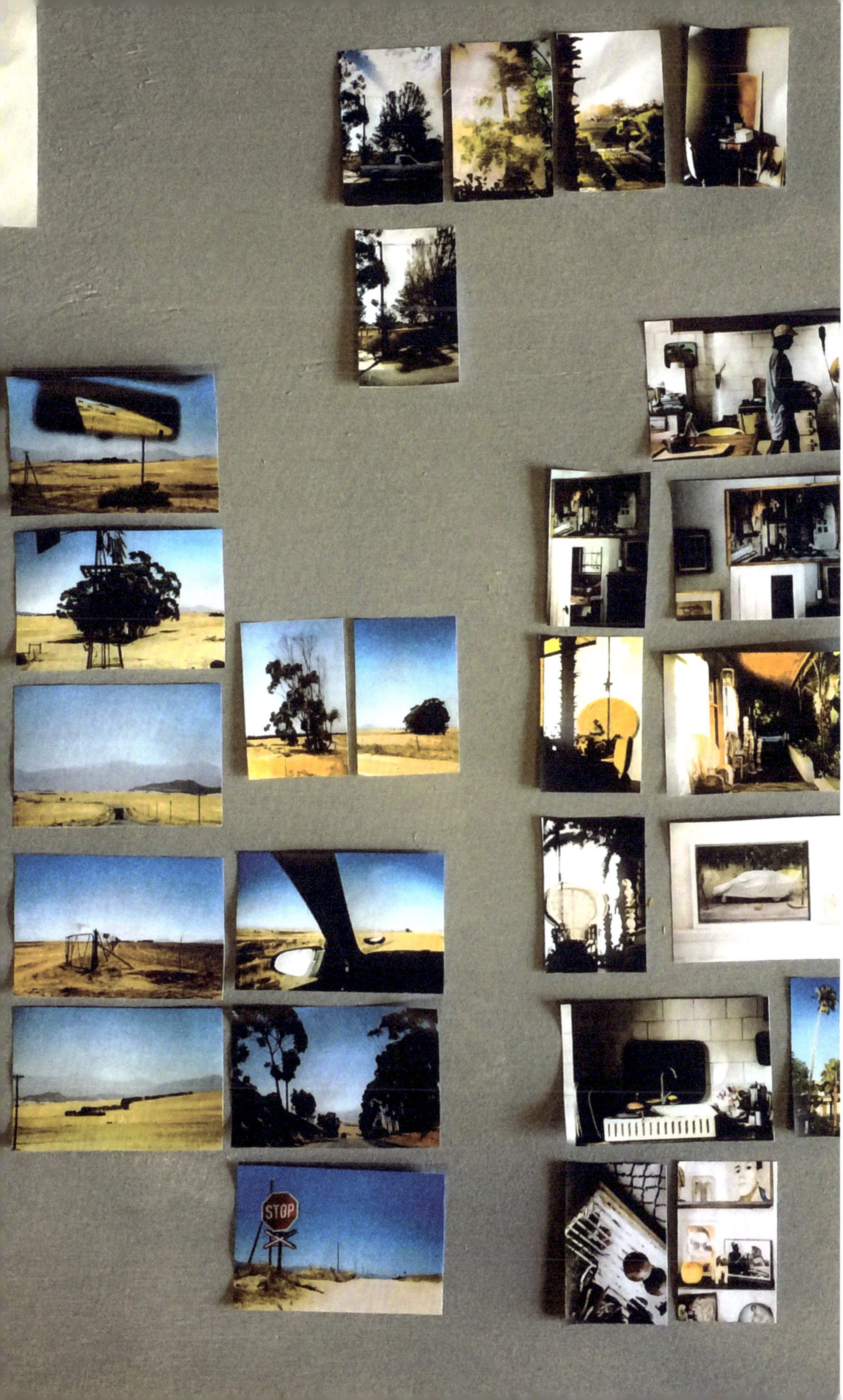

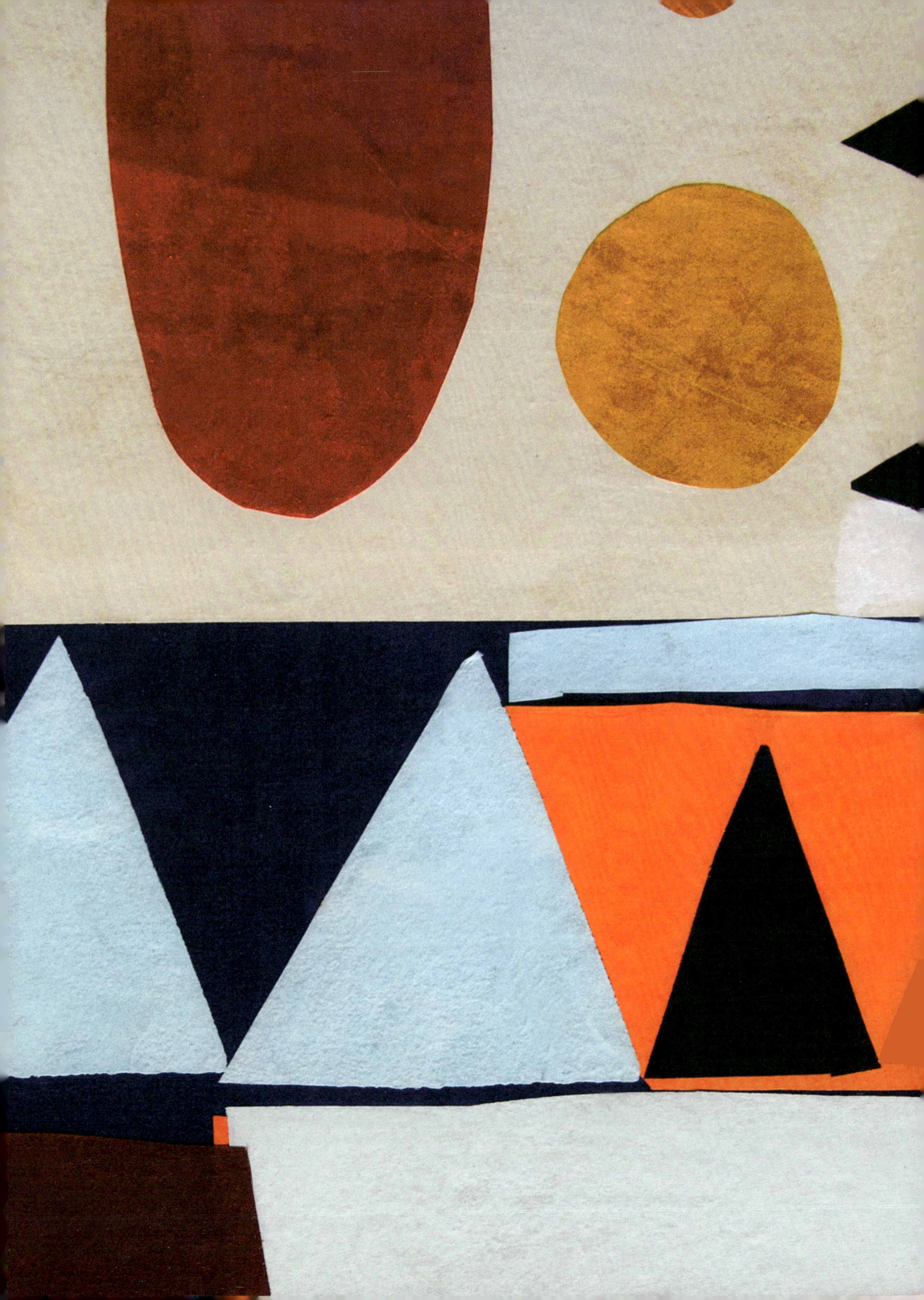